FRIEDRICH HECKER
TWO LIVES FOR LIBERTY

Friedrich Hecker as a revolutionary icon. Exhibit "Mit Feder und Hammer" (1983), Western Historical Manuscripts, University of Missouri – St. Louis.

SABINE FREITAG

FRIEDRICH HECKER
TWO LIVES FOR LIBERTY

translated from the German and edited by
Steven Rowan

St. Louis Mercantile Library
University of Missouri – St. Louis
St. Louis, 2006
Distributed by University of Missouri Press

This book was made possible by the
John A. A. Hecker Fund
at the
St. Louis Mercantile Library,
University of Missouri – St. Louis.

This English edition has been translated from the original German publication
Friedrich Hecker, Biographie eines Republikaners
©1998 by Franz Steiner Verlag GmbH

Printed with the permission of Franz Steiner Verlag GmbH

English language translation and Translator's Preface © 2006 by
The Curators of the University of Missouri

Published in the United States of America
by the
St. Louis Mercantile Library
University of Missouri – St. Louis
One University Boulevard
St. Louis, Missouri 63121

Freitag, Sabine.
Friedrich Hecker : two lives for liberty / Sabine Freitag ; translated from the
German and edited by Steven Rowan.
p. cm.
ISBN 0-9639804-7-5
1. Hecker, Friedrich, 1811-1881. 2. Revolutionaries—Germany—Biography.
2. Germans—United States. 4. United States—Politics and government—
1849-1877. 4. Germany—History—Revolution, 1848-1849.
I. Title. II. Rowan, Steven W.

DD205.H37F7413 2006
943/.4607/092

Designer: Jerry Maschan
Typesetter: Adrian Creative Services
Printer: Chelmsford Printing, Inc.
Printed and Bound in Hong Kong
Typeface: Palatino
Distributed by University of Missouri Press

DEDICATION

The family of John A. A. Hecker
dedicates this translation in memory and honor of him

CONTENTS

HECKER IN GERMANY

HECKER IN AMERICA

Translator's Preface

This translation of Dr. Sabine Freitag's biography of Friedrich Hecker was made possible by the John A. A. Hecker Fund at the St. Louis Mercantile Library at the University of Missouri – St. Louis. This fund was created in honor and memory of John Arthur Alexander Hecker, who was the youngest child of Friedrich Hecker's son, Erwin Hecker. The Fund was established by John A. A. Hecker's daughter Gladys Hecker Myles; his grand-daughter Marjorie Myles Ivey; his grandson James Hecker Myles and Jim's wife Andrea Jay Myles; and Jim's and Andrea's children Stephanie L. Myles and Carolyn A. Myles. Their support of this project in tandem with the dedication and diligence John Neal Hoover, Director of the St. Louis Mercantile Library at the University of Missouri – St. Louis, has resulted in a biography that may give Americans insight into the life of Friedrich Hecker, who was the emblematic hero of the German Revolution of 1848 and who spent the latter half of his life in the United States as an extremely active American citizen.

In 1999 when I wrote a biographical article about Friedrich Hecker for the new *American National Biography*, I was stating the truth when I said that at that time there was no complete biography of this politically involved German-American. In part, this was because he lived in a typically rural American setting, in Summerfield, Illinois. It was also because most of the key source material for a biography rested in a blue trunk in the basement of George S. Hecker, the grandchild of Friedrich Hecker's son Arthur. In the 1980s, George Hecker donated these materials to the Western Historical Manuscript Collection at the University of Missouri – St. Louis, where they were ultimately joined with other Hecker documents previously held by the Missouri Historical Society.

It was my task to organize and catalogue all these Hecker materials. Most of the papers represented an effort by Alice Hecker Reynolds, the daughter of Fredrich Hecker's son Alexander, to fashion from family sources a biography of her grandfather as an American; however, these efforts had never borne the intended fruit. A grant from the Federal German Archives in Koblenz made it possible to microfilm the Hecker collection, making it available to German researchers, who had already been alerted by an article on the collection published in the *Zeitschrift für die Geschichte des Oberrheins* by Prof. Dr. Franz X. Vollmer of the Pädagogische Hochschule of Freiburg im Breisgau. Dr. Vollmer and I were brought together by the energy and insight of my old Freiburg friend Renate Liessem.

When I organized the Hecker collection, Germans often asked whether I myself intended to write Friedrich Hecker's biography. The reason that I declined lies before you in this translation of Dr. Freitag's work. She has orchestrated her sources far better than I ever could have, and her diligence has made often-obscure materials sing with the political and cultural story of two continents. As is often the case with biographies of German-Americans, her work is potentially a window that may be looked through from either side, so that a German might use it to see America, and an American might use it to see Germany – as well as an America that he or she might not know.

I was able to complete this translation only with the able editorial assistance of Amy Branch, then a graduate student in English at the University of Missouri – St. Louis, as well as my former student Elizabeth Bowling, nee Sims. Gregory Ames, Curator of the Barriger Collection at the St. Louis Mercantile Library at the University of Missouri – St. Louis, provided additional editorial assistance. In keeping with standardized English monographs, I have condensed Dr. Freitag's extensive footnotes. Also for the sake of brevity, I have not included the author's summary of her method of research which relates to the book's original dissertation format. Responsibility for this condensation is my own.

SR

Author's Foreword

This study was accepted as a dissertation in history at the Johann Wolfgang Goethe University [Frankfurt a. M.] in the winter semester of 1995-96. It was slightly shortened and reworked for German publication.

My special thanks go to Professor Peter Wende, who oversaw my doctoral work, and to Professor Lothar Gall, who was the second reader.

Many people and institutions have contributed to the completion of this study. I have profited greatly from the advice of Steven Rowan of the University of Missouri – St. Louis. I am thankful to Katharina Becker, Barbara Wolbring and Walter Altvater for much encouragement and for their critical review of this extensive manuscript. I would like to thank George S. Hecker, Friedrich Hecker's great-grandson, for permitting me to see documents that have remained in the possession of the family. Gretchen and Jim Bohman provided me with hospitality in St. Louis. Roland Paul enlightened me on a trip through Illinois about Belleville's German community. Andreas Daum substantially eased the difficult time shortly before publication with his trans-Atlantic courier service and some important references.

Of those working in the libraries and archives I have utilized, these are to be mentioned in particular: Fred Baumann of the Manuscript Division at the Library of Congress in Washington, D. C.; Lou Ann James of the Belleville Public Library in Belleville, Illinois; Margret Heilbrunn of the New York Historical Society; Daniel Kress of the Staatsarchiv des Kantons Basel-Stadt; and Mrs. Jeschke of the Bundesarchiv, Aussenstelle Frankfurt a. M. Further thanks go to the assistants at the National Archives in Washington, D.C.; the Missouri Historical Society in St. Louis, Missouri; and the Generallandesarchiv and the Landesbibliothek in Karlsruhe.

The *Hessische Graduiertenförderung* has made a substantial contribution to the completion of this work by providing a two-year stipend. Publication was made much easier by the cheerful and unbureaucratic financial support of Mr. Heinrich Vetter of Mannheim and the *Mannheimer Versorgungs- und Verkehrs-AG (MVV)*. I want to thank them both.

I must thank to the German Historical Institute in Washington, D.C., for accepting this work in its series *Transatlantische Historische Studien.* I owe the editor of the series, Petra Marquardt-Bigman, special thanks for the enthusiasm with which she adopted the manuscript in such a brief time.

London, December 1997

Sabine Freitag

INTRODUCTION

When the people ask, "Does Hecker still live?"
You should say, "Yes, he lives still,"
He hangs on no tree, from no rope,
But only on his dream of a free republic."[1]

Everybody knows about Hecker. Even those with little knowledge of the revolutionary events during the years 1848 and 1849 know the name because of a cult that began when Hecker was no longer living on German soil. Hecker became a part of the folklore remembered from the German democratic movement, which came to a sudden end 150 years ago after having barely blossomed. The Hecker cult is still significant as a social and political phenomenon, and anyone interested in it will learn a great deal about the social roots of the Revolution of 1848 and the dominant political sense of its core supporters.[2] Yet when looking for the "real" Hecker, one has to start by carefully distinguishing between his own biography and the cult that developed about him, particularly about his name, even if in the end one concedes that the two cannot be separated, because the cult inevitably influenced the biography. Spurred by public opinion and civic virtue, Hecker's efforts as a political citizen to make his radical self-creation real, show there was little distance between his own style of life and his external pose.

It might be true that, because of the personality cult, Hecker's importance for the revolution of 1848 has been exaggerated. Rudolf Muhs, for one, after extensive investigation, determines Hecker's accomplishments to be rather small in comparison to many other men's. Hecker's early departure from the revolutionary process through his swift emigration to the United States in September 1848 prevented him from being associated in any way with the revolution's failure; at least he avoided discrediting himself. He was no longer put to the test like Lorenz Brentano, who was briefly entrusted with erecting a republican government in early summer 1849, or Amand Goegg, who was responsible for an essential part of the mobilization of the masses through organizing associations. There can be little objection to this. However, saying that "a scholarly Hecker biography would contribute little to the study of the Revolution" is not compelling. It is precisely through the description and comparison of Hecker's political activities in both Germany and America that we can sharpen our historical knowledge of the radical democratic movement, of the dominant understanding of republicanism before the German Revolution.

This book has no interest in excessively promoting Hecker's importance to the German Revolution of 1848-49. For this reason Part I concentrates more on Hecker's political development, the biographical and intellectual influences that formed him, than on the course of events in Baden, thus necessary correcting the one-sided notion of Hecker, "the man of deeds," and his role in the "myth of the German Republic" projected on him by contemporaries as soon as he left the National Assembly. Amidst an actual, existing republic, Hecker's later life in the United States of America – which had been an attractive alternative to him even before the Revolution – again provides insight into the republican assumptions about German leaders before their emigration, as well as their continuing self-perception and political presumptions. It is also important to know whether judgments about political developments after 1848-49 were formulated from the point of view of a citizen of the American Union or a subject of some European monarchy. Finally, the political emigration of the German Revolution to the United States, the story of a tiny intellectual elite that constituted a mere fraction of the grand stream of German emigrants at the start of the 1850s, is an extension of the history of the Revolution itself, although admittedly outside German borders. Exquisite care was taken within Germany's borders to ignore the continual republican critique from emigrants across the ocean. Particularly after the foundation of the *Reich,* for example German historians held that Hecker had resigned himself to a self-contained life as a farmer in the American Midwest after the failure of the German Revolution. But in a way the memory of an alternative form of state emigrated along with the republican elite, and with them any constructive republican opposition – opposition that later was almost utterly lacking in Germany. When Hecker visited Germany in 1873, he remarked to a friend, "Republicans lurk on only as isolated specimens living in dark caves, like the last dinosaurs, and democrats are thinly sown upon the ground, visible only now and then like birds of passage." When he publicly offered this criticism, the National Liberal press saw him as someone who did not recognize the signs of the times, a man returning from a magical slumber of twenty-five years to a world that he obviously did not understand. He was never forgiven for withholding praise of "Germany's greatness."[3]

With Hecker one has to deal with the perennial question in historiography of whether the German democratic and republican tradition has grown from its own roots or is only a "variety of liberalism," its radicalized, more consistent ultimate extension, so to speak. Hecker was certainly one of the intellectual elite of Baden; but he did not belong to that Praetorian Guard of autonomous theoreticians such as Gustav von Struve, Arnold Ruge or Julius Fröbel, whose political concepts were used by Peter Wende to demonstrate the coherence of their radical democratic theory. Rather, Hecker's life story demonstrates a continuous development from constitutional liberal into a democratic radical, combining elements of pre-Revolutionary liberalism with a coherent republicanism, and pursuing the second direction ever more decisively over time.

In this context, Hecker's republicanism did not end with the demand for a republican form of state and administration, but went on to define a citizen of a republic, with specific preconditions. Rather than succumbing to seduction by Struve, Hecker went through his own process, as Heinrich Scharp sought to show in his neglected thesis of 1923, contradicting the notion long made socially acceptable by Ludwig Häusser. Hecker was socially more conservative than Struve in many ways, and his proverbial stubbornness spoke against too great an influence by Struve. This book asserts that men such as Adam von Itzstein and Carl von Rotteck were much more important for Hecker. In any case Hecker resembled such "technicians of politics" as Robert Blum and Karl Vogt, for whom the practical use of political theory was to provide themselves with a usable basis for argument. In contrast to the intellectual Struve, Hecker was a man of deeds, more interested in questions of practical application, and any theoretical superstructure was often lacking in stringency. In his eclectic procedure Hecker adapted anything that seemed useful.[4]

The influences that molded Hecker were so numerous – typical for the pre-Revolutionary period – that it is difficult to assign each element its proper weight. Among them were geographic influences such as the nearness of France, which embodied among other things the *Code Napoléon*, and the example of Switzerland, a league of frugal citizens who truly combined prosperity and personal virtue and who served as models for many. Theoretical influences also showed in Hecker's clear openness to the Enlightenment of the eighteenth century, often derived through Rotteck or Schlosser's historiography. However, Hecker always subordinated theoretical arguments to practical intentions. To be sure, he did declare that the first goal was realizing principles; but in him one cannot find the abstraction from reality often found with such an orientation. "He did not succumb to the analysis of philosophical questions," Friedrich Münch, Karl Follen's brother-in-law, recalled of his fellow farmer Hecker. "He was an infidel of the highest degree and completely satisfied with the view that life was composed only of energy and matter, and he neither demanded nor recognized anything further." Hecker's work in the Baden State Assembly or the concepts of civil-service reform that he later developed in America, both of which are addressed in this work, specifically demonstrated his interest in forming political institutions. In addition he was particularly interested in political mechanisms protecting the due-process state that he sought to establish. He involved himself in concepts of reciprocal control, protection against the abuse of power and the erection of committees and boards that would in the last analysis not only bring about an efficient and frugal public administration, but also create the kind of high-quality political institutions that a democratic constitutional state essentially depended on for existence. Demonstrating his practical understanding as a jurist, Hecker once asserted that lawyers were irreplaceable in legislation because they knew from experience how to tell what a law was worth in practice.

If Hecker himself had ever mentioned who influenced him the most theoretically, it is obvious that the name of Carl von Rotteck would have passed his lips. In America Hecker later described this man as his great teacher, although he did not copy him slavishly and always made his own decisions. Hecker's support of the general right to vote, for example, opposed Rotteck's defense of a suffrage based on property. In terms of the law of reason, what Hecker gained from Rotteck was classic pre-Revolutionary liberalism – the drive to increase political participation and to protect against arbitrary rule – which remained with all liberals once their differing conceptions of socio-economic questions were subtracted. Hecker never really discarded Rotteck's dualism of government and the governed. He did not see direct democracy as an expression of radical popular sovereignty worth striving for, but rather desired a popular sovereignty filtered through representation, restricted by the division of powers and basic rights. Starting with the liberal axiom of the individual's autonomy and one's inviolable sphere of rights, Hecker rallied again and again for human rights that protected this area from intervention by the state, especially in his criticisms of German conditions. In this popular sovereignty, nothing was abstract and absolute. Rather it was a simple numerical concept – the sum of sovereign individuals. In America Hecker was always "one of the two million sovereigns of Illinois," and he could not have made a more pregnant response to the question of whether he would visit Bismarck in Berlin during his visit to Germany than when he said, "What are you thinking about. ... how can I as a republican sovereign visit the servant of a sovereign?"

Hecker shared with the liberals – and in this the radical democrats did not differ – a high regard for a constitution. To him it was the prime condition for the potential state, and before anything else, the politics of a republic had to measure itself publicly according to its principles. But the constitution was not an unalterable holy of holies. It had "nothing to do with heaven, nothing with the interior of the person, nothing with the conscience." Instead, "its realm is of this world, it is the law that defines ... the state." Thus, a constitution always had to be capable of revision in the light of new experiences, in keeping with the needs and demands of the times, as Jefferson and Paine had formulated it, and as Hecker himself repeated in self-defense in the *Rising of the People in Baden for the German Republic in Early 1848 [Erhebung des Volkes in Baden für die deutsche Republik im Frühjahr 1848]*. The integrity of the constitution was the point of leverage and support for pre-revolutionary liberalism, and Rotteck's dualism had nourished the belief that this constitution was threatened by a police state that infringed on the citizen's guaranteed rights. "We, the liberals, are the conservatives," Hecker once declared in the Second Baden Chamber. "We desire the integrity of the constitution, we want to make it into truth. We do not desire to intervene in the crown's prerogatives, but on the other hand, we do not want to lose a single right. We hold fast to the rights that the constitution grants to the people and will not waver from that by a hair's breadth." The integrity of the constitution could be guaranteed only through the use of force, and every imbalance to one side had to be put aside. Hecker also spoke in America on behalf of the preservation of this balance between the various powers, campaigning against presumptuous executives such as President Andrew Johnson or President Ulysses Grant, or against legislatures desiring to extend their control beyond propriety at the cost of the executive, as in the conflict between President Rutherford B. Hayes and the American Congress. In this relationship between the citizen and the constitution that Dolf Sternberger calls "constitutional patriotism," – the identification with the process of the state that is seen as the precondition for one's own existence – there lay for Hecker a personal, concrete call for action. For him the preservation of the state and the protection of the constitution were the supreme commandments, and his proposal of a citizen militia in 1848 and his participation in the American Civil War show most strikingly what this meant for a "political citizen" such as himself.[5]

Hecker drew the moral motivation for his patriotism from the teachings about virtue in humanism and the Enlightenment, which, in turn, were based on the political theory of antiquity. The ideal of citizen participation, meaning commitment to the common good and the surrender of private, individual desires and interests, was part of his republicanism. It constantly went beyond mere thinking and demanded concrete action. Hecker's patriotism, on the other hand, was nothing more than civic virtue that arose from the common good and was directed at the state – entirely in keeping with the teachings of Rotteck and Welcker's *Staatslexikon*. Hecker had little difficulty combining his individualistic liberal values with an obviously pre-individualistic, collectivist republicanism. He was a particularly good test case of what Paul Nolte has recently demonstrated as Baden's communal liberalism.[6] Only ten years after the Revolution, when speaking of the radical democrats, Julius Fröbel described them as a "combination of modern ideas with old, historical republicanism," an orientation toward a model of a community's future created by the active political participation of its members, which was then applied to the idea of the order of the state. Whatever the case was with "experienced republicanism" in Baden communities, there was no doubt that this model had great relevance, not least because in the end the virtues of enlightenment and education were thought to depend on a morality defined by freedom. Nolte rightly notes the eminently political implications of this concept, which implies a political community that should culminate in a homogeneous civil society constituting itself of those of its members oriented toward the common good. Many pre-Revolutionary liberals referred to this concept for merely strategic and rhetorical reasons, but for Hecker this "doubled" republicanism – the moral challenge for a change of one's own political life and the genuine accomplishment of a reform of state and government – became a "morality," as it was strikingly formulated in one memorial speech.[7]

"Can one really blame the patriot if he advances from absolute monarchy to a republic?" Hecker asked the Second Chamber of Baden during discussions on political amnesty in March 1848. "Could you blame such a man who, perhaps inspired by *the study of classical antiquity*, having chosen the republic as the best form of the state, breaks into a cheer for his republican ideas? You cannot." Hecker praised Mannheim during his German tour of 1873 as the city where he received his first "impressions of liberty," where he heard of Gaius and Sempronius [Gracchus], where he read of the last Roman [Cato the Younger] who, "because he did not wish to experience the end of liberty, pressed the dagger into his own breast." This was more than a histrionic homage to his old hometown; it was a reference to the origin of his republican ideal through enlightenment and education. The descriptions of the Greek polis, but even more of the Roman Republic, provided him with those images and presumptions with which he illuminated Rousseau's concept of popular sovereignty. There was little heed to

Benjamin Constant's warning not to confuse ancient and modern liberty. Hecker was proud to make it his way of life to be a complete political citizen in the republican sense.

Nolte is right to argue that this concept of the political citizen, aiming at an ever-greater number of active participants, also had as its goal a politically homogeneous community into which everyone might be accepted who distinguished himself by selfless commitment for the common good. This concept was placed under severe pressure after 1840 through socioeconomic changes and realities. Growing social inequality made the realization of a planned society and a state based on civic virtue and equal political participation seem increasingly impossible. The radicals alone would have defended their plan earnestly, even without hope of success. But although the preconditions for realizing this political model of the future no longer appeared possible in Europe, particularly after the Revolution of 1848-49, many Forty-Eighter emigrants of a radical republican persuasion believed it would still work in America. Hecker, in particular, saw his views confirmed through his experiences in the frugal milieu of independent farmers in the American Midwest. Twenty years later he would be confronted with the developments of a capitalist market economy based on competition and unequal capital accumulation that had already marked the horizon in Baden in the 1840s. And his many years of experience in America in the meantime made it unmistakably clear that the United States was neither a Greek polis nor the Roman Republic. But Hecker unwaveringly continued to judge his new homeland according to the internalized standard of his ideal republicanism. He did not do this either naïvely or blindly, but with a consciousness of a political order that was as desirable as ever, and that had to be pursued. Again and again he applied this model to American conditions, and his model of explanation and interpretation continually showed his study of antiquity. Failings such as the corrupt American bureaucracy or the rising domination of materialism were branded as the great perils of the republic that would in the end lead to its fall. The solutions offered by Hecker were taken from his analysis of ancient sources, in the best case refreshed by authors such as Montesquieu or Jefferson. The call for virtue and frugality, for example, returned again and again, particularly in the 1870s, times that were as difficult in the United States as in Europe.

As for many other pre-Revolutionary liberals, history was for Hecker a *magistra vitae*, a mistress of life, not be interpreted but merely deeply studied to draw out its teachings. Hecker did so his entire life. In history, he once said in the Baden Second Chamber, "the comprehending man ... draws counsel ... in the great complexities and processes of life, because everything that is has already been, if only in another outer form." Even in his later years, Hecker was proud of never having interrupted his classical studies. Contemporaries praised his stupendous knowledge and his easy use of it. It is no surprise that Hecker emigrated so quickly and directly to a settlement in the American Midwest famous for its "Latin Farmers" – the classically educated German republicans who had already emigrated from Germany in the 1830s due to dissatisfaction or persecution. They intended to continue their study of antiquity alongside their agricultural pursuits, realizing the ideal of a landowning and hence independent citizen. This highlighted another facet of Hecker's republicanism. Coupled with the ownership of land as a foundation of civic virtue, derived from antiquity and favored by Jefferson, Hecker stressed a frugal life without the corrupting luxury that would endanger the republic. This played as great a role as the assumption that one could only preserve virtue on the land, far from the corruption of cities.[8]

Until late into the 1870s Hecker believed that neither his republicanism nor his orientation to the middle class – also a result of reading Aristotle – was threatened by industrial development; he persisted in the progressive optimism of the Enlightenment. "Time carries heavy swords," he wrote to a German friend in Chicago on the eve of the American Civil War, "a story is starting to unroll that is without equal, the century appears to want to industrialize. I am happy to be alive ... that I may experience the development of things." For Hecker industrialization meant rising prosperity and the opening of markets to world trade, both of these should set in motion a worldwide democratization. Here he was following Adam Smith, Kant and Thomas Paine. His faith "in a solidarity of democratic principles and interests" caused him to see a great opportunity in the opening of markets and in the homogenizing force of world trade. In Mannheim in 1873 he said that every bale of goods coming to Germany from America spread the message of the republican form of state and its economic prosperity. Economic exchange, the mutual relations between individual states, would make the monarchical form of state impossible over the short or long term because the exchange of thought followed the exchange of goods. "The new means of transportation of the new trade life cannot be digested by monarchism," he asserted after his return from Germany. "They devour it, until the king is only a tolerated puppet with crown and scepter on the throne, and the sword is with the people." When he was confronted by discussion of a new press law in Germany, he shook his head in disbelief. "In this age of rapid national and international transportation and exchange of ideas from mouth to mouth, it is entirely unbelievable that anyone still believes it possible to put the human spirit into such a pitiful straight jacket and suffocate it."[9]

Even in the case of the founding of the German *Reich*, Hecker hoped that the internal market that would arise would take over this democratizing function within the country. He felt betrayed in many of his hopes by Bismarck's later protective tariff policy, under which American expansion also suffered. "Bismarck has trumped nonsense with his mad seesaw of protective tariff for industry in addition to protection for agrarians," Hecker bitterly wrote to a friend.[10] The fact that Hecker completely identified at the end of his life with the economic imperialistic course of the Republican Party, even contributing to publicists' grandiose promotions for constructing the Panama Canal under American leadership, had something to do with this basic conviction of democratization.

This presumption could not be brought entirely into harmony with his republicanism, however. Prosperity could degrade into luxury, and luxury in turn endangered the republic. In many places it became obvious how much the formation of a class society as a result of industrialization produced the usual conflicts, and how hard it was to be oriented to a model that did not keep up with the times. But, in contrast to most liberals in the German *Reich*, Hecker believed that in America he could continue to hold onto the commitment to the middle class that had been shared by liberals and radicals alike before 1848.[11] His hope for a prosperous, independent, stabilizing middle class that would find its way in an industrial society – a society whose core as ever would be farmers as small, independent entrepreneurs and into which the workers in urban centers would somehow find their way by means of the American slogan "help yourself" – always seemed more possible in America than in Germany.

Here again a correction of the popular interpretation of Hecker is necessary. At the Heidelberg assembly of 1848, his eagerly cited statement that he wanted "Freedom, the whole freedom for all, *in whatever form of state it is to be achieved. But no freedom for the privileged or the rich alone; I am, if I would name it in one word, a Social Democrat,"[12] has led many in a false direction. If Hecker had remained in Germany or returned there, it is certain that there is one party in which he would not have been found: the Social Democratic Party of August Bebel and Wilhelm Liebknecht. For him socialism was a continuation of the monarchical system under a different label. A regulatory, order-producing state intervening from on high in all areas of life violated both Hecker's principle of the "most free self-determination" that distinguished the "republican." It also violated the right to property, always significant to him.[13] As a measure against the danger associated with the formation of a class society, a conscienceless industrial plutocracy and an impoverished proletariat, it is no accident that Hecker praised associations in America, as well, because they corresponded most closely with his own presumptions of self-determined initiative and organization. In the late 1870s he was still speaking in favor of farm cooperatives of families desiring to settle in the American West. But even here the individualism associated with ownership remained central. The families exclusively worked their own land and organized solely for the purposes of better supply and marketing potential. For Hecker it was a failing of Germans that they sought their total salvation from the government, the state, instead of acting on their own behalf as happened in the United States.

Hecker's perennial fostering of associations had a theoretical element. In the Chamber debates of 1848 and earlier, Hecker dealt with the theme of associations. It has long been assumed that this demonstrates Struve's influence and his inclination to the French socialists. But what Hecker defined as "socialism," the "most equitable possible prosperity of all," was not to be accomplished by state intervention in growing concentrations of capital and deepening mass poverty. The social question was not to be answered by the state at all, but through self-organization by citizens. "Cooperation" was the "great idea" of the times, and "associations [Genossenschaften]" were a form for its realization.[14] Of these terms, Association [Assoziation] is the older word, and Genossenschaft was only regularly used in the second half of the nineteenth century, but Hecker used both concepts before 1848. Hecker was a jurist, as was the case with many Forty-Eighters. His plea on behalf of associations did not derive from French socialists, from whom he borrowed only occasionally; rather it derived from the legal scholarship at German universities concerning Germanic and Roman law.

Two characteristics made the law of associations, combined with Old Germanic freedom since Montesquieu, so attractive. First, there was the national momentum of a German law or "people's law,"[15] idealized as a law arising from the people themselves and not imposed on them in an fashion, as Roman law had been. Second, the gathering of equals that was presumed in associations had a democratic principle; the members, equal in duties and rights, could together accomplish their common goals more effectively. Even if a representative organ were created to represent interests to the outside world, the common power still remained in the hands of all members.

It was not far from the right of association to justifying communities of opinion, or parties. For Hecker associations were so obvious a means of political pressure that there was almost nothing for which associations could not be formed, for or against. It remains for the reader of this study to discover what strange blossoms his enthusiasm brought forth.

In contrast to German historical research, American historical research has occupied itself heavily with the political emigrants of the revolution of 1848-49, called the Forty-Eighters.[16] It was always clear that this small political elite did not really represent the great emigration storm of the 1850s, which left the old homeland for economic reasons. The Forty-Eighters had superior educations, an edge that contributed to many of the political exiles becoming outstanding representatives for the interests of German-Americans in the course of their American lives. Whether directly through political office or indirectly through their journalistic activity in German-American newspapers, the emigrated Forty-Eighters contributed as a group to German-Americans' disproportionately strong voice in American politics. This fact led earlier research to overestimate the influence of German votes in Abraham Lincoln's election, and only more recent investigation has corrected this presumption. The commonplaces of "liberty and unity" brought from Europe by the political emigrants had been assumed until now to be sufficient reason for their great engagement in American politics. It was believed, for example, that their struggle against slavery was the struggle against injured egalitarianism, and that their commitment to the American Union in the Civil War showed their concern for the establishment and defense of unity. These evaluations can be seen now as superficial; in fact subtler motivations played a role. One of the tasks of this study to present Hecker's German and American lives together and show where there were continuities, revisions or breaks in his thought. The political concepts that Hecker pursued in Germany have therefore been chosen with an eye toward recurring themes in his American years, to show Hecker's closeness to or distance from American politics.

The Forty-Eighters came from a European context, and they brought their European presumptions with them to the United States. It is a thesis of this study that pre-Revolutionary liberals found a very great deal to like in the ideology of the nascent Republican Party, because there were similarities and parallels of a principled nature. Their struggle against the slave aristocracy in the South was therefore less about black emancipation than about white emancipation because it was intended, above all else, to secure the expansion of the white middle class. It was concerned with eliminating an economic system that not only was diametrically opposed to Northern concepts of free labor, but also established a two-class society of a few very rich upon a broad mass of the dependent poor. This would have prevented what the Forty-Eighters saw as their ideal, which they believed was virtually achieved in the American West: the erection of a politically stable middle class.

For European refugees, the attraction of the Republican Party lay in its specifically middle-class sensibility, stressing autonomy, the elevation of free white labor, the "right to rise" repeatedly proclaimed by Lincoln and the winning of personal property. After the Civil War, when this ideology was threatened by the formation of a class society, a portion of the Republicans split off – including Carl Schurz and Friedrich Hecker – in order to combat the political system that had been established in the interim and that made these expectations increasingly impossible for the middle class, for men such as themselves. It was only logical for men such as Schurz and Hecker, who saw the protection of the middle class as crucial, that in the face of these efforts any guarantee of freedmen's rights in the Southern states had to yield.

Other connections can be shown between Hecker's European origins and his American engagement. The extreme hostility to officialdom that Hecker brought with him from Baden over his experiences with the "Blittersdorf System" – he once remarked in a motion concerning officials that there were "offices from which a sort of legitimate suspicion cannot be separated"[17] – resulted in America in his efforts for an American civil-service reform, which remarkably enough became a life theme for Schurz as well as Hecker. According to Hecker a reform of officialdom had to lead to transforming the state administration into something civil and make officials what they should be, which was servants of the state and not an extended arm of monarchs or corrupt republican governments. This would not only bring an end, purely for economic considerations, to an administration that was as costly and inefficient in America as in Germany; through the introduction of the productivity principle, the naming of officials would also be made as free as possible from arbitrary control by parties or presidents. At the same time Hecker expected reform to better chances for advancement for people of his own nationality.

The most surprising continuity between European liberalism and American engagement was Hecker's "American *Kulturkampf*" ["Cultural War"]. His vehemently promoted demand for a strict division of church and state rested on the idea that a conflict of loyalty existed between the citizen and the Catholic, who was dependent on Rome; in this conflict the state always found itself in the weaker position. This concern was further determined by Hecker's republican presumptions. The state had to be able to count on the undivided loyalty of its citizens who had to be educated and trained in such a way that they saw the interests of the state as their own. The school must achieve the education for citizenship without the church's influence.

> In a republic with democratic principles such as the Union, every citizen is not just called but obligated to participate in the administration of the concerns of the people, to govern and to administer. The republican constitution presumes this, and her existence rests on the intelligence of the citizens... A free school system, promoting spirit and research, is of ten times greater importance in a republic than in a monarchy.[18]

When Hecker believed strict separation to be threatened by the growing influence of the Catholic Church and the increased establishment of parochial schools in the United States, he launched a *Kulturkampf* whose intensity caused some amazement even among his contemporaries. His hostility to the Catholic Church, bordering on a pathology, was motivated in his later years by something further: the fear of the manipulation of uneducated masses, who as "voting cattle" would support the traditionally pro-Catholic Democratic Party. Here he became a direct apologist for the Republican Party.

Hecker also showed himself in complete agreement with the heritage of German liberals in his discussion on the vote for women. His lecture on this subject, presented in the largest cities of the Union, was not different in the least from corresponding lectures of German professors in the old Fatherland.

***

When Hecker died few of the National Liberal newspapers were ready to attribute him any significance for Germany. However, in the United States he was honored as one of its best citizens as well as a fighter for German-American interests. In America it was presumed that Hecker played an important role within the group of exiled Forty-Eighters and that he had taken an enthusiastic part in all the decisive political conflicts of American politics from 1848 on: the founding of the Republican Party, the

Civil War, the Liberal Republican reform movement and the later presidential campaigns, in each of which the Republicans won. On top of that he
remained a concerned polemicist for the cultural needs of German-
Americans and committed himself as decisively against nativism as he did
against efforts at temperance or the introduction of Sabbath legislation. For
him everything was politics. Even as a lecturer he believed himself to be
actively in the service of enlightening the people, just as he did it in
Germany in the 1840s. And so, when the many-volumed *Deutsch-Amerikanische
Conversations-Lexicon,* edited by Alexander Schem, appeared in the early
1870s, seeking to unite all the names and concepts of sigificance for
German-Americans, the article on Friedrich Hecker was as large as the one
following it on G. W. F. Hegel. One could get the impression that Hecker
was indeed more important in this land of political pragmatism than that
great philosopher.[19]

It is a matter for discussion whether or not Hecker's sense of independence, the same sense that led him to America, was always politically wise.
"The man could certainly act *[Handeln],* but he was born for neither negotiation *[Verhandeln]* nor mediation *[Unterhandeln],"* commented a memorial
that was actually on his side politically. This simply repeated what Ludwig
Häusser rightly said long before, when he remarked that Hecker's essential
weakness was that he had a poor understanding of "subordinating himself
to the party majority and its tactics."[20] This political arrogance unquestion-
ably dictated a large number of Hecker's personal life-decisions, resulting
in disadvantageous entanglements. Hecker himself would more likely have
described this not as arrogance but as a marked sense of liberty, and would
have attributed it to a strict commitment to principles. This element of his
character, this uncompromising orientation to principles, this application of
a model of virtue even to the point of giving up or denying personal needs,
is not entirely subject to a psychological interpretation, any more than his
perennial attitude of reacting to political and personal crises with precipitate and ill-considered action. Launching the volunteers' march was the
most famous example, to be sure. But his journey to Algeria in early 1847,
his great physical exertion at farming in the first years of exile, his voluntary
participation in the American Civil War, finally his walking out of the
Liberal Republican convention, clearly redolent of the pre-Parliament – all
vouched for Hecker's impatience and hotheadedness. He displayed a rigid,
ascetic self-control alongside complete loss of control. While Hecker was
primarily saturated with the ideas of the Enlightenment, he overwhelmingly played the role of a secularized romantic.

As his friend Caspar Butz rightly noted, "He was a man of complete disbelief in regard to religion."[21] Although baptized a Catholic, he received no "Christian" education even in his childhood years. The need for a religious emphasis was fulfilled for him, to overstate it somewhat, in his political faith. The doctrine of republican virtue was his morality, and his hope for a republic was his confession of faith. "I am a faithful, unimprovable adherent to the republican form of state and cannot doubt it,"[22] he once wrote to Carl Schurz. He was very proud of the coherence of the life he had lived, even when his arrogance and stubbornness drew upon him the accusations of the German National Liberals that he had basically never been a politician, or if a politician then a very poor one. Hecker had as little regret about his emigration to America, the offspring of consistency, as his fellow exile, Franz Sigel, who specifically emphasized in his will: "It is my wish that I shall be buried … on American soil, in the country of my choice."[23] The United States of America was also Hecker's country of choice, a land in which, like his teacher Rotteck, he wished to see "the main demands of a pure theory" realized. Although Hecker was not blind to the inadequacies of his adopted homeland, the republican institutions that he found there were crafted in such a way that he was guaranteed an individual and political liberty that could easily motivate his love of country and his civic virtue. "I have never regarded it to be a misfortune that I have been thrown onto these coasts," Hecker wrote to Schurz two years before his death: "Over there I would have been continually abused in my sense of independence, or put in a monarchical jail for safe keeping. Besides, my snout was too deformed for a muzzle."[24]

1 This is the first verse of an anti-Hecker song written by reactionary students but later adopted by democrats as a theme song for their own cause.
2 On the Hecker cult, see Peter Assion, "Der Heckercult. Ein Volksheld von 1848 im Wandel seiner geschichtlichen Präsenz," *Zeitschrift für Volkskunde* 87 (1991), 53-76; idem, "'Es lebe Hecker! Stoßet an!' Die Popularität und Verehrung Friedrich Heckers von 1848/49 bis zur Gegenwart," Alfred G. Frei, ed., *Friedrich Hecker in den USA. Eine deutsch-amerikanische Spurensicherung* (Konstanz, 1993), 117-34.
3 Rudolf Muhs, "Heckermythos und Revolutionsforschung," ZGO 134 (1986), 422-41. The number of political refugees going to America has been estimated at between three and four thousand; for a closer definition of this group, see Jörg Nagler, *Fremont contra Lincoln. Die deutsch-amerikanische Opposition in der republikanischen Partei während des amerikanischen Bürgerkrieges* (Frankfurt, 1984), 292-93. FH to Charles Söhner, Wildbad im Schwarzwald, 18 July 1873, FHP, box 3, folder 38.
4 Peter Wende, *Radikalismus im Vormärz. Untersuchungen zur politischen Theorie der frühen deutschen Demokratie* (Wiesbaden, 1975). Heinrich Scharp, *Friedrich Hecker, ein deutscher Demokrat*, Ph. D. diss., Frankfurt a. M., 1923. Caspar Butz, "Erinnerungen an Friedrich Hecker," *TWP*, part 2, 8 May 1881. Wende, *Radikalismus*, 33.
5 Friedrich Münch on FH, *TWP*, 5 April 1881. FH, GL, 1870, 208 ("Blätter und Blüthen"); Butz, "Erinnerungen," part 2. From the address on the separation of state and church held on 8 January 1874 in St. Louis, printed in the *TWP*, 9 January 1874. VSB, 68. öS (14 May 1844), 236.

⁶ See Paul Nolte, "Bürgerideal, Gemeinde und Republik. 'Klassischer Republikanismus' im frühen deutschen Liberalismus," *HZ* 154 (1992), 609-56; idem, "Gemeindeliberalismus. Zur lokalen Entstehung und sozialen Verankerung der liberalen Partei in Baden 1831-1855," *HZ* 152 (1991), 57-93; idem, *Gemeindebürgertum und Liberalismus in Baden 1800-1850*, Kritische Studien zur Geschichtswissenschaft, vol. 102 (Göttingen, 1994); see also Sabine Freitag, "Schwarzwälder Republik von Thiengen als Polis," Ius commune, vol. 22 (1996), 367-79.

⁷ Julius Fröbel, preface to *Theorie der Politik, als Ergebnis einer erneuten Prüfung demokratischer Lehrmeinungen*, vol. 1 (Vienna, 1861). Nolte, "Gemeindeliberalismus," 225.

⁸ *VSB*, 39, öS (16 March 1848), 220; my emphasis. Hecker's farewell address to Mannheim, delivered on 26 August 1873, printed, among other places, in the *Neue Badische Landeszeitung*, 26 August 1873, FHP, box 4, folder 41; also reprinted in the *TWP*, 13 September 1873, and the TISZ, 15 September 1873. See Benjamin Constant, "De la liberté des anciens comparée à celle des modernes," in idem, *De l'esprit de conquête et de l'usurpation* (Paris, 1986), 265 ff. VSB, 70. öS (18 May 1844), 301. See Hecker's remarks on this in GL, 1874, 526; also the record of a lecture in the *TISZ*, 27 December 1872. Hecker "never completely neglected scholarship even in his American farmer life." He himself described his life as that of a "private tutor" (FH to Charles Söhner, Summerfield, 7 December 1875, FHP, box 3, folder 38).

⁹ FH to Georg Schneider, Lebanon, St. Clair County, Ill., 16 May 1859, Georg Schneider Papers, Chicago Historical Society, Chicago. Hecker's farewell address, as above. FH to Charles Söhner, 14 November 1872, FHP, box 3, folder 38. Hecker's second letter from Germany of 7 June 1873, printed in the TISZ, 30 June 1873.

¹⁰ FH to Charles Söhner, Summerfield, St. Clair County, Ill., 4 January 1880, FHP, box 3, folder 38.

¹¹ Cf., for example, Struve's ideal of the middle class, Wende, *Radikalismus,* 118-19; in general, Lothar Gall, "Liberalismus und 'Bürgerliche Gesellschaft.' Zu Charakter und Entwicklung der liberalen Bewegung in Deutschland," *HZ* 220 (1975), 324-56; on the ancient topos of mesoi and the idea of the middle class in early liberalism, also Nolte, "Gemeindeliberalismus," 214-15.

¹² Cited by Karl Obermann, *Einheit und Freiheit. Die deutsche Geschichte von 1815 bis 1849 in zeitgenössische Dokumenten* (Berlin, 1950), 241; see also Peter Wende, "Radikalismus," in *Geschichtliche Grundbegriffe*, vol. V (Stuttgart, 1984), 121. The statement is not a verbatim citation, but it agrees with what he had said in the Chamber.

¹³ FH, "Das farbige Stimmrecht," *WP* (n. d., 1880), FHP, box 9.

¹⁴ *VSB*, gS (18 December 1847), 120-21.

¹⁵ See Georg Beseler, *Volksrecht und Juristenrecht* (Leipzig, 1843); idem, "Ueber die Stellung des römischen Rechts zu dem nationalen Recht der germanischen Völker. Aus der Rede des Hrn. Verfassers beim Antritt seiner Professur in Basel, dasselbst erschienen 1836," *Paränesen für Studierende. Zweite Sammlung. u Rechts- und Staatswissenschaft*, Karl Hermann Scheidler, ed. (Jena, 1842), 126-36.

¹⁶ The two "classics" are Adolf E. Zucker, ed., *The Forty-Eighters. Political Refugees of the German Revolution of 1848* (New York, 1950); Carl Wittke, *Refugees of Revolution: The German Forty-Eighters of America* (Philadelphia, 1952); a more recent collection of essays on this is Charlotte L. Brancaforte, ed., *The German Forty-Eighters in the United States* (New York, 1989).

¹⁷ "Begründung der Motion des Abgeordneten Hecker auf Vorlage eines Gesetzes, die Verantwortlichkeit der Minister und der obersten Staatsbeamten betreffend," *VSB, 13. Beilagenheft, Beilage Nr. 1 zum Protokoll der 85. ÖS am 11. Juni 1844*, 129-47.

¹⁸ FH, "Warum wird der erste Angriff von Seiten der Vaticanler auf das Freischulensystem gemacht," *WP* (n. d., 1875), FHP, box 9.

¹⁹ See Alexander J. Schem, ed., *Deutsch-amerikanisches Conversations-Lexicon. Mit specieller Rücksicht auf das Bedürfnis der in Amerika lebenden Deutschen*, vol. 5 (New York, 1871), 233 ff.

²⁰ Häusser, *Gegenwart*, 358.

²¹ Butz, "Erinnerungen," part 2.

²² FH to Carl Schurz, Summerfield, St. Clair County, Ill., 7 October 1871, Schurz Papers, Manuscript Division, Library of Congress, Washington, D.C.

²³ See the transcript of the "Last Will and Testament of Franz Sigel," Sigel Papers, New York Historical Society, New York, N.Y.

²⁴ FH to Carl Schurz, Summerfield, St. Clair County, Ill., 25 June 1879, Schurz Papers.

Gustav Körner of Belleville, Illinois, in 1836, Hecker's dueling opponent as a student in Germany and political ally in America. Saint Louis Mercantile Library at the University of Missouri – St. Louis. Background contrast altered by Western Historical Manuscripts, University of Missouri – St. Louis.

HECKER IN GERMANY
I
THE EARLY YEARS

"Where ever did you get that big mouth?" – The Parental House.

Friedrich Karl Franz Hecker was born on 28 September 1811 "at a quarter to eleven o'clock" in Eichtersheim, Baden. He grew up in secure financial and social conditions. Little is known of his parents, but according to Hecker's own statements his father played a decisive role in his life. Hecker would learn from his father how to protest and to commit himself to altering political relations. In Eichtersheim (today the community of Angelbachtal in the Kreisgau district), the royal Bavarian court councillor Josef Hecker held the position of a seigneurial district officer for Baron von Venningen. In 1809 he married Wilhelmine von Lueder, daughter of Baron Friedrich von Lueder, prefect for Palatinate-Simmern in Castellaun. In 1815 the freethinking Josef Hecker was one of the signatories to a critical opposition address to the grand duke of Baden, which, as it later emerged, he actually authored. The cause of this defiance was a new income-tax system that withdrew privileges from the nobility but also appeared to tax the peasantry unjustly. On 2 November 1815 many members of the lowland nobility had gathered in Sinsheim, where the address, which resembled "not a complaint [but] rather a libel," was read aloud and adopted. It criticized the ingratitude of the grand duke of Baden and the profligacy of his court, complained about the decadence of the officialdom and asserted itself to be the defender of the people as a whole by pointing out the oppressed situation of the rural population. The address was intended primarily to defend the economic special interests of the nobility and reinforce its demand for the return of its privileges; yet the arguments that were brought to bear are interesting. There was a demand to consider that small states could maintain themselves only if they introduced more liberal constitutions than larger, monarchical territorial states. Thus there was a demand for the immediate calling of a state assembly. Ultimately, the address said, there was no other means to protect against the arbitrary acts of the government:

> If the subject is not happy there [in smaller states] then he will either
> promote their dissolution and incorporation into larger neighbors, *or he*

will emigrate. The governments of the League of the Rhine have in any
case turned away the hearts of their subjects through excessive demands.

Thirty-three nobles besides Josef Hecker signed this address, including
the Baron von Venningen, who was ejected from court and state service as
a result. In contrast, Josef Hecker, who had managed to incorporate a great
deal of his civic sensibilities into this address, suffered no consequences for
his authorship; his eventual pension was quite generous. Josef Hecker openly plays in the Sinsheim address on the theme of the right to emigrate as a
means of removing oneself from an unloved or useless ruler when the father
of one's country would not deal with the real needs of his subjects. Naturally
Josef Hecker never suspected that his first-born would eventually choose
this route. Emigration was to be the last resort of a subject who could not
succeed in altering conditions positively, through introducing and securing
a "good constitution" and calling a state assembly. Emigration was also not
to be confused with desertion, but merely assured the subject's right to
choose a constitution under which life promised him more. In short, the
address did not rashly promote emigration, but rather questioned the his-
toric claim of lifelong, unbroken subject loyalty to a monarch. The reference
to a subject's free choice to emigration was intended to bring rulers to reason. The threat of an internal dissolution of smaller states and their incorporation into more powerful states was formulated with the same intention.[1]

Josef Hecker supported his son's efforts throughout his life. Even in his
old age, a few years before his death, he spoke in his son's defense at
Friedrich Hecker's trial for high treason. "You know of course," Hecker
wrote to his sister in Mannheim after their father's death in the summer of
1858, "with what pleasure he ... read and read again every little newspaper
notice where my name was given. He often preached to me that he saw in
my life a mirror of what he had pursued in his younger years and what was
hindered in his own development through the pressure of circumstances."
Other contemporaries who knew Josef Hecker likewise believed in this
unlimited approval, Caspar Butz, recalling a conversation with Josef Hecker
in Mannheim in the 1850s, reported, "He was very proud of all his sons,
especially of his American son."

Concerning Josef Hecker, Butz also wrote, "To some extent he sounded
to me like a chronicle of the Great Revolution and the Napoleonic times. The
old man had experienced much. ... There was a certain cynicism in him, of

which his own son was never entirely free." This cynicism was paired with a peculiar humor. Hecker's father often reproached his son with the question, "Boy, where ever did you get that big mouth?" And Hecker knew exactly where he had gotten it. He recalled, "Who had always told me about the Federal Diet and the dreadful political business in the German *Reich* but he? My gorge rose even as a child, and I also think I often made real use of my mouth!" In later years Hecker always stressed the oppositional spirit that marked his father's house, perhaps not least in searching for the origins of the political attitude that had accompanied him all his life.[2]

At the age of nine Hecker entered the Karl Friedrich Lyceum in Mannheim, which had operated on egalitarian principles since 1807. It was a non-confessional institution arising from the amalgamation of the Catholic and Protestant gymnasia with the Calvinist Latin School. Hecker found in Mannheim his "elective home town." Due to its mercantile spirit, it breathed a different atmosphere from both the government residence of Karlsruhe and placid Eichtersheim, where his parents continued to live. On Hecker's graduation in August 1830, the administration of the Grand-Ducal Lyceum issued him a remarkable certificate.

> With very great ability and intense zeal he made such progress in the elementary subjects that he was able to be listed as among the best students of the second division, and in rhetoric, where his achievements were particularly excellent, he was among the most outstanding of the entire class. Furthermore, his conduct, so far as we could observe, was lawful and decent.[3]

The Heidelberg Professors and an Independent Teacher

Three months after leaving the Mannheim Lyceum, Friedrich Hecker registered on 30 November 1830 at the Ruperto-Carolina University in Heidelberg as a law student. Along with criminal law, procedure, German law and legal history, he was interested particularly in public law. At the beginning of the 1830s a series of significant jurists taught at Heidelberg, the majority of them inclined to natural law and keeping a critical distance to the rising historical school of law. Among them was the teacher of Pandects, Anton Friedrich Justus Thibaut.

Thibaut, a student of Kant, was a partisan of the late phase of the Law of Reason school. He had held a professorship at Heidelberg since 1806, and on the eve of the political restoration in Germany in 1814, he wrote a memorial, *On the Necessity of a General Civil Code for Germany [Über die Nothwendigkeit eines allgemeinen bürgerlichen Gesetzbuches für Deutschland]*, which became famous due to Thibaut's dispute with Savigny. In this work Thibaut called for a common German codification, modeled somewhat on the [Prussian] *Allgemeines Landrecht*, but even more on the French *Code civil*, which had already been adopted by the states of the League of the Rhine. Behind Thibaut's demand lay the idea that such a legal Code for all of Germany would promote the unification of the nation, which was then divided into many states and cities. It would serve as a guarantee against the anti-Napoleonic reaction that Thibaut already feared. And above all else, it would raise the law itself from the dusty, dead region of learned tradition "into a living political possession of the nation."

In direct response, Friedrich Karl von Savigny declared to Thibaut in his book, of the same year, *On the Calling of Our Times for Legislation and Legal Scholarship [Vom Beruf unserer Zeit für Gesetzgebung und Rechtswissenschaft]*, that all laws and positive codifications were "inorganic," that the object of legal scholarship was predetermined by the historicity of current law and could not be changed into a positive law by the abstractions of the Law of Reason. Law was a product of the "spirit of the people," a cultural heritage made up of custom, scholarship and practice. The *Code civil* was for Savigny a hated inheritance from the French Revolution. At the end of his treatise he identified academic legal scholars with legislators, because they alone were in the position to develop this organic law properly. Thus Thibaut was not altogether wrong in his response fear of anti-revolutionary reactionaries.

Grounded in the free civic sense, Thibaut's demand for a common legal code as a guarantee of national unity and liberty found in Hecker a convinced follower. In the Baden State Assembly long before 1848, when Representative Bassermann, referring to an earlier motion of Representative Welcker, took up again the idea of unity though a national parliament, Hecker did not hesitate a minute to support this idea and declare that unity for him was "precisely the unity of public law." Hecker then made a motion that, along with a national parliament and the unity of public law,

> a unity of private law should also be introduced throughout the entire German nation – a common civil law and common trade legislation.

> If the nation is to be externally strong and powerful even with its cur-
> rent internal divisions, there is only one means to unite the nation, by
> saturating it with one and the same law. Law is the milk of education
> and general enlightenment, and only a community of law can unify the
> nation indeed. [4]

Like his teacher Thibaut, Hecker rejected Savigny's elitist view of a
learned class of jurists, which he feared as yet another guardianship of the
people and as a denial of something that had only just been expressed by
the French Revolution, namely, spontaneous legislation by the people as a
new manifestation of a sovereign political will.

At Heidelberg, Hecker also heard lectures by Karl Salomo Zachariä von
Lingenthal. Like Thibaut, with whose support Zachariä was called to
Heidelberg university in 1806 as Ordinary Professor, Zachariä had made a
public name for himself even before 1815 and had experienced as a writing
and judging adult the Old Regime and its collapse. In 1808 Zachariä drew
attention with his classic presentation, *Manual of French Civil Law* – Baden
had just adopted the new Civil Code, the *Code Napoléon* – the first scholarly
systematization of this law in German. Zachariä then changed from private
law to public law, where he likewise drew respect as a jurist.

In his defense of the *Code Napoléon*, with its guarantees of personal
equality and individual freedom, Zachariä was not particularly different
from Thibaut. One must therefore look further to explain Hecker's outspo-
ken dislike of Zachariä. One might initially classify Zachariä as a liberal for
demanding a reform of criminal law, for supporting public and oral court
proceedings, and for struggling on behalf of a general freedom of occupation. But both enlightened and conservative policies were intermingled in
his teachings on the state. He was deemed by contempories to be perceptive
when he became the first publicist of a party state in Germany with his early
essay of 1823, *On a Hereditary Monarchy with a People's Representation [Über
die erbliche Einherrschaft mit einer Volksvertretung]*. He saw two parties at
work in the constitutional monarchy, one royalist and one democratic. He
desired that the formation of a government depend on whichever party was
the strongest at the time. He presented this view in 1839 in the second edition of his *Forty Books on the State*. The realist in him justified the advantage
of combining monarchy and popular representation, rather than a purely
representative system under German conditions, because "too dramatic dif-

ferences in property and origin make forming a political consensus difficult." For this reason he did not want the prince excluded from the political
process. Zacharia "held the exclusive formation of a government to be too
risky in view of the weak party organization in the Chambers." He was one
of the few jurists in Heidelberg to reject rational liberalism and the constitu-
tion-making of the Enlightenment when considering the question of founding a state, categorically declaring that the state arose historically *de facto*,
and people were legally obligated to obey it. [5]

From Hecker's point of view, Zacharia, with all his penetration as a
political theorist, committed a deeply unpatriotic error in 1810 by publishing *The State Law of the Federated States of the Rhine and the Law of the Rhenish
League*, a book that catered entirely to the interests of those then in power.

But Hecker's hostility toward Zacharia was based, it appears,
primarily on Zacharia as a person. Robert von Mohl and Karl Gutzow had
already portrayed Zacharia as a pedant, a cynic and a skinflint. Zacharia
served from 1820 to 1825 as representative of Heidelberg University in the
First Chamber and successor of Thibaut, who had surrendered his seat.
Thereafter he served another two years as representative in the Second
Chamber for the district of Heidelberg-Land. It could have been Zacharia's
role as a representative in the First Chamber that caused Hecker, for whom
the function of representing the people ranked very high, to despise him.
Particularly when he served in the First Chamber, Zacharia defended the
prerogatives of the crown and the privileges of lords, for whom he happily
prepared "richly endowed legal opinions." In the State Assembly of 1822,
while serving as spokesman for the aristocracy, Zacharia made the unforgettable statement "that promoting the braking principle is the true purpose of
the First Chamber, and that only in this way can the peril be avoided by
which the motion principle embodied in the Second Chamber endangers
the whole community." And it was in this particular Assembly that
Zacharia did not hesitate to speak against eliminating compulsory labor for
lords, and for the reintroduction of censorship, despite the fact that freedom
of the press was guaranteed by the constitution at the time.

In letters printed in a German-American newspaper in 1867, published
a year later in Germany as a book, Hecker denounced Zacharia as a renegade and traitor to the people. This must be understood in the context of the
rising euphoria of German nationalism after 1866:

A famous professor of state law in Heidelberg committed treason against Germany with a systematic "law of the Rhenish League." After a good dinner with even better wine, this same man, as a member of the First Baden Chamber, on the occasion of the military budget, shouted out, "I am voting for everything, I vote for even a million more. Baden must become a conquering people, we must conquer, conquer, conquer!"[6]

Elsewhere there is further mention of Zachariä, just as partisan: "Zachariä, the great jurist, ... and others brought the Rhine League's subservience to paper, writing Your Majesty's most subservient and servile dog-system of Rhenish League Law." For Hecker, Zachariä remained a symbol of the spineless renegade, favoring only whatever promised him the most advantage. Caught up in the euphoria of the *Reich's* founding and conscious of German national pride, which was also making waves in America, Hecker mentioned Zachariä for the last time in 1871 in the same breath with Gentz and Kotzebue, calling him in markedly pungent language a "literate licker of princely boot soles."[7]

The most lasting juristic influence on Hecker in Heidelberg was certainly the criminal law specialist Karl Josef Anton Mittermaier. Hecker heard German private and trade law, criminal law and civil and criminal procedure from him. Together with Hecker's personal experiences attending jury proceedings in Paris, Mittermaier's lectures convinced him of the importance of public and oral trials, Mittermaier above all others had promoted public and oral procedure at an early date, from the very start of the Second Chamber, and somewhat later he advocated the advantages of the jury system. Mittermaier's work questioning the practical needs of criminal law and procedure corresponded precisely to the demands later formulated in the Second Chamber for a reformed legal practice. Practical experience, statistical investigations and comparative analysis of different legal systems in Europe – Belgium, England and France particularly, but also America – and sociological and even psychological aspects were included by Mittermaier in his writings and lectures, and from them his demands for legal reform were derived.

After Mittermaier spoke out against the death penalty because he had demonstrated statistically that it had no intimidating effect, Hecker argued a number of years later entirely in his teacher's vein. In debates over the death penalty in the Chamber, in the context of a new criminal code, we find Hecker's usual combination of theory with a serious effort to find a practical, reasonable and humane resolution. First he made use of contract theory, calling on natural law for a plea for the abolition of the death penalty. In his speech of 21 June 1844 he declared to the Chamber,

> I will not hold the Chamber with a long speech, but I will start with the remark that I was the only one in the commission to declare himself against the death penalty. I consider life to be an inalienable good; the reason I hold that is obvious, and I will not give in to deep philosophical and religious speculation over this. But if life is an inalienable good, then man does not bring it with him into the social contract on which the state rests. Life is not an object of the social contract. And if one brings to that contract only what man can alienate and renounce without giving up his individuality, then the state has no right to pass over the limits of the social contract and rob him of the inalienable good that man has not made an object of the contract.[8]

As a practical jurist Hecker then went on to demonstrate that the death penalty was not even needed from "the point of view of necessity," because "if one wishes to render the criminal harmless toward the injured society," then one could neutralize him through lifelong imprisonment or deportation. The death penalty was also not useful because it excluded every possibility of improvement, and "man to some extent takes the place of divine justice." As the practice of countries with the most barbarian penalties had shown, the death penalty was also not an adequate means of intimidation, and the notion that an innocent person might be robbed of his life just because a judge erred was to Hecker too great a risk. Finally, said Hecker, the death penalty was not even a penalty, "because in the instant it is applied, it ceases to be a penalty."

Hecker also revealed parallels with Mittermaier's treatment of legal history, since Hecker, using "legal history as a quarry for understanding past points of view in order to explicate and develop the current law. But these points of view had to withstand review by his – practical – reason; he had in fact no philosophical view of what constituted historical development." Hecker proceeded in the same way in debates about a new criminal procedure, a new criminal code and even about justice in general.

He defended new forms of adjudication hitherto unknown in Germany so long as he was convinced of their usefulness and practicality. Just as Mittermaier was possessed by the democratic idea of true participation of the citizen in judgment, Hecker never lacked the courage for something entirely new in legal practice, unlike most other deputies. He was not attracted by eternally fiddling with what was already there, but rather by basic reforms. Typical of this was his call to the Chamber, "What is the purpose of this endless experimentation! Let's do something thorough for once!" Years earlier he had likewise implored the Chamber belligerently, "As long as one does not take the position in favor of a radical reform of the law, there will be no help for the people, just piecework and fixing up."[9]

Mittermaier, who had important American friends with whom he corresponded extensively on constitutional questions, was probably the teacher who most thoroughly acquainted Hecker with the American constitutional system. When the Baden Second Chamber came to debate Bassermann's motion on creating a national assembly in 1848, Mittermaier stated the wish to orient it entirely in the direction of the American federal constitution.[10] As a constitutional liberal Mittermaier certainly believed in the possibility of adapting American constitutional institutions to German conditions, particularly the form of the federal state, without having to violate the monarchical form of state. But independent of this problem, American institutions were particularly important for Mittermaier in relation to jurisprudence. He drew some of his proposals and suggestions for change from the American model, and Hecker did the same.

Besides law lectures Hecker also attended lectures by the historian Friedrich Christoph Schlosser, who had come to Heidelberg University in 1817. The treatises of "brave old Schlosser" provided a wealth of citations for Hecker to support in America his own opinions on small-state life, the spirit of subservience and the lack of a sense of community among Germans. He even had the fascicles of Schlosser's *World History* sent to him in America as soon as they appeared. In Schlosser, he encountered a historian who thought little of the dominant historical-critical method of nineteenth-century historiography and consciously avowed the rationalist method of the late eighteenth century. Hecker explicitly defended Schlosser's moralizing historiography, which Schlosser's critics rejected as subjective. Writing and studying history, according to the pragmatic Schlosser, had to fulfill the purpose of moral education, whose purpose lay in moral and civic enlightenment and training. What this meant for Schlosser's own historical procedure was that he rejected both the esthetically calculated, rhetorically refined historiography of a Johannes von Müller, oriented chiefly to evoking emotions, and what he held to be the misunderstood objectivity of Leopold von Ranke's historical method. For Schlosser a historian's work was not completed by "learned rooting around in sources and documents," although he did not question the importance of the basic study of sources. The empirically researched facts had to be applied to moral questions, and that meant nothing more than communicate one's own views; in short, to judge. It was only through the application of the system of values possessed by the historian, only through the orientation of the past to moral questions – one could also speak of a practical contemporary interest – that one could claim to have gained knowledge. By openly expressing value judgments, Schlosser possessed the advantage of a rational control. What seemed to be objective historiography hid its judgment behind the narrative, whose selection could appear to be arbitrary and whimsical if it were not made clear with what criteria – precisely value judgments – it sought out and assembled.[11]

Schlosser was interested in the progress of realizing political freedom in history, which he always understood as the development of the democratic idea. He attempted to choose and judge historical events in terms of their connection to this concept. For that reason he confessed quite openly in his *History of the Eighteenth Century* that he presumed the course of events could be understood as well known; everything therefore depended on how the historian chose and placed the facts and judged them. Schlosser was influenced by Kant, among others, in organizing historical events according to the idea of reason, which is why it was possible for him to write a "universal history." At the same time this assumed that the development of man as rational being did not perfect itself through the individual but through the human race as a whole, and that in the course of this "an intention of nature in history beyond the conscious motivations of acts" must be revealed. Despite this, one cannot say that Schlosser completely accepted Kant's philosophical conception, precisely because he attributed a large importance to the conscious motivations of individuals. Schlosser did not want to reduce history to a mere "external active application of general rules," subsuming historical facts under general maxims of philosophy as a pure ends/means rationality or as the securing of material interests; he also wanted to pay attention to the spiritual characteristics of the actors, to their "intellectual or contemplative characteristics." The true moral quality of a historical judgment arose for Schlosser only through ascribing intellectuality and the active competence resulting from it, producing signposts in each case for social orientation and practical contemporary interest.[12]

Schlosser's radicalism emerged in his sharp condemnation of all those forces that hindered or braked the progressing process of mankind, such as the nobility or the clergy. And it is no surprise that Schlosser, an author of historical works who never achieved the popularity of Carl von Rotteck, showed special sympathy to developments in the United States. In his *History of the Eighteenth Century*, when treating the Declaration of Independence and comparing the French and American revolutions, Schlosser declared "The Declaration of Independence was masterfully composed, particularly remarkable because it states the rights of the citizen inalienable in all types of states, if one believes in the principles to which the Congress confesses here." Unfortunately, Schlosser continued, the people's masterful concept in Europe, where everything was in ferment, had a "dreadful influence." Although only a few "scoundrels" in Europe abused the enthusiasm of the people for liberty, critics of the French Revolution unjustly made the American declaration of liberty and independence responsible for the French Revolution and rejected it as thoroughly as they had the French Revolution itself. Schlosser regretted this situation. He spoke frequently elsewhere of Rousseau and Thomas Paine, who "erected a democratic or, as we would say today, a radical principle" and thus precipitated a movement in the people that could not be stopped. Schlosser named authors who were of central importance to Hecker.

The extent to which Hecker used Schlosser's historical approach when dealing with historical events and figures may be seen with special clarity in Hecker's later historical efforts, particularly his lecture on Lincoln and Cromwell. His selective use of historical events and figures to demonstrate his own views, his moral judgment of the subjects in question and his historical standard, which presumed the progressive democratization of conditions over time, very much recalled Schlosser, but not Schlosser alone.[13]

Carl von Rotteck was not a teacher whom Hecker could encounter in Heidelberg, but he still influenced Hecker profoundly. Hecker came to know this professor in Freiburg in the 1830s, and in an article in the *Gartenlaube* he later elevated this meeting as central to his entire development. Rudolf Muhs is justified in seeing this as Hecker's legitimizing his own acts after the fact, a scenario in which "the 36-year-younger Hecker … received the political blessing of the old patriarch of the opposition."[14] This is because the "old" Hecker had a particularly strong inclination to self-dramatization. Yet, his own autobiographical intentions aside, it is also clear that Hecker's repeated references to Rotteck into his last days were part of a political program, for it is obvious that the two men shared many things in their constitutional politics.

Rotteck represented the classical concept of a dichotomy between government and the representatives of the people.[15] Because the constitution introduced in Baden in 1818 had, for reasons of state, been granted "from above," it was not to be understood as a "declaration of abdication by the patriarchal sovereign state." The liberals never acknowledged this constitution to be a universally accepted foundation for a new political order; rather they saw it as an instrument with whose help the state could be gradually turned in a liberal democratic direction. As a result, they could not see themselves as an integral part of either the state or its government. They essentially saw the mission of the people's representation to be protecting against sovereign arbitrariness and expanding political participation, necessarily a position of opposition to the government. Rotteck, under Rousseau's influence, portrayed this position of popular representatives in his early writing *On State Assemblies* (1819), saying "Estates … are a committee representing (that is, in nature and truth, without poetic metaphor) the people (or a part of them) united in a state, commissioned to practice the rights of this people (or a part of them) over and against the government." Thus one of the principal missions of the representatives of the people was "to defend the people's rights against the government."

Here Rotteck formulated a concept of popular representation and of the popular representative arising from obvious, necessary opposition to the government. Instead of understanding popular representation as an integral part of the state's government and comprehending how to participate in structuring and elaborating the state through the progressive forces within the government, Rotteck defined the chief function of popular representation as controlling the government, in permanent opposition. Lothar Gall says that, under Rotteck's leadership, there developed a friend/foe ideology in the consciousness of the Baden liberals, according to which all the forces in political life divided into two parts, the fundamentally anti-government "Progress Party" and the servile, pro-government "Stasis Party," two camps between which, to Rotteck's view, there could never be a compromise – a thesis promoting political radicalism.[16]

This superheated concept of popular representation, ready for no compromise, could be seen in Hecker from his early sharp attacks on servile renegades and members of the government to the statements that he made in Swiss exile. There – beaten, pursued and isolated – he protested to Adam von Itzstein, "I was a true ambassador of the people, and I am still that today!" It was an easy matter for Hecker, already under Schlosser's influence, to adopt Rotteck's typical "moralizing history." In Rotteck's rational perception of history, the general development of mankind was in keeping with reasonable principles, rejecting historical right.[17]

As Paul Nolte rightly emphasized, Hecker's sharp condemnation of servile officials and aristocratic groups also fed off another view that he took from Rotteck: his orientation to the ideal of citizen participation. Rotteck conceived striving toward freedom to be the essential principle of his time, and he interpreted this as a consistent orientation to an increasingly democratic and in the final instance republican, form of state. The realization of the freedom principle and a republican form of socio-political order belonged together. Relying on the doctrine of virtue found in the Enlightenment and humanism, and developed from the traditions of antiquity, a republic based on liberty could be preserved, as history teaches, only if its citizens were virtuous. This meant that they sacrificed personal, individual wishes and interests to strive for the well-being of their communities and, ultimately, of the state. Even in the case of collisions between private and general *interests*, Rotteck said in his article on "community spirit" in his *Staatslexikon*, one should cease pursuing particular interests in order to promote the common good. Rotteck saw this attitude to be the true "principle of life," the "sole guarantee" of the prosperity of the community.

Independent of the political implications of this assumption aiming to create a political community of equal citizens, the connection of ethics and politics is decisive. When turned into political terms, common interest becomes civic virtue, describing a moral relationship to the state. This means neither the thoughtless pursuit of abstract law nor motivation through sensual stimulation. It is, as Carl Theodor Welcker also said in the *Staatslexikon*, the "strengthened, self-sacrificing, stubborn and courageous subordination of drives and strivings for the sake of higher purpose," hence an act of will, a reasonable decision, a political attitude. Virtue, both personal and civic, should be promoted through "spiritual and moral development, education and practice, through enlightenment." This was why education had such pride of place in all liberal concepts. But personal and civic virtues were bound to the existence of freedom. Only freedom could produce the "all-sacrificing striving for the civic community" that "dignified participation in a higher whole to which one feels himself belonging and subordinated to." This alone should explain Rotteck's and finally Hecker's opposition to the Baden government, to the First Chamber of the State Assembly and to officialdom. When measured according to the standard of the participatory civic ideal, these institutions were vigorously criticized because they pursued only particular, egotistical interests and did not aim their efforts at a superordinated, common good. Baden realities were still far from being able to unify government and governed, the lawmaker and those subjected to the law.[18]

If one keeps in mind Rotteck's synonymous use of "republican" and "free," it does not appear too speculative to compare the positive image of America that Rotteck presented in his *General History* to Hecker's longing for America, which Hecker said began in the early 1830s. Rotteck, with his unrestrained enthusiasm for America as "the land of liberty," was one of those liberals who stylized the United States as the land in which a theoretical ideal had found its practical realization, a view less influenced by American events themselves than by German developments. "The principal demands of a pure theory," Rotteck said in his *General History*, "which places itself in such hostility to historical right in Europe, are seen there in enviable fulfillment." In his chapter on the American Revolution, Rotteck conceived of the just struggle of the colonists against the "unnaturalness of the relationship" between colonies and mother country as a "deed of the maturing of America." With almost religious exaltation he stressed, "To be sure it was not ideas alone that made America free. … It was God who protected it and made it triumph, who awoke men of higher spirit in advice and deed and blessed their heroism." However, since Rotteck also believed that the stability and functioning of a republic and hence the preservation of a condition of liberty, depended on the virtue and enlightenment of the people; he therefore had to emphasize above everything else the virtuous, enlightened and developed character of the colonists. "Concord, patriotic commitment, noble zeal for freedom … made the American people capable and worthy of freedom," he asserted.

Through reference to Thomas Paine and Benjamin Franklin, Rotteck further raised a bridge to the liberal demands that he sought to achieve. Everywhere in America there reigned security of property and person; the Constitution was a clever balancing act between the claims of the various federal states and the central government; no laws passed were permitted to violate the basic rights of freedom of religion, freedom of the press, and the right of petition. Here Rotteck connected the participatory, collective-oriented concept of civic virtue with liberal, individualistic presumptions. Like Schlosser, Rotteck praised above all else the formulation of the Bill of Rights. And like Hecker after him, he had no problem combining the liberal presumptions of an autonomous, atomistic individual and his legal sphere, which guaranteed individual, inalienable rights, with a political orientation to action for the common good. This, of course, was with the exception of slavery, which did not yet correspond to the common principle of legally guaranteed equality and freedom. But for Rotteck it was only a matter of time; America showed all signs of becoming Europe's better heir.[19]

In the concluding chapter of the ninth volume of his *General History*, Rotteck sketched America's overarching mission for the general development of mankind. He described it, based on his presumption of a Europe grown weak with age and rejuvenated in America, as a struggle of two systems, historical right and the right of reason. Because of the Eastern threat, Europe might "sink back into the bonds of rigid historical right." Liberty, however, would be found elsewhere, for, as the last sentence of the *General History* declared, "Europe will only see the holy flame that it has preserved until now (namely the idea of natural right, unquenchable in every human breast) shining from afar, from the opposite side of the Atlantic."[20]

It is from this presumption that Rotteck stresses, as he already had in an earlier volume of his *General History*, the legitimate right of emigration, the right to choose a better constitution. "[F]or the resident of the Old World there lay in the unmeasured regions of the New … [a] secure place of refuge for oppressed right and for the outlawed love of liberty." The supporters of historical right, more strongly influenced by Romanticism, saw America as a land without history and thus without culture; they preferred to leave to the play of nature the unmeasured distances of a land so richly endowed by creation. In contrast, the rationalistic liberals of the pre-Revolutionary period, influenced by the Enlightenment, saw America as the land of guaranteed liberty, the model land of the future. Here Hecker followed Rotteck completely.[21]

Years of Study and Wandering: Mannheim and Paris

After five semesters at Heidelberg University, Hecker spent a semester in Munich in the summer of 1833. Before he departed for Munich, the Grand-Ducal University Office in Heidelberg issued him a certificate

> confirming that he registered on 30 November 1830 at the university here as a student of law, remaining here to the present time, and – with one exception – when he was punished by career arrest for one and fourteen days because of a duel actually carried out – otherwise conducted himself according to the academic laws and decently. He was not under investigation by us for participating in banned student associations.[22]

The duel, mentioned in almost lapidary style, had an extensive impact on Hecker's own biography. His opponent was no less than Gustav Körner, who would soon play a leading role in the storming of the Guardhouse in Frankfurt in April 1833 and would emigrate to America after the failure of his attempted *Putsch*. There Körner became lieutenant governor of Illinois in 1852, in turn Hecker's party colleague and then opponent in his later American years. The Heidelberg duel arose from an argument among students one night. Hecker challenged Körner, as yet unknown to him. They met in the Hirschgasse, and, in the end, a maneuver of Körner's caused by Hecker's ineptness wounded Hecker between the thumb and index finger. The injury was severe enough that to require stitches. This did not reduce Hecker's respect for his dueling partner, because when he later came through Frankfurt in 1845 following his expulsion from Prussia, Hecker met Körner's brother at a festive banquet arranged for him and Itzstein. Hecker greeted him heartily and extended his hand, saying with a laugh, "See here, your brother left me this memento!" The duel with Körner was not to be the last for the "crass" Hecker. Josef Hecker's favorite story, which grew rather exaggerated over time, consisted largely of portrayals of his sons' student adventures – Karl did not concede second place in this to his older brother – "and how they were brought home scraped and poked after their duels."[23]

One experience directly connected with his student period was Hecker's encounter with the system of surveillance that continually over-saw the individual moves of students. Even for a brief visit to his parents in Eichtersheim from 14 March to 20 April 1833, the law student needed con-firmation that he had "resided [there and] conducted himself with out-standing morality." When Hecker left Munich University in August 1833, he received once more a

> Moral testimony on departing the university … concerning his conduct at the university here from [27 April 1833] to the present attesting that he conducted himself in a manner without complaint and in keeping with the statutes. He was not suspected of membership in any associa-tion not allowed by His Royal Majesty.

Back at Heidelberg University, Hecker was invited by the Justice Ministry in Karlsruhe to take the written and oral examinations on 26 May 1834. He passed the state examination there and was promoted to *Doctor juris, summa cum laude,* at Heidelberg the following month, during Mittermaier's term as dean. He continued on to a two-year law practicum at the *Landamt* in Karlsruhe. As early as September 1834 he was declared qualified "for written procedure law, for advocacy before the Superior Court, and for state service."[24]

In September, 1835, Hecker traveled to Paris to extend his practical experience. His intention for this journey was solely for juristic training; he desired

> to go to Paris to further his theoretical and practical training, to work in the office of a local advocate, as well as to study the sources of French law, and to learn the procedure of trials in civil and criminal cases, requesting that the period of his residence in France count as part of his practical probation.

Hecker's residency in Paris expanded more than his juristic knowledge.

Alongside the public trials, which left a lasting impression, Hecker also attended the French National Assembly. Until February 1836, besides public court sessions, he also heard the lectures of State Counsel Dr. Gerando on administrative, civil, commercial and criminal law and the legal conferences of the advocates. In November 1835 he attended a "European Historical Congress" [Congrès Historique Européen].[25] In later debates of the Baden Second Chamber, Hecker addressed juristic questions in an entirely practical manner, referring to his foreign experience.

At the end of February 1836, Hecker returned to the Landamt in Karlsruhe, but he left state service as soon as his probation ended. He returned to Mannheim and sought to establish himself as an advocate and procurator for the Aulic Court of the Lower Rhine. His admission lasted little more than a year, because, as a document of the Aulic Court of 5 October 1837 declared, "at this time there is no need to increase the number of Aulic Court procurators."[26] On 28 December 1838 Hecker was finally named an advocate and procurator at the Grand-Ducal Superior and Aulic Court of the Upper Rhenish Circle.

Gustav von Struve came to the Aulic Court as an advocate at the same time, but contact between the two men remained slight until the mid-1840s, when Hecker defended Struve in his trial for violations of the press law. While the Livonian noble had problems settling in socially in Mannheim, Hecker easily made himself at home. A few months after his mother's death, in October 1839, Hecker married Marie Josefine Eisenhardt, the daughter of a prosperous Mannheim merchant. In 1842, at the age of 31, he was elected to the Mannheim municipal council. He had become a member of the exclusive Räuberhölle gentlemen's club, and in the same year he entered the Baden Second Chamber as deputy of the 35th electoral district, Weinheim-Ladenburg, after some dispute over the election. Hecker's election was the result of agitation by Itzstein; along with other politicians of the liberal opposition, Itzstein had invalidated the first election and finally won new elections. As a result of Hecker's election, the liberal opposition was increased by one eloquent fighter, who quickly would so aggravate his political enemies through many an abrasive statement that the conservative deputy Friedrich Rettig asked the president of the Chamber to "put a pillow in front of Deputy Hecker, so the blows of his fist on the podium can no longer be heard."[27]

His Political Foster Father

The names of Hecker and Struve are often mentioned in a single breath, and it is assumed that they were personally close, working from a similar political understanding. It is therefore often overlooked that Hecker's actual political foster father was Adam von Itzstein. Itzstein introduced Hecker to the realities of political life and for a long time had the greatest political influence on him. Hecker often described his relationship with Itzstein, who was two years older than his own father, as a father-son relationship. Their mutual sympathy and concern continued their entire lives, through all the political confusion until Itzstein's death in 1855. Shortly after his election to the Baden Second Chamber in 1842, Hecker began to continue Itzstein's combative heritage in his own right, while the old man withdrew more and more from intense debates. And after the failure of the revolution, Hecker often asked Itzstein to spend the last years of his life with him on his farm in free America.

Itzstein himself repeatedly pointed out the differences between Hecker and Struve, particularly during the revolution, and – when the liberal opposition appeared not to understand it – cried out in complaint, "We have Mr. Struve to thank for this!"[28] All his life Itzstein had an extremely tense, cool relationship with Struve. The passing over of Struve in the Chamber elections of 1847 was a result of Itzstein's encouragement along with that of Mathy and Bassermann.[29] This intensified Struve's hostilities to the "halfways" into ever-greater bitterness. Hecker grew nearer to Struve's political views and demands, not deliberately, but largely because his strategic concept was that of any leftist Chamber deputy: to achieve his political demands within the Chamber. During the period of the Revolution itself, Hecker sat between chairs, so to speak, torn between his old loyalty to Itzstein and Struve's repeated view – entirely correct – that virtually nothing could be accomplished via the Chamber. Hecker's parliamentary exhaustion in early 1847, which led him to give up his seat, meant that this conflict would no longer be hidden.

Itzstein met Hecker at the earliest in 1839 and at the latest in Mannheim. He knew from the outset how to bind the younger man to himself.[30] Itzstein's tactical calculation, his well-tempered diplomacy in organizing a liberal opposition, could hardly have fallen on deaf ears with Hecker. Since the end of the 1830s Hecker had been a regular participant in political meetings at Hallgarten,[31] where he would have met Itzstein, but he also appears to have visited Itzstein often outside this gathering, accompanied by his wife and child. Political gatherings were not a secret but also were not public; the Hallgarten meetings were therefore reduced from several days to single days in order to avoid entries in the hotel register that would be compromising for participants. At these meetings a common strategy was developed for the assemblies of several German states, and Itzstein sought to make systematic contact with deputies from the eastern and northern states, specifically Robert Blum, Otto von Watzdorf, Julius Dieskau and Count Eduard von Reichenbach. The filing of similar motions in several assemblies at once appeared to be a tactic agreed to in Hallgarten. Participants also agreed to petitions and other arguments within the Chamber after common discussion in advance. Thus Hecker remarked in his 1844 publication, *Ideas and Proposals for a Reform of Courts,* that he was leaving out specific points in order not to interfere with a petition by Itzstein that would contain those propositions. The resignation of the Baden minister von Blittersdorf in 1844 can be seen as a partial success of the agitation of the Hallgarten circle, which also arranged for the publication of the secret acts of the Vienna Conference. In general, however, one may agree with Rudolf Muhs, who concludes about the Hallgarten circle and its later dissolution, "Hallgarten was marked by a concern for coordinating the opposition, not for its radicalizing. Itzstein's true service to German liberalism is that he was able to keep the conversation going so long."[32]

Hallgarten did offer Hecker the opportunity to join with noted liberal opposition politicians. This was also the political purpose of a journey to Saxony and Prussia, represented as a vacation, which he took with Itzstein in 1845. The two had traveled for a similar purpose in 1840 to Leipzig, there to meet Robert Blum. This time they had planned to meet with Robert Blum and the Silesian Count Eduard von Reichenbach in Leipzig; another meeting with Reichenbach was scheduled for Berlin. Leisler, a lawyer from Nassau, was supposed to join them there. A continuation of the journey to Königsberg was supposed to make possible a meeting with Johann Jacoby.[33] The political purpose of this journey did not remain a secret to the Prussian police, and there followed the expulsion of the two men by Police Counsel Hoffrichter at five in the morning of 23 May 1845, without a stated reason, with the order to leave the Prussian states and return home at once.

The unexpected public response to this expulsion, which was above all else an affront to liberal hopes for German unity and the right of the freest possible movement between the various German states, made Hecker and Itzstein not only popular, but virtually martyrs overnight. Their expulsion was turned into a "concern of the German people," "an injury to the personal and civic liberty of the Germans, an attack against the people as a whole in these individuals." Hecker himself stressed this presumption in his letter of complaint to the Baden State Ministry in Karlsruhe, published in the press, in which he said there that Prussia had

> broken for them the ancient and holy statute of international law that promises protection to the stranger, the guaranteed right of the Federation that a German citizen may move freely from state to state without hindrance ... No German citizen has free passage and security in the Kingdom of Prussia any more; he may be expelled if he is merely unwanted, expelled from a German land, expelled from a Customs Union land, excluded from all personal and commercial intercourse. His personal rights are obliterated whenever they require his personal presence; he is without public or private rights, not a recipient of the protection of a visitor, banned and a stranger on German soil.

People were particularly upset because the expulsion had been ordered by Prussia, the very state of which much was expected for the future of Germany, a state thought to be at the "heights of culture." The freedom of movement was "ancient national law," "which everyone has a right to claim as a person and particularly every free man in a civilized state." It could not permit expulsion, the critics said, just because someone was seen as a "republican or non-Christian." Not even "conviction, intellectual direction or effort" should lead to "being treated like a criminal." Naturally one should not have any illusions about the reason for the expulsion, a leaflet continued; there was no denying that these were deputies with republican views. But the anonymous author of the leaflet asked the reader to consider that these deputies had never exceeded the limits of legitimacy. Prussia, instead, that had to demonstrate what it thought "of constitutions and national estates."

Hecker and Itzstein never received the compensation they felt their good name deserved, either from Prussian or from Baden officials. But their spirit of Southwest-German particularism, already marked, seemed to intensify.[34]

¹ Excerpt from the *Tauf-und Geburtsbuch der Gemeinde Eichtersheim Bezirksamt Wiesloch vom 2. Jahrgang 1811* §290, transcript of 24 November 1843, FHP, box 1, folder 2. On Hecker's origins and ancestry, Friedrich Walter on Hecker's father in *Mannheimer Geschichtsblätter* 7(1908), and Gustav Rommel, "Friedrich Heckers Vater," ibid. 32 (1931), 136-42. (Georg) Josef Hecker (*12 December 1777 in Endigen am Necker, †9 June 1858 in Mannheim); the mother Wilhelmine von Lueder (*12 December 1784, †1839) was an aunt of the Bavarian minister of finance and war Ludwig von Lueder, see Paul Strack, *Friedrich Heckers Herkunft*, Breiträge zur Familien- und Heimatkunde in Baden, no. 2 (Grafenhausen bei Lahr/Baden, 1959); on the evolving titles of an episcopal, later royal Bavarian court councillor, see Strack, *Herkunft*, 12, 14. Willy Andreas, *Geschichte der badischen Verwaltungsorganisation und Verfassung in den Jahren 1802-1818*, vol. 1 (Leipzig, 1913), 409-11. Karl Obser, ed., *Denkwürdigkeit des Markgrafen Wilhelm von Baden*, vol. 1 (Heidelberg, 1906), 424.

² Trial, beginning on 22 August 1854, in GLA 276/3431 and GLA 275/3432; FH was sentenced to prison for life. Josef Hecker suffered considerably for his son's reputation as a traitor, see the incidents in Strack, *Herkunft*, 13. FH to his sister, St. Clair County, Ill., 18 July 1858, printed in Hansmartin Schwarzmeier, "Auswanderungsbriefe aus Nordamerika," ZGO 126(1978), 303-69, here 327. Butz, "Erinnerungen," part 2. The conversation took place a year before Josef Hecker's death, in 1857. FH to Ernst Keil (n.d., n.p.), GL 1872, 391. See, for example, FH, *Gepfefferte Briefe über Kleinstaate und Kleinstaaterei. Geschrieben im Frühjahr 1867* (Mannheim, 1868), 60.

³ On Mannheim, Friedrich Walter, *Geschichte Mannheims vom Übergang an Baden (1802) bis zur Gründung des Reiches* (1907; repr. Frankfurt a. M., 1978), esp. 169-72. "Direction des großherzoglichen Lyceums, Mannheim," 24 August 1830, signed by Nüßlin, FHP, box 1, folder 2.

⁴ Registration certificate, FHP, box 1, folder 2. Scharp, *Hecker*, 19, using Hecker's Latin autobiography, law faculty, Heidelberg. On Thibaut, see in general *ADB*, 37 (Leipzig, 1894; repr. Berlin, 1971), 737-44.

⁵ Scharp, Hecker, 22. *Allgemine politische Annalen*, vol. 9, 201-48; cf. Brandt, *Restauration*, 60, n. 141. Karl Salomo Zachariä, *Vierzig Bücher vom Staate*, vol. 4 (Heidelberg, 1820-32); here, 2nd ed. (Heidelberg, 1839-43), vol. 3 (Heidelberg, 1839), 230 ff.; cf. also Brandt, *Restauration*, 59-60. *Vierzig Bücher*, 2nd ed., vol. 1, 1. Buch, 4. Hauptstück; cf. on this also Michael Stolleis, *Geschichte des öffentlichen Rechts in Deutschland (1800-1914)*, vol. 2 (Munich, 1992), 171.

⁶ Karl Salomo Zachariä, *Das Staatsrecht der Rheinischen Bundesstaaten und das Rheinische Bundesrecht* (Heidelberg, 1810); also idem, *Jus publicum Civitatum, quae Foederi Rhenano adscriptae sunt* (Heidelberg, 1808). "Zachariä," *ADB*, 44 (1898), 646-52, here 648. FH, *Gepfefferte Briefe*, 40.

⁷ Hecker praised the *Code civil* in the Second Chamber and accepted it as a model, as well as the *Code d'instruction criminelle* and the *Code de procédure civile*, for example VSB, 27. öS (17 December 1844), 200; 76. öS (5 July 1844), 202; 83. öS (8 June 1844), 280; 87. öS (14 June 1844), 292. TISZ, 10 August 1871.

⁸ Scharp, *Hecker*, 24. Klaus Lüdersen, "Karl Joseph Anton Mittermaier und der Empirismus in der Strafrechtswissenschaft," Wilfried Küper, ed., *Heidelberger Strafrechtler im 19. und 20. Jahrhundert* (Heidelberg, 1986), 101-15, here 108. VSB, 92. öS (21 June 1844), 97-98.

⁹ VSB, 92. öS (21 June 1844), 98. Lüdersen, "Mittermaier," 112. VSB, gS (18 December 1847), 143. VSB, 75. öS (29 May 1844), 10.

¹⁰ See VSB, 43. öS (24 March 1848), 309.

[11] Scharp, *Hecker*, 25. FH, *Gepfefferte Briefe*, 60; cf. also ibid., 52, where FH names Schlosser in a context with his own teacher Schlözer. FH's order to a book dealer, Summerfield, St. Clair County, Ill., 28 March 1873, original in the Mannheim Stadtarchiv, Kleine Erwerbungen, 127.

[12] Friedrich Christoph Schlosser, *Geschichte des 18. Jahrhunderts*, vol. 3, 4th ed. (Heidelberg, 1853), 528; idem, *Universalhistorische Übersicht der Geschichte der alten Welt und ihrer Cultur, 3 Teile in 9 Abteilungen* (Frankfurt am Main, 1826-34), here Teil I, 1. Abteilung, 26.

[13] Gölter, Schlosser, 167 and 174. Hildegard Meyer, *Nord-Amerika im Urteil des Deutschen Schrifttums bis zur Mitte des 19. Jahrhunderts. Eine Untersuchung über Kürnbergers "Amerika-Müden"* (Hamburg, 1929), 42. Schlosser, *Geschichte des 18. Jahrhunderts*, vol. 3, 3rd ed. (Heidelberg, 1844), 529 ff. Ibid., vol. 3, cited here in Gölter, Schlosser, 145-46. Cf. FH, *Reden*, 71-91.

[14] FH, "Erinnerungen aus meinem Leben, 1. Wie die geheimen Wiener Conferenzbeschlüsse an das Tagelicht gezogen wurden," GL 1869, 552-54, here 553.

[15] Lothar Gall, *Der Liberalismus als regierende Partei in Baden* (Wiesbaden, 1968), 24ff.

[16] Gall, *Liberalismus*, 25, 36. Carl von Rotteck, *Ideen über die Landstände* (Karlsruhe, 1819), cited in Gall, *Liberalismus*, 26. Carl von Rotteck, "Abgeordneter," Rotteck, Welcker, eds., *Staatslexikon*, vol. 1 (Altona, 1834), 110.

[17] FH to Adam von Itzstein, Muttenz, 28 May 1848, Itzstein Nachlaß, Bundesarchiv, Abteilungen Potsdam, Zug-Nr. 168/58. Cf. Emil Ganter, *Karl von Rotteck als Geschichtsschreiber* (Freiburg, 1908), 108.

[18] Rotteck, "Gemeingeist, Gemeinsinn," *Staatskexikon*, vol. 6 (Altona, 1838), 448-59, here 450. Carl Theodor Welcker, "Bürgertugend, Bürgersinn," *Staatslexikon*, vol. 1 (supplement to the 1st ed.) (Altona, 1846), 748-758, here 750.

[19] FH to Emma Herwegh, Muttenz, 11 July 1848, printed in Marcel Herwegh, ed. *1848 – Briefe an und von Georg Herwegh* (Munich, 1896), 247. Carl von Rotteck, *Allgemeine Geschichte vom Anfang der historischen Kenntniß bis auf unsere Zeiten*, 9 vols., 1st ed. (Freiburg, 1812-27), here vol. 8, 9th ed. (Freiburg, 1833), 394. Rotteck, *Allgemeine Geschichte*, vol. 8, 1st ed. (Freiburg, 1826), 579, 591, 592, 624-25, 628.

[20] Rotteck, *Allgemeine Geschichte*, vol. 9, 9th ed. (Freiburg, 1833), 540, §27. Rotteck, *Allgemeine Geschichte*, vol. 1, 1st ed. (Freiburg, 1812), 327.

[21] Rotteck, *Allgemeine Geschichte*, vol. 7, 9th ed. (Freiburg, 1833), 136.

[22] See registration certificate, University of Munich, 27 April 1833, FHP, box 1, folder 2. Testimonium morum, Heidelberg, 14 March 1833, Grosherzogl. Universitaets Amt, ibid.

[23] Thomas J. McCormack, ed., *Memoirs of Gustav Koerner, 1808-1896. Life Sketches at the Suggestion of His Children*, 2 vols. (Cedar Rapids, Iowa, 1909), here vol. 1, 179-81. Cf. Scharp, *Hecker*, 9; similar Häusser, *Gegenwart*, 357. Hecker's brother, Karl Friedrich Franz Hecker (*6 November 1812, † 28 October 1878), Strack, *Herkunft*, 15. Caspar Butz in conversation with Josef Hecker, Butz, "Erinnerungen," part 2.

[24] Certificate, Eichtersheim im badischen Neckar, Kreis Amtes Wiesloch, 20 April 1833, signed by Schüßler, the mayor. Großherzoglich Badisches Justiz-Ministerium, Karlsruhe, 9 September 1834. 1 August 1833. Justiz-Ministerium, Karlsruhe, 11 April 1834. Diploma, Heidelberg University, 16 June 1834, FHP, box 1, folder 2.

[25] Land Amt Karlsruhe, 28 September 1835, FHP, box 1, folder 2; cf. also the petition for permission for this journey to the Justice Ministry in Karlsruhe on 30 June 1835 and to the grand-ducal government of the Middle-Rhine Circle on 20 July 1835; Permission of the Justice Ministry, all FHP, box 1, folder 2. An unpublished work, *Ein Wort der Berechtigung über Frankreichs Magistratur und Barreau* (1836), came from this journey; cf. Muhs, "Heckermythos,"

428. See, for example, his remarks, *VSB*, 51. öS (19 April 1844), 21; ibid., 57. öS (27 April 1844), 193. Generally on Hecker's residence in Paris, see Scharp, *Hecker*, 27-28.

[26] Hofgericht des Unterrheinkreises, Mannheim, 5 October 1837, signed by Jägermann, FHP, box 1, folder 2.

[27] Justiz-Ministerium, Karlsruhe, 28 December 1838, FHP, box 1, folder 2 and Hofgericht des Unterrheinkreises, Mannheim, 7 January 1839, FHP, box 1, folder 2. Gustav Struve, Gustav Rasch, *Zwölf Streiter für die Revolution* (Berlin, 1867), 277-78. On his marriage to Marie Josefine Eisenhardt, see Strack, *Herkunft*, 9, 10. Walter, *Mannheim*, 277-78. On Itzstein's election agitation 1842-46, cf. Josef Roßkopf, *Johann Adam von Itzstein*, Ph. D. diss. Mainz, 1954, 149; Nolte, "Gemeindeliberalismus," 407; on the special circumstances of Hecker's election, see the debates in sessions of the Baden Chamber: *VSB*, 12. öS (17 June 1842), 294-97; *VSB*, 14. öS (23 June 1842), 5-7, 21; *VSB*, 26. öS (25 July 1842), 298-99. *VSB*, 23. öS (29 January 1844), 318.

[28] FH to Adam von Itzstein, Belleville, 14 June 1850, Itzstein Nachlaß, Zug-Nr. 168/58. Roßkopf, *Itzstein*, 152, also Hans Blum, *Die deutsche Revolution 1848/49. Eine Jubiläumsausgabe für das deutsche Volk* (Florence; Leipzig, 1898), 90.

[29] Cf. Roßkopf, *Itzstein*, 151.

[30] Adam von Itzstein was godfather for all three Hecker children born in those years, Arthur, Erwin and Malwina, see Strack, *Herkunft*, 10.

[31] See on the following particularly Roßkopf, *Itzstein*, 134-39; with extensive explanations of the proceedings and various combinations at the meetings, Siegfried Schmidt, "Der Hallgartenkreis 1839-47. Zur Genese des bürgerlichen Parteiwesens im deutschen Vormärz," *Wissenschaftliche Beiträge der Friedrich-Schiller-Universität Jena* 13 (1964), 221-28; Hecker's article in the *GL* 1869, 552 ff.; see as well the thoroughly researched article by Rudolf Muhs, "'Wie die geheimen Konferenzbeschlüsse an das Tageslicht gezogen wurden.' Zur Publikation des Schlussprotokols von 1834 und zur Rolle des Hallgarten-Kreises fur die vormarzliche Opposition," *AfS* 26 (1986), 321-343.

[32] FH to Adam von Itzstein, Belleville, Ill., 22 October 1853, Itzstein Nachlaß; here he mentions that his eldest son Arthur still had lively memories of Hallgarten. FH, *Ideen und Vorschläge zu einer Reform des Gerichtswesens* (Mannheim, 1844), 14. Thorough on this is Rudolf Muhs, "Wiener Konferenzbeschlüsse," 331; the knowledge of these acts was also the reason Hecker gave for rejecting the budget in 1846, see *VSB*, 76. öS (14. September 1846), 165; cf. also *VSB*, 28. öS (24. Februar 1848), 308. Muhs, "Wiener Konferenzbeschlüsse," 342.

[33] Roßkopf, *Itzstein*, 139-45. See Peter Schuppan, *Johann Jacoby und seine politische Wirksamkeit innerhalb der bürgerlichen-demokratischen Bewegung des Vormärz (1830-1846)*, Ph. D. diss., Berlin/East, 1963, 370, n. 12, based on the Robert Blum Papers.

[34] This event even aroused attention in America, see Körner, *Memoirs*, vol. 1, 180. See the debate in the Baden Chamber on the expulsion, *VSB*, 26. öS (26 July 1845), 18-32; on the petitions, cf. also August Heinrich Hoffmann von Fallersleben, Adam von Itzstein, in Eduard Duller, ed., *Männer des Volkes*, vol. 5/6 (Frankfurt am Main, 1848), 174-75. *Ein freies Wort über die Ausweisung der badischen Abgeordneten v. Itzstein und Hecker aus Preußen* (Leipzig, 1845), 7, 8, 9, 11, 14, 17, 20. Hecker's complaint to the Baden State Ministry, Karlsruhe, Mannheim, 27 May 1845, printed in Fallersleben, *Itzstein*, 170-71; also in *Mannheimer Journal*, no. 148, 3 June 1845, 589-90.

Friedrich Hecker speaking in the Second Chamber, Grand Duchy of Baden, about 1846. Friedrich Hecker Papers, Western Historical Manuscripts, University of Missouri – St. Louis.

II

POLITICAL CONCEPTS

The Social Contract – Constitution – Popular Representation

Unlike Julius Fröbel, Gustav von Struve or Arnold Ruge, Hecker never attempted to present his political views in a theoretical treatise. If one wished to give a survey of his basic principles, it would be necessary to distill his political presumptions from the plethora of his Chamber speeches, his motions in the assembly and his articles for the daily press. This shows us how much he was a "child of his times," because his concepts of constitution and the state reflected in classic style the many influences that generally determined political thought in the pre-Revolutionary era. He was, as Heinrich Scharp correctly remarked, "not so much a creator or awakener as a bearer and an expression of the ideas and themes of his time."[1]

Hecker knew two methods of argument, as a rule. On the one hand, keeping with the matter under discussion, he started "from the standpoint of principles," making theoretical presumptions his foundation. On the other, as a practicing jurist, he used the standpoint of "positive law," and he interpreted the law or constitutional passage in question in his own sense. As a rule, however, he made use of theoretical considerations only insofar as it appeared useful to him in achieving specific political goals.

Because Hecker's 1845 publication on *The Situation of the German-Catholics in State Law* used a whole string of theories and principles of state to defend religious freedom, a glance at the views on the law of reason that obviously dominated him is necessary. Ideas from Aristotle's *Politics*, Locke's *Two Treatises on Government*, Montesquieu's *Spirit of the Laws* and *Persian Letters*, Rousseau's *Social Contract* and various writings by Kant showed up time and again in Hecker. He thought of the state as something "given, formal," marked by a contract. In the area before or outside the state, in which man was in fact already man but not yet a citizen, all of those inalienable human rights were to be found that cannot be touched even by the state. These extra-state rights described roughly the home, hence the family, the area of religion (liberty of conscience), as well as the right to physical security – an addition found neither in Aristotle nor in Rousseau, but which had significance for Hecker in connection with the debate on the death penalty. This showed that he was not slavishly dependent on specific predecessors but was continually on the lookout for new and better arguments in his own eclectic process.

Upon entering the state, according to Hecker, a person makes what are called minimal concessions, either giving up some alienable rights in favor of the state constitution, or restricting them to promote the supreme, social purpose of the state, which was to secure the existence of the state itself. Hecker thought of the human being entirely in Enlightenment terms, a creature whose nature aimed at perfecting its potential and who joined into a political association, the state, because he understood that perfection would be less possible in isolation than in a community. This "drive to sociability, to common effort, is inborn." For that reason, the political formation of a state came from exactly the same origin as the right of association. "Since the individual person," Hecker argued, drawing on Aristotle and Rousseau, "is not so perfect or gifted that he is in the position to achieve all achievable goals by means of his isolated personality, he must be conceded the right to unite, and with it the possibility to intellectual development and perfection. This perception has united people into society, into the state, even when," Hecker followed Aristotle, "a special drive for sociability and association has not been recognized as being present." Hecker derived the general right of association from the nature of human beings. Whoever denied this right and assumed that the rule was isolation obviously denied the foundations of the state, and further the family, prescribing for man a lonely "Troglodyte's life."

The rights of the individual were reduced by the state to the extent "that the purpose of self-preservation of the state commands it." Everything, in fact, that could endanger the existence or survival of the state found its limitation in the "emergency right of the state." Someone who entered the state association became "a member of the state" and is obligated to "essential duties toward the state society," "obligations received through the social contract" that were compensated through the securing of rights. "Because right and duty are correlated," Hecker saw, "the lasting foundation of the state [rested] alone on this true mutuality of all in right and duty." This contract theory was the basic presumption of Hecker's concept of the state.

When arguing a question, Hecker always adjusted it to the actual conditions in Baden. Like Rotteck in his *Ideas on the State Assembly*, Hecker interpreted the Baden Constitution on the basis of positive legislation with an entirely strong position for the Second Chamber. For Hecker, the Baden Constitution was a representative one, and this was distinguished in the election law. There the concept of a "constitutionally restrained monarchy" and the basic principle of the equality of rights were expressed. "Until the appearance of the Constitutional Charter of 28 August 1818, Baden was an absolute monarchy," the constitution, which for Hecker was nothing more than a prescription for the relationship between the government and the ruled, expressed the rights and duties of all members of the state. The fundamental principles of the former absolute monarchy became void. "A new state has taken the place of the earlier one, and all true political rights can only be judged according to the statements of the new basic contract." This new basic contract made a new public law. If one paid attention to the old laws, Hecker explained, Baden would have a "double political code or a double basic state contract," an untenable situation for political practice. And the liberties and rights guaranteed by the new constitution could only be altered or restricted by means of new legislation, and possible only with the consent of the estates.[2] Like many liberals of his time, Hecker thus assumed the basic alterability of the constitution, as an ever closer approach to democratic and, in the end, republican conditions.[3]

As early as 1843 Hecker had the opportunity to publish an article about the Baden Assembly of 1842 in *Twenty-one Sheets from Switzerland*, a work that, as he wrote to the "Literary Exchange" in Zürich, could easily have had a sequel.[4] The occasion of this article was the furlough conflict that led to the dissolution of the Chamber, and new elections. Along with reprinting the ministerial rescript, which made manifest the government's attempts to influence the elections, Hecker was able to register his view of the political position and mission of the estate assembly. Like Rotteck, Hecker denied the rights of the First Chamber. Also like Rotteck, Hecker countered objections that spoke of the estates in terms of the "idea of feudal estates," at worst, or "postulate state assemblies" at best. Hecker interpreted the First Chamber as an anachronism from the start, representing individuals against the general interest of the people. He raised the Second Chamber to the level of true representative of the people. In his motion for ministerial responsibility, he brought this view to the lowest common denominator, saying, "After its organization, the Second Chamber is the representative of the people; from its exclusive election, it represents the people's interests, desires, ideas, the demands of the time; it is the moving element."[5]

Hecker was pleading as soon as the early 1840s for a very broad electoral basis. All the way to the pre-Parliament he remained true to his demand for as large a primary electorate as possible. There he later moved to have one representative for every 50,000 souls, not for every 70,000 voters as originally proposed. But his argument remained basically the same as in earlier years because one was could not call together the entire people, but had to represent it through deputies, "the number of representatives [must be] as large as possible." The broader the basis of primary voters, the more liberal and uncorrupted the election of electors would be, and the more difficult it would be for the government to influence elections.

If one should again make the civil right to vote dependent on property alone, determined by a census – something that was often demanded even in Baden – it would be "a declaration of war on fundamental human rights." "The rich and propertied are not the only ones who rescue the endangered fatherland," he reminded readers in his article of 1843,

> and if the poorer citizen is good enough to shed his blood for the common good, he must also be good enough to participate in general state assembly matters, for blood counts more than money, and a true representative system is present only when all citizens participate in popular representation.

For Hecker the same was true for the right to be elected. Property and tax payments alone should not determine the election of deputies, but also "the weapon of intelligence," with which the lawyer, the physician, the scholar and the artist might bestow their representation on one "whom good fortune has not favored with a more extensive education."[6]

Immediately after his election as deputy in August 1842, Hecker left no doubt how strongly he held the rights assured the estates through the constitutional charter. Hecker joined the long-standing pre-Revolutionary discussion of Kant's distinction between decrees and orders that were not laws because they only rested on the decision of the regent in a particular case, and could be altered.[7] Hecker called his colleagues to recall the competence of the Chamber, saying, "Gentlemen, all of you know that according to the constitution, no law can come into being without the approval or cooperation of the Chamber." On the other hand, he continued, it was the government's right to issue orders insofar as they did not contradict the constitutional rights of the Chambers. But if one considered the nature of such orders, "which the government has a right to issue on its own authority," a simple double nature was revealed.

> The government can issue regulations, that is, commands, when they give detailed application to principles already expressed in laws that have come into existence with the cooperation of the Chambers; the government has the power to regulate execution and detailed application.

In other words, a law became law for Hecker only through the concurrence of the Chambers; consequently, binding force could derive only from a law. Naturally, as Hecker magnanimously conceded, the government had a series of powers given by the constitution. But he insisted on a right of the Second Chamber to recall government orders. Taken to its full implication, this would have meant that only the Second Chamber could interpret what was an order and what was a law. To Hecker there was a great "temptation" on the part of the government either to issue entirely new laws without the approval of the Chambers or to introduce laws that "mutilate, hem in or in part or entirety destroy those laws approved by the estates." For that reason it was the supreme mission of a watchful People's Chamber to take care "that the police legislation and the right of oversight be practiced only within constitutional limits" and "to keep watch that a separate legislation does not creep into our state without our approval, lest the citizen no longer know what laws to keep."

When Deputy Sander made a motion concerning deputies' responsibility for their statements in the Chamber, Hecker obviously supported irresponsibility and immunity with the argument that it contradicted the nature of the representative constitution to deny the Chamber the "right of the *free word*." "We are not speaking here as free persons; rather, everything that we say is in our capacity as deputies, an expression of the common will of the people." Because of this, deputies could not be treated as private persons. Because the Second Chamber was, for Hecker, the "true expression of the common will of the people" from the very beginning, the simple right of approving laws became the sole right to make laws; a decree of the government became a generally applicable and binding law only through the approval of the Chamber.

Hecker similarly interpreted the right of the Second Chamber to approve taxes. He dealt with the question in the preface to his petition to deny the budget:[8]

> To put the matter simply and nakedly, the question is this: can the government fill positions stricken by the Chamber against its will? In other words, does the Chamber have the right to strike particular positions within the budget? Does it have this right absolutely or not? ... does the Chamber have the right to strike on its own authority under the given conditions, and is the government bound to such actions?[9]

Hecker's response reminds one of Rotteck. If the Chamber did not have the right to strike positions on its own authority, but only the right to approve, one could no longer speak of a right; for it was no right if the government could independently give out positions as it pleased with or without approval. Instead, the Chamber assumed only a merely advisory function. Whether this advice is accepted or rejected depended on the judgment or good will of the government, and in each case the government would not be bound to it. "If that were so, then we would be mere provincial estates or postulate-estates and no longer a state assembly."[10] The deputies could simply go home. Conversely, Hecker reasoned, if the right of approval were recognized, then the right of approving the budget also had to be recognized. As the course of events would show, achieving a denial of the budget by the Chamber would create many problems, and its failure would drive Hecker to the limits of parliamentary possibilities.

Freedom of Conscience and Religious Tolerance –
The German-Catholics and Thomas Paine

The conflict involving the position of the German-Catholic religious community caused Hecker to take a public position for the first time on the freedom of conscience and religious tolerance. The history of the German-Catholics began with an open letter by the Silesian chaplain Johannes Ronge to Bishop Arnoldi of Trier on 1 October 1844. In this message the chaplain protested the display of the Holy Robe in Trier Cathedral, an event that was orchestrated by the Catholic clergy as a mass pilgrimage, and was oriented particularly to the poorer parts of the population. Celebrated by liberals as a "second Luther," for going to war against crude works-righteousness and the cult of relics, Ronge was excommunicated by the Roman Catholic Church. In response, he and a fellow excommunicant, the vicar Johannes Czerski, established German-Catholic congregations in Silesia. By early 1845 these were more than a hundred strong. In Mannheim a congregation of German-Catholics was called into existence on 29 July 1845, including among its founders Hecker's brother-in-law Eisenhardt. A few months later, on 28 September, Ronge came to Mannheim in person, accompanied by Rudolph Dowiat, the Turner, and there was a festive gathering that Hecker and Bassermann also attended.[11]

The majority of the German states, as well as Catholic Austria, saw the German-Catholic movement as a threat endangering the security of both the state and the Roman Catholic Church. Oppressive and restrictive measures were introduced in Baden, leading to a conflict between the government and the Second Chamber that broadened into a principled discussion of the freedom of conscience, belief and opinion. The liberal deputies in particular were aware that the Trier pilgrimage had been set up by the clergy and nobility primarily for the lower social classes. The propertied and educated bourgeoisie was virtually uninvolved.[12]

Debates in the Second Chamber on 15 December 1845 addressed this question. The subject of German-Catholics was brought up in connection with the motion of Deputy Zettel on freedom of religion. Hecker, who had no religious convictions at all, declared the cause of the German-Catholics to be a triumph of reason and its realization in history. According to Hecker's analysis, tradition and historical right could not prevent the rise of the democratizing process or the self-determination of each individual citizen:

> The day when the first new-Catholic congregation formed was the dawn of a great moment in our historical phase. For the first time reason came into its rights against historical right, and the great truth emerged that the stream cannot be held back, whatever the tradition of millennia has established and however much the grand tradition of liberty has been oppressed.[13]

A series of writings appeared, defending the German-Catholics and expressing the liberals' varying desires and hopes. The projections varied, depending on whether each author sought an extension of the rights of liberty or hoped for national unity. For example, in his publication of 1845 on *The Mission of the German-Catholics*, Georg Gottfried Gervinus saw the German-Catholic movement as growing from the "core of the middle class," and he pled for a super-confessional union of German-Catholics and Protestants as a preliminary to German unification. Here, Gervinus said, was an opportunity to create the foundation for a new German national state "on the agreement of spiritual education and religious reconciliation."[14]

In his own publication of 1845, *The Situation of the German-Catholics in State Law with Special Reference to Baden*, Hecker took a different path, but one that was characteristic of him. This position was immediately obvious from the choice of a motto from Thomas Paine's *The Rights of Man*.

> It is only under governments built on presumption and false principles that one is not permitted to contemplate or research governmental systems and principles or show their various qualities and faults, without being branded a lampooner and a rebel.

In this publication Hecker again used the law of contract to distinguish two spheres, the private and the political, the sphere of people and the sphere of the citizen. For Hecker there is no doubt that religion belonged in the area before, or outside, the state. He saw the liberty of conscience as an inalienable right; restricting religious confession merely "hinders the fulfillment of civic duties." Religion was, in Kant's sense of the word, something entirely "interior." The state had to restrict itself to the area of external appearances, and man "comes into consideration only as a member of the state, not as the confessor of a religion." For Hecker, the most reasonable example of this statement was the declaration of the Bill of Rights, amending the American

Constitution, "that Congress shall make no law establishing religion, or for-
bidding its free exercise." According to Hecker,

> The separation of Church from state, the principle of religious liberty, is
> most practically solved there; and American authors ascribe the swift
> blooming, the prosperity and development of their land to this full lib-
> erty of religion and its influence on civic life.

Hecker's belief that the enormous prosperity of the United States
resulted from a free constitution was one of his central themes during the
Revolutionary period. The United States had drawn an important lesson
from history, namely, that intermingling church and state only conjured up
eternal conflicts to the disadvantage of both; "the bloodiest and most
destructive wars were soon religious ones, and religion was used as the
cover for other views."[15] Hecker formulated it somewhat more specifically
in 1845, drawing from Rousseau, Montesquieu and Tocqueville by speaking
of constitutional patriotism as a secularized religion, the uniting strength of
the state.[16]

> The United States recognized that the unifying force of the state was
> not in the unity or equality of the religious conviction of the citizens,
> but instead in the thoughts of all having the state as their point of uni-
> fication, while simultaneously diffused in religious matters, and pre-
> cisely because the confession of every religion was permitted, all the
> residents of a state region found their point of unity in the state, it
> becoming their common highest good.[17]

It was no accident that Hecker mentioned love of country in the context
of religion, for patriotism took thoroughly quasi-religious forms even when
oriented to a secular institution, the state. According to Montesquieu, the
"love of the republic" – an attachment to existing institutions, as Hecker
saw it – was a feeling open to everyone in the state, regardless of class or
education. It was not the consequence of perceptions. As stated in the
Staatslexikon, patriotism did not mean dependence on the accidental land of
one's own birth, but rather in the

> nobler sense ... the most intimate community with the land and the
> people where one has *citizen rights* – a community that expresses itself
> in the most loyal dependence on this land and people, expressed in
> total commitment, so that one makes the concerns of the whole one's
> own concerns and continually subordinates his personality to the
> generality.[18]

Patriotism contained components of both emotion and action. It was a political feeling transformed into deeds that were not precisely command- ed and could not be produced by unthinking obedience to abstract laws. The state itself must with good laws create the reason why one could "love it in a reasonable way."[19] Hecker's struggle for these "good laws" was moti- vated by his perception of this mutual causation. Constitution and laws must be created in such a way that the citizen could perceive in them the guaranteed realization of his own determination. But this assumes that one could love every state that fulfilled these conditions, suggesting that such a land might be other than the one in which one was born.

Hecker saw religion, represented for him by the Catholic Church, as the great competitor to his concept of the citizen. He shared Rousseau's skepti- cism that one could ever be both a pious and good citizen at the same time, because contradictory obligations would hinder this. But the individual was not alone in perpetual conflict; conflicts between states that defined themselves by their faith were also preordained.

Hecker's statement in the Chamber showed that, for him, America was the best example for successfully achieving separation of church and state:

> It has been asserted that North America is in chaos because of freedom of religion. I spoke only yesterday to a North American diplomat to whom I presented what you said, and three months ago I spoke with a North American preacher. Both assured me no person knows anything about this chaos. ... North America operates from entirely practical principles in this case. It has grown great on our bloody experiences, and it has adopted into its constitution the principle that every person can combine with others of his faith without disturbance. If one does not identify state with church, all the members of the state have only one common focus for their external lives, and this is the state.[20]

In the field of positive law, Hecker drew on paragraph 18 of the Baden Constitution, which defended freedom of religion by assuring "every resi- dent ... undisturbed liberty of conscience, and equal protection in consider- ation of his manner of worship."[21] To Hecker the explication of paragraph 9, referring to the "three ... confessions" present in the country, was simply a historical statement; at the time of the composition of the Baden Consti- tution, there were in fact only three confessions. This historical statement was to be distinguished from the political axiom of religious freedom, which marked progressive development in accommodating new conditions.

For Hecker the separation of church and state also encompassed the separation of church and school. In his view school instruction should promote enlightenment, by educating citizens.[22] His excessive dislike of Jesuits, which would reach almost grotesque proportions in America, stemmed from his presumption of their influence on education and instruction. He believed there was only one thing to do in response, "I do not fear anything, even from the Jesuits," Hecker declared, turning to the government bench in the Chamber,

> if you give us your guarantee, which is the best dam against their ultramontane and Jesuit traditions and machinations ... A principle means against the Jesuits is enlightenment and education, and, further, good school instruction – no convent schools, no boys' seminaries or Merciful Sisters. A second principle means that does not taste of the police state is freedom of the press, association and assembly.

This demand explained Hecker's engaged attitude in the Second Chamber on questions of upgrading public school teachers, altering the schooling system, or academic freedom at the universities. Shortly after entering the Second Chamber, he bewailed the pitiful state of teachers, in whose flourishing everyone had an interest, because everyone owed his first education to this group. A year later, Hecker supported Deputy Bissing's motion demanding the emancipation of the schools from the church. Hecker stressed that the church restricted academic freedom, and that a teacher's calling was entirely different from that of the church. The teacher had to make his pupils "aware of the rights of citizens and the foundations on which these rested, as well as of constitutional life," hence educating them into citizens. When raising the pay of teachers was debated a few months later, Hecker supported it without further question, despite already high financial burdens on the state of Baden from the military budget, railroad construction and the promotion of investment for trade and industry. "Whoever wants to have an intelligent people," he stated shortly and sharply, "cannot spare the means that lead to it." "We have to educate citizens," on that is founded "the entire basis of the state ... the entire wellbeing of the state [depends] on the intelligence and preparation of the individual."[23] Through public education, Hecker already aimed at a republican form of state.

What was proper for the public schools could only be just for academic freedom at the universities. All of the restrictions and restrictive decrees at the universities – and here Hecker spoke of his own life – served only to trouble the intellectual self-determination of studying youth. In the severe restrictions on young teachers, Hecker recognized the government's effort to hinder precisely those forces that could guarantee rejuvenated and intellectually animated life at the universities.

We must permit freer breathing space for youth in the few years in which they can obtain a broader intellectual direction and are not yet pressed by the cares of life, so that we do not raise slaves but rather people capable of determining their own will.[24]

Behind this demand stood once more the idea, arising from the Enlightenment and important for the pre-Revolutionary era, of educating citizens in individual self-determination. Only such people could develop a consciousness that was morally oriented to common interests. For Hecker two considerations came together here: on the one hand, education to citizenship, and on the other, the entirely practical demand for general, popular education as a guarantee that even lower classes could "climb up" and participate in prosperity. The latter concept found its place in perhaps an even more radical form in the Offenburg Program's "education for everyone."

A Matter of Honor – Attorney for the People

When Friedrich Hecker was elected to the Second Baden Chamber in 1842, he had already been practicing as a lawyer in Mannheim for some time. Even his political opponents in the parliament could not deny that he brought "significant additions to the parliamentary struggle"[25] with a mixture of eloquence and dialectical tactics peculiar to his profession."A talented, tireless, ever-aggressive lawyer's eloquence, a fresh, lovely, often stormy way of fighting, supported by the energy and ruthlessness of his young and winning individuality" made him "very qualified to be leader of the opposition," wrote Häusser in an article of 1848. Häusser went on to say, "It cannot be ignored that he was, along with Sander, the most significant juristic talent on the opposition's side. His proven talent as a lawyer, if applied with judgment, worked well for him." This, to be sure, was before Häusser's search for blame a few years later, in which he recast admirable lawyer's talent as hateful "lawyer radicalism"[26] that spread clear revolutionary tendencies throughout Baden.

For Hecker the mission of the lawyer greatly resembled that of a people's representative. A brief glance should therefore be given to the political implications associated with this profession, as well as to Hecker's expressions of his own self-understanding. Hecker belonged to the legal profession "by choice and inclination," and he had "not chosen [it] because of material interests." On what Hecker knew of his own juristic training and professional practice, much is found in an article that Hecker contributed to the second edition of the *Staatslexikon*. Indeed, the editors, who had already accepted an article on the same subject,[27] felt compelled to remark in a footnote to the second article, "The high importance of the subject seemed to

warrant accepting this second article." The piece is saturated with principled views on the state, society and legal consciousness.

Hecker believed the position and status of a lawyer depended on the
intensity of free institutions in a state. An active public life appeared indispensable to the existence of a prestigious lawyer class. The lawyer was "the
mediator between scholarship and practice." As the "legal friend of the people," he played an essential part in the progress of legislation, "insofar as,
despite all his respect for the law, he [indicated] its lack of applicability to
the present in the phenomena of life"; that is, he forced and supported progressive, new legislation, taking changed circumstances into account. The
lawyer was therefore supposed to be the practical conduit for progress, having a better understanding of the times than those who were not familiar
with legal traditions.

Hecker did not see the mission of the lawyer as restricted to the sector
of private law. For him the juristic mission in politics included the mutual
dependence of civil and public law. If the civil law lay in fetters as far as the
law of property, wealth, marriage and family were concerned, then public
law could not recognize any "citizen bestowed with free rights." In other
words, every state constitution not only found its expression in public law,
but also conditioned all modifications of private law. Here Hecker appeared
not to go so far as Julius Fröbel, who wanted to dissolve private law completely into public law by constituting a true people's state. According to
Fröbel, the civil law, or private law, could no longer be sanctioned as an area
distinguished from the political, public law, and would actually be suspended. Hecker, however, paid attention to the mutual dependence of the two
legal spheres. "The spirit of the public, legal constitution of an individual
state blew through all private legal relationships," he said. And since he
believed this, he was able to formulate the eminently political mission of the
German lawyer class.

> The lawyer in Germany is called to oppose the systematic enslavement
> of a splendid nation; to teach, defend, and encourage his fellow citizens
> to be citizens aware of their rights; to raise them out of their stupor and
> awaken their awareness of rights, to oppose pretense and contempt for
> citizens; to fight every violation of the law, and every stroke of cabinet-
> justice, every legalized murder, with an elevated voice and, finally, to
> call them before the incorruptible tribunal of public opinion.[28]

Many assumptions underlay this passage. Clearly, Hecker shared with
other radical democrats the presumption that the condition of political reality in Germany had its foundation in the individual's imperfect level of
awareness. He stressed the fictional but popular historical assumption that

in earlier times there had once been a free German people who were aware of their rights and were later rendered dependent by an alien force. Borrowings from the concept of "Germanic liberty" were clear here. According to that theory, nobility, clergy and bureaucracy had degraded the law and justice into the possession of a caste and patrimony instead of elevating it to the people's common property. Legislation had been formulated not from clear principles but according to changing needs and interests, so that law and justice became a "Riddle of the Sphinx for the people."[29] Cases were foreordained in which the citizen would violate some criminal law or other without knowing it. For this reason lawyers had to assist the citizen, enlighten him, and also reawaken the people's "shaken" consciousness of right.

Much of the enlightenment function attributed to lawyers recalled the elitist concept of other radical democrats, such as Arnold Ruge and Julius Fröbel, as well as Gustav von Struve. They saw the people's incapacity and lack of enlightenment as so great that it legitimized a theoretical elite which could claim leadership as long as the consciousness of liberty and rights was incompletely developed in the people. American historians have thus explained the outstanding position of the Forty-Eighters among Germans in the United States, through this claim to leadership that they brought along with them from Europe and that was later to blame for conflicts within German-American leadership. Hecker's article on the legal profession also theoretically legitimized the existence of an "intelligentsia" that was called to leadership because of greater fundamental preparation. Of course, there was the danger of lawyers becoming too elitist and isolated, using their knowledge in an authoritarian way. For this reason Hecker once again drew on the concept of civic virtue, derived from ancient and neo-humanist traditions.

Civic virtue was a selfless activity, motivated by morality and directed solely toward the common good. Hecker presented the virtuous lawyer as "fighting in the first rank" but, at the same time, anchored him entirely among the people and belonging to them totally. In order to hinder corruption in the profession, Hecker knew only one means, an appeal to that professional honor recognized by all sides in a communicative association. "The most effective means to hold down abuse and impropriety," he wrote, "has always been the discipline of comrades, as history shows." In contradiction to Montesquieu, German pre-Revolutionary liberals thus paralleled the concept of virtue and the concept of honor. Honor was the spur to social recognition through commitment to the common good, in the interests of the state. In this early context Hecker used the established concept of "honor of labor" as a basis for motivation. Citizens were attracted by commitment to the common good and were spurred "not to prove unworthy of it." France, in particular, was for him an example of this mechanism. There the spirit of the public served as the corrective for judging actions in public matters, and each leader was accountable to this public for his office. "Reputation and honor" were thus the highest human goods, along with "existence and support." Hecker would demonstrate in America how highly he valued reputation and honor. His actions would echo Article 13 of the Offenburg Program, which said, "We demand the abolition of all privileges. *To each the respect of his free fellow citizens is his sole advantage and payment.*"[30]

His demand for honorable and virtuous labor for the community bound Hecker with a particular image of humanity shared by liberals before the Revolution of 1848. Entirely in keeping with Rousseau's notion that man was not evil, but was only made evil by circumstances, Hecker was certain that only a free constitution could make free men possible. Freedom bred virtuous men, just as despotism bred only "slaves" and damaged morals. "Take anyone and suspend the presumption of goodness [*praesumtio boni viri*], declare him immoral and degraded, and he will become so." Hecker also drew on the tradition of the Enlightenment and appealed to the better side of people, to their unending possibility for development, which would result in a rise in morality. This morality was the core of his "concept of civic virtue." "It is an old truth that, if one entrusts anyone with a noble activity, if one sees himself entrusted with a certain moral greatness, there is a great incentive not to disappoint this public trust." The lawyer was to be rewarded for his commitment for the common good by the recognition of his fellow citizens.

The fact that Hecker was drawing on sources from antiquity was shown elsewhere. When a discussion arose in the Chamber about awarding medals, Hecker was obviously opposed, saying that they would merely cost money, increase vanity and represent no recognition from the people. In contrast the granting of laurel wreaths or cups in antiquity did show this recognition by the people because "in antiquity, whoever became unworthy of laurel wreaths lost them, but here we see many men continuing to bear their medals with pride."[31] For every lawyer, every official, the respect of his fellow citizens should be the determining incentive for moral, virtuous action for the common good.

Community and Sense of Community – Associations, Corporations and Societies

In his writing and in speeches in the Chamber, Hecker often touched on the Old-Germanic law of associations and corporations, as it was formed and accepted in the legal struggle between Romanists and Germanists in the nineteenth century. It was obvious that, when he emphasized the necessity of forming workers' associations as a means of overcoming the social question during the Revolutionary period, he drew more on the old idea of community known to him from studying Germanic legal procedure than on his incomplete acquaintance with French socialists, which he perhaps received only in the later 1840s via Struve and Fröbel. The fact that Hecker combined political concepts with the idea of association emerges from a letter Hecker sent to Julius Groos the Heidelberg publisher of his pamphlet on the German-Catholics. In this letter Hecker made it clear that his work arose primarily from the right of assembly and only secondarily from the theme of religious tolerance. It was his intention, Hecker told the publisher,

> if this little work has a positive reception, to deal with the great questions of the day … in brochures of this sort, in which I would next deal with the right of association and assembly. It all depends on the reception of this work, which will certainly set court publicist pens into action.[32]

In the search for sources of a Germanic idea of right, the conflict between Germanists and Romanists started with the presumption that Germanic law could not attain the abstract concept of personality of Roman law, but rather continually placed the mutual relationship of individuals to one another in the center.[33] In Germanic law the individual always counted for more as a member of the community than he did in his purely abstract, isolated individuality. In his article in the *Staatslexikon*, Hecker stated this juristic distinction in an almost classic manner:

> While the idea of association always shines through everywhere in German law, with the individual primarily considered as the member of the community or corporation, the idea of individual rights goes through the whole of Roman law. … Everywhere in Roman law the individual citizen appears in his exclusive legal sphere, for him alone, while in Germanic law the citizen always appears in relation to his family or communal society.[34]

The attractiveness of the idea of association in Germanic law, as communicated in an idealized form through legal science doctrine in the nineteenth century, was caused by a markedly nationalistic, as well as democratic dynamic. When the historical tradition and the development of communal right were stressed, a nationalistic dynamic was emphasized. The Germanic past was interpreted as a form of right derived directly from Germanic conditions, the second great form of right, alongside the right of lords. Communal law was declared a true people's law, shaken only by the reception of Roman law. In opposition to this, Roman law was seen as the possession of a caste. The law increasingly was administered by the emperor and his jurists alone, with the people utterly excluded. Preserved only in an artificial language via Byzantine compilations, it became solely the property of the learned, "the doctors," originating "outside of the people," as the jurist Georg Beseler stressed in his Basel inaugural address in 1836. It was this Beseler who later attempted, in his 1843 book *People's Law and Jurists' Law* [*Volksrecht und Juristenrecht*], to take the juristic fictive character from Germanic associations and attribute to them a real existence.[35]

The law of association was shaped by a democratic as well as a nationalistic dynamic. While "rulers' law" was established only by the prince or king, and was exercised over individuals, the association was thought to bind each member with all others, dealing with them together as a single living unit. Here, as with the law of lords, the concept of mutual rights and duties applied. But in the association a new "old" form of gathering together was found. This was a joining of equals together, and the full powers that were vested in the association as a whole were transferred, with the approval of all members, to a few people or to a single person. This person or persons then acted as a deputy. But common power did not mutate into a personal power, because the common power was thought to remain in the hands of all members. In ideal terms, the association continued, united, willing and acting over any common property, while at the same time restricting the "economic activity of the individual in favor of the whole." Seen from outside, the association in many ways restricted the "individual will" of the member who submitted to it; but it also represented and protected him against the outside world. The association represented the whole and constituted itself as a single subject of law by assembling all members as bearers of the unity of the group. This was despite the fact that the association's essential nature was both a unity and a plurality of many individuals. With such a whole there might be the threat of dissolution into individuals and their "special interests." But membership in the association did not mean that all individual interests dissolved and disappeared. A part of those interests remained untouched by the whole. The common will, conceived as unanimous, was actually a resolution passed by a majority.[36] Conceived as a single legal person – a group that was, in contrast to Roman law, capable of rights, hence capable of representation – the association was unaltered in its identity despite departure or change of membership, although changes in the whole might occur due to cumulative changes in membership.

In his work *The Situation of the German-Catholics in State Law*, Hecker used the distinction between Germanic and Roman law, developed in the disputes between the Romanists and the Germanists, to justify the association of German-Catholics independent of the state. Like many other jurists, he held fast to the concept that the introduction of Roman law had been nothing other than the transfer of alien legal concepts onto a people entirely foreign to this law. "The product of other national outlooks and political institutions was grafted, for the advantage of the rulers, onto a people whose character and state institutions were worlds apart from the Romans."[37]

In order to defend the viability of a free right of association that was politically significant, free and independent of the state, Hecker, who otherwise paid little attention to historical origins, had to stress here the law that grew historically, that is, the law of association, which arose from an idealized Germanic past. The justification for "forming associations," he said in his work, was a

> principle saturating the whole of Germanic national life, but which was suppressed by Roman views. A proud, hard civic consciousness surrounded every Roman citizen with a massive sphere of lordly rights. The Roman citizen, a full-fledged individual, was viewed more on his own and less in connection with others. [The principle of association] has arisen once more in recent times. We see associations arise in all the situations of civic life, in trade and crafts, in science and art, and to suppress them would be to block a vital vein. Associations are being formed everywhere, even in opposition to existing legislation in order to influence it by legal means.[38]

Hecker joined the right of association to the concept of a group that, precisely because its members had joined together in mutual agreement, could collectively have more impact on the state than could an individual. Certainly the right of association had its limit in having to choose goals that did not endanger the state. But the state should have the right to dissolve associations only when they threatened the state. In Hecker's argument, openness was the controlling organ to demonstrate that an association's goals were no danger to the state. Associations and openness belonged together, and they should be in constant interchange with each other. Hecker tolerated secret societies neither in Germany nor in America.

The rediscovery and emphasis of Germanic rights and the associational legal form supported efforts at political, as well as non-political, association. Jurists and public law specialists such as Welcker, Rotteck, Zachariä, Mohl, Stahl and – following their reception and interpretation – Hecker, as well, intensively occupied themselves with it. The idea of association was, as Hartwig Brandt stressed, "one of the key, stimulating concepts of the epoch"; it theoretically justified not only a new social form, but also a new, politically useful form of organization.[39]

For Hecker, the concepts of the right of association could be found in all sorts of associational self-administration and solidarity for worker and craft groups. Yet he made association law the sole positive law on which to rely in the pre-Revolutionary period, when he demanded legal association-building and popular assembly. Hecker and other jurists and specialists in state law interpreted this law of association as broadly as possible. A clear example of this was Carl Theodor Welcker's article in the *Staatslexikon* on the concept of "Association," in which he immediately subsumed the concepts of "society, community, people's assembly (address to the people, collective petitions), right of association."[40]

The law of 26 October 1833 stated as positive law the unrestricted right of association. Hecker recognized as fact that "now, by the authority of the right of association, the choice of goal and means by which temporary advantages, spiritual or moral development and perfection may be achieved remains open to the members of the state." For these purposes, people might form societies.

> Every association, the unification of a majority of individuals to achieve a common purpose according to certain principles and according to certain forms among which such are applied, forms a body, a legal personality. It does not require any special recognition by the state; this would contradict a free right of association, because the association could only come into existence through state permission and would not exist if state permission were denied. Yet, in contradiction to the law of 26 October 1833, a society can come into existence only with state permission. These freely formed legal personalities, due to their nature and legal situation, necessarily have the obligation to order their social situations through certain associational organs and to take care to choose a chairman, establish a location, regulate their assemblies and gatherings, all in public. This is in the interests of the state and is public due to state oversight.[41]

Hecker had in mind not only the problem of the German-Catholics at the time, but also the right to form any association at all. This right rose to ever greater prominence in the 1840s and was transformed into a larger scale in the first weeks of the Revolution, particularly after the second Offenburg assembly. If one reads Hecker carefully, he seemed to borrow from Tocqueville when speaking of the freedom of association. Tocqueville very precisely described the mechanism between a democratic form of state and the liberty of association. Tocqueville, like Hecker, started from the idea that the right of association was an inalienable right, and that it was absolutely necessary in democratic states.[42] In America the formation of political associations offered a democratic form of protest to support necessary alterations and reforms. Hecker was not alone in making continual use of this tool after coming to the land of unrestricted association. For him there was virtually no political or social problem that could not be addressed by forming an association. One of the reasons that Hecker, along with many other Forty-Eighters, could fit so easily into the American party system was his positive attitude toward forming associations. The Forty-Eighters knew, at least in theory, that no other means led so efficiently to the realization of commonly formulated goals.

Military Patriotism – The Citizen Militia

When, in the March days of 1848, calls to arm the people and erect a citizen militia grew ever louder, the Baden Second Chamber resolved to respond. Under pressure from the revolutionary mood in the country, the Chamber drafted a provisional citizen militia law. As early as 2 March 1848 Hecker and other deputies accepted an amendment to the expanded Mannheim Demands in order to thank the grand duke for approving a draft of the law to arm the people, and to express their expectation,

> that that arming will be carried out immediately, the choice of officers conceded to the people, and the military organization so erected that in need this arming of the people will serve to defend the fatherland against any external enemy; hence that, in times of peace, the burdening of the citizens through too great an extension of the military of the line may also fall away.

The draft law presented by the government did not, however, correspond to the Chamber's expectations. As a result Hecker was entrusted with redrafting it. In a few days and nights he drafted a provisional citizen's guard organization. It was discussed in the Chamber on 28 March 1848 and – due to the limited time available because of the impending Frankfurt pre-

Parliament – was adopted "by all voices" in the same session. This draft, marked by the widest possible democratic principles, was clearly derived from two-prongued idea. A general arming of the people, with the parallel eventual dismissal of the standing army, would serve as the "true" representation of the people. For Hecker this representation might be either a united national parliament or the second chamber in a constitutional state.[43] Because the representation of the people communicated the people's will, the decision to use the citizen's militia should also depend on the people themselves, that is, on its representatives, the Second Chamber.

The duty of the commission in whose name Hecker spoke and debated as its reporter on 28 March consisted of transforming the entire military system so "that a general arming of the people, similar to institutions in Switzerland," should occur. The expression "national guard" had been replaced by the term "citizens' guard" with the intent

> to express that all citizens should be armed. But we have also believed we must move beyond the narrow-minded position of particularism. Every German can be accepted, and so we have practically put the *idea of a free citizenry* into this law.

Because this law solidified only a transitory situation, and would be replaced with a future general military system, Hecker wanted to create with his citizens' guard system the foundation for later dissolving the armies of Germany into a citizens' guard.[44]

Hecker's concept of a citizens' guard foresaw an army aimed against both external and internal enemies. Hecker carefully avoided speaking any longer of "securing of the throne and the people," unlike Carl Theodor Welcker's article on the military in the *Staatslexikon*, whose proposals Hecker otherwise usually followed. Hecker added the following to the second article of his draft:

> The defense of the country, the constitution and the rights and freedoms secured by laws against internal and external enemies are the duty of the citizens' guard. We have seen the armed people as the solid protector of their own freedom and rights. We have not understood the guard simply as a security watch, as in Württemberg. We have not seen our soldiers simply as Corpus Christi soldiers. We have thought of the armed citizen as the defender against all attacks, from inside and outside.

Because Hecker expected the complete replacement of the line army by the citizens' guard, with the standing army either eliminated or dissolved into the people's army, he also saw national defense as part of the function of the citizens' militia. For him a militia was more than "a material condition for a comprehensive mobilization of the general right of resistance to the existing state." Hecker operated on the presumption that the free citizen identified with the constitution and would have to make its protection and defense his central concern. Like many pre-Revolutionary liberals, drawing on the historical idea of antiquity refreshed by Montesquieu and Tocqueville, Hecker could think of no more engaged defender than the citizen himself. He regarded moral motivation – a morality that was created by upbringing and education and that generated the political "feeling" of love of country – as more important than military efficiency created through disciplined drill. For that reason, Hecker did not hesitate in his draft to extend the competence of the citizens' militia to the greatest possible degree. The government's original draft of the law, rejected by the Chamber, wished a militia "only to maintain domestic order" and foresaw its use within individual communities, for local purposes. With his draft law Hecker approached a republican form of state and a union of confederated federal states. By accepting "all Germans," he foresaw the erection of an organically organized army that would cover the entire country and would be in a position to mobilize and defend against internal and external enemies.

Hecker clearly did not wish to leave the calling of the armed forces to state authority alone; he therefore incorporated restricting clauses. These expected the armed forces to be used only through an "act of legislation, and only for a limited time for war service." If the estates were not assembled, the estate standing committee could act through a provisional law, but the estates had to be called within ten days to confirm the law. If this confirming law were not approved within fourteen days, the provisional law then lost its effect. Hecker's justification for calling the representatives of the people the instant that the citizens' guard was to be mustered demonstrated his concern about the arbitrary use of the men by the state. For Hecker the participation of the estate standing committee was a guarantee "that the blood and property of the citizens will not be put in danger arbitrarily." Adoption of this Article 55 was sharply criticized by the government, as was to be expected, and Deputy Schaaf was correct when he complained that, from his point of view, "This shifts all the responsibility from the government to the estate standing committee."

In exceptional and emergency conditions, ministerial responsibility and civic virtue were of decisive importance in Hecker's construct. Ministerial responsibility, perennially demanded by Hecker and other deputies,

ensured that members of the government were held responsible to the popular representation for the quick, autonomous decisions that times of crisis
required. "As free a position as possible" was also taken on the training of
armed personnel and the election of their officers. With one exception, election as an officer should remain open to every citizen, "each and all;" the
sole exception was the commander of the legion, whose election by the officers still required state confirmation. Hecker took into account any objection
against amateurism in military leadership by including a restricting clause
expecting the leader of the army to have technical qualifications. For that
reason he explained the restrictions in the Chamber debates:

> There can be no doubt that in the case of war the commander himself
> will obtain the necessary technical knowledge, or if peril is at the gates,
> the people will seek out such leaders as are in a position to lead it
> according to the rules of the art of war. I have been elected a colonel of
> the guard in Mannheim. But I tell you, I would hold it to be a derelic-
> tion of duty to lead the force before the enemy before I had obtained the
> technical knowledge. On the other hand, one trusts the correct tact and
> healthy sense of the people that it would seek out such a leader in case of
> war who had such technical qualifications that it would not fall into peril
> or endanger its existence through the commandants it had elected.[45]

Hecker presumed moral integrity and responsible action in both ministers
and military commanders.[46] In keeping with the people's representation as
the controlling organ over ministers, he proposed to establish military
courts that would judge disciplinary violations of guardsmen and give
judgment through an oral process, without further recourse. These military
courts were to be jury courts, thus including citizens in judgment, as well.

On the question of the cost of armament, the commission was confronted with the difficulty that the necessary money could not be covered by the
treasuries of the state or communes, let alone by the funds of the corps
themselves. The ultimate solution was to appeal wholly to the patriotism of
the citizens. "We expect from the patriotism of our fellow citizens that the
individual guardsman should bear the costs of his arming himself." It was
only when the individual was unable to raise the funds that the corps treasury or the commune should contribute, in a limited fashion, and this was
restricted by conditions of eligibility. There would be no substitutes, and citizens who were incapable of bearing arms or who were sick were to contribute with their wealth to arming "on behalf of those without means."

Hecker saw the obligation to pay according to income to be "the idea of the income tax brought to practical life." When Deputy Peter proposed that contributions by sick persons should be voluntary, Hecker typically insisted on his own concept of social justice. "He [the rich sick person] could have brought on his gout with oysters and guzzling champagne. We cannot be so sentimental that we should let the wealthy get away free. Poor sick people are free."[47] Along with the disabled and the elderly (55 or older), wage workers with small children, mayors occupied with communal business, members of the estates for the duration of the assembly, ordained clergy, those obligated by state business and common criminals (this would be of great personal importance for Hecker in the American Civil War) were all exempted from the citizens' guard rule. In the case of the criminals, Hecker believed that they lacked the moral requirements for civic virtue. Above all else, this idea of civic patriotism, which Hecker employed to motivate and discipline the citizens' guard, would determine his own participation in the American Civil War. The fact that not everyone who participated in that war was motivated by the same degree of patriotism would prove one of Hecker's most painful wartime lessons.

Hecker's idealistic concept of the relationship between the citizen and the state, what he himself called the "idea of free citizenship," was demonstrated particularly well in his concept of the citizens' guard. The citizen, who was politically committed to the commonwealth, recognized that his own liberties depended on the free institutions of the state. If these were endangered, the security of his own existence was also imperiled. The inviolability of the state must be sustained because it represented an elementary condition of the existence of the free citizen. But in the final analysis the state arose out of voluntary association. The citizen himself participated as legislator in the blessings of a free state or community, whose "good laws" provided its members with equal rights and liberties and supplied them with certain basic goods. The citizen remained committed to these laws alone. To exclude egotistical motivations, this commitment must be made with official recognition by fellow citizens, the people. Civic virtue was the moral impulse to the general welfare, to which special interests were subordinated. Special interests could play no role if the citizen were actively, that is, politically, engaged by the state. Material attractions, which had no moral value, were to be excluded.

Hecker derived specific demands for his citizens' guard from these principles. First of all, a paid army never had the same motivation as a citizens' army, particularly not when the soldiers who were paid for their services did not participate in the blessings of the state or did not possess the rights of citizens. Second, there could be no substitutes, because whoever would not personally defend his honor and liberty did not value them, and should lose them, and they no longer have value for him; as stated in the *Staatslexikon*, one loses "all higher point of view for the honor and liberty of country or citizen."[48] Finally, physical toughening through military exercise contributed to the concept of civic virtue because without physical toughening, moral courage, self-control and discipline weakened. Reasonable self-control could be supported or advanced only through physical toughening. This would make it easy to understand Hecker's support for the Turner movement in America.

If we summarize the chapter just completed, what is surprising is that concepts of liberal, individualistic origins combined with collectivist, communitarian ones in Hecker's theoretical borrowings. Man, at once atomistic and unbound, joined with others to found a political system that would in turn help to secure his autonomous development. The inalienable rights attributed to the individual appeared to be grounded in natural law; they were rights that the state could not deny because a person did not submit them to the state contract. In the relationship between the citizen and the state, Hecker's participatory ideal of the citizen came to the fore. The "political" citizen was to set aside the pursuit of individual interests if they conflicted with the interests of the state. In order to develop patriotism at all, the state, as well as its laws and institutions, must be made in such a way that the original purpose of foundation could be realized as completely as possible. Hecker's political demands could be understood under the rubrics of ideal participatory citizen, constitution and community or state through its actively committed members; they all advanced increasing democratization, ever greater political representation and participation. Examples of this included eliminating the aristocratic First Chamber, increasing the competence of the Second, expanding the primary voter base and making legal practice a civic matter.

[1] Scharp, *Hecker*, 2.
[2] FH, *Deutschkatholiken*, vi, 4, 6, 18, 19-20, 21, 23-24 (civic duties), 33, 34 (equality of rights), 39, 60, 61, 69, 70, 71.
[3] Cf. FH, *Ministerialverantwortlichkeit*, 129-47.
[4] FH to "das Literarisches Comptoir" in Zürich, Mannheim, November, 1842, Stadtarchiv Mannheim, Kleine Erwerbungen, 127.
[5] FH, "Der badische Landtag von 1842," in Georg Herwegh, ed., *Einundzwanzig Bogen aus der Schweiz* (Zürich; Winterthur, 1843), 33-55, esp. 41 ff. FH, *Ministerverantwortlichkeit*, 136.
[6] Jucho, ed., *Verhandlungen des Deutschen Parlamentes. Officielle Ausgabe, 1. Lieferung* (Frankfurt am Main, 1848), 38. Cf. on the following, FH, "Der badische Landtag," 38, 39.
[7] See Kant, *Metaphysik der Sitten, Rechtslehre, Staatsrecht*, § 49.

8 *VSB*, 39. öS (17 August 1842), 330. *VSB*, 21. öS (23 January 1844), 262, 263; emphasis in the original. Budget vote on 1 August 1844, cf. VSB, 119. öS, 319. Only 7 voted against the budget, with 49 in favor: Itzstein, Bassermann, Mathy, Gerbel, Hecker, Richter and Sander, cf. ibid., 327.

9 *VSB*, 119. öS (1 August 1844) 320.

10 Ibid., 321.

11 This letter first appeared in Robert Blum, ed., *Sächsische Vaterlandsblättern*, cf. Wolfgang Schieder, "Kirche und Revolution. Sozialgeschichteliche Aspekte der Trierer Wallfahrt von 1844," *AfS* 14 (1974), 419-54, here 429; also Nolte, "Gemeindeliberalismus," 254-262; cf. on this *Katalog der ständigen Ausstellung, Bundesarchiv Abteilung Rastatt Erinnerungsstätte für die Freiheitsbewegungen in der deutschen Geschichte* (Koblenz, 1984), 150 ff. Cf. Ludwig Mathy, ed., *Aus dem Nachlaß von Karl Mathy. Briefe aus den Jahren 1846-1848* (Leipzig, 1898), 44. Nolte, "Gemeindeliberalismus," 256; Walter, *Mannheim*, 294-98.

12 In his review Bruno Bauer spoke of Ronge as a "hero of the bourgeoisie" and of the "horror" the bourgeoisie expressed over the "spectacle at Trier." Bruno Bauer, *Die Bürgerliche Revolution in Deutschland seit dem Anfang der deutsch-katholische Bewegung bis zur Gegenwart* (Berlin, 1849), 11; cf. also Schieder, "Kirche und Revolution," 428-29.

13 FH in the debate on the motion of Deputy Zettel on the freedom of religion, *VSB*, 9. öS (15 December 1845), 147.

14 Georg Gottfried Gervinus, *Die Mission der Deutschkatholiken* (Heidelberg, 1845), and idem, *Die protestantische Geistlichkeit und die Deutschkatholiken* (Heidelberg, 1846), 54; cf. also Schieder, "Kirche und Revolution," 429. Gervinus, *Mission*, cited in *Katalog der ständigen Ausstellung*, 107.

15 FH, *Deutschkatholiken*, title page, 3, 5, 23, 24-25; cf. on this Hecker's statement in *VSB*, 55. öS (13 August 1846), 96-106. See also Hecker's argumentation in the debate over the furloughing of Pastor Künzer, *VSB*, 36. öS, 5 March 1844, 328.

16 Cf. Tocqueville, *Demokratie*, vol. 1, 135 ff. Rousseau, cf. "On civic religion" *Social Contract*, chapter 8; Montesquieu, "What is Virtue in the Political State," *On the Spirit of the Laws*, book 5, chapter 2.

17 FH, *Deutschkatholiken*, 25-26; Benjamin Constant is cited for this on p. 26, "ruling through division."

18 Cf. Murhard, "Patriotismus," *Staatslexikon*, vol. 12 (Altona, 1841), 385-419, here 387, my emphasis.

19 Ibid., 390.

20 *VSB*, 55. öS (13 August 1846), 102.

21 FH, *Deutschkatholiken*, 61; in debates in the Chamber, Hecker referred to Article 16 of the *Bundesakte*, see *VSB*, 75. öS (13 August 1846), 101.

22 FH, *Deutschkatholiken*, 68; by confessions, FH meant specifically Catholics, Reformed and Lutherans. Cf. ibid., 27.

23 *VSB*, 33. öS (5 August 1842), 177; 55. öS (13 August 1846), 105; 23. öS (29 January 1844), 312; 45. öS (26 March 1844), 267.

24 *VSB*, 70. öS (18 May 1844), 301; he mentions as examples the suspicions against Carl von Rotteck's son and the lamentable resignation of the Heidelberg professor Kapp. *VSB*, 71. öS (20 May 1844), 322.

25 Ludwig Häusser, "Baden vor den Ereignissen von 1848," *Die Gegenwart*, vol. 2 (Leipzig, 1849), 321-59, here 357.

26 Häusser, *Denkwürdigkeiten*, 115, 116; also Vollmer, "Nachlaß," 363 n. 31; Weech, *Hecker*, 167. When Sander died in 1845, it was Hecker who held the memorial oration for his dead friend in the Chamber, cf. *VSB*, 25 November 1845, 1. Protokollheft, 5-6. Häusser, *Gegenwart*, 357.

27 *VSB*, 65. öS (10 May 1844), 115-16. FH, "Advocat. Der deutsche Advocatenstand," *Staatslexikon*, vol. 1, 2nd ed. (Altona, 1845), 355-69. Hecker was one of the 21 new authors working on the second edition, including Struve. "Advocat" in ibid., vol. 1, 343-55.

[28] Wende, *Radikalismus*, 80; FH, "Advocat," 355-56.

[29] Wende, *Radikalismus*, 64-65; FH, "Advocat," 356.

[30] FH, "Advocat," 363, 365. Wende, *Radikalismus*, 165. *VSB*, 65. öS (10 May 1844), 119. Carl Theodor Welcker, "Infamie, Ehre, Ehrenstrafen," *Staatslexikon*, vol. 8 (Altona, 1839), here 320-323. FH, "Advocat," 356; on the "feeling for honor," cf. also *VSB*, 65. öS (10 May 1844), 118. Cf. Ernst Rudolf Huber, ed., *Dokumente der deutschen Verfassungsgeschichte* (Stuttgart, 1961), vol. 1, 262, my emphasis.

[31] FH, "Advocat," 357, 359, 366; *VSB*, 12. öS (7 January 1846), 233.; he refers to a work by the jurist Steinacker, *Aufgabe des Advocatenstandes* (Braunschweig, 1841).

[32] Der Obergerichtsadvokat und Prokurator Dr. Friedrich Hecker an den Universitäts-buchhändler Jul. Groos in Heidelberg, Mannheim, 21 November 1845, Mannheimer Stadtarchiv, Kleine Erwerbungen, 736.

[33] Cf. Georg Beseler, "Ueber die Stellung des römischen Rechts zu dem nationalen Recht der germanischen Völker. Aus der Rede des Hrn. Verfassers beim Antritt seiner Professur in Basel, dasselbst erschienen 1836," Karl Hermann Scheidler, ed., *Paränesen für Studirende. Zweite Sammlung. Zu Rechts- und Staatswissenschaft* (Jena, 1842), 126-36.

[34] FH, "Advocat," 358.

[35] Georg Beseler, "Ueber die Stellung des römischen Rechts," 128, 132. Beseler's student Otto von Gierke, *Das Deutsche Genossenschaftsrecht*, vol. 2: *Geschichte des deutschen Körperschaftsbegriffs* (Darmstadt, 1954), 5-56; cf. idem, *Deutsches Privatrecht*, vol. 1: *Allgemeiner Teil und Personenrecht* (Leipzig, 1895; repr. Munich; Leipzig, 1936).

[36] Gierke, *Genossenschaftsrecht*, 46, 47, 50, 51; statement of majority might be through acclamation, force of weapons, etc.

[37] FH, *Reform des Gerichtswesens*, 3.

[38] FH, *Deutschkatholiken*, 72.

[39] Brandt, *Restauration*, 56.

[40] Cf. discussions about this law in *VSB*, 55. öS (13 August 1846), 104 ff. Welcker, "Association," *Staatslexikon*, vol. 2 (Altona, 1835), 21-53, here 21.

[41] FH, *Deutschkatholiken*, 73, 74.

[42] On Hecker's reading of Tocqueville, cf., for example, *TISZ*, 13 March 1874, where he describes his early lively interest in Tocqueville; cf. Tocqueville, *Demokratie*, vol. 2, 279 ff. Tocqueville uses the word "association" in conjunction with the word "society," obviously joining it with the British/American tradition of freedom of association. Ibid., vol. 2, 285.

[43] *VSB*, 33. öS (2 March 1848), 64. The entire citizens' guard system, as adopted by the Second Chamber, is printed in *VSB*, 44. öS (28 March 1848), 354-61; citation ibid., 347. Article 93, dealing with transitory directives, foresees that the law will go out of effect as soon as "the imminent law on the obligation to military service with the melding of the standing army with a general arming of the people is promulgated," *VSB*, 44. öS (28 March 1848), 361. He speaks in the draft of "estates," cf. *VSB*, 44. öS (28 March 1848), 361.

[44] In fact the commission consisted of only Mathy, Itzstein and Hecker after other deputies preferred not to take part in the discussion, cf. *VSB*, 44. öS (28 March 1848), 329, 331, 332, 335, 337. Debate continued late into four evenings.

[45] Welcker, "Heerwesen, Landwehrsystem," *Staatslexikon*, vol. 7 (Altona, 1839), 589-607, here 598, emphasis in spread type in the original. Ibid., 329, 330-31; my emphasis. Wende, *Radikalismus*, 86. *VSB*, 44. öS (28 March 1848), 330, 331, 344.

[46] Ibid., 342.

[47] *VSB*, 44. öS (28 March 1848), 331, 335.

[48] Welcker, "Bürgertugund, Bürgersinn," *Staatslexikon*, supplement to the 1st ed., vol. 1 (Altona, 1846), 748-58.

D.ʳ FRIEDR. HECKER

(am 20 April 1848.)

Hecker at the battle at Kandern, 20 April 1848. Friedrich Hecker Papers, Western Historical Manuscripts, University of Missouri – St. Louis.

III

Radicalization and Revolution (1847-48)

The Rejected Budget

The year 1847 is notorious for the growing separation between liberals and democrats. At the Durlach meeting at the end of November 1846, the entire liberal opposition, with the exception of Hecker, gathered one last time for common discussions; it is not known whether Hecker's absence was incidental or on purpose. The sharpening of differences was due in part to the failure of efforts in the state assembly, which had undertaken to pass many things, but could realize only a fraction of them. In turn, Hecker's radicalization must be understood as a "reaction to the failure of all reform attempts on the part of the moderate liberal opposition." His attempt, along with other deputies, to increase the power of the Chamber by rejecting the budget failed, although obvious inadequacies in the finance ministry could be demonstrated. "Where are any of our rights?" Hecker asked, challenging the Chamber in September 1846 by describing in detail what had happened to elections, the freedom and autonomy of the communes, freedom of religion and, finally, the right to approve taxation.[1] The blocking of important bills by the right wing of the Chamber and the government bench had hindered any constructive work.

At the start of March 1847, Hecker was one of the first deputies to withdraw from the Chamber in protest. By giving his electors only an inadequate explanation of his motives, he increased the confusion. In a letter to Deputy Sebastian Straub, a fellow lawyer and at the time still one of his good friends, Hecker spoke particularly of his physical exhaustion and of the impossibility of getting the opposition to act together. "Perhaps," he said hopefully, "my step will make our people more considerate of one another, will cause more solid and warmer cooperation, and then much will be accomplished. These robberies, jealousies and belittlings cannot go on; everything that has been held together so carefully by Itzstein is falling apart."[2]

It was above all Itzstein and Struve who tried to move Hecker to return

to the Chamber. But Hecker reacted to his stress, the source of his physical
exhaustion, with a trip through France to Algeria, ignoring Itzstein's suggestion that he take only a short journey to Naples and Sicily to recover. He
repeated this pattern often in the course of his life, running away to an unfamiliar world in order to gain control of his distress, dissatisfaction and
physical overexertion. Hecker himself said little about this journey. In the
corridor of the prefecture in Marseilles, where every traveler bound for
Algeria had to visit to have his passport checked, Hecker met Caspar Butz,
a traveling salesman. The young German from Hagen, in Westphalia, was
on the way to Algeria on business, and he became Hecker's companion
aboard the steamer *Charlemagne*. It was the beginning of a friendship that
would last the next 34 years, until Hecker's death in 1881. While Butz went
about his business in Algeria, Hecker traveled far into the interior, to Médéa
in the Atlas Mountains. There were not yet any railroads in Algeria, which
had been held by the French since 1830, so Hecker rode horseback from
Blida across the Atlas Mountains, "managing to ride himself into a dreadful
saddle sore, which tormented him for several days. ... Covered with dust,
dead tired, lame in the loins and barely capable of walking," "the blond-
bearded Baden deputy" finally returned to Algiers from his desert adventure, winning little sympathy from his new friend, "because whoever had
the injury" did not have to be "concerned about the ridicule."[3] After this
adventure Hecker decided that he had recovered sufficiently and returned
home.

He had been gone from Mannheim almost two months, but his disappointment over what had not been accomplished remained. "Hecker felt,"
a contemporary sought to explain, "that he had run the narrow racetrack of
the Chamber as far as the 'word' reached. He had 'said' everything that
could possibly be 'said.'" Now a close cooperation began with Struve, who
had himself never won a seat in the state assembly. While Struve organized
extra-parliamentary agitation, Hecker advanced things in the Chamber. The
first general extra-parliamentary demonstration took place between sessions of the assembly in autumn 1847. On 12 September 1847 what became
the famous Thirteen Articles were passed at the Zum Salmen inn in Offenburg.
The formulation of this program was generally ascribed to Struve. He was
certainly responsible for some of the demands there, such as a progressive
income tax and the amalgamation of labor and capital (Article 10). Struve
dealt with these questions in a more theoretical manner than Hecker.
Despite this, such demands were not foreign to Hecker; he had already supported a progressive income tax in the Chamber in another context.

In addition, the Offenburg Program formulated the general demands of the entire liberal opposition, such as releasing the Baden state government from the decrees of 1819, 1831, 1832 and 1834, a notion that Hecker had been demanding in the Chamber for years and that was tied directly with the agitation of the Hallgarten group. Similarly, demands for liberty of conscience and teaching (Article 3), jury courts (Article 11) and an educational system supported by the community, equally accessible to all (Article 9), were all early themes in Hecker's publications and Chamber statements. Liberal demands for freedom of the press (Article 2), swearing of an oath by the military to the constitution (Article 4) and representation of the people in the German League (Article 6), were all so much part of the canon of liberal opposition demands since the establishment of the Baden Second Chamber that they represented simple, well-known demands. Unlike the program that Struve presented half a year later in the pre-Parliament, here there was no direct reference to erecting a republic. Despite that, a few days after the assembly, the pro-government *Mannheimer Morgenblatt* accused Dr. Hecker, Struve and Eller, the organizers and chief speakers of the Offenburg assembly, of preaching revolution as agitators and promoting rebellion.[4] In response the three men were compelled "to pursue a complaint before a court for slander and injury of honor against the responsible editor of the *Morgenblatt*,"[5] a rather symbolic effort with no success.

As early as 10 October 1847 a "counter-gathering" of the moderate liberals met in Heppenheim. The form of organization that they adopted contrasted with the Offenburg assembly, particularly their exclusion of the public. The Heppenheim meeting was "a pure blue-ribbon assembly without the public to evaluate things as they were." The fact that Itzstein was also there can be seen as a measure of his dislike of Struve, but might also speak for the fact that the fronts had not yet hardened so completely as usually assumed.

There is Great Urgency – Events Until the Pre-Parliament

To be sure, the differences between the liberals and the democrats had visibly sharpened in the course of 1847. But within the Chamber there were combinations that permitted no simple attribution to one side or the other. On 9 December 1847 the state assembly convened again, Struve had still not won a seat, and Hecker managed to be reelected only with the support of the liberals. He was not present at the opening of the Chamber, nor at the official reception by the grand duke. On 18 December the Second Chamber's address of thanks and response to the grand duke's throne speech was discussed. When three members of the Chamber presented a petition to discuss the address of thanks in secret session, it was of course Hecker who vehemently opposed exclusion of the public from Chamber activities. One could not obliterate the "great right of the public"[6] for three private persons, because this was one of the most important constitutional rights. Public court proceedings, public popular assemblies and finally, in this case, public sessions of the Chamber belonged together, as far as Hecker was concerned, combining to correct and control abuses. He saw them as the sole legitimate forum of political dispute.

Yet the debate of 18 December is notorious for other themes. Because the throne speech of the grand duke dealt with the failed harvest, as well as with the difficult economic and social conditions in Baden, the social question had unexpectedly been raised by his mentioning growing poverty among broad segments of the population. Hecker saw in the most recent developments the possible extinction of the middle class, and he feared that "and in the end … there will [remain] only two types of people, the dominating rich and the hated, persecuted and abused proletariat." Hecker's answer to the social question relied on the idea of association, which would hinder the formation of a two-class society and strengthen the middle class. The drive to associate, the foundation of every theory of social contract, formed the central impulse of the movement. Hecker believed in eliminating the restrictive barriers the police state put up against the efforts of workers, crafts and occupational groups. The state needed to protect associations, giving them a helping hand without upsetting free competition. Only associations of workers, a united administration, and their joint participation in achieved profits could provide a genuine alternative to the ever-growing one-sided capitalist factory system. Hecker desired state aid only in the form of initial assistance to an otherwise free and independent administration of these associations. Even while he was making "socialist noises," he had not given up the old liberal idea of a passive state that would not intervene in the economy:

> Awaken the great idea of *association* in the crafts. Tell the craftsman, "Bring together your small capital; associate yourselves in *corporations* [*Genossenschaften*] in the same way that guilds of the Middle Ages emerged; obtain raw materials in common, and draw as a group the profit that the individual cannot when he gets raw materials."[7]

Hecker believed in societies of "small" merchants that could send one of their number to Amsterdam for purchasing; aid associations [*Hülfsassociationen*] that obligated themselves to gather the products of worker assocations and market them economically; loan associations [*Leihassociationen*] that could provide the crafts with needed money at a reasonable rate. A series of such associations must "cover the land." He envisioned the foundation of craftsmen's banks after the Scottish model, so that "the idea of socialism [might] become practical through a mass of interwoven associations." Hecker prophesied a great, growing struggle against the unequal distribution of capital. If there were no response to the rising misery, he said,

> then the sole liberated element will hoard capital in keeping with the egoistic nature of people, in opposition to the other elements, and it will cause the society, deeply wounded in its dignity, to say, "This war must come to a decision through raw force."

The socialism that Hecker described is not to be confused with communism. The fact that Hecker never compromised individual property is shown by his Chamber statement regarding ownership, still the foundation of civic society, which was accepted without objection in the same session. But he was not able to pass all of his proposals through the Chamber. Two weeks later, in debate over the introduction of a new craft regulation system, he emphasized what he saw as the correct combination of an economy that was independent of the state, and the simultaneous, autonomous development of associations.

> I want support from the state's side, not through granting money, but through support of free development. I want true material support from others. Alongside such associations as I have described, there are other associations that will make it possible for the oppressed and disadvantaged to find support.

Strong associations would operate effectively against the "supremacy of capital." In Hecker's opinion, two words typified the possibility of resolving the "bad relationship of capital and labor," a phrase that had already been formulated in the Offenburg Program; these words were freedom and union. Hecker understood the latter as particularly necessary in the economy. Neither the state nor the police should regulate crafts; rather the crafts should do it themselves. The state should guarantee "natural free development," and "all guardianship on behalf of the state" should vanish.[8] Here Hecker joined two ideas: first, the economic liberal concept of *laissez-faire*, according to which the state should guarantee security against outside influence but not intervene in internal economic developments, and secondly, the medieval concept (loaded with modern overtones) of associations of workers, craftsmen and businesses, which organized and sustained themselves.

In all of these discussions Hecker had sought to prevent intervention by government or state in trade and crafts. In a later debate he likewise rejected support for three Baden factories. He argued that the already over-burdened taxpayer could not be asked to pay for bad speculation. And, in the end, one was only helping capital and not workers. Along with Bassermann, he opposed state support; he hoped indealistically that the factories could be restructured with interim help and pass partly into the hands of the workers, providing a real model for a self-organized coopera-tive. Mathy, who feared social trouble from the mass layoff of 4000 workers, finally managed to pass the government motion. Instead of the originally demanded temporary credit of 1.5 million Gulden, however, bonds were issued in the amount of 500,000 Gulden each for the sugar factory in Waghäusel, the spinning and weaving mill in Ettlingen and the Kessler machine factory in Karlsruhe, with the interest paid by the state.[9]

On 12 February 1848 there was debate on Deputy Bassermann's motion for a representation of the German estates in the Federal Diet. The idea of a German parliament mentioned in the motion was certainly not new; but it was spark enough for stormy discussion. "I tell you," Hecker prophesied, "this motion will mark an epoch in German history."[10] It expressed what all educated members of the people felt and regarded as necessary. Concerning Bassermann's motion, Hecker now drew from his fund of argument the category of historical necessity and development. Associations were the first level and the legal state was the last. "What is the main idea of the times among the Germanic peoples? This idea, which begins with the crafts and passes on to politics, is the idea of federalism and fraternity in law."[11] Above all, Hecker saw the need for a single national rep-resentative to the outside world.

In the revolutionary days of February and March 1848, discussions of the technical administrative concerns of the state were slightly expanded to

include repeated petitions for such long-standing demands as freedom of
the press, jury trials and a citizens' defense system. Even before the
February Revolution in France became known, Hecker was seized by a militant, irritable tone. It was Mathy who played on the formula, popular with
liberals and radicals alike, the denial of reform as a cause for revolution. It
was not excessive freedom of the press, but rather the repression of this freedom that called into life the movements of recent times. Because these
movements had achieved no results with tameness, it was about time that
they "tried wildness; but that could not be restricted to an assembly hall."[12]
Only news of Paris events would show how much some people wished to
prevent revolution at any price, while others saw revolution as an advancing principle, in whose wake they hoped to realize the demands that had so
long resonated in public discussion. Yet others wanted to make use of the
blessing of the moment to gain everything at once, undivided. Through the
Chamber statements of Bassermann, Welcker and Mathy, Hecker could easily rest in the belief that they were essentially in agreement. All of them
were of the opinion that there should be fundamental change. And yet, they
were somewhat surprised by the sudden outbreak in Paris. There was little
time to think about a strategy or plan a procedure; every day brought new
dispatches and parallel concessions from the government.

In Baden the first spontaneous, emphatic phase of popular assemblies
and proclamations commenced. During this period Hecker swung between
his duties as a deputy in the Chamber and his attempt to organize a peaceful revolution. He was stormily greeted at every popular assembly, and in
the March Days his influence reached an enormous scale. Even Häusser
stresses that Hecker showed that no one was preparing a powerful blow.
The revolutionary atmosphere lifted Hecker up enormously, stimulating his
spirit. "All of the influences around him determined his wavering opinion;
hence, he changed his appearance to adapt to the settings and effects."[13]

On 27 February 1848, under the impact of the news from Paris, the first
mass meeting was held under Itzstein's presidency. Hecker himself was
absent due to illness. From this popular assembly came what was known as
the Mannheim Demands, calling for freedom of the press, jury trials, arming of the people and representation of the German people in the Federal
Diet. Only two days later the government announced its intention to
approve the first three demands, and only Hecker and Brentano remained
unconvinced. Hecker said, "One would not have the efforts of our own people, but rather the corpses of Frenchmen and Italians to thank" for these

promises, and Brentano warned, "Today is a day in which we have become richer by one promise, but who guarantees its realization?"[14] Mathy, Bassermann and Welcker chose to be satisfied with this result, looking forward to a national assembly. Despite the general movement, Hecker seemed to want to remain within the limits of constitutional possibilities. When Struve entered the Chamber at the head of an enormous mass of people on 1 March to proclaim the Mannheim Demands and make a speech, Hecker, who had arranged his actions in advance with Mittermaier, the president of the Chamber, advanced toward Struve, took his petition from his hand, and threatened to leave the Chamber should Struve open his mouth. Any speech by Struve, who was not an elected member of the house, would have violated the bylaws.

As announced, Hecker, Brentano and other deputies added eight additional demands to the four Mannheim Demands, referring them all to an advisory committee. Almost all of the demands that Hecker had supported in the course of his parliamentary work appeared in this expanded version: a law for the responsibility of ministers, another on other state officials, popular sentencing "through a proper participation of citizens," independence of judges, "regulations … for a more just distribution of the burdens of the state and the communes, and the supervision of crafts and simple work." This last point seemed to originate with Hecker, who stressed how honorable it was for the Baden Chamber to be the first that "included a social question in its resolution."[15]

At the start of March, 51 Southwest German liberals gathered in Heidelberg to consider further actions and the organization of the pre-Parliament. Hecker brought Struve with him to this assembly. Bassermann and Mathy brought along the Heidelberg professor Gervinus, who, like Struve, was not a deputy in the Chamber. Because only a protocol of the results was filed, the record of this Heidelberg assembly, particularly the speeches given there, is problematic. Responding to the demand that important political offices should be filled with persons of public trust, the president of the Justice Ministry resigned on 7 March. There was said to be an attempt to offer this position to Hecker or Alexander von Soiron,[16] but a switch to the government side was impossible for Hecker.

The call for a general arming of the people grew louder everywhere. There was likewise widespread demand for a distribution of weapons at state cost, but this was supported neither by the Chamber nor the government. Even Hecker and Brentano declared themselves against issuing weapons at state expense. Hecker argued that it was the duty of every citizen to obtain a weapon at his own expense, guaranteeing that it could not then be recovered by the state, as had happened in the Napoleonic wars. Days earlier Hecker had advanced swearing in of the military to obey the constitution, because "it is necessary to show that they [mean] it honestly." In the middle of March, Hecker had been named colonel of the Mannheim citizens' guard.[17]

As debates progressed in the Second Chamber, the call grew ever louder in the extra-parliamentary assemblies to establish a republic. One of these extra-parliamentary agitators was Fickler, the stirring editor of the radical *Seeblätter*. More and more news reports accumulated about the departure of armed volunteers from Paris, sent in support of a German republic. In fact Hecker had received a letter from the German poet Herwegh in Paris, offering his aid; but Hecker declined the offer by leaving the letter unanswered. "We don't want to draw any foreigners into the country, because we can handle our affairs ourselves," Hecker announced in the Chamber. "Help from outside would bring us liberty, but they will also present us a bill for it." When discussion of the German Legion from Paris revived, Hecker approved the government's plan to allow them across the Rhine in small, unarmed units, to support them at state expense and then to send them home, an offer that some legionnaires actually accepted. Hecker even encouraged other German states to extend credit to the Grand Duchy of Baden to resolve this problem by providing support.[18] However, this was actually for the benefit of German workers, not the French.

On 16 March the deputies debated a motion that Brentano had presented for amnesty for political prisoners, certainly influenced by the rumor of workers approaching from Paris. It is interesting how freely the liberal opposition still supported political amnesty, quite the opposite of its later position in the National Assembly. Hecker pled for the greatest possible extension of political amnesty, all the way to the day when the final version passed the Chamber. Political amnesty was generally applied to men such as Jordan or Eisenmann; but Chamber members also thought back to the expulsion of Hecker and Itzstein from Prussia, which was a sin against German unity. Obviously no one was thinking yet of high treason, or rebel volunteers; the Chamber was united in believing that all "common crimes" were exempted from political amnesty. But Hecker believed that voicing the form of state in which one believed should never again be regarded as a political crime. The origins of Hecker's republicanism in his study of ancient writings was nowhere so clear as here, demonstrating what Julius Fröbel later said about radical democrats' combining modern ideas with an "ancient historical republicanism." There can be no doubt that Hecker was talking here about himself:

> Can anyone blame a patriot when he advances from an absolute monarchy to a republic? Can you blame such a man who, perhaps enthused by the study of classical antiquity, has held the republic to be the best form of state, if he breaks out in jubilation over his republican ideas? You cannot. These are people with no criminal intent.[19]

On 19 March there was a mass rally in Offenburg attended by Soiron and Welcker as well as Hecker and Struve. According to rumor Hecker was supposed to have brandished a pistol during the preparations, threatening Fickler against proclaiming the republic. Another rumor in Offenburg held that 51 Southwest German liberals had secretly expressed their support of the republic, but Itzstein, Kapp, Bassermann and Welcker issued a denial. Brentano and Hecker declined to join them, not wanting to bind themselves by such a statement. One of the Offenburg resolutions foresaw the formation of local associations in every community to arm and educate citizens, an absolute necessity in the theoretical plans of most Forty-Eighters in order to win over capable and patriotic citizens. All local associations were placed under a general country association, with Hecker named as its head. At the Offenburg rally Hecker once more insisted that the pre-Parliament was the legal way to achieve democratic goals.[20]

When it came to debating Bassermann's motion in the Chamber on 24 March, Hecker expressed the idea, later promoted in the pre-Parliament, that it was urgent for the nation to find a gathering place; in three weeks it would already be too late. His republican rhetoric became obvious here as well:

> There are persons who do not grasp the time in which we are living. We are living in the middle of a great revolution that arose from the ocean and will sweep to the Urals ... Saguntum went to its ruin while they argued in Rome! That's how it will be with us. I do not want to stop the discussion, but the nation has to have a gathering place, a place of assembly, because we are in the midst of an adjournment. It would be wrong to dispute a long time about full powers. It would be the begin-

ning of ruin. We are not where we should be after half a year. I am saying that, when it is a question of saving the country, things must be
done quickly, and an assembly must proclaim itself the constituent
assembly of the *Reich*.[21]

In view of the short time, Hecker proposed that the various estate
assemblies should come together and work out a German constitution,
whose revision would be reserved to the legislative bodies that were created. Hecker's recommendation carefully took into account the fact that the
members of the governments of the individual states should enter negotiations only with the people's constitutionally elected representatives and
not, as Bekk put it, with "arbitrarily and spontaneously gathered masses."
For this reason Hecker announced that the Offenburg Resolutions by
Brentano, Richter, Welte, Sachs and Kapp and himself should be elevated
into a motion, taking the constitutionally proper path through the chambers. This never happened, due to the precipitate events in April.[22]

Hecker did not appear at the Heidelberg meeting on 24 March, to
Struve's great disapproval. Instead he stayed at home in Mannheim to work
on his new military system, while Struve spoke at a meeting in Freiburg.
When discussions were held in the Chamber on the new military system,
even conservative deputies conceded, under the circumstances, that the
government's proposal and the Chamber commission entrusted with it
should both be set aside and an entirely new proposal be considered. Before
Hecker presented his proposal to the Chamber, he discussed it with Mathy
and Itzstein. There was insufficient time to discuss thoroughly the military
system in its new form, due to the pre-Parliament in Frankfurt; it was therefore unanimously passed in the same session. Häusser commented in his
retrospective, "So the chambers and the government allowed Hecker to
impose on them a law for a citizens' guard."[23]

The Necessary Gathering Point –
The Pre-Parliament and Its Permanence

Adam von Itzstein had taken over coordinating and organizing the pre-
Parliament, inviting "all members of German estate assemblies, and besides
these men, several men who have the trust of the people and can help the
assembly by word and deed." Because the United State Assembly of Prussia
planned to meet on 2 April, shortly after the gathering of the pre-

Parliament, it was an open question whether many deputies would come to Frankfurt from there. Itzstein believed he would have a large number of Prussian deputies because the pre-Parliament had precedence, and because the beginning of a state assembly was engaged only in formal questions; but this did not happen.

Not keeping entirely with the order of business, Gustav Struve sought to read out a composed petition immediately after the opening of the assembly. This petition encountered great opposition within the pre-Parliament, possibly indicating that the demands expressed in it were seen as revolutionary and that the majority present was not willing to accept them. Still, this petition was not entirely shocking, or even surprising. President Mittermaier had charged the gathering that "freedom of expression" must rule in the pre-Parliament and that "no one [should shrink] from even the boldest of words or the boldest of petitions." Struve had simply taken Mittermauer at his literal word. It is probable that such petitions were to be expected, whether the views in them were shared or not. A few days before, in response to Bassermann's demand for a national assembly, the same Mittermaier, as president of the Baden Second Chamber, had oriented himself to an American-style constitution, "if things are to go well," with the condition that "the ideas on which this federation rests ... be applied to monarchy." Hecker later asserted that the entire assembly had "the American Constitution [waving] before its eyes." But this appears overstated, in view of the many participants like Deputy Bassermann, who saw in Struve's petition only a "sentimental fantasy of the brotherhood of the peoples."[24]

As with the Offenburg Program, only a few points in Struve's petition were radical; these included, for example, demands for progressive taxes on income and wealth, as well as the elimination of imbalances between labor and capital. The final point demanded the elimination of hereditary monarchy and the introduction of a federal constitution along the lines of the free states of North America. All of the other demands, such as securing of property and persons, liberty of belief, elimination of privileges, introduction of a unified economic region, freedom of the press and public and oral jury trials, corresponded to liberal concepts. For that reason Mittermaier's interjection that many points introduced by Struve would be discussed later, with other petitions, was entirely justified.

The first problem with Struve's petition was that the majority of the pre-Parliament would not have voted for its content under any circumstances. Second, the petition offended the organizational principles of the pre-Parliament. The pre-Parliament was not there to discuss any fundamental principles or questions of constitution, only to establish procedures and forms of organization for elections to the National Assembly. These organizational questions ultimately took up the broadest possible room, and it was in the pre-Parliament's interest to deal first with the question of its own self-comprehension. Only Struve's last demand, that the assembly should remain together "until a freely elected parliament [can] lead Germany's destiny,"[25] dealt with the pre-Parliament's discussion of its own political status.

Hecker chose to discuss the same point in his first speech. Many objections arose declaring that the pre-Parliament had no power to legislate because its composition was not representative. It could not even be said to express the public opinion of all Germany. Its only purpose consisted in organizing the National Assembly as quickly as possible.[26] Hecker suggested that taking this last purpose seriously did not mean dissolving after forty-eight hours in order to save the time and money that reasonable negotiation would demand.

> Something different is expected. It is expected that we remain permanently together until the National Assembly meets ... If we do not remain together and do not use the sole threat we possess legally, which is that of remaining together, then we have set the cause of freedom back fifty years.[27]

The Committee of Seven had worked out a preliminary draft of the matters to be negotiated even before the pre-Parliament met. This program envisioned consultations about a federal head with responsible ministers. But for Hecker this was "not logically sustainable." First, the fact "that we are in the middle of a revolution" had to be addressed. Hecker believed that this required an autonomous confession by the pre-Parliament of its own mission, to which a statement of human rights such as those expressed in Struve's petition, and similar to the American Declaration of Independence, could be joined. But instead of this, the pre-Parliament capitulated its own autonomy recognizing and demanding a federal head without equipping itself with powers or rights. The pre-Parliament did not even possess "the honor to be a people" that saw itself as sovereign, and expressed its sovereignty before any other act. If the pre-Pariament were actually serious about declaring itself powerless, Hecker reasoned, any further action would be wrong; one could debate neither the Committee of Seven program nor any other petition. According to Hecker, the pre-Parliament, in awareness of its own role, needed to constitute itself as a revolutionary instrument independent of the governments, and equip itself with special rights. Then it could be made a visible symbolic rallying point for the people. "We must oppose the powerlessness and dissolution of the German Federation and the German governments – as common defenders of the nation" Hecker stated in his second speech on the necessity of permanence. In such important moments it is of the greatest importance that the nation has a central point." Hecker might have had Mirabeau in mind when he spoke. In his closing plea he also called on the words of his former teacher Mittermaier, declaring that it was necessary for the pre-Parliament to conceive of itself as "the executive of the nation," and declare itself permanent. Hecker's plea was a challenge to carry on and complete the revolution by revolutionary means, which by no means had to be violent. At the same time his perennial distrust of the old powers could be seen, powers whose influence he did not regard as dead and whose revival he did not wish to see. In any case Hecker was willing and ready to spend more than two days in session. His speech formally proposed to disregard time and money, because experience had shown that the shorter the debate, the poorer and more confused the result.[28]

Hecker's motion to make the assembly permanent failed by 369 votes to 148. The majority of the pre-Parliament declared itself in agreement with the Federal Diet, which was still a legitimate authority that sustained the connection to the individual states. The Left, in particular, criticized recognizing the Federal Diet. But in order to sustain some influence after this declaration of bankruptcy of revolutionary momentum, members of the Left such as Zitz, Itzstein and Jacoby sought at least to obligate the Diet to shed its unconstitutional emergency resolutions before it took up its new mission. Then, they believed, the Diet could "remove the men who worked to conjure up and apply it from its bosom" unconstitutional measures.[29] Hecker demanded the stronger version using "before" and "until," but he lost to Bassermann's milder form that only wanted to insert an "insofar."

Since Struve had declared Zitz's motion the last attempt to work with the assembly and remain in it, this motion's failure was a call to walk out. This demonstrative walkout, consisting of Hecker, Struve and about forty other members, did not yet signal a resort to arms. Because the Federal Diet conformed with the demands of the pre-Parliament on the same day, and because many members of the Federal Diet in fact took the occasion to depart independently, Itzstein's mediation succeeded in getting the walk-outs to return. It was surprising, however, that the small leftist minority remaining behind in St. Paul's Church was unable to prevent any further resolutions while the walkout was taking place, because they regarded it as necessary by parliamentary procedure to accede to the majority. They simply continued to debate. This was, in fact, an error for both sides.

Both the republican leftist minority and the constitutional monarchical majority wanted to turn the proceedings as quickly as possible in its own direction, paying no attention to the opposite party. This was entirely obvious in the Committee of Fifty election, which Hecker in later exile called "a boring narcotic essence ... hence a permanent non-permanence." Hecker, who narrowly missed committee election, appeared in fifty-first place, with 100 votes against 62. Naturally, Hecker later bitterly declared that "not a single man of republican action and decision was elected," obviously counting only those who left the assembly with him in protest. The four members of the Committee of Fifty with the most votes belonged to the republican minority. Wiesner, one of the two Austrians present and later a defender of Hecker in the National Assembly, received the greatest number of votes, with 457, immediately followed by Itzstein, with 443, then Robert Blum, with 435, and finally Johann Jacoby, with 396.[30]

Hecker's contemporaries were the first to speculate on what would have happened if he had been elected to the Committee of Fifty: "As members of the committee, Hecker and Struve would have had trouble participating in the proclamation in the highlands of Baden," Häusser supposed. Veit Valentin accepts this evaluation, asserting, "Contemporaries already thought it to be un-statesmanlike that, despite the express will of the assembly to form a politically balanced Committee of Fifty, the pre-Parliament proceeded to vote the two leading opposition members out rather than in." And a contemporary in sympathy with the republican members emphasized the necessity of Hecker's demands in the pre-Parliament.

> More correctly than others who were otherwise his intellectual superi-ors, Hecker, within a few hours with a healthy glance, had figured out the assembly's spirit, capability of will, truth of the cause and situation. He saw that there was now little soil in the assembly for what he want-ed on behalf of Germany, certainly even less in a new assembly after

another four weeks of waiting. He knew his enemy, who had sown the weeds, although he did not yet know about the plan of operation or the instructions of the Holy Lodge in Wilhelmstrasse in Berlin.[31]

The proceedings of the pre-Parliament showed clearly how Hecker wanted to bring the revolution to a conclusion in a "legal revolutionary" manner. Only a complete exchange of the old powers together with the establishment of a new parliament as a political center seemed adequate to him, guaranteeing that the existing structure of rule would be genuinely eliminated. Proclaiming the permanence of the pre-Parliament would naturally have also been a step closer to his constitutional ideal, a republic. What he wanted from the pre-Parliament, and his reason for forestalling those who demanded the immediate introduction of the republic to the pre-Parliament, did not materialize. In fact, the opposite occurred. Hecker feared correctly that a delay of four weeks would result in the evaporation of the euphoric enthusiasm of the first Revolutionary days.

While Hecker was working in Frankfurt to have the Pre-Parliament declared permanent, the enthusiastic Josef Fickler was in Strasbourg discussing future actions with two emissaries sent ahead by Herwegh. In the company of these two men, Fickler stated at a meeting in Achern on 2 April that the republic should be proclaimed if the Pre-Parliament could not decide to do so. Karl Mathy regarded Fickler as the most dangerous of agitators on the basis of reports that he had heard from several sides about Fickler's attitude. As late as 7 April, two days after Fickler and Struve presented a memorandum to Welcker, the new Baden representative at the Federal Diet, demanding that the grand-ducal government permit the communes to vote on constitutional monarchy or a republic, Fickler complained in Strasbourg because Hecker had not yet declared himself for the republic. In the meantime the population of Baden had been upset by the stationing of federal contingents from Württemberg, Bavaria and Hessia along Baden's borders to protect against the volunteer columns that were advancing from Paris. On 5 April 1848 the appearance of the Württemberg quartermaster in Donaueschingen resulted, within a day, in a mass meeting of more than 6000 persons. This assemblage demanded, among other things, the removal of foreign troops from Baden; otherwise, the proclamations stated, it would be necessary to meet force with force.[32]

On 7 April the Baden Second Chamber began debates on the volunteer troops and by extension, on the necessity of foreign troops on Baden territory. Hecker, just returned to the Chamber from the pre-Parliament, opposed the need for troops, as did Brentano, Richter and others. "What do the seething people in Silesia, in Prussia, in Baden demand?" Hecker asked in the Chamber.

> Is it soldiers? No, it is real aid, and while the people demand savings in pensions, salaries and the pressing burden of the military, you send it the Eighth Army Corps with 63,000 foreign troops along the country's border.[33]

The Chamber appeared little impressed by Hecker's objections. The motion of Deputy Bissing approving the government's action was passed with only eight votes, including Hecker's against. Hecker's opponents later asserted that he spoke entirely on his own behalf in this session because his planned uprising depended as much as possible on keeping the military out of Baden. His statements in this session of the Chamber, his last in this forum, could be understood that way; but perhaps they were marked by his smarting defeat in Frankfurt and his need to make a clear confession of faith.

> In a time like the present, every honorable man who does not secretly maneuver like Talleyrand must question himself and come clean about what form of state he sees as the sole salvation if the state dissolves into anarchy. If he says that he sees the republic as the best form of state, he has my favor more than someone who lies about the kingdom, or monarchy, or who wants to create a monarchy that is merely his puppet, to be thrown away in the end. I respect only the man who openly supports what is true. I have always hated political hypocrites. Even more, I have contempt for them.[34]

One day after Hecker's speech came the fateful arrest of Josef Fickler by Karl Mathy at the Karlsruhe railroad station. Even Bassermann was amazed that a "purely private man" would let himself be moved to such an act. Juristically Fickler's arrest was illegal. But this did not alter Mathy's later public statements nor his effort to gain the support of the president of the Chamber, Mittermaier, who responded after his fashion by pleading illness and then distancing himself from Mathy's acts. Fickler's arrest was probably the precipitating cause for Hecker's sudden departure for

Constance via the secure soil of France and Switzerland. Lorenz Brentano, who had not been initiated into Hecker's plans, repeated this in the National Assembly. And eyewitnesses reported that "when Fickler was arrested ... [Hecker] said, 'Now they will also come for me and the Chamber will approve my arrest.'" The only person who seemed entirely satisfied with the proceedings was Karl Mathy. The day after Hecker's flight, Mathy wrote to Mittermaier from Mannheim, "The positive development of things in the last two days already bears good fruit. The natural course of events needs only to be helped along, and then everything will be good. Struve has already vanished, [and] Hecker, as I hear, was not to be found in the place where honor, according to his own concepts, would call him,"[35] that is, in the Chamber.

The Man of Sudden Impulses

Hecker's volunteers' march, the first of a series of Baden rebellions, has never lost its romantic halo. Two circumstances have contributed to this. The first is Hecker's popularity as a "true man of the people." The second is the revolutionary euphoria that prevailed in the first days of April.

The course of the uprising has been described many times. On 12 April Hecker proclaimed the republic in Constance, and the ensuing six-day march across the Black Forest toward Karlsruhe was supposed to grow into a true mass movement. According to contemporaries, this march differed considerably from the two later marches. In each of his proclamations issued during the march, Hecker required the men who joined to supply themselves with provisions and money for six days, in order to avoid burdening the poor country population. In retrospect, the fact that there was virtually no looting made this first rising appear relatively harmless. Hecker's own idealized notion of the course of the French Revolution – influenced by his reading of the Paris letters of Georg Forster, whom Hecker called an "ingenious man" – also fed in him the conviction that revolutionary undertakings were possible without plundering or violent outbreaks. In the Chamber on 9 March 1848, speaking of plundering, Hecker said,

> The French Revolution gave us a grand example, the likes of which we have hardly ever experienced. In those civic storms, there was no plundering or any other mischief, and when it did happen, the poor people intervened, judging with lynch justice those who abused the great

cause of liberty for personal advantage. They shot down offenders on the spot, while everyone shouted, "*Voleurs, voleurs!* Thieves, thieves!" That was a great act by this class of the people, although they were poor and needy, disapproved of the plundering of their fellow citizens.[36]

It was Hecker's error to presume his own high moral aspirations in others, however. He fell into this misconception ever more frequently, convinced that "the poorest person [would be] purified in the hour of peril," and that "He sloughs off the dross that burdens him." The fact that the towns through which Hecker's volunteers passed supported him, even while contributing almost no men to the march, is demonstrated by petitions from Constance and Schopfheim to the National Assembly supporting Hecker's admission to that body.

Despite Hecker's consistent rejection of two offers from Emma Herwegh to unite with the Paris Legion under Herwegh's command, he was still accused of high treason. To the disapproval of such participants as Theodor Mögling or Gustav von Struve (who later joined with Herwegh's Legion), Hecker remained convinced that he could not accept foreign help. Behind this was his belief, which lasted almost until the end of the march, that it would not come to a military confrontation. There was also his view, previously expressed in the Chamber in February, that a people must win their own liberty. But the possibility that Herwegh's legion could pose the problem of high treason for Hecker, is demonstrated by the rumor that emerged asserting that Hecker had "shot Herwegh in pure rage" after the failure of the march.[37] It was not yet clear that the volunteers' march would be condemned, given the revolutionary situation.

The failure of the volunteers' march could be blamed on either the terrible stormy weather or the peasantry, which cheered the men as they marched by, but then turned back to working their fields. Much more decisive, however, was the problem of coordination, along with the fact that most villagers awaited the right command to join. In other words, the march failed as a result of a question of authority. Hecker knew how the people awaited a written command, so in the first days of the march he therefore wrote not only his proclamations, but also innumerable letters to the mayors of the communes. Only when the mayors supported his approach did he find recruits waiting for him. But if, as frequently happened, the mayor was skeptical or opposed, especially when mayors consulted Karlsruhe, the cause was hopeless. The mayor and council in Stockach, for example, decid-

ed to decline the march access, and "most of the others," as Baron von
Andlaw described with approval, "wanted to cover themselves with an
order from the authorities before they would allow their people to join."
Mayor Fischler of Möhringen delayed any participation, drawing the communal council to his side and telling its members that the "people demanded a command from an authority." In stark contrast, Huetlin the mayor of
Constance, declared the entry of the city into the republic without even con-
sulting the commune, arguing the decision had to be made at once.

While Hecker was proclaiming the republic in Constance, the commandant of the Baden division, Marquis Max, was temporarily replaced by
General Friedrich von Gagern, then in Dutch service. The Baden deputies
Bassermann and Buhl were among the most engaged supporters of
Gagern's sudden summons, and the general did not even have time to gain
leave from the Dutch king for this assignment. But contemporaries were the
first to see this sudden change of leadership as a political error that could be
erased only by a splendid military victory. Calling the "foreigner" Gagern
irritated Baden officers and soldiers, and the Badeners were placed between
Hessian and Württemberg soldiers to prevent their going over to the other
side at the later Battle of Kandern. In truth, Friedrich von Gagern himself
apparently presumed that events would not come to military conflict.
Andlaw validly assumed, "Gagern demanded neither advice nor information and repeatedly declared, 'This is more a political than a military matter.'" The conservative Andlaw, who was no friend of Hecker's, God knows,
went on to say,

> It is plausible that Gagern wanted to convince Hecker to turn back
> by using his brothers' friendship to *Hecker* by promises of support, cer-
> tainly a guarantee of immunity, if not actually specific benefits ("The
> Bekk Government had already offered Hecker the justice ministry in
> March 1848").[38]

Hecker himself, who had heard the many complaints of the Baden soldiers, admitted that he was counting on having the troops defect to him.
"You would not hold me to be so stupid as to think that my little band
would win against the troops; but I knew the troops would come over to my
side at once." Hecker assured two representatives of the Committee of Fifty
of this. In response to the amnesty that the two men offered, Hecker extend-

ed "amnesty to the 34 German princes in the name of the German people, if they withdraw to private life within 14 days."[39]

In the first few days after the volunteers' march became known, no one imagined the drama it would achieve at its conclusion. It was not until 17 April 1848, for example, that there was "a presentation on behalf of the high government concerning the revolutionary undertakings of Hecker and Struve." Budgetary matters, such as the improvement of invalid homes had been under debate. The Baden interior minister, Bekk, declared, "It is with regret that I must say that a member of this very house is to be found among the rebels. He has surely been brought to this step through unfortunate confusion. This is all the more to be regretted, because this is a man with otherwise outstanding intellectual qualities." Deputy Alexander von Soiron filed a ready-drafted resolution for the Chamber to distance itself in the sharpest terms from Hecker's undertaking and discourage all participation. Soiron's decisive act was not without a private resonance; he had been one of Hecker's wedding witnesses. In general, however, as Interior Minister Bekk confirmed, there was an unexpectedly great reluctance in the Chamber to take "any extraordinary steps against one of its own members." After the declaration, they went back to the regular order of the day, and a day later, for example, they had a thorough discussion of Itzstein's exposition of the budget.

It was only the fatal result of the march that sharpened the tone of condemnation. Moments after General von Gagern's discussions with Hecker, Gagern had been killed by a hostile bullet. The president of the Second Chamber, Mittermaier, spoke only of a "theater of civil war and criminal horror," and Interior Minister Bekk had "the honor of presenting for approval the provisional law of the 25th of the month declaring the Lake Circle and the Upper Rhine Circle as retrospectively in a state of war." It was the unexpected death of Gagern that became the welcome instrument of the "liberal reaction," which stigmatized the volunteers' march as a violent uprising, anarchy and high treason. Privately friends wondered about Hecker's mental condition.[40]

After the defeat of his volunteers on the Scheidegg at Kandern, and his own flight into nearby Switzerland, Hecker was presented with an accomplished fact; the use of force had given his volunteers' march a new face. He must have clearly foreseen that the language of weapons, not planned but ultimately used, would provide ammunition for his political enemies. To this extent Robert Blum was right when he wrote to his wife from Frankfurt, at the start of Hecker's efforts, "Hecker and Struve are real fools, charging through the Forest like stuck oxen, making victory terribly difficult for us." Now, for the first time, there was a personified bogeyman of the revolution. Hecker, who had been merely a vague enemy for the liberals, was transformed into a true leader of the revolting lower classes.[41] At the same moment, the monarchical governments were for the first time able to calm themselves about the masses' readiness for revolution. The Federal Diet had its military competence tested with success, and the revolutionary potential in the Baden population appeared much lower than originally presumed.

Myth of the German Republic – Hecker in St. Paul's Church

It was not the volunteers' march alone that established Hecker's reputation as a myth of the German Republic; rather, that reputation was nurtured in the conflict over his election as a deputy of the National Assembly and the final rejection of this election by the Assembly majority.

On 8 August 1848, debate on the report of the Committee for Legislation and Justice, concerning several petitions for amnesty for political criminals, was on the National Assembly's agenda.[42] Many of the petitions came from the Southwest German region, including such places as Constance and Schopfheim that had come into direct contact with the volunteers' march. A series of these petitions included, with a general demand for amnesty, a demand that Hecker's election as a deputy of the National Assembly be recognized and that he be summoned there at once (On 7 June 1848, during his exile in Muttenz, Hecker was elected in due form, by an absolute majority, as a deputy in the fourth Baden electoral district, Thiengen). At first an attempt was made to distinguish clearly between the question of this election and the general discussion of political amnesty; however, the course of the debate showed that this was impossible.

The National Assembly's Committee for Legislation and Justice had already marked the petitions "response negative" on 15 July. Because their subject was events specifically in Baden, a majority of the petitions, in the view of the committee, did not concern "a crime committed directly or immediately against the whole of Germany," but rather "an immediate and autonomous assault on the Grand Duchy of Baden." Hence the competence as well as the decision should lie with the individual state, in this case the government of Baden and not with the National Assembly. The committee's report clearly reflected the position and self-perception of the majority of the National Assembly.

Most deputies believed that the National Assembly's mission was to establish the unity and liberty of Germany through a general constitution, declare the basic rights of the German people, and secure the "principles of the constitutions of the individual states essential to general liberty." The National Assembly, advised the committee, was empowered to intervene in states only when "such an intervention into the legal competence of the individual states proved unavoidable in carrying out its own mission."[43] Such a reason did not apply to the Hecker coup, in their view.

Furthermore, the Grand Duchy of Baden was the only state in Germany that had responded immediately to revolutionary demands and had called elections to the National Assembly. Those elections were an expression of the entire German people. As a result, Hecker had acted not against the old, unjust feudal state, but against the new order, which was based on liberty; in short, against everything that the National Assembly represented, according to the understanding of its majority. It was even suggested that Hecker had attempted to subordinate the general will, which was already clearly stated in the elections, to his individual will.

The committee and the deputies in joining this opinion called on the right of revolution that had produced the National Assembly; however, they stressed their conviction that the general will of the people was completely expressed in its elected representatives. Since the pre-Parliament had convened and the Committee of Fifty had been elected, the "right of revolution had ceased, and the obligation of reform" had begun. It was feared that an amnesty granted too early to refugees persisting in their revolutionary commitments would provoke "a repetition of civil war." Widenmann, the committee reporter, argued that "amnesty would be only a stimulant to new disturbances."[44] Because none of the refugees had themselves petitioned the National Assembly for amnesty, the committee moved to return to the routine agenda, declining to discuss the matter further.

Adam von Itzstein, who was in close contact with the exiled Hecker, read aloud a statement from Hecker immediately after the committee report. Hecker did not request amnesty for himself, but instead for all of the men who participated in the volunteers' march, whose arrest injured not only themselves, but also their families. With this Itzstein declared that he had told Hecker in a letter on 29 July 1848, "I hold it to be good that you do not ask for any amnesty for yourself, and as soon as you decide, you should express this during the discussion on this question." Itzstein had written this even though he knew that he would have little success. As Itzstein told Hecker:

Perhaps there are many who would be ready to declare amnesty if it were not a matter of Hecker, who is feared by them but loved by the people. For that reason, I fear negative rulings, because you cannot imagine what spirit rules the all-too-numerous Right. They will overturn your election, as well as the amnesty.[45]

Itzstein attempted to keep the men supporting Hecker's political amnesty away from Struve and Heinzen's entourage, sheltering them from what those two men had "written in exaggeration of their ideas."[46] Once more, Itzstein's distaste for Struve and Heinzen was clear.

Because amnesty depended decisively on the question of whether Hecker was recruiting volunteers on the border to invade Baden anew, as the committee and the Baden government assumed, Deputy Ludwig Simon, a lawyer from Trier, read aloud Hecker's declaration that sought to expose the rumors as reactionary propaganda. Hecker expressly distanced himself from these rumors.[47] For strategic reasons or from personal distrust, however, the majority of the National Assembly did not believe his declaration.

Simon, a member of the extreme left of the Donnersberg faction and later a member of the Rump Parliament, was one of Hecker's most active supporters in the National Assembly. He sought with all his strength to convince the deputies in St. Paul's Church that the Baden uprising was not aimed at the National Assembly at all, but against the princes. Addressing the argument that, at the time of the rebellion, there was no more republican feeling in Baden, he used the result of the Baden elections to the National Assembly, which had to be interpreted by ordinary standards as an expression of the people:

> Look at the list of names of the Baden deputies among us. Out of twenty deputies, seven, at the most are of constitutionalist principles, and even these seven are not of the purest constitutional water. It is even asserted that some [Mathy?] would have joined Hecker in better times. ("Applause and laughter from the gallery.") Hence, of the twenty deputies from the Grand Duchy of Baden you have at the most seven constitutionalists. I now ask you whether it is a matter of only Hecker's peculiar will, or whether there might have been republican convictions in the people as a whole. I call your attention to the fact that State Counsel Mathy was not elected in Baden, nor Mr. Bassermann. ("Great disturbance in the Center. Some voices: 'Out of place! Those are person-

alities!' The president restored peace with his bell. ... ") I am speaking of the attitude of the Baden people and am judging it through elections ... Peace and order have been restored in Baden, but in such a way that whoever supports Hecker or the republic has been silenced.[48]

Simon expressed a painful truth to which the Center responded with great distress. One of Hecker's most eloquent defenders was his friend Lorenz Brentano, Mannheim lawyer and Baden Chamber deputy. He personally represented the connection between events in Baden and Hecker's rebellion. Brentano insisted that skepticism about the Baden government's response to the demands of the people was justified. In response to the argument on behalf of the pre-Parliament, which was so persuasive with the moderate side of the National Assembly, Brentano demonstrated how much the individual governments could vary from the proclaimed principle of personal liberty of citizens.

> I come now to the arrest of a Baden citizen by a private person. Gentlemen! On 8 April, a private person dared, against the command of the Baden constitution, which guarantees the legal defense of personal liberty, I say, a Baden private person dared to arrest a Baden citizen on the charge of state treason. ... Wonder why, if such things happen, ... great doubt arises whether a monarchical government has the true and perfect intent to keep its promises? ... We have here, gentlemen, the simplest explanation of the republican coup in Baden. Fickler's arrest happened on 8 April, and on 9 April Hecker went to the highlands, there to proclaim the republic.[49]

Brentano thus made use of the old argument that the reactionary arbitrary rule of most governments was responsible for the outbreak of rebellion. As Brentano knew through Itzstein,[50] Hecker's very readiness to enter the National Assembly was proof that he was not contemplating a new rebellion. Still, the success of the Left proved very modest; the amnesty proposal was rejected.

Baden Interior Minister Bekk wrote to Karl Mathy on 10 August 1848, "The vote on amnesty now has also indirectly decided Hecker's election." He was right. A letter of the Karlsruhe ministry of 14 June 1848 informed the president of the National Assembly, Heinrich von Gagern, of the election results. Gagern first assigned the matter to the Credentials Committee, whose duty it was to examine elections. However, because no one could find fault in the legally immaculate election, the Credentials Committee sent the discussion to the plenum of the National Assembly, pleading non-competence. The deputies were then notified of the election on 1 July 1848.[51]

The debate on the question of Hecker's reception as a deputy in the National Assembly, which began two days after the discussion of amnesty, confirmed the open divergence between a constitutionalist legitimist major-ity and a democratic republican minority. For the majority of the deputies, the National Assembly might have arisen from the revolutionary move-ment, but it had long since consciously left this path. The proverbial fear of revolution among the majority in St. Paul's Church culminated in the debate over Hecker's person. A motion adopted by 350 votes to 116 estab-lished a committee for the sole question, which foretold invalidating the Thiengen election and prescribing new elections. All of this combined to establish Hecker's reputation in the "Myth of the German Republic," as Deputy Simon of Trier never tired of stressing. In Frankfurt, there were sev-eral scenarios, such as Hecker renewing the invasion of Baden or his appearing at the doors of St. Paul's Church with the immunity of a duly elected deputy.[52]

The strategies of argument of the two parties of deputies in St. Paul's Church, were as divergent as their opinions of Hecker's reception. A sub-mission from the Baden ministry to President von Gagern, signed by Alexander von Dusch, preempted the arguments of the constitutionalist lib-erals and the Center-Right coalition. It contained both a report on the results of the election and the statement that Hecker's "treasonous undertakings against Baden, against all of Germany, [lie] so obvious to the whole world that no further emphasis is needed in this situation from a political stand-point." The report's evaluation of the Thiengen election presented the great-est problem for the Baden government.

> Just the casting of votes in favor of a traitor, in favor of an enemy cur-rently threatening the border of Germany with armed partisans, gives the matter a peculiar character. It presents the question of whether such a district, where the majority of the electors has placed itself on the side of a traitor, should lose the right to vote altogether, or whether legal success should be denied to such a criminal vote, as is only right, so that the majority of the electors be reported only after all ballots cast for Hecker are removed. The grand duke's government believes that this

matter, as well as the general principle touching Hecker's position, cannot be regarded as a simple state matter alone, and therefore passes the decision to the National Assembly.[53]

This text quickly impressed the Left, saying as it did, that in this case "the National Assembly should haul out of the fire the chestnuts that the Baden government allowed to get a bit hot in its confrontation with its own people." (The analogy is that of Deputy Vogt from Giessen.) Equally astonishing, however, was the frankness with which the Baden government confessed that it saw the election of a "traitor" as a treasonous act by the entire district, and considered withdrawing the right to vote as a result. "The notion that one could commit the crime of treason by handing in his ballot," Vogt responded in debate, exceeded "all the definitions of high treason that old Metternich and consorts declared. It goes further than anything in the days of the worst reaction. It is completely unworthy."[54]

Friedrich Hecker was never officially notified of his election. For that reason he attempted to bring the matter to a decision himself through a letter of 20 June 1848 to the president of the National Assembly. At the same time he desired to testify to the lawfulness of his actions. The letter, which was read out in the National Assembly, demonstrated the same strategy of argument as the first pages of his self-justifying text, *The Rising of the People in Baden for the German Republic in Early 1848*. Hecker appealed to the high calling of a representative of the people, whose first duty was "expressing the will of the sovereign people." He sought to make a clear distinction between, on the one hand, the governments still in existence, and, on the other hand, the new power of popular representation as an expression of the sovereign people. The accusation of high treason had been derived from "yesterday's principles," which were, for that very reason, no longer relevant for the deputies in St. Paul's Church. Old principles would degrade the National Assembly to mere organs of the government, and the deputies would thus commit treason against the real principle to which they owe their legitimacy and existence as representatives of the people, namely, the people as source of both power and right. This was a departure from the traditional basis for law.

You stand with us, who have raised our weapons for the sovereignty of the people on the soil of the revolution. You have denied monarchical power with your resolutions, and we have provided these resolutions with weapons as a means of execution. That does not alter the matter in the least. ... With one word, there is in principle no difference between the speaking, decreeing revolution and the armed revolution.[55]

The petitions supporting Hecker's election entirely followed this reasoning. Thus Julius Fröbel as president and Friedrich Kapp as secretary of the Congress of German Democrats in Frankfurt demanded calling Deputy Hecker to Frankfurt "as a mark of respect for the will of the people and *as a sign of trust in itself.*" The question had expanded into a matter of principle, distinguishing the factions over central questions of popular sovereignty and the right of revolution, and calling into question the very competence of the National Assembly. Personal animosity toward Hecker played virtually no role in the deputies' judgment.[56]

Formally speaking, Hecker's election was in order. At the time of the debates in St. Paul's Church, he had not yet been convicted by any court, which would have been the sole possible hindrance to election. At this point, even in the case of a trial, the result would have been hard to predict, as the jury trial in Freiburg against Gustav von Struve after his failed attempt at rebellion in September 1848 later documented. There, Struve was acquitted because "according to the opinion of the jurors, the Baden uprising [was] a part of the revolution." Deputies Nauwerk and Zitz argued in precisely this manner, using the right of revolution. Nauwerk referred to it by saying, "We had a revolution, and different forms of high treason developed there." Deputy Zitz seized this argument by stressing a distinction between the old, princely state, which was unjust, and a new, legal state, brought into being only by revolution and established through popular sovereignty.

> Hecker is no traitor. Since the March Days, the people are sovereign. Thus, to commit treason one must commit a crime against the sovereignty of the people. The Assembly itself will judge whether Hecker rebelled against the power of princes.

Itzstein argued in the same way.[57]

But the moderate deputies conceived of the right of revolution and the sovereignty of the people entirely differently. Deputy Plathner from Halberstadt referred to the pre-Parliament and its participants, who had declared in agreement "that only the called constituent National Assembly is to decide the common constitution of Germany." The entire German nation declared its will in the resolutions of the pre-Parliament. Just as the German nation was sovereign in its totality, so the deputies in their totality were sovereign as representatives of the German nation. Just as one could not see the electors of Thiengen as the totality, Hecker could hardly represent a totality. Rather, he tried to subject the population of Baden to his own will. In short, "That was not a revolution, but a rebellion, and therein lies the difference." The Prussian deputy Simon from Königsberg also conceded that the National Assembly derived from the revolution, but he vehemently resisted the conclusion of the deputies Wiesner from Vienna and Vogt from Giessen that it was still identified with the revolution; this would make it a revolutionary tribunal. Simon said that, if there were "no difference between the speaking, decreeing revolution and the armed revolution," then "Hecker's demand to be accepted into this assembly was entirely justified." But then the National Assembly would have to concede the choice of means as entirely secondary. Between "the work in St. Paul's Church and the undertaking in the Baden highlands" there would, in principle, be no difference. In Simon's eyes, receiving Hecker would signal a complete disavowal of the National Assembly, and it would make the Assembly an "absolute impossibility."[58]

The refusal of the majority of the National Assembly to seat Hecker as a deputy, with a deputy's immunity, and its assertion that the Assembly was no court of law and that Hecker could be called to account by a Baden court independently of his mandate, documented a complete renunciation of the revolutionary principle. Instead of being integrated, the extra-parliamentary republican opposition was excluded. Hecker was the most popularly cited example of this renunciation. His increasingly radical rhetoric after the rebellion certainly contributed. Copies of his *Volksfreund* were cited in St. Paul's Church, with some effect, to prove that he was not ready to disown either his deed or his attitude. Similar use was made of his electoral manifesto, which encouraged electors to choose "men of the republican deed" such as Gustav von Struve, Theodor Mögling, Dr. Kaiser from Constance, Andreas Willmann or Friedrich Doll, "all of them fugitive volunteers," according to the committee reporter.[59]

Hecker was not surprised by the result of the debates on his reception. For him, a seat in St. Paul's Church would have meant a return to parliamentary work. His plans to emigrate could have been altered at this point. His reception was not completely beyond possibility. This was shown by

the election of Deputy Peter, who had been installed during Hecker's rebellion as provisional governor of the Republic in the Lake Circle and yet was
later able to take his seat as a legitimate member of the National Assembly.
The reelection of Hecker in Thiengen on 26 October 1848, when he was
already in America, demonstrated once again the consciously perverse attitude of one Baden district, which accepted non-representation in the
National Assembly in order to express repeatedly its republican convictions. The sovereign electorate of Thiengen expressly wanted to distance
itself from the opinion of the "persecuting, stupefying government." It
demanded amnesty for all the politically persecuted languishing in cells or
in exile, and it finally demanded Hecker's reception into the National
Assembly with the comment that "world history ... is the world court,"
and "such talent and such good consciousness of the welfare of the people
shall no longer remain estranged from the National Assembly." But neither
this petition nor repeated elections altered the majority conviction of the
deputies in St. Paul's Church, who rejected their demand.[60]

Things Look Dark – Exile in Muttenz

As Hecker explained to Itzstein in a letter, he had a declaration published in the *Frankfurter Journal* at the start of May. In it, he took a position
about the events on the Scheidegg in Kandern, particularly opposing the
accusation of having treacherously murdered General Friedrich von Gagern
during an argument. After a detailed account of the episode, he concluded,
"No man of honor, even if he is my political enemy, would ever believe that
a republican is, that I am, capable of tolerating a murder, even as a
bystander, let alone promoting it or defending it; for that I pledge my life."
Over time, the Gagern legend proved more and more untenable, and some
witnesses had to be doubted as having obviously been bought. Even conservative contemporaries began to recognize that General von Gagern fell at
the very beginning of the skirmish, in honorable struggle. But the murder
rumor had so much life that Hecker was confronted with it almost thirty
years later in America.[61]

Hecker took up quarters in the Zum Schlüssel inn in Muttenz on 23
April 1848. The grand duke's Baden ministry wrote a letter dated 25 April
1848 to the governing council of Canton Basel-Land asking for Hecker's
extradition. The response was noncommittal, and the request did not have
the desired result; the Swiss side was determined to plead ignorance and

make it clear that involvement in domestic political matters was forbidden.[62]

Hecker had many visitors in Muttenz. His family – specifically his wife Josefine, who was very pregnant at the time, his three children and his father – remained in Switzerland for weeks at a time. Among deputies of the National Assembly, Karl Vogt, Karl Nauwerk and Johann Jacoby visited him, some of the same people who spoke on his behalf during the amnesty debate and the debate on the Thiengen election immediately following. There were regular complaints to the grand duke's ministry about these "pilgrimages," very frequent "short-term border crossings" between the grand duchy and Switzerland. The governing council of Canton Bern would later feel compelled to remark on it after Hecker's departure for America, writing rather indignantly,

> There should be no aspersions here that the refugees received support in Muttenz; on the contrary, it should be noted that among those pilgrims, as Your Excellency's note chooses to call them, there were to be found exemplars of the first German chambers, and even members of the German National Assembly, to whom entry into Swiss territory could not have been forbidden without violating neighborly hospitality. It is, however, also a fact that these visits were made to the very leader of the first Baden revolt, who had warned with all decisiveness against a second coup, and who withdrew himself from any involvement in it by voluntary banishment.[63]

Hecker did advise Struve and others against a renewed rebellion in Baden. His political activities in exile were restricted to publishing his *Volksfreund* and writing his self-justification, *The Rising of the People in Baden*. His publication of the *Volksfreund* caused a glut of citations against Superior Court Advocate Dr. Friedrich Hecker for violations of the press law; an indictment was launched against each issue, each ending with Hecker's conviction *in absentia*. Because "the sample issue, as well as the name of the publisher and editor," left no doubt "that the paper will take a thoroughly hostile direction against the existing state order," read the official formulation, "in keeping with a decision of the grand duke's state ministry at the highest level … all passport officials are ordered to seize every issue of the *Volksfreund*, printed and published by F. Hollinger in Rheinfelden and edited by Hecker." In each case the alleged violations were "insulting the government," "promoting treasonous activities" and "offending majesty."[64]

On 4 July the refugee Hecker and his wife, along with United States Consul George H. Goundie, celebrated American Independence Day on a spur of the Wartenberg, which was, according to an eye-witness, "decorated" on this occasion "with [one] Swiss, two Baden and one American flag." Hundreds of onlookers streamed in from Baden and Basel, but they were disappointed when Hecker made no speech on the Wartenberg. Instead, on their return to the drill field at Muttenz, the crowd was received by Struve, who "occupied [the public] with stories of the liberty of America and Switzerland." When the "Wartenberg group" finally arrived at the drill field, Hecker gave in to demands and made a brief speech. Because he was forbidden to speak on current political matters, he dealt chiefly with the differences between the American republic and a constitutional monarchy. Hecker then gave thanks for the flag presented to him, and the gathering went back to the inn without "any discussion of armed attack on Baden," as was believably noted. Thus ended Hecker's first public celebration of American independence. Many would follow, some of them considerably more spectacular than this first one on Swiss soil.

Despite his respect for Switzerland, Hecker longed to break out of his inactivity. Nothing was more intolerable to Hecker than things' standing still. Theodor Mögling recalled that Hecker in the course of his exile longed to emigrate to America, and Gustav von Struve also knew that for Hecker "the idea of emigration was not foreign ... even earlier." Hecker himself indicated his decision to emigrate in a letter to Emma Herwegh. "Things look dark, esteemed lady. Liberty shrouds her head and I am pulled toward home, to the homeland for which I have longed for 14 years, to the American West."[65]

Hecker's choice of new homeland documented his conscious decision for a republican form of state. A day before his final departure, he wrote a letter to Karl Brenner, a radical participant in the Independence Day celebration on the Wartenberg and later government councilor, summarizing his motivation. "You already know through Goundie that I am traveling to the Union with him to put an end to this pointless life of drifting, restore my health and get to know that great people on the other side of the ocean, that true republic, in its organic inner life."[66]

On 5 September Hecker traveled from Muttenz to Strasbourg with his friends Schöninger, Doll and Itzstein. The *Frankfurter Journal* reported that Itzstein had attempted mediating a reconciliation of Hecker with Struve and Heinzen, but failed. Struve and Heizen were reported to have criticized his decision and had differing views about future political actions. Itzstein corrected these false reports, saying Hecker had not even sought to contact Struve and Heinzen.

There were many receptions in Hecker's honor in Strasbourg, and the inn where he stayed was constantly crowded with visitors. One day before his departure for Le Havre, Hecker gave a farewell address. This speech was marked by disappointment over the further course of the Revolution. He stressed that every revolution that shifted from "deeds ... to debate" would be consumed by the tactics of those it opposed. Hecker was certain that a people first had to destroy the enemy power completely, bringing the "revolution [to an end] by all revolutionary means" and organizing themselves provisionally in order to begin discussions over the new form of state. Instead, the German Revolution of 1848 had given in to "negotiation and mediation, long speeches and groundless nonsense." But no agreement with monarchy was possible, since self-preservation was a prince's highest goal.

Hecker's farewell address also underlined the importance of making the pre-Parliament permanent. It would have formed a necessary rallying point, issued decrees by power of revolutionary will and created new foundations, "passing [what was created] on as a heritage to a constitutional convention." As ever, Hecker was convinced that "a rising in mass would have brought the Revolution to victory without a stroke of the sword; the standing army, whose discipline was in shreds, would not have opposed the people in a revolution in mass," but would have joined it. The people, however, "did not have the courage to go with the words." There had been a lack of willingness to sacrifice. They had set their hopes on the Parliament, and now they expressed disappointment with the result. It was now up to his audience, Hecker said, to float the ship of the people's state once more and take its outlawed sons aboard.

Alien to any personality cult, Hecker could not be happy hearing his name celebrated. He had chosen to leave the "consuming illness of exile" that damned him to be an inactive observer of events. He was traveling to join that "mighty citizen-people who first lit the lamp of liberty for all the peoples of the Old World, making their own image in free institutions." He hoped to be able to act for his fatherland there.[67] If the people could make a decision for a republican deed, he said, he would be back on German soil within two weeks. This pledge of return was no empty promise; Hecker would fulfill it in 1849. By then he had already become an American landowner and would use the opportunity of his European visit to take his family back with him to America.

1 Bassermann, *Denkwürdigkeiten*, 25; Scharp, *Hecker*, 94. Wende, *Radikalismus*, 214. See Hecker's speech in *VSB*, 12. öS (7 January 1846), 236-37; ibid., 76. öS (14 September 1846), 236-37.

2 Peiser, *Struve*, 48; Mathy, *Nachlaß*, 18; Scharp, *Hecker*, 93. FH, *Erhebung*, 40; see also Helmut Eckert, "Heckerbriefe," *ZGO* 93 (1941), 279-85, here 279. FH to Sebastian Straub, Mannheim, 20 March 1847, printed in *ZGO* 93 (1941), 281.

3 See Adam von Itzstein to Sebastian Straub, Mannheim, 17 April 1847, printed in *ZGO* 93 (1941), 283. Zucker, *Forty Eighters*, 283; Hildegard B. Johnson, "Caspar Butz of Chicago – Politician and Poet," *AGR* 12, no. 6 (1946), 4-5. Butz, "Erinnerungen," part 1.

4 Constance mayor Hüetlin to Karl Mathy, Constance, 24 March 1847, Mathy, *Nachlaß*, 17-18. Peiser, *Struve*, 52 ff.; Heinrich von Andlaw, *Der Aufruhr und Umsturz in Baden, 4. Abteilung* (Freiburg, 1850-51), 111 (with a reprint of the Offenburg Program); also in Ernst Rudolf Huber, ed., *Dokumente zur deutschen Verfassungsgeschichte*, vol. 1 (Stuttgart, 1961), 261-64 (with the Heppenheim Program of the liberals). Wende, *Radikalismus*, 117-18. *VSB*, 76. öS (14 September 1846), 165; the Mannheim demands are repeated, ibid., 33. öS (2 March 1848), 63; see also Welcker's commentary on the conclusions, ibid., 64. Nolte, "Gemeindeliberalismus," 298 ff. Johann Peter Grohe, Struve and Hecker owned shares in the *Mannheimer Abendzeitung*.

5 *Mannheimer Abendzeitung*, no. 253; cf. on that Andlaw, *Aufruhr*, 111-12; also Peiser, *Struve*, 55.

6 Ludwig Bergsträsser, "Die parteipolitische Lage beim Zusammentritt des Vorparlamentes," *Zeitschrift für Politik* 6 (1913), 598. Bassermann, *Denkwürdigkeiten*, 13. Scharp, *Hecker*, 104; on the Mathy-Struve conflict, see also Adler, *Literarische Geheimberichte*, 168-69; on Struve's hindered election, Bassermann, *Denkwürdigkeiten*, 29. *VSB*, gS (18 December 1847), 92-93.

7 Throne speech printed in *VSB*, Eröffnungssitzung (9 December 1847), 4-5. Ibid., gS (18 December 1847), 120, my emphasis.

8 *VSB*, gS (18 December 1847), 121, 122. *VSB*, 10. öS (14 January 1848), 191.

9 Discussion in debates on 15, 27 and 28 January 1848. *VSB*, 16. öS (28 January 1848), 283. See Manfred Pohl, *Südzucker 1837-1987* (Frankfurt am Main, 1987), 32.

10 *VSB*, 23. öS (12 February 1848), 126; see also Bassermann, *Denkwürdigkeiten*, 31.

11 *VSB*, 23. öS (12 February 1848), 126.

12 *VSB*, 28. öS (23 February 1848), 268.

13 Bassermann, *Denkwürdigkeiten*, 64; see also the letter from Heinrich Hoffmann to FH, Frankfurt am Main, 25 March 1848, Nachlaß Häusser, Fsg 1/104, Bundesarchiv, Außenstelle Frankfurt am Main. Hoffmann warns Hecker to use his great influence to encourage moderation. Häusser, *Denkwürdigkeiten*, 115, 118.

14 Bassermann, *Denkwürdigkeiten*, 40; J. Baptist Bekk, *Die Bewegung in Baden vom Ende Februar 1848 bis zur Mitte des Mai 1849* (Mannheim, 1850), 59, 108-9; Peiser, *Struve*, 96. See Andlaw, *Aufruhr*, 91. *VSB*, 32. öS (1 March 1848), 45. Ibid., 31. öS (29 February 1848), 32.

15 "Begründung der Motion des Abgeordneten Hecker über die Unvereinbarkeit gewisser Aemter mit der Stellung eines Abgeordneten," *VSB*, 7, Beilageheft, Beilage Nr. 2 zum Protokoll der 25. öS (30. Juni 1846), 197-210. The extended version ibid., 33. öS (2 March 1848), 64-65; this citation is point 4.

16 Bassermann's narrative and the resolutions, *Denkwürdigkeiten*, 65 ff. See Jucho, *Verhandlungen, Anlage A*, Heidelberg, 5 March 1848, viii-ix. Karl Obermann, *Einheit und Freiheit. Die deutsche Geschichte von 1815 bis 1849 in zeitgenössischen Dokumenten* (Berlin, 1950), 241; see also Peter Wende, "Radikalismus," *Geschichtliche Grundbegriffe*, vol. 5 (Stuttgart, 1984), 113-33, here 121. On the demand for resignations, see point 12 of the expanded version in the Chamber, *VSB*, 33. öS (2 March 1848), 64. Andlaw, *Aufruhr*, 107.

17 Bekk, *Bewegung*, 97. *VSB*, 35. öS (9 March 1848), 102; Bassermann, *Denkwürdigkeit*, 77. Mathy, *Nachlaß*, 209.

18 Peiser, *Struve*, 108. *VSB*, 39. öS (16 March 1848), 221. Bekk, *Bewegung*, 127, and the note attached. *VSB*, 43. öS (24 March 1848), 298.

19 *VSB*, 39. öS (16 March 1848), 220; Welcker wanted it extended to 8 March, Brentano until 4 March. Julius Fröbel, *Theorie der Politik, als Ergebnis einer erneuerten Prüfung demokratischer Lehrmeinungen*, vol. 1 (Vienna, 1861), here, preface, p. v. *VSB*, 39. öS (16 March 1848), 220.

20 Gustav Freitag, *Karl Mathy. Geschichte seines Lebens* (Leipzig, 1870), 253. Bassermann, *Denkwürdigkeiten*, 78 ff.; Andlaw, *Aufruhr*, 136; on the fact that Hecker spoke against the republic in Offenburg, see also Bekk, *Bewegung*, 121 ff., 145. The resolutions of the Offenburg meeting in Andlaw, *Aufruhr*, 116-18, see also 136.

21 *VSB*, 43. öS (24 March 1848), 305, 317-18; see on this also Bekk, *Bewegung*, 84, p. 85, n., that Hecker "appears still not to have planned rebellion."

22 Bekk, *Bewegung*, 122. For the announcement see *VSB*, 43. öS (24 March 1848), 306; also Peiser, *Struve*, 108.

23 Struve, *Zwölf Streiter*, 15. Hecker, *Erhebung*, 27, n. 28. Andlaw, *Aufruhr*, 126 ff.; Bekk, *Bewegung*, 99-100, 124 ff. Discussion and publication of the military system, *VSB*, 44. öS (28 March 1848), 330 ff. Bassermann, *Denkwürdigkeiten*, 92. Häusser, *Denkwürdigkeiten*, 112.

24 Adam von Itzstein, *VSB*, 43. öS (24 March 1848), 318. Petition in Jucho, *Verhandlungen*, 6-7. Wende, *Revolutionsbegriff*, 59. Jucho, *Verhandlungen*, 4. There was a series of petitions and drafts of a Magna Carta of human rights, Ludwig Häusser, *Gegenwart*, 703. *VSB*, 43. öS (24 March 1848), 306-12, cited here, 309. Hecker, *Erhebung*, 22. Bassermann, *Denkwürdigkeiten*, 148.

25 Jucho, *Verhandlungen, Antrag*, 7.

26 Thus Robert Blum, Jucho, *Verhandlungen*, 11; in fact there were only two Austrians and 141 "substitute Prussians" present due to the summoning procedure, because the United Prussian Assembly had summoned its deputies at precisely this time.

27 Jucho, *Verhandlungen*, 15. The speech, with a commentary, is also in Peter Wende, ed., *Politische Reden 1792-1867*, vol. 1 (Frankfurt am Main, 1990), 292-95; commentary, 777-80. My own emphasis.

28 See Jucho, *Verhandlungen*, 1, 15, 65-66, 67. Mittermaier's opening address, ibid., 3: "We act as executors," also ibid., 5, 57. *VSB*, 32. öS (1 March 1848), 58.

29 See Häusser, *Gegenwart*, 699; Jucho, *Verhandlungen*, 85, 113; Zimmermann, *Revolution*, 405-6, 410-11.

30 See Jucho, *Verhandlungen*, 144-45, 161. See the Häusser article in *Die Gegenwart* (Leipzig, 1848). FH, *Erhebung*, 24.

31 Häusser, "Das Vorparlament," *Die Gegenwart*, 703. Veit Valentin follows Häusser precisely, Valentin, *Geschichte der deutschen Revolution von 1848-1849*, vol. 1 (Cologne; Berlin, 1970), 478 and n. 41. Zimmermann, *Revolution*, 392.

32 See Bekk, *Bewegung*, 130, 124; Peiser, *Struve*, 115. Eimer to Karl Mathy, Lahr, 3 April 1848, Mathy, *Nachlaß*, 168. See Peiser, Struve, 121-22. Welcker issued his memorandum in Karlsruhe on 7 April, possibly one of the reasons for Fickler's arrest; Scharp, *Hecker*, 179; also Bekk, *Bewegung*, 132. Franz Wigard, ed., *Stenographischer Bericht über die Verhandlungen der deutschen constituierenden Nationalversammlung zu Frankfurt am Main* vol. 2 (Frankfurt a. M., 1848-50), 57. Sitzung (8 August 1848), 1452-53. Karl Mathy to K. J. A. Mittermaier, Frankfurt a. M., 10 April 1848, Mathy, *Nachlaß*, 185. Bekk, *Bewegung*, 136-37; on address ibid., 140; cf. also Andlaw, who also printed the proclamation, *Aufruhr*, 138.

33 See Bassermann, *Denkwürdigkeiten*, 124 ff.; Bekk, *Bewegung*, 137-38. *VSB*, 47. öS (7 April 1848), 50.

34 Mathy, *Nachlaß*, 181. *VSB*, 47. öS (7 April 1848), 50.

35 On the episode and its impact, Bassermann, *Denkwürdigkeiten*, 123-26; Bekk, *Bewegung*, 33-34, 142, 146. Mathy's explanation in *Nachlaß*, 183; Peiser, *Struve*, 122. See his explication on this in *VSB*, 65. öS (13 may 1848), 122. *Neues Tageblatt*, Stuttgart, no. 155b, 6 July 1873. Freitag, *Mathy*, 263. Karl Mathy to K. J. A. Mittermaier, 10 April 1848, Mathy, *Nachlaß*, 184. Mathy is playing here on Hecker's concept of republican honor.

36 GLA 276/3431; GLA 276/3432. Bekk, *Bewegung*, 148; Scharp, Hecker, 97; FH, *Erhebung*, 80; cf. also the Hecker proclamations dated Constance, 12 April 1848, Stockach, 13 April 1848 and Geisingen, 15 April 1848, printed in *VSB*, 53. öS (17 April 1848), 180, "with provisions for six days and with adequate money." Andres Lück, *Friedrich Hecker. Rolle, Programm und politische Möglichkeit eines Führers der radikal-demokratische Bewegung von 1847/48 in Baden*, Ph.D. diss., Berlin, 1979, 226, n. 94. FH, *Gepfefferte Briefe*, 57; FH also tolerated Forster's change to the French side in this passage. *VSB*, 35. öS (9 March 1848), 112.

37 *VSB*, 43. öS (24 March 1848), 318. Hecker, *Erhebung*, 56; also Mögling's *Bericht*, 83, 89 (second meeting with Emma Herwegh), renunciation of foreign help, Peiser, *Struve*, 127; Mathy, *Nachlaß*, 163; also Emma Herwegh, *Geschichte der deutschen demokratischen Legion aus Paris. Von einer Hochverrätherin* (Grünberg, 1849). Peiser, *Struve*, 128; also *VSB*, 39. öS (16 March 1848), 221. Mathy to Franz Buhl, 1 May 1848, Mathy, *Nachlaß*, 223.

38 Andlaw, *Aufruhr*, 142, also 141, 143-44, 145-46. Bekk, *Bewegung*, 145, 146-47, 148, 157. Peiser, *Struve*, 129; also FH, *Erhebung*, 58. Buhl was later favored by the Baden government as the leading replacement candidate for Hecker's seat as deputy in the National Assembly, see Mathy, *Nachlaß*, 30. Andlaw, *Aufruhr*, 147. See ibid., emphasis as spread type in the text; two deputies in the Committee of Fifty, Spatz and Hecker's friend Venedey moved to "forget the event."

39 Bekk, *Bewegung*, 155; also ibid., 154; also Peiser, *Struve*, 126; Freytag, *Mathy*, 264; Emma Herwegh, *Demokratische Legion*, 33; Andlaw, *Aufruhr*, 140. Mathy, *Nachlaß*, 162-64; FH, *Erhebung*, 49.

40 *VSB*, 53, öS (17 April 1848), 179. Bekk in *VSB*, 53. öS (17 April 1848), 181; Soiron's motion, ibid., 82. Strack, *Herkunft*, 10; the date of the wedding was 24 October 1839. Bekk, *Bewegung*, 151-52. *VSB*, 54. öS (18 April 1848); not a word about FH in this session. Ibid., 55. öS (28 April 1848), 216-17. Cf. Gottschalk to Karl Mathy, Schopfheim, 6 May 1848, Mathy, *Nachlaß*, 250, 252.

41 FH to Itzstein, Muttenz, 16 May 1848, Itzstein Nachlaß. Robert Blum to his wife, 13 April 1848, cited in Ludwig Bergsträsser, ed., *Das Frankfurter Parlament in Briefen und Tagebüchern* (Frankfurt am Main, 1929), 352. Wolfgang Siemann, *Die deutsche Revolution von 1848/49* (Frankfurt am Main, 1985), 74.

42 *Stenographischer Bericht*, vol. 2, 1415 ff.; on the following also brief and telling: Herbert Reiter, *Politisches Asyl im 19. Jahrhundert. Die deutschen politischen Flüchtlinge des Vormärz und der Revolution von 1848/4 in Europa und den USA* (Berlin, 1993), 147-53. In addition a petition had been filed on 29 May 1848 by the Austrian deputy Wiesner from Felsberg, calling for a "complete amnesty for all political crimes and nisdemeanors committed until now," *Stenographischer Bericht*, 1422 and his speech, ibid., 1432.

43 *Stenographischer Bericht*, 1416.

44 Note the name of the source, here Deputy Biedermann [="decent"] from Leipzig, ibid., 1431, 1420, see also 1417.

45 On 28 June 1848 Hecker had a list of the names of all political refugees staying in Birsfeld. Among them were carpenters, tailors and shoemakers as well as two physicians, a communal councilor and a notary, the list in Martin Leuenberger, "Muttenz: die erste Station in Friedrich Heckers Exil," Frei, *Hecker in den USA*, 43-59, here 54. Adam von Itzstein to Friedrich Hecker, 29 July 1848, Hecker Papers, box 1, folder 5; printed by Vollmer, "Nachlaß," 367.

46 See *Stenographischer Bericht*, 1422; Widenmann, the bill's reporter, had read Struve and Heinzen's *Plan zur Revolutionirung und Republikanisirung Deutschlands* to document the continued and unaltered radical position of the "rebels," ibid., 1420.

47 See the statement of the Baden government, also on the rumors, Bekk to Mathy, 5 July 1848, Mathy, *Nachlaß*, 327/28, 330. *Stenographischer Bericht*, 1430. See FH's explanation in the *Frankfurter Journal*, see n. 214 below, and the reference by Deputy Simon, *Stenographischer Bericht*, 1430.

48 On Simon, *ADB*, vol. 35, 379-80. *Stenographischer Bericht*, 1430.

[49] Ibid., 1437.

[50] See Itzstein to Hecker, 24 March 1848, FHP, box 1, folder 5; printed in Vollmer, "Nachlaß," 360 ff.

[51] Mathy, *Nachlaß*, 365. *VSB*, 76. öS (9 October 1848), 162. See *Stenographischer Bericht*, 29. Sitzung (1 July 1848), 658-60.

[52] See *Stenographischer Bericht*, 58. Sitzung (10 August 1848), 1496-1501. *Stenographischer Bericht*, 659. See Bassermann, *Denkwürdigkeiten*, 165-66; Bekk, *Bewegung*, 179. *Stenographischer Bericht*, 181. Sitzung (5 March 1849), 5587. Itzstein to FH, Mannheim, 9 June 1848, FHP, box 1, folder 5; printed in Vollmer, "Nachlaß," 364-65.

[53] The letter was dated 14 June 1848; it was presented again in *Stenographischer Bericht*, 58. Sitzung (10 August 1848), 1476. Of the 142 electors, 134 had appeared. "Of them 77 voted for the former deputy of the Second Chamber of the Baden estates, Friedrich Hecker, but 56 for Deputy Franz Buhl of Ettlingen, one for Baron von Andlaw in Freiburg." See *Stenographischer Bericht*, 29. Sitzung (1 July 1848), 658.

[54] *Stenographischer Bericht*, 58. Sitzung (10 August 1848), 1492. Verified by a letter by Karl Mathy to Ludwig Häusser of 13 June 1848, a day before the official government letter to the National Assembly, cf. Mathy, *Nachlaß*, 302. *Stenographischer Bericht*, 1491.

[55] Adam von Itzstein to FH, 9 June 1848, FHP, box 1, folder 5, printed in Vollmer, "Nachlaß," 365. Printed in *Stenographischer Bericht*, 58. Sitzung (10 August 1848), 1476-77; also *Der Volksfreund*, no. 9, 25 June 1848, GLA 234/1660.

[56] Ibid., 1477-78, with a long series of further petitions; my own emphasis; even Hecker's opponents had to recognize that petitions for him "were numerous," ibid., 1488. See, for example, Deputy Simon of Königsberg, *Stenographischer Bericht*, 58. Sitzung (10 August 1848), 1489.

[57] See on this evaluation, Reinhold Reith, *Der Aprilaufstand von 1848 in Konstanz. Zur biographischen Dimension von "Hochverrath und Aufruhr." Versuch einer historischen Protestanalyse* (Sigmaringen, 1982); on the Struve trial, Mathias Reimann, *Der Hochverratsprozeß gegen Gustav Struve und Karl Blind. Der erste Schwurgerichtsfall in Baden* (Sigmaringen, 1985). Reiter, *Politisches Asyl*, 151; cf. also Peiser, *Struve*, 180. *Stenographischer Bericht*, 29. Sitzung (1 July 1848), 660. See ibid., 58. Sitzung (10 August 1848), 1484.

[58] Ibid., 1485-86, 1488.

[59] Ibid., 1482. The call to election is printed in the same place.

[60] Bekk, *Bewegung*, 161; also debate about Deputy Peter (*VSB*, 71, öS [17 June 1848], 63 ff. See the statement of several communes of the fourth electoral district (Thiengen) to the National Assembly, printed in *Der Volksfreund*, no. 15, Sunday, 20 August 1848, 59. See also the anonymous brochure, *Die Wahl von Thiengen und die deutsche Nationalversammlung. Den unerschrockenen Wahlmännern von Thiengen gewidmet von einem Abgeordneten der deutschen Nationalversammlung in Frankfurt am Main* (Frankfurt a. M., 1848).

[61] FH to Itzstein, Muttenz, 28 May 1848, Itzstein-Nachlaß. FH's explanation in 3rd supplement to the *Frankfurter Journal*, no. 134, Sunday, 14 May 1848; see also the announcement and summary in the 2nd supplement to the *Frankfurter Journal*, no. 130, Wednesday, 10 May 1848. *Frankfurter Journal*, no. 134, ibid.; see also the statement of volunteer Georg Benz, who testified that Hecker negotiated with Gagern for about nine minutes, then returned to his people and, upon being asked what Gagern had said, responded, "Gagern demands that the column put down its weapons, and on asking whether they wanted to do it, the column responded, 'no,' on which the column began moving again toward the mountain." It was only after they had been divided into three lines by Lieutenant Willich that the shooting began, testimony, Lörrach, 16 May 1848, signed by Oberamtmann Exter, Heckers Hochverratsakte, GLA 276/ 3431, pp. 125-33. "Ein charakteristischer Brief Friedrich Heckers," *DAG*, 3 (1903), no. 3, 47-48.

[62] Martin Leuenberger, "Muttenz: die erste Station in Friedrich Heckers Exil," Frei. ed., *Hecker in den USA*, 43-59; the message is found in the Staatsarchiv des Kantons Basel-Landschaft (StaBL), Politisches D1, Deutsche Flüchtlinge. On the reception in the press of the extradition request, see also supplement to the *Frankfurter Journal*, no. 129, Tuesday, 9 May 1848. Even Mathy regarded the ministry's request to be politically unwise, since the response could be foreseen, see Mathy to Häusser, 15 May 1848, Mathy, *Nachlaß*, 262.

[63] See the travel permit for Josefine Hecker and her three children, FHP, box 1, folder 7; the permit "to go to Muttenz in Switzerland and reside there" and "in all circumstances to be allowed to return here as our proper community member and to find irrevocable reception," was given for a year, dated Mannheim, 15 June 1848. StaBL Politisches D1, Deutsche Flüchtlinge, Präsident und Regierungsrat des Kantons Bern als eidgenossische Vorort an den deutschen Reichsgesandten F. Raveaux, 4 November 1848, cited in Leuenberger, "Muttenz," 46.

[64] Bekk, *Bewegung*, 177; particularly the papers in GLA 234/1660. GLA 234/1660, Großherzogthum Baden Justizministerium, Strafrechtspflege / Hochverrat und Aufruhr, against the publisher Hollinger and the editor Hecker, here the decree of the grand duke's State Ministry of 19 (June), no. 1322. See, for example, the sentence of the grand duke's Aulic Court of the Oberrheinkreis, 27 September 1848, in which Hecker is condemned "to one year of workhouse punishment as well as taking on the costs of investigation and punishment," GLA 234/1660.

[65] Report of Lieutenant Gisin, head of the Baselbieter Landjäger-Corps, Liestal, 5 July 1848, to the president and council of the canton, StaBL Politisches D1, Deutsche Flüchtlinge, cited after Leuenberger, "Muttenz," 50. Leuenberger, "Muttenz," 52-53. Theodor Mögling, *Briefe an seine Freunde* (Solothurn, 1858), 128. Vollmer, "Nachlaß," 393. Struve, *Zwölf Streiter*, 21. FH to Emma Herwegh, Muttenz, 11 July 1848, printed in Marcel Herwegh, ed., *1848 – Briefe an und von Georg Herwegh* (Munich, 1896), 247.

[66] Goundie did not accompany the refugees on their journey, but he did have an active part in their reception in New York. FH to Karl Brenner, Muttenz, 4 September 1848, from the private archive of the Brenner family, Stadtarchiv Basel Stadt, Sig. PA 565 D 3g.

[67] Otto Wiltberger, "Die deutschen Flüchtlinge in Straßburg von 1830-49," *Freiburger Abhandlungen zur mittleren und neueren Geschichte*, 17 (Berlin; Leipzig, 1910), 188. Second supplement to the *Frankfurter Journal*, no. 247, Monday, 11 September 1848, title "Vom Oberrhein, 8. Sept." Struve and Heinzen had the brochure *Plan zur Revolutionierung und Republikanisierung Deutschlands* printed by Johann Ulrich Walser in Birsfelden, a brochure banned even in Switzerland, cf. Leuenberger, "Muttenz," 45. See "Adam von Itzstein, Mitglied der Nationalversammlung, Frankfurt a. M., den 12. September 1848," published in *Frankfurter Journal*, no. 249, Wednesday, 13 September 1848. Facsimile of the flier in Hans Blum, *Deutsche Revolution 1848-49* (Florence; Leipzig, 1897), 240-41. It bears the title, "Heckers Abschied vom deutschen Volke. Gedruckt und zu haben in der Vereinsbuchdruckerei, Neue Kirchgasse No. 2."

HECKER IN AMERICA
IV
EXILE AND NEW HOMELAND (1848-54)

This Side of the Ocean and That

A few days after his farewell address in Strasbourg, Friedrich Hecker took ship in Le Havre for Southampton, accompanied by his cousin Heinrich Tiedemann and his friend Schöninger. On 20 September he left Southampton on the steamship *Hermann* bound for New York. Hecker traveled as a second-class cabin passenger. "As much as they offered me first class at no extra charge," he wrote to his wife, "I have become a true democrat and will oppose such aristocratic distinctions where I can."[1]

Also on board the *Hermann*, there was the liberal political scientist and jurist Franz Lieber, who had already left Germany for political reasons in the 1820s. Lieber was a close friend of Karl Josef Anton Mittermaier, Hecker's earlier teacher in Heidelberg and later president of the pre-Parliament. Lieber's sympathy for the Revolution and a German republic had caused him to leave for Germany at the first word of the Berlin disturbances, in order to see things with his own eyes. His eldest son, Oscar Montgomery, only seventeen years old, had rushed ahead to Berlin to participate in the barricade battles in the first days of March. Hecker described his new, helpful acquaintance as an "extremely educated, lovable man who gave me a mass of recommendations, and with whom I shall always exchange letters."[2] In fact Hecker had an active correspondence with Lieber over the following years. At its center was the most important American question of the 1850s, slavery. It is hardly puzzling, therefore, that one of the three letters of introduction that Lieber wrote out for Hecker was to the lawyer Charles Sumner in Boston.[3] Sumner was one of the most committed fighters for equal rights, a sharp critic of the Southern system and of slavery. As United States senator from Massachusetts, he became a central figure among opponents of slavery within the Republican Party in the 1850s.[4]

When Hecker arrived in New York on 5 October 1848, he discovered at once that he did not need any letters of introduction. Thousands of German-Americans had gathered to greet him at New York's harbor, accompanied by many Americans and a series of officers of the municipal administration. Hecker was not only the first, but also the most popular political refugee of the Revolution to set foot on American soil. The first news of the revolutionary movement in Europe, and especially in Germany, had provoked the warmest support of the German-American population. As early as the beginning of April, there was a revolutionary celebration in New York, and on 8 May a mass procession of thousands of people "passed along Broadway for hours." On 29 May 1848, an address of sympathy was composed to the National Assembly, signed by 494 Germans in New York and accompanied by $3500 for the "poor survivors of the martyrs of the young freedom of Germany." Reports and narratives, some written by Hecker, Sigel and Mögling themselves, and published in Switzerland, had already been published in the *New Yorker Staatszeitung*. The essential facts about the first Baden uprising were widely known. The American consul in Switzerland who befriended Hecker, George H. Goundie, had not only financed the crossing of refugees with donations sent to him from America, but also sent ahead reports about Hecker's planned travels in the United States so that timely arrangements could be made to receive him.[5]

"I have been received like no European since Lafayette," Hecker wrote euphorically to his wife. Deputies of a committee of German republicans greeted him while he was still on board his ship and accompanied him to the Shakespeare Hotel, where free rooms awaited him and his company. Hecker answered in German the German address that was presented the next day, and in English "as well as I could" the address that was in English.[6] On 9 October 1848 New York Germans organized a mass assembly at Tammany Hall. Here Hecker repeated the declaration that he had composed in Strasbourg, saying that he had come to get to know a true practicing republican government and to prepare himself for a second Revolutionary uprising. At the same time he noted how the Frankfurt Parliament had great interest in the constitutional system of the United States.[7] He thus maintained at the outset the notion that he was not an immigrant but a man seeking help, whose sojourn in America was temporary.

Only two days after arriving in New York, however, he wrote to his wife, detailing how she should plan her own voyage to New York, what provisions she should bring with her and whom she should inform when she arrived in New York. In this letter Hecker made a special effort to persuade his father to come over, as well, for the passage had no special perils for older people. He assured his wife that news of his family's arrival in New York would reach him "in a couple hours, even in the furthest West" through the electric telegraph. In this letter he also indicated his preferred goal, the Midwest.

The men then proceeded west and south. Honors were renewed in Newark and in Philadelphia, where Hecker spoke at a dinner for the Philadelphia workers' association. The party reached Cincinnati on 22 October via Baltimore and Louisville. Here the emigrants made the acquaintance of German writer and jurist Johann Bernhard Stallo, who received "the travelers with a speech masterful in form and content." Stallo and Hecker began a close personal, as well as public and political, friendship that would not end until the 1870s, due to political divergence. Whenever Hecker was in Cincinnati for presentations or election campaigns, he usually stayed in "Judge Stallo's" house.[8]

On 31 October 1848 Hecker, Schöninger and Tiedemann arrived in St. Louis. While in Swiss exile Hecker had received an address of greeting and pledge of support from Dr. Ferdinand Häussler, chairman of the "St. Louis German republican committee." An address and resolutions unanimously passed by "thousands of local German citizens" at a "mass meeting" on 15 April 1848 accompanying the written message. One finds in them an expression of particular disappointment over the course of the Revolution, especially fate of the pre-Parliament. Men such as "Gagern, Jordan, Bassermann, Mathy" and others who had held the highest reputation among German-Americans, had committed what could only be called a "breach of faith with the cause of freedom" and with "cowardly treason to the cause of the German people." In contrast, the writing continued, Hecker, "along with Struve and other honorable patriots making up the republican minority in Frankfurt, did not fail the trust we place in them."[9]

In St. Louis Hecker had the opportunity to publish a call to the Germans of America and the American friends of a German republic, in which he calls for the formation of revolutionary associations and a monetary fund for the German Revolution. On 28 December there was a gathering of several thousand people in the rotunda of the courthouse. Hecker's speech there was "received with stormy applause." His presence precipitated the formation of a support society and the planning of an address to Germans in the old fatherland.

What was good for the Germans of St. Louis must naturally be right for the Germans of Belleville, Illinois, about 14 miles on the other side of the Mississippi. And so there, on 6 January 1849, under the presidency of the mayor, Hecker addressed his second great rally in the St. Clair county courthouse. He gave a lively description of the oppression that Germans had endured for years in their homeland, portraying the population's growing resistance and the March Days in Baden. He stressed once again his belief that an error had been made when the rapid concessions offered by the governments had been accepted so quickly, giving the governments valuable maneuvering time. Only a revolution pressed with greater decisiveness could have saved the cause of liberty. He also repeated here his analysis of the absurd construction of a German union of sovereign states under one head; union, he believed, would make sense only in a federative system of republican states after the model of the United States or of Switzerland. Money was gathered at this rally, as well, and the $200 collected was put together with the $200 profit from a bazaar organized by German women in Belleville, for transmittal to the Central Democratic Association in Berlin.

Everywhere in the country, not merely in St. Louis or under Hecker's inspiration, revolutionary societies arose. Some of them saw it as their mission to equip volunteer partisans and send them to Europe to take an active part in the struggle for liberty. Others were satisfied with collecting money, while still others turned simply to "symbolic" support in the form of addresses.[10] Privately, Hecker remained little convinced that such actions would be effective – quite the contrary.

Shortly after his arrival in St. Louis, Hecker learned about the best areas for settlement and the general conditions of life. He wrote to his wife:

> The lots in the city [of St. Louis] are enormously expensive. The farms in the immediate vicinity are the same. Only in the flourishing neighboring state, or a few miles from the city is it cheap. For $2000, 5000 guilders, you can get a lovely farm .... We are looking at a farm where there is public land, so that all our friends may settle nearby. If monarchy wins in Germany, we still have nice farms and we can found a town. If the republic wins and they call me back, then we have a nice little property here that can be rented out, getting more valuable all the time, guaranteeing the children a secure existence. As things stand now, I do not believe in a return.[11]

By November Hecker had already moved from St. Louis to Belleville, setting up his temporary quarters in George Neuhoff's hotel. There, he made contact with German immigrants who had chosen this as their homeland in the 1830s. The best known of these was Gustav Körner, Hecker's former duelling foe from his Heidelberg student days. Körner recalled in his memoirs that, as soon as they met, Hecker remarked on his desire to get a farm as close to Belleville as possible. For that reason they set out in the following days to look at farms for sale. They traveled as far as the northern reaches of Monroe County, but despite many sufficient pieces of land, Hecker could not quite make up his mind.

Through the efforts of Dr. Roman, a land broker, he found what he wanted, a farm three miles southeast of Lebanon. The farm was about 300 acres, a part of it fertile prairie soil, the rest woodland. The rooms of the brick farmhouse were deteriorated, but the price was right, and so Hecker decided on this farm, which he was to occupy for the rest of his life. With this farm Hecker obtained land that had already been cultivated, a tactic that many immigrant guides recommended. Cultivated land was certainly more expensive that unoccupied "Congress Land." But the new arrival was spared the trouble of having to clear it, and he could also expect crops from the very beginning.[12]

Closeness to Belleville was a factor in Hecker's choice. Since the 1830s there had been a strong wave of academically trained German immigrants with republican convictions, particularly from the areas of Darmstadt, Frankfurt am Main and the Palatinate. Like Hecker, they sought first to secure their existence by buying functioning farms. Few of these "soft-handed farmers" succeeded, and after a few years they returned to the cities and resumed bourgeois careers. Belleville in particular profited from this, and an intense cultural life developed, influenced by the German academic tradition.[13] With the influx of Forty-Eighters, who had been much more intensely involved in politics in the old country than were "Thirtyers" and who were therefore readier to play an active political role in the United States, Belleville became prominent in American politics. From the start of the 1850s, the Forty-Eighters' republican tone dominated the German-American press in Belleville, which was soon noticed in other states. This republicanism, oriented to models from ancient history and saturated with the liberal principles of the era before the Revolution, was almost identical to Hecker's rhetoric. For that reason it is hardly strange that Hecker's public efforts always found the broadest support here, where they shared the same basic principles.

Not all of Belleville's residents were charmed by Hecker's presence. In the course of time a conflict over ethnic leadership would develop between the more politically moderate "Grays," who were long familiar with American institutions, and the newly arrived more radical "Greens" of the late 1840s and early 1850s. The conflict was already evident shortly after Hecker's arrival in Belleville in letters of the "Gray Thirtyer" Theodor Erasmus Hilgard, from West Belleville, to his friend in the Rhenish Palatinate, Philipp Heinrich von Kraemer. Gustav Körner had introduced

Hecker to Hilgard.[14] To Hilgard, a generation older and a bourgeois liberal to his core, Hecker's unrestrained, effervessent and radical political position was horrifying. Hilgard wrote to his friend,

> You will wonder not a little, by the way, if I tell you that we now have the essence of all German agitation [*Wühlerei*], that is to say *Hecker*, right here in Belleville! Fortunately, there is nothing to agitate [*wühlen*] here, because American Germans do not allow themselves to waste their time in enthusiastic rallies and hot declamations about Germany's liberation from the tyrant's yoke ... Hecker sits quietly in an inn here, alongside two companions (*Tiedemann* and *Schöninger*), and studies the American Constitution and legislation. A more *practical* republic, it is hoped, will make his views milder and more positive. Namely, he will learn what our German heroes of liberty in general do not know or have not yet taken to heart, that the true republican must, before all else, *submit to the majority*, even when it appears to him that it is a hundred times wrong. ... I can therefore ... find a great enjoyment in his activity up to now, although he also has good and pleasant qualities. He perhaps is among the few with whom personal ambition is not the chief motivation. If I am not successful in bringing him to more moderate views, we will never be good friends.[15]

Hilgard and Hecker presumably never did become good friends. Because Hilgard preferred to stay far from politics, the two men never had much chance to meet in the times that followed. Further, Hilgard decided in the mid-1850s to leave America and return to Heidelberg.[16]

Soon after the mass meetings in St. Louis and Belleville, Hilgard actually saw his planned moderating influence on Hecker wither away, and he confessed to his friend that Hecker was "agitating" in Belleville, as well:

> He has managed to establish a large association in St. Louis, whose purpose it is to collect money to support *republican* efforts in Germany to teach the Germans through addresses, etc., about the advantages of the republican form of state!! *Hecker* is a devilish rascal who easily seizes those who have no understanding, as blind as they are, with his rhetorical talent and his enthusiasm – and the masses, as we know them, are without understanding everywhere.[17]

Just as the political influence of the Forty-Eighters was fated gradually to replace that of the Thirtyers, so there was a pro-Hecker atmosphere in

Belleville from the beginning despite Hilgard's views. The English-language newspaper the *Belleville Advocate* greeted Hecker's decision to settle in St. Clair County with the warm assurance that "on no spot in the wide world could he have chosen an asylum where a warmer grasp of the Republican hand is ever ready for liberty's devoted friend." And the *Belleviller Zeitung*, newly founded in January 1849, reported with enthusiasm Hecker's purchase and settlement near Lebanon in St. Clair County.[18]

In the meantime the German National Assembly had adopted the constitution that had been discussed so long and disputatiously at the end of March, 1849, offering the German emperor's crown to the king of Prussia. The delegation that traveled to Berlin with this petition on 3 April received a noncommittal response at first, but on 28 April 1849, there was a final, negative response. In the sequel, Prussia refused to adopt the constitution and dissolved its assembly. In Baden the government accepted the *Reich* constitution, but continued civil disruptions and the desertion of garrisons at Rastatt and elsewhere to the democratic people's movement caused Grand Duke Leopold to flee Karlsruhe on 14 May. On the recommendation of the Karlsruhe city council, a provisional state committee, under the leadership of Lorenz Brentano, took over government business for the time being. A constituent state assembly was to work out a new constitution.

The news reaching Hecker about the new rising in Baden caused him to return to Germany at once. It is possible that he was moved to do this by a letter from the twelve members of the revolutionary state committee dated 16 May 1849, asking Hecker's wife Josefine to inform her husband of the resolution of the committee "to call the man of the people, Hecker of Mannheim, to return to our Fatherland at once and take his place in the state committee."[19] Whether or not Hecker received this letter in time is obscure.[20] On the morning of 15 June, he left Belleville in the company of seven other men from the German community. Hecker's departure led him this time through Chicago, where Adolph Engelmann joined the group. On 27 June the steamer *Cambria* left New York with the nine men on board. But by the time Hecker arrived in Strasbourg with his friends on 15 July, Baden revolutionary troops had already been defeated by two Prussian army corps as well as a federal corps. Many of the freedom fighters fled to Switzerland, and Hecker himself returned to Le Havre after the surrender of Fortress Rastatt on 23 July, never having set foot on German soil. In Le Havre he met his wife Josefine and his three children Arthur, Erwin and Malwina.[21]

Caspar Butz, his earlier acquaintance from his Algerian journey in 1847, was among the friends who met Hecker in Le Havre. Butz had just decided to turn his back on Europe and try his mercantile fortune in the New World.

In his memoirs Butz described that he shared walks in the evening with Hecker on the harbor walls of Le Havre, awaiting the arrival of the steamer *Seine* that was to return them to New York. Butz doubted whether Hecker could have turned the Baden movement into a general German rising, even if he had arrived at the right moment. And Hecker appeared to agree with him. Butz recalled, "He felt that his European life was at an end, and he turned his gaze across the ocean, where he had already lived for almost a year." There survives a farewell letter from Hecker to a friend in Switzerland that repeated this view and that gave clear expression to Hecker's decision to turn away from Europe at last, despite the fact that so many friends still doubted the finality of this decision years later.[22]

> I look across to the far West and my woodland solitude with true long-ing; filled with disgust and bitterly disappointed, feeling the earth of Europe, weak with age, under my feet. In rash flight, I put behind me 6000 English miles to see a revolution put down that had had such powerful resources. Baden was left in the lurch by all the others and left to bleed to death alone. All of the heads of the republican party were there, and yet everything was at an end in four weeks. This demon-strates that the mass of the people lacks true revolutionary enthusiasm and the necessary force, while the leaders lack the genius and iron will to conjure up enthusiasm and effort. With bitter feeling I take the end of the pencil and erase twelve years of valiant, restless action and strug-gle from my life, starting over at 38, working and creating in the small world of a Western farmer.[23]

In the Small World of a Western Farmer – Country Life

"No European is fit and able to become a pioneer." Hecker noted this saying in his edition of Traugott Bromme's *Rathgeber für Auswanderungslustige* [*"Advisor for Those Desiring to Emigrate"*], which he later gave to Caspar Butz in Le Havre after "having studied [it] thoroughly enough." Butz took this saying to heart and never attempted to run a farm, like most Forty-Eighters. The political tendency of Traugott Bromme's little emigration guide must have pleased Hecker; it said that the German press misunderstood the importance of emigration. "In its pride over its own value," wrote Bromme, "it is continuously occupied with the raising of sensibility and of the bour-geoisie, expecting all salvation to come from political institutions." The German press specifically forgot the political truth that human happiness and well-being could only be produced from "material principles, that the health of the state and peoples rests *on this alone*, and that true liberty *can* only be derived from those who are materially secure and not from those who have to struggle for the future in sad concern." In other words, just as Hecker did in his *Erhebung*, Bromme favored a particular relationship, in the form of the state, among property, individual happiness and prosperity. In public opinion in the 1840s and 1850s, America stood for a social form in which the mass impoverishment of broad social groups that increasingly predominated in Germany was not present, a form where effort could free a person from the seemingly eternal curse of poverty. For that reason the enemies of emigration criticized America the most; it was a republic, a system so utterly opposed to the guardian state, and yet, or precisely because of that, marked by such astonishing prosperity.[24]

How was it that Hecker advised anyone who had not grown up on a peasant property not become a farmer, while choosing this activity for himself? A romantic notion, fueled by the rosy account of Gottfried Duden, beguiled the minds of many people who tired of Europe. They wanted to express their hatred of European tyrants by felling trees on their own land, axes in hand. Many, unaware of the necessarily brutal labor of an American farmer, let themselves be seduced by romantic reports into America's West, where they often failed as a result of unexpected difficulties. Critical contemporaries, such as Gustav Körner, Friedrich Münch, and, later, Friedrich Kapp and Hecker, armed with the knowledge of the situation, took it upon themselves to combat this problem with education.[25] Hecker himself consciously decided on the life of a Latin Farmer and would soon be one of the very few political refugees to succeed at it, and even achieve a certain prosperity.

Hecker's farm lay near the settlement of Summerfield, which had been occupied chiefly by Mennonites from the Palatinate and Bavaria. Because this settlement consisted of broadly scattered, isolated farms, a true center to the village did not yet exist, and Hecker's mailing address was "Postoffice Lebanon" in his first years. His own address, "Padfield's Grove Settlement," bore the name of the first settler in the area. To get to Hecker's farm from St. Louis, one first had to take the ferry over the Mississippi, travel by postal coach from there to Belleville, and then continue by the same means to Lebanon. It was another three or four miles to Hecker's farm on foot or by wagon if arrangements had been made for a pick-up. Over the years the net of railroads extended ever farther. As early as 1857 the Ohio-Mississippi Railroad reached Lebanon, stimulating rapid growth in the area. In Hecker's last years there was at least a direct rail connection with St. Louis through a station in Summerfield itself.[26] In 1858, Hecker wrote to his sister in Mannheim:

When I came here I rode for hours across the wild prairie in grass so high that a horse and rider could not be seen. Now everything is cultivated, and farm borders on farm. You could have bought the whole of Lebanon for a thousand dollars; now it is a really flourishing town. A tract of land that was offered to me in Chicago for $6000 was later sold in 1856 for $172,000.[27]

Through the mid-1850s Hecker dedicated himself almost exclusively to building up his farm. The work was new to him and strenuous beyond all measure. More than once he stressed in his letters that his political past and hard physical labor in the field caused him to age prematurely. But, despite his arduous life, Hecker's contacts to Germany never broke off entirely. American Consul Goundie kept him up to date on the residence of other refugees, and political friends wrote to him in America. Through reports from German newspapers, which were thoroughly cited in German-American papers in the United States, he stayed informed on developments in Baden and knew of Itzstein's flight to Switzerland, his subsequent retirement to Hallgarten and his abstention from all political activities. Hecker repeatedly invited both his "adopted father" Izstein and his own biological father to come to his farm, shake the dust of Europe from their feet and participate in his "half-backwoods life," closing the evening of their lives on free soil in a free country. Josef Hecker wrote to Adam von Itzstein of his son's invitation, "I am not uninterested, since living as a pariah here is no piece of cake. First Lieutenant Riegel has already insulted me three times on the open street, and you have experienced what has happened to us."[28]

Hecker had plenty of time to think about his past during field labor. In his letters to Itzstein, he expressed political justification and self-stylizing, but also resignation.

I look at myself as a man marooned or dead, whose duty it is to drink from the stream of the past while he is still alive and to look on his own past life as a strange saga. … It is now my joy to make something of myself through the industry of my hands and to see my children, half wild by the standards of the Old World, become adults. If you saw my Arthur now, how I give him the command to saddle his horse and ride miles across the prairie to carry out his mission, and how the boy comes back and reports, you would love it. This autonomy, at an age when over there [in Germany] a boy can barely go out on the street, can only be obtained here. … *I have come to the conviction that permanent democrat-*

ic liberty is possible only in agrarian states, and I am happy always to have opposed the industrialists and merchants in the Chamber. Back to politics again![29]

Two things were significant in this letter. First, Hecker's statement that democratic liberty was in the long run possible only in "agrarian states" refers to the context of his pre-modern thought; influenced by ancient writers, whose ideas he thought were confirmed by American practice, he did not pay attention to genuine American conditions. Before the Civil War it was still possible for him to have the impression in the "agrarian" structure of Midwestern America that there, through equally distributed property, the formation of a two-class society – rich industrialists and an impoverished proletariat – was being hindered, and that a broad, prosperous middle class was in the lead. He saw as confirmation of the liberal tradition's concept that the inalienable rights of life and liberty could be adequately achieved only through the possession of property. Hecker naturally now thought particularly of landed property. But property of all kinds, he believed, created the conditions for securing the "nutritive estate," suggesting that every person could provide the basic necessities for himself and his family. After the Civil War, when there was discussion about making it possible for former slaves to own land to avoid their becoming wage workers on their former plantations, such considerations became extremely important. Experience had taught the more insightful politicians of the North that colored people had a great interest in owning and cultivating their own land. Liberty for the former slaves meant working without controls.[30] Hecker would plead for a "migration" of freed slaves to Texas and Colorado, where there was enough free and uncultivated land available. For Hecker the inheritable ownership of land not only provided a necessary foundation for a virtuous life and the practical securing of existence, but also was a symbol for the confirmation and preservation of personal autonomy and independence.

Second, and of apparently equal political and private significance to Hecker were his remarks on the education of his children. Arnold Ruge once formulated the circular concept that "the free form of state requires free persons, but it is only the free form of state that reliably produces free people."[31] Hecker avoided this circularity by presuming that his children would receive adequate exposure and development in America, which was already supplied with a free constitution. This idea appeared so often in his letters that one may assume a personal motive behind it. The guardian state, which could not be changed, could produce only slaves. Hecker therefore wrote proudly to his sister:

> Because I belong to a great nation here, I can compare it to your little-state system in every way, and only then can I see what it means to be a great nation. The whole horizon of our children is different. They speak of California and the St. Lawrence torrent, of Florida and Oregon, as if they all were a mere ten hours away. ... I thank fate for leading me to this coast, where my children have a real future. What could I have raised over there? Oppressed servants, irritated lawyers, small-time merchants or lifelong bureaucrats and the like.[32]

The monotony of life in the country was continually interrupted at Hecker's farm by visits, which Butz recalled in his memoirs.

> In the first years after the German rebellion, Hecker's farm was the political Mecca toward which many exiles journeyed as pilgrims, certainly not always to Hecker's advantage. Former members of St. Paul's Church, officers of the revolutionary Baden army, the banished from all countries, visited him ... His hospitality was without limit, and everyone was received in a friendly manner.[33]

Friedrich Doll, for example, a fellow fighter in the Baden movement, reached the United States in 1853 and stayed at Hecker's farm, where he died a year later in an accident. Distressed at the dreadful loss of his friend, Hecker wrote to Heinrich Börnstein in St. Louis. "Destiny does not tire, seeking me out me in the stillest, furthest corner of the earth."[34]

Although the political refugees who came to the American West made up only a fraction of the great wave of emigration of the early 1850s, Hecker was well informed about the residence of Revolutionary comrades. He wrote to Itzstein:

> Refugees still come almost every week to the West, members of the Parliament among others. Hoffbauer is a physician in Iowa, Schmitt has a teaching institution in St. Louis, Dieskau from Annaberg edits a journal there, Schlöffel and Reichardt are innkeepers in Philadelphia, Zitz is farming, ... [illegible] is a pastor in Newark, etc.

And Hecker himself was, by his own confession, a "worked-out peasant who has ruined himself with plowing, sowing, mowing, tying up fruit trees, planting corn, etc., like no servile peasant in the Old World."[35]

When Carl Schurz wanted to visit Hecker for the first time on his farm in the autumn of 1854, several friends in St. Louis had forewarned him about Hecker's distressing state. For that reason, as he later reported to his wife, they advised him,

> that I should make every effort to get him to change his way of life if it not yet too late. They ascribe his illness to the reckless overexertion with which he works his farm, and they believe that he cannot live long if he continues, even if he manages to survive his current crisis. ... They tell amazing stories here about the zeal with which he does his new chores, as if he wanted to dampen the fire that burns within him through the distress of physical labor.[36]

When Schurz came to the farm, he found Hecker, who had become extremely nervous, in a bad mood, plagued by a recurring fever,[37] negligently clothed, irritated and overworked. Hecker's "sanguine choleric temperament" often threw him from one extreme to the other "in the most contradictory manner," Schurz told his wife. On top of this, he was plagued by memories from the past:

> The powerful, unrestrained physical exertions, the bitter perversity with which he has exposed himself to the dangerous influence of the climate, all have broken down his strength, and his current isolation has conjured up in him the darkest visions of life.[38]

Hecker's bad mood and complaints were a shock to Schurz, who was young, engaged and dedicated to an American career. The almost legendary revolutionary hero had degenerated into a hard-bitten peasant. Moderate and pleasant, Schurz would often have the pleasure of Hecker's rages in the course of his life; however, this did not prevent the two men from having a politically fruitful friendship, if not a close private one.

Despite all of the disappointments, Hecker's agrarian efforts did bear fruit over the years. Not a full year after Schurz's visit, Hecker wrote confidently (in English) to Franz Lieber's youngest son, Hamilton, for whom he had arranged purchases of land in St. Clair County.[39]

> We were busy from Dawn to Dark, and have all the crop savely in and sheltered. barley and oats splendid. Fruits ... abundant, grapes wonderful. ... There is great emigration to Missouri from East, and I think

we did well to buy in time and have made a good speculation. I hope to see you in the fall in our great West.[40]

Hecker did not err in purchasing land. In truth, the stream of immigration from the East continued, and Illinois experienced its greatest period of population growth between 1850 and 1860.[41] He also wrote to his sister with great satisfaction over this development:

> I have built a house in Lebanon and rented it very well. If I can get the money together, I will put houses on all of my lots there, because with the growth of the town [there is] always a shortage of houses, and a good rent can be had.[42]

Hecker's fame as a successful farmer rose over the years. This is clear from how often he was asked advice in connection with questions of emigration and settling in the American West. Occasionally his responses appeared as open letters in German-American newspapers. One of these from later years, appearing with the title, "Friedrich Hecker on Colonization," showed how well informed Hecker was on other regions of settlement in the Union, the productivity of their soils, and their climate. Along with his usual advice, this letter was also animated by his ideas on association. He called for settlement as a community, but not merely "on account of social life and mutual assistance." Here he was considering the common purchase and use of tools for house and field, as well as the advantage of bulk purchase, which a cooperative of ten to twenty families could realize by avoiding a middle man. Here again his idea of free association arose, this time in an Americanized form and naturally under the presumption that each family owned and worked its own land. By recommending a *Gehöft-Gemeinde* in keeping with the model of Switzerland, Tyrol and Austria, Hecker thus clearly distanced himself from the American "principle of isolation"[43] in agriculture, which presumed freedom of movement of individual farmers; he favored instead the village communities common in Germany. In general, independent land use by the individual farmers was hailed as a major American accomplishment. Hecker, on the other hand, advocated the placement of houses in long rows, with the fields stretching behind, making the region of the community clear. Eventually he advised people to send only men and grown sons into such settlements initially, to bring the work to the point where women and children could come without concern.

Although Hecker propagated the idea of cooperation, independence remained central to the self-perception of most farmers in the Midwest. The general independence and autonomy of the farmers could not be denied, and Hecker himself admired it; after all, he was, in his own words, "not made to be a political adventurer." He "eschewed the humiliation incumbent on chasing offices, and lawyers in America mostly worked next to the gallows."[44] His rejection of political office, which will be dealt with here later, was all the easier for him because – in contrast to many other Forty-Eighters – he did not depend on it. He preferred to be politically active without expecting personal advantage. Everything indicated that Hecker intended to incorporate the ancient ideal of a people's tribune, who considered public matters only for social honor,[45] into his republican faith in land ownership as the foundation of citizen virtue. The fact that Hecker had no interest in political office won him great credit from the German-American population, and he was seen as seeking "the fame of utter selflessness and pure love for the people." Recalling his weaknesses, the same writer said, "His failings are *only* failings of temperament; he is an old hothead and has his whims. But he is a 'mad head and a heart of gold.' He could have had many profitable offices already, but he rejects those and remains behind his plow."[46] Another passage concluded, "How sad that Hecker's determination not to accept any public office is so unshakably solid. He would be the man. ... But it does not work, for the most relevant of all reasons: He does not *want* to."[47]

Passing the Plate for the Revolution

Hecker's apolitical farmer life was interrupted in its first years by European political refugees, who came not as immigrants but as visitors intent on collecting money in America for a new revolution. Gottfried Kinkel reached New York in September 1851 with this purpose in mind, representing a London exile group. Kinkel was formerly professor for artistic, cultural and Church history at Bonn, a participant in the campaign for the *Reich* Constitution and the Baden-Palatine revolution and the teacher of Carl Schurz. Schurz had liberated him from a Spandau prison, where he was serving a life term. On the advice of Schurz, Kinkel began a propaganda tour for a German national loan. The original plan came from Giuseppe Mazzini, who hoped to amass enormous sums and create a revolutionary fund through the sale of what were called revolutionary loans in small denominations. Repayment would come after the establishment of an Italian republic. Kinkel, with similar aims, had his money administered by a revolutionary committee in London. He intended to establish branches of this committee in the United States that would continue to sell revolutionary loans after his return. It might have been a dubious idea; but Kinkel, who was as brilliant a speaker as Hecker, knew how to portray a new revolutionary upheaval as a likely event, in view of the unstable situation in France.[48]

The reaction of Forty-Eighters to Kinkel's plan betrayed the political mood within this group. Hope for a return to Germany and an alteration of the political situation there survived, but disillusionment had arisen in the meantime. There were critics of the plan from several angles who expressed themselves in a savage newspaper polemic. Karl Heinzen, a radical ex-revolutionary notorious for his calls to assassinate tyrants,[49] wrote to the New York *Deutsche Zeitung*, "Mr. Kinkel might be little uplifted over our unfriendly greeting. We are even less uplifted over his speculations and believe it harmful to support him."[50] And Heinrich Börnstein, who described the entire undertaking as "Passing the Plate for the Revolution,"[51] opposed the project with his *Anzeiger des Westens*, "from the very beginning," as he confessed,

> because I had no faith or trust in a revolution brought about by money gathered in begging. I was convinced that revolutions could only be brought into being by an enlightened ruler or a great statesman … or from below through a powerful idea permeating the entire people, an irresistible pressure for liberation from an intolerable situation as had happened in France in 1789. Nowhere in history had a great revolution moving all of mankind ever been brought into being with money, particularly money that had to be collected by begging.[52]

According to Börnstein the first mission was to "educate" the people thoroughly and bring them to the point at which they actually wanted a new revolution.

Friedrich Kapp, another Forty-Eighter, saw the situation with the same chilly realism, and even less orientation to the future. He wrote directly to Kinkel.

> The cause that you have taken over appears to me to have too little guarantee. It will and must dissolve into an illusion. I know America and the chances of a European revolution. In the best case it has no support among German-Americans. … I believe that the essential difference between us lies in the fact that I see the reason for our defeat in ourselves, while you over there [in London] place the guilt for our miserable existence more or less outside of us.[53]

Enthusiasm nevertheless reigned among most Forty-Eighters. Gustav von Struve, for example, supported Kinkel's plan. And Kinkel's propaganda tour led him from New York – where he was received as enthusiastically as Hecker three years earlier – via Philadelphia and Baltimore to Washington, where he was presented to President Millard Fillmore, and where Congress also honored him.[54] Then the professor from London traveled westwards, finally reaching St. Louis via Albany, Chicago and Davenport and entering Belleville on 17 December. He was greeted formally there as well.

On the first evening there was an unofficial gathering in the barroom of Winter's inn, at which Hecker was present. The "cannibalistic drinking and screaming on behalf of the German Republic" seemed to have edified him as little as another German visitor, who was extremely surprised that Hecker "would expend his speaking gifts, compelling to those of a certain persuasion, on such a still-born child as the revolutionary loan of the firm of Kinkel & Co." Other speakers

> provided the brave people of Belleville with their democratic commitment and their glibness, calling to mind the next elections. They had no clear notion of what cause they were talking about. This was not the case with Hecker. He appeared to be honorable through and through, and he could not be misled about the situation in Europe. Despite this, he participated in this charade. Either he thought he was fulfilling an obligation to a friend, or he sank for a moment in the obsessive glow of the old days and forgot the disappointments of the past through a fantastically decorated present.[55]

But Hecker was in a difficult situation. His support, in particular, was expected, or his original agitation in Belleville would appear entirely unbelievable.

A day after Kinkel's arrival there was an official meeting in the courthouse. The mayor, Mr. Abend, greeted Kinkel in the warmest manner. After Kinkel gave what eyewitnesses called an all too rhetorical and pathetic presentation on the German national loan, Hecker took the podium with a "soul-stirring speech."[56] As would so often to happen in the future, the report in the newspapers on his appearance was part of an effort to present the Germans of the town as a closed and engaged group, united in its support of the Revolution in Europe. The *Belleviller Zeitung* assured its readers "that more was happening in this town than in many towns, where Germans were divided into their usual factions." Concerning Hecker, it was said in certain exaggeration that he supported "the enterprise with the full decisiveness of his nature."

Hecker has not spoken in public for two years; but his splendid spirit, rested in the isolation of farmer life, broke out all the more powerfully when he saw his proper element, an enthused crowd, before him. We have heard many famous speakers, but this storming power of eloquence has never appeared before us. ... In these few days a relationship of personal friendship and recognition has developed between him and Kinkel that passes far beyond their common party interest.[57]

When the honored guest departed town the next morning "on Kinkel's argosy to conquer the golden fleece of the German-Americans, the tale of passing the revolutionary plate was hardly at an end." Impressed by Kinkel's supposed pecuniary successes in the economic wonderland of the United States, the "left red wing" of the German emigrants in London loosed one of their apostles to cut off another piece of the American financial cake for German Revolution. Amand Goegg, former member of the provisional state committee under Brentano's leadership, organizer of the extensive system of associations in Baden and principal leader of the third Baden rebellion, left London two months after Kinkel, heading for New York. The peculiarity in Goegg's enterprise lay in its creation of a German Revolutionary League, whose financial basis differed from Kinkel's loan. Friedrich Hassaurek, another Forty-Eighter, later described it as he could best recall.

There were about three million Germans here in America. If each of them paid only a cent a week, that would be three million cents a week. Three million cents are $30,000 a week, or $1,560,000 a year. Half a dozen German princes could be tossed off their thrones for that. Perhaps they could just buy out the smaller ones, the *duodecimi*. With that much money you could print convincing, electrifying pamphlets that could be spread from Switzerland across Germany and distributed there.[58]

The Revolutionary League wanted to concern itself particularly with the distribution of revolutionary agitation tracts. Goegg, however, was by no measure the gifted speaker that Kinkel was, and his speeches were seen as not only dry, but also marred by his severe Baden accent. "The Revolutionary League fared nowhere near so well as the national loan. Also the cream had already been tapped from the revolutionary milk,"[59] Friedrich Hassaurek ironically formulated it two decades later. In order to get Goegg a hearing, the *New Yorker Abendzeitung* tried a trick to make the cause a little more attractive. The newspaper said that it was a necessity for the German Revolutionary Party to unite behind a single head overseas, as the Italians had done with Mazzini, and proposed Friedrich Hecker for this. To demonstrate that Hecker was the right man for the expected demands, the newspaper repeated his Belleville speech for the German national loan and noted its undiminished revolutionary position. Hecker's withdrawal from political activity, it was asserted, was only temporary. Here, as in later years, it was clear how useful the German-American press found Hecker's popularity to be.

> Hecker has demonstrated in his most recent meeting with Gottfried Kinkel, a dramatically enthused and exciting speech to the assembled Germans and Americans, that he is still the man of old, that his patriotic heart still beats in the same right place. Hecker and no other must be the provisional head of the Revolution.[60]

The article continued by saying that brothers in Germany would receive with jubilation the news that Hecker was again fighting for the good cause. Hecker himself did not respond to this suggestion, however. In private he also met with Amand Goegg, and later he published a letter to him in which he sought to make clear his position "outside all fractional divisions and personal unclarities." Hecker praised Goegg in this letter for his capacity to avoid personal bitterness in his speeches and addresses in America, which would only serve the enemies of the cause; only in this way could any unity of the divided forces be achieved. Combining his own fate with world events, Hecker went on in his letter to explain the disunity of the various groups, brought about by the life of political refugees in exile and the conflicts arising from that life; Hecker blamed it on the sudden shift from political action to inactivity and lost influence. All ideas and plans currently being developed by the exiles, he wrote, could never unite an absolute majority behind them unless all forces swore to one common struggle. As yet, they were far from that.

In responding to Goegg's question, Hecker was noncommittal about what path should be taken or would lead to the goal. But he knew that the path of choice must include at least a tolerance for all working for the common cause, whatever the means. He "who shares our goal, he can be like Lessing's Nathan [the Wise], a person who honestly wishes and moves straight ahead." When Kinkel called the plan for a national loan into being,

Hecker had been happy to support it, since he knew from his own experience how important it was to have the means at hand at the moment of real struggle. Continuing to use his own defeat in April 1848 as a counter-example, Hecker added, "If I had only had $50,000 at my disposal, much would have happened differently." He could not guarantee that the money gathered would still be there when needed or would be used correctly when the decisive moment came. But he consoled himself with a glance at history, saying that the beginning of a new era had never been set with mathematical precision. For that reason, if Goegg's Agitation Society wanted to take a route different from Kinkel's, Hecker supported it. "The more ways, the better." After all, who knew who bore "the genuine ring?"[61]

Hecker thus withdrew into the position of a reconciler and negotiator, sparing himself all possible conflicts with other refugees. They had made his exile in Switzerland irritating. For that reason, he proposed in an open letter that all those who could not warm themselves to the national loan should go with Goegg's Revolutionary League. All patriots, he concluded in a visionary and ultimately implausible strain, would find themselves together through the common goal. Hecker was not ready for any other concessions, and he distanced himself from demands that he should loudly promote American intervention in Europe for a German republic. The slogan of radical forces, "intervention for non-intervention," expressed the concept that, whenever a popular uprising sought the creation of a republic, the United States should hinder monarchical intervention and act as general protector of all republics. Men such as Hecker and Friedrich Hassaurek made no secret of their opinion of this; they considered American liberation and reform of Western Europe absurd and completely impossible.[62]

The third member of the club seeking American funds at this time was Lájos Kossuth, leader of the Hungarian national movement. Kossuth presented himself on American soil at the same time as Gottfried Kinkel to raise new money for the defeated Hungarian revolution. Kossuth, however, did not appeal specifically to Germans, but to all Americans. He did not hesitate to promote his cause at American, German or Irish gatherings. Kossuth's financing system was by far the most practical, even if it was marked by the vanity of its leader. Neither shares of a national loan nor monthly contributions for a revolutionary league were proposed, but rather the sale of "Kossuth Notes," beautifully printed with Kossuth's picture. These certificates were issued for one, five, ten or a hundred dollar cash payments. After a successful revolution and the establishment of an independent Hungary they were to be usable as currency and even payable in gold at all government cashiers in the new state.

Kossuth was accorded as enthusiastic an American reception as Kinkel. He was likewise heard in Congress and also traveled via St. Louis to Belleville. There he expressed to Gustav Körner his desire to meet Friedrich Hecker, and Körner indirectly informed Hecker of this. But because the invitation had not come directly, Hecker stayed away, and the two men never met. The *Belleviller Zeitung* reported Kossuth's amazement at Hecker's complete isolation, as well as criticism of Hecker's restraint, and Hecker's relationship to Kossuth changed. While Hecker praised Kossuth to the skies in 1849, he mentioned him years later only in a negative way. It is possible that Kossuth's pomp and self-promotion in the United States – he traveled with a court of 56 persons and he sent his companion Ferenzs Pulsky ahead to prepare for his arrival – fostered Hecker's later distaste. In 1859, at the time of the Sardinian-French war against Austria, Hecker opposed Kossuth as an enemy of the Germans, since Hecker, an enemy of Napoléon III's politics, preferred victory for Austria, while Kossuth was understandably against Austria and cooperated with Napoléon III. Hecker had received information about this from his London friend Karl Blind,[63] who had his information, in turn, from Mazzini.

Hecker himself attempted only once to explain what, among a constellation of possible reasons, accounted for his negative attitude toward Kossuth.

When he [Kossuth] came here with his court, we saw him land in New York, answering the friendly handshakes of Americans and the hearty greetings of the Germans with a cold, dismissive response. The further he went toward the West, we learned, the more he understood that the sensation-seeking natives merely gawked at him like a remarkable elephant. From that moment he became ever more German, ever friendlier, in the end promoting noble Germanic enthusiasm. But we still read at the bottom of his heart his hatred of Germans and, hence, did not stand in his waiting room.[64]

The agitation tours of Kinkel, Goegg and Kossuth meant a revival of political orientation to Europe. But just as the three delegates were basically disappointed at the results of their tours, even in financial terms, so the Forty-Eighters became increasingly aware that a new revolution in Europe was "not simply around the corner." Hecker even exhorted his political comrades to abstain from their utopian dreams and their "sick longing" for revolution.[65] Carl Schurz later recalled Hecker's clear position on this. Hecker was "one of the few of his convictions," Schurz wrote,

> who clearly recognized his error in judging what was possible and gave up the illusion-addicted planning that failed revolutionary movements usually pursue. From that time on, established in America, he belonged to his new homeland with the same loyalty of conviction and honor that he had belonged to his old one, and likewise honored it with his name.[66]

America itself soon forgot the era of passing the plate. The country's internal conflicts soon totally occupied not only the Americans, but increasingly the Forty-Eighters as well.

[1] FH to Josefine Hecker, New York, 7 October 1848, printed in *The American-German Review*, April/May 1960, 18-19, here 18. On Tiedemann, see Adolf E. Zucker, ed., *The Forty-Eighters: Political Refugees of the German Revolution of 1848* (New York, 1950), 348; Vollmer, "Nachlaß," 378, n. 119; Wittke, *Refugees*, 331-32; cf. also the *Tiedemannakten* GLA 221/454/455; GLA 234/1660; GLA 234/2010, particularly interesting is a letter of his father, Prof. Tiedemann, to the grand duke of Baden requesting amnesty for his two sons Heinrich and Friedrich, Munich, 2 September 1858, where he describes their seduction by the "demagogue" Hecker.

[2] FH to Josefine Hecker, New York, 7 October 1848, 19.

[3] See on Lieber *DAB*, 11 (New York, 1933), 236-38, with literature references; *ADB*, 22 (Munich, 1885; repr. Berlin, 1970), 27; Ruetenik, *Deutsche Vorkämpfer*, 211-17; *Der Deutsche Pionier*, 5, no. 6 (September, 1873), 203-7; Tolzmann, *German-American Literature* (Metuchen, NJ; London, 1977); Gustav Körner, *Das deutsche Element in den Vereinigten Staaten von Nordamerika (1818-1848)* (Cincinnati, 1880), 166-67; Alfred Vagts, *Deutsch-Amerikanische Rückwanderung. Probleme – Statistik – Soziologie – Biographie*, Beihefte zum Jahrbuch für Amerikastudien, no. 6 (Heidelberg, 1960), 156-63. Franz Lieber to Charles Sumner, ab the steamship *Hermann*, 27 September 1848, FHP, box 2, folder 16. The two other letters of introduction were to Mr. Bingham in Michigan and Timothy Walker in Cincinnati, FHP, box 2, folder 16. Stefan von Senger und Etterlin, *Neu-Deutschland in Nordamerika. Massenauswanderung, nationale Gruppenansiedlungen und liberale Kolonialbewegung, 1815-1860* (Stuttgart, 1991), 373; Wolfgang Hinners, *Exil und Rückkehr. Friedrich Kapp in Amerika und Deutschland, 1824-1884* (Stuttgart, 1987), 41. Günter Moltmann, *Atlantische Blockpolitik im 19. Jahrhundert. Die Vereinigten Staaten und der deutsche Liberalismus während der Revolution von 1848/49* (Düsseldorf, 1973), 71, n. 48; Nagler, *Politisches Exil*, 277-78; 270, n. 16.

[4] Sumner was a friend not only of Franz Lieber but also Karl Josef Anton Mittermaier. See *DAB*, 18 (New York, 1938), 208-14; on Mittermaier, see above, chapter 1, part 2. See the Lieber letters, 1851-58, FHP, box 2, folder 17. There is a single Hecker letter in the Franz Lieber Papers in the Huntington Library in San Marino, Cal., addressed to Franz Lieber's second son, Hamilton. Hecker worked for Hamilton as a land buyer.

[5] Moltmann, *Blockpolitik*, 73, 75, 80, 81, 95 and 95 n. 29. *NYSZ*, 22 and 23 September 1848, cf. also Wittke, *Refugees*, 36-37; including citations from FH's *Erhebung* and from the second edition prepared by Theodor Mögling in Strasbourg. On the continuous reports of the revolution in New York newspapers, see Wittke, *Refugees*, 39, n. 38. The *Freiheitsverein* in Philadelphia sent $318.50 to Goundie to support refugees of the Baden uprising then in Switzerland, see in general on the reception, C. F. Huch, "Die Deutsch-Amerikaner und die deutsche Revolution,"

DAG, 11 (1911), 37-38; also G. H. Goundie to FH, Bethlehem, PA, 16 October 1849, FHP, box 1, folder 9; also Vollmer, "Nachlaß," 403.

6 FH to Josefine Hecker, New York, 7 October 1848, 19. For a thorough account of the discussions and resolutions of the New York officials, see *NYSZ*, 7 October 1848; the American consul in Frankfurt, Graebe, wanted to "play down the great reception given this republican expelled from St. Paul's Church, as a private matter among only some Germans. He feared that the prestige of his country among the liberals would suffer. During his visit with Heinrich von Gagern and in an article for the *Oberpostamtszeitung* Graebe insisted that his government had nothing to do with Hecker's reception." Cf. Moltmann, *Blockpolitik*, 84 n. 85.

7 *NYSZ*, 14 and 27 October 1848; cf. Wittke, *Refugees*, 36-37. The American government was the only one officially to recognize the National Assembly.

8 FH to Josefine Hecker, New York, 7 October 1848, 19. Wittke, *Refugees*, 37. On Stallo, Körner, *Das deutsche Element*, 217-25; Bruce Levine, *The Spirit of 1848* (Urbana; Chicago, 1992), 184. *Friedrich Hecker und sein Antheil an der Geschichte Deutschlands und Amerikas* (Cincinnati, 1881), 26. See Körner, *Memoirs*, vol. 2, 557.

9 Friedrich Schnake, "Geschichte der deutschen Bevölkerung und der deutschen Presse von St. Louis und Umgebung," *Der deutsche Pionier* vol. 4, no. 4 (September, 1872), 234. The printed resolutions of the German meeting on 15 April 1848, resting only on the news of Hecker's conduct at the pre-Parliament, and the letter from Dr. Ferdinand Häußler, St. Louis, 12 May 1848, are in the FHP, box 1, folder 5. See also Körner, *Das deutsche Element*, 349.

10 Cf. *Friedrich Hecker und sein Antheil*, 27; also, "Aus einer Rede Heckers, gehalten zu St. Louis im Februar d. J. bei einer Geldsammlung für den Centralausschuß der deutschen Demokraten in Berlin," *Der Volksfreund. Eine Wochenschrift für Westfalen/Lemgo*, no. 31, 3 August 1849, 128-29 (part 1); no. 32, 10 August 1849, 132 (part 2). Körner, *Das deutsche Element*, 350. *St. Louis Republican*, 8 January 1849. On Hecker's appearance in Belleville, Körner, *Memoirs*, vol. 1, 529-30. *Belleville Advocate*, 1 February 1849; *AW*, 20 January 1849; see Marlin J. Tucker, *Political Leadership in the Illinois-Missouri German Community, 1836-1872*, Ph.D. diss., University of Illinois-Champaign, 1968, 93; on *Frauenvereinen* also *BZ*, weekly, 20 January 1849. See Levine, *Spirit*, 84-85.

11 FH to Josefine Hecker, St. Louis, 9 November 1848, printed in the *Rheinische Blätter. Unterhaltungsblatt zur Mannheimer Abendzeitung*, no. 132, 20 December 1848.

12 Körner, *Memoirs*, vol. 1, 529. See, for example, Carl Ludwig Fleischmann, *Wegweiser und Rathgeber nach und in den Vereinigten Staaten von Nordamerika* (Stuttgart, 1852), 144. The contracts bear the dates of 2 and 28 February 1849 and name a payment of $2400. One contract also names Gustav Körner as witness and guarantor. See materials in FHP, box 2, folder 23.

13 Oswald Garrison Villard, "The 'Latin Peasants' of Belleville, Illinois," *JISHS* 35, no. 1 (March, 1942), 7-20, here 7; on Belleville, see also *History of St. Clair County, Illinois* (Philadelphia, 1881), 62-67. Study forthcoming by Andreas Daum; see also his "Celebrating Humanism in St. Louis: The Origins of the Humboldt Statue in Tower Grove Park, 1859-1878," *Gateway Heritage* 15, no. 2 (Fall, 1994), 48-58.

14 On Hilgard, see Körner, *Das deutsche Element*, 255-59; Ruetenik, *Deutsche Vorkämpfer*, 175-76. See Tucker, *Political Leadership*, 94.

15 Theodor Erasmus Hilgard to Philipp Heinrich von Kraemer, Belleville, Ill., 23 December 1848, in Theodor Erasmus Hilgard, *Briefe an seinen Freund Philipp Heinrich von Kraemer 1835-1865*, Wolfgang Krämer ed. (Saarbrücken, 1935), here 142-43; emphasis in spread type in the text. Hilgard plays here on the current term of "*Wühlerei*" ["rooting around"] for the radical democratic forces in the revolution; cf., for example, Heinich Hoffmann, *Handbüchlein für Wühler* (1848).

16 See the obituary in the *BZ*, weekly, 27 February 1873. Hilgard visited Belleville only once more, in 1861.

17 Hilgard, *Briefe*, 156 (Belleville, Illinois, 8 January 1849), emphasis in the text.

18 *Belleville Advocate*, 22 February 1849; cf. also Tucker, *Political Leadership*, 92. *BZ*, weekly, 10

March 1849.

19 FHP, box 1, folder 10. A further decree of the state committee, Karlsruhe, 17 May 1849, says: "Citizen Hecker, currently living in North America, is ordered to return to the Fatherland and place himself at our disposal." *Regierungsblatt* no. 31, 18 May 1849; see Sonja-Maria Bauer, *Die Verfassungsgebende Versammlung in der Badischen Revolution von 1849. Darstellung und Dokumentation* (Düsseldorf, 1991), 128.

20 Karl Blind recalled that Hecker later told him that this letter did not reach him in time, so that he started out for Europe on the basis of vague news reports, Karl Blind, "Aus Europa, London Ende März," *WP*, daily, 21 April 1881.

21 FH was accompanied by his friend Schöninger as well as by Thomas Mayne Reid, a veteran of the Mexican War, and Hermann Gritzner, cf. Wittke, *Refugees*, 38. On Engelmann, see Körner, *Memoirs*, vol. 1, 540; also Tucker, *Political Leadership*, 93; Ruetenik, *Deutsche Vorkämpfer*, 169-71; Nagler, *Politisches Exil*, 278. Wittke, *Refugees*, 38. See *Hecker und sein Antheil*, 21-22. A daughter whom Hecker never saw was born in August 1848, died in January, 1849; see the register of Josefine Hecker in Hecker Papers, box 1, folder 2. The eldest son Arthur Joseph Gabriel (*6 November 1842, † 2 January 1926); Malwina Müller or Miller, née Hecker (*6 November 1845); Erwin Hecker (*12 December 1846, †9 April 1885). Further children of the Heckers: a stillborn girl(†25 July 1840); Gabriele (*2 September 1841, †1843); born in America, Alfred Hecker (*4 December 1852, †14 February 1887); Alexander Hecker (2 March 1854, †25 May 1895), cf. some details in Strack, *Herkunft*, 10.

22 Butz, "Erinnerungen," part 2. "How long will you wait, Germany, to call back one of your best sons from distant America?" Gustav von Struve was still asking in 1865; see Struve, "Friedrich Hecker in Amerika," *GL*, 1865, 56-59, here 59; reprinted in Struve, *Zwölf Streiter*, 33; see also Theodor Mögling's letter to Hecker where he declares himself amazed that Hecker was now mixing in American politics, although he should always desire to return home, Mögling to Hecker, Wildbad, September, 1856, FHP, box 1, folder 6; also Vollmer, "Nachlaß," 393.

23 Here cited according to *Hecker und sein Antheil*, 22-23. Unfortunately it was never recorded to whom this was written. It is also cited in excerpts and translations in Wolfgang Haaß, *Friedrich Hecker – Leben und Wirken in Dokumenten und Wertungen der Mit- und Nachwelt* (Angelbachtal, c. 1981), 78, 80; *Die Grenzboten*, 8. Jahrgang, 2. Sem., vol. 3 (1849), 408-9; Roland Paul, "'Freie Erde und freies Vaterland.' Friedrich Hecker in den USA," Frei, *Hecker in den USA*, 22-23; Wittke, *Refugees*, 38; Zucker, *Forty-Eighters*, 48; *GL*, 1881, 265; anonymous, *Die republikanische Parthei Badens und ihre Führer, beurtheilt und gerichtet in der schriftliche Hinterlassenschaft von Hecker, Struve und Brentano* (Mannheim, 1849), 9-10; see also Hecker's letter from Le Havre of 30 July 1849 in the anonymous publication, *Eine Nothwendigkeit für Deutschland. Worte aus voller Brust an die Ehrlichen aller Parteien. Mit einem Briefe als Vorwort von Fr. Hecker* (Herisau, 1849); see on this also Muhs, "Heckermythos," 426.

24 Traugott Bromme, *Rathgeber für Auswanderungslustige* (Stuttgart, 1846); Gustav von Struve created a guide of his own on the basis of Bromme, *Wegweiser für Auswanderer* (Bamberg, 1866). Bromme, *Rathgeber*, 1-2 (emphasis in spread type), 6. FH, *Erhebung*, 5-11; Butz, "Erinnerung," part 2. Hannah Arendt, *Über die Revolution* (Munich, 1965), 26.

25 FH to an unnamed acquaintance in Germany, Postoffice Lebanon, St. Clair County, Ill., 28 April 1857, Stadtarchiv Mannheim, Kleine Erwerbungen 127, Sig. 28,316. Gottfried Duden, *Bericht über eine Reise nach den westlichen Staaten Nordamerika's und einen mehrjährigen Aufenthalt am Missouri* (Elberfeld, 1829). [English translation, Gottfried Duden, *Report on a Journey to the Western States of North American and a Stay of Several Years Along the Missouri (During the Years 1824, '25, '26, 1827)*, James W. Goodrich, ed. (Columbia, MO: State Historical Society of Missouri; University of Missouri Press, 1980).] On failures, see Ernest Bruncken, "German Political Refugees in the United States during the Period from 1815-1860," *DAG*, 3 (1903), no. 3/4, 33-48, here 35. Körner, "Antwort auf Gottfried Dudens Schrift, 'Beleuchtung des Duden'schen Berichts,'" written in 1834, reprinted in *DAG* 16 (1916), 280-333; see for example, Friedrich Kapp, "Lateinische Bauern" in *Aus und über Amerika* (Berlin, 1876), 291-306.

26 Paul, "Freie Erde," 21; cf. especially the supple descriptions of Carl Köhler, *Briefe aus Amerika. Ein lehrreicher Wegweiser jeden Standes* (Darmstadt, 1852), 145. Köhler worked for two months on Hecker's farm and reported it in his letters; English excerpts from the letters in Frederic Trautmann, "Eight Weeks on a St. Clair County Farm in 1851 – Letters by a Young German," *JISHS* 75, no. 3 (Fall, 1982), 162-78. Köhler, *Briefe*, 114; in the purchase documents (Hecker Papers, box 2, folder 23) are to be found the names Thomas, Temperance, William and Mahala Padfield. At the start of the 1870s the river was crossed by a large bridge [Ead's Bridge], see "Riesenüberbrückung des größten nordamerikanischen Stroms," *GL*, 1874, 582-85. *BV*, 3 April 1857. See the planning of a special train to Summerfield station for Hecker's burial, *WP*, daily, 27 March 1881.

27 FH to his sister, Lebanon, St. Clair County, [Ill.], 8 November 1858, printed in Schwarzmaier, *Auswanderungsbriefe*, 329-30.

28 FH to Adam von Itzstein, 28 August 1851, Itzstein Nachlaß. Also Hecker to his sister, Postoffice Lebanon, 18 July 1858: "since with the hard labors I have gone through, along with the blows of fate, age knocks on my door before its time." Printed by Schwarzmaier, *Auswanderungsbriefe*, 328. FH to Itzstein, 14 June 1850, Izstein Nachlaß. On Riegel, see Nolte, *Gemeindeliberalismus*, 281. Josef Hecker to Adam von Itzstein, Mannheim, 29 December 1850, Itzstein Nachlaß.

29 FH to Adam von Itzstein, Belleville, 28 August 1851, Itzstein Nachlaß, my own emphasis.

30 See Eric Foner, "Land and Labor after the Civil War," in idem, *Politics and Ideology in the Age of the Civil War* (Oxford, 1980), 97-127.

31 Arnold Ruge, "Die Religion unserer Zeit," *Akademie, Philosophisches Taschenbuch* (Leipzig, 1848), 83, cited from Wende, "Radikalismus," 210.

32 FH to his sister, Lebanon, St. Clair County, 8 November; reprinted in Schwarzmaier, *Auswanderungsbriefe*, 329.

33 Butz, "Erinnerung," part 2.

34 On Friedrich Doll, see Vollmer, "Nachlaß," 370 n. 56. On his accident on the farm, see interview with Franz Sigel of 22 February 1887 in Sigel Papers, also FH to Heinrich Börnstein, 21 February 1854. In this letter, Hecker asks for publication in the *AW* of his eulogy of Doll, since Börnstein had been a good friend of Doll. Doll shot himself due to careless handling of a hunting rifle. "The black legions will not hesitate to dirty the noble dead with their spirits; the press will know how to encounter this claptrap." Original in the Stadtarchiv Mannheim, Kleine Erwerbungen.

35 FH to Adam von Itzstein, Belleville, 28 August 1851, Itzstein Nachlaß.

36 Carl Schurz to his wife, St. Louis, 2 October 1854, in Carl Schurz, *Lebenserinnerungen*, vol. 3 (Berlin, 1912), 113-14; English translation in Joseph Schafer, ed., *Intimate Letters of Carl Schurz, 1841-1869* (Madison, Wisc., 1928), 132-33.

37 Schurz speaks of a "congestive fever." In his first years Hecker appears to have suffered often from malaria, and Köhler also found him ill with malaria in 1851, see Köhler, *Briefe*, 119.

38 Carl Schurz to his wife, 5 October 1854, in Schurz, *Lebenserinnerungen*, vol. 3, 116, in English translation by Schafer, *Intimate Letters*, 135-36. Schafer's account is even more thorough: "When he complains, he accuses; when he censures, he damns outright. He feels old, believes it is no longer worth the trouble to live. ... He looks at everything with the eyes of his dejected spirit and complains bitterly about disillusionments where he never needed to have been deceived." Interpreting this encounter is Hans L. Trefousse, "Carl Schurz und Friedrich Hecker," in Frei, *Hecker in den USA*, 97-106; Muhs uses this encounter as proof for his judgment that "Nothing constructive can be reported" about Hecker in America, see Muhs, *Heckermythos*, 427, n. 24.

39 On Hecker's purchases on behalf of Hamilton, see the contracts with both names, FHP, box 2, folder 23, 160 acres purchased from Hermann Griesmaier, 3 March 1855, signed Hecker "in the name of Hamilton Lieber."

40 FH to Hamilton Lieber, Post Office Lebanon, St. Clair County, 26 August 1855, Franz Lieber Papers, Huntington Library. Hecker also bought land for himself in Missouri.

41 See James M. Bergquist, *The Political Attitude of the German Immigrants in Illinois, 1848-1860*, Ph.D. diss., Northwestern University, 1966, 21: Illinois (1850) 38,451; (1860) 130,804 = growth of 92,353; Missouri (1850), 45,120; (1860) 88,487 = growth of 43,367.

42 FH to his sister Henriette Cron, Lebanon, St. Clair County, 8 November 1858, printed in Schwarzmaier, *Auswanderungsbriefe*, 330; cf. also Paul, *Freie Erde*, 24.

43 This was the opinion of another pioneer of the region, Friedrich Münch, "Das Landleben in Deutschland und hier," Missouri, September 1855, printed in the *BZ*, weekly, 3 November 1855.

44 FH to Ernst Keil, *GL*, 1869, 416.

45 On this cf. his article on the "Advokat" in the *Staatslexikon* and above.

46 *TIS*, 18 April 1872, emphasis in spread-type.

47 *TIS*, 13 May 1872, 2; emphasis in spread-type.

48 Rosemary Ashton, *Little Germany: German Refugees in Victorian Britain* (Oxford; New York, 1989), 159, 161. Louis Napoléon then stood in open conflict with the French National Assembly, and a coup d'état was not out of the question. In fact Napoléon's coup of December 1851, which occurred during Kinkel's tour in the United States, reduced this hope to a minimum.

49 After the failed April uprising, Struve made contact with Heinzen in Strasbourg, and the pair published two works together, *Schilderhebung der deutschen Republikaner im April 1848* and *An die Männer des gesunden Menschenverstandes in Teutschland* (Strasbourg, 1848). Heinzen and Hecker had criticized each other intensely during Hecker's exile in Muttenz, and Heinzen continued his tireless criticism after Hecker reached American soil. Hecker himself took to calling Heinzen a "superstinker," letter to Charles Söhner, 19 July 1873, FHP, box 3, folder 38, but he otherwise ignored Heinzen's criticism. Heinzen's *Pionier*, whose columns he filled almost single-handedly, was often cited in other German-American newspapers because of its exotic radicalism. On Heinzen see Carl Wittke, *Against the Current: The Life of Karl Heinzen (1809-1880)* (Chicago, 1945); Zucker, *Forty-Eighters*, 302-3; Vollmer, "Nachlaß," n. 113; *DAB*, vol. 8 (New York, 1932), 508-9.

50 Carl Heinzen, *New Yorker Deutsche Zeitung*, 16 September 1851, here cited after Wolfgang Hinners, *Exil und Rückkehr. Friedrich Kapp, Amerika und Deutschland* (Stuttgart, 1987), 54; see also the bitter commentary on Gottfried Kinkel in America in Karl Heinzen, *Teutscher Radikalismus in Amerika. Ausgewählte Abhandlungen, Kritiken und Aphorismen aus den Jahren 1854-1879*, 3 vols. (Milwaukee, 1898), here vol. 1, 63-67.

51 On Börnstein see Zucker, *Forty-Eighters*, 280-81; Bruncken, *Political Refugees*, 36-37, 57; Henry Saalberg, *The Westliche Post of St. Louis*, Ph. D. diss., University of Missouri-Columbia, 1964, 249; Steven Rowan, *Germans for a Free Missouri* (Columbia, MO, 1983), 37-38. Heinrich Börnstein, *Fünfundsiebzig Jahre in der Alten und Neuen Welt. Memoiren eines Unbedeutenden*, 2 vols. (Leipzig, 1884), here vol. 2, 124 [partial English-language edition is Henry Boernstein, *Memoirs of a Nobody: The Missouri Years of an Austrian Radical, 1849-1866*, Steven Rowan ed. and tr. (St. Louis, MO: Missouri Historical Society, 1997), here 151].

52 Börnstein, *Fünfundsiebzig Jahre*, vol. 2, 127 [idem, *Memoirs*, 155].

53 On Kapp, Hinners, *Exil*; Zucker, *Forty-Eighters*, 307-8. Friedrich Kapp to Gottfried Kinkel, 15 January 1852; printed in Hans-Ulrich Wehler, ed., *Friedrich Kapp. Vom radikalen Frühsozialisten des Vormärz zum liberalen Parteipolitiker des Bismarckreiches. Briefe 1843-1884* (Frankfurt am Main, 1969), 68.

54 See *Deutscher Zuschauer*, cited in *BZ*, weekly, 11 March 1852, stating, "Kinkel worthily represented the Revolution from the German point of view." Senators Shields and Douglas in particular greeted the revolutionary. See on the following Körner, *Memoirs*, vol. 1, 573-77; Schafer, *Schurz*, 70-71; Ashton, *Little Germany*, 159-60; Börnstein, *Fünfundsiebzig Jahre*, 124-35 [*Memoirs*, 150-61]; on Kossuth, Börnstein, *Fünfundsiebzig Jahre*, 134-45 [*Memoirs*, 162-71]; Bruncken, *Political Refugees*, 33-36; Levine, *The Spirit*, 86-87; "Die 'Achtundvierziger' in Amerika. Rede gehalten von Friedrich Hassaurek beim Stiftungsfeste der deutschen Pioniere in Cincinnati am 25. Mai," *TIS*, 28 May 1875, 2-3; Wittke, *Refugees*, 96 ff.

55 Moritz Busch, *Wanderungen zwischen Hudson und Mississippi, 1851 und 1852*, 2 vols. (Stuttgart; Tübingen, 1854), here vol. 2, 83-86; ibid., 84-85.

56 Körner, *Memoirs*, vol. 1, 577; Körner presided over the meeting.

57 *Deutsche Tribüne*, cited in *BZ*, weekly, 1 January 1852. Kinkel and Hecker met for the first time in Belleville.

58 Börnstein, *Fünfundsiebzig Jahre*, vol. 2, 134-35 [*Memoirs*, 162-64]. Besides Amand Goegg, this wing also included Arnold Ruge and Josef Fickler, see Wittke, *Refugees*, 100. Zucker, *Forty-Eighters*, 297. Zucker, *Forty-Eighters*, 300-1. "Die 'Achtundvierziger' in Amerika, Rede gehalten von Friedrich Hassaurek," 3; the account by Börnstein agrees down to the smallest details.

59 "Die 'Achtundvierziger' in Amerika, Rede gehalten von Friedrich Hassaurek," 3.

60 "Es lebe der amerikanische Revolutionsbund. Friedrich Hecker," *New Yorker Abendzeitung*, cited in *BZ*, weekly, 19 February 1852.

61 FH to Amand Goegg, Lookingglaß Prairie bei Lebanon, 10 April 1852, reprinted in *BZ*, weekly, 22 April 1852. "I had tried something similar before," FH wrote [*ibid.*]. It cannot be decided whether he meant by that the revolutionary fund proposed by him in his speeches in St. Louis and Belleville in 1848-49 or the "Voluntary Loan to the Benefit of the German Republic." It speaks against the latter that the issuance of this certificate of debt on 21 September 1848 coincided with the beginning of Struve's coup. This loan was endorsed by Struve and Karl Heinzen "in the name of the Society of German Republicans" and was raised by Johann Philipp Becker; thus FH had no role in the sole loan raised during the Revolution. See description and history of this loan, Eckhardt Wanner, "Freiheit, Bildung, Wohlstand: die badische Revolution," *Die Bank* 12 (1993), 738-41.

62 Among the radical forces were men such as Theodor Pösche, Charles Goepp and Eduard Schläger, the principal speaker at the Wheeling Congress, cf. on all of them Bruncken, *Political Refugees*, 35-36; Hassaurek, "Rede," 3. On the Wheeling Congress from 19 to 22 September 1852, where 16 supporters of Goegg's undertaking demanded American intervention under the motto *E pluribus unum*, see Wittke, *Refugees*, 102-4.

63 Börnstein, *Fünfundsiebzig Jahre*, vol. 2, 138; Hassaurek, "Rede," 3. Körner, *Memoirs*, vol. 1, 584. *BZ*, weekly, 19 February 1852. FH, *Antheil*, 23. Julius Fröbel's evaluations of Kossuth, whom he had met first in New York and later in London: "The man has always been an unpleasant personality to me, whose comic vanity never was able to fill me with confidence," Julius Fröbel, *Ein Lebenslauf. Aufzeichnungen, Erinnerungen und Bekenntnisse*, vol. 2 (Stuttgart, 1891), 34. Saalberg, *Westliche Post*, 245-47. Karl Blind and Hecker developed a friendship and a correspondence over decades, see Blind's letters in the FHP, box 2, folder 18; there is only one Hecker letter in the Karl Blind Papers (Add MS 40125 f 120) in the the manuscript collections, British Library, London. On Blind's information and his link to Mazzini, see particularly Julius Fröbel, *Ein Lebenslauf*, vol. 2, 32-33. See Vollmer, "Nachlaß," 373, n. 82; Rudolf Muhs, "Ein Talent in der Wichtigmacherei. Karl Blind," in Sabine Freitag, ed., *Die Achtundvierziger. Lebensbilder der deutschen Revolution 1848/49* (Munich, 1997), 81-98.

64 Newspaper clipping AGRICOLA (n.d., 1859), *BZ*, *WP* or *AW*, FHP, box 4, folder 42; see also the nativist tendencies of some senators in response to Kossuth, Levine, *Spirit*, 155.

65 There can be no definitive statement of the amount of money gathered, only estimates, see Schafer, *Schurz*, 70-71. Kinkel deposited the loan money in a bank in London. Exiles such as Karl Blind sought to exploit this money for various newspaper projects between 1857 and 1861, but all failed due to Kinkel's opposition. See, for example, the letter from Karl Blind to Gustav Struve, London, 6 January 1857, in Struve Nachlaß; also Ashton, *Little Germany*, 160. Amand Goegg later received control of the money when Kinkel accepted a chair in Zürich. A portion went to support August Bebel's Social-Democratic Party and its journal, see on this also Wittke, *Refugees*, 106-7. *NYSZ*, 18 March, 22 June 1852; 19 January 1854.

66 Carl Schurz to Emil Preetorius, New York, 26 September 1881, reprinted in Schurz, *Lebenserinnerungen*, vol. 3, 19-20.

152

Friedrich Münch of Marthasville, Missouri, Hecker's political ally, as a member of the pro-Union Missouri Legislature, November, 1861. Courtesy of Dorris Keeven-Franke of Washington, Missouri.

Carl Schurz, Hecker's political friend and frequent commanding officer in the Civil War. Exhibit "Mit Feder und Hammer" (1983), Western Historical Manuscripts, University of Missouri – St. Louis.

V

THE BEGINNINGS OF THE REPUBLICAN PARTY IN ILLINOIS (1854-60)

Excursus: A Society in Crisis – Debates over the Kansas-Nebraska Bill

The founding of the Republican Party in America in the 1850s was a multi-layered process, a reaction to several entirely different political challenges. These challenges included the expansion and legitimation of slavery in the new territories, as well as such questions as the banning of alcohol, Sabbath restrictions and the rise of nativist secret societies. The complex origins of the party meant that its founding in various states proceeded neither synchronically nor under the same auspices. The formation of the Republican Party spanned the full course of two years from the time Senator Stephen A. Douglas presented the Kansas-Nebraska Bill to the United States Senate in 1854 to the final nomination of John Charles Frémont as presidential candidate in 1856. Organization in the various states depended on differing local conditions as well as on varying constellations of party politics. Before we can consider the participation of German-Americans, in general, and of Friedrich Hecker in particular – including with him, the situation in Illinois – it is necessary briefly to sketch the domestic political situation before the Civil War. The concrete references in Hecker's speeches on behalf of the Republican Party may then be placed in context.[1]

The ideology of republicanism was generally accepted in American political life in the decade before the Civil War. Every large party called on the heritage of the American Revolution and the Constitution, and even in the 1850s, the ideas and values of the eighteenth century continued – individual liberty, legal equality and a government restricted by law. New to the scene was the fear of possible conspiracy from within threatening these values and the political system itself. The general recognition of republicanism did not lead to skepticism about the party system; on the contrary, the legitimacy of parties found continually broader approval. As William Gienapp writes, "by the last decade before the Civil War, anti-partyism was, at least in its traditional form, a dying tradition. Instead of being viewed as threats to republican government, parties were now considered both inevitable and good."[2] There was no question that two large, continuously opposed factions were generally regarded as guarantees of stability for the American system of checks and balances in governmental institutions.

On 4 January 1854 the Democratic United States Senator from Illinois, Stephen Douglas, as chairman of the Senate Committee for Territorial Matters, presented a bill whose goal was to simplify the political organition, settlement and economic development of the new territory of Nebraska. Politically new territories were still almost completely unorganized, and Senator Douglas's declared intention was to suspend the Indian frontier, give emigration and civilization the chance "to roll onward until it rushes through the passes of mountains, and spreads over the plains, and mingles with the waters of the Pacific." The politically explosive part of Douglas' proposal was his conscious suspension of the 1820 Missouri Compromise, reconfirmed as recently as 1850, which established that slavery should not be extended to territories beyond the north latitude of 36° 30′.

In 1850, as a result of the efforts of Senator Henry Clay, an agreement had been reached to receive California into the Union as a free state, since it had rejected slavery in a referendum, and to receive New Mexico and Utah as new territories without defining their positions on slavery. An agreement simultaneously had been made with the slave states for a new Fugitive Slave Act, intensifying conditions for the interstate return of runaway slaves. Slavery remained a matter for the individual states to administer if they were received into the Union as slave states, while the federal government administered the territories.[3] When it came to the legal status of slavery in the territories, Douglas now proposed the territories themselves decide whether to permit slaves or to forbid them. He justified with the winged slogan of "popular sovereignty" his demand that residents of the territories settle this question themselves. The vote in California had reassured him that this principle would work to the advantage of Free-Soilers in the long run; even if slave owners brought their slaves with them, they would be overwhelmed by the massive arrival of free settlers from the North. However, Nebraska, like Kansas, lay north of the latitude 36° 30′, which meant that adopting the bill would implicitly overturn the Missouri Compromise. It was obvious that Douglas's bill was a concession to Southern senators, whose support was needed to pass a such a law. But these senators further demanded that slave owners specifically be allowed to settle the new territory with their slaves, an explicit suspension of the Missouri Compromise. Douglas modified his bill in response, presenting a new Kansas-Nebraska Bill to the Senate on 23 January. President

Franklin Pierce's private support of the bill was generally known,[4] and the Senate passed it on 3 March. After a long, intense debate, the House of Representatives passed the bill on 22 May. President Pierce signed the law a week later, on 30 May 1854.

The reaction to Douglas' bill was immediate. Within a day opponents of slavery answered the revised bill of 23 January with the "Appeal of the Independent Democrats of Congress to the People of the United States," composed by congressional members Salmon Chase, Joshua Giddings and Edward Wade from Ohio, Charles Sumner and Alexander De Witt from Massachusetts, and Gerrit Smith from New York. This group accused Douglas of openly breaking a contract. Believing that the new law would hinder the flow of independent settlers from Europe and free workers from the East Coast into the West, they prophesied the outbreak of despotism and tyranny in the territories. They argued that no free worker or farmer would choose to settle alongside slaves and compete with their labor. They claimed that, if Congress ever were to pass a homestead bill, as planned, it would be worthless in the new territories. They made a nationwide appeal for public demonstrations and resolutions, specifically requesting that "the enlightened conductors of newspapers printed in the German and other foreign languages … direct the attention of their readers to this important matter." This direct appeal to German-Americans showed the importance of their support. For one thing the Germans, in contrast to the Irish, were more inclined to go further west and settle as farmers than they were to stay in Eastern cities.[5] For another, three of the authors of the appeal came from Ohio, a state where German votes were important for their reelections. By the end of March the enemies of Douglas's bill with German-American support had conjured up two- to three-hundred large protest meetings.

The first primarily German meeting of this sort, although not clearly planned as an all-German event, took place on 29 January 1854 (Thomas Paine's Birthday) under the presidency of Georg Schneider, Francis A. Hoffmann and Georg Hillgärtner in Warner's Hall in Chicago. Hillgärtner and Schneider were both the sort of "enlightened conductors of newspapers printed in the German language" whose support Chase, Sumner, and their congressional allies sought.[6] After meeting and voting a resolution, the three men, who had all sympathized with the Democratic Party up until then, telegraphed their Democratic Congressional representative, John Wentworth, in Washington.

At first protest against Douglas's Bill was local, but it spread as debates in the Senate clarified the possible law's impact. On 2 March 1854 Whig

Senator John M. Clayton of Delaware proposed an amendment to Douglas's bill. Since emigrants' hostility to the Kansas-Nebraska Bill was all too clear, Clayton wanted to restrict to American citizens exclusively the right to vote and the capacity to hold office in the territories. Recent immigrants would be entirely excluded by Clayton's amendment from participation in territorial popular sovereignty, which was of decisive importance in the political creation of the territories, and Clayton's amendment was seen as punitive. In general, citizenship required five years of residence in the United States, and in the state where one wished to vote at least six months' residence. There were fewer restrictions in the territories, however, such as a shorter time for naturalization, in order to make settling more attractive and ensure rapid development. The Senate adopted Clayton's amendment by 23 to 21, but opposition of the House of Representatives removed the amendment from the final law. The House thus recognized an issue that was continually raised by anti-Douglas speakers and newspapers during the Senate debates, "that slavery and the rights and welfare of immigrants were fundamentally incompatible."[7]

Clayton's proposed amendment intensified immigrants' resistance to the Kansas-Nebraska Bill. On the evening of 16 March 1854, on the initiative of Eduard Schläger, editor of the *Illinois Staatszeitung,* the first large specifically German protest meeting took place at South Market Hall in Chicago. It was not so much the moral aspect of slavery as it was the injury to the interests of free labor that was stressed. Speakers also dwelt on the specter of an ominous "slave power" an idea that increasingly gripped the free North. The extent to which free labor and freely workable soil were key to German-Americans was shown by the fact that the chief speaker, Francis A. Hoffmann, condemned the Clayton amendment in the strongest terms. The meeting's official resolutions left nothing to desire in openness and directness. Already under the influence of the "Southern conspiracy" theory, the committee formed to draft these resolutions declared that the South's current attempt to introduce slavery to the territories and to extend the predominance of the slaveholding interests in the Union was "not a solitary measure, but a logical consequence of similar previous acts and an ominous prophecy of further attack upon Northern liberty." The Democratic Party and its leaders were depicted as utterly dependent on the South. The committee's first resolution proceeded not only to condemn Douglas's bill but also to propose the reduction of slavery to what it had once been, "a local institution existing by sufferance." The committee declared that people hiding under the cloak of popular sovereignty actually intended to introduce slavery to new regions. Advocates of popular sovereignty were the greatest enemies of freedom and true republicanism, because their attack on free labor was in truth an attack on the freedom-loving and independent spirit of the North. Clayton's amendment was an attempt to oppress free immigrants, making them virtual slaves without political rights and without any recourse against the influence of slaveholders. The committee declared:

> We perceive a spirit particularly inimical to us Germans. Pioneers of the West that we are, we have lost our confidence in, and must look with distrust upon, the leaders of the Democratic Party, in whom we hitherto had confidence enough to think that they paid some regard to our interests.

and announced that a new organization should be created to keep a closer watch over German interests, if only "to prevent the present organization from being any further an instrument of *slave power*." One resolution rejected Douglas himself as an ambitious and dangerous demagogue of whom it was necessary "to rid ourselves of him as quick as possible."[8] An additional resolution said in a nutshell, "Resolved, that we consider the political career of Senator Douglas is terminated."[9] This last addition, along with other sharp statements against Douglas, resulted in a large group of participants' forming a parade at the end of the meeting and passing through the German quarter to Court House Square, where they burned Douglas in effigy. In the case of Chicago, at least, the most militant opponents of the Douglas bill were recruited from the ranks of wageworkers fearing a reduction in work opportunities and advancement in the territories due to expansion of slavery.

More importantly the first large German-American mass demonstrations were directed against the Democratic Party, the very party to which the overwhelming majority of German immigrants had belonged since the 1830s. There were historical reasons for the pre-1854 affinity of most Germans to the Democrats. Generally regarded as friendly to immigrants, the party had pressed the interests of settlers by supporting a homestead bill, had stressed at least verbally its enthusiasm for European freedom, had sought to avoid or modify puritanical demands for prohibition or Sabbath rest laws and had continually portrayed itself as the party for popular rights and the people. The Democratic Party saw itself as the heir of Jacksonian Democracy, committed to the true American ideals of the Declaration of Independence and the interests of farmers and the lower middle class. In contrast, the Whig party, which arose from a fusion of small groups in opposition to President Andrew Jackson's policies, was regarded as the party of the Southern aristocracy, large landowners and the upper middle class. Economically the Whigs represented the interests of the prosperous classes. Their electorate consisted primarily of merchants, factory owners, bankers and land speculators, while the Democratic Party stood more for the interests of the "working classes" and had as voters both wageworkers in towns and small farmers and settlers in the West. From its inception the Whig party was also marked by a strong awareness of American nationality, expressing displeasure over "foreign elements" and demanding rapid assimilation or Americanization. Nativist dynamics were always associated with this party, as demonstrated by the fact that the Whigs never attempted to win votes among the Germans.[10]

With its strident tone, the South Market Hall meeting was uncharacteristic of the majority of German-Americans. There can be no confusion about the views of most Germans concerning the Nebraska Bill, of course; out of 88 German-language newspapers, 80 opposed it and only 8 approved. But a moderate tone dominated the press during the first months of the conflict, influenced by the steadfast loyalty of the older emigrants, the "Grays," to the Democratic Party. This group still had a stronger influence over the German-American press. Pastor Franz Hoffmann in particular, tied to the party since the early 1840s, did not want to see the Kansas-Nebraska conflict as a party test. Gustav Körner, who had risen to lieutenant governor of Illinois, the highest office achieved by an foreign-born immigrant in Pierce's days, maintained a similar viewpoint. In an article that he wrote in the *Belleviller Zeitung* on 23 March 1854, he said that the Nebraska Bill was a mechanism for professional politicians to create an unprecedented, artificial uproar among the people. Körner further said that the South Market Hall meeting placed the issues of free land and territorial access over all other matters, and that the preference for states' rights typical of the Democratic Party, which contrasted with the Whigs' preference for federal power, would realize America's economic potential and bring supremacy in world trade. Old-line Democrats, Gustav Körner among them, believed that every republic that had ever been formed ultimately lost its republican and democratic character by adopting centralization. These Democrats insisted on strong, autonomous state politics, and they chose to see the Nebraska Bill as an attempt to take slavery out of the national forum and return it to the states and territories. Decentralization, they believed, would better serve local peculiarities and interests. In fact state and even local concerns, for them, played a much larger role in forming a party than did national consensus.

> The decentralization also reflected the priorities of party leaders. Whatever their hopes of winning a national election were, politicians, even those with national aspirations, were tied to state organizations; controlling the state governments took precedence.[11]

For voters before 1854, party loyalty was usually a decision for life. The relationship between a voter and his party grew over the years, and separation from the party was often a long, trying process, with the voter torn between his loyalty and his dissatisfaction with the changing principles of the party. In contrast to the long-established Thirtyers, the young Forty-Eighters had no experience with American party membership – Hecker, for example, did not become an American citizen and hence able to vote until 1854. The Forty-Eighters had not developed a party loyalty that could cause them to hesitate. There were also no personal reasons binding them to a particular party. The "Grays," on the other hand, held to the Democratic Party out of habit as well as personal interest.[12] The problem of party loyalty also afflicted the Whigs, and events would show that the speed with which the new Republican Party formed in the various states depended on the extent and speed with which Whigs and "independent" Democrats were ready to leave their old party and adhere to a new one. Most of them did prefer to elect anti-Nebraska legislators in the federal and state elections and replace those representatives who had voted for the Bill, but they did so under the belief that they would not leave their party.

It was only after the Kansas-Nebraska Bill became law that the moderate tone of the *Belleviller Zeitung* changed. The paper had stressed that the great majority of the population of the United States did not want the law at all, but in fact hated and rejected it, since it annulled the Missouri Compromise and made it possible for slaves to be moved to free soil. But the decided Free-Soil position was much more pronounced among the German-American population than was any moral condemnation of slavery in itself. It was settlement policy and "the doctrine of the primacy of westward expansion," not abolition, in which immigrants, and particularly Germans, were most interested. For almost all Catholics, including German and Irish, the "peculiar institution" was a God-given establishment, one of the oddities of the new country that they never considered opposing. Catholic newspapers preferred to ignore slavery, and the same may be observed in the strict religious communities of German Lutherans. Used to strict social order and authority, they felt little sympathy for the fanatical agitation of radical abolitionists, who managed only to shake the Constitution and endanger the Union. In their circles these immigrants placed greater value on demonstratively withholding contact with Anglo-Saxon fanatics.

For the Catholics – in 1860, 30,000 of the 130,000 Germans in Illinois were Catholics – it was unthinkable to make common cause with people whose puritanical style of life demanded numerous restrictions, of which Sabbath legislation and a ban on alcohol were the most egregious. The increased involvement of anticlerical Forty-Eighters, with their "shrill anti-clericalism," did not exactly inspire trust among Catholics. [13] The attitude to slavery might also have had a geographic source. As a rule, the closer one lived to the border of slave states, or – as was the case with many in south-ern Illinois – if one had previously lived in a slave state, the more modulat-ed was one's their attitude toward slavery. Most radical abolitionists came from states on the East Coast. There was always a difference between peo-ple in the majority, who supported reestablishing the Missouri Compromise, and those who wanted to abolish slavery completely, as a moral evil. Between the question of humanity and the question of material and eco-nomic interest, it was the latter that set the political agenda.

Douglas's bill was not the sole point of dispute in the social and political dissensions of the 1850s. Between 1845 and 1854 America was con-fronted with the greatest wave of immigration in its entire history; 2,939,000 new arrivals reached American soil in this period, a number amounting to 14.5% of the total population in 1845.[14] The sudden, broad expansion of a secret Protestant organization directed against Catholicism and immigra-tion disturbed not only large numbers of immigrants, but also many politi-cians from various Northern factions. The members of this organization called themselves Know-Nothings, from their mutual promise to respond to all inquiries with the sentence, "I know nothing." The official name of the group was the "Order of the Star Spangled Banner." Established in New York, the city most strongly impacted by immigration, the organization it played no significant role until the middle of 1853. A change of leadership within the order brought with it more aggressive propaganda, leading to massive growth of the secret league. By the end of 1854 each state in the North had its own organization, with a strong basis in many small, local associations.

From the very beginning the Know-Nothings drew most of their adherents from Protestant New England and isolated enclaves of Puritan descendants in the West. Only adult men born in America with no ties to Catholicism, political or personal, were accepted as members. As is the case with any secret society, the Know-Nothings were hierarchically structured and practiced a fully articulated system of rituals. These activities especially, to say nothing of the stimulus of exclusivity, attracted the curious. The relationship of the organization to Protestant immigrants was ambivalent. Some members were ready to work with Protestant immigrants, while the more radical Know-Nothings sought to exclude all immigrants. There is no doubt, however, that Catholicism was the Know-Nothings' chief nemesis, and here their enmity struck Irish Catholics in particular.

The immediate spur here for nativists was the perennial conflict over the school system. As a rule Catholics rejected the American free-school system and committed themselves to founding parochial schools, a point of conflict to which Hecker would dedicate great attention in the 1870s. In addition the visit of Archbishop Gaetano Bedini, who toured the United States from June 1853 to February 1854 to settle disputes over the legality of Catholic Church's freedom from property taxes in America, poured oil on the nativists' fire. Nativist fanatics stormed about a papal invasion whose vanguard was Nuncio Bedini. Hysterical conspiracy theories, suggesting that the pope was involved in destroying American republicanism were as virulent and powerful as the supposed agitation by the scheming slave power. Because nativists swore to an intensified form of Protestant values, they conceived of American civilization as a political continuation of the Reformation. For them America was a permanent protest against every form of absolutism; one of these was seen to be the Catholic Church.[15]

Nativists shared this conviction with most of the political refugees of 1848, who perceived the Catholic Church as merely the ally of reactionary states. For both those groups the Catholic Church was the declared enemy of true republicanism. Nativist defense of Protestant values, however, led to a demand for Anglo-conformity. There was a sensitive reaction to the fact that many immigrants showed no great inclination to Americanize. On the basis of opposed social and religious values and ways of life, tensions between nativists and immigrants were inevitable. To puritanical New Englanders, immigrants' views on keeping the Sabbath and on using alcohol were a thorn in the side. "The besotted Irish Catholics functioned as their primary negative reference group." The disproportionate participation of immigrants in violent crime, rowdyism and poverty in the large towns – in 1860 New York City, for example, 80 percent of those living on poor relief were "foreign born"[16] – also led nativists and religious temperance supporters to promote a ban on alcohol because they saw it as the chief reason for social problems. Germans, on the other hand, could only see the temperance movement only as an attack on their personal freedom, and they protested heartily against it.

Clear political demands arose from this for the nativists. The Whigs, many of whom became Know-Nothings, had long complained about the growing influence of immigrants in politics, particularly in large cities. Catholics in particular, it was asserted, were always able to elect a legislature in their favor by voting as a "bloc" under the influence of the Church and the leaders of the Democratic Party. Nativists feared the decline of the American tradition, and for that reason they advocated restrictions on the right to vote. "Americans should rule America," asserted a widely distributed anonymous tract. Drawing on their Protestant ethos, nativists criticized the existing political parties as corrupt and irresponsible. Throughout the whole of 1855, the Know-Nothings, in their incarnation as the new American Party, won great success in city, communal and district elections. They represented to a great extent the interests of the Free-Soil movement and promoted the restoration of the Missouri Compromise. To be sure, many slavery expansionists hoped that Know-Nothing ideology would help restrict the movement of immigrants to the territories; but the Know-Nothings did not seize the point. The emergence of the Know-Nothings made the political spectrum before the presidential election of 1856 even more complex. The Democratic Party initially saw them as a series of individual phenomena. "Rivalries among the various factions of the opposition – Whigs, Anti-Nebraska Democrats, Free-Soilers and *Know-Nothings* – meant that politics would vary considerably from state to state." German-American newspapers, for their part, reacted to the Know-Nothings with a call for people to register and participate in the elections.[17]

A third political movement that specifically distressed Germans was the effort to ban alcohol. Temperance agitation had begun in Illinois in 1853, and in February 1855 a prohibition law was passed by the state legislature, modeled in its strictness on the Maine Law.[18] In June an Illinois referendum was scheduled to ratify the law. The months between passage and plebiscite brought Germans into direct confrontation with the temperance supporters. Chicago's saloon keepers, most of them German, responded to an attempt by city government to close all the beer gardens and saloons; they marched as a body on city hall, with such vehemence that their conflict with the police on 21 and 22 April ended in what were called the "Lager Beer Riots."

The June referendum in fact led to the law's defeat. Both counties and wards of large cities with a large populations of Irish or Germans expressed themselves overwhelmingly against the law. In the region of Chicago occupied by Irish and Germans, 91 percent of the votes opposed the law. Hecker's home county of St. Clair in southern Illinois showed itself almost as unanimous with 82.8 percent in rejection. The town of Belleville made its opinion known as well with 88.8 percent against. The German press, particularly the *Belleviller Zeitung* and the *Illinois Staatszeitung*, built opinion against the law through continuous articles. German arguments were multifarious, reaching from criticism of the excessive power of sheriffs or constables, who could arrest drunks on their own authority, to the dependence of the local economy on beer and whiskey production – Germans had had an essential role in the expansion of beer brewing – and the necessity to protect the "home market." A subtler argument was that the "temperance humbug" was "nothing more than a nursery for hypocrisy, and as such it brings mankind immeasurable injury." This argument played on the idea of "European dualism" between the class of clerics, nobles and moneyed aristocracy on the one hand and the working, thinking and socializing people on the other. The German press dedicated more attention to its concerns over the temperance question and the Know-Nothings than it did to such themes as slavery and the Nebraska Bill.

This deep resonance among Germans against the prohibition law would later mislead American politicians about the influence of the "German vote."[19] More immediately, however, such a shift in theme merely benefited Stephen A. Douglas. His speeches turned from the Nebraska matter to the anti-immigrant phenomena of Know-Nothings and temperance. Douglas told a friend he had great expectations of succeeding in making nativism the central theme. "That will bring the Germans and all other foreigners and Catholics to our side," he confidently wrote in the autumn of 1854. Yet when Douglas visited Belleville a year later, in the autumn of 1855, he had a cool reception. Simply condemning the Know-Nothings and temperance did not suffice to change long-term German-American opinion on his position on the Nebraska question. On the contrary, the voters had become more critical.

The formation of state Republican Party organizations had already begun in Michigan and Wisconsin. In Illinois the process was somewhat delayed by the dilemma of opaque party distribution. In the north, and particularly in Chicago, the state had a strong Free Soil faction. The counties in central Illinois constituted a fortress for the Whigs, while the south, with its high percentage of Germans, boasted a solid Democratic vote. The mainstream Democratic Party continued to stand behind Douglas, but it fell increasingly under the suspicion of being the party of the South. Nativist Whigs showed a solid front against Douglas, and they might have been open to coalition with "independent" Democrats and a general anti-Nebraska coalition; however, they still believed themselves capable of winning through a split in the Democratic Party, which, in the two-party system of 1854 would have meant a strengthening of their own ranks. An anti-Nebraska meeting held in the Illinois capital of Springfield on 5 October 1854 failed in its attempt to establish a new common party, due to resistance from Whigs. Abraham Lincoln was the most prominent exponent of this attitude. Even in November 1854, Lincoln still believed in the survival of his own Whig Party.[20] The independent anti-Nebraska Democrats were just as disinclined to join the Whigs. They worked with the Whigs in elections for Congress and state offices, electing a strong anti-Nebraska legislature, but they were not yet ready to found a new party. They still hoped, in the autumn of 1854, to be able to avoid splitting the party by making an attack on Douglas's leadership instead.

The German press was well aware of this dilemma. The fracture among Democrats over Douglas made clear the problems that also confronted the German-American population. The *Belleviller Zeitung*, for example, narrowed the dispute to one point, and when asked whether to return to the ranks of the Democrats or take an independent, tentative position, opted for the latter. In response to the demand by several German meetings to found an independent German party, an article on 16 October 1854 stressed that the German-Americans were too weak. If no other party arose with which one could ally wholeheartedly, then the only alternative was to preserve as independent a position as possible and hope for a new, better party constellation in the future.

Other voices spoke more decisively. "Papa" Münch, Missouri's most popular Thirtyer, had already declared in August 1854 that German-Americans must orient themselves to events in Michigan, where a fusion of Whigs, Free-Soilers and Democrats had created a Republican Party on the state level. Germans should join such a party, said Münch. In the meantime, in Chicago, Georg Schneider and Georg Hillgärtner distanced themselves in September 1854 from their resolutions of March and no longer supported a separate German party; rather they endorsed a genuinely broad American freedom party in which all should find a place. Their hopes would not be fulfilled until the end of 1855:

By the end of the year ... there were still no signs of further Republican organization. ... "Republican" was still only a name loosely applied to the opposition to Douglas; the term might even have widely different connotations even in different parts of Illinois.[21]

The Frémont Campaign: Preliminaries

The year 1856, with its approaching presidential election, compelled all of the anti-Nebraska forces in Illinois to coalesce. In most Northern states people had rallied around the banner of the new Republican Party, while in others it had been around the American Party of the Know-Nothings. Problems had not been resolved, and the antipathy between Democrats and orthodox Whigs remained virulent. Old-line Democrats such as Gustav Körner held back, waiting for confirmation of their Nebraska policy by the Democratic National Convention in Cincinnati in July before they would make a final decision.[22]

Twenty-five journalists and newspaper publishers called for a common meeting in Decatur, Illinois, to discuss and organize journalistic conduct for the upcoming campaign. The organizer of this meeting was Paul Selby, publisher of the *Morgan Journals* in Jacksonville, but there were also editors of German-American newspapers present, particularly Georg Schneider of the *Illinois Staatszeitung* and Franz Grimm of the *Belleviller Zeitung*. Abraham Lincoln also participated unofficially in the meeting as an "outsider." The meeting elected the moderate Charles Ray of the Chicago *Tribune* as president and Schneider as a member of the resolution committee. The committee in turn asked Abraham Lincoln to assist in composing a resolution acceptable to all. The resolution had to overcome the dilemma that persisted between two important electorates and future party groupings. The Germans and the Know-Nothings were in agreement in opposition to the Nebraska affair, but they excluded one another from any coalition for obvious reasons. The future Republican Party needed both groups if it hoped to win Illinois. It was thus a clever play to elect to the resolution committee both Charles Ray, who knew how to keep the Chicago *Tribune* out of nativist discussions, and Georg Schneider, publisher of one of the most important German-American newspapers. Abraham Lincoln was also included as a known moderate and pro-German Whig who, in 1856, was increasingly becoming the leader of the anti-Nebraska coalition; his presence indicated a desire to work together.[23]

Concerning the question of slavery, the Decatur resolution began with moderation by recognizing the legal rights of the existing slave states and assuring them that there was no intent "to disturb or upset our brother states in the peaceful enjoyment of their rights." The resolution accepted the Fugitive Slave Act, but it demanded the restoration of the Missouri Compromise and stressed – "in agreement with the expressed opinion of Thomas Jefferson – that areas obtained since the adoption of the Constitution had no constitutional right to demand reception into the brotherhood of states." In other words, any constitutional obligation of Congress to accept new states was denied. If Congress did choose to weigh the application of a new state, it had "to consider the impact of such an admission on the current and future flourishing, on the rights and security of the states of the Union as a whole and in particular and decide according to their best knowledge." "Our general government" had to make this judgment through discussion "ensouled through and through by the spirit of freedom," under the presumption "that [it] recognize *freedom* as the rule, *slavery* as the exception, made and determined as such – and that it never approved *property in human beings* as one of its principles nor as a principle in keeping with them."

Alongside these general statements a direct resolution against nativist defamations was also adopted. It doubtless came from the German editors, particularly Georg Schneider, and it moved Lincoln to say, "Gentlemen, the resolution introduced by Mr. Schneider is nothing new. It is already contained in the Declaration of Independence, and you cannot form a new party on proscriptive principles." Immediately after the anti-nativist resolution, however, another was adopted about the Know-Nothings' concern over the influence of the Catholic Church:

> Resolved, ... that we should welcome the banned and emigrants of the Old World; that, while we are for the broadest tolerance in all conditions of religious belief, we wish to reject all attacks on our public school system, or on any other of our teaching institutions, or our state policies from the side of adherents to any religious body.[24]

The Decatur Conference ended its work by naming a committee to compose an invitation to the state convention to meet on 29 May 1856 in Bloomington and make preparations for it. Clearly this convention was to take up organization of an Illinois Republican Party and nominate a state ticket, although its organizers still shied away from the name "Republican" due to their bad experience at the meeting on 5 October 1854.

After the Decatur meeting Charles H. Ray wrote to Senator Lyman Trumbull that a similar resolution on the Germans' concerns must be adopted in Bloomington. "[T]here should be some distinct ground assumed on which 20,000 anti-slavery German voters of this state stand, or we shall lose them in a body. They will go over to the enemy, and we are beaten." The battle for the German vote had begun. The fact that this vote was regarded as crucial was made clear by the hotly contested municipal elections in Chicago in March 1856. There the Democrats had won the mayoral election hands down because the candidate presented by the Free-Soilers had also been the nominee of the Know-Nothings, and the Democrats only needed to refer constantly to the nativism of the Republican candidate.[25] This showed that Germans placed the problem of nativism higher than their own Free-Soil interests.

The Bloomington Convention represented a broad spectrum of anti-Nebraska forces ranging from moderate and conservative Whigs to anti-Nebraska Democrats to a few German delegations. When the convention opened, 270 delegates were present, far fewer than the organization had hoped for. More than 30 of the state's 112 counties were not represented; surprisingly, many of these counties were from southern Illinois. There was one major exception, to be sure; St. Clair County sent two delegates, Gustav Körner and Friedrich Hecker. The unequal distribution of representation meant that most persons attending the Bloomington Convention had been selected by informal elections. Drafting a platform took place under the same auspices as in Decatur, although this time no German was elected to the committee. Because both German and nativist votes were needed to bring together a majority coalition, ethno-cultural references were avoided in the platform; instead, common views on the slavery question were stressed. With a view to the Germans, the question of temperance was ignored. By an amendment to the resolution, German-Americans were also assured of the party's intention "to proscribe no one, by legislation or otherwise, on account of religious opinions, or in consequence of place of birth."[26] Composing a ticket for Illinois was marked by attempts to compromise between Whigs and Democrats. The convention nominated William H. Bissell, veteran of the Mexican War and Democratic representative for St. Clair County, for governor, and the German Pastor Francis A. (Franz) Hoffmann for lieutenant governor. Bissell enjoyed great respect in the German community of southern Illinois, but he had a Catholic wife, which allayed fears that he might be a Know-Nothing. Hoffmann had been promoted as a candidate for lieutenant governor by the German press before the convention. As a Lutheran pastor he could help win the votes of more conservative Germans, who were skeptical about the participation of Forty-Eighters in the Republican Party's campaign. Of the eleven electors nominated, the candidates were equally distributed between Whigs and Democrats with one exception: Friedrich Hecker. Hecker was elected as the only "free" delegate to be presidential elector at large, serving alongside the most prominent Whig, Abraham Lincoln. The delegation elected in Bloomington to represent Illinois at the national convention called for Philadelphia included the two most influential editors of German-American newspapers in the Midwest, Georg Schneider of the *Illinois Staatszeitung* and Franz Grimm of the *Belleviller Zeitung*. German-American newspapers – at least those inclined to the Republican cause – declared themselves very satisfied with a state ticket supplied with so many Germans. Officially, out of concern for the Whigs, the name "Republican Party" was still not used, but rather that of the "Anti-Nebraska Convention."[27] Still, the nomination of delegates to for the national convention now made Illinois's participation quite clear.

Hecker's selection as state elector at large was without doubt a mark of honor, connected to a certain political influence. The indirect selection of the American president by electors, chosen by the people and gathered together in the capital of each state on the first Wednesday in December, originally left the decision of candidate free to each elector. In form, this claim to autonomy was preserved. But because they were nominated by state conventions that also named a specific presidential candidate, electors were in principle obligated as the executors of a nomination that came from the delegates of the national convention. Naturally Hecker's selection as elector carried political implications; it was "a position obligating him to make political speeches at various places." Georg Hillgärtner, now the publisher of the *Iowa Staatszeitung*, also saw the following intention behind Hecker's naming.

> Think of Friedrich Hecker, the proudest of Germans, as a presidential elector! If he enters the field for the Republican cause, for freedom of speech, individual liberty, freedom in the territories, free Kansas and opposition to the slaveholder oligarchy, what German will go against him? Every German man who loves freedom is inclined to recognize Hecker as his leader and serve under him, certainly never against him. Whoever opposes him will hardly be able to call himself a "Democrat." And Hecker has finally been lured out of the isolation in which he had

sought asylum from the absurdity of the world, onto the field of battle.[28]

Hillgärtner would prove wrong about the electoral attitude of Germans, but not about Hecker's own engagement or the motives with which the "independent" Republican took up the obligations of a potential elector of the president. There were many Forty-Eighters "on the stump" in the election year of 1856, but none was so active as Friedrich Hecker. American Republicans thought themselves very fortunate to have brought the Baden revolutionary hero out of hiding and back into political life, and to have won him for their cause. The *Democratic Press* of Chicago, which went over to the Republicans early despite its name, celebrated Hecker as "perhaps the most influential German in America."[29]

The national convention took place on 17 June 1856 in Philadelphia's Musical Fund Hall, which had about 2000 seats. In addition to journalists and politically interested spectators, 565 delegates came to nominate the presidential candidate for their new "fusion" party. New York City provided the largest group, with 90 delegates. Illinois was represented by 33 delegates, including the Germans Georg Schneider and Hermann Kreismann of Chicago, Franz Grimm, Friedrich Hecker and Gustav Körner (a Republican since Bloomington), who came on the invitation of Lyman Trumbull. A possible candidate for president had already emerged at the end of the Bloomington Convention. He was John Charles Frémont, of whom little more was known beyond his discovery of a number of new routes to the West Coast as a surveyor, and his resulting nickname, "The Pathfinder."

With his nomination the Republicans followed a tactic similar to that of the Democrats, who nominated James Buchanan rather than the too-divisive Douglas at their national convention in Chicago.[30] A Pennsylvania politician, Buchanan had been living at a secure distance in England at the time the Kansas-Nebraska Bill was passed, so he was untouched by the political conflicts of the previous two years. John Charles Frémont himself had the invaluable advantage of an un-political past. He could not be accused of ever having expressed himself even once on the controversial themes of the day. Once launched successfully into the world, the image of the "Pathfinder" would offer a positive back-drop on which others could project all important and necessary attributes of a president. Most of the delegates in Philadelphia knew very little about Frémont, particularly his personal views on slavery and other political themes.

Among the true propagandists who groomed Frémont's image from April 1856 onward were his closest advisor, the ex-Democrat Francis P. Blair,

Jr., and the nativist Nathaniel P. Banks. They portrayed Frémont as a man of
great strength of will, ready to act. Their campaign to launched the candidate showed clearly how much a president was "made," and how much his
nomination was a "triumph of image over achievement." Personal conversation revealed Frémont himself to be shallow, quiet and undecided, and
Republicans who sought from him any leadership for the national campaign found little support. Frémont's restricted himself to receiving various
delegations in his home in New York; he wrote no public letters and made
no significant statements throughout the campaign. He was thought to be
so sensitive, in fact, that his wife preferred to open his letters and protected
him from negative newspapers articles. In this way he became the first,
although not the last, presidential candidate of whom it could be said that
any real political understanding was not his, but rather his wife's.

Jessie Benton Frémont, daughter of Missouri's noted United States
Senator Thomas Hart Benton, was the person who polished her husband's
image, together with John Bigelow of the New York *Evening Post*. An embel-
lished biography that she wrote for this purpose appeared in almost every
Republican newspaper. A German translation in the *Belleviller Zeitung* was
the source from which Hecker derived most of his information on Frémont
for campaign speeches. The German Republican press itself sought through
name-dropping to raise Frémont's popularity among the German-
American population. For example, the *Belleviller Zeitung* published an 1850
letter from Alexander von Humboldt to Frémont in which the German
scholar praised the "Pathfinder" with the comment, "Here is the witness of
a man who is worth more than the entire Democratic Party taken together."
This private letter from Humboldt rose to the status of a campaign document for the Republican Party.[31]

Since Frémont was utterly lacking as a leader, others had to get the
Republican electoral machine rolling and maintain it. There were classic
election campaign obligations to fulfill. Money had to be raised, election
writings had to be circulated and large rallies had to be organized. For any
prospect of victory outside the free Northern states, where victory was certain, the Republicans had to win all of the disputed states except
Pennsylvania, or Pennsylvania and two or three other states, depending on
the number of electoral votes. California was immediately conceded as too
Democratic, so the party shifted its focus to Pennsylvania, convinced that
loss there would mean the loss of the election. As a result the election efforts
of the party's central authority in New York concentrated on Pennsylvania,
while Connecticut, Indiana and particularly Illinois were left to shift for

themselves.[32] The speakers' bureau created for the party was so disorganized that mistakes were chronic. While New York had more speakers than it could use, other states had none. Conversely, popular speakers such as Hecker were used in several states where there was a considerable German population. In the course of the campaign Hecker spoke not only in Illinois but also in the Pennsylvanian cities of Philadelphia and Erie, as well as in New York and Buffalo.

Illinois party leaders were on their own for the duration of the campaign, with no hope of either money or reinforcements for their team of speakers. Every voice that could be used was all the more important.[33] Two of the most active organizers in Illinois were Abraham Lincoln and Elihu B. Washburne. Both of them asked Hecker for help. Hecker's efforts with Elihu Washburne would continue to grow in the course of the senatorial campaign of 1858. Hecker's first public appearance in 1856 was in Mascoutah, near Belleville, on 28 June. Listeners were less occupied with substantive themes than with the joyful fact that Hecker was back on the political stage:

> For eight years Hecker has lived on his farm in total seclusion from all political effort. With the energy that restless men have, he has thrown himself into the arms of this new activity, and out of a wild prairie he has created a noble, flourishing little place. ... The disinclination that a large part of the emigration at first felt against any involvement in American politics was almost entirely a result of the dreadful experience across the ocean. But this withdrawal could not last long. The times are too important. A crisis of more than local significance, a crisis that is of the greatest importance for the development of general liberty, calls into the first rows of battle the old fighters for human rights, equality and prosperity for all. The call has not gone unanswered.[34]

In fact old warriors arose from all quarters. Lorenz Brentano, thought lost in the broad prairies of the American West, reported by letter from his farm in Michigan. It would not be long before he, less successful as a farmer than Hecker, returned to the civilization of metropolitan Chicago. Gustav von Struve interrupted his own labors on his *World History* and left Staten Island, where he lived with his wife Amalie, to announce to the Germans that, if he had the right to vote, he would vote for Frémont. Carl Schurz sought to spread the same attitude among Germans in Wisconsin. Judge Stallo sought to convert the Germans of Cincinnati, and Pastor Hoffmann, although his nomination as lieutenant governor had to be withdrawn, did not fail to tour all the larger towns of the North. Georg Schneider in Chicago did the same, while Friedrich Kapp, Julius Fröbel and Franz Zitz did their best in New York. Hecker and Körner took their home state of Illinois as their assignment. "Papa" Münch and Heinrich Börnstein even beat the drum in Missouri, although Frémont was not even on the ballot in that state. The collaboration of "Grays" and "Greens" in this campaign was astounding, but it in fact happened.

> So we see the elite of our emigration along with the elite of the earlier emigration, whose names have a good sound to unprejudiced Germans in America, ... united at the same work, united for liberty against the aristocratic power of the slaveholders and their characterless Northern satellites.[35]

In two published letters Hecker gave an account of his decision to mix again in politics. The first letter was addressed to Christian Esselen, editor of the radical *Buffalo Telegraph*, who had invited him to a mass meeting in the name of the local Republican committee. Hecker wrote the second letter to Theodor Dietsch, an acquaintance from the revolutionary period and currently editor of the *Cincinnati Volksblatt*. Dietsch had asked Hecker to speak to the Germans of Cincinnati about the "burning questions of the day."

> If I have felt myself moved at the moment to cut my moorings and row out into the thankless sea of public life, this was chiefly because I see in the present crisis – the repressed question of the extension of slavery – an opportunity for the German-American population to rise from the humiliation in which, in part due to its own fault, it has found itself. Taking a solid, decisive position on this issue will open the way to a better future.

The same argument was found in Hecker's letter to Esselen. Hecker was once more using his argument a lawyer's role in alarming and enlightening the people. Here his horror over the contempt that Anglo-Saxons felt for the Germans was even plainer. It was high time to lift the consciousness of the Germans, Hecker said, so "that even the most rotted-out native [had] to see what spiritual agitation had seized this mass, whose great number had arisen since 1848." In other words, Hecker wanted to wage war against the stolidity of the German "voting cattle." No longer would they be given over to gross party politics as cannon fodder. Care should be taken "that the hateful distinction between 'Dutch' and "American" resolve itself into the term "American citizen." Hecker had

> no illusions that the "God-damned Dutchman" will vanish as if touched by Merlin's magic dust, but it will be at least a beginning. so that they do not continue to see us merely as "voting cattle." They will seek the German vote more militantly. They will have to show more than a mere handshake beforehand, and contempt afterward. The election will no longer suffice.

Hecker was by no means blind to the justified accusation of the Democrats that Know-Nothings made up a majority of Republicans. Grown distrustful through experience, Hecker also saw the possibility "that they would misuse us again and with our help achieve secret ends, even against us." But knowing the significance of the German vote for the Republican Party, he could threatened the party with withdrawal, "if we see that they are cheating us, that their lack of principles have real impact, then an honorable man will rip up his ticket to prevent such a two-tongued party from winning the election."

Hecker knew about both the Know-Nothings and their agitation within the American Party, an influence that was hard to estimate in this campaign. Like Pastor Hoffmann two years earlier, Hecker – who had no experience with party membership – stressed that, in the end, it was not party affiliation but principles that mattered. These principles had been clearly stated at the state convention in Bloomington and at the national convention in Philadelphia. Germans, with the "history of two continents" before their eyes, could join only the party that represented the "principles of all true republicans of all times." "We German-American refugees," he declared, "cannot favor the expansion of slavery. We would be cursing our past, the flag for which we fought and for which our brothers died. We would dishonor the graves of those murdered by courts." Hecker told Dietsch in precise terms the principles to be defended:

> We are for whole, full republican freedom; against slavery; against aristocracy; against centralizing pressures that weaken so much of the power of the people when central authority grows in strength. We are against corruption (according to Franklin's statement in the Pennsylvania legislature, public offices should provide that love of country, dependence on republican institutions, their continuation,

strengthening and fortification that would open a solid area of influence as the finest salary for their bearers), against every restriction of
republican equality and human worth through distinction on account
of birth or religion; against every restriction of social freedom through
unnatural laws of prohibition, which are laughable and unenforceable.[36]

This was the first version of Hecker's confession of faith, which he
repeated at every election rally. After Mascoutah he traveled to all of the
surrounding towns of St. Clair County. Due to illness, Hecker was unable to
accept an invitation to a mass rally in Belleville on 12 July, where William
Bissell, candidate for governor, and Gustav Körner were to speak. On 3
August 1856, however, he spoke in Belleville at the Turner Festival, a week
later at Waterloo in Monroe County and three days later at a meeting of the
Republican Club in Belleville. Hecker remained in Belleville overnight.
Around 10 o'clock that night, as the Turners of the place gave him "a sere-
nade with music and torches," his house was burning down a few miles
away.[37]

Initial news of this misfortune was stark. "[Hecker's] house, including
the kitchen down to the cellar level, and part of the furniture, burned
between one and three. The fire was accidental. The destroyed property was
only partly insured." Whoever studied the newspapers with attention could
read of such accidental fires all the time. There was also arson by wandering vagabonds, who were often persecuted by severe local laws and took to
setting fires as a response. As a rule these were not politically motivated
attacks. And so it was only ten days later that a change in interpretation
occurred about what had at first been an accidental house fire. Under the
headline, "The Border Ruffians in Illinois! Hecker's House Set Afire," the
Belleviller Zeitung published a letter from Hecker to the *Illinois Staatszeitung*
in which he expressed suspicion that the house had been set afire. "When
we heard the first news of the burning of Hecker's house," Georg Schneider
wrote in his introduction to the letter, "we had no doubt the fire had been
set. We did not speak our mind openly because we wished to await further
news."[38] That news arrived, in the form of Hecker's letter, on 14 August,
three days after the misfortune, and it confirmed suspicions. The letter was
genuine. Besides his suspicion about arson, it expressed Hecker's wish that
the *Illinois Staatszeitung* publish his communication because so many letters
and invitations had been destroyed to which he now could not respond.
Further, he announced his decision to suspend his stump tour, for obvious
reasons.

It cannot be established whether Hecker wrote this letter merely for propaganda purposes for the Republican Party. It does appear very likely that the house fire was set, but the question remained, by whom? Here the field was wide open for speculation. Although Hecker carefully spoke in another letter from the same time "only" of an "accident," in the letter to the *Illinois Staatszeitung* he was certain.

> *I am solidly convinced that the fire was set* … just as everyone in the house and the neighborhood is also convinced. Completely unknown fellows asked whether this was my house and whether I was at home. The fire broke out while I was on a stump tour through Monroe and St. Clair Counties, holding a speech in Belleville discussing the questions of the day … I showed the burn to a builder, and he is also convinced that the fire was set. If it had not rained so much, if the shingles and roof had been entirely dry and if the wind had blown, the whole family and guests would have become victims of the flames, because the fire broke out while all were in the first, deep sleep (about midnight) … Kansas seems to have moved eastwards.[39]

This last sentence of Hecker's letter makes clear how much he was obliged to the Republican rhetoric of this campaign, and the degree to which he agreed with the myth of "bleeding Kansas" that was constructed by Republican propaganda. Troubles arose in the territories mostly when border areas were being settled. As a rule violence in the territories should not be seen as an immediate expression of the divergence between Southern and Northern states. In contrast to Nebraska, whose organization went forward peacefully, there were continual conflicts in Kansas. But they were so locally limited that only diffuse rumors reached the East Coast. These rumors were then used to create the fixed idea that the organization of Kansas was primarily a battle between the North and the South for the control of the region. "Border Ruffianism," a fancy term for invasion by hired Southern rowdies from bordering states to drive out peaceful settlers, was one of the most ominous, paralyzing themes promoted by the Republican Party in the campaign of 1856. There was true armed conflict on 21 May 1856 in the "free-state" town of Lawrence between troops of the sheriff, who took a clear pro-slavery position, and local citizens, who had been arrested without cause. This led to some plundering and vandalism, and the Republican press sounded the alarm. The first reports of events in Lawrence, particularly in the *Chicago Tribune* and the *New York Tribune*, were based on wild, completely unfounded speculation. It was these images – not their later corrections, which came out rather slowly – that gave readers in the North an impression of an attack on Lawrence.

In addition there was an assault on Senator Charles Sumner by the Southern Congressman Preston Brooks on 22 May 1856, which fueled reports of the South's supposed readiness to use force. According to one contemporary, it was "not merely an *incident*, but a *demonstration*." The assault on Sumner, which followed a speech delivered in the Senate against the South, was shock enough. But it bestowed added believability to fragmentary, uncertain and often contradictory rumors from Kansas: "Bleeding Sumner and Bleeding Kansas were powerful Republican symbols in the 1856 presidential campaign. … No theme received greater emphasis from party spokesmen in … 1856…." Southern aggression became fact to the Northern states.

By alleging arson, Hecker joined the trend and gave a particular interpretation to Kansas events. The *Illinois Staatszeitung* added its own commentary, picking up on Hecker's most provoking sentence. "And so it is," the editor confirmed,

> Kansas is moving eastwards. The Democratic border monsters set a fire at an opponent's house while he was gone, giving his helpless family over to the flames! To these arsonists it is no merit that no life was lost … Nemesis will strike the party that uses such means to reach its goals and seeks to set aside its enemies through murder in Kansas and arson in Illinois. They have achieved one goal immediately, which was to remove Hecker from the public eye … . The smoking ruin of this house should be a lasting sign of what they can expect from the party of slaveholders to all German citizens.[40]

Some moderate, if unheard, newspapers warned that, "when the real facts are made public, this excitement in Kansas will be found to be all moonshine." The editors of the *Belleviller Zeitung* therefore printed Hecker's letter and commentary at full length, restricting themselves to the concluding skeptical remark: "We do not know upon what special conditions the imputation [comes] that some 'Democratic' fanatics committed this border ruffian act, and hence we do not wish to endorse what is given here, but the matter is certainly *suspicious*."[41]

The matter was debatable, or rather believable, because readers of German-American newspapers had been witness to an entire series of accusations since the moment Hecker actively entered the campaign. It must have been one of Hecker's strangest experiences to discover that America's much-praised freedom of the press often degenerated into mud wrestling during political campaigns. On the one hand, Republican papers could barely restrain their praise of his "outstanding talent" and the "masterwork of his popular eloquence." On the other hand, once one negative claim was released, there was a hail of endless reciprocal accusations as Democratic and Republican papers exchanged blows. Criticizing or denigrating Hecker, meant invalidating some quality peculiar to him, and attacks on his personal integrity were always popular. One anonymous hate-letter against Hecker in the *New Yorker Staatszeitung*, written in response to his published letter to Esselen, went even further in its accusations. Hecker was said to have taken the war chest with him to America in 1848, and he was accused of joining the Republican camp only because the party paid richly for his help. Hecker was so offended that, short as he was of time, he sent an immediate reply, entitled, "An Even 'More Open Answer' to Mr. M. H. B., Who Did Not Even Sign His Full Name," published in the *New Yorker Abendzeitung* and diligently copied by many other papers. Hecker blamed the attention paid to him by the press as well as the accusations heaped upon him on how influential his critics felt his speaking ability and electoral support to be. Because the burning of his house had become a party matter, and because the Republican Party valued Hecker's help, some members sought to compensate part of his loss and, at the same time, get him back on the stump. He had already agreed on a tour of the East Coast when a letter arrived from Abraham Lincoln shortly before his departure asking for his help in Springfield and offering him financial support to rebuild his farm:

> Could you not be with us here on the 25th of this month, when we expect to have a large mass meeting? We cannot dispense with your services in this contest, and we ought, in a peculiar way, to give you some relief in the difficulty of having your house burnt. I have started a proposition for this, among our friends, with a prospect of some degree of success. It is but fair and just; and I hope you will not decline what we may be able to do.

Whether and how money came cannot be proven. It must be assumed that Hecker received some support from the Republican Party.[42]

The Frémont Campaign: Hecker's Address to the German-American
Population of the United States

Because Hecker could not accept all invitations and was even less inclined to travel after the burning of his house, the *Belleviller Volksblatt* published a portion of his "Address to the German Population of the United States by Friedrich Hecker" in each of its weekend editions, starting in the middle of August. This extensive work, intended to be separately published as a pamphlet and excerpted in many German-American newspapers, contained in its full form all the arguments and assertions that Hecker included in his speeches. It was also a typical document of the rhetoric of that campaign.

The very structure of the "Address," which never could have been presented as a speech because of its length, shows how much Hecker had thought about the specific situation of German-Americans. Before dealing with the "great questions of the day," Hecker commenced by illustrating the German-American situation in even more extensive form than in his letters to Esselen and Dietsch. Because the Republican Party had absorbed a powerful nativist wing, it was inevitable that ethno-political questions be mentioned in election speeches to foreign-born audiences. Hecker stressed how important it was for Germans to win a respected place in American society through clear political action. The rules, he said, were easy. Germans should choose only the party "of which it may be assumed" that it represented in the purest form "eternal, immutable and inalienable human rights [and] republican American principles, as established in the Declaration of Independence." Naturally Hecker promoted the Republican Party and could do so with a clear conscience thanks to Georg Schneider's influence on the Bloomington Convention's platform. Hecker also stressed that alliance with Know-Nothings had been clearly rejected at the Philadelphia Convention. As long as the Republican Party did not act against the platform adopted at its conventions, it was possible to work with it with confidence, without false motives and suspicions.

Hecker did not deny any accusations that the Republican Party was infiltrated by Know-Nothings. But he saw no reason to break into panic as a result.

> If we take a look at this fearful hubbub in general and in detail, Know-Nothingism is as old as the world. But it has never achieved anything beyond the temporary disruption of peace and prosperity in a republic.

> It cannot involve republics in ruinous conflicts because it is contrary to
> the true principles of equality contained in humanity and in
> Christianity. Know-Nothingism is an aristocracy of birth, hence intoler-
> able in republican institutions, especially in a land whose population is
> gathered from all nationalities and … to prosper cannot do without
> settlement by an immigrating stream of people. … Know-Nothingism
> existed in ancient Rome, and it contributed to the ruin of the republic.
> The *homines Italici nominis dic Socii et Latini* ["Men of the Italic name
> called allies and Latins"] fought against the narrow-hearted efforts of
> Rome itself to keep them in legal subordination. Civil wars of the
> [Swiss] Confederation rested on the same foundation.

Hecker denied that Know-Nothingism would have a long life. He was
convinced that, even if the current naturalization law were altered in favor
of the Know-Nothings, it would have to be altered again in no time at all in
favor of the foreign born. A republic such as the United States of America
could not afford such a law because America was a trading nation, and trading partners would note these developments. The further development of
the Know-Nothing movement would prove Hecker right. After their beginning successes in 1855 and the election year of 1856, when the American
Party nominated Millard Fillmore as its presidential candidate, this group
vanished from the political stage, at least as a distinct factor. A group
hostile to foreigners could not be an attractive political party over the
long term.

In his "Address," Hecker cleverly shifted the problem of nativist attitudes to the positions of the parties. The sole open anti-foreign resolution of
which he knew came from the Democratic Party. It was the Clayton amendment to the Kansas-Nebraska Bill, which would have restricted the right of
immigrants to vote in the territories and thus settle there. It appeared para-
doxical, Hecker continued, that even "Master Douglas, father of the
Nebraska Bill, guiding star of the Nebraskans … offers the expansion of
slavery with one hand and with the other assures equality and liberty to the
foreign-born." Douglas indeed had spoken out against the Clayton amendment. In 1851 he had spoken of the Missouri Compromise as an "act of
peace," while now he had nothing more urgent to accomplish than to overthrow that compromise. "Make sense of it who can" Hecker quipped, allowing this contradiction to stand in his pamphlet, since all he needed was
proof that a legal extension of slavery in the new territories could not agree
with the prosperity of immigrants. In other words, he portrayed the

Nebraska Bill as a law aimed indirectly against the interests of immigrants. When considering Hecker's argument, however, we must recall that the number of slaves in the territory was so small that there was in truth no reason to be concerned, and that the issue was useful as an electoral theme only through exaggeration.

Hecker was able neither in his speeches nor in this article, as widely distributed as it was, to avoid the problem of temperance. He referred to the "remarkable coincidence of turbulent questions" and suspected that a political maneuver was behind it. "It is precisely in this time of strife, when the Missouri Compromise is being set aside, that there is agitation over temperance and Know-Nothingism." In principle he believed temperance legislation would never pass, due, he hoped, to healthy human reason. "I refer to the decisive defeat of the Maine Law in our healthy state of Illinois, of which I am proud to be a citizen. All fanatical "isms" have failed when confronting the fresh sense of the intelligent, hard-working and advancing population." We can read criticism in Hecker's remark that a social restriction or ban often works "more irritatingly than even a political one" because it touches personal needs. It was no secret to him, either, that the German-American population was more concerned about a ban on alcohol than it was about the slavery question. "To many people a political insult, such as a limitation on the right to vote, is not so continually present, bothering them hourly and daily, as a limitation affecting life at home or in society."

Hecker's other arguments against temperance belonged to the common canon. They span from the accusation of hypocrisy ("if the priest drinks alone, the congregation soon boozes in the square") to economic considerations. "Such a law intervenes so deeply in internal production, in agriculture and international trade that it cannot have a long life. Don't worry!" Because economic development was a central concern for Hecker and, as he saw it, all Americans, he resolved the problems of both temperance and Know-Nothings with the same schema: No one wanted a law against his own prosperity. Know-Nothingism and temperance, he declared, were issues that overarched the party.

In the meantime Hecker learned on his own the mechanisms and strategies of presidential campaigns, including efforts of each party to accuse the others of violating the Constitution. The Constitution, he asserted, was like the Bible and had always been used for "party needs." But Hecker also knew from his personal experience that no American party, not a single American, wherever he stood, would seriously place the Constitution in peril. Neither the Republicans, nor the "morally" engaged

Forty-Eighters, who had come to love the American Constitution so much as a result of their own experiences, could be accused of such frivolity.

> And we foreign-born, especially those of us of German birth, vindicate the same dependence; the same love for this eternal document ourselves. Those among us who have not a foot's worth of the homeland in which we were born to call our own except the headsman's block on which our head will fall, or a few square feet of temporary or lifelong prison; who have no homeland other than this republic; who have studied and supported it overseas, marveling with elevated hands at this splendid structure of a free and equal humanity; who have measured the weight of opinions formed there against the real scale of public life here – for us there is no other thought than to protect this holy asylum of mankind.

It cannot be said whether Hecker had forgotten in the meantime that he had emigrated with intent and not gone into exile. But it is obvious that he was dealing here chiefly with the right of Forty-Eighters to exist on American soil. He wanted to show that patriotism had nothing to do with the land of one's birth but was motivated by the presence of a free constitution.

It is possible that Hecker was recalling the man who essentially formed his vision of America, Carl von Rotteck. Rotteck's illumination of the Declaration of Independence, which consciously rejected the monarchical principle, and the Constitution, which surrounded the republic with a series of protective institutions, was seminal. It was with Rotteck's help that Hecker now brought a moral condemnation of slavery into his argument. But his condemnation was now more strongly influenced by political considerations, because slavery endangered the very existence of the state.

> The name of that noble, great historian and statesman Carl von Rotteck is certainly known to men of German and American origin. I recall as freshly as if it were yesterday that some time before his death I spoke with him about this glorious Union, its support and survival. The only concern that he expressed was over the slavery question, that its survival and expansion would have as destructive an influence over the course of years as the history of all slaveholding republics teaches.[43]

What followed in Hecker's "Address" was an excerpt from Rotteck's writings running for pages on the problem of slavery. This was intended to show his German-American audience "how men not belonging to this country but still committed in their hearts to its prosperity, flourishing and survival, thought on this question." Hecker was seeking to show how even those born abroad could have an interest in the prosperity of the American nation, could be good citizens because they knew how to appreciate the blessings of a free constitution. By appealing to Rotteck's authority, Hecker brought an exclusively German dimension to his text, because hardly a single American speaker could have quoted Rotteck. Hecker cited important passages in which Rotteck warned that "only one great sin" stood like a thorn in the eye of the "friend of liberty and progressive mankind, with all its admiration of the American Constitution," namely "despotic Negro slavery." It was, Rotteck declared, "a branding of the nation, a reason for shame and an injury to every honorable and enlightened American, … a cancerous tumor every day eating away more from your fatherland and its otherwise so great Constitution."

Hecker called on Rotteck's authority to demonstrate that the decline of the Roman Empire was an example of the irreconcilability of slavery with the "moral principle of liberty in the rule of reason." And Rotteck held that ancient Roman slavery was virtually "innocent" when compared to American. Rotteck had seen the Missouri Compromise of 1820 as an honest attempt to limit the expansion of slavery, and likewise the ban on importing slaves after 1808. Hecker adopted from Rotteck the assurance that in the end "such a capable constitutional structure and national force as is the North American" would help to eliminate Negro slavery entirely. According to Rotteck, "The victory will be won through the love of country and honor, through the energy and the free means of North American citizens."

This passage made clear once more the source of Hecker's positive concept of an American citizen. Through his reception of Rotteck he made his own the model of a republic borne chiefly by patriotism and civic virtue. If he argued here in moral terms, then he did so less because he was an enemy of slavery from experience, than because slavery contradicted his own concept of citizenship. It made impossible pure patriotism, which presumed free men. Slaves could develop no love for a state that forbade them all possibility of political participation. Hecker's "Address" introduced Rotteck's name introduced to the Midwest, a land that the Freiburg professor never saw with his own eyes, but whose political conditions he believed capable of realizing "the chief demands of a pure theory." His pupil Hecker held fast to the notion that this pure theory with the social design associated with it could in fact be made real.

The threat to dissolve the Union was another "scary ghost" exploited by the Democratic Party's press. In response, Hecker restricted himself to the classical objections of American Republicans. He outlined the widely held Northern theory of a gradual expansion of slavery, pursued "systematically" by the South since 1850. With little difficulty he could identify the Southern aristocracy with the old European aristocracy, using the basic theory that "every power seeks its own expansion," he painted a picture of an implacable South not brought to heel in time.

The presumption that the primary peril for the American republic did not come from the outside, but from an inner corruption, was so generally accepted that it is not clear when it first took concrete form. The notion that a privileged class of Southern plantation owners conspired to win increasing control of the national government usually needed no further defense. "Americans were so accustomed to thinking in terms of conspiracies that Republicans devoted only limited effort to proving the existence of this conspiracy and focused instead on urging the necessity of concerted action against it." Because Hecker had to expand these conspiracy theories somewhat, he must have assumed that his German readers and listeners were not entirely unfamiliar with them.

Despite the threats, Hecker did not believe in the real possibility of the South's separation from the North. He enumerated a number of reasons for this, all having to do with the South's declining economic power. If Calhoun, the "eminent political talent" of the South, had succeeded in the 1830s with his nullification theories, an extreme version of states' rights asserting that federal laws could be declared invalid within the boundaries of individual states, then the "Great United Republic" would have degenerated into a "league of states without a core." It would have approached European conditions, "like the German *Reich* at the time of its collapse, like that separate league [*Sonderbund*] project that failed as a result of the healthy sense of the people of Switzerland." In the place of a solid and efficient Union, Hecker continued, there would be a "plethora of dissident state sovereignties." But there were a sufficient number of patriots in the South, he believed, who understood enough of economic and commercial interests to prevent a separation by all possible means. Statistical data would reinforce Hecker's assertion that secession was extremely dangerous. The low population density of the South and the long coasts of the Southern states made it too easy to attack and too difficult to defend, contrary to appearances.

If Hecker exploited history for his arguments here, he also copied the practice of both Democrats and Republicans in identifying his party with the traditions of the founding fathers. He thought that adopting values derived from history meant that he was influenced by Adams, Madison, Jefferson, Franklin and Washington. In this context Hecker once again oriented himself to that image of ancient republics presented by the humanistic tradition of the eighteenth century, asserting that wherever slavery arose, whether in antiquity or in modern times, the results were perennially the same. For that reason lessons could be drawn directly from antiquity. His ancient witnesses were historians such as Appian and Livy. From them he took principles "that apply to our own times almost word for word." First, "that the expansion of slavery withdraws space from the same number of free beings as there are slave beings." This idea directly applied to the Free-Soil ideology of the North. Second, "slaveholding must bear with it and feed a large number of persons, the house slaves, whose real work has no relationship to what is needed." This proposition stressed that slavery was an inefficient form of economic production. Third, "much of the effort of humanity is devoted to useless luxury articles [and] slavery makes possible a great concentration of goods in one hand." This criticism of one-sided capital accumulation echoed Revolutionary objections to the unequal distribution of property and soil in Europe, and pointed to luxury as an injury to virtue. Hecker also referred here to an idea in his pamphlet *The Rising*, the presumption, arising from the bourgeois work ethic, that all persons should have "useful occupations producing things of value." Slave owners as such did not. Fourth, "in times of war or internal disruption no secure use can be made of this mass of persons held in servitude to defend the country." This last notion underpinned Hecker's old concept of patriotism and the citizens' guard. It played on the notion that slaves could never be loyal, patriotic defenders and soldiers as long as they were denied participation in civil and political rights, were not full-fledged citizens of the state and did not identify with the interests of the state or see its preservation as their highest goal. Instead, there was a danger that they would be misused as the weapon of interests that were hostile to the state, as happened with the rebellion of Spartacus and again with Marius and his alien troops.

"Slavery was always the coffin of republics," quipped Hecker. Montesquieu's *Spirit of the Laws* testified that slavery had ruined republics over the course of time. In "this product of deep historical study, this immortal work of one of the most ingenious thinkers," Montesquieu asserted that slavery resulted in a general coarsening of morals; the master received all manner of bad habits from his slaves and gradually became used to "rejecting all moral virtues." Thomas Jefferson expressed the same view in his *Notes on Virginia*. "The practice of tyranny," Jefferson wrote, not only injured the morals of parents, but also had a negative impact on children, who copied the attitudes of their parents. And along with the morals and virtue of a people, the will to work vanished. "Because under a warm sky no one wants to work for himself when he can have another work for him. This is so true that rarely does one see slaveholders work." Here Hecker indirectly returned to economics by morally condemning slavery. And it was less a concern for the welfare of colored people that he expressed than it was a concern for saving white morality, the white will to work and white interests. Hecker never forgot that he was writing for a German-American public.

Hecker properly defended the Republic program of restoring the Missouri Compromise. It was, he said, "the first means of rescuing the territories from being overwhelmed with slaves"; unchecked, the presence of slaves would "burden and eject free labor" from the territories. According to Hecker, the troubles of American politics had arisen over time because both parties had continuously strayed from the great principles of the Declaration of Independence and the Constitution. Alterations in these principles had all been for the worse. Such changes occurred when legislators discarded a clear statement of elevated principles and replaced certain "fundamental truths" with an increasingly complex system of sophisticated laws to protect slavery. Hecker thought that Tacitus was right in saying *corruptissima respublica plurimae leges* ["the most corrupt state has the most laws"]. Here again, Hecker was consistent. Pre-Revolutionary liberals had already declared that simplifying laws and making them comprehensible, with a content that was dedicated to the welfare of all, was mandatory. The Fugitive Slave Act, however, was just the sort of corrupt, sophisticated law that Hecker objected to, injuring general interests and supporting special ones. Hecker denied that the law could be supported by the simple principles of the Constitution. He asserted that the crimes and punishments that it ordered that were not mentioned in the Constitution. And he objected that the validity of this law depended on the competence of Congress – although he felt that the autonomous competence of the individual states to make decisions was otherwise already set too high. Just as Hecker once had wanted the competence of the Second Chamber clearly expressed, he now demanded a clear statement of the American Congress's power concerning the territories, with recognition by all the states.

Either Congress has no power to mix in the local legislation in the territories, or it has power. If it does not have it, then Mr. Douglas's whole new Nebraska Bill is invalid; if it has it, however, then all the prior talk about self-government and squatter sovereignty is vain wind and smoke, and Congress has the power to test the constitutionality of laws passed by the people of the territory and to decide what is to happen.

At the close of his "Address," Hecker came to the genuinely "classical" part of his Republican strategy. Here he sought to illustrate the effects of the expansion of slavery from a statistical and economic position. This process was peculiar to Republican propaganda in general, because a statistical comparison of North and South naturally could only fall to the North's advantage. The same numbers were always in circulation for this purpose. Hecker drew them from extensive material in "newspapers, brochures, pamphlets of all parties, along with negotiations, reports and speeches in Congress." He showed that the North was smaller in extent than the South, but that a smaller area supported twice the population. While there were still large stretches of the South lying fallow or unused, due to the restriction of immigration there, only a little uncultivated land lay available in the North. Only the black population was growing in the South. The largest number of foreign-born Americans resided in the North. Yet, in the lightly populated state of South Carolina, there were twice as many paupers as in the densely settled state of Illinois. Hecker brought these phenomena down to a single common factor: "The immigrant knows all too well that he cannot place a homestead alongside slave labor." If territories were assigned to slave labor, immigrants would have no further prospect of building a new existence in the United States The number of immigrants bringing enough capital to buy land in the densely settled free states for a high price would be few. A decline in immigration numbers would be inevitable.

Here Hecker struck the central concern of most foreign-born Americans, namely, the hope for the progressive settlement of the West. Free land and free immigration had been the secret of the rapid blooming of the younger, free, Western states. Hecker's message was that the West must remain open to free settlers. Even rich farmers did not have enough land to divide among all of their children. Established and new settlers had to be interested opening new areas so that enough space would be available. "The son goes West as a pioneer, a bearer of civilization and liberty into the land where once the scalp-hunting Indian and trapper swarmed as a hunter." Hecker was concerned not merely with the territories, but also their effect on all Northern states. Any restriction of free labor in the existing free states, he continued, would inevitably result in the rapid growth of pauperism. In short, tearing up the Missouri Compromise was a "national misfortune" from both a political and an economic point of view. Its suspension would be a blow against the interests of the middle class. The emigrants from slaveholding states to new territories, claimed Hecker, were "almost exclusively small landowners and craftsmen, lower middle class that could not withstand competition of large plantations or slave labor, and therefore are compelled to emigrate." It was a fact "that the greater planters always sought to round out their holdings and buy out smaller landholders, exactly as aristocracy of all sorts in Europe do." This unequal pattern of property ownership had to be fought with all possible strength, so that "the political strength of the middle class, which remains the core of the state" should not sink. Hecker's wish to strengthen the middle class was still deeply rooted in his pre-industrial economic presumption of small businesses, independent merchants, farmers and craftsmen. For him everything depended on the concept of free labor and free soil – and perhaps on the dream of Jefferson, as well, of a simple, agrarian and earnest life, offering the opportunity for survival and enhancement.

> Small landholding would become worthless and hopeless, and rising through one's own labor more rare; only where labor is free and honored is any chance to advance possible, promising and rewarding. Only where free labor is respected, where work is an honor, does the working man continue in the pride of his entire moral and civil value.

Hecker saw a decline in respect for civil work when an entire class of persons looked on labor as an unworthy occupation. In contrast, he saw the Republican Party as the protector of that "irresistible force [drawing] the poorer, free whites and the lower middle classes from the South into the territories." The party was, in his eyes, the protector of free labor on free soil, guaranteeing that labor would continue to be honored and that "hard work would be worth it."[44]

Hecker's "Address" offered a glimpse into the development of the Republican Party. First the Republican Party in 1856 was obviously still in the process of development, and not yet complete. In its first years the party's members were clearly more motivated by hostility to specific groups and political themes than they were by positive identification with the party. Hecker's own history would show how long it took to develop positive party loyalty; his dogmatic Republicanism would not be evident until the 1870s.

Whatever the Republican Party would become after the Civil War, however, economic orientation was not yet a central party concern in its formative phase of the 1850s. The beginnings were there, in the ideology of free labor; but the Republican Party defined itself more in the 1850s by its stand *against* something than through a clear program *for* anything. The party program opposed the expansion of slavery, but in most cases this was not to promote the welfare of slaves; rather it was to secure the emancipation of the white middle class.

Precisely this issue was made clear in the last installment of Hecker's "Address." It was easy for Hecker to identify in principle with a Protestant work ethic that corresponded to his own liberal, pre-Revolutionary concepts of economy and society. The idea of social mobility and readiness to accomplish things; the notion that "work ennobles"; the belief that, through one's own effort, self-discipline and restraint, one could advance – these concepts resurfaced in Republican rhetoric whenever there was talk of the "dignity and nobility of labor." Combined with the of-repeated slogan of the "right to rise,"[45] the concept that every man should have the opportunity to rise economically or socially as far as his abilities and talents could take him. Thus far the Republican Party held fast to the American Dream – precisely as did the Democratic Party. The right to rise belonged to everyone except, obvious, the great landowners and factory owners who did not share Republican values and therefore were condemned in Republican election speeches as Southern aristocracy. The white middle class promoted by Republicans was to embrace all levels of American society, the small independent farmer of the Midwest just as much as the small shipowner, merchant and entrepreneur of the towns, or even the wageworkers of the large cities. This last group was specifically included because the concept of a bettering of one's situation through one's own efforts – the dream of one day earning enough money to buy a farm in the West, and becoming an independent farmer – seemed most easily transferred to them. It was, in other words, simply a matter of time before this group would rise into the autonomous middle class.

It also appears to have been the case that Republicans in America, like the liberals in Germany, were mistaken about the future of the capitalist, competitive economy. On the one hand they praised the growth of an autonomous middle class, its courage at new undertakings and its innovations and economic development. On the other hand they preserved the almost anachronistic republican ideal of the founding fathers. Work, property and virtue were a dream of society that was already dissolving, if it had ever existed in this form. Republicans were thus blind to the growing concentration of wealth in the North and the way that approaching industrialization made social mobility and economic advancement impossible for many.

The Frémont Campaign: Where would Robert Blum Stand Today? Where Trützschler? – Successful Losers

Although most newspapers expected that Hecker would be unable to continue speaking because of the burning of his house, he appeared on the East Coast within six weeks of the fire. On 1 October he spoke in Erie, in northwestern Pennsylvania, a crucial region for the Republicans. One day later he spoke alongside Friedrich Münch (alias "Far West") of Warren County, Missouri, at a meeting in Buffalo. Hecker then traveled with Münch to New York City, where the two men were expected at the Astor House on 4 October. The largest German mass meeting in New York up to that time was scheduled for a few days hence. On Tuesday evening, 7 October, between seven and ten thousand Germans from New York and the neighboring cities of Brooklyn, Williamsburg, Hoboken and Jersey City were gathered in the Academy of Music. They had answered the invitation of the German Republican Central Committee of New York, whose president, Friedrich Kapp, led the meeting. At 7:30 p. m. the hall was so full that no one could find a place. More than five hundred Turners from various parts of the city opened the meeting with a march, including not only Hecker and Münch but also Gustav von Struve, Gustav Körner, Julius Fröbel, Franz Zitz, Friedrich Hassaurek and Reinhard Solger. "Without any advanced discussion," Gustav Struve later wrote, "we [Struve and Hecker] went to work for the election of Frémont and against Buchanan in 1856."[46]

After the overture by the orchestra and the address of greeting by President Kapp, Struve was introduced to the crowd as the first speaker of the evening. His arguments and themes did not differ from the usual Republican rhetoric; he referred to the slave power conspiracy and declared that the Republican Party was obligated to return the Constitution to its original purity. After Struve, Münch mounted the tribune. Like Hecker, Münch was one of those people moved to participate in the election only by the current political situation. For him it was more than a question of "achieving an ordinary political party's goals, an ordinary party's victory." He declared the party must move "the entire political situation of our country along an entirely different, new path. ... [I]t is a question of the spiritual rebirth of an entire people (applause). Where it is a question of reconquering freedom, national honor and human rights once more." As a confirmed freethinker, Münch was perhaps the most moral opponent of slavery at this gathering.

Hecker mounted the tribune as the third and last speaker to give the most extensive address of the evening. The structure of his speech was a shortened version of his text in the *Belleviller Volksblatt*. Hecker began with remarks on the problem of the Know-Nothings and temperance, then demanded a basic investigation of the question of who represented the true democratic principles of the founding fathers. He cited extensively the writings of "Washington, Jefferson, Morris, Mercer and others,"[47] to show "that the fathers of the republic had always been against slavery." He ended with his familiar statistical comparison of North and South. "Hecker left the stand amid a hurricane of applause," an American newspaper reported. It took a half hour before the overfilled hall was emptied. "Thus ended the greatest and most important meeting citizens of German origin ever held upon the Western continent."[48]

From New York Hecker went on to Philadelphia. Here he spoke with Julius Fröbel and Reinhold Solger in Independence Hall. Hecker began his speech with the statement that he had had the opportunity to meet Frémont in New York and ask him for his position on the naturalization question. The candidate of the Republican Party

> assured him that, if the presidency fell to him, *he would never approve an extension of the period for naturalization or any other restrictive bill; rather, he would heartily support every effort to give greater legal protection overseas for immigrants who had taken out their first papers.*

Hecker appeared convinced by this answer, adding, "If Frémont's eyes lied, then there is not a single honorable man in this meeting tonight."[49]

While Hecker was still on the campaign trail in the East, Abraham Lincoln visited Belleville on 18 October. Lincoln's speech showed how uniform Republican rhetoric was. He also condemned "slavery and its evils [and] vindicated the cause of free labor, that national capital ... which constitutes the real wealth of this great country, and creates that intelligent power in the masses [that is] alone to be relied on as the bulwark of great institutions." He accused the Democratic Party of attempting to degrade free labor. Speaking in a town occupied primarily by Germans, Lincoln also had to direct a few words particularly at them. "This associate of Hecker," the reporter of the English-language *Belleville Advocate* later wrote,

> referred to the Germans and the noble positions taken by them in just and dignified terms. When he called down the blessings of the Almighty on their heads, a thrill of sympathy and pleasure ran through his whole audience. They all rejoiced that clap-trap, false issues and humbugs are powerless with the great hearts of Germany in America. Lincoln and Hecker were inscribed on many banners.[50]

The future president of the United States did not appear at all uncomfortable at being connected politically with the living symbol of the German Revolution.

Although the Republican Party had the greater number of German-speaking talent on its side, the election results did not entirely reflect this. Nevertheless, the results were striking for a party that had barely had time to organize itself adequately. The electoral participation was 83 percent, 7 percent higher than the previous election. Democrats won all Southern states except Maryland, which went to the candidate of the American Party, Fillmore. Of the Northern states, the Democrats won Pennsylvania, New Jersey, Indiana, Illinois and California. The Republicans won the eleven other free Northern states, gaining only Connecticut from the "uncertain" states. While Frémont received virtually no votes from the South, Fillmore received virtually all his votes from that region and few from the North. In New York, Frémont had almost 80,000 more votes than Buchanan. Buchanan won in Illinois, but at the same time the Republican candidate William Bissell won the governor's office, so that Gustav Körner could speak of a "half victory" of the Republican Party in Illinois.[51] Bissell, known as a rather conservative anti-slavery man but also liked by the Germans, won his victory with the aid of the Whigs. The high vote count for the Know-Nothing candidate, Millard Fillmore, in the hard-contested states of Pennsylvania, Indiana and Illinois demonstrated that the Republican Party could succeed in the next campaign only if it won the large nativist and conservative vote still loyal to the American Party. That meant drafting a more moderate, conservative platform, which would in turn disappoint the more radical forces.

In Illinois participation in the election was stronger in the north and Chicago than in southern Illinois. Despite that, the Democrats succeeded in the north, as well. For example, the almost entirely German Seventh Ward of Chicago voted Democratic. It was obvious that the Republican Party received almost no support among German Catholics; they were, as Marlin Tucker writes, "perhaps more fearful of Know-Nothings in Illinois than of negroes in faraway Nebraska." But such attribution cannot be entirely unambiguous.

> The divisions in the German community to some extent followed religious lines, with Protestant Germans more likely to vote Republican while their Catholic countrymen remained Democratic, although German Catholics were probably not as intensely hostile to Republicanism as were their Irish co-religionists. Apparently only the more radical Germans, typified by the Turners, voted solidly for Frémont.[52]

The latent tension between nativists and Germans remained a large problem for the Republican Party. Depending on how strong a role nativist themes or the temperance question played in the local arena, Germans could be either won or scared away.

In an article looking back on the campaign, the *Illinois Staatszeitung* in Chicago stressed the participation of the Forty-Eighters. Through their involvement in American affairs, the political landscape had been basically changed. "Where would Robert Blum stand now? Where Trützchler?"[53] the newspaper asked its German readers. For Hecker and those of his conviction, at least, the answer was not difficult.

A House Divided Against Itself Cannot Stand – Lincoln, Douglas and the Germans

After the presidential campaign peace initially returned to American life. The Democratic Party and its new president, Buchanan, appeared to have the rudder solidly in hand, and many people came to think that the better-organized, more experienced party had properly won the presidency. In his inaugural address, traditionally given on 4 March of the year following the election, Buchanan declared he had no intention of seeking reelection. Even his opponents could not accuse him of a self-seeking desire for power, because the one-term principle was thought by many to guarantee against creeping corruption. Buchanan stressed that he had the well being and interests of the country at heart, declaring himself a decided Union man. He confirmed at the same time that the Kansas-Nebraska Bill was "right in principle," adding "that this territory must be added to the Union as a free or slave state depending on how the people decide in the course of adopting a constitution." He thus supported Douglas's principle of popular sovereignty.

Buchanan also touched on two points that particularly concerned the foreign-born. First, he stressed that his government would "put an end to the squandering of public lands" and would take care "that our children will be able to establish homes," clearing the way for a much-needed homestead law. Second, he asserted that "the current naturalization laws and the democratic equality of adoptive citizens and natives [must] be sustained." Most immigrants could not ask for more. Buchanan's government could also claim an additional plus for itself that negated a major propaganda theme of the Republican Party, in that the situation in Kansas was stabilizing. The severe intervention of the new Democratic governor of Kansas Territory, John W. Geary, was already bearing fruit in early 1857, to the regret of the Republican Party.[54]

Republicans knew all too well they lacked three vital things: a national leader behind whom the party could rally and organize itself, a true party platform that was not composed of phrases of opposition and a magical formula of the right combination of voters to secure the party a majority in the next presidential election.[55] Two days after Buchanan's inauguration, the decision of the Supreme Court of the United States in the case of the slave Dred Scott gave the Republican Party the chance to define itself more clearly than had previously been the case.

Dred Scott was born in a territory of the United States where slavery did not legally exist, his mother having been taken into this territory by her owner. Scott, together with his wife, had lived with the approval of his master in territory where, according to the Missouri Compromise, slavery was banished "forever." According to the views of many, residence in a free state alone made him free. But the lawyers of his owner opposed this, declaring that "the ban on slavery in that territory by the federal central power was contrary to the Constitution, hence null and void."[56] The court agreed with defendant's counsel and declared that the Constitution expressly protected property, including slaves, even when it was moved to another territory. The court's decision also stressed that Congress had no power to limit the right of property legislatively. In the wider sense, this ruling hid within it the interpretation that Congress had no right to determine whether slavery should be introduced or banned in the territories. Slaves could be taken wherever they were not banned by positive legislation. In keeping with these findings, the ruling concluded by rejecting the legality of the Missouri

Compromise and declaring it unconstitutional.

Grounds for criticizing this decision were obvious. Clearly the ruling must be seen as not just a juridical, but also a political act. The decision of the Supreme Court to declare the Missouri Compromise unconstitutional struck the Republican Party at the core of its self-perception. The party had condemned the suspension of the Missouri Compromise in both state and national conventions in 1856 and had demanded its restoration. In addition there was a moral aspect of the ruling that would only increase with time, namely, the express definition of slaves as property. The introduction of the moral aspect of slavery into a political discussion hitherto dominated by pragmatism altered the climate of conflict. This change would first become palpable in the 1858 speeches of Lincoln.

Because there was a clear majority of free-state men in Kansas, the Southern wing of the Democratic Party sought to use President Buchanan to obtain congressional recognition of what was called the Lecompton Constitution. This document, which anticipated Kansas's admission as a slave state, was a draft produced by a pro-slavery convention in Lecompton, Kansas, at the start of November 1857. The Lecompton Constitution established that residents of the territory could vote only on the question of being with or without slavery, and could not reject the constitution as a whole.[57] This proposal was an expression not of the will of Kansas residents, but rather that of a part of the Buchanan Administration. Douglas saw the Lecompton Constitution as a travesty of his demand for popular sovereignty because documents drafted in this form denied the possibility of the majority of the electors at the ballot box to vote for their own constitution. Douglas, who had received a commitment from Buchanan that there would be a fair popular referendum over the future constitution of Kansas, raged at the betrayal and felt that he had been outmaneuvered. At the head of a small group of Democrats aided by Republicans, he sought to hinder the adoption of the Lecompton Constitution in the Senate. His struggle brought him high approval among Republicans, many of whom thought they were now fighting for a common cause. There were even attempts to draw Douglas into the Republican camp, but without success.

Douglas felt he could not afford to miss this opportunity to campaign for German votes, as well, as he intended to run for the Senate in the forthcoming Illinois elections. He began with a visit to his old friend, Francis A. Hoffmann, and had his anti-Lecompton speech translated into German, distributing more than three thousand copies. Even the *Belleviller Zeitung* showed itself favorable to his consistency in defending popular sovereignty, praising him in December 1856 after his Senate speech. Heinrich Börnstein and Carl Bernays of the *Anzeiger des Westens* in St. Louis promoted Douglas as a new, common anti-slavery man. Horace Greeley, powerful publisher of the New York *Tribune*, supported Douglas as the new fusion candidate of the Republican Party. Douglas' peculiar position, with Republican support and some Northern Democrats on one side, and hostile Southern and Administration Democrats on the other, would give the upcoming senatorial campaign in Illinois special significance. For that reason the New York *Tribune* commented in August 1858, "Perhaps no local contest in this country ever excited so general or so profound an interest as that now raging in Illinois."[58]

Members of the Republican Party in Illinois saw themselves confronted with the alternative of either taking Douglas's side and giving up their autonomy, or giving their own party a more distinct profile with a platform that was clearly distanced from Douglas's positions. The decision was obvious to Gustav Körner and Friedrich Hecker. Körner could not return to the Democratic camp, and in April 1858 he decided to support Abraham Lincoln as the chief representative of the party in Illinois. Lincoln had been the most engaged organizer of the Republican Party in the presidential election of 1856. Hecker likewise endorsed him, since he could not overcome his personal dislike for Douglas. Seeing Douglas accept the Dred Scott Decision, he presumed that Douglas would remain bound by popular sovereignty on all decisions of this sort, and accept the unconstitutionality of the Missouri Compromise. This was an injury to the most promoted goal of the Republican Party, the Missouri Compromise's restoration.

At the Illinois state convention of the Republican Party in Springfield on 16 July, it was "resolved, that Abraham Lincoln is the first and only choice of Republicans in Illinois for United States Senator and successor to Stephen A. Douglas." Republicans had sent delegates from 95 counties. Among more than 1400 delegates there were about a hundred Germans. Körner was elected president of the assembly. Caspar Butz from Chicago, Hecker's old Algerian acquaintance and political party comrade, was nominated as a representative of the 57th District for the Illinois Legislature. Naturally Hecker actively supported Butz's nomination, and he did not fail to give the audience at an election rally in Chicago his testimony, "from years of friendship," that Butz "has always stood true and consistently loyal and immutable for the cause of the people and liberty, … and that in him Chicago will have that rarity, a conscientious, an honorable man in the legislature." It was at the Springfield convention this same Abraham Lincoln presented his famous "House Divided" speech, with Hecker in the audience.

> A house divided against itself cannot stand. I believe this government
> cannot endure, permanently half *slave* and half free. I do not expect the
> Union to be dissolved – I do not expect the house to *fall* – but I *do* expect
> it will cease to be divided. It will become *all* one thing, or *all* the other.
> Either the *opponents* of slavery, will arrest the further spread of it, and
> place it where the public mind shall rest in the belief that it is in course
> of ultimate extinction; or its *advocates* will push it forward, till it become
> alike lawful in *all* the States, old as well as new – *North* as well as
> *South*.[59]

Lincoln's speech marked the beginning of the senatorial campaign in
Illinois. The two combatants, Lincoln and Douglas, appeared in seven
mutual debates, confronting each other directly and making speeches in
turn. Lincoln's intention had already been clear in his "House Divided"
speech to make distinguish between Douglas and the Republicans, mini-
mizing as much as possible Douglas's opposition to the Lecompton
Constitution, which had won him so much credit. "Lincoln is a talented
man," wrote the *Belleviller Zeitung*, which reprinted his speech in full in
German translation.

> One of the best and sharpest speakers in the state and hence Mr.
> Douglas's most dangerous opponent ... This is no ordinary stump
> speech but rather a well-developed address with razor-sharp logic such
> that a talented politician and statesman like Lincoln can give. We rec-
> ommend it to the close examination of readers.[60]

In this election the choice between Douglas and Lincoln went far
beyond the usual measure of political pragmatism. Douglas held that the
introduction of a moral argument against slavery into the political debate
was questionable and wrong. For him the preservation of the Union was a
much more central concern than slavery. He viewed slavery as a matter of
local significance whose resolution could be decided only on the local level.
For him popular sovereignty was the only viable solution; the decision was
left to the residents, because they had to live with the result. Douglas
believed his own position to be national, and by no means pro-slavery.
Slavery did not disturb him morally; it disturbed him because it disrupted
the Union. It was precisely his pragmatic position on everyday politics, and

his desire not to endanger the Union, that caused him to exclude the moral question entirely. In response to Lincoln's objection that slavery had been constitutionally abolished in many states, Douglas answered that slavery had usually been abolished in those states where it had been shown to be economically inefficient. Yet by underestimating the national reaction to the moral dimension of the slavery question, Douglas sowed "the seeds of his own political repudiation, for he satisfied neither those who regarded slavery as immoral and desired its restriction, nor those who looked on slavery as a good and sought to guarantee its expansion."[61]

Douglas's conscious indifference to the moral aspect of slavery offered Lincoln a fulcrum for distinguishing between Douglas's position and his own, which he declared to be the Republican position. He needed to establish this distance from Douglas precisely because they differed hardly at all on other matters. Lincoln supported the same principles as Douglas concerning local self-government. In his "House Divided" speech Lincoln therefore repeated that sentence from Douglas's anti-Lecompton speech in the Senate that gave proof of Douglas' neutrality on the moral question of slavery. But he gave it another accent by taking it out of its context. Douglas had declared in the Senate on 9 December 1857:

> If Kansas wants a slave-State constitution she has a right to it, if she wants a free state constitution she has a right to it. It is none of my business which way the slavery clause is decided. *I don't care whether it is voted down or voted up.*[62]

Republicans concentrated on the sentence, "I don't care," although it was clear that Douglas was speaking here only in terms of the slavery clause in the Lecompton Constitution. He was declaring that his opposition did not rest on this single clause, but that he was opposed to the whole constitution, because it did not even approximately represent the will of the people, whether the slavery clause was adopted or declined. Despite this, Fehrenbacher writes, Lincoln believed "that the phrase was an accurate summary of popular sovereignty,"[63] at least as far as Douglas grasped it.

Lincoln's argumentation was elegant and very attractive to men such as Hecker, who was used to arguing in moral terms, as will be shown more completely elsewhere. This was because Lincoln started with the presumption that there were questions on which no one could take a neutral position. Lincoln suggested that Douglas's moral ambiguity not only permitted the further survival of slavery, but actually made its expansion possible.

Douglas's assertion that public politics had to exclude moral questions would already have given citizens this impression. Under such a philosophy, Lincoln argued, there was in the end no reason to oppose slavery, because personal moral judgments in particular could not be applied. This lulling to sleep of public opinion eliminated the only thing that could prevent the expansion of slavery. Douglas's indifference was thus seen by Lincoln to be an attack on public opinion. Because Lincoln believed that there could be no neutral position on this question, he interpreted Douglas's declaration as a pro- slavery statement. Douglas's denial of any moral aspect of slavery created an atmosphere, as Lincoln had declared already in Springfield,[64] in which it would be increasingly easy for the Supreme Court to render a second Dred Scott Decision. And once Douglas had persuaded people that slavery was not morally wrong, there would no longer be any reason to ban it.

Lincoln's coherent understanding of the Declaration of Independence and the equality of all persons stated there could never admit the concept of slaves as property. If slaves were human beings, they must participate in those basic rights that their definition as human beings granted them, whatever other rights were granted or withheld from them. Lincoln's adherence to these assumptions was bound up with another presumption that was consistent with Hecker's own, namely "that there is a natural right to improve one's own condition." The immorality of slavery lay for Lincoln in its contradiction of this right. Lincoln was one of those who saw as the basis of the prosperity of the United States the concept that everyone had the opportunity to make his own happiness. For Lincoln, Jefferson's ideal of equality was joined to the concept of equal opportunity for economic advancement. If Southerners pointed at the wageworkers of the North and argued that their own slaves were better cared for, it was precisely this possibility for workers in the North to rise into independence that distinguished them clearly from slaves. "[T]he general rule is otherwise … the poor, honest, industrious, and resolute man raises himself, that he may work on his own account, and hire somebody else." This process, Lincoln declared in a speech in Cincinnati, "is that improvement in condition that is intended to be secured by those institutions under which we live, is the great principle for which this government was really formed." Lincoln, like Hecker in 1856, saw the interdependence of black and white rights, and he was convinced that the refusal of particular rights for colored people would, in the long run, endanger the protection of white rights. He also stressed the negative influence of becoming accustomed to bad morals. The German-

American press saw Lincoln's appeal to the Declaration of Independence to be his special argument.[65]

In order to be successful the Republican Party needed to win not only German votes but also the "Fillmore votes" from 1856. Most of these Fillmore supporters, whose American Party had dissolved after the defeat, were against slavery but had kept a distance from the Republicans, whom they viewed as too radical. A further complication was that some of them continued to look positively on Know-Nothing principles. Lincoln was confronted with a dilemma. He needed these votes, which came primarily from the counties of central Illinois, because they could serve as the deciding factor in the state legislature's selection of a senator. In 1856, however, liberalized naturalization laws had been a Republican Party platform, to the distress of conservative Whigs. In 1858 Lincoln had to backpedal and market himself to these conservative Whigs as a conservative Unionist, keeping himself from seeming too radical an abolitionist.[66]

Some Germans reacted negatively to attempts by the Republican Party to make concessions to "old line Whigs" or, even worse, the Know-Nothings. Upset, Hecker wrote a letter to Elihu Washburne making clear to the Republican congressman the catastrophic results that promoting such a fusion would have among the Germans of the party. All of the German-language newspapers, claimed Hecker, would promote boycotting the election if the Republican ticket rested on a fusion with the American Party, which was tainted by the Know-Nothings. That was the last thing that the party needed, because without German votes it did not have a chance. Hecker's analysis of the attitude of the German-American press was correct. Articles with titles such as "The Position of the Germans to the Parties" in the *Belleviller Zeitung* described the Germans' dilemma. Editors of Republican papers tried to point out "that nativism is just as strong in the Republican Party as in the so-called Democratic," and thus was a problem of all parties; Germans therefore had no alternative but to adhere to the Republican Party in spite of nativism. It represented German interests at least in part, and "lacking an even better party, that is, a party pursuing our goals even more directly and practically, the Republican Party is our means to an end, nothing else."[67] At the same time newspapers left no doubt that they would show their backs to the Republican Party as soon as it openly professed nativism.

Madison and St. Clair counties, which together supplied only 6 of the total of 100 members of the legislature in Springfield, were strongly contested districts due to the nearly even participation of Germans and Whigs.

Lincoln planned to use Hecker in some undecided districts and wrote to Gustav Körner for that purpose.

> I have just been called on by one of our german republicans here, to ascertain if Mr. Hecker could not be prevailed on to visit this region, and address the germans, at this place, and a few others at least. Please ascertain & write me. He would, of course, have to be paid something. Find out from him how much.

Gustav Körner did not seem very interested in using Hecker in central Illinois, where he would find a public different from that in his home county of St. Clair. On the contrary, Körner thought that Hecker did more harm than good with his polemical rhetoric. Körner replied that Hecker could only reinforce those who were already convinced, but that he could not win over political opponents.

> But, and this is strictly between ourselves, I am not inclined to think that his presence will do much good. At least, this is my experience. While well calculated to animate friends, he cannot conciliate opponents, and amongst the Catholics and even orthodox protestants he is considered as the very anti-Christ. We lost more by his exertions in the adjoining counties, where they only knew him by reputation, than we gained. In St. Clair, where his noble personal character was known, it was otherwise.[68]

Lincoln accepted Körner's rejoinder and conceded that he had heard of some problems. "Many Germans are anxious to have Mr. Hecker come," he wrote to Körner, adding, "but I suppose your judgment is best. I write this mostly because I learn we are in great danger in Madison. It is said half the Americans are going for Douglas; and that slam will ruin us, if not counteracted."[69] But as likelihood of Lincoln's defeat increased, the campaign could not do without the red-haired anti-Christ. Elihu Washburne, a loyal friend of Lincoln and a solid Republican congressman, wanted Hecker to commit at once to several speeches. Washburne had taken Hecker's complaints about the Know-Nothing drift of the Republicans seriously, and he obviously never shared any of Lincoln's or Körner's fears. On the contrary, in one letter he assured Hecker that a hearty reception was being prepared for him, and that Germans from all parts of the district would come in.[70]

As planned, Hecker gave a speech in Chicago on 25 October 1858 lasting over two and a half hours, which the *Illinois Staatszeitung* could only publish in excerpts two days later due to its enormous length. "We are of the opinion," the introduction of the newspaper read,

> that Hecker's speech lasting two and a half hours on Monday evening was the most trenchant and effective speech this "farmer from southern Illinois" ever gave in the United States. We have seldom seen such an energetic translation of American politics into the language of European feeling, of pure humanity of the old fatherland, displayed before us. Hecker often reminds us of [Ulrich von] Hutten.

This praise was nothing more than election propaganda, of course; the editors of the *Illinois Staatszeitung* were among Hecker's good friends. Along with Georg Schneider, Caspar Butz provided many partisan articles. What was described by Hecker's two friends as "such an energetic translation of American politics into the language of European feeling" was for long stretches nothing but a political assault on Douglas and his dreadful "assassination and crime." Hecker, for example, had "studied him in the congressional debates, I pursued him on his journeys as if after a hunted animal that I want to kill." And behold, he had discovered that it was all a rotten game, that Douglas had not stood "for a single day at the side of the free people" but had always been nothing but "the servile toady of the most prideful aristocracy of the entire earth."

Because Hecker was aware of Douglas's revived popularity, he was as concerned as Lincoln about reducing the attractiveness of the "Little Giant." In his speech Hecker sought to minimize Douglas's opposition to the Lecompton Constitution by stressing the similarities between Douglas and Buchanan: "Both of them endorse the Dred Scott decision, and that is enough." Douglas likewise became the personification of the conspiracy theory. Hecker asserted that Douglas had planned everything, step by step, all the way to the Kansas-Nebraska Bill. "*But of all his tricks, this was the greatest scoundrel act he had ever brought to pass.*" One could expect nothing better of someone who was, after all, a slaveholder in Mississippi, as Hecker falsely accused him; it could not be in the interests of such a man to declare the territories free of slaves.

> Now [Douglas] comes and praises himself for his opposition to the Lecompton Swindle, with his defense of "popular sovereignty." Where did Douglas ever respect this "popular sovereignty"? As the fruits

grew on the poisoned tree of the Nebraska Bill, as the border ruffians appeared with knife and pistol at the first elections in the region and imposed a border-ruffian legislature on the people, did Douglas ever protest these unvirtuous doings? Oh, God help us. He merely said coldly, "I don't care a bit whether slavery is voted *in* or voted *out*."

Although the troubles in Kansas were long past, Hecker obviously thought their impact was still great enough to be rhetorically exploited. Douglas and "Bleeding Kansas" belonged together, Hecker suggested in his speech. One would have expected from an earnest and concerned representative, certainly from the "chairman of the Territorial Committee," that he would energetically oppose such a "border-ruffian assembly, this convention with its cheats" arisen from "blood and violence," as Hecker described the Lecompton legislature.

Not so Douglas. He said, "These border ruffians do not concern me. I oppose the Lecompton Constitution not for this reason, but for another." He wants to achieve reelection with his anti-Lecomptonism. ... When the border ruffians came over, one would think that the great inventor of popular sovereignty would declare himself against them. "But no," Douglas declares, "no harm can come to the border ruffians; that is popular sovereignty."

Hecker recalled that the governors of territories continued to be named by the president. He stressed that speaking against slavery had become an unconstitutional activity through the Dred Scott decision, and that was what Douglas' popular sovereignty looked like now. In conclusion the Latin Farmer from Summerfield drew, as the commentary of the *Staatszeitung* declared, "a striking parallel between the times of Tiberius and our own." According to the *Illinois Staatszeitung*, his conclusion was

among the most beautiful that we have ever heard in political speeches, the comparison of Tiberius, who ruined the best Romans in the name of the Roman Republic, with Douglas, who deals a fatal blow at liberty and popular sovereignty in the innocent garb of "popular sovereignty," was as rich in pathos as it was annihilating for him to whom the comparison was applied.

That was also the opinion of Hecker's friends, who could not deny his impact. Once more the rhetoric of ancient republicanism was shown to be generally known and familiar. Hecker's republicanism was the republicanism of many emigrated Forty-Eighters, who had grown up with the same education.

It is amazing that Hecker did not adopt and elaborate on Lincoln's moral argument. He regarded the Declaration of Independence and the egalitarian principle declared there to be his holiest principle. He did make brief mention in Chicago of the enlightened eighteenth century and the "esteemed abolitionists" Jefferson, Washington, Madison, Monroe, Patrick Henry "and the other great men of the revolution." On the whole, however, he remained true to his argumentative strategy of 1856. Other than his polemic against Douglas, Hecker devoted the most time to, and placed the most emphasis on, the argument for free white labor, not any concept of equality. He discussed the negative impact of slavery on the situation of the white population, and the emancipation of the white class, rather than the colored people remained central.

In the only high moral moment in his discussion of slavery, Hecker borrowed the economic perception of the right to rise that Lincoln had derived from the inalienable rights of the Declaration of Independence. Even in Chicago, Hecker was not about to omit an economic and social comparison between the Southern and Northern states. "The speaker," the commentary summarized Hecker's arguments,

> placed the joyful comfort of the farmer and craftsman in the free states in contrast to the oppressed nature and life of the *free whites* in the slave states. And these slaveholders, these Imperial barons of the South, who place the *white worker* lower than their slaves, are Douglas's friends and supporters.

In his speech, however, Hecker showed "the dreadful consequences that must arise from the concentration and restriction of *Northern population*," when he "warned of the *European proletariat*" as an example. In other words, slavery was particularly significant for its impact on free white labor. Even when Hecker came to speak of the "dreadful and demoralizing influences that the existence of slavery, life among and next to it would exercise *on the white man of the North*,"[71] and on the connection between diligent work and the recognition of labor, he showed that he was more obligated to concepts of free labor than to any principled distinction of right or wrong. His explication of the peril to "white morals" was central to his own model of civic virtue. For that reason Hecker remained tied to the economic and political interests of German-American settlers more strongly than was Lincoln.

Hecker traveled from Chicago to Galena, where he gave what was surely a similar speech on 27 October. The next day he spoke at Freeport, where a debate between Lincoln and Douglas had taken place on 27 August. Still, his efforts would have as little success as they did in 1856. After the campaign the Democrats had the majority in this assembly, and Douglas was confirmed in his office as United States Senator with 54 votes to 41 (some Republicans were absent from the voting). According to James Bergquist, the Republicans could have won more German votes if they had not made so many concessions to the nativists. Gustav Körner saw the situation in a similar way. After the election he told Lincoln he considered rapprochement with the nativists to be the greatest error the Republican Party had made, whether or not they reached a majority.[72]

This defeat caused leading Republicans to listen to German-American concens more carefully. Whatever is asserted about the participation of Germans in the election of Lincoln in 1860, historians agree that it was the loud protests of Germans within the Republican Party that prevented it from drifting to the nativist side. Men such as Körner, Hecker and Schurz, who made his first campaign tour in northern Illinois in 1858, contributed to this.[73]

Still, Hecker was deeply disappointed by the results of the senatorial election, as was Elihu Washburne. Washburne sought to lift Hecker's spirits:

> your influence on your … german friends was greater than any of us had a right to anticipate. The german vote in our County gave the republican a splendid victory as you saw it has been followed up this spring in Galena by the election of a Republican mayor and eight out of ten aldermen, a result … precedent for our city … . In 1860, I tell you Hecker, the final struggle between liberty and slavery in this country is to be faught and how many hopes centre on your countrymen. Their influence and their votes must be … in that great struggle on the side of human freedom – it cannot[,] it must not be … on the side of bondage.[74]

Washburne was one of those Republicans who clearly distanced himself from nativist tendencies and hoped for the support of Germans, or at least Protestant Germans. Because he could not count on the support of German Catholics, Washburne did not feel threatened by Hecker's anticlerical rhetoric. But Washburne was not able to obtain Hecker's commitment to active participation in the upcoming presidential campaign of 1860. Washburne also could not have known that there was already a discussion among Germans about possible 1860 candidates that gave Washburne himself some chance at the candidacy. At least Georg Schneider and Hecker agreed that Washburne – and not Lincoln – who would be a good candidate for president, and Gustav Körner could be nominated for a second term as lieutenant governor. "As far as my view on Washburne and Körner," Hecker wrote to Goerg Schneider in May, 1859,

> I am completely in agreement with you about the choice of persons. Lincoln has lost so often that this could be done with success. Wheat will not grow for anyone in Egypt, and on Washburne's behalf you can say that he not only conquered the old Hunker castle of Galena, but that he cannot be outbid by anyone in the entire northwest corner. He also has the right manners to win people. His conduct is friendly, cordial without slipping into the common.

Hecker promised Schneider to commit himself to Washburne and Körner, but he was simply not ready to participate in the campaign to any larger extent. There was "something depressing in the manner in which politics is practiced here; it is unfortunately cold calculation, no noble enthusiasm. One could easily register the whole of politics in the book of debit and credit."[75]

Not just Schneider and Hecker thought about Republican presidential candidates acceptable to the Germans. As early as 1859 two other candidates emerged: Edward Bates from Missouri and William H. Seward from New York. A prominent politician from Missouri, Bates was favored by the Germans there, with the exception of Carl Dänzer, who had founded the influential *Westliche Post* in St. Louis in 1857. Bates's problem was that he had presided over the American Party Convention in 1856 that nominated Millard Fillmore, and maintained contacts with known nativists. Bates had also showed himself reluctant when called upon to become a convinced Republican. As a result he was unacceptable to many Germans. In addition, the strong wing of radical abolitionists hated him.[76] He wanted to resolve the slavery question over the long term through colonization, and he believed that the moral question of slavery ought to be restricted to the territories and was essentially a state problem.

The Germans' favorite candidate was Seward, who had consistently pursued Free-Soil politics since the early 1850s and was a decided opponent of slavery. As early as August 1859 the *Belleviller Zeitung* demanded the preparation of a "German Republican Manifesto" that would name Seward as the favored presidential candidate clearly and unmistakably.[77] Neither Seward nor Bates could unite the entire Republican Party behind him, however. While Bates was too conservative, Seward appeared too radical to the nativist wing of the Republicans.

In order to unite on a single candidate and plan informally for a clear anti-nativist plank in the national platform, some Germans from the East Coast and the Midwest gathered in the Deutsches Haus in Chicago on 14 May 1860, two days before the official national convention of the Republican Party. They were responding to an invitation from the Republican Committee of New York for a preparatory caucus. Because Hecker did not participate in this meeting and was not a delegate to the convention, the results of that meeting will be briefly summarized. Differences between Germans of the East and the West emerged, over both expectations for the Republican platform and the choice of a presidential candidate. The resolutions that were passed could only be presented at the national convention by Gustav Körner, Carl Schurz or Carl Bernays, who were delegates and belonged to the platform committee. Their influence was reflected in the passage of a platform whose thirteenth article promised protection for a homestead law, and whose fourteenth article declared "that the national Republican Party is opposed to any change in the naturalization law." German members expressed satisfaction with this, and nativists were disappointed. German convention participants could not exercise much influence over the choice of a presidential candidate. The nomination of Lincoln, a man who was moderate enough to be acceptable to the more radical forces and conservative enough to convince the Whigs, did not come from the majority of the German participants. To be sure, Gustav Körner supported Lincoln's election from the beginning. But Schurz had worked as hard for the nomination of Seward. As Eric Foner tellingly quotes a contemporary, Lincoln was "the second choice of everybody."[78] This also appeared to be the view of the overwhelming number of German-American Republican newspapers.

The Republicans had learned from their experiences in the previous campaign, and this time they went to work better organized. On 23 June 1860 Hecker received a message from the newly organized Republican State Central Committee in Chicago,[79] to which Gustav Körner belonged. Hecker was called upon to assist actively. Perhaps it was this message, or perhaps it was private pressure from Schneider, Butz, Körner or Schurz that compelled him to make some election tours. This central committee call was a circular sent to known, loyal party members in Illinois. It demanded the cooperation of all Republican clubs and committees in the state with the new umbrella association. For this reason the circular included a form on which the names and addresses of all members of the committee or club were to be entered and returned to Chicago. Each recipient was also exhorted "as a zealous and working Republican" to promote the creation of a committee or club where none existed and to report on the development of this club from time to time. Above all, the central committee was interested in receiving nominations for every office, from the "basis," from that of president of the United States (although this was naturally already settled for the current campaign) down to sheriff and postmaster in one's own town. Only "the best and strongest men" should be put forward.

Körner and Hecker made campaign appearances in St. Clair, Madison and other nearby counties and made many tours into the critical areas of German settlement around Springfield in central Illinois. There was a great Republican rally in Belleville on 28 July 1860 that quickly took on the character of a popular festival, lasting all day and into the night. The chief speakers of the day were Francis P. Blair, Jr., from St. Louis, who spoke to the public in English, and Carl Schurz, who gave his speech in German. Hecker, who was named one of the vice presidents on the morning of the rally, originally did not wish to speak, but the stormy demands of the crowd, numbering between six and eight thousand, led him to say a few words after a torchlit procession that evening. Carl Schurz closed the rally in both English and German. Schurz, who rose to become the most important German speaker in this campaign, orated along with Abraham Lincoln in Springfield a few days later. In the middle of September Hecker gave an address in the St. Louis Opera House.[80]

Lincoln won the election, his victory resting on the support of earlier Fillmore votes in the uncertain states of Pennsylvania, Illinois and Indiana. Recent research paying closer attention to local ethnic composition has revised earlier investigations, which asserted that it was German votes in particular that made Lincoln's election possible. It must in fact be presumed that Lincoln could have won the election even without his doubtless large German majority in 1860. Still, some general statements can be made about his election and his relationship to the German voters.

"The significance of the German vote lay not so much in its actual as in its supposed importance," Marlin Tucker writes, proposing that the assumption that Lincoln was elected due to a high German vote arose from the large participation of German speakers in the campaign, for between 80 and 100 Thirtyer and Forty-Eighter speakers are estimated to have been involved. In 1860 Hecker was rather the exception in his hesitation. Schurz in particular traveled for months through the uncertain states making election speeches. In the same way Georg Schneider, Caspar Butz and Hermann Kreismann worked in northern Illinois. Pastor Francis A. Hoffmann, this time successfully nominated and finally elected as lieutenant governor, had Chicago well in hand. Börnstein and Bernays, converted at last to Lincoln, covered the St. Louis region. Theodor Canisius, editor of the *Illinois Staatsanzeiger* which has been purchased by Lincoln, courted the favor of Germans in the region around Springfield. The fact that these men, as Tucker writes, "willingly played an American game *as Americans* by American rules and for American prizes" was shown later, when Lincoln handed out offices. None came away empty-handed.[81]

On the whole the organizational efforts of the Republican Party in 1860 meant that Democratic slurs against them as a nativist party slowly lost their effect. Further, the presidential candidate fielded by the Southern Democrats, John C. Breckinridge, Buchanan's vice president, was no charismatic opponent. The rhetorical strategy of the Republicans to appeal to the self-interest of free workers and settlers through their free-labor and Free-Soil ideology, of which Hecker was a good example, appears to have born fruit among the new immigrants of the 1850s. These newcomers were voting for the first time in 1860 and had formed no party loyalty. Perhaps, as the American historian Eric Foner comments, Illinois was in fact the only state whose electoral conduct supported the traditional claim of a great German influence on Lincoln's election.[82] But the argument of a unified American German vote for Lincoln is a fiction. German communities were complex entities made up of varied and, in part, hostile interest groups. The temporary unity of Germans in matters of temperance or nativism usually dissolved once the goal was achieved. The religious background of communities, the local origin in the old homeland, and the length of residency in the United States all influenced the voting attitude of not only the Germans, but other immigrant groups as well. Moreover, Germans were in the minority in almost all states as far as voting numbers were concerned. In Illinois their number was only a sixth of the total population, and in Wisconsin only an eighth. Through their politically experienced speakers and newspaper editors, this immigrant group was able to get a hearing. The problem was that the votes of the Germans showed no direct agreement with the political ambitions of their speakers.

1 On the following, see particularly William E. Gienapp, *The Origins of the Republican Party 1852-1856* (New York; Oxford, 1987); Eric Foner, *Free Soil, Free Labor, Free Men. The Ideology of the Republican Party before the Civil War* (New York, 1970); Stephen L. Hansen, *The Making of the Third Party System: Voters and Parties in Illinois, 1850-1876* (Ann Arbor, Mich.,1980); Victor B. Howard, "The Illinois Republican Party," *JISHS* part 1, 64 (Summer, 1971), 125-60, part 1, 64/3 (Fall, 1971), 285-311; Walter Kamphoefner, "St. Louis Germans and the Republican Party, 1848-1860," *Mid-America* 57 (April, 1975), 69-88; F. I. Herriott, "The Germans of Chicago and Stephen A. Douglas in 1854," *DAG* (1912) 381-404.

2 Gienapp, *Origins*, 5.

3 On the following, see particularly Levine, *Spirit*, 152-54. James Malin, "The Motives of Stephen A. Douglas in the Organization of the Nebraska Territory: A Letter Dated Dec. 17, 1853," *Kansas Historical Quarterly* 19 (November 1951), 352, cited by Levine, *The Spirit*, 153. Cf. on this Hans Rudolf Guggisberg, *Geschichte der USA*, 2 vols. (Stuttgart, 1975-76), here vol. 1, 108; Willi Paul Adams, ed., *Die Vereinigten Staaten von Amerika* (Frankfurt am Main, 1977), 100-1; Tucker, *Political Leadership*, 144-46.

4 Foner, *Free Soil*, 124-26. Levine, *Spirit*, 153.

5 The call is printed in Herriott, *The Germans*, 389-90. See Guggisberg, *Geschichte der USA*, vol. 1, 106. Foner, *Free Soil*, 29. A corresponding law was passed with Republican support in 1862. *National Era*, 24 January 1854.

6 Tucker, *Political Leadership*,147; Zucker, *Forty-Eighters*, 61-62; Bergquist, *Political Attitudes*, 139. Zucker, *Forty-Eighters*, 305, 339-40; Ruetenik, *Deutsche Vorkämpfer*, 318-20. *DAG* 7 (1907) 65 ff. and *DAG* 12 (1912) 516ff.; Arthur Cole, *The Era of the Civil War*, 30, 123, 143 ff. A protest note signed by several hundred Germans was delivered to Lieutenant Governor Gustav Körner on 17 February 1854; see Tucker, *Political Leadership*, 148 based on a report of the *Chicago Daily Democratic Press*, 20 February 1854.

7 Levine, *Spirit*, 155-56; Tucker, *Political Leadership*, 148-49; Herriott, *Germans*, 390-91. Tucker, *Political Leadership*, 148-49. Bergquist, *Political Attitudes*, 141, 145.

8 Herriott, *Germans*, 396-97.

9 Edward Schläger, together with Bernhard Domschke and Philip Wagner (both Forty-Eighters, the latter chairman of the German Revolutionary Society in Boston), edited the *Neu England Zeitung*. Levine, *The Spirit*, 202-5; Zucker, *The Forty-Eighters*, 337. Herriott, *The Germans*, 393 ff. The resolution is printed ibid., 396-97.

10 Bruncken, "German Political Refugees," part 2, 44.

11 Chicago was the first place in Illinois to show vehement reaction to the Nebraska Bill, among both Germans and Americans, see Howard, "Illinois Republican Party," part 1, 126-27. Carl Wittke, *The German Language Press in America* (Lexington, 1957), 139; also Bruncken, "German Political Refugees," part 2, 45; also Tucker, *Political Leadership*, 152, 157. *BZ*, weekly, 2 March 1854. See Foner, *Politics*, 44-46. Gienapp, *Origins*, 6.

12 See Bruncken, "German Political Refugees," part 2, 45.

13 *BZ*, weekly, 1 June 1854. Bergquist, *Political Attitudes*, 81. Tucker, *Political Attitudes*, 164. Foner, *Free Soil*, 231; "The pro-slavery attitudes of Boston's Irish was notorious"; also Kamphoefner, "St. Louis Germans," 84-86. Bergquist, *Political Attitudes*, 59 ff., 66-68, 84. I have adopted "shrill anticlericalism" from Kamphoefner in referring particularly to Börnstein, but which can easily

be applied to other Forty-Eighters, see Kamphoefner, "St. Louis Germans," 84-86.

[14] For the Know-Nothing movement in Illinois, see Cole, *Era of the Civil War*, 136-41; and the "classic" Fehrenbacher, *Prelude to Greatness*, chapter 1; Eric Foner, *Free Soil*, chapter 7; Gienapp, *Origins*, 92-102; Tucker, *Political Leadership*, 164-65; Bruncken, "German Political Refugees," 47-48; there is an outstanding collection of documents in Edith Abbott, *Historical Aspects of the Immigration Problem, Selected Documents* (Chicago, 1926), here Section V, "Public Opinion and the Immigrants," 697-859. Illinois doubled its population between 1850 and 1860 from 851,470 to 1,711,951 residents, see Tucker, "Political Leadership," 165.

[15] Bergquist, *Political Attitudes*, 66-67. Levine, *Spirit*, 188-90. Foner, *Free Soil*, 228.

[16] Levine, *Spirit*, 107, on the nativism of some senators during the 1840s and 1850s. Gienapp, *Origins*, 98; Begquist, *Political Attitudes*, 75-77. Foner, *Free Soil*, 231.

[17] Foner, *Free Soil*, 229-30; Bergquist, *Political Attitudes*, 70-71. Levine, *Spirit*, 107. Gienapp, *The Origins*, 102. *BZ*, weekly, 28 August 1855. The same strategy was followed by such as Heinrich Börnstein's *AW* in St. Louis, which carried just such a call on every front page of the newspaper; see Kamphoefner, "St. Louis Germans," 79.

[18] See Gienapp, *Origins*, 45.

[19] See Tucker, *Political Leadership*, 167-68. Gienapp, *Origins*, 292. Tucker, *Political Leadership*, 168; Bergquist, *Political Attitudes*, 45, 178. See the article on the front page of the *BZ*, 10 April 1855. *BZ*, weekly, 6 March 1855. Issues of the *BZ* dealing with the Know-Nothings, for example, 10 April, 3 June, 24 June and 28 August 1855. See also Tucker, *Political Leadership*, 169; Kamphoefner, "St. Louis Germans," 70; Bergquist, *Political Attitudes*, 181. Foner comes to the same conclusion, *Free Soil*, 227.

[20] Douglas to Sheahan, 14 September 1854 in Robert W. Johannsen, ed., *The Letters of Stephen A. Douglas* (Urbana, 1961), 330. *BZ*, weekly, 25 September 1855. Gienapp, *Origins*, 104-6, 122; on Michigan, see Foner, *Free Soil*, 127-28. Howard, "Illinois Republican Party," part 1, 131, 133 , 135, 146, 147, 153; The same problems appeared in New York.

[21] A meeting in Peoria from 29 to 31 May 1854 was to unite Germans in southern Illinois, but only 17 delegates appeared, although the meeting had been announced in almost all the German-language newspapers, see Bergquist, *Political Attitudes*, 149-51 *BZ*, weekly, 16 October 1854. Münch wrote under the pseudonym "Far West," here in *AW*, St. Louis, 19 August 1854. *ISZ*, 20 September 1854, see Cole, *Era of the Civil War*, 124. Bergquist, *Political Attitudes*, 192-93.

[22] Körner, *Memoirs*, vol. 2, 2; cf. also Gienapp, *Origins*, 290; Bergquist, *Attitudes*, 203; Foner, *Free Soil*, 246.

[23] Gienapp, *Origins*, 288-89; Tucker, *Political Leadership*, 170 ff.; Paul Selby, "The Editorial Convention, February 22, 1856," *McClean County Historical Society Transactions*, 3 (1900), 30-43; idem, "The Editorial Convention of 1856," *JISHS*, 5 (1912), 343-49. American historians are inclined to see this meeting as the actual foundation date of the Republican Party in Illinois; see also Fehrenbacher, *Prelude to Greatness*, 44; Howard, "Illinois Republican Party," part 2, 296-98. Otto R. Kyle, "Mr. Lincoln Steps Out: the Anti-Nebraska Editors' Convention," *Abraham Lincoln Quarterly*, 5/1 (1948), 25-37.

[24] Franz Grimm printed the resolutions in German on 11 March 1856, "Erklärung der Editoren-Convention zu Decatur," *BZ*, weekly, 11 March 1856. Abraham Lincoln at the Decatur Conference, here cited in Zucker, *Forty-Eighters*, 339.

25 As a decided anti-Nebraska man, Trumbull made the switch from the Democrats to the Republicans in 1855; *DAB*, vol. 19 (New York, 1936), 19-20. Charles H. Ray to Lyman Trumbull, 21 March 1856, in Lyman Trumbull Papers, Illinois State Historical Library, cited in Tucker, *Political Leadership*, 171; cf. also Gienapp, *Origins*, 292. Ray calculated that a strong anti-Know-Nothing resolution would draw in "The Germans, English, Protestant Irish, Scotch, and Scandinavian vote – in all about 30,000 – more than double the K. N. strength," Charles Ray to Elihu Washburne, 4 May 1856, in Washburne Papers, Library of Congress, Manuscript Division, see also Foner, *Free Soil*, 246. Gienapp, *Origins*, 292.

26 Gienapp, *Origins*, 294-95; also J. O. Cunningham, "The Bloomington Convention of 1856 and Those Who Participated in It," *Illinois State Historical Society Transactions* (1905), 104-7; Howard, "Illinois Republican Party," part 2, 302-6; Arthur C. Cole, *The Era of the Civil War* (Springfield, 1919), on this 149-50.

27 Hoffmann had to withdraw his nomination because he had not fulfilled the conditions of naturalization. He was renominated in 1860 and could then take the office, see Bergquist, *Political Attitudes*, 207, 211, 226; Foner, *Free Soil*, 246. Tucker, *Political Leadership*, 179; the office of lieutenant governor of Illinois was being temporarily filled in 1856 by John A. Wood from Quincy. See *BZ* for 20 and 27 May 1856. *BV*, 31 May 1856. See Howard, "Illinois Republican Party," part 2, 304.

28 Butz, "Erinnerungen," part 2. Georg Hillgärtner, *Iowa Staatszeitung*, Dubuque, quoted in *BV*, 28 June 1856.

29 *Chicago Daily Democratic Press*, quoted in *Illinois State Journal*, 12 June 1856; the *Illinois State Journal* was the most influential Whig organ in the capital of Springfield, particularly for its later support for Abraham Lincoln.

30 Tucker, *Political Leadership*, 171. Bergquist, *Political Attitudes*, 220.

31 Gienapp, *Origins*, 324, 341, 376, 377. Article from *Neue Zeit* on "Johann Carl Fremont," reprinted in *BZ*, weekly, 8 and 15 July 1856. "Humboldt über Fremont," Alexander von Humboldt to John Charles Frémont, Sans Souci, 7 October 1850, *BZ*, 22 July 1856.

32 Gienapp, *Origins*, 378, n. 10, 379.

33 The financial situation of the young Republican Party was dreadful, Gienapp, *Origins*, 380-81.

34 Gienapp, *Origins*, 379 n. 15. The organizational work of Lincoln and Washburne can be extracted from their correspondence in 1856, see Basler, *Collected Works*, vol. 2, 332 ff. Bergquist, *Political Attitudes*, 228; see also the correspondence between FH and Lincoln in Basler, *Collected Works*, vol. 2, 376. See in general the letters from Elihu Washburne to FH between 1858 and 1881 in FHP, box 2, folder 19, and FH's letters to Washburne in the Washburne Papers, Manuscript Devision, Library of Congress, Washington; Washburne was regarded as extraordinarily friendly to Germans. *BV*, 5 July 1856.

35 See Brentano's letter from Michigan in the *Kalamazoo Telegraph*, 25 July 1856; Wittke, *Refugees*, 206. On Schurz see Josef Schafer, *Carl Schurz: Militant Liberal* (Evansville, 1930), 104-5. On Struve and Brentano, see *BZ*, 5 August 1856: "Gustav Struve und Lorenz Brentano für die republikanische Partei." On Struve in New York, see his introduction to *Diesseits und Jenseits des Oceans*, 1 ff.; on Stallo, see Levine, *Spirit*, 185; in general also chapter 15 ("The Battle for the

German Vote") in Wittke, *Refugees*, 203-20. On the fact that FH was not the only one to return suddenly to the public eye, see *ISZ*, quoted in the *BZ*, weekly, 25 November 1856, on the return of the Forty-Eighters to politics. *BV*, 5 July 1856.

36 FH to Th. Dietsch, Postoffice Lebanon, St. Clair County, Ill., 15 July 1856, FHP, box 4, folder 42; partly published in *BZ*, 5 August 1856; FH to Christian Esselen, Belleville, 7 July 1856, FHP, box 4, folder 42. FH to Charles Söhner, Postoffice Lebanon, St. Clair County, Il. , 25 July 1856, FHP, box 3, folder 38. FH to Christian Esselen, 7 July 1856. Compare FH's letters to his statements on the "Advokatenstand" in Germany.

37 See the announcement in *BZ*, weekly, 29 July 1856; FH's speech is reviewed in *BV*, 9 August 1856. Speech on 9 August 1856, see *BZ*, 19 August 1856. Speech on 11 August 1856, reviewed in the *BZ*, weekly, 19 August 1856. Report of the *BZ*, weekly, 19 August 1856.

38 *BV*, 16 August 1856. On the "vagabond laws," see Schnake, "Deutsche Presse," 108; also Friedrich Münch mentions vagabonds, *BZ*, weekly, 28 October 1856. *Ibid.*, 26 August 1856. Georg Schneider, *ISZ*, quoted in *BZ*, weekly, 26 August 1856.

39 See the letter to the editors of the *St. Clair Tribune* reacting to a false report of his speech on 16 August 1856, no. 27, FHP, box 4, printed in *BZ*, weekly, 2 September 1856. *ISZ*, quoted in *BZ*, weekly, 26 August 1856.

40 Gienapp, *Origins*, 168-69, 299-302, 348-53. Thus newspaper reports spoke of a large number of dead, and the Free-Soiler leader Pomeroy was supposedly lynched along with another person. In fact no one was injured, see Gienapp, *Origins*, 298, also 302, 352. Stephen Emery to Hannibal Hamlin, 27 May in the Hamlin Papers, quoted in ibid., 362; emphasis in the original. *ISZ*, quoted in *BZ*, weekly, 26 August 1856.

41 The Democratic *Chenango American*, 29 May 1856, quoted in Gienapp, *Origins*, 298. *BZ*, weekly, 26 August 1856; emphasis in the text.

42 FH would have press battles in the 1870s with Oswald Ottendörfer, the editor and later owner of the *New Yorker Staatszeitung*. The "Offene Brief an Friedrich Hecker" *New Yorker Staatszeitung*, 21 July 1856, signed with the intitials M. H. B. The rumor of extensive party money was false; see Strack, *Friedrich Heckers Herkunft*, 14, showing the wealth of the father; Josefine Hecker also brought property into the marriage, and the confiscation of the house took place late. It is possible that Josefine Hecker brought money with her to Switzerland; in FH's *Volksfreund* there was an official transfer of the rights to the newspaper and its money; Theodor Mögling officially administered the revolutionary funds, see "An die Leser des Hecker'schen Volksfreundes," *Der Volksfreund*, 22 October 1848, 129-30. The contract of transfer, dated Rheinfelden/Muttenz, 1 September 1848, "Wer gründete den Hecker'schen Volksfreund und Wer hat zunächst das Eigentumsrecht an demselben?" *Der Volksfreund*, 26 October 1848, 136. FH to the *New Yorker Abendzeitung*, 25 July 1856, quoted in *BZ*, 12 August 1856. Abraham Lincoln to FH, Springfield, 14 September 1856, printed in Basler, *Collected Works*, vol. 2, 376. Daniel Hertle reported in 1857 that a lovely new brick house had been built in the place of the old house, see Daniel Hertle to Ludwig Heidenreich, 2 April 1858, Stadtarchiv Speyer, Best. 191-1; see Paul, *Freie Erde*, 24.

43 FH, "Ansprache an die deutsch-amerikanische Bevölkerung der Vereinigten Staaten von Amerika," *BV*, weekly, no. 26, 16 August 1856 (introduction); no. 27, 23 August 1856; no. 28, 30 August 1856; no. 29, 6 September 1856; no. 30, 13 September 1856; no. 31, 20 September 1856; no. 33, 4 October 1856 (conclusion).

44 Rotteck, quoted in *BV*, no. 27, 23 August 1856. Rotteck, *Allgemeine Geschichte*, vol. 8 (Freiburg, 1828), 628 Montesquieu, "Comment les lois de l'esclavage ont du rapport avec la nature du climat," *De l'esprit des lois*, book 15, chapter 1. Thomas Jefferson, *Notes on the State of Virginia*, quoted in "Ansprache," *BV*, no. 28, 30 August 1856. Gienapp, *Origins*, 365. FH, *Erhebung*, 8. On the use of statistics, see Foner, *Free Soil*, 43.

45 Naturally there were radical abolitionists within the party who stressed the moral aspect of slavery and advocated a humane treatment of colored people, but "Welfare of blacks had never been a strong sentiment in the free states," Gienapp, *Origins*, 363. The terms used in FH's "Ansprache" are "intelligent, hard-working, striving," see *BV*, no. 26, 16 August 1856. See most extensively Foner, *Free Soil*, 11 ff.; Gienapp, *Origins*, 356; aso the views of Abraham Lincoln, Gabor S. Borritt, "The Right to Rise," in Cullom Davis et al., ed., *The Public and the Private Lincoln: Contemporary Perspectives* (Carbondale, 1979), 57-70; idem, *Lincoln and the Economics of the American Dream* (Memphis, 1978).

46 See reports from the newspaper pool, *BV*, 11 October 1856. On the New York meeting see Bruncken, "Political Refugees," 52; Herriott, *Germans*, 160; Julius Fröbel, *Ein Lebenslauf. Aufzeichnungen, Erinnerungen und Bekenntnisse*, vol. 1 (Stuttgart, 1891), 556-57; Levine, *Spirit*, 218-19; Friedrich Münch, "Friedrich Hecker," *TWP*, 5 April 1881. Zucker, *Forty-Eighters*, 343-44, 357; Vollmer, "Nachlaß," 380, n. 132; also Manfred Köhler, "'Aus dem Lande des Republikanismus, der Sklavenbefreiung und des Nützlichkeitsprinzips.' New Yorker Briefe des Mainzers Manfred Zitz an Julius Fröbel, 1851-1865. Mit einer Skizze seiner Lebensgeschichte," *Mainzer Zeitschrift*, 84/85 (1989/90), 167-99. Bruncken, "German Political Refugees," part 2, 52; Herriott, *The Germans*, 160. Gustav Struve, *Zwölf Streiter*, 22.

47 English and German versions of his speech in FHP, box 4, folder 42.

48 In the FHP, box 4, folder 42, there is an undated newspaper clipping with speeches by Hecker, Struve and Münch in English and German, see the collaborating reports in the *NYC*, 8 and 10 October 1856; *New York Daily Tribune*, 8 October 1856; *New York Daily Times*, 8 October 1856. Friedrich Münch's speech in German was also printed in the *BZ*, 28 October 1856.

49 Fröbel later distanced himself from the speeches held by him in America in his memoirs, Julius Fröbel, *Ein Lebenslauf*, vol. 1, 556. FH's speech of 11 October 1856 in Philadelphia, FHP, box 4, folder 42.

50 *Belleville Weekly Advocate*, 22 October 1856; see also Basler, *Collected Works*, vol. 2, 379-80.

51 On Körner, see Gienapp, *Origins*, 417.

52 Tucker, *Political Leadership*, 184; only about 20-25 percent of German Catholics voted for the Republican Party, see on this Bergquist, *Political Attitudes*, 238. Gienapp, *Origins*, 426.

53 See "Die 48ger," *ISZ*, quoted in *BZ*, weekly, 25 November 1856.

54 "Die Antrittsrede des Präsidenten Buchanan," *BV*, 6 March 1857. "Circular des republikanischen National-Comités," *BZ*, weekly, 25 August 1859.

55 See the article "Die Republikanische Partei," *Davenport Demokrat*, quoted in *BZ*, 15 May 1858.

56 "Der Dred Scott-Prozeß," *BV*, 6 March 1857; see further articles on this case in *BV*, 20 March 1857 and 3 April 1857.

57 Robert W. Johannsen, ed., *The Lincoln-Douglas Debates of 1858* (Oxford; New York, 1965), 8-11; Tucker, *Political Leadership*, 199; David Zarefsky, *Lincoln, Douglas and Slavery in the Crucible of Public Debate* (Chicago; London, 1993), 17-39; David F. Ericson, *The Shaping of American*

Liberalism: The Debates over Ratification, Nullification and Slavery (Chicago; London, 1993), 117-74. Bergquist, *Political Attitudes*, 247.

[58] Tucker, *Political Leadership*, 201. *BZ*, weekly, 24 December 1857. Zarefsky, *Lincoln*, 180. *New York Tribune*, August, 1858, quoted in Johannsen, *Lincoln-Douglas Debates*, 3.

[59] *BZ*, 20 May 1858. *Illinois State Register*, 12 June 1857, cited in Cole, *The Era*, 155. See more thoroughly below: Hecker's speech in Chicago, *TISZ*, 27 October 1858, FHP, box 4, folder 42. More detail in the printed pamphlet, *Platform der Republikaner von Illinois, niedergelegt in der Republikanischen Staatsconvention, gehalten in Springfield, Illinois, 16. Juni 1858, nebst den Reden der Herren Abraham Lincoln und G. Körner gehalten während der Convention. Gedruckt in der Office der Alton Freien Presse* (Alton, Illinois, 1858), 5. Republican ticket printed in the *TISZ*, 27 October 1858. FH's speech in the Metropolitan Hall in Chicago on 25 October 1858, *ISZ*, 27 October 1858, FHP, box 4, folder 42. Basler, *Collected Works*, vol. 2, 461-69; Johannsen, *Lincoln-Douglas Debates*, 14-21; Herbert Mitgang, ed., *Selected Writings of Abraham Lincoln* (New York, 1992), 62-71. It was distributed in German in the pamphlet mentioned and in German-American newspapers, such as *BZ*, weekly, 8 July 1858. Abraham Lincoln, "House Divided" speech at Springfield, 16 June 1858; quoted here according to Mitgang, *Selected Writings*, 62; emphasis by Lincoln himself, who entered it on correcting the galleys, see Zarefsky, *Lincoln*, 43.

[60] The joint appearances took place in seven election districts where neither Lincoln nor Douglas had made a major speech in some time (Ottawa, 21 August; Freeport, 27 August; Jonesboro, 15 September; Charleston, 18 September; Galesburg, 7 October; Quincy, 13 October; Alton, 15 October); all of these "joint debates" are printed in Johannsen, *Lincoln-Douglas Debates. BZ*, weekly, 8 July 1858.

[61] Douglas's speech in Alton, 15 October 1858, Johannsen, *Lincoln-Douglas Debates*, 299. See also ibid., 7.

[62] Lincoln's speech in Springfield, 16 June 1858, Johannsen, *Lincoln-Douglas Debates*, 16; see also Lincoln's speech in Alton, 15 October 1858. Douglas, Senate speech, 9 December 1857, *Congressional Globe*, 35th Congress, 1st session, 27, part 1, 18; my emphasis.

[63] Fehrenbacher, *Prelude to Greatness*, 181; see precise examination of the "moral argument" in Zarefsky, *Lincoln*, 166-97, here 172.

[64] Lincoln's speech in Springfield, 16 June 1858, in Johannsen, *Lincoln-Douglas Debates*, 17-18.

[65] Zarefsky, *Lincoln*, 176. Lincoln's speech in Cincinnati, Ohio, 17 September 1859, quoted after Basler, *Collected Works*, Supplement, 43-44. Lincoln's speech in Edwardsville, Ill., 17 September 1858, Basler, *Collected Works*, vol. 3, 95. *BZ*, 2 Sepember 1858.

[66] See Zarefsky, *Lincoln*, 46.

[67] FH to Elihu Washburne, Lebanon, St. Clair County, Ill., 26 September 1858, Washburne Papers. "Die Stellung der Deutschen zu den Parteien," *BZ*, weekly, 30 September 1858. Ibid., weekly, 30 September 1858; cf. ibid., 7 October 1858.

[68] Abraham Lincoln to Gustav Körner, Springfield, 15 July 1858, Basler, *Collected Works*, vol. 2, 502. Gustav Körner to Abraham Lincoln, 17 July 1858, Lincoln Manuscripts, Library of Congress, quoted here by Tucker, *Political Leadership*, 218.

[69] Abraham Lincoln to Gustav Körner, Springfield, 25 July 1858, Basler, *Collected Works*, vol. 2, 524.

[70] Further letters in FHP, box 2, folder 19, document how good FH's relationship with

Washburne was. Washburne believed until the end in Lincoln's victory, and so he was deeply disappointed at the result of the election. Washburne's response to FH's letter of 2 October 1858; FHP, box 2, folder 19; this letter also has the invitation to the election rallies where FH was to speak. Elihu Washburne to FH, Galena, Illinois, 12 October 1858, FHP, box 2, folder 19.

[71] FH's speech in Metropolitan Hall, Chicago, *ISZ*, 27 October 1858, with a commentary and supplement.

[72] Confirming FH's speeches in Galena and Freeport, see Washburne to FH, Raynham, Massachusetts, 28 March 1859, FHP, box 2, folder 19. Tucker, *Political Leadership*, 208-9; Johannsen, *Lincoln-Douglas Debates*, 12. Bergquist, *Political Attitudes*, 269. Gustav Körner to Abraham Lincoln, 4 April 1859; Robert Todd Lincoln Papers, MSS Library of Congress, also quoted in Tucker, *Political Leadership*, 222; see also the commentary in the *BZ* of 3 March 1859.

[73] Tucker, *Political Leadership*, 218; Bruncken, "German Political Refugees," no. 2, 56. On reducing and restraining of nativist tendencies in the Republican Party by German members, see Kamphoefner, "St. Louis Germans," 81; Bergquist, *Political Attitudes*, 417-20.

[74] Elihu Washburne to FH, Raynham, Massachusetts, 28 March 1859, FHP, box 2, folder 19.

[75] "Egypt" consisted of the counties in southernmost Illinois that had hitherto voted solidly Democratic. "Hunker" was a slang term for Whigs. FH to Georg Schneider, Lebanon, St. Clair County, Illinois, 16 May 1859, original in the Georg Schneider Papers.

[76] Zucker, *Forty-Eighters*, 285. On Bates, see Tucker, *Political Leadership*, 225-28.

[77] Both quotes, *BZ*, weekly, 25 August 1859.

[78] Herriott made an error by holding FH attended, see F. I. Herriott, "The Conference in the Deutsches Haus, May 14-15, 1860," *Transaction of the Illinois State Historical Society for the Year 1928* (Springfield, 1929), 101-91, here 180. James M. Bergquist, "The Forty-Eighters and the Republican Convention of 1860," Brancaforte, ed., *The Forty-Eighters*, 141-56; see also Bergquist, *Political Attitudes*, 300. See the commentary on the meeting in the Deutsches Haus on 14 and 15 May 1860 in the *Rochester Beobachter*, quoted in *MB*, 10 June 1860; see also the commentaries from the *Buffalo Telegraph* and the *Albany Beobachter* criticizing Missouri German support for Bates and stressing the active participation of Caspar Butz, Carl Dänzer, Gustav Körner and Carl Schurz. I draw on additional newspaper material that reinforces Bergquist's conclusions. The resolutions are printed by Herriott, "Deutsches Haus," 189. "Plattform der nationalen republikanischen Partei, angenommen am 17. Mai 1860 auf der Chicago Nationalconvention," *MB*, 20 May 1860. On the meeting in the Deutsches Haus and the Republican National Convention in Chicago, see also Foner, *Free Soil*, 257-60, 213-14. Tucker, *Political Leadership*, 231; also Bergquist, *Political Attitudes*, 283.

[79] Circular bulletin by N. B. Judd, Chairman of the Republican State Central Committee, Chicago, 23 June 1860, FHP, box 2, folder 22.

[80] Butz and Schneider were present at the meeting in the Deutsches Haus and at the Republican National Convention. Bergquist, *Political Attitudes*, 311-12. *WP*, 15 September 1860; see Saalberg, *Westliche Post*, 97, 117.

[81] A review of the discussion and its conclusion would go beyond the limits of this work, but see the very useful collection of articles from the birth of the "Dodd-Smith Thesis" to its modification through studies of the individual states in Frederick C. Luebke, ed., *Ethnic Voters and the Election of Lincoln* (Lincoln, 1971). W. E. Dodd in his essay in 1912 proposed the thesis that

the states of Illinois, Indiana and Iowa would have gone to Douglas in 1860 without German votes, and that the Germans unanimously supported their liberal "spokesmen," particularly the "Forty-Eighters." Donald V. Smith also presumed solidarity of immigrant groups in his study of 1932 and argued for a powerful Republican "voting bloc" based on united attitudes of voters. The election results in the individual states do not support such generalizations. One of the first critics was the Schurz biographer Joseph Schafer in 1941, who showed that only a sixth of the Germans in Wisconsin voted Republican. Further investigations showed that Germans in Iowa, Indiana, Ohio and Michigan also were not united enough as Republicans to give Lincoln the majority in those states. Jay Monaghan confirmed Schafer's conclusions in 1942; he also stressed the German preference for the Republican Party, but he placed their influence on the national election results in question. Hildegard B. Johnson finally confirmed for Minnesota in 1947 that the majority of Germans there voted Republican, but they were not a large enough group to decide the election. Tucker, *Political Leadership*, 238-40. Jörg Nagler, "'Ubi libertas, ibi patria' – Deutsche Demokraten im Exil," Frei, *Friedrich Hecker*, 65. Bergquist, *Political Attitudes*, 322; on Schneider's nomination as United States consul in Elsinore, see also *BZ*, 19 September 1861; on the whole Tucker, "Struggle for the Spoils, 1860-1863," *Political Leadership*, 238-69; also Otto Scheider, "Abraham Lincoln und das Deutschtum," *DAG* 7 (1907), 65-75, here 69; Arthur C. Cole, "President Lincoln and the Illinois Radical Republicans," *The Mississippi Valley Historical Review* 4/4 (March, 1918), 417-36, here 431 ff.

[82] For precise results, Bergquist, *Political Attitudes*, 321 ff., Foner, *Free Soil*, 259, n. 71.

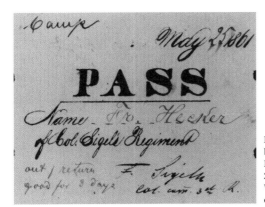

Pass issued to Private Fr. Hecker as a member of the Third Missouri Volunteer Regiment commanded by Col. Franz Sigel, 25 May 1861. Friedrich Hecker Papers, Western Historical Manuscripts, University of Missouri – St. Louis.

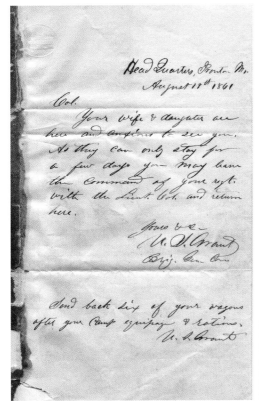

Letter from Brigadier General Ulysses S. Grant to Colonel Friedrich Hecker, Ironton, Missouri, 18 August 1861. Hecker's absence gave rise to the "mutiny" of officers of the regiment. Friedrich Hecker Papers, Western Historical Manuscripts, University of Missouri – St. Louis.

Head Quarters, Ironton Mo
August 16th 1861

Col.

Move very Cautiously forward
keeping as well informed of the
position of the enemy as possible
and should he be between you and
Farmington when you arrive at
Fredericktown, push back in that
direction—, sending me word.

You can have better opportunity of
knowing the practicability of
moving on to Brunot then I
can and must exercise a due
amount of discretion.

U. S. Grant
Brig. Gen. Com

To
Col. F. Hecker
Comd'g 24th Ill. Vol.

Letter from Brigadier General Ulysses S. Grant to Colonel Friedrich Hecker, Ironton, Missouri, 16 August 1861, directing him in combat. Friedrich Hecker Papers, Western Historical Manuscripts, University of Missouri – St. Louis.

VI

HECKER AND THE CIVIL WAR (1861-1865)

The Hecker Rifles Regiment (The 24th Illinois Volunteers)

With Lincoln's election, the conflict between the Northern and Southern states sharpened. Literally not a single voter had cast a ballot for Lincoln in 10 of the 15 Southern states. Barely two months after his election, what had long been feared took place. On 20 December 1860 South Carolina was the first state to declare that the union with other states known as the "United States of America" be dissolved. In the secessionist capital city of Charleston, at least, this was greeted with incredible transports of enthusiasm. Between 9 January and 1 February 1861, the states of Florida, Mississippi, Alabama, Georgia, Louisiana and Texas declared their secession. These seven states, now seeing themselves as sovereign, associated themselves on 8 February 1861 by adopting a constitution of the Confederate States of America – a slightly modified version of the old Union.

Until Lincoln's entry into office on 4 March 1861, outgoing President Buchanan showed himself to be indecisive and hesitant. In his inaugural address President Lincoln declared that the peril of a civil war and also its prevention, rested in the hands of the Southern states. On 12 April 1861 there followed the attack on Fort Sumter, a federal fort in Charleston's harbor whose provocative position supposedly placed the sovereignty of the Southern states in question. The Confederates demanded the fort's surrender, and when this was refused, bombardment began on the morning of 12 April. This attack marked the beginning of the American Civil War. Two days later, on Sunday, 14 April, Lincoln issued a proclamation calling 75,000 men to arms in order to return that Southern splintering, as he called it, which had taken place contrary to constitution and law, to the Union. In Belleville Lincoln's proclamation was received as a clear intention on the part of the federal government to recover federal property and to eliminate public enemies. The German newspapers called upon all Americans, whatever their origin or party, to rush to the aid of the supreme official of the country. However much one was tied to the old homeland, now it was time to help their adopted fatherland.[1]

When recruiting began in Missouri – there had been no levy in Illinois, and there would never be any obligation there to serve – Hecker did not hesitate, at fifty years of age, to cross the Mississippi with his oldest son Arthur and enlist as a private in the 3rd Missouri Volunteer Regiment of Colonel (soon Brigadier General) Franz Sigel. "He said there was no peace for him at home, and he wanted to share our fate," Daniel Hertle reported Hecker's words on his arrival in St. Louis.

Although the suppression of the Baden rebellion by Prussian troops was known in America, the Germans in America had exaggerated Sigel's military ability to mythic proportions. Personally complex, he was still so beloved among German soldiers that there was a special pride in the statement, "I fight mit Sigel."[2] Sigel, who had been living in St. Louis as a teacher of mathematics and geography, promoted the recruiting of volunteers at the outbreak of the war. He was given considerable credit for keeping Missouri in the Union through the use of his troops in the capture of Camp Jackson. This encampment ordered by Missouri's pro-Confederate governor Claiborne Fox Jackson, had been seen as a threat to the federal arsenal in St. Louis.

The speech Hecker that would make at the time of the ceremonial presentation of the flag to his own regiment revealed his motives for taking an active part in the Civil War. First, since his "days as a child and a youth he had had only one principle before his eyes," the principle of liberty, which he must constantly pursue. For that reason it was unavoidable that the "Southern aristocracy be broken … for liberty to flourish." For Hecker as for many Forty-Eighters, the struggle against the South was similar to the struggle against European aristocracy. Aristocrats must be cast aside not only because of the immorality of slavery but also because, even in America, they represented a limiting, hierarchical system that produced inequality and would always undermine democratic development. When Hecker later marched through the South with his second regiment, he wrote very telling lines to Struve:

> I would never have believed that America afforded such marvelous scenery as I saw in Maryland, Virginia, Kentucky, Tennessee, Alabama and Georgia. … if one says what could have become of this beautiful country *if free white labor had made it fruitful*, only then does one recognize the full curse of slavery.[3]

Free white labor meant independent, autonomous farmers, who would give political stability to the United States as part of a prospering middle class.

After everything that Hecker had said in his election speeches, consistency demanded opposing this particularly inefficient economic system, which called forth the same political and social ills as the aristocratic class in Europe. Hecker could no more tolerate the "peculiar institution" in the long run than he could accept the First Chamber of the Baden State Assembly.

A second motive for his involvement was also obvious. Here the situation Hecker had foreseen in theory was actually taking place; the existence of the state was in peril, and the moment had come for every good citizen to sacrifice private and personal interests to his higher obligation. The state was threatened by a Southern confederation that, according to Hecker, was simply a minority pursuing its own interests at the cost of communal well-being. Many years after the Civil War Hecker described the situation tellingly in a letter. "The South ... could not secede because the Union was a permanent contract that could not be arbitrarily, unilaterally broken by a minority. This was breaking the backbone of the Union." As in the 1840s, Hecker thought in terms of a social contract, which he transferred with his emigration to American conditions. For him the United States was the only country that actually derived from a formal contract. The state came into being through that contract, and the state's foremost goal was its own – and thus the contract's – preservation. This was why the contract had been made, and every citizen had to act to ensure its preservation.

Hecker took command of his own volunteer infantry regiment on 6 June 1861. Recruiting for this Hecker Rifles Regiment had begun in Chicago in May 1861 without Hecker's knowledge, but certainly with the support of his Chicago friends Caspar Butz, Lorenz Brentano and Georg Schneider. Because Illinois did not have to supply any regular troops, each volunteer group needed special recognition from the president of the United States. Even before Hecker knew of the existence of a regiment in his name, Lincoln "through a special order of 30 May," had accepted the incomplete unit "as an independent regiment." Hecker would later assert that the formation of the regiment had never been entirely proper, because more soldiers were listed on the muster rolls sent to Washington than had actually been recruited at that point; organizers, he said, "had only used my person and my name to bring a regiment together."[4]

When Hecker was finally informed of the existence of a Hecker Rifles Regiment and offered the command, he at first declined. The *Chicago Sonntagszeitung* reported that he had "second thoughts, due to the modesty of a true man, whether he could fulfill the expectations of the brave men honoring him with the command." In fact Hecker hesitated to because of his

1848 concept of a citizens' guard, which held that every honorable man must evaluate his own military ability and, if the given situation demanded, yield command to another, more gifted officer in order to guarantee the security of the soldiers and prevent the senseless waste of human life. This corresponded to Hecker's own choice to serve as a private soldier under the command of Sigel, whom he regarded as a well-trained and experienced soldier. Caspar Butz later gave a very credible report of why Hecker finally accepted command. He was moved to change his mind, Butz said, by of an old German veteran who stormily declared he would remain true to Hecker and be his obedient soldier. "What hours of reasoned argument by his friends could not do, was accomplished by a moment's impulse to serve loyally."[5]

Hecker later asserted that he had accepted election as colonel in the belief that he would be able to lead a regiment "of trained, courageous, energetic, fraternally bound officers and like-minded soldiers." He would lead "into battle an unconquered corps of men bound to live and die together with harmony of conviction." "They would not regard money or food as the highest good," but "would embrace every discipline in voluntary subordination and the spontaneous fulfillment of duty, without which an army is only a consuming horde." Hecker returned to Sigel's Regiment in St. Louis to "take leave of my unforgettable friends of the 3rd Missouri Regiment." He then planned to "dedicate all my energy to the organization of the [new] regiment, which I would lead into camp for this purpose."[6] He could not have known what an error it was to accept this command, and what a "true living hell" he was entering.

At the moment of its flag's dedication, Hecker's regiment already had an established group of officers. Captain Thomas Lang had functioned as commandant until Hecker's appearance. The number of soldiers was small at first, although it would increase in the first months of Hecker's command through continuing recruitment throughout Illinois. From the beginning there were serious supply problems, due to the confusion of the sudden outbreak of war and the rapid recruitment of troops. Colonel Hecker would soon experience these problems first hand. His first concern was to make up for the lack of privates. "I foresaw that if I did not move immediately to a camp outside town and keep my recruits there, the regiment would dissolve in a beer explosion. I pitched my camp several miles outside Chicago." Hecker wrote to Georg Schneider from this camp in Gary.

My dear friend! We are lacking nothing but more men. You and

Brentano should do what you can to send us men. You have committed my honor and existence, you say, so that I will win. Everything is all right in Springfield after my response to the governor and the supreme war officials; they promise to fulfill my requisitions, which has happened in part, so that my future is a little brighter … Finally my pressing request is that this regiment, called into life by your zealous impulse, should grow through effective recruitment.[7]

From Gary, Hecker's regiment, with only 260 soldiers, was ordered by a command from Springfield on 17 June to Alton, where a camp was to protect the mouth of the Missouri. Since the regiment was far from the full size presumed by the order, Hecker later reported, it was only through a pressing request from General McClellan, who was then inspecting the unit, "that the regiment was mustered in, despite the small number of soldiers, so that the collapse of the whole undertaking was prevented." Discipline was Hecker's greatest problem after poor supply, he added, "I was convinced that introduction of effective discipline and filling out of the regiment were impossible in the vicinity of the city [Chicago]." Under the command of General Pope, an almost complete brigade, including Hecker's regiment, was moved from Alton to St. Charles in Missouri by steamboat, although troop transport was usually by rail.[8]

Because President Lincoln had adopted Hecker's regiment as independent, the question arose who should pay to care and equip it. Did the regiment lay directly under the orders of the War Department in Washington or, like other Illinois regiments, depended on the officials in Springfield? Hecker received no answer to his written inquiry about this open question:

The people are lying under the open sky, clothed in what they owned, left with what they had brought with them for food. After untold trouble, trips to Springfield, and representations everywhere, we finally received blankets, rations and tents. I had to struggle for everything we got … I do not know to this day how and when the regiment went from an independent regiment to the 24th Illinois; I never received any report on it. I repeatedly sought weapons and paraphernalia; we only received backpacks and cartridge pouches months later. If the pride of the residents of Cook County and the brave, patriotic city of Chicago had not cared for providing the men with uniforms, we would have dissolved.[9]

The bad supply situation was not a problem for Hecker's regiment alone; it was general. The *Westliche Post* expressed the hope that the situation would improve with the appearance of General John C. Frémont, who had just returned from Europe to take over the command of the Western Department.[10] Frémont, whose presidential candidacy in 1856 had so engaged the Germans, still enjoyed trust as a man of action and imagination, particularly among the politically active Forty-Eighters. Gustav Körner, for example, allowed himself to be enrolled in Frémont's staff as aide de camp to resolve organizational problems.

In July Hecker traveled to Washington to describe the situation to President Lincoln and Secretary of War Simon Cameron. The president issued an order to secure at least the vital weapons supplies. But when the delivery was made to the troops, the guns were "smoothbore muskets of such outstanding quality that , if one was actually able to ram the bullets down, they were more a peril to the living in general than to the enemy after three or four shots." Supply would remain a great problem throughout the following months. There is no doubt that Hecker committed himself diligently to his people's needs, as Butz demonstrated. Because Lincoln, supreme official of the country, was Hecker's old party comrade, the Illinois farmer thought nothing of writing directly to call attention to the condition of his troops. In September 1861 Hecker wrote to Lincoln and described the catastrophic situation of his soldiers, who had entered the struggle with "nobel [*sic*] patriotic feelings," had left their families and were performing their functions without complaint, but who did not even have adequate shoes. Any patriotic heart must break in such circumstances, wrote Hecker. Constant moving about had exhausted his men, illness was bound to increase, and his soldiers had not yet even received their pay. "Major General Fremont, his staff officer … promised me to provide for the pay," he wrote to Lincoln,

> I entertained them [the soldiers] with the hope of pay from week to week. The best way to break the health and … spirit of a good body of men is to betray them in their hopes. I address myself Sir personally to you, we have no confidence in anybody else. From your authority we hope and expect the relief from this.[11]

Hecker's proper complaints were later exploited by the German-American press to call attention to the dreadful state of administration in Washington and the half-hearted waging of the war. The *Louisville Anzeiger* wrote:

The splendid Hecker Regiment knows how contemptibly the administration treats its *best* troops, because it has not had 24 hours of rest in
four months and despite that has only received $10, that is ten dollars.
Our entire administration is not worth a straw.[12]

In a letter marked "private" to Georg Schneider and Lorenz Brentano,
Hecker thoroughly portrayed the fact that much of commanding a regiment
consisted of administrative obligations. This letter also repeated Hecker's
views expressed in his 1848 plan for a Citizens' Guard, that one should willingly renounce command in favor of a more experienced soldier. The letter
confirmed Hecker's position that, if one could not or would not pass command to another, one was at least obligated to obtain the knowledge necessary for command:

> I am not unaware of the significance of the position into which I have
> been thrown, and my sole worry is that I understand nothing about tac-
> tics. With the continuous trouble with which the administration of a
> regiment is burdened, I cannot study. That the people are thrown into
> the fire without understanding anything is a hard business. I am happy
> to sacrifice my hide, and I am ready day and night to go through hell,
> but not everything is settled that way. If I knew a man such as Sigel, I
> would be happy to lay the command in his hands. Mihalotzi is a good
> soldier, but it appears to me that his education does not reach to being
> a regimental commander; for the administration of a regiment, it is nec-
> essary to get along with officials, and the commander has to handle a
> pen as well as a weapon. Sigel is the best at that, and far above most
> American military leaders.[13]

Because the Southern states maintained a defensive posture, it was up
to the troops of the Northern states to advance into the South. In the East
they pressed in the direction of the Confederate capital of Richmond, and
the disastrous defeat at Bull Run immediately destroyed the illusion of a
quick victory. The forces in the West, meanwhile, advanced south along the
Mississippi. From the end of July until his arrival in Colesburgh, Kentucky,
in the middle of October, Hecker's regiment was ceaselessly in motion. It
passed through the whole of Missouri on marches and expeditions from
north to south. It moved from Cape Girardeau on to Fort Holt, and finally
to Camp Dennison on the Ohio. After a few days they moved into Kentucky.
The continuous movements and marching quickly ruined shoes and cloth-
ing, and a large portion of Hecker's men became sick from continuous liv-

ing in the open, and from contageous diseases brought on by the swamps. At one more than 300 of his total of 560 soldiers were ill. Hecker wrote, "I do not believe that any regiment of the western army was as tossed about as the 24th Illinois." To make matters worse, there was technical, administrative confusion. "I had the honor of belonging to no fewer than sixteen different brigades and other large units since the end of July."[14]

Small skirmishes were all that Hecker was involved in during his command of the 24th Illinois, but even these virtually fruitless engagements were reported in detail in the German-American press. The commitment of Germans to a rapid and uncompromising conduct of the war was embodied in Hecker's person. Time and again such papers as the *Belleviller Zeitung* printed articles by Hecker, in which he complained about the "snail-like progress of the war." But Hecker's problems with his command were of a more internal nature, even leading to a public breach within the regiment. From the beginning of his command Hecker was determined to have order and discipline. As naïve, inexperienced and possessed by patriotism as he was, he presumed that if everyone completely fulfilled his function and mission, in keeping with his competence, "the inner administration and technical training of a regiment would be easy." No one had fulfilled his duty if he merely believed that his obligations were done after a few hours of drill.

> I was convinced that we would endure defeats everywhere if we did not aspire to European discipline. However, I had to endure regiments on the march moving like disorderly herds, falling out at every brook and stream; raiding houses, stalls and orchards while company officers of the infantry commanded from horseback; camping along with women; still cooking and eating at the announced time of muster, so that if the time were set for 4 a. m., the columns were only ready for marching three hours later.[15]

His own papers give proof of Hecker's strict regime. His orders of the day for his troops in Marble Creek, Missouri, called for the arrest of drunken soldiers, their emprisonment until trial, a ban on the sale of alcohol to soldiers and officers and a ban on passing the night outside camp. With the exception of licensed washerwomen, no females were tolerated within the camp.[16]

Trouble came during a maneuver ordered by Brigadier General Ulysses S. Grant, under whose command Hecker's regiment stood at the time. Grant sent Hecker an order on 16 August 1861 to move his men forward and to keep him informed of the enemy's movements. Hecker's troops were encamped in Marble Creek, twelve miles from Grant's headquarters in Ironton. He immediately had the bugler blow for muster:

> I had ... to win a position in which I myself could have held out against even the most overwhelming enemy. My study of the maps and the reports of scouts made it possible for me to choose such a position. *I reached the position through a forced march.* Things happened on this march as described above; 25 valiant fighters could have driven this unruly mob to distraction. I made the most extreme efforts to establish and keep order.

Hecker's "most extreme efforts" and his manner, described by even Caspar Butz as "harsh," must have convinced some of his officers after this march to accuse him of being a "man-eater." [17]

Two days later, on 18 August 1861, Hecker heard from General Grant that his wife and daughter had arrived at headquarters to see him. He left for Ironton. During his absence there was a meeting of his officers in camp in which they complained about Hecker's conduct. The resolution that they composed said that Hecker "should not reprimand officers in the presence of non-commissioned officers or privates, should not act against non-commissioned officers with weapons or otherwise with force" – a point that is not completely surprising in view of Hecker's frequent challenges to duels in Germany and was even indirectly conceded by Hecker in a later declaration. Finally, "he should not compel officers to resign." The last had actually happened. An officer on his staff, Jacob Poull, had owned a brothel in Chicago. A soldier in Hecker's regiment had participated as a clerk in a trial against Poull in Chicago in which Poull had been fined $50 in January 1860. Hecker admitted he had told Poull "that he would see to it that he received no officer's commission, because he was not happy to wear the same uniform as a whore-monger." Hecker believed the man's presence to be incompatible with his regiment's discipline. In article 4 of his draft of a Citizens' Guard system in 1848, Hecker had written,

> Excluded are all who 1) have received a physical punishment; 2) have been condemned to a penalty involving public infamy, namely due to theft, embezzlement, fraud, forgery or flight to avoid payment; 3) are found in police custody; 4) declared incompetent.[18]

To be sure Lieutenant Poull had not been condemned for theft or embezzlement. But the monetary fine for keeping a brothel appeared to Hecker to be a "penalty involving public infamy." In Mannheim in 1848 he seems even not to have considered mentioning owners of brothels.

Hecker, who had never quite recovered from the trauma of betrayal in 1848, was always ready with conspiracy theories. He saw the meeting as a mutiny by his officer staff, although the greater part of his men assured him in writing of their undiminished loyalty and expressly distanced themselves from the gathering. After his return Hecker informed his new superior, Brigadier General Benjamin Prentiss, who had just replaced Grant, of the unofficial gathering of his officers. Hecker asked Prentice whether a court of inquiry could be granted him and whether he could remove the officers from service if the accusations against him were found to be groundless. The investigation ordered by Prentiss affirmed Hecker's conduct and found the complaints groundless. Prentiss then sent Hecker to General Frémont, who was to decide on the removal of the seven officers who were the principals engaged in the meeting and the resolutions. Hecker, who felt that the break between himself and some of the officers could not be repaired, offered Frémont his resignation. Frémont rejected it and instead provided Hecker with a letter on 27 August 1861 authorizing the reorganization of his regiment, advising Prentiss to remove the seven officers. By Official Order No. 53 on 29 August 1861, Prentiss removed from the regiment "upon the recommendation of Colonel Friedrich Hecker," Major Julian Kune, Captains Lang and Augustus Mauff, First Lieutenants August Gerhardy and G. A. Busse and Second Lieutenants Jacob Poull and E. F. C. Klokke. In his letter to Prentiss, Hecker justified these removals with the comment that the officers were intolerable to the regiment. He cited as his authority the order from General Frémont for the completely reorganization of his regiment. Hecker wrote to Prentiss, "The same order confers on me the power to present to you the names of the officers for dismissal, whose presence renders it impossible for me to hold an effective command." In an earlier letter, he had accused the officers of mutiny and resisting his orders. In the present justification Hecker accused the officers of almost never being with the regiment on grounds of illness or some other reason, and he complained that in the case of three of the seven officers, "none is able to give a report in good English, and Jacob Poull scarcely in German."

Dismissing the officers in this manner avoided a military court. Unfortunately, there was an administrative problem with Hecker's demand.

He had received permission from General Prentiss to dismiss the officers, but he soon had to accept the reversal of this order by Brigadier Generals Grant and Sherman, and restore the officers. When asked later why he did not submit the matter to a military court as attempted mutiny, Hecker said that he had tried several times to have general courts-martial, but had received no response. He had once had to take an arrested person along with him for weeks because he was not able to get him judged according to military law. Constant movement undermined any court proceedings. There was also the fact that the majority of the men had declared their loyalty to him; Hecker saw the seven offending officers as exceptions. He had already told Prentiss in his first letter, "The vacancies so created I shall fill immediately with able men, so that the service shall not suffer, and submit a list to you." On this list stood the names of soldiers of whom Hecker had proof of undivided loyalty, demonstrated at the time of his threat to resign. This group had clearly distinguished itself from the mutinous officers, declaring that they would also leave the army if Hecker resigned.[19]

The seven dismissed officers complained to Major General Frémont about Hecker's procedure and declared that they did not recognize a dismissal that was not supported by any higher military level.[20] Hecker had acted "without the shadow of right or justice" in dismissing them from the regiment on his own authority, they said. Hecker cited the order supported by General Prentiss.[21] The officers' complaints passed to the War Department in Washington, where Hecker believed one of the officers had good connections, and ultimately reached Secretary of War Simon Cameron.

What was hard for Hecker to understand was that the fact that entire controversy was less about the situation itself than it was part of a confrontation between the War Department and General Frémont, with whose leadership Washington was increasingly dissatisfied. This was particularly the case following Frémont's abortive emancipation proclamation of 30 August 1861, after which his freedom of action had been limited.

Frémont had been installed as military commander of the Western Department. But the War Department thought his leadership style imperiled, rather than guaranteed, the military security of Missouri. He appeared to scatter his troops (including the eternally marching 24th Illinois) rather than concentrate them and bring them effectively to bear against the secessionists. Washington held Frémont responsible for the disaster at Wilson Creek in Missouri, where the Union commander, Brigadier General Nathaniel Lyon, lost his life because Frémont had not sent him enough troops. Frémont was also the target of personal controversy, he treating local

politicians unwisely and tactlessly, and violating army rules with gusto as
he pleased. Lincoln was particularly upset by Frémont's "proconsular arrogance." Frémont's staff had swollen to a crowd of 28 persons – including
directors of music, police, and the mails – that would have sufficed for an
army of 100,000 men. "Here rules chaos," Gustav Körner wrote from camp
to his wife Sophie as well as to Franz Sigel; Frémont's love of drama aroused
suspicion. To Sigel's horror, Frémont's politically involved wife Jessie was
also beginning to act like Amalie von Struve, attempting to penetrate the
last domain ruled by men alone, the military.[22]

On 30 August 1861 Frémont issued a proclamation for Missouri. As
commanding general, he took over administrative power in Missouri, "proclaimed martial law, decreed the death penalty for partisans caught behind
Union lines, confiscated the property of all Confederate activists in Missouri
and declared their slaves free." Two reasons appear to have moved Frémont
to this step. First, he wanted to discourage both the numerous partisans and
the civilian population of Missouri who supported them. Secondly, he
wanted to bring over to his side the radical opponents of slavery within the
Republican Party. Frémont's proclamation was received with particular
enthusiasm by those German-Americans upset at Washington's slow pros-
ecution of the war. However, the proclamation upset Lincoln's careful
diplomatic attitude and ruined his attempt to keep an uncertain Kentucky
within the Union. At first Lincoln sought in a private letter to Frémont to
have him reissue or modify the proclamation, which he described in a separate letter to a friend as *"purely political*, and not within the range of military law, or necessity." Further, Lincoln forbad Frémont to shoot partisans
"without my advanced approval," because if he executed every imprisoned
partisan without distinction,"the Confederates would surely in retaliation
shoot the best of our own people in their hands, and so on, man for man, *ad
infinitum*." Frémont rejected Lincoln's demands in a letter of 8 September.
The president responded with an official letter to the general on 11 September, published in translation by the German-American press. This order
rescinded the proclamation clauses on the confiscation of property and the
freeing of slaves, a ruling in keeping with the law passed by Congress on 6
August declaring that confiscation of property, including slaves, would
only take place when that property immediately served the war efforts of
the Confederates. The German-American press defended Frémont's proclamation and criticized Lincoln, who it said sought to undermine Frémont's
authority. There were also demonstrations of sympathy for Frémont upon
the publication of Lincoln's measures.[23]

The events in Hecker's regiment were handled as they were because of a convergence of conflicts surrounding Frémont. One order issued by the War Department required the restoration of the dismissed officers and specifically revoked Frémont's command for the reason that he was not empowered to take such a step at that time. At the same time Hecker was ordered that the officers provisionally placed, but not yet officially confirmed by Governor Richard Yates of Illinois, be mustered out of the regiment and placed in other regiments. Hecker concluded, "That meant nothing more or less than the departure from the regiment of friends of the colonel, and the return of all his enemies." When officers Klokke and Lang presented Hecker with Frémont's revised order of 17 September, commanding their restoration, Hecker composed a horrified letter to Frémont. He expressed his suspicion that he had been entrusted with the organization of the 24th Illinois merely to boost recruiting among the German-American population with his important name; then did everything possible was done to get rid of him. Little real value was placed on his leadership. That was Hecker's subjective opinion, which he repeated in another letter to Governor Richard Yates of Illinois, stating exactly the same suspicion along with his request for confirmation of the new list of officers.[24] He wrote a further letter to the president as well.

Hecker never received a reply to his objections from either Governor Yates or President Lincoln. Requesting the right to make an oral report of the episode, he traveled to Washington himself at the start of October. His visit was unsuccessful, and the order to receive the discharged officers back into his regiment was simply repeated. In response the *Louisville Anzeiger* expressed its suspicion that "the order to dismiss [the seven officers] derived from Frémont, and binds our War Department to nothing, as long as Frémont can be given a shove by not recognizing his command."[25]

Brigadier General William Tecumseh Sherman, who had succeeded Frémont, with Brigadier General Robert Anderson, commander over the 24th Illinois Regiment, agreed with Hecker's reasons for removing the officers. But once Hecker received his order from the War Department, they bowed to the higher authority and acted to restore Hecker's dismissed officers to the regiment. Ulysses Grant, admired by Hecker during the Civil War years as a "decent, gallant, brave general and a man of honor," also spoke positively of Hecker's leadership qualities, but he stayed out of the whole problem because it was not his business.[26]

The War Department's decision in Washington fell "entirely against Hecker," the *Belleviller Zeitung* informed its readers three days after the event. In truth Hecker was compelled by a special order to place the dismissed officers back in their positions on 19 October before the assembled regiment, and dismiss the officers provisionally replacing them. "I had the honor – despite all my convictions that the uniform of the United States was being mocked if persons wore it who had been punished in public court for keeping a disorderly house – to install the aforementioned gentleman formally as a fellow officer." Hecker's friend Caspar Butz, who had heard of the decision directly from Washington, knew what an insult this was to a man like Hecker. For that reason he wrote to Franz Sigel, under whose command Hecker would have preferred to serve, to ask whether Sigel could do anything for the colonel.[27]

In the meantime Hecker confirmed the restoration of the officers in a letter to Secretary Cameron. He complained once more about the moral character of some of these officers, particularly the Chicago brothel owner Poull.[28] In his letter to Cameron, Hecker conceded formal errors on his part; it had been an error not to inform the War Department at once of the conditions in his regiment, for example, or inform it of the planned dismissals in order to receive confirmation. He was as certain as ever that the War Department would never have hesitated to dismiss the men if there had been a complete explanation. Hecker still felt that it was not too late for such a step. But Washington did not agree.

At the start of November Hecker returned to his farm, suspended from duty on account of illness and desperately in need of peace. There he received the news a bit later that the disputed officers now sought their own dismissal because they were being "received by the soldiers with icy coldness." Hecker immediately drew up a list of officers to take the vacant places. He sent the staff physician, Dr. Wagner, to Springfield with the list and asked him to return once the list had been confirmed by the governor. Hecker waited four weeks for a positive answer. None came. Hecker wrote to Yates again to say that, if his personal presence were necessary, he would come to Springfield. He received no reply to this letter either. Hecker was convinced that this silence was "conscious neglect" and that the worst of nativists were at work in Springfield. In the meantime he composed a letter to Elihu Washburne, the sole representative in Washington whom he still trusted. In this English-language letter he reviewed all of the events once more, and he asked Washburne to discover in Washington the meaning of his treatment, which was a true puzzlement to him.

I have from the beginning been the object of unrelenting chicane and persecutions. Let me know the reason of it, tell it to me frankly; if you do no know it you can find it out. ... My experience of former years did teach me that discipline is the soul of military bodies. I insisted on a very rigid system of it, but not half way as it is in European armies. I was throughout against the marauding and plundering on marches, I insisted to be surrounded by educated, intelligent, faithful, reliable officers. ... What is the reason? If they do not want my services why not tell it plainly. I shall willingly resign then, I do not stick to this colonelcy. I left a happy home, a comfortable life, induced by no selfish motive I acted as a man who has for long years studied the civil wars of ancient and of modern times; I expressed my opinions frankly. Is there, perhaps, the sin? Or is it because I am styled an abolitionist? [...] from you, always so friendly towards me, I hope the solution of this mistery of persecution. Will you tell me the full truth?[29]

Washburne could do little to clarify Hecker's concern. Caspar Butz encouraged Hecker in his notion that nativists were at work. Butz was agitating in the press about the fate of the Hecker Rifles just as he had about Frémont's removal in Missouri and Sigel's later resignation. All of these episodes served merely to show Lincoln's lack of ability and reinforced demands that he remove some of his advisors.[30]

Guilt for the debacle of Hecker's regiment must be sought on both sides. Hecker's explosive nature contributed to this unedifying conflict, and he apologized after the fact in his farewell address to his regiment for his possibly misunderstood attitude. But the administrations in Washington and Springfield also failed to provide Hecker with an opportunity to explain and defend himself. Hecker appeared offended beyond all measure. He had never been dealt with in such a manner, even by the highest officials of monarchies where he was mortally hated.

And they do that to a man who did not rush to the flag as an adventurer, a soldier of fortune, from need or as a mercenary. My enthusiasm has been obliterated to the foundation. It has been made clear to me that the Dutch have no homeland here, but at most may be granted some toleration. By comparison the toleration edicts of the popes for the Jews are true jewels of humanity.[31]

On 20 December 1861 Hecker submitted his resignation. Oddly enough the Springfield officials responded this time by return mail; only three days

Colonel Friedrich Hecker. Saint Louis Mercantile Library at the University of Missouri – St. Louis.

later, on 23 December 1861, he received notice that his request was granted.

Of all the accusations that he unjustly leveled in his agitation and in the presumption of a conspiracy against him, the administrative delay of his petitions and submissions was certainly a genuine irritation, and hard to explain. Richard Yates, an enthusiastic war governor, had never hesitated to promote American volunteer units. Hecker had sent in triplicate a list of his officer nominees – all copies vanished. When Adjutant General Mather, the right hand of Governor Yates, later entered active service and was replaced by Adjutant General A. C. Fuller, Hecker's submissions were found, covered with dust, in a corner of Mather's Springfield offices. Even the lieutenant governor of Illinois, Frances A. Hoffmann, who often represented Yates in Springfield, indirectly admitted errors in an open letter. Hecker responded by accusing Hoffmann of neglecting his duty. Hoffmann, as "second official of the state," had an unconditional interest in rapidly carrying out the appointments. Hecker declared after his resignation that the conduct of officials, their conscious delay and their belittling, which could be exceeded only by their corruption, had essentially discouraged him from service. They had "obliterated the greatest enthusiasm" of an independent man. In this struggle one "asks in vain for the principles he is fighting for … And I do not serve for money."

The German-American press, on the whole, was of the opinion that an injustice had been done to "a man of honor." Whether this injustice was committed by the governor of Illinois or by the federal government, the balanced judgment of the *Buffalo Demokrat* declared, "we cannot give any ruling … in view of the many contradictory reports."[32]

Colonel Friedrich Hecker's snuff box and the bullet it deflected at the Battle of Chancellorsville, May, 1863. Friedrich Hecker Papers, Western Historical Manuscripts, University of Missouri – St. Louis.

ILLINOIS VOLUNTEERS.

HEAD-QUARTERS.

Springfield, Ills.,   October 28ᵀᴴ 1862.

To all to whom These Presents Shall come, Greeting:

Know Ye, That *Frederic Hecker* having been duly

APPOINTED COLONEL OF THE 82nd REGIMENT ILLINOIS VOLUNTEERS

I, RICHARD YATES,
GOVERNOR OF THE STATE OF ILLINOIS,

FOR AND ON BEHALF OF THE PEOPLE OF SAID STATE, DO COMMISSION HIM TO TAKE

Rank as *COLONEL* from the *TWENTY-THIRD* day of *OCTOBER* 1862.

He is, therefore, carefully and diligently to discharge the duties of said Office, by doing and performing all manner of things thereunto belonging; and I do strictly require all Officers and Soldiers under his command to be obedient to his orders; and he is to obey all such orders and directions as he shall receive, from time to time, from his Commander-in-Chief, or superior Officer.

In Testimony Whereof, I have hereunto set my hand and caused the **GREAT SEAL OF STATE** to be affixed. Done at the City of Springfield, this *TWENTY-EIGHTH* day of *OCTOBER* in the year of our Lord one thousand eight hundred and sixty-*TWO* and of the independence of the United States, the eighty-*SEVENTH*.

Rich Yates
Governor

O. M. Hatch
Secretary of State.

Registered Book *A*, Page *343*.

Allen C. Fuller
Adjutant General.

Commission of Friedrich Hecker as Colonel of the 82nd Illinois Volunteers, 23 October 1862. Friedrich Hecker Papers, Western Historical Manuscripts, University of Missouri – St. Louis.

A New Command (The 82nd Illinois Volunteers)

After Hecker's resignation Caspar Butz visited him on his farm in the winter of 1861-62.

> The compelled inactivity oppresses him, as the world around him glows with the flames of war. I asked him whether he would not like to enter the field at the head of another regiment. He declared himself ready, but he could not stamp soldiers out of the field on his farm. I responded that his friends would do that for him.[33]

In fact Butz and other friends of Hecker were in Chicago to act not only for him, but also for Franz Sigel, whose resignation was seen by Germans as a response to unreduced nativism in the American military. Amid the general disappointment over the "snail's pace of the war" and Butz's agitation against Lincoln and his administration, Hecker's resignation from active service seemed proof of the military's contempt for German services. For that reason, Caspar Butz, Georg Schneider, Anton Hesing and Lorenz Brentano, all collaborators of the *Illinois Staatszeitung*, sent a letter to the Congressmen Lyman Trumbull, Isaac Arnold, Elihu Washburne and Lovejoy Browning. They complained about the treatment of German officers and soldiers in the American Civil War, as well as other problems. This memorandum at Butz's initiative and appears also to have been composed by him. A first sign of success of these German protests was that President Lincoln received a German-American delegation from New York to discuss Sigel's situation (Sigel's promotion to major general eventually took place in July, 1862, following intense German pressure). The extent to which these efforts to advance German officers depended on a round robin between the Forty-Eighters in Chicago, St. Louis and New York and the congressmen in Washington was shown in a letter from Brentano to Hecker, in which Brentano reported on discussions that took place after he visited Hecker's farm. Brentano informed Hecker of a letter from Congressman Isaac Arnold, who was acting on behalf of the promotion of August von Willich and Augustus Mercy and who also tried to have Hecker recalled to join Frémont's staff. Brentano knew that Schurz was acting on Hecker's behalf as well. Other Hecker friends, including the physician Philipp Weigel, who had come with him to St. Louis in 1848, and Emil Preetorius, later the publisher of the *Westliche Post*, had acted on Hecker's behalf and petitioned General Frémont. They had received from him a thoroughly positive answer, "Not only because I like to do what would gratify yourselves but also because I regard Hecker as my personal friend and agree with you both in thinking that he has been unjustly treated, regretting to see his good service lost to the country." Frémont continued by saying that he was restricted "from above" as far as his staff was concerned, and that it was best to ask Colonel Körner, who was still in his service as aide de camp, whether he could get an appointment through the president. "Should it then be referred to me I will write immediately to the president and express my desire that it should be done."[34]

On 22 September 1862, five months after this letter and five days after the Battle of Antietam, came Lincoln's Emancipation Proclamation. This order declared freedom for all slaves in those states and regions still in rebellion against the United States as of the beginning of the new year, 1863. Lincoln's earlier new call for volunteers had made possible the creation of a second Hecker regiment. As soon as he was asked, Governor Richard Yates gave his confirmation, and on 26 September 1862 a new regiment, the 82nd Illinois Volunteers, was organized in Camp Butler near Springfield. It was formally mustered into United States service on 23 October. As was the case with the 24th Illinois, the 82nd consisted primarily of Germans, but there were also some Swiss, Americans and Norwegians, mostly recruited from the area around Chicago. There was also a "Jewish company, specially formed for the Hecker Regiment by rich Jews of Chicago."[35]

Those who knew Hecker were aware that he could hardly be kept at home after the Emancipation Proclamation. During the period of the new levy in August 1862, a general amnesty had been proclaimed in Baden for participants in the Revolution of 1848. Hecker's relatives obviously had little idea how much he had integrated himself into American conditions and how little he was interested in returning to Germany. Even as arrangements were being made for a new Hecker Regiment in Chicago, Hecker's wife Josefine received a letter from her mother in Mannheim, expressing her hope to be able to see her "Americans" soon settled back on German soil:

> I saw with great disapproval from your last letter that Fritz wants to participate in it again and risk his life, so necessary to his children, and his health. God protect him and save his family. Amnesty brought great joy even to Fritz's opponents.[36]

But Prospects for peace were not good in August, 1862. Another German friend of the family, who had a more balanced view of the situation, wrote

Hecker's oldest son Arthur in September that he had heard that Hecker

> has already exchanged the comparative peace on the farm with the rat-
> tle of war again; this news did not much surprise me, as I had thought
> to myself when I read about the president's two levies that he would
> not be able to stay home … With the excitement reigning in the United
> States, the news of your papa's amnesty probably had little impact.
> Here in Mannheim in particular it was received with great rejoicing,
> and it was hoped that all the refugees now overseas would return.

Despite all expectations, Hecker was not among them. Other emigrants,
such as Franz Sigel, had also long since made their commitment to the
United States.[37]

Hecker's new regiment would be placed under the command of Major
General Joseph Hooker of the XI and XII Corps, Army of the Potomac. For
Hecker the theater of war moved east, to Virginia. Eugen Weigel, son of
Philipp Weigel of St. Louis and adjutant of the regiment, informed Hecker's
son Arthur by letter of the monotony of camp life there and the influence of
war conditions. In December 1862 he wrote "from lousy Virginia":

> I can tell you that there is not much going on here. It might once have
> been a beautiful country, but now everything is destroyed and burned
> out. The only thing one can still buy here is horses. Your father bought
> one the day before yesterday for $20 … It appears that we will be stay-
> ing here for a long time. I just wish you were here with us.[38]

On 26 November, in Sigel's camp in Fairfax near Washington, Hecker
met Gustav von Struve again. It was their second meeting since the campaign of 1856, and it was to be their last. Struve recalled this meeting two
years later in the *Gartenlaube*.

> How much things have changed since the days we unfurled the banner
> of freedom in the Baden highlands! Franz Sigel had become a major
> general of the United States and commanded a whole army corps. In
> Europe we had fought against the existing powers, while in America
> we stand on the side of the constitutional authorities.

In the dawning new year, Struve returned to Germany as the American consul for the Thuringian states. At the beginning of February 1863 Hecker left

his regiment, sick from typhus, to recover in Philadelphia under the care of his brother-in-law Dr. Heinrich Tiedemann.[39]

An end to the monotony of camp life was brought only by the start of the early-year offensive under General Hooker, the "rising man" about whom Butz had warned Hecker. At the end of January "Fighting Joe" had replaced Major General Ambrose Burnside. In April he sought to move the front, which had stalled in Virginia between the troops of the Southern General Robert E. Lee and the Union. The Confederates had laid a net of trenches 40 kilometers long along the Rappahannock River near Fredericksburg, but it was not Hooker's intention to challenge it. Hooker had an army twice the size of Lee's. His plan was to leave a third of his army, 40,000 men, under Major General John Sedgwick, along the old line of battle, where the troops there had dug themselves into position. This force would harrass Lee with feints so that Hooker himself, with the bulk of the army, could draw upriver, pass around Lee's troops to the west and attack them in the rear. The plan was either to cut Lee's troops from their supply lines or to compel their withdrawal to the Confederate capital of Richmond, ending the constant threat to Washington. Threatened by both sides, General Lee would be compelled to attack in one direction or another, breaking through in order to avoid encirclement. Hooker, certain of victory, told his people, "Our foe must either seek craven flight or leave his cover and give battle on our own terrain, where certain annihilation awaits him."[40] On 30 April 1863, 10,000 cavalry and 70,000 infantry, including Brigadier General Carl Schurz's 3rd Division and Hecker's 82nd Illinois, moved up the Rappahannock. They halted surprisingly soon at Chancellorsville, 13 kilometers west of Fredericksburg.

Hecker's 82nd Illinois was in the 3rd Division of the XI Corps of the Army of the Potomac. Commanding the 3rd Division was Schurz, who had returned from his post as American minister at the Spanish court to join the ranks of the Union army's "political officers." The XI Corps stood under the command of Major General Oliver O. Howard, a professional officer with West Point training and the reputation of a brave soldier. He had lost an arm in the Battle of Fair Oaks and was a "monogamous, Congregationalist abstinence man bearing the nickname of the *Christian Soldier*"[41] With barely 12,000 men the XI Corps formed the extreme right flank of Hooker's troops. Lee, who was aware of Hooker's movements, decided to leave behind a troop of only 10,000 men under Jubal Early to face Sedgwick. He then moved westward on 1 May with the 50,000 men available to him, to guard against Hooker's main force, toward the "Wilderness," as a region of thicket, underbrush and crippled oaks south of the Rappahannock was called. Hooker's troops meanwhile had fallen into unknown terrain. The various columns had come to a standstill, and the advance had been stalled, preventing the construction of a unified front. The XI Corps was extended far ahead and was completely separated from the rest of the army. When Hooker became aware of Lee's movements, he had his troops halt and take a defensive position. This caused the XI Corps to halt, as well. But because Hooker mistook his enemy's ensuing movements as a retreat, in keeping with his dream of a Confederate "craven flight," he persisted in inaction. Had he known Lee's true strength at this moment an attack like the one that he had originally planned would have been an easy play.

Lee had been informed by spies that Hooker's right wing was hanging "in the air," without an adequate connection to the main army. Lee decided to keep a small force of 15,000 men in front of Hooker's main body to feint an attack. Meanwhile Lieutenant General Thomas J. "Stonewall" Jackson set off on an 18-mile march along the open enemy flank with 30,000 infantry and artillery. Although protected by the thicket of the Wilderness, Jackson's drawn-out columns would have been extremely vulnerable at this moment. But Hooker fatally saw the movement as his enemy's withdrawal. Lee, who intended to attack as soon as he heard the thunder from Jackson's assault on Hooker's right wing, received confirmation at 5:15 on the evening of 2 May that Jackson had drawn up his forces in the thickets and was about to unleash a merciless attack on the badly protected Union right wing. That included Schurz's 3rd Division with Hecker's 82nd Illinois.

Carl Schurz later wrote in his memoirs that he had not been fooled by the enemy's maneuvers. Informed by his own observers, he told his superiors of the exposed position of the XI Corps, but neither Howard nor Hooker credited his fears. Hooker's sudden halting of the troops had been a clear blunder. On his own authority, Schurz decided to reinforce his position to the west with some of his regiments. "In the absence of orders," he reported,

> but becoming more and more convinced that the enemy's attack would come from the west and fall upon our right and rear, I took it upon my own responsibility to detach two regiments from the second line of my Second Brigade, and to place them in a good position.[42]

Howard even confirmed Schurz's action shortly thereafter.

But Jackson's attack on the regiments of the right wing on the evening of 2 May was an utter surprise. Panic broke out among the Union forces, particularly the regiments of the 1st Division under Major General Charles

Devens. Howard had turned most of his troops to the south because he thought that an attack through the woods, which he considered the impenetrable thicket, was impossible. Most of the Union soldiers were preparing to cook supper or had settled down to rest as Jackson and his men prepared a front three kilometers wide and three divisions deep. The Confederates fell on the Union troops, who were turned southwards, from the rear. Despite the wild confusion that broke out with this twilight action, some brigades managed to resist the Confederate attack for a time, and force it to stall. Hecker's brigade was posted in the second line, but while he was trying to get his troops to advance to the first line, he was halted and stymied in his advance by fleeing Union soldiers running through his ranks, pursued hotly by the Confederates. Hecker's regiment could form a front only with difficulty, "as the scattered men of the First Division were continually breaking through our ranks." Colonel Hecker, as Schurz described, had grabbed the flag of his regiment and stepped forward with a loud hurrah to get his troops to hold ranks, but this was impossible in the confusion, and Hecker ended up on the firing line. While he rode along the line of his regiment, encouraging his soldiers, he was shot in the upper thigh. Despite this the second line managed to fight the enemy to a standstill for a time, according to Schurz's report.

> As the enemy emerged from the woods, the regiment of my second line stopped him with well-directed and rapid fire. ... Colonel Hecker, of the Eighty-second Illinois, fell wounded, from his horse while holding the colors of his regiment in his hands and giving the order to charge bayonets.

Losses on both sides were extremely high.[43]

Hecker described the Battle of Chancellorsville from his own point of view in a letter to Gustav von Struve. He praised his men's conduct and described his own attack and the attempt to motivate his soldiers. But he also recognized the enemy's efforts. "These rebels are real soldiers. They came like a swarm of bees careless of their lives. Powder and whiskey were found in their canteens. They handle their artillery splendidly." And about the XI Corps, later so severely criticized, he wrote,

> No corps in the world of such a small number and such a position could have held the enemy. The best proof is that Hooker had to unlimber his artillery, forty pieces, and apply his entire disposable force to bring to a standstill an enemy who was already exhausted by hours of

attack and running … What he was not able to accomplish with this mass could hardly be expected of a weak corps, overrun due to his and Howard's errors. I am nonpartisan. No one says of me, nor can say of me, that I did not hold my ground.[44]

The wounded Hecker was taken by soldiers of Buschbeck's Brigade into their entrenchment but was then left behind at his own insistence in order not to delay the brigade's retreat. He passed through enemy lines riding on a wounded horse. He was then brought to a field hospital during the night and given medical care. An ambulance of the 3rd Division finally carried Hecker to Washington, where he was handed over to his brother-in-law, Dr. Heinrich Tiedemann, and his sister Charlotte, who took him back to Philadelphia.

Although Hooker had much the larger force, he was unable to react adequately to the rapid, shocking collapse of his right wing. The entire following day, which Hecker passed in an ambulance wagon, Hooker permitted Lee's troops to storm through the burning woods, attacking his main force and pressing it back to the Rappahannock. Only the arrival of the report that "Uncle" John Sedgwick had taken the weakly held heights at Fredericksburg on his third assault on 3 May, so that he stood in Lee's rear, prevented Hooker from being completely overrun. Lee then left a small force to watch Hooker's front while he turned to meet Sedgwick's approaching troops, defeating an uncoordinated attack at Salem Church on 4 May with 21,000 rebels. The losses of the Battle of Chancellorsville were high for both sides. The Army of Northern Virginia lost almost 13,000 men, 22 percent of the soldiers involved in the battle. The Union troops showed 17,000 dead, about 15 percent of their total army. "Stonewall" Jackson died on 10 May as a result of wounds received on 2 May when he was brought down by two shots from his own sentries during an inspection tour. One arm had been amputated, and a lung infection finally weakened him so much that he could not recover.

In his official report, which appeared in the newspapers, Hooker blamed the XI Corps for the failed operation at Chancellorsville. Nativist undertones against the "dutch corps" could not be ignored. The "running dutchmen" were accused of cowardice and failed patriotism. The accusations enraged the Germans. When Hecker saw Hooker's report, he wrote a letter at once to Caspar Butz with an enclosed map clearly showing the tactical errors. Schurz also responded to incorrect accounts by speaking of his own report to General Howard, telling him to correct his position.

The Eleventh Corps, and, by error or malice, especially the Third

Division, has been held up to the whole country as a band of cowards. My division has been made responsible for the defeat of the Eleventh Corps, and the Eleventh Corps for the failure of the campaign. ... I am far from saying that on May 2 anybody did his duty to the best of his power. But one thing I will say, because I know it: These men are no cowards!

Convinced that his narrative was the closest to the actual events, Schurz asked that his report be published. He made the same request of Secretary of War Edwin M. Stanton, who had succeeded Cameron in February 1862. A little later he wrote Lincoln a letter with the same contents. A German-American protest meeting was held in the Cooper Institute in New York against the unjust, nativist accusations of Hooker and the *New York Times*.[45] Hecker was meanwhile recovering from his wounds with his brother-in-law in Philadelphia.

Hecker did not return to his regiment until early July, on the last day of the Battle of Gettysburg. There survives a private report of Gettysburg by Hecker's adjutant Eugen Weigel. Weigel's letter made clear the personal horror of so great a battle. It also gave information about Hecker's return to the regiment, and his "madness about intrigues":

Lieutenant Colonel Salomon has performed splendidly and is much loved. For that reason he contrasts favorably with the old man [Hecker], because he is always cool and quiet, while the latter is always out of control and makes a heathen spectacle. Since [Hecker] has been back he has fallen once more into his madness about intrigues, and he thinks everyone in the world wants to be rid of him. ... Our people have had to endure dreadful problems.[46]

After the battle, Union troops pursued the rebels from southern Pennsylvania through Maryland into Virginia. Hecker's own regiment left its position on Cemetery Hill near Gettysburg at 5:30 p.m. on 5 July in order to continue in the direction of Emmitsburg, "but on account of the horrible roads and darkness that prevailed, we encamped near a creek (name unknown) at the hour of 11:30 p.m." From then until his arrival in Warrenton Junction on 25 July, Hecker's regiment marched an average of 30 miles a day. On 25 September the XI Corps, severely decimated and still under the command of Howard, received orders to go to Lookout Valley at the foot of Lookout Mountain near Chattanooga, Tennessee, as part of the Army of the Cumberland. Hecker was commanding one of the three brigades of Schurz's 3rd Division, although he still held the rank of colonel. This 3rd Brigade consisted of his own regiment, the 82nd Illinois, together with the 80th Illinois, the 75th Pennsylvania and the 68th New York. The 3rd Division's 1st Brigade was commanded by Brigadier General Hector Tyndale and the 2nd Brigade by Colonel Vladimir Krzyzanowski. All three brigades of Schurz's 3rd Division were involved on the night of 28-29 October in an operation that was distinguished by misunderstandings and became known less for its military significance than for the court of inquiry later convened in response to Hecker and Schurz following the publication of the official report by Major General Hooker. This was the night skirmish at Wauhatchie.[47]

That night rebels had gone over to the attack against the 2nd Division of XII Corps under the command of Brigadier General John Geary at Wauhatchie. Two divisions of Howard's XI Corps were camped only two miles away. As the attack proceeded, Schurz received the order from General Hooker, who commanded XI and XII Corps, to rush to Geary's support with the brigade that was closest. Schurz set out with Tyndale's 1st Brigade and ordered both the 2nd Brigade under Krzyzanowski and the 3rd under Hecker to follow. While still underway to Geary, Schurz received the order from Lieutenant Paul Oliver of Hooker's staff first to take the hill held by the rebels along the road to Geary in order to secure the way for the other brigades. This was done successfully. Krzyzanowski's brigade went first, followed by Hecker's brigade. When Krzyzanowski received the order to halt, Hecker's brigade passed him by, as Hecker had received no such command.

After Hecker passed Krzyzanowski, Hecker received from Major Howard of major General Howard's staff the order to halt at the next crossroad, about 150 yards distant. On arriving at this crossroad, Hecker formed his troops, as ordered, in a battle line aimed at Smith Hill. At this point General Hooker came riding back on an inspection tour, and he asked for their position. Hecker reported himself as the 3rd Brigade, 3rd Division, XI Corps, and he told Hooker the position of the two other brigades.[48] In the meantime Major Howard had ridden to Schurz and explained the positions of the two brigades and their placement under the command of General Hooker, who feared a rebel attack from the left side of the two hills – a justified fear, as Hecker remarked in his report. After taking the hill Schurz rode back to Hooker to report. When Hooker learned that his original order to aid Geary had not been accomplished, he expressed his displeasure with Schurz in clear terms. Hooker repeated his original order, and Schurz now gave Hecker's and Krzyzanowski's brigades the command to advance toward Geary. The 2nd Brigade was placed in such a way as to protect Hecker's flanks as he passed by. Hecker's brigade was able to complete their march to Wauhatchie without major incident, where they reached Geary's 2nd Division on the morning of 29 October at 5:30 a.m., to great jubilation. The 2nd Brigade under Krzyzanowski arrived at 7:00.

The entire action was not very spectacular, and very little damage had been done. The skirmish between the rebels and Geary's troops had already calmed down shortly after the meeting of Hecker and Hooker, and it ceased entirely shortly thereafter. There was at first no reason for further criticism or excitement about this episode. Hecker's letters to Struve on 21 December and Elihu Washburne on 14 December 1863 mentioned the Battle of Wauhatchie and described how Federals had stormed enemy positions on the hills. In comparison with the later Battle of Chattanooga, which Hecker regarded as "Grant's masterpiece," Wauhatchie was entirely insignificant. The marching routes of the 3rd Brigade only reported the usual maneuvers and marches reported by Struve in his letter and in complete agreement with the official report. At the end of November the brigade finally took its winter quarters at the foot of Lookout Mountain,

> where we await shoes, clothing, tents, etc., to fight the last battle after the winter rest. If I were not of tough wood, I would long have been gone ... Mr. Reb was also nice enough to leave my hide unshorn and to shoot cleanly past me.[49]

But the rest that Hecker expected would be disturbed in January 1864 by the publication of General Hooker's official report of the night operation at Wauhatchie. Various newspapers printed the report, and Hecker accidentally came into possession of it in a copy of the *Cincinnati Commercial* of 5 January 1864. Hecker could not tell whether the report had been published with the permission of the War Department in Washington or not. No sooner had he seen the report, than he wrote in great distress to Carl Schurz, citing the relevant passage.

> The brigade dispatched to the relief of Geary, by orders delivered in person to the division commander, never reached him until long after the fight had ended. It was alleged that it lost its way, when it had a terrific infantry fire to guide it all the way; and that it became involved in a swamp, where there was no swamp or other obstacle between it and Geary which should have delayed it a moment in marching to the relief of its imperiled companions.

In his letter Hecker then gave his version of the episode on the night of 28-29 October. He said that he had held strictly to the order given him personally by Hooker and that as soon as he received the order from Schurz, on his return, to advance, he had marched away at once. Already sensitized by Hooker's nativist report on the Battle of Chancellorsville, Hecker interpreted the passage in Hooker's new report as a personal attack on his honor. Because his brigade had been the first to arrive at Geary at dawn, he had no doubt that the unit criticized was his own, although the brigade was not specifically named nor anyone else, even Schurz as division commander. "I never in my whole military life failed to do my duty," the offended Hecker wrote to Schurz,

> and so far as courage and valor are concerned, nobody has doubted it or shall doubt it. As I have been reproached without foundation in a public document, all transactions in this case, of course, are of a public character; I therefore most respectfully ... demand a court of inquiry[50]

Hecker's passion in Germany for duels was exceeded in America by his passion for investigatory commissions and military courts. But in this last instance it was a "question of honor."

Schurz allowed himself to be convinced by Hecker's view of things. He wrote to Major General Hooker the same day using almost the same words as Hecker to criticize the same passage of the report, and adding a corrected version of the episode. Schurz wrote that it would have been impossible for Hecker and his men to reach Geary before the end of the skirmish after being halted by Hooker himself, and from a position that was so far from Geary's camp. Nor could Hecker be made responsible, because he had strictly obeyed an order. "I obeyed and executed it [the order] without delay," Hecker later said before the court of inquiry, because "during an attack of the enemy the battle-field is not the place for asking questions about the orders."

It must have been clear to Schurz that the accusation in Hooker's report did not apply to Hecker, but to himself. For that reason he accepted responsibility. "If, indeed," he informed Hooker, "somebody must be blamed, I would rather claim the blame entirely for myself, than permit it to fall, even by construction, upon my subordinate commanders and their men, who bear no responsibility in this matter and have always executed orders with promptness and alacrity." Hecker's request for a "public exoneration from the censure inflicted on him and his brigade by (Hooker's) report or a court of inquiry" was enclosed with Schurz's letter. Joseph Hooker wrote two days later to Brigadier General William D. Whipple that he would support such an investigation. At the same time he expressed his astonishment over why Hecker in particular felt attacked by the report. "It is not known," he wrote to Whipple, "for what reason Colonel Hecker makes this application, or why he should connect his brigade with it."[51]

The court of inquiry, took place between 29 January and 15 February in Major General Hooker's headquarters under the presidency of Colonel Adolph Buschbeck of the 27th Pennsylvania Volunteers. Schurz and Hecker were present. Hecker had at first requested that the two cases be brought before the court separately, because Schurz had been under different command that night, but after a brief consultation the court decided that the matter could easily be clarified by a shared investigation. The report presented by the court was fair and balanced. The only weak point was the unexplained halt of the 2nd Brigade. At the same time the commission stressed its view that General Hooker was justified in the criticism expressed in his report if one considered that his order was the proper one in this situation. The assault on Geary was a night attack, which no one had expected. It was right to go to the aid of General Geary's relatively small command as quickly as possible, since one had to assume that the enemy had the larger force. Hooker had a right to expect his orders to be carried out correctly, and he was correspondingly horrified when that was not the case.

Hecker's case was the easiest for the court of inquiry, because it was obvious that Hooker had not expressly mentioned him individually in his report.

> So far as the conduct of Colonel Hecker is concerned, it is not deserving of censure. It is apparent that the strictures contained in General Hooker's official report were not intended to apply to him or his command. In the opinion of the Court, the strictures were not deserved by the conduct of Colonel Hecker, or any part of his command.

Hooker had, however, given Schurz a specific command to help Geary at once. The commission found that Schurz was not guilty of any failure to obey, because it had been his intention all along to carry out this order. He had merely veered from that intention because further and different orders arrived that he felt were superior. Schurz was not responsible for the misunderstanding.[52]

The relief and restoration of honor that Hecker and Schurz had sought was achieved with this verdict. Yet while the court was in recess, Hecker wrote to Major General Howard to ask for immediate honorable release from military service.[53] The reason that he gave was his state of health, which had suffered greatly over the last few months; he also had to see after personal matters on his farm. This is not beyond belief. As Caspar Butz recalled, Hecker was actually in rather poor health. Major General Howard approved Hecker's application, and in his accompanying letter to the adjutant general in Washington, gave the additional reason that Hecker had been passed over several times for promotion. This agrees with Struve's conclusion that Hecker left active service due to injured dignity.

It is possible that Struve, who knew Hecker's sense of dignity, was best situated to understand his desire for promotion. Hecker had become colonel through the election of his soldiers, according to the rules of volunteer regiments. He would have had to be officially named brigadier general by the highest authorities in Washington. Hecker probably never desired anything more in his life than an official promotion. It would have been a repayment for his patriotism as well as a personal compensation for his defeat at Kandern. He would have regarded it as deserved official recognition for a citizen who had committed himself selflessly to the common good and the preservation of the republic. Finally, the military title of a brigadier general would have made a great impression in Germany.

The extent to which Hecker hoped for promotion was evident in a letter to Elihu Washburne composed in December 1863, hence before he became aware of Hooker's report. Weighing his chances of promotion, Hecker explained to Washburne that he was one of the longest-serving colonels. Yet he had always been passed over even though he currently commanded a brigade. Washburne was to inform him if his name appeared on the list of those nominated for "promotion to the rank of Brigade-General." If this were not the case, then Washburne should understand that Hecker wished to withdraw to private life, because he did not want to experience another person taking over his command.

When Hooker's report was published, Hecker had to assume that his hope for promotion was finished, or at least very imperiled. This was the reason that Hecker forced an investigation so intensely, to have the case clarified by a court. Hecker knew from experience, as his letter to Washburne showed, that promotions were taking place at that moment. In fact, on 31 January 1864 a list went to the War Department signed by Major General George H. Thomas of the Army of the Cumberland, to which Hecker's regiment had belonged since September, and endorsed by senators and representatives from Ohio. The names of nine colonels were on this list had already commanded brigades for the prescribed amount of time and were now ready for promotion to brigadier general. Hecker's name was among them. But while Major General Thomas could provide the necessary information for seven candidates, he had to confess about Hecker and another colonel, "[they] have not been in this army a great while & I am not prepared to speak specially of them."[54] Hecker's hopes were thus not groundless, but he seemed to lack an adequate spokesman.

Hecker's letter to Governor Yates of Illinois two days after the end of the court of inquiry also showed how much the "matter of honor" meant to him. Hecker gave Yates the details of the episode and the result of the investigation, asking the governor to work for a restoration of his military honor of his soldiers in proper form. Hecker was forbidden by the articles of war and military law to act publicly on his own behalf. In a memorandum of the Springfield administration on 27 February, Yates remarked about Hecker's letter that two officers, Hirschback and Loomis, were to be asked how the matter would be best handled, and "carefully" in any case. Finally a telegram from Governor Yates reached President Lincoln seeking the promotion of Friedrich Hecker to brigadier general in retrospect, since his resignation had already been approved. Yates mentioned Hecker's active efforts for the Republican Party in Illinois and stressed his military accomplishments. He also felt the promotion was completely justified as a sign of public recognition that would particularly please the German population of Illinois. Jesse Dubois, an auditor of the Illinois Legislature who, as a Republican politician, depended on German votes, also wrote to Lincoln after he had heard of Yates' action to support Hecker's promotion: "I think this step … would be very judicious and an act of simple justice to a most excellent man & officer. It has been looked for, desired and demanded a long time by public sentiment." As was the case with the governor's letter, Dubois' letter was forwarded by Lincoln to the War Department.[55] But no promotion was ever granted.

[1] See the call and the German commentary on it, *BZ*, weekly, 18 April 1861. On the enthused reception, see also Jörg Nagler, *Fremont contra Lincoln* (Frankfurt a. M.; New York; Bern, 1984), here 18-21; approximately 176,000 to 216,000 soldiers of German birth served as volunteers in the Northern army, while 70,000 fought on the Confederate side. See Saalberg, *Westliche Post*, 93-94, 104.

[2] *BZ*, weekly, 18 April 1861, 22 August 1861. On Yates' excessive zeal, see *DAB*, vol. 20, 599-601, here 600. See the newspaper interview with Sigel from 1887 in the Franz Sigel Papers, New York Historical Society, New York. Daniel Hertle, *Die Deutschen in Nordamerika und der Freiheitskampf in Missouri* (Chicago, 1865), 84. Marcus Junkelmann, *Der amerikanische*

Bürgerkrieg, 1861-1865 (Zürich, 1992), 87; Steven Rowan, James Neal Primm, eds., *Germans for a Free Missouri* (Columbia, MO, 1983); also article in *BZ*, weekly, 22 August 1861.

3 *WP*, 26 June 1861. FH to Gustav von Struve, Lookout Valley, Tennessee, 21 December 1863, *GL*, 1865, 58; my own emphasis.

4 A letter of FH, *BZ*, weekly, 19 October 1871. FH to Richard Yates, Colesburgh, 24 September 1861, FHP, box 2, folder 24; it was only in the course of later troop formation that the Hecker-Jäger-Regiment became the 24th Illinois Volunteer Regiment; in all Illinois raised almost 150 regiments during the war. See *BZ*, weekly, 23 May 1861; the naming of some officers to command the regiment provisionally until its colonel would arrive. "Eine Erklärung Friedrich Heckers. Mein Ausscheidung aus dem Dienste. Ein Beitrag zur Geschichte des hiesigen Heerwesens," *ISZ*, quoted here from *Der Westbote*, weekly, 30 January 1862, FHP, box 2, folder 42.

5 *Chicago Sonntagszeitung*, quoted in *BZ*, weekly, 13 June 1861. Butz, "Erinnerungen," part 2.

6 "Eine Erklärung Friedrich Heckers"; see also "Die Abschiedsproklamation des Obersten Friedrich Hecker an sein Regiment, St. Clair Co., Ill., 8. Januar 1862," *AW*, weekly, 8 January 1862. *Chicago Sonntagszeitung*.

7 "Eine Erklärung Friedrich Heckers." FH to Capt. Schneider and L. Brentano, Gary, 27 June 1861, Georg Schneider Papers, Chicago Historical Society.

8 "Eine Erklärung Friedrich Heckers." Details of the troop movements and marches of the 24th Illinois Volunteer Regiment in *Records of Event. Compiled Records showing service of Military Units in Volunteer Union Organizations, Illinois (21st-26th Inf.),* microfilm 594, roll 17, National Archives, Washington. *WP*, 19 July 1861, also quoted in *BZ*, weekly, 1 August 1861.

9 "Eine Erklärung Friedrich Heckers."

10 *WP*, 19 July 1861, also quoted in *BZ*, weekly, 1 August 1861.

11 On this meeting also Otto Schneider, "Abraham Lincoln und das Deutschthum," *DAG*, 7 (1907), 65-75, here 69; also Hecker's letter to Ernst Keil, *GL*, 1869, 416. "Eine Erklärung Friedrich Heckers." Butz, "Erinnerungen," part 2.   FH to Abraham Lincoln, Camp Dennison, 20 September 1861, FHP, box 2, folder 24, preliminary drafts.

12 *Louisviller Anzeiger*, quoted in *BZ*, weekly, 10 October 1861, emphasis in the original.

13 Mihalotzi later succeeded Hecker because he was neither one of those dismissed by FH nor one of the officers promoted by him on the spot. G. Mihalotzi to General D. C. Buel, 17 November 1861, FHP, box 2, folder 24. FH to Georg Schneider (and Lorenz Brentano), Camp Pope, 14 July 1861, Schneider Papers.

14 "Eine Erklärung Friedrich Heckers."

15 *BZ*, weekly, 22 August 1861. "Gerechte Klagen Heckers," *Louisville Anzeiger*, quoted in *BZ*, weekly, 10 October 1861; the same quote again in *BZ*, weekly, 31 October 1861. "Eine Erklärung Friedrich Heckers."

16 Sigel was at work on a comparison of the "standing army versus army of the people," and he supplied his proposed structure with commentaries, including sections on suppressing the abuse of alcohol in the regiment, see Sigel Papers; the sketches derive from approximately the mid-1850s; the Papers are not adequately catalogued. See the regimental orders of 7 and 8 August 1861, FHP, box 2, folder 24.

17 See the complete order, Brigadier General U. S. Grant to Col. FH, Headquarters, Ironton, MO, 16 August 1861, FHP, box 2, folder 24. "Eine Erklärung Friedrich Heckers." After his resignation an article entitled "Die neue militärische Wirksamkeit Friedrich Heckers," in which Hecker's conduct was defended, and where it becomes clear what episodes led to the "maneater" accusation. *WP* or *AW*, no date, c. February 1862, FHP, box 4, folder 42.

18 Brigadier General U. S. Grant to FH, Ironton, MO, 18 August 1861, FHP, box 2, folder 24. Hecker's farewell in *Der Westbote*, weekly, 30 January 1862, FHP, box 2, folder 42 "Eine Erklärung Friedrich Heckers." Hecker later sent a notarized transcript of the trial to Secretary Cameron. See *VSB*, 44. öS, 28 March 1848, 354.

[19] See the letter signed by 12 captains and lieutenants, Captain Eduard Salomon to Col. Frederick Hecker, Marble Creek, 21 August 1861, FHP, box 2, folder 24. Captain Eduard Salomon to Col. FH, as above; see the list of officers and soldiers recommended by Hecker, Headquarters of Division, Fredericktown, MO, 29 August 1861, Official Order no. 53 signed by General B. M. Prentiss, FHP, box 2, folder 24. FH to General B. M. Prentiss, Fredericktown, MO, 29 August 1861, FHP, box 2, folder 24.

[20] Captain Thomas Lang (in the name of the other officers) to the Adjutant General of the U. S. Army, 20 September 1861, FHP, box 2, folder 24.

[21] FH to Frémont, Camp Dennison, 20 September 1861, FHP, box 2, folder 24.

[22] Tucker, *Leadership*, 283; James M. McPherson, *Für die Freiheit sterben. Die Geschichte des amerikanischen Bürgerkriegs* (Munich, 1988), 340-41, 343. Körner, *Memoirs*, vol. 2, 168-81. Franz Sigel to Caspar Butz, 7 December 1861, Sigel Papers; the entire letter printed in Nagler, *Fremont*, 263-64.

[23] McPherson, *Für die Freiheit*, 342; see also Nagler, *Fremont*, 21. Thorough treatment by Nagler, *Fremont*, 21-26; see on that also the article "Unsere Lage," *BZ*, weekly edition, 22 August 1861. See Lincoln to Frémont, 2 September 1861, Basler, *Collected Works*, vol. 4, 506; Frémont declined to do this, see ibid., 507; see also the commentary of the *ISZ*, "Lincoln sucht Fremont auf dem Privatweg zur Modifikation seiner Proklamation zu bewegen," quoted in *BZ*, weekly, 26 September 1861. Lincoln to Orville H. Browning, quoted in Basler, *Collected Works*, vol. 4, 530-31, emphasis in original. Lincoln to Frémont, 2 September 1861, ibid., vol. 4, 506; here quoted in McPherson, *Für die Freiheit*, 343; emphasis in the text. See the printing of the Lincoln letter in the *BZ*, weekly, 26 September 1861, also for example the article "Ferner Verhandlungen über Fremont's Proklamation," *WP*, quoted in *BZ*, weekly, 19 September 1861. "Herr Lincoln und General Fremont," *ISZ*, quoted in *BZ*, weekly, 26 September 1861; "Fremont's Proklamation vom 30. August modificirt," ibid., 26 September 1861; "Fremont und seine Feinde," *New Yorker Demokrat*, quoted in *BZ*, weekly, 10 October 1861. *ISZ*, quoted in *BZ*, weekly, 26 September 1861; *WP*, quoted in *BZ*, weekly, 19 September 1861. The principled conflict that developed between Lincoln and Frémont and the German opposition, eventually resulting in the founding of a new party, Radical Democracy, finally nominating Frémont as its presidential candidate, cannot be pursued here; see Nagler, *Fremont contra Lincoln*; also Tucker, *Political Leadership*, 287, 306-333. Nagler, *Fremont*, 37-42. Resolution of the meeting in St. Louis, *WP*, weekly, 13 November 1861, quoted in Nagler, *Fremont*, 38.

[24] "Eine Erklärung Friedrich Heckers." FH to Frémont, Camp Dennison, Kentucky, 20 September 1861, FHP, box 2, folder 24 (transcript and drafts), The Frémont order bears no. 207, 17 September 1861, St. Louis. FH to Richard Yates, Colesburgh, 24 September 1861, FHP, box 2, folder 24. A first letter to Yates is dated 22 September 1861; the originals of the Hecker letters are in the Richard Yates Papers, Illinois Historical Society, Springfield, IL.

[25] "Eine Erklärung Friedrich Heckers." *Louisville Anzeiger*, quoted in *BZ*, weekly, 24 October 1861.

[26] Frémont's responsibility for the 24th Illinois Volunteer Infantry Regiment ended on 22 September 1861, see his telegram to Hecker, 22 September 1861, FHP, box 2, folder 24. Brigadier General Sherman to FH, 29 September 1861, FHP, box 2, folder 24; and Sherman to FH, 4 October 1861, ibid. See the command of the Adjutant General Office, Washington, 14 October 1861 to Brigadier General W. T. Sherman, Commanding the Department of the Cumberland, Louisville; there it is commanded that the decision by Frémont was not ratified, but rather that the officers must be restored (signed Thomas A. Scott, acting as Secretary of War), FHP, box 2, folder 24; see also the account in the *BZ*, weekly, 24 October 1861. "Eine Erklärung Friedrich Heckers." Grant obviously got on well with Hecker, see Daniel Hertle, *Die Deutschen in Nordamerika*, 84-85. Brigadier General Grant to FH, head Quarter Department, Cairo, 17 October 1861, FHP, box 2, folder 24.

[27] *BZ*, weekly, 17 October 1861. See his report, FH, Headquarters, 24th Reg., Ill. Vol., Colesburgh, Ky, 19 October 1861 to the Department of War, Adj. General Office-Washington D.

C.: "I, in front of the regiment, reinstalled them to day in command," FHP, box 2, folder 24. "Eine Erklärung Friedrich Heckers." See FH to Franz Sigel, 11 September 1861, Sigel Papers: "You will have received my letter in which I move you to arrange the incorporation of my regiment in your division. It is the desire of the entire regiment. We now have prospects of attacking the rebels near Columbus, and we certainly would not want to miss that, but that does not hinder our incorporation into your brigade … As much as I am happy with Brigadier General Grant, I would prefer a command under you." Caspar Butz to Franz Sigel, Chicago, 21 September 1861, Sigel Papers. Butz was the real agitator in the cause of Frémont against Lincoln.

28 FH to Simon Cameron, Secretary of War, 21 October 1861, FHP, box 2, folder 24.

29 *BZ*, weekly, 31 October 1861. FH to Brigadier General Buel, commander of the Department of the Ohio, 21 November 1861, FHP, box 2, folder 24. "Eine Erklärung Friedrich Heckers"; Friedrich Hecker, "Offene Antwort an Herrn Francis A. Hoffmann," St. Clair Co., 10 February 1862, ibid. FH to Elihu Washburne, Lebanon, St. Clair County, Ill., 9 December [1861], Washburne Papers.

30 Tucker, *Leadership*, 292; also *BZ*, weekly, 22 August 1861. See, for example, Butz's article in the *ISZ*, quoted in *BZ*, weekly, 31 October 1861.

31 "Die Abschiedsproklamation des Obersten Heckers an sein Regiment," also "Eine Erklärung Friedrich Heckers."

32 *Buffalo Demokrat*, quoted in *ISZ* [n. d., January-February 1862] in FHP, box 4, folder 42. "Eine Erklärung Friedrich Heckers"; Francis A. Hoffmann, lieutenant governor of Illinois, "Offener Brief an Fr. Hecker" [n. d., circa start of February 1862], FHP, box 4, folder 42; FH, "Offene Antwort an Herrn Francis A. Hoffmann," as above. Tucker, *Leadership*, 263; due to Yates' alcoholic problems, Hoffmann often had to take his place as "acting governor." This substitution can be established using the Yates Papers for September-October 1862 and April-May 1863, but his replacement by Hoffmann is likely for earlier periods as well. Repeated reports of corruption in the administration of the army in the anti-Lincoln press, for example *Chicago Tribune*, 26 October 1861. See excerpt of the confirmation of 23 December 1861, Special Order no. 41, Headquarters, Department of the Ohio, Louisville, Kentucky, signed by General Buel, FHP, box 2, folder 24. "Eine Erklärung Friedrich Heckers."

33 Butz, "Erinnerungen," part 2.

34 Caspar Butz, Georg Schneider, A. C. Hesing, Lorenz Brentano to Lyman Trumbull, Isaac Arnold, Elihu Washburne, L. Browning, Chicago, 8 January 1862, Sigel Papers. Also see the letter from Isaac Arnold to FH concerning Arnold's efforts for Franz Sigel's restoration, Washington, 4 December 1862, FHP, folder 29; Arnold was highly dependent on German votes. See Lorenz Brentano to FH, Chicago, 20 May 1862, FHP, box 2, folder 29; also printed in the appendix of Nagler, *Fremont*, 268. Major General John Charles Frémont to Dr. Philipp Weigel, Emil Preetorius and Felix Corte, Headquarters, Mountain Department, Wheeling, Va., 17 April 1862, FHP, box 2, folder 29.

35 FHP, box 9 (oversized documents), 28 October 1862, Springfield, Illinois, Illinois commission of Frederick Hecker as Colonel of the 82nd Regiment, Illinois Volunteers, signed Governor Yates, 23 October 1862. Report of Emil Frey, printed in the *Highland News Leader*, 14 September 1877, FHP, box 2, folder 28. Report of Eugen Weigel, *TWP*, 2 July 1893, Scrapbook of Eugen Weigel, FHP, box 3, folder 32.

36 The amnesty law was dated 7 August 1862; while Hecker fell under the amnesty law, the Grand Duchy did not issue a general and unconditional amnesty for Struve, "condemned to death *in contumaciam*." Margaretha Eisenhardt to Josephine Hecker, Mannheim, 30 August 1862, FHP, box 2, folder 29.

37 H. Rinker to Arthur Hecker, Tauber-Bischofsheim, 28 September 1862, FHP, box 2, folder 29.

38 Eugen Weigel to Arthur Hecker, Head Quarters, 82nd Ill. Vol., Camp Sigel near Fairfax, Va., 3 December 1862, FHP, folder 29.

39 The movements of the 82nd Illinois are listed in detail in the Records of Event, Microfilm 594, roll 26, National Archives, Washington; on 15 November 1863 the regiment had entered

Fairfax, coming from Arlington and Alexandria. Gustav von Struve, "Friedrich Hecker in Amerika," *GL*, 1865, 57. Since the Thuringian states refused him entry, Struve settled in "relatively free Coburg," where he published his book *Diesseits und Jenseits des Ozeans* (Coburg, 1863-64), which was thought of as a "communication on the relations between America and Germany," see Vagts, *Rückwanderung*, 175. See the reports on the illness by Paul B. Goddard, Philadelphia, 6 February 1863, and by Francis G. Smith, Medical Officer, 24 February 1863, FHP, box 2, folder 26.

[40] Caspar Butz to FH, Chicago, 12 October 1862, FHP, box 2, folder 26. On Chancellorsville, see McPherson, *Für die Freiheit*, 627-35. *The War of the Rebellion: Official Records of the Union and Confederate Armies*, 128 vols. (Washington, 1880-1901), here series 1, vol. 25, part 1, 232.

[41] McPherson, *Für die Freiheit*, 631.

[42] Carl Schurz, *The Reminiscences of Carl Schurz*, vol. 1 (New York, 1907), 670 ff. I think his official report composed shortly after the battle is a better source, see Report of Carl Schurz to Major General O. O. Howard, Virginia, 12 May 1863, *Official Records*, series 1, vol. 25, 647-058; Report of Brigadier General Alexander Schimmelpfennig to Carl Schurz, 10 May 1863, ibid., 662-63; Report of Lieutenant Colonel Edward S. Salomon to Alexander Schimmelpfennig, May, 1863, ibid., 663-64. Also see criticism of Hooker's decision by American officers, McPherson, *Für die Freiheit*, 629. Schurz to Howard, *Official Records*, series 1, vol. 25, 652.

[43] See the report of Lieutenant Colonel Adolph von Hartung, *Official Records*, vol. 25, 665. Schurz to Howard, *Official Records*, series 1, vol. 25, 655-56. In his report, Schurz gives his losses at 23 percent, *ibid.*, 658. Hecker lost 150 of his total of 450 soldiers.

[44] FH to Gustav Struve, 58.

[45] On its title page of 5 May 1863, the *New York Times* blamed the German-American soldiers exclusively for the defeat at Chancellorsville, see on the conflict also Wilhelm Kaufmann, *Die Deutschen im amerikanischen Bürgerkrieg* (Munich; Berlin, 1911), 344 ff. [English translation by Steven Rowan, *The Germans in the American Civil War* (Carlisle, PA: Kallmann, 1999), 212]. Wittke, *Refugees*, 236-37; Hans Louis Trefousse, *Carl Schurz: A Biography* (Knoxville, 1982), 132 ff. Butz, "Erinnerungen," part 2. Schurz to Howard, *Official Records*, vol. 25, 658. Carl Schurz to E. M. Stanton, Secretary of War, Camp near Stafford Court House, 18 May 1863, *Official Records*, vol. 25, 659. Carl Schurz to Abraham Lincoln, 28 May 1863; Lincoln MSS, Library of Congress, Washington. Nagler, *Fremont*, 119-20.

[46] On the "Gettysburg Campaign," see the report of Carl Schurz to Major General O. O Howard, 20 August 1863, *Official Records*, series 1, vol. 27, 727-32; report of Col. Frederick Hecker to Col. G. von Amsberg, 21 August 1863, ibid., 732-34 (comprehends the movements of the Hecker Regiment from 28 June to 21 August [Warrenton Junction]). In this report, Hecker stresses that his report on Gettysburg was based on information from Lieutenant Colonel Edward Salomon, who led the 82nd Illinois Regiment until Hecker's return. From 4 July on, Hecker speaks as "we." He was back with his regiment at the latest then. Franz Hennes' supposition that he returned once more to Illinois to raise new troops is incorrect, see Henne, Frei ed., *Hecker in den USA*, 95. The illness certificate found in Hecker's military papers in the National Archives is by Hecker's brother-in-law Tiedemann, dated 6 June, and it speaks of a convalescence period of 30 days. Two months passed between his wounding on 2 May and the Battle of Gettysburg. See on this the Letter Records of the Volunteers, National Archives, Washington (File Mark W 493 [VS] 1867) with information for his claim of a pension, indicating Hecker's presence with the regiment for that month; on Hecker's direct return from Philadelphia to Gettysburg, see newspaper reports in FHP, box 4, folder 41. Eugen Weigel to his parents, Head Quarters, 82nd Reg. Ills. Vols., Boonesborough, Md., 9 July 1863, FHP, box 3, folder 31.

[47] Report of FH, 21 August 1863, 733, as above, with the precise route of march to Warren Junction. See organization in *Official Records*, series 3, vol. 32, 552. *Original Records*, series 1, vol. 31, part 1, 83; losses of the "Chattanooga-Ringgold Campaign"; see also FH to Struve; the march route described in this letter agrees with the official reports by Carl Schurz to Howard

published in the *Official Records*. *Official Records*, series 1, vol. 31, part 1, 97-99; 110-213.

[48] A map of the area with the location of the troops is in *Official Records*, series 1, vol. 31, part 1, 212 (Appendix E). Also see Col. FH to Richard Yates, White Side, Tenn., 17 February 1864, Yates Family Papers, a copy of the letter is in FHP, box 2, folder 26; on events, see the thorough report of Hecker as Appendix C, Lookout Valley, 12 February 1864, *Official Records*, series 1, vol. 31, part 1, 201-6.

[49] See FH to Elihu Washburne, Lookout Valley, Tennessee, 14 December 1863, Washburne Papers; letter from Friedrich Hecker to Gustav Struve, 58. See Intineraries of the First Brigade (Brig. General Hector Tyndale) and the Third Brigade (Col. Frederick Hecker), 1-30 November, *Official Records*, series 1, vol. 31, part 2, 383-84 (no. 107). Letter from FH to Gustav Struve (n. 8); see on that also Carl Schurz to Lieutenant Colonel Meysenburg, Lookout Valley, 22 December 1863, *Official Records*, series 1, vol. 31, part 2, 381-83 (no. 196). Letter from Friedrich Hecker to Gustav Struve (as in n. 8), 59.

[50] Due to the continual movements, many reports on battles and operations were only written and filed in winter quarters; Hooker's official report on the night battle at Wauhatchie, dated 6 November 1862, was only published in January, 1864, see also Trefousse, *Schurz*, 143. FH to Richard Yates, White Side, Tenn., 17 February 1864, Yates Papers. Report of FH, Tenn., 10 January 1864, *Official Records*, series 1, vol. 31, part 1, 180-81.

[51] Carl Schurz to Major General Joseph Hooker, 10 January 1864, *Official Records*, series 1, vol. 31, part 1, 182-84; Schurz sent a copy of this letter to Hecker, now in FHP, box 2, folder 26. The letter of complaint to Schurz written by Colonel Orland Smith of 20 November 1863, demanding an investigation of Hecker, found in Hecker's military papers, increases the impression that it dealt with Hecker's troop. Colonel Orland Smith headed the 2nd Brigade of the 2nd Division; see *Official Records*, series 1, vol. 32, part 3, 552; Henne, *Hecker*, 210. FH's submission to the court of inquiry, Appendix C, Lookout Valley, 12 February 1864, *Official Records*, series 1, vol. 31, part 1, 201-6, here 206. Hecker makes clear in his letter to Yates, "Maj. Gen. Schurz (at whom the blow is aimed, and by mistake fell on myself also)," see FH to Richard Yates, as above. Carl Schurz to Joseph Hooker, 10 January 1864, *Official Records*, series 1, vol. 31, part 1, 184. Joseph Hooker to William D. Whipple, 12 January 1864, *Official Records*, series 1, vol. 31, part 1, 179-80, here 180.

[52] See in detail, No. 37, Record of a Court of Inquiry, and accompanying documents, *Official Records*, series 1, vol. 31, part 1, 137 ff. See Appendix D, 206-11, further ibid,, 209-11.

[53] FH to Major General O. O. Howard, 12 February 1864, Hecker military papers, National Archives (see Henne, *Hecker*, 210).

[54] Butz, "Erinnerungen," part 2. Butz as well had written to Senator Lyman Trumbull in March, 1863, with the request that Hecker be promoted to Brigadier General, see Caspar Butz to Lyman Trumbull, 11 March 1863, Lyman Trumbull Papers, Library of Congress, Manuscript Division; printed by Nagler, Fremont, 269-70; there is only one Hecker letter to Trumbull, of 20 March 1872. Struve, "Hecker in America," *GL*, 1865, 59. FH to Elihu Washburne, Lookout Valley, Tennessee, 14 December 1863, Washburne Papers. Major General Thomas to the War Department, Office U. S. Military Telegraph, 31 January 1864, Sig. T46 CB (=Letters received by the Commission Branch) 1864, microfilm 1064, roll 126, National Archives, Washington.

[55] FH to Richard Yates, as above, Executive Office, 27 February 1864, ref. Hecker, Col., Whiteside, Tenn., 17 February 1864, Yates Papers. Richard Yates to Abraham Lincoln, Executive Office, Springfield, 11 May 1864, see also Henne, *Hecker*, 211. Jesse K. Dubois to Abraham Lincoln, Springfield, Illinois, 19 May 1864, Sig D 781 CB (=Letters received by the Commission Branch of the Adjutant General's Office, 1863-1870), 1864, microfilm 1064, roll 87, National Archives, Washington. "Respectfully referred by the President to the Hon. the secretary of war," 25 May 1864; see n. 180.

Quod Bonum Felix Faustumque Sit.

SUB AUSPICIIS

Illustris Civitatum Americanarum Rei Publicae Unitae et Civitatis,

Quae Collegium Nostrum Probavit Missouriensis, Nos

Collegii Medici Humboldtiani

Curatores nec non Decanus Ceterique Facultatis Professores

Virum Nobilissimum atque Doctissimum

Fredericum Hecker.

Honorarium Medicinae Doctorem

Creamus, hoc ipso Diplomate Renunciamus Eidemque Omnia Jura et Privilegia Doctoris

CONFERIMUS.

CURATORES.

(signatures)

PROFESSORES.

(signatures)

SANCTO LUDOVICI,

Sub Facultatis Sigillo

XIV DIEA... MENSIS A... MDCCCLXVIII.

Honorary Degree awarded in 1868 to Friedrich Hecker by the Humboldt Medical College of St. Louis, signed by the faculty, including refugees of the 1848 Revolution. Friedrich Hecker Papers, Western Historical Manuscripts, University of Missouri – St. Louis.

VII

RECONSTRUCTION (1865-1876)

The Time of Great Questions

"Rebellion draws to a close," Hecker wrote from his farm in December 1864 to Elihu Washburne in Washington. The victory of the Union armies grew ever clearer, and Hecker was already thinking about the end of the war and the postwar order. History was his teacher for this.

> Then comes the time of great questions, and I hope our legislators in Washington will study the history of the reconstruction of Rome, England, France and Germany after the revolutions were over, not to commit the same faults and not to endanger the future of this great Republic by a hasty, reckless and unprincipled reconstruction, and to leave it to the old proverb *die providentia et hominum confusione regnat res publica* ["The state is ruled by the accidents of the day and the confusion of men"].[1]

Since his return to private life Hecker had kept intensely involved in the progress of the war through letters from his lieutenant, Rudolph Müller, and through newspaper reports. In his own turn he reported the course of the war to Europe in letters. Some of his letters were published, because there was a lively interest in personal description and opinion on the war. Hecker appeared to have his eye particularly aimed at the results of the war; he had little interest in other political events. His friend Caspar Butz had called to life a large German-led opposition party, Radical Democracy, which once more raised the pro-German John Charles Frémont as candidate in the approaching presidential campaign of 1864. But Hecker appeared not to participate in any way in this undertaking. He thought little of the whole project, which had an early end with Frémont's withdrawal in September 1864. Hecker declined an invitation from John Austin Stevens, Jr., to a planned meeting of Radical Democracy in Cincinnati because he did not want to contribute to splitting the Republican Party, and he particularly did not want to endanger the Union through such a political split. Despite his own displeasure, and perhaps in hopes of a retrospective promotion, he preserved his loyalty to "Old Abe" and the president's central idea of preserving the Union. Hecker did not act personally on behalf of Lincoln in the campaign year of 1864, but this was for reasons different from those Forty-Eighters who compromised themselves through their "schismatic" support of Frémont. Only Carl Schurz, Gustav Körner, Francis Hoffmann and Fritz Hassaurek went on campaign tours for Lincoln against the Democratic candidate George McClellan.[2]

In the meantime the transformation of the military situation was working to the advantage of the president. The capture of Atlanta by Union troops in early September was the beginning of a series of military successes. The victories of the Union leaders Sherman, Farragut and Sheridan made possible Lincoln's reelection on 8 November, something that he himself considered impossible a few months before. To cut off the Confederates from supplies and food, Union troops left destruction and desolation in their wake. On 1 April 1865 the Confederate front was broken. General Lee abandoned the burning Confederate capital of Richmond, which Union troops entered on 3 April. Lee found himself resisting a power of 130,000 Union soldiers with 28,000 Confederates. His capitulation on 9 April 1865 essentially ended the war, although it would in fact be another two months until all large Confederate units surrendered their weapons. Exactly five days after the capitulation, President Lincoln fell victim to an assassin during a visit to the theater in Washington. The actor John Wilkes Booth, a fanatical supporter of the South, killed the president with a pistol shot. In a letter that Hecker wrote to a friend in Germany three months after Lincoln's murder, he condemned the crime as an act of revenge by Southern conspirators. But he also stressed how much the conclusion of the Civil War by a Union victory meant the victory of republican institutions, which relied on the people alone and not on the person of the president. Hecker saw the Union's victory entirely as the victory of his own political convictions.

> We have emerged from this dreadful struggle a powerful warrior people on land and sea. Our industry has grown in powerful dimensions. Inventions have followed in rapid succession that made possible an expansion of basic production using old men and boys, while our sons were fighting the battles. Just as the Romans once could say, "*civis Romanus sum*,["I am a Roman citizen"]" we may express with pride, "I am an American." Do not mistake the scale of this victory of republican institutions. When Lincoln was so shamefully murdered, two friends

visited me who were worried about the future, because the murder took place at the time of highest crisis. "The people lives. The people has not been murdered. Have no concern for the future." And so it has come to pass. What crises would such an event call forth in states and towns elsewhere![3]

When the American Civil War is considered in the context of foreign-born participants, the question always arises whether the war accelerated or delayed assimilation. A direct answer to this question seems impossible. Jörg Nagler speaks for delayed assimilation when he considers the campaign for Radical Democracy and the attempt of many ethnic leaders to represent a unified German community. This is opposed to the usual assertion that the Civil War contributed to the final assimilation of the Germans. One factor to be included is the fact that there was not always a congruent relationship between the leadership layers of the Thirtyers and the Forty-Eighters. These leaders' political actions often cannot be understood as representing the mood of all German-Americans. Certainly personal experience also played a large role in individual cases. Hecker's view of the Union after the war was at least ambivalent. He was visibly proud of having contributed to the preserving the nation and freedom, but at the same time his experience with nativism during "three years in the camps" had convinced him "that no matter how self-sacrificing foreigners are, neither roses nor recognition bloom there." He allowed his personal disappointment to fade only in his perennial comparison of the pride of a Roman citizen. This stressed what was more important for Hecker, namely, his role as a political citizen. He was not "merely a German," but in a much more inclusive sense a citizen of a republic and, as such, responsible for protecting its republican institutions. Although experience had long since taught him that the United States did not embody the classical republican ideal, he kept returning to his ancient model and an idealized vision of the future; it was for him the most desireable political order. He consciously applied his model to American conditions time and again. Even the American Civil War was for him an example of how a republic gained control of its own problems, as well as an example of how much "strength and power" could come from "our republican institutions."[4]

Hecker had no illusions about the decisive changes brought on by the war. The conclusion of a civil war challenged the state in the same way as the end of a revolution. In an English-language letter, Hecker reflected on the results of the war as early as May 1862, after his first resignation.

We are in a state of transition. This rebellion [will] end, our body politic will take a new career. New and unforseen [sic] organic changes will be necessary; new formations will spring up new or altered principles will lead us, as it is the consequence of all revolutions and has been since the beginning of the world. Our financial, military and administratif [sic] system, our internal improvements, and of course the administratif [sic] division of the territory will require the care of the legislator.[5]

Hecker greeted these necessary changes. He believed that his republican virtues and his orientation to principles, although sometimes stiff, would not be threatened or endangered by industrial growth and economic expansion. He promoted the formation of a modern state, which now moved rapidly forward with the end of the war. Hecker had always associated industrialization with expanding world trade, and in turn world trade with the process of democratization. American conditions, however, would change more rapidly than Hecker could have imagined. The Civil War and mobilization for it led both the South and the North to construct modern, central states. The partially private financing of the war created a new class of finance capitalists in the North who increasingly wanted to control not only the economic but also the political course of the country.[6] This meant political power in the future would be concentrated in a few persons.

At first the new president, Andrew Johnson, appeared to continue the policies of his predecessor. There were surprising parallels between him and Lincoln. Both were born and raised in poor circumstances, received a partial education, and did not manage to rise politically until their fifties. As the *Belleviller Zeitung* described it, Johnson embodied the most important aspects of the American ideology of social advancement. He was "a true self-made man after the heart of the American people. By his own force of will, through an inborn drive for the heights, he raised himself from the lower sphere that had been bestowed on him by his birth."[7] The radical wing of the Republican Party expected from Johnson an uncompromisingly paternalistic Southern policy, as well as improvement in, and a reorganization of government administration. But these hopes would not be fulfilled.

Because Congress did not reconvene until eight months after his entry into office, Johnson initially had a free hand for carrying out his own policies. The new president wanted rapid reintegration of the South into the Union and a rapid normalization of relations, with extremely easy preconditions. Johnson did not heed the demands of Radical Republicans for a strong central power with extensive executive prerogatives to realize an effective Reconstruction. Nor did he share their commitment to the political equality of black people. His interests were for a reunified Union government and a strict restoration of the Constitution in the South. As a result, reconstruction for him meant restoring the South to unrestricted participation in political rights as quickly as possible. This was most apparent in the reinstatement of suspended voting rights for the Confederates. In his vision of a reconstructed South, the freedmen played no special role. "White men alone must manage the South" he summarized. As he stated in his annual message in December1867, he was convinced that colored people had a lower "capacity for government than any other race of people ... Whenever they have been left to their own devices they have shown a constant tendency to relapse into barbarism."[8]

In a proclamation on 29 May 1865, Johnson declared amnesty for all Confederates who declared their loyalty to the Union and their readiness to support emancipation. This declaration also encompassed the restoration of all property rights in the South with the exception of slaves. Only Confederates whose property amounted to more than $20,000 had to ask the president for special amnesty. At first this was seen as a device for the exclusion of the Southern elite. But Johnson was soon seen as the South's friendly protector against the ultra-fanatics of the North. Because all Southern federal and local offices were vacant and had to be refilled, Johnson's government possessed unlimited opportunities for patronage. The president named governors, who in turn were able to fill up to 4000 positions with their own people by August 1865, everything from judges through mayors down to constables.[9] These positions were not filled with loyal Union people but, understandably, mostly with Southern notables. This happened not only for reasons of regional politics, but also to secure the support of local populations.

When the 39th Congress assembled, few members agreed with Johnson's Reconstruction policies. Many had already disagreed with Lincoln's mild conditions for peace.[10] Such abrupt decisions as the emancipation of the slaves had not corresponded to their views of a long-term democratization of the South. But with the war's end, the policy of Congress moved in a different direction. The new rights of the freed slaves needed to be protected under all circumstances. The Southern aristocracy must be broken permanently. The competence of the individual governments must be restricted and that of the federal government expanded. The way must be prepared for a totally new South.

Conflict between Johnson and the majority of the Republican Party also arose from the fact that the party had been formed on an anti-slavery platform and for that reason insisted on complete emancipation, assuring "civil rights for the negro." When President Johnson vetoed a Freedmen's Bureau bill and a civil rights bill in early 1866, both sponsored by Senator Lyman Trumbull, a final break with his own party was unavoidable. As the *Belleviller Zeitung* had predicted only a few months before this episode, the Republican Party passed through a "process of division and transition." As the paper suggested, the only new aspect of the matter was "that the leader of the party, the president, was the first to desert the flag and more or less desert to the party position of the defeated opponent." Hecker shared the majority view of American and German-American Republicans. He wrote to his former major, Frey, in Basel.

> There is no more infamous traitor than our drunken tailor [Johnson]; he is worse than Tyler and the conditions in the South are chaotic. Once the army is gone, anarchy will reign. Perhaps that is good, like a chronic process. The rebels are bolder than in their time of glory, and the candidates for office mount the stump in their gray uniforms, certain of success. Loyal Northerners and colored people are being killed like blackbirds. Fortunately Congress is holding back the storm and has clubbed the modern John of Leyden colossally. So long as Congress does not recess and leave the scoundrel a free field.[11]

Johnson's impeachment was applauded without restraint in the German press. The *Illinois Staatszeitung*, the *Westliche Post* and the *Belleviller Zeitung*, which criticized the excessively powerful president as a "king in a frock coat," bet everything on getting rid of him. "Not one of all the presidents besides Accidental President Andrew Johnson was so malign as to reverse or mutilate the rights of the people," judged the *Belleviller Zeitung*. In an article in the *Illinois Staatszeitung*, Hecker exercised his juristic talents in a legal and historical comparison between impeachment in England and in America, showing that an impeachment could "take place even when the incriminating act or procedure did not come near justifying a penal indictment." He came to the conclusion "that in England a public officer accused as Andrew Johnson could be impeached at once and removed from office." In Hecker's earlier efforts to establish ministerial responsibility, he had sustained the idea that "the king can do no wrong" for reasons of the theory of state, but an elected president, who was nothing but the supreme officer of the state, was by that very fact no monarch, and therefore owed an accounting to the people.[12]

Public dissatisfaction with Johnson's lack of cooperation produced a clear two-thirds majority in both houses for Johnson's radical opponents in the Republican Party in the congressional elections of 1866. The impeachment against him only fell one vote short of the two-thirds majority needed in the Senate, but the result did not seem to disappoint the Republicans dramatically. They knew that a presidential election loomed ahead and the problem would resolve itself then.

Hecker did not participate in the 1868 presidential campaign for Ulysses S. Grant, although he esteemed Grant personally. During the presidential campaign the Republican Party primarily exploited the theme of Reconstruction, once again raising questions of the complete emancipation of slaves and the treatment of white Southerners. The party thus avoided all of the long-standing divergences within the ranks – divergences that would emerge again. Carl Schurz was doubtless one of the most engaged and successful speakers for the party in this campaign, and he presided for a time over the convention that nominated Grant as presidential candidate. The Republican platform was still dominated by the war and its conduct; four of the ten planks dealt with repayment and reduction of the national debt, the credit worthiness of the United States and corruption. Protection of the civil rights of naturalized citizens received equal mention with the promotion of European immigration to the United States, "which in the past has contributed so much to the wealth, the development of resources and the growing of strength of this nation." A special plank dealt with veterans of the war. No one, it declared, deserved greater honor than

the brave soldiers and sailors who persisted in bearing the burdens of campaigns and sea service, placing their lives in peril in the service of the country. The bounties and pensions legally granted to these brave defenders of the country are commitments that should never be neglected.

In the future, whether someone had served in the war or not would play a large role in the granting of offices.

Carl Schurz presented two amendments at the Republican convention in Chicago that predicted his own future political course, and Hecker's, as

well. The first appealed to the "spirit of magnanimity and reconciliation" to
receive "once more into community with loyal people" those Americans
who had served the rebellion but now honorably and earnestly strove for
peace. Schurz demanded the "suspension of disenfranchisement and
restriction of legal rights placed on rebels, to the extent that the spirit of disloyalty would die out and thus the security of loyal people would not be
endangered." The second motion stressed an unlimited recognition "of the
great principles laid down by the Declaration of Independence as the true
foundation of a democratic government."[13] Both resolutions passed unanimously. No one suspected that the first would be the foundation of a new
political movement of its own.

In 1868 it appeared that almost all Thirtyers and Forty-Eighters were on
the road for Grant. Nothing indicated that four years later most of them would
join Schurz and Hecker in a new political camp. Friedrich Hassaurek spoke
at German meetings in Cleveland and praised the party of Union, freedom
and human rights. Franz Sigel, Friedrich Kapp and the German historian
and publicist Hermann von Holst spoke at the Cooper Institute in New York.
Gustav Körner, who feared that Democrats could undermine the work of
Radical Republicans in Congress and for whom Reconstruction was a central campaign issue in 1868, accepted selection as an elector on the Grant
ticket and only barely escaped assassination at an election rally in Quincy.

Hecker, in contrast, permitted himself to discuss the election only in
writing. As always, such letters were printed as propaganda in the newspapers; nothing seemed more effective than the views of a well-known
personality.

> I am voting for Grant and Colfax, not only because I know both of them
> personally – I came to know the straightness, honor and good-hearted
> solidity of the former when I served under him as colonel of the 24th
> Infantry Regiment – but because the election of Seymour and Blair
> would be the same thing as a revolution, inciting the spilling of blood
> and state bankruptcy, along with the ruin of all private conditions. If
> the Germans there (in central Ohio) have ever seen what a civil war is,
> they would never doubt for whom to vote.[14]

Hecker's views in this election were still determined by his Civil War
experiences. The enormous attraction of the "hero of Appomattox," the general to whom Lincoln owed the successful conclusion of the Civil War, was

the basis of Grant's clear victory. The *New Yorker Abendzeitung* announced, "Every citizen who means well to his republic will give his vote this autumn to the savior of the Union." Following the nomination of the Democratic opponents, the *Belleviller Zeitung* wrote, "Seymour against Grant in 1868 is as much as a Democratic surrender, a dissolution of the Democratic Party."[15] Grant won in Illinois with a secure majority of 56 percent of the votes, more than 50,000 votes. With him a new political order entered office, and the advancing industrial age altered the political landscape.

A Good and Thrifty Administration – Civil-Service Reform

One person who would profit from the result of the presidential campaign was without a doubt Carl Schurz. By 1867 he had moved to St. Louis as co-publisher and part owner of the *Westliche Post*. Initially he had pitched his camp in a hotel in the city, and he informed Hecker in detail of his arrival and of his intention first to buy a house and then to visit the old colonel in person as soon as he had the time. "My dear general," Hecker greeted Schurz from his farm eighteen miles away, "for you to enter the *Westliche Post* will do it good. I am glad that you have moved here, where I have long wanted to see you." Hecker then assured him with an astonishingly good prediction of the future course of events,

> You have a real career ahead of you in St. Louis in every way. From there you are assured a seat in the halls of Congress, and you are a real necessity for the Germans in St. Louis and Missouri. Being so close, I hope to be able to see you once again at my place.[16]

Hecker would be right in his assertion. Within two years Schurz held the highest possible office for a foreign-born person, serving as United States senator for Missouri. It was not without calculation on his own behalf that Schurz spent the last five or six weeks of the 1868 Grant campaign doing campaign tours in Missouri. He knew that there would be a Senate election the following year and that the reelection of Senator Henderson was doubtful because he had voted against Johnson's impeachment. In addition, Missouri was under the influence of the Radical Republicans, a faction to which Schurz still felt he belonged, despite growing differences. Hecker in any case congratulated Schurz with all his heart.[17]

Schurz took his seat in the Senate on 4 March 1869, the day President

Grant entered office. No sooner was Schurz in office than he was plagued
by every possible petitioner and office seeker. The German senator had
never before had a clear idea of the number of these unwelcome pests. At
least he could be sure that Hecker was writing him of his own accord and
without any special interest. He let Hecker know it. "I learned something
from your letter," Schurz wrote to Hecker.

> In most of them I find nothing but "oppressed head of the family, wife
> and 12 children," ruined health that can only be repaired in Germany,
> etc. And all of these splendors are "placed in my hands in confidence."
> It has been maddening, and it just does not stop. There is not a
> moment's peace until the last office hour. I tried occasionally to be
> unpleasant about it, but it does no good. I have now armed myself with
> resignation and put up with what cannot be avoided.[18]

Schurz's experiences with "*Ämterjäger*," as the German-American press
called office-hunters, were significant and made his interest in fundamental
civil-service reform grow. He dedicated his first major speech in the Senate
to this theme. "Moving under his shadow" Hecker was also seized by the
desire to "muck out the Augian Stables."[19] In the period that followed, the
correspondence between Schurz and Hecker rotated around civil-service
reform. Naturally Hecker followed Schurz's speeches and efforts in the Senate
with particular interest, and he was not shy with either praise or criticism.

After Grant's election as president, the radical wing of the Republican
Party pushed through a rigidly paternalistic Reconstruction policy. The
patronage system bloomed, restricting voting rights for some Southerners.
The Radical Republicans acted to protect freedmen, whose political rights in
the South were otherwise in peril. Union troops were still stationed in the
South to protect the efforts ordered from Washington. Grant responded to
such phenomena as the Ku Klux Klan with harsher laws and military measures. The Ku Klux Klan bill passed on 20 April 1871, for example, not only
gave federal courts extensive jurisdiction in apprehending acts of violence,
but also authorized the president to decree an emergency in districts with
an active Ku Klux Klan. In those areas the president was permitted to suspend *habeas corpus*, and put down excesses by military force. In contrast,
Schurz and other senators promoted reconciliation and reintegration. They
criticized the increasingly obvious centralization of government and growth
in federal power. Schurz spoke against the anti-Klan legislation, convinced

that most acts attributed to the Klan were in fact symptoms of general disturbance arising from social changes in the South. Such incidents, Schurz
maintained, were never violent or numerous enough to justify excessive
centralization of government or the violation of the rights of states. Hecker
was likewise disturbed by the president's policies, and he endorsed Schurz's
position. Schurz appreciated this support, responding,

> Before everything else it is necessary that these things come to an end.
> After all that has happened in this Reconstruction story, it is not so
> much a matter of what means to use in these states but that no further
> time be lost … Now we must turn to the future. … Once the Fifteenth
> Amendment is adopted, it appears to me, it is high time to give former
> rebels an interest in cooperatively building the future. That, also, is a
> measure for peace. As far as the annexation of Santo Domingo, I have
> to confess myself a decided opponent of the measure, and I have had a
> very open argument with Grant over it. We have no colonial system,
> and we cannot have one. … One South is enough, and we will have
> only trouble with this second one. The vital strength of the republic lies
> in moderation; we must not exhaust this vital strength through
> unhealthy appendages. Concede I am right on this![20]

Schurz's demand for a general amnesty in the South earned Hecker's
applause. Hecker wrote to him,

> I already gave you my opinion on the question of amnesty a year and
> a day ago. *You* have taken the correct position, the *national* one, and the
> others have taken the *particularist* position. But the prior one is winning,
> and quickly. Amnesty and the northwest are the same thing for anyone
> who has an ape's eyes. You may laugh at my German professorial rhap-
> sody, but give me some credit for my sixty years and my wasted life.[21]

The conflict over Santo Domingo increasingly widened the gap
between Schurz and President Grant. In his Senate speech on 28 and 29
March 1871, the German senator condemned Grant's policies without
restraint and declared that Congress alone had the right to declare war. "I
confess to you, it made me worry about your position in Washington,"
Hecker confided to Schurz even beforehand, anticipating Schurz's uncompromising proceeding in the Senate. Doubtless Hecker was remembering

his own struggle against the "Blittersdorf System." But his enthusiastic support of Schurz's reform plans once more gave him the opportunity to act on behalf of "good laws." Hecker's old lust for lawmaking had revived.

On 20 December 1870, having worked on it all summer in St. Louis, Schurz presented his civil service bill for the first time. He refiled this bill on 27 January 1871. Concerning Schurz's December speech, Hecker wrote to him,

> There are moments in the life of peoples when raising and resolving certain questions is epoch-making. Here a profitable field has been offered you ... You have broken a path, and struck a nest of wasps (robbing insects). But wasps' stings are supposed to be good against rheumatism, so forward, charge! It is a privilege to cut into the rotten parts of the party, and the more ruffled they are, the more they will feel in their bones and corns that we are on the eve of forming a new party.[22]

Again Hecker was making a correct prediction, a year and a half before the founding of the Liberal Republican Party. To be sure, this movement was not predominantly German-American. But Schurz was still one of its most outstanding exponents, and Hecker identified with his efforts. Schurz in return was glad of Hecker's fatherly support and reported to him the progress in Washington.

> You can imagine that my position is a very difficult one. The parties are not used to any free criticism and will not get used to it as long as patronage exists. I am often enough among Republicans who secretly shake my hand for my attacks on the existing system. But almost none of them has the courage to join the struggle with me in the open. Naturally that does not confuse me. Whether one wants to or not, he still hears, and I know that I have a thankful audience outside the Senate. I tell you that party business is dreadfully rotten, and nothing will help it but a heroic cure.

Five months later, in September 1871, men with similar views gathered in Nashville, Tennessee, at the first meeting calling together both Democrats and Republicans. The plan passed in Nashville foresaw the creation of what were called Reunion and Reform Associations to discuss reform principles and goals during the oncoming winter. Participants planned to confront the old Republican Party with the results, and perhaps influence it, so that the coming Republican National Convention would adopt a liberal platform and prevent Grant's renomination. Schurz told Hecker, "My success in Nashville met all my expectations. You will soon see the fruits in the form of a 'Reunion and Reform Association' that unites men of both parties." Hecker had already read Schurz's Nashville speech in the newspapers and responded joyfully to the senator.

> I wanted to write you right away concerning your Nashville speech. The Chicago speech was the baby to *this man*. "You are a glory of the Lord God." Know that I said to our statesmen … and several other friends who were there, "Schurz's speech was the best I have read since the days of old Calhoun." That was no small compliment; an old horse-hair brush like me cannot make them. To me the speech was new oil poured into the old lamp, and I immediately wrote my lecture "Officials in a Principality and a Republic" … I, an old warhorse against officialdom who was tearing at the hide of Blittersdorf in 1842 and who fought the prominent proletariat, who has always ridden the same old horse here – I'm completely in agreement with yours and Jenckes' proposals.[23]

The congressman from Rhode Island mentioned in this letter, Thomas Jenckes, had proposed a civil-service bill four years before Schurz, based on the British model. It foresaw a system of competitive examinations and life tenure for officials. Schurz had adopted this model with some modifications, which struck at the heart of Grant's policies and the Republican party machine, and gone to war with it. As foreseen, there was severe criticism of this model from the Republican Party. The American press had difficulty overcoming its distrust that an alien institution on a European model was being imposed on the American administrative system. The press underscored the anti-democratic implications of such a proposal and saw in the permanent appointment of officials the growth of an aristocracy of office-holders, entirely independent from the will of the people. Critics warned that the proposed examination system would permit only a small elite to have access to office in a time when only a tiny percentage of the population was able to graduate from college. Those who would prevail would be fools anyway, "who have crammed up a diploma at Yale, but know nothing of practical affairs." The advocates of emancipated slaves also saw the measure as discriminatory; civil-service reform "would effectively bar the whole colored population from office."[24]

It was against precisely these objections formulated in the American press that Hecker composed his lecture on "The Official in Principalities and in a Republic." He made it his task to explain both the European and the American systems of officials, showing the weaknesses of both systems and presenting a means for their improvement. Hecker wanted foremost to show Americans and German-Americans that it was not a question of imposing a European system on American conditions, because the European system appeared to him as inadequate and wrong as the current American one. Hecker had already corresponded with Carl Schurz about his ideas. He wrote to Schurz that, in contrast to Schurz and Jenckes, he worked "from the motto that the highest principle even in officialdom has to be popular election." Hecker thought of designing a "civil-service practice with thorough examinations, as in Switzerland, or in the ancient republics."[25] "I am only sketching," Hecker zealously concluded his exposition to Schurz.

> You understand me. I would like to hear your views, your criticism. The matter is close to my heart. The people are good and on the way; they need only encouragement. My lectures serve only to vindicate the republican form of state, shoveling the sewage [of the opponents] in their faces, not perfuming what smells rotten here, but sticking our noses right in it, also saying where I think the broom is. I have always been a faithful, incurable adherent of republics and cannot doubt them even if it stinks like all Mephisto's hell.[26]

Hecker worked for the new reform movement through his lectures. At the start of December 1867, he presented his lecture on reforming the civil service, exposing "the civil-service failings of both monarchies and republics with ruthless strictness and truth."[27] As was the case with all of the other reformers of the Liberal Republican movement, Hecker also stressed that he was not pursuing a party cause or his own interests but rather the common good of the society and of republican institutions. This was probably true in Hecker's case, but it was not always the case with the other politicians who joined the movement, as would be evident.

Hecker's conception of the European civil-service system had changed little since his days in the Baden state assembly. He criticized the sterility of most official effort and the one-sided dependence of state servants on the prevailing power. He believed that the peril of a caste or aristocracy of officials was greater in Europe than in America; but the appearance of secret societies such as the Know-Nothings or the Ku Klux Klan was an unmistakable sign to him that the wrong use of the civil service system could produce a "closed bureaucratic caste." In Europe, the choice, naming, promotion, removal and paying of officials, the most important crown prerogative, continually supported the ruler's purposes and thus opposed civil liberty and development. Hecker stressed in his lecture that European officialdom depended on the crown and had deteriorated into an extended arm of monarchical rulers. Here he saw a problem. The members of the American Congress did not have adequate knowledge of European conditions to recognize that suppressing and abusing civil liberty were inherent in this system; they did not adequately see its possible misuse.

What Hecker did see as worth copying in the European model was the legally established regulation of the relationship between the official and the executive. The official had to have a "dignified" and "secure" position to be safe from executive abuse. There must also be legal guarantees against abuse of the power over the people that was entrusted to the official, that is, a control of their conduct. Obtaining an office should be tied to "certain qualifications or conditions," Hecker demanded. He criticized the enormous concentration of power of the president in the American system, with more than 41,000 appointments. The mere approval of the Senate was no longer an adequate control of these appointments. "The officers will always see only the president who named them as their lord, master, benefactor and dispenser of grace, depending on *him*, not on the many-headed Senate."

In connection with this discussion, President Grant had proposed calling an advisory board to prepare proposed appointments for him. Hecker criticized this proposal not only because the board would be named by the president alone, but also because the president was not bound to the board's advice. Such a committee would simply take the place of the entire Congress as an easily manipulated instrument. The president's power would only seem to be reduced, because the place of recommendations from the entire Congress (House and Senate) would be taken by recommendations of "a handful of creatures of the administration, and the president would have the alibi of reduced responsibility." "This entire commission for examining and naming officials is merely two irresponsible court societies for presidential laziness and irresponsibility." With such institutions, the "king in a frock coat" would be closer to reality than fifty years earlier. Hecker naturally continued his criticism to include an attack on the function of the president as commander in chief of the armed forces, as well as on the military spirit cultivated at West Point. The reduced standing army was still not a citizen army, Hecker stressed. He remained true to his old citizens' guard system, maintaining that only a civic guard was enthused by patriotism. When Hecker argued for a decentralization of administration based on the growing population, he was also pleading for a decentralization of military training. Military educational institutions in the states should take the place of "dangerous West-Pointism."

Whether it was the European naming of officials or the American patronage system, the manner in which officials were placed in their function, the question of how these functions themselves were defined and their relationship to the people were so close to his heart because he saw this as the practical application and securing of a political system. A good and thrifty administration should offer as little opportunity as possible for corruption.

> One rules through and with officials. One separates them, insofar as they are set apart from the mass of the people, and places them closer to the source of dispensing grace. The right to office has always been the most important crown prerogative, and patronage is a cancer on the very life of a republic. The right to office gives premiums for obedience, and distinction for pleasing usefulness. The perfect, ordinary act of monarchical power, even in a republic, is to depose an otherwise capable official for daring to have an opinion that displeases the dominant system.

Hecker believed that the demand for reform was spread everywhere. The suspension of slavery had been a start, and completing the reform of public service would be the capstone. It was necessary to show clearly that "the people [managed] its laws and treasure through its servants." Here, as well, Hecker reached back to the republics of antiquity.

> In a republic all the strength lies in the people; all power rests there. That power does not act, does not tend to a center. Nor does it arise out of it. It works peripherally, like the nerves in a human body. Officials are merely the responsible executors of the people's will; they are subject to the people in their service, to the people that pays them.

Hecker's proposals all had as their goal the prevention of that "cancer of the republic," the patronage system. To reduce the concentration of power in the hands of the president was to secure the sovereignty of the people and the existence of the republic. Hecker saw the cause of the malady arising from two sources: first, the manner in which officials were paid, and second, the lack of control over officials once they were named. The American system of fees, percentages and bonuses was, he said, "only an advanced institution of thievery." What was forbidden in Europe was permitted in America, specifically, to do business with taxes, often enormous business. Set salaries for municipal, county and federal officials and a ban on further business were thus the first step to improvement. Much of this recalls what Hecker had written in the 1840s on lawyers' fees.

The control of financial administration was a continuation of this idea. Hecker proposed effective prevention of fraud and misconduct by municipal or county officers through "frequent, unexpected visitations of offices and treasuries," combined with the publication of a detailed accounting at short intervals – quarterly, semi-annual and annual. Even after two years no thread of Ariadne would lead one through the labyrinth; this was the reason that "Bismarck and the government [of Prussia] insists on a three-year budget." To detect impropriety, Hecker wanted to call into existence an institution like the one already in operation for theft: a grand jury of accounts, "called or selected by the citizens ... whose purpose it is to check accounts, supervise officials and occasionally audit the auditors." In Hecker's view this authority should "never consist of members of only *one* party, but should also have minority representation, because members of the political minority would pursue misuse and crime with greater zeal." The intimidation that would come from such oversight was not to be underestimated. The practical Romans had had just such a "vigilance committee," "whose strictness [acted against] consuls, senators and knights, as well as thieves and pimps." According to Hecker, that censor "was the last instance of control over the officials. Such an oversight could not harm our state legislatures." In addition, the United States was a country of associations. People form associations for all sorts of purposes. Why not "organize a jury association against theft and tax abuse?"

When considering federal officials, Hecker joined in precisely with the demands of Jenckes and Schurz. The spoils system had to be altered in the interests of the nation's dignity and that of the president. When the highest official was surrounded by office-hunters, it was not the most capable who achieved office, but the rudest, those with the longest breath in the struggle for appointment. In his lecture also Hecker pled for public training institutes that anyone could attend, countering elitism with opportunities for "even the poorest and least well provided."

> Whoever comes from such institutions of education with a diploma in those matters has a presumption that he could fill a position as an official. He will not shrink at all from an additional examination. Rather, he will be proud to prove that he has stored up intellectual treasures.[28]

In other words, in the place of favoritism or arbitrary choice, capability and professional knowledge should decide – the principle of bourgeois accomplishment should decide.

Carl Schurz had great interest in Hecker's thoughts and proposals on civil-service reform. He wrote to the Baden reformer,

> I would be very happy, if you would send me a thorough critique of Grant's civil-service plan. Can I also have your lecture on civil service, if you are ready with it? Your views on the matter are of special value to me. Could you also inform me where and how I may find the documents, discussions in European assemblies and reports you draw on in your letters?[29]

Hecker was happy to oblige Schurz. He was literally revived by the desire to draft laws, make reforms, and improve corrupt republican institutions. Once more he was trying to conjure up political virtue, where personal interests had long since penetrated and conquered party operations. Butz recalled that he had "seldom seen Hecker in a better mood. He bubbled with wit and spirited ideas."[30] Typical for Hecker's good mood was the end of a letter to Schurz in which he sketched his conception of civil-service reform.

> Well, there you have a full four pages again. You would say that old people love to talk. Do you know why? Because they have experienced much, and they have not forgotten everything. Unlike Tithonos, who had the beautiful Eos as wife, but who forgot what was important, which is to keep at least the heart young.[31]

Temperance, Weapons Trade and Corruption –
Organizing a Reform Party

Since the days of its foundation, the Republican Party was an imperiled coalition of political elements, some of them diverging. The band holding them together had been the common agitation against the expansion of slavery; now, with the Civil War's end and the political dislocations of Reconstruction, it had dissolved. Once the slavery question moved from the center of political dispute, the old disputes of the 1850s, which had been necessarily set aside or had continued as merely local questions, returned to prominence with new urgency. The altered political and economic conditions of the country gave reforms of all types new intensity. Among these were the revival of temperance agitation in Illinois and Wisconsin,[32] discussions on tariffs and currency and the question of organized labor in the expanding industrial cities of the East and the Midwest.

Temperance agitation was without a doubt one of the phenomena that most endangered the fragile association of German-Americans with the Republican Party and made many of them vulnerable to a new reform movement. As early as the start of 1867, the temperance movement had a new beginning with a meeting in Farwell Hall in Chicago under the leadership of the Republican Reverend Hatfield, who declared all Chicago saloons to be establishments of Satan. The new United States senator for Illinois, Richard Yates, now "tested by alcohol," was blowing the same horn when he joined the temperance movement in February 1867, making the goals of the movement his own in a dramatic speech in the Senate. This time German-Americans went to the barricades arm in arm with Irish-Americans. Articles on temperance agitation outnumbered all other themes in German-American newspapers.

As in the 1850s, it was the obvious alliance of temperance and nativism that disturbed Germans. Thoughts were already being voiced about forming a new party, and even returning to the Democratic Party was not mocked. Despite all fears and protest, a temperance law passed both houses of the Republican-controlled Illinois legislature in January 1872. Men such as Caspar Butz and Friedrich Hecker were alerted. Butz wrote to the new governor of Illinois, John M. Palmer, who had signed the bill and gave it the force of law. Butz made it unmistakably clear that Germans now had no doubts about the growth of nativism within the Republican Party. Hecker was completely upset and thought up a strategy of his own that was all the stranger when one considers how much he hated the spy world of Metternich and how much he prized personal liberty. Under the title "German-Hating" he published a call "to the Germans of America!" "German as well as English papers" were asked to copy the article. In this statement he declared that the deepest motive of the current temperance movement was "hatred against the German element and its power," arising from the foundation of the German *Reich* and the growing self-awareness of German-Americans. When the Republican Party was founded, the German element had demanded guarantees against the Know-Nothings; but now it appeared that these had been temporary. The new tone of nativism demanded a new answer from the Germans. Hecker's trust in associations provided a key to the resolution. In order to tear the "mask from the face" of hypocrisy, he proposed,

> To found associations in every town, every village or township, with the mission of using every reliable, respectable means to discover who among temperance supporters and busybodies are secretly or half-publicly addicted to opiates, hashish, chloroform, brandies, cordials or similar alcoholic drinks. Those names will be published through the associations in the press, in public placards and postings. The associations should also dedicate themselves to the general moral conduct of these false saints and tend to their unmasking.[33]

One day after this call, the *Illinois Staatszeitung* printed the commentary of the *Anzeiger des Westens* of St. Louis in which Hecker's proposal was published. The *Anzeiger* said that they could not follow the "old man" all the way. "This time it seems to me that the old people's awakener has gone a little too far," the *Anzeiger des Westens* told its readers. It would "burden the people with too much work" if, besides doing their business, reading their newspapers, signing protests and sending letters to newspapers – in short, performing all of their domestic, civic and political obligations – "that they also had to play secret policeman and sniff out the lifestyle of their fellow citizens." In the place of "moral policemen and keyhole-lookers," there were effective means in this republic against temperance nonsense. Freedom of the press was still unrestricted, and in the end no German was compelled to vote for a particular candidate "who does not state unequivocal opposition to all temperance-law efforts." The *Anzeiger* praised Hecker's efforts to fight nativists and "water-nuts"; before activating a detective system, however, it wanted to "try the usual open democratic means," which could achieve much once they were used.[34]

Hecker apparently took this criticism to heart and satisfied himself with the usual means of political agitation. One day after the critique by the *Anzeiger*, the *Illinois Staatszeitung* published "with pleasure" another article by Hecker on "The Range of the New Temperance Law." It contained a "telling argumentation from the old freedom-fighter perceiving the temperance law from an entirely new angle." This "Hecker Manifesto," as it came to be called in the press, could be had for free in English and German at Emil Dietzsch's shop in Chicago, and it was supposedly widely distributed,"especially among the English population." The document was so popular that the *Chicago Tribune*, one of the leading papers of the reform movement, discussed it in their issue of 8 March, in part criticizing and in part endorsing it. Hecker seized the opportunity to write a second article, "The Temperance Law and the *Chicago Tribune*," which essentially repeated the first article and stressed what he had said before. He had composed this second article "on the unconstitutionality of the [temperance] law to submit to the gathering in Springfield on the 14th of the month, which I could not attend in person because earlier commitments for lectures have drawn me elsewhere."[35]

Hecker, as ever, insisted on the need to pressure the members of the legislature in Springfield. The *Illinois Staatszeitung* and other German newspapers had been so thoughtful as to provide a list of those representatives in Springfield, Republican and Democratic, who voted for the temperance law. Hecker stated "that all returning members of the legislature who had not acted against the law now had an opportunity to disapprove of it, both clearly and understandably." Naturally this was joined to the threat to withhold the German vote. Hecker's demand made it clear to legislators that no one could expect to continue in office who voted for this law. Even after widespread criticism of his "surveillance association," Hecker continued to be convinced of the efficiency of associations. He proposed that associations be formed in each county to gather in crowds in Springfield as a "living mass petition"[36] and demand that the law be suspended. This reminds one of the beginning of the 1848 volunteers' march in Constance.

The law as passed was aimed primarily at the sale of alcoholic drinks by illegal or unlicensed sellers, and it prescribed severe penalties for the seller, not the customer. A customer could accuse a seller entirely anonymously without giving his own name, the specific drink sold, or the place. Wives suffering from their husbands' drinking would report not the hus-

band but the publican, if he sold alcohol to someone already drunk or contributed to making him drunk. In the long run this personal liability law,
which also provided a higher tax burden for the publican, would have
reduced the illegal corner bars and thus the public sale of alcohol. It also
meant strong regulation and control by the state, because every new publican
had to post a bond and name two respected citizens who would guarantee
his place.

Hecker thought this law was extremely presumptuous; by comparison,
he said, the persecution of witches had been a "pious shell-game. The law
would raise a jubilant cry from the monarchical press of Europe: "Look at
the much-praised republic! Such tyrannical laws are impossible with us!
Don't emigrate to such a country!" Hecker quoted the *Norddeutsche Allgemeine
Zeitung* and stressed that this sort of legislation would be regarded in
Europe "as an insult to the American people, and there would be talk of
how low America's morale had sunk to need such laws." A year later, during his tour of Germany, Hecker was still saying that such temperance laws
injured respect for the United States.

In Hecker's eyes the temperance law was an arbitrary act against a particular branch of business whose ruin would affect other trades and branches
of agriculture. It was "not about bars but about the subjugation of the majority by a fanatical minority." For that reason Hecker felt himself "justified in
opposing this temperance law not in the interest of the bar owners, but in
the interest of constitutional liberty." He saw civil liberties violated because
this law in one paragraph granted the master and the factory owner the right
to fire drunken workers or apprentices, while workers did not have the
same rights against their employers. A further objection was that when only
a small number of inns had a near monopoly, the rich could always afford
a real drink, while the poor were condemned to secret drinking. In short,
"the law is a declaration of war against the *middle class* and against *poverty*."

For Hecker, who produced his own wine, and who knew the brewing
industry in America had largely been founded by Germans, there was a significant difference between the Germans' moderate enjoyment of wine and
the limitless American lust for whisky.

> When I landed on these coasts 24 years ago, I [saw] more dreadful
> drunkenness in one city, New York, as well as in cities under the liquor
> law, ... than in all of Europe through my entire life. Here there is gross
> consumption of brandy as well as the local manner of stepping to the

bar and downing drinks one after another. In Europe one sits, talks and entertains. In general I have seen that people here operate only in extremes, either drinking senselessly or declaring themselves totally abstinent, at least publicly. Decent, social drinking is hardly known by this people, and Horace's *medium in rebus* ["moderation in things"] appears lost to the American drinker.[37]

Concerning German culture and German influence on American society, the introduction of beer and wine drinking through the Germans was no small advance. At least this was Hecker's view of the numerous German breweries in the Midwest. Once "beer and wine took the place of hard liquor," he said, exaggerating the calming influence of Germans, the usual riots and scandals that had been the order of the day in every part of the Midwest vanished.

In early 1872 Hecker took the opportunity, along with his usual speaking engagements, to accept many invitations to speak against the temperance law in German communities in the surrounding towns of St. Clair County. His special acquaintance in distant New York, Father Oertel, who always kept a close eye on Hecker's anti-Catholic tirades, published in the *Katholische Kirchenzeitung* a report of one speech by Hecker given at the "invitation of the saloonkeepers of Peru [Illinois]," and for which he was well paid. In this anti-temperance speech Hecker claimed that priests had hatched this law "in order to get the people into their claws and rule them spirit and body." That was just old Hecker's way of speaking, Father Oertel told his readers, because the German freedom fighter well knew "that we Catholics (Jesuits and Ulramontanes) have nothing to do with Puritanical temperance legislation." No doubt Hecker, when speaking against temperance, also made polemic warnings against the "black hordes," although they had nothing whatsoever to do with temperance, in view of the many German and Irish Catholics. The purpose of such irresponsible rhetoric was to win Germans over to the reform movement by all means possible. For that reason Hecker wrote to Schurz about his anti-temperance agitation, "I have completely exploited the stupidity and silliness of the boors and priests, do-gooders, in short the whole zoo of our legislature. The German everywhere is ready to be done with the Lord-God-making and the waterfools. They will all join with us in the great reform movement."[38]

Hecker loved disputing with Father Oertel. He left the Father's accusations unanswered and wrote an open letter to the *Illinois Staatszeitung* in which he declared that Father Oertel had committed a mortal sin by spreading an untruth in his *Kirchenzeitung*:

> It was not the saloonkeepers of Peru who invited me to hold a lecture, but rather the Turner Society and other citizens, and in fact messrs. Ackermann and Metzger ... to speak about Lord-God-making, Sabbath-bats and other bigotry, as well as that tail of the ox-godling, temperance.

To Oertel's accusation that he was well paid for his lectures, Hecker answered rather calmly, "As long as the priests let themselves be paid for the hard work of baptizing, anointing, burying and preaching, I do not intend to hold my lectures for nothing."

Temperance agitation was not the only occasion causing tension between German-Americans and the Republican Party during the Grant administration. With President Grant's knowledge, large amounts of weapons had been purchased by agents in America during the Franco-Prussian War, and delivered to France. When German-Americans discovered this, a storm of protest broke out. There was a mass demonstration "against the weapon-mongers" on 19 January 1871 at the Turner Hall in Chicago. The chief speakers were Hecker's friends Georg Schneider and Caspar Butz. Butz was already upset with Grant for personal reasons, because, under Grant, he had suffered the same fate as Schneider under President Johnson, and had lost his office. Butz regarded this as an insult, and Georg Schneider pointed out in his own speech the additional insult that the weapons sold to France came from the Civil War. He described the dilemma of German-Americans and Germans in highly dramatic terms. These were "in part weapons carried by German soldiers to put down the rebellion. The same weapons have been sold to commit an intellectual assassination of the German people, which alone stood by the Union with sympathy and untold sums of money when America was in need." Because the weapons sales had been known since September 1870, Schneider's criticism was also aimed at Carl Schurz, who should have protested long before:

> It would certainly have been proper for our German representative in the federal Senate to oppose this delivery of weapons. It would have been proper if the senator, the man of 1848 and 1849, had recalled that Germans still exist. He should have gone to the first steamer and asked,

"Where, for what purpose, why?" In a serious time Germans demand serious men. No church politics. No phrase politics. He does not represent Missouri alone. If that man, however high he stands, forgets his mother, forgets the Germans, then criticism will fall without mercy.[39]

There were similar protests in St. Louis and Cincinnati, other fortresses of German population, in January 1871. In Cincinnati Hecker's old friend Judge Stallo spoke, making a clear definition of the relationship of German-Americans to their old motherland and to their adopted fatherland. "For that reason we protest as American citizens, as Germans and as republicans," he declared in his speech. As an American citizen he had lost trust in his government, which shook a threatening fist at England while itself subverting neutrality. As a German he felt the same insult as Georg Schneider,

that the muskets with which our brave countrymen recently defended the Union have now been pressed into the hands of the French with the intent of shooting down the brothers of those who fell here by the thousands in the struggle for unity and freedom.

As a committed republican he shared the hope of many Germans, including Hecker, that although at that moment "there is no real republic either in Germany nor in France," it was Germany and not France that would achieve "the domination of the spirit from which republics are born." But with its sale of weapons to France, America was committing "fratricide in a double sense," first against Germans who had bet their lives so bravely on the preservation of the Union, and second against the spirit of republicanism, on whose foundation the Union itself was based and on which Germany would soon be based.[40] The first password of the German-Americans was "through unity to liberty."

German-American self-consciousness was clear in such rhetoric. Both the founding of the *Reich* and Germans' efforts to preserve the Union, factors that would continue to be stressed into the twentieth century, contributed to its rise. The resolution passed at the Chicago meeting arose from this awakened self-consciousness. It declared "that we, representing a large part of the American population, claim our right to have a say in the administration and thus protest the proceedings of the government so far." This demand by German-Americans for a right of participation was one of the most important elements of the reform movement. The obvious hostility to foreigners rampant in the old Republican Party elevated German-American criticism of the Grant Administration. There was a strong impression that the practice of overlooking German officers for decoration or promotion, evident in the Civil War, was now being confirmed in public administration.

Despite all of the protests, Carl Schurz was not ready in early 1871 to stop departing steamers and ask them "Where, for what purpose, why?" It was more than a year later, on 13 and 15 February 1872, with the support of Charles Sumner, that he raised in the Senate the issue of weapons sales to France. The storm had long since passed, but the clear intent of Schurz's maneuver was not hidden to anyone, particularly not to his political opponents; it was an attempt to unite German-Americans behind his reform policies and the new liberal party. The theme of the weapons trade served this purpose for him, although he did not believe there had been any real injury either to relations between the United States and Germany or to international law. Schurz wrote that to Hecker, "I have not the least concern about our relationship with Germany or the Geneva arbitration. Bismarck appears decided to ignore the entire matter. In fact, I am completely convinced." Hecker was of the same mind. He was likewise thinking about the useful effect on the new reform movement. In the "debate over the weapon-mongers," he wrote to Schurz, "these lame-footed administration poodles have been more useful than everything that happened before." He laconically added, "and they have been too dumb and ordinary besides."[41]

Hecker's lectures and speeches in late 1871 and early 1872 stood entirely under the banner of the new reform movement. "If only I were done with my lecture tour," he wrote to Schurz impatiently and then announced that he had "worked over [Grant] everywhere and with success."

> There is a meeting in Jefferson City on the 24th, as you know, and the ball will get rolling. The main thing is to put the right man on the carpet at the right time. They will surely see it as settled that Cratz-Brown [sic], who attracts support and is to be trusted, is not a candidate. [Charles Francis] Adams is a "splendid gentleman and Yankee," but will draw little support in the Northwest or the South. Palmer has made himself dead to the Germans and Irish in Illinois through his silly signing of the temperance law. And this law collapses the [Grand] Old Party in Illinois.[42]

The state convention of Liberal Republicans met in Jefferson City,

Missouri, on 24 February 1872 and voted to call a national convention in Cincinnati at the start of May. There a presidential candidate was to be nominated who could also be supported by the Democrats. Among the demands this meeting made were revision of the protective tariff (the overwhelming majority favored free trade); civil-service reform; the decidedly friendly reintegration of the South demanded by Schurz and others, with the suspension of remaining restrictions; local self-government – that is, autonomy of local administration – and the one-term-principle for the president. Although Hecker was a decided supporter of the one-term-principle, he paid little attention to it in his speeches, because others had treated it adequately in various newspapers. Hecker also tended to avoid detailed discussions of free trade and protective tariff, which required extensive study, because he did not want to defend assumptions or principles ignorantly.[43]

Hecker's central themes were civil-service reform and local self-government. Both were directed against the centralization of the federal government and the concentration of power in the hands of the president arising that had arisen during the war. Both themes were also at the heart of Hecker's concept of republicanism. He was committed to communal self-government and to the reduction of bureaucracy and officialdom. In his condemnation of centralizing tendencies, Hecker once again took "lessons from history" and applied them in his familiar, direct manner to American conditions. Thus he explained in a letter to his fiend Charles Söhner in Indianapolis,

> After all the civil wars in antiquity and in later times, the same phenomena appeared, the worst of which was that people became used to centralization through military effort and came to expect the same from civil life, ignored the perils for freedom.

For Hecker centralization was an almost unavoidable but nevertheless wrong result of the Civil War. It was "promoted by railroads, telegraphs, etc.," and "profoundly [extended] the power of the executive branch."[44] Concerning local self-administration, he defended the creation of townships, technical administrative districts that permitted closer oversight and thus control of administration. Township organization for him embodied the basic idea of the American republic.

> Because the people rules itself, and each knows best what suits him and is necessary, the law is interested in dividing the counties into small

administrative districts like *little republics*, related to the county officials
in the county seat in the same way that the county of St. Clair is related to the state of Illinois, and it in turn to the Union.

The entire Union rested on this "grand splendid principle of freedom."
"Centralization is the password for all monarchies, decentralization the
basis of all republics."[45] For Hecker this demand for local self-government
was part of civil service reform, because the control of public money by citizens became more difficult with the increase of residents.

As early as 1872 Hecker discussed with Schurz the further organization
of the reform movement. He already had his eye on a presidential candidate
he thought was qualified – Lyman Trumbull, United States Senator for
Illinois. Trumbull had first been a Democrat, then an anti-Douglas
Republican, a supporter of Lincoln, and now, since being driven from the
camp of regular Republicans by Grant's policies, a convinced supporter of
the new movement. Like Hecker, Trumbull had contributed to civil-service
reform by advocating that federal offices with a local character, such as postmaster, be elected by the people and excluded from the "naming machinery" in Washington. How much Hecker expected from Trumbull and the
new reform movement could be seen in the fact that he offered his support
voluntarily this time. He wrote to Schurz,

> If you think that Trumbull will agree to run on the platform of the new
> party, I will fly into action at once. Because I know how he and all you
> practiced politicians are, it is enough to me if you send me a white piece
> of paper with an = (nothing), meaning none, meaning he does not want
> to. Otherwise send a white sheet with any sign at all (meaning yes).

Gustav Körner later wrote in his memoirs, "No one went into this Liberal
Republican movement more enthusiastically than [Hecker]." At the beginning of April an article on corruption by Hecker was printed in the *Westliche
Post*. This article once more made it clear how much Hecker was oriented to
classical republicanism in his explanation of particular political phenomena.
Also expressed here was Hecker's uninterrupted, unrestrained support for
the foundation of a new reform party of both Democrats and Republicans,
which lasted until the national convention in Cincinnati.[46]

The phenomenon of corruption was for Hecker an expression of private interest, which he linked to the progressing economic development of

America. "Corruption, the hunt after profit, excessive advantage, corruption as a whole is the inevitable result of the industry and trade of today." The result was that politics was seen as a trade, and even patriotism was subjected to the calculation of personal advantage. As much as Hecker approved trade as an opportunity and process for democratization, he feared just as much as that a capitalistic, market-oriented, free economy would harm his concept of republican virtue. The reason for the gradual decline of republics was private egoism, because actions were no longer oriented to the common good. As Hecker declared in a "classical" manner, corruption was the result of bad passions that were no longer motivated by virtue, frugality and selfless love of country. Such passions restricted society. As a deterrent to degenerate and corrupt parties, he proposed that, "all patriotic men loving their country and liberty should unite and associate to bring about better conditions as best they can. That is the history of all reformations. *Reformations... are disguised revolutions.*" His answer to his own objection that a new party would also become corrupt spoke for his application of a cyclical model of ancient republics. The new party would also be covered "with the primal scum of humanity," he said.

> Fine, it will be that way. Just as the needs of the time call new laws into being in place of the old, the law of national life will call ever newer parties into being. ... Or do you hypocrites prefer throwing the flint into the corn and permitting the nonsense to go on. Or singing hymns to absolutism?

At this point Hecker no longer believed in a "purification of the party within the party." The old party, he wrote, had had enough time "to clean out the Augian Stables," but had not done it. The sole possibility that he favored was therefore the association of all "patriotic, honest people of both old parties into a common goal, the well-being of the country." Hecker carefully declared to Schurz, when discussing possible cooperation with the Democratic Party, it could end like the opera [*Die Zauberflöte*, "The Magic Flute" by Mozart], in which "the Moor fears Papageno and Papageno fears the Moor." Hecker appeared to have known what a hard task reformers were letting themselves in for, in cooperating with the Democrats. He knew the fear of the Liberal Republicans of being taken over by the Democrats, and conversely the pride of the Democrats as a great party that resisted "being pulled along in the wake of the little Liberal Republicans." He also knew that his optimism must sound like euphoria. But other reformers were just as incautious: "The anti-corruption movement is moving forward splendidly everywhere," Carl Schurz wrote Hecker. "I have no doubt that we are in the position of sweeping out the whole foul nest next fall."[47]

The criticism of the reformers gradually shifted from the Grant administration to the person of the president himself. Hecker also made this shift.[48] An example of the increased attacks on Grant was Hecker's great "reform speech" in the *Vorwärts* Turner Hall in Chicago on 15 April 1872. For the first time Hecker profited from the restraint that he had shown during the 1868 campaign. He informed his audience why he had not participated then. First of all, "he had not believed General Grant had the statesmanlike qualifications for the office of president," because "he had not been pleased by Grant's ambiguous position in Johnson's entourage." Second, he had been bothered "that General Grant had permitted himself to be heaped with presents from all manner of people, and this at the very time when his election was being promoted."[49] Hecker stressed that he harbored no personal dislike of Grant; but he accused the president of abuse in the distribution of offices in which Germans were not adequately cared for. That was more water under the mill wheels of Germans in Chicago, in view of their demand for more participation in power. In addition Hecker felt that Grant had remained too much a soldier and had become too little a statesman. Hecker was convinced that the transition from militarism to constitutionalism would have demanded a rare man such as George Washington. In short, Hecker's efforts in Chicago were aimed, as was the case with other speakers, to prevent a renewal of Grant's term in office and to put a halt to centralization.

Hecker already told Schurz in March about organizing activities.

> I have just written to Körner that we want to issue a call for organization and assemblies. We must … step into the open. If [Körner] does not act, I will do it myself with my old freebooter manner.

Gustav Körner, who like Hecker supported his good friend Lyman Trumbull, did not wait long.[50] The two men published a call in the *Belleviller Zeitung* for all liberal Republicans in agreement with the new principles to gather in Belleville on 18 April to prepare for the Cincinnati convention. The naming of 25 delegates, led by Körner and Hecker, was done because it was assumed "that it is possible that a delegation certified by a county assembly would appear with more authority than one that came on its own to participate in the convention. But this election of delegates should by no means be interpreted as meaning that others will not be welcome or not have the same rights in the great popular army of the reform party." It was hoped, the article concluded, "that everyone able to leave business for a few days should join the delegation."[51] In truth the openness and casualness of forming delegations in Cincinnati would shortly prove to be one of the meeting's greatest problems.

The Liberal Republicans and the Cincinnati Convention[52]

When the Liberal Repubicans gathered in Cincinnati on 1 May 1872 their composition was as heterogeneous as it had been in the Frémont campaign in 1856. Professional politicians and amateur reformers, intellectuals, newspaper publishers and editors traveled to the convention with varying expectations as former Free-Soilers, free traders, protectionists, Republicans and Democrats. The sole band that held them together was their opposition to Grant's reelection. Because there had been no standard for calling delegates, the states were represented in varying strengths. The high participation of Germans was surprising. Among the 661 registered participants there were 84 Germans, a proportion of 12.7 percent. After Lyman Trumbull's early withdrawal, Schurz, who had made an agreement before the meeting with the chairman of the Democratic Party, August Belmont, to have the Democratic National Convention follow the Cincinnati meeting and confirm the candidate of the Liberal Republicans, favored the independent politician Charles Francis Adams. Adams, the son of President John Quincy Adams, was known neither for nativism nor temperance and thus was an acceptable presidential candidate for the Germans. Because Schurz was elected president of the convention, he could influence the nominations only indirectly. He did praise Adams in his speech, but he made no decided effort to nominate him. According to his own account, Schurz as a German-American wanted to avoid taking too strong a position. To the surprise of many participants, the convention nominated not Adams but Horace Greeley, publisher of the New York *Tribune*. This occurred after several ballots and by a small majority. As the *Belleviller Zeitung* wrote, "His selection was more an accident than the result of mature consideration."[53]

The distress among Germans was intense because Greeley was known as a temperance man and a protectionist. Many saw the root of his nomination in the opaque composition of the delegations. All the delegates had all traveled there on their own resources. Delegates were not bound to any instructions, they also did not form voting blocs of any faction, and most of them voted according to their personal judgment or taste. It was easy for Körner, Schurz and Hecker to be misled about the delegates' potential vote, due not so much to political naïveté as to excessive confidence in Adams' victory. Greeley had considerable sympathy among Southerners and, in contrast to the "frosty Adams," he also had adherents among workers in the large cities. In addition, among the conference participants was a group of 68 delegates from New York, most of them protectionists, whose over-representation might have been responsible for Greeley's selection. Schurz, Butz, Körner and Hecker believed themselves to have been cheated by professional politicians from the Democratic camp. Hecker blamed it all on the vice-presidential candidate Gratz-Brown and the Democratic politician Francis P. Blair, Jr. "Depend on it," he wrote to his friend Wilhelm Rapp after the nomination, "that Democrats of the worst sort will support *this* ticket. … Schurz was completely duped. The whole thing was calculated to get rid of him and to strike the Germans a blow (and how!)."[54]

After the shock of seeing a temperance man nominated, Hecker needed a drink. Together with Butz he left the meeting even before the nomination of the vice president, as he later boasted. The former officer of an Ohio regiment whom Hecker knew from the Civil War, ran a wine tavern in Cincinnati. Here Hecker and Butz drank "at least one good round to their disappointment." In the evening the two men returned to Stallo's house. In the meantime Schurz and Körner had also arrived, and Schurz was sitting at the piano playing Chopin's funeral march, a scene that the pro-Grant press loved to portray to its readers. "We all felt that a great historical moment, perhaps filled with great potential, had been missed without recovery," Caspar Butz said on later recalling the atmosphere in Stallo's house. Hecker described it shortly after the nomination. "It was like when an illegitimate birth is announced in a bourgeois household. There is an addition to the family tree, but no one wants to give congratulations." They discussed what to do. Körner, Butz and Schurz had no faith in Greeley but faith in a victory for the reform party, and so they decided to support the campaign, although not with total enthusiasm. Stallo made plans to attempt to nominate another candidate at the upcoming Reunion and Reform Convention, and he promised to work for the movement until then. Hecker, however, did not want to give a good face to a bad game and declared to his friends that he would not raise a finger for this "water-idiot" from New

York. Whoever wished to visit him this summer would find him at his farm. Hecker was true to his word and returned to Summerfield that very evening, "sick and profoundly embittered over the result of the convention," as the *Illinois Staatszeitung* reported.[55]

Greeley was no candidate for the Germans, and Hecker's commitment against the "temperance nonsense" excluded any support for the New York publisher on his part. "When a party celebrates its birth in such a manner, what can we expect of its life career?" he wrote in disappointment to his friend Söhner. The decisive question had been nominating the right candidate, but this had been fundamentally fouled:

> Besides the fact that it is not known whether Greeley is more a fool or a philosopher, besides the fact that the Honorable Gratz-Brown is a swindler without morals or character and a wire-puller for the Blair clan, it appears to me that the worst elements of the Democratic Party will at once endorse the nomination and make up the sum, Grant plus Greeley = rotten cheese and rancid butter. I want no part in this experimenting.[56]

Hecker's prophecy would be fulfilled. At the start of June the nomination of Greeley was confirmed at the national convention of the Democrats in Baltimore. As Hecker had feared, there was no question that the Democratic Party welcomed the split in the Republican Party, and professional politicians were trying to exploit this movement for their own purposes. Francis P. Blair, Jr., the Democratic politician from Missouri mentioned in Hecker's letter, expressed the hope to a friend that the Republicans might be beaten with the help of the Liberal Republicans and the Germans who had joined them, toward whom care should be taken as an electoral tactic alone. For that reason he and Gratz-Brown, who had been elected governor of Missouri in 1870 with the common help of the Liberal Republicans and Democrats against the Radical Republican candidate, and who was thus a good example for functioning cooperation, went to Cincinnati to prevent the candidacy of the independent Adams. Hecker's suspicions about the "wire-puller" corresponded surprisingly well to the truth, even considering the fact that Hecker was, as Butz once wrote, a "good hater," and that a "conspiracy theory" corresponded best to his form of political explanation.[57]

Because Greeley's views on temperance and his hostility to free trade were generally known, the electoral themes of the Liberal Republicans shift-

ed to the peaceful reintegration of the South, which the candidate had
demanded early and vehemently. In the question between free trade and a
protective tariff – Republicans with a Whig past inclined to protection,
while those from the Democratic camp favored free trade – the resolution
was passed to allow each congressional district to vote on it. Civil-service
reform remained a theme, but it was not enough to win the votes of
Germans, who cared more about nativism and temperance than about
Reconstruction or civil service. For that reason the regular Republican press
was able to exploit the nomination of the "original arch-temperance man."
With Mr. Greeley's nomination the Germans get a kick," said the *Illinois
Staatszeitung*. Against the "liberal" theme of peaceful reconciliation the
Republican press raised the accusation of treason against the cause and
goals of the Civil War. For that reason they liked to publish letters by
German Republicans such as Franz Lieber and Franz Sigel, who remained
in the rows of the old party; they did not share the views of the Liberals on
general amnesty but rather warned against it. Franz Lieber above all criticized the "peculiar nature of Greeley's nomination in Cincinnati" and the
"illegitimate marriage of Republicanism and Democracy."

The Republican press saw their opportunity with Greeley's nomination
and did not hesitate to pay closer attention to German interests. The foreign
vote gained in importance. At the Illinois Republican state convention in
Springfield on 22 May 1872, some of the German-Americans who remained
in the party – such as Anton C. Hesing and Hermann Raster of the *Illinois
Staatszeitung* – were able to win adoption of a plank against the temperance
law passed in January. According to this, "all ... legislation for the cure of
any of the disorders of society, whether irreligion, intemperance or any
other evil" was unconstitutional. German-Americans were thus able, as Jörg
Nagler has properly stressed, "successfully to practice ethnic politics
against a large part of the Republican Party." Raster, as a member of the
platform committee of the Republican National Convention, managed to
have a similar plank approved at the start of June in Philadelphia, over the
opposition of numerous New England members who sought to minimize
the significance of German votes. Opponents asserted that the Germans
who had left the Republican Party would vote for Greeley anyway, but the
adoption of the Republican plank won a mass of German votes that would
otherwise have been lost to the Liberal Republicans. Raster, who was pursuing his own interests and wished to demonstrate the great influence of the
Illinois Staatszeitung, had pressured the convention. "Unless you adopt that

resolution," he told the gathering, "I shall put on my hat, walk out of this convention, and also go with Schurz." Raster won. Asked about the content of what was called the "Raster Plank," he later declared that the resolution meant "the right to drink what one pleases," and "the right to look upon the day on which Christians hold their prayer meetings as any other day."[58]

Through the adoption of Raster's plank, the influential *Illinois Staatszeitung* remained in the Republican ranks. Vehement mud slinging against Schurz and his schismatics followed, and gained in strength. This was the harbinger of an increasing tendency in the 1860s, namely the divergence of the Thirtyers and the Forty-Eighters as a common ethnic pressure group in American politics.

Raster himself had already attacked Schurz in March 1872 over his tardiness in dealing with the weapons-sales question, accusing him of personal interest. Schurz was aware of Raster's attacks, but he assured Hecker that they did not bother him.[59] Hecker presumed that Raster would soon let loose on him as well, because he had declared himself in favor of Schurz's cause. This would certainly have been the case if Hecker had continued to work for the Liberal Republican movement after Greeley's nomination. He soon became a welcome source of quotations for the Grant press, however. His protests against the "Greeley-Swindle" were published chiefly in the *Anzeiger des Westens*, a St. Louis newspaper favoring the reform movement but opposed to Greeley. They served as indirect propaganda for the Republican Party. The fact that Hecker's commentaries continued to be copied showed how he was still treasured as a morally solid character and a political great. But the star of the Forty-Eighters, and with them their political influence, was beginning to fade. This decline was due to a new German immigration after the end of the Civil War. Politically less involved and more materially oriented, these newcomers were already far removed from the Revolution of 1848 and could make little of the heroes of yesterday.[60]

The *Illinois Staatszeitung* was always ready to mention Hecker's decision to fight the "Cincinnati nomination with all his energy, campaigning against it if necessary even from his sickbed." The commentator was happy for his own cause.

> We would expect nothing different from our brave old Hecker. He joined the Liberal movement out of honorable faith in a pure and noble content, and had only the well being of the people as his aim. We warned him against the tricks and stupidities of the band that he briefly

joined. And now he knows well how well founded our warning was.[61]

Hecker's one-sided treatment by the *Staatszeitung* attracted the protests of other newspapers. The *Chicago Union* sought to expose the tactics of the Grant press and pointed out that, even if Hecker were against Greeley, it did not mean that he would vote for Grant. But what the *Union* criticized above all was that Hecker himself had not protested this one-sided and misleading use of his name. The paper could in the end do nothing but refer its readers to Hecker's principled critique of both presidential candidates.

After Greeley's confirmation by the Democratic National Convention, a last attempt was made to raise an opposition candidate. Initiating this effort was Oswald Ottendorfer, publisher of the *New Yorker Staatszeitung*, who was a great exception among the Forty-Eighters in having remained a Democrat since the 1850s. More than a hundred persons, particularly opponents of the protective tariff, attended the Fifth Avenue Conference, to which Hecker was invited but could not come due to illness. The conclusion was finally reached that the time to nominate a new candidate was past, and the chances of victory were too small. If the conference had been able to unite on a candidate, it is possible that Hecker might have continued to support the reform movement. Judge Stallo, one of the German participants along with Friedrich Hassaurek and Carl Dänzer, also distanced himself from the movement at this point. In various public speeches, Stallo later took a position to the reform movement. Hecker understood well. Hecker wrote,

> The Greeley swindle becomes thinner every day, like Soup-Caspar in *Struwelpeter*. Greeley has run so often and lost that he will survive this time, too. But I am sorry for old Körner. Tomorrow Stallo speaks in St. Louis. I am curious to hear him. He then comes over to me to rest for a few days. What I am happy about is that I don't have to make speeches. There is not much honor to be won in the campaign.[62]

With Hecker's declared neutrality and the critical distance of many earlier supporters, the reform movement lost much of its original promising momentum. Other than the *Westliche Post*, which stood under the influence of Emil Preetorius and Carl Schurz and bravely remained true to Greeley, hardly any German-American newspaper was openly for the New Yorker; perhaps for the movement, but not for its candidate. Criticism from its own ranks and conflict among individual members of the reform movement doubtless contributed to its weakening. For the first time, Hecker did not vote in St. Clair County for a president. "He could not vote for Grant; he did not want to vote for Greeley." But he did defend Körner's candidacy in some articles and asked his countrymen to vote for him. Many German-Americans followed his example and voted for neither presidential candidate. In articles such as "The Obligation to Vote," Hecker reflected on the rights and duties of the citizen and spoke of voting as a right but no command; every citizen had to make use of it according to his conviction. As Hecker said in a letter to Charles Söhner, the fact that Greeley in the end "presidented himself to death" only confirmed his expectations. The reelection of Grant in the meantime could not shake Hecker's faith in a functioning republic. He finally judged the Liberal Republican movement as he did the Civil War; for him it had a signaling character, because it forced aside all those with autocratic desires:

> Greeley was beaten and how! A few days before I was still telling Körner and Butz, "He will receive fewer votes than any other presidential candidate before him." That was not hard to foresee. ... We now have Grant back on our necks, and he is dumb enough to succeed himself. I am not afraid of the Caesarean worm, however, since anyone who wanted to play Caesar would be slipped the steel, would gobble the bullet. Things are not so far developed with the American people, and Grant is made as little as possible from that leather they make Caesar puppets. ... Once is good! The intriguers, the whited sepulchers and the moral dung heaps have been so completely rooted out that those in the [White] House will never dare more. A new party made of better elements has been shown to be a necessity and the sooner it appears, the better, and the bolder the victors will be. In addition, there will be a bunch of men gathering in the next Congress, for whatever motive, following every step of the administration and exposing their doings.[63]

The result of the election was clear. Grant won every state north of the Mason-Dixon line and, with 55 percent of the voters he achieved the largest majority in presidential elections between 1836 and 1892. Some tendencies could be seen in these results. Foremost was that the Republicans had been successful with the plea that Reconstruction was in danger. Their mention of the violent excesses in the South, the tactic of "waving the bloody shirt," had awakened the impression that the time for reconciliation was still not ripe. This "unripe times theory" proposed by historians rests on the assumption that the Republicans better understood, and could make better use of, the public mood by appealing to the interests of material prosperity and a "booming, optimistic postwar world," than the reformers could by appealing to reconciliation, virtue and self-reliance. [64]

"The Best Men"[65] – Hecker, Schurz and Protecting the Middle Class

In American scholarship consideration of the Liberal Republican movement takes up considerable space. This movement is seen as the reaction of a particular social group to the political, economic and social changes in the decade after the American Civil War. In addition the movement gives us information about how this group saw its own chances in postwar America. Scholarship has generally pursued two distinct lines of interpretation, depending on the conscious goals of the reformers, lines that do not exclude each other and in fact often cross.

Some historians have placed greater weight on the "reunionists" of the movement and their efforts to end the country's division with political care and mildness. General amnesty and peaceful reintegration of the South were intended to restore national harmony and put an end to sectional bitterness. This approach included the demand for "local self-government." The demand for political autonomy on the local and state level rested on the idea that political leadership must be returned to the "natural leaders" of the region in order to achieve regional recovery.[66] The rigidly paternalistic policy of the Grant government could never succeed in binding educated Southerners into the political decision process as people interested in the common good, it was argued. For that reason there was talk against "tyrannical military laws," and the carpetbaggers were stigmatized as corrupt Northerners for reasons of personal gain who were uninterested in reconciliation, because they personally profited from the division and Grant's Southern policy.

Other historians stress the "reformationist" character and the high moral claims of the Liberal Republican movement and understand the movement as an attempt by a tiny intellectual elite to introduce moral criteria to politics and put an end to the crass materialism and political vices of the Grant government. Within this effort civil-service reform was the attempt to secure personal integrity and the sense of virtues of the old republic of the founding fathers in each officer – a virtually anachronistic undertaking in view of the rise of industrialization and "machine politics" in the large cities. Most reformers never tired of stressing that they were disinterested, selfless spokesmen for the common good.

The latter assertion, at least, has been increasingly placed in question by recent research the more one interprets the demands of the Liberal Republicans in terms of industrial development and the formation of a class society. The reform movement was, as Eric Foner shows, an example of an increasingly conservative middle-class consciousness, "the outcry of a middle-class intelligentsia alarmed by class conflict, the ascendancy of machine politics, and its own exclusion from power." As an almost exclusively urban phenomenon, the movement struggled against both the proletariat of the cities and the industrial plutocracy that manipulated it, arguing against railroad magnates, grand capitalists and iron and coal rings that were strangely involved with labor unions. Liberals feared that powerful bosses, in conjunction with the labor unions, would be able to exercise their own interest-bound politics and power, bypassing the Liberals entirely. The most popular example of the combination of capital and workers and its defeat was the indictment of "Boss" William M. Tweed in 1870 for corruption and election manipulation in New York. Reformers working with journalists of the *New York Times*, merchants, jurists and financiers of the city, brought about Tweed's fall and the fall of his established Democratic political machine through the formation of a "Committee of Seventy." "The Tweed Ring symbolized the symbiotic relationship among corruption, organizational politics, the political power of both railroad men and the urban working class, and the misuses of the state." Tweed, an Irish lawyer who had been elected to the New York Legislature in 1867, had the entire administration of the city solidly in his hand within two years by entering combinations with railroad magnates such as Jim Fisk and Jay Gould, maintaining close connections to unions and establishing an unofficial welfare system. Tweed saw to it that municipal money was available to care for workers, support Catholic schools and build Catholic churches, which won him the loyal support of a large voting bloc of workers. What particularly upset liberal reformers was the fact that not even sentencing Tweed to prison reduced his popularity among the workers.

This unholy combination of entrepreneurs, speculators, large investors, interest groups and labor unions revolted middle-class reformers. In a letter

to Hecker, Schurz spoke of a "great moral revolution that has brought the
Tammany fortress down in New York," and which he hoped would "spread
across the entire national territory."[67] For most reformers the goal was to bar
this liaison's powerful influence on politics and create or expand political
access for people of their own origins and education, thus increasing their
sphere of influence. This would be achieved by civil-service reforms, based
on the principle of individual accomplishment, providing a certain independence from the patronage system. The way would be made free again
for the rise of the middle class against the expanded power of the *nouveaux
riches*.

Eric Goldman has seen the motivation of the reformers as a combination of "disinterested idealism and status consciousness." Almost none of
the reformers, Goldman stresses, had relations to industry, and most of
them sensed "that they were displaced persons in the America of Ulysses S.
Grant." Their status consciousness as the "natural elite, with the elite's prerogatives of fixing standards," saw in civil-service reform the possibility of
a break in the alliance between big capital and the workers. In its place they
would make a government "composed of 'gentlemen' whose service provided its own rewards, and supported by sober, industrious ... middle class
persons who take over ... the proper standards of conduct."[68] This middle-
class ideology corresponded precisely to the model of most Forty-Eighters
from Germany. If their radicalism in Germany consisted in their wish to
realize the republican form of state, their social presumptions revolved
around a stable middle class, which was in turn the *conditio sine qua non* for
their republic. Even moderate liberals who were able to make their peace
with a constitutional monarchy favored the expansion of this middle class.

In connection with the reform movement as a reaction to class conflict,
what the historian Eric Foner shows on the relationship between the class
and race prejudices of the reformers is also interesting. With their disappointment over the development of Reconstruction, with industrialization
and continually diverging interests, Foner sees race prejudice increasing to
the same degree as fear of the proletariat. "Class and racial prejudices reinforced each other, as the reformers' concern with distancing themselves
from the lower orders at home went hand in hand with a growing insensi-
tivity to the egalitarian aspirations of the former slaves." Charles Francis
Adams, the man most favored as a presidential candidate by the Germans
in Cincinnati, had already expressed himself against universal suffrage in
1869: "Universal suffrage can only mean in plain English the government of

ignorance and vice: – It means a European, and especial Celtic, proletariat on the Atlantic coast, an African proletariat on the shores of the Gulf, and a Chinese proletariat on the Pacific." Carl Schurz likewise answered the accusation of Radical Republicans that peaceful reconciliation and the promotion of local self-government in the South would actually mean reestablishing Southern authority and selling out freedmen's rights: "There are many social disorders which it is very difficult to cure by laws." Hans L. Trefousse, Schurz's biographer, who to my mind underestimates the elements of Schurz's European origins and thought that can be well integrated into this movement, has a hard time explaining Schurz's change of heart concerning the freed slaves:

> Of all his many switches in politics, his [Schurz's] desertion of the blacks – for [that was] what it was, whether he recognized it or not – was the most difficult to explain. That he genuinely believed in racial justice is certain; … But the circumstances of his election in Missouri, and presumably the Germans' lukewarm attitude toward the freedmen, soon made him invent all kinds of excuses for his course of apparently caring more for the restoration of the political rights of former Confederates than the protection of those of the blacks.[69]

Most of the reformers, including Horace Greeley, took the position that the government had already done enough for the freed slaves, and it was now up to them to take their future in hand. Conversely what James McPherson establishes about the radical abolitionists of the 1850s is no wonder, namely that this group remained primarily in the ranks of the regular Republican Party in the 1870s because they worked consistently for the realization of slave emancipation and saw liberal reconciliation as a danger. In their eyes civil-service reform meant absolutely no equality of opportunity for colored people and was never intended to provide it.[70]

These generalities were naturally modified in individual cases. When we ask about the motivation of reformers in supporting the movement, a look at their political origin is interesting. Most reformers who were from the Democratic and Free-Soil camp and switched to the Republican Party in the 1850s in the struggle over the expansion of slavery moved into the reform movement in favor of free trade and against the protective tariff, and they held to states' rights over federal rights. Most Liberal Republicans were also blind to the changed conditions of the later nineteenth century,

remaining attached to orthodox Manchester liberalism. When they were
confronted with an industry based on exploitation, their only answer was to
refuse all intervention, whether in the private form of unions and craft
groups or in the public form of state regulation. On the other hand, most
Republicans with a Whig past[71] remained in the regular camp and supported
economic expansion under a strong central government, tied to monopolies
in certain industrial branches and state protection to shield home industry.

Regarding Hecker's position within the reform movement, it can be
established that he was personally not one of the excluded aspirants for
office who hoped for a change in their own situation from the reform movement. He sought no office. However, if not for himself personally, he hoped
that Germans in general would gain a larger right of participation – he
accused Grant of neglecting Germans when distributing offices – and an
easier access to office if office distribution were based on talent and accomplishment, not on patronage. Civil-service reform would not only reduce
corruption but also make it easier for gifted *foreigners* to reach office.

There was also Hecker's orientation to the historical tradition of ancient
republics, from which he appealed to virtue as the necessary presumption
for a functioning democracy. The demand of the reformers for moral
responsibility in government and administration could easily appear as a
conjuring up of a virtue that had long since gone out of fashion in the
Gilded Age. A few years later, when Hecker mentioned the "sentimentality of 1872" to Schurz, he appeared to have come to understand how
anachronistic and idealistic this effort was in the view of a rapidly changing
economic and social reality. Despite all of the associated propaganda, the
assertion of the *Illinois Staatszeitung* made sense: "His noble, trusting heart
… [has] made him believe that the Cincinnati assembly marks the beginning of something better." In one article Hecker saw himself as a naïf "who
was serious about reform." His republican ethos conjured up the virtues
that the founding fathers had regarded as necessary, and he referred to the
history of ancient republics, with their cycles of corruption and purification.
He clearly saw the reform movement as one of purification. The reform
movement was also meant to secure the middle class that Aristotle himself
saw as the absolutely necessary precondition of a prospering republic.
Convinced by the republican form of state, Hecker saw his economic and
social ideal in the free economy of a middle-class society. Precisely like
Schurz, whom Eric Foner calls "one of the most articulate spokesmen for the
free-labor ideology before the war," Hecker was no radical abolitionist in

the 1850s. In the Free-Soil and free-labor ideology of the Republican Party he favored what was basically white emancipation, for both autonomous farmers and workers who would eventually make it to independence. Just as he had defended white emancipation and expansion against an economic system that threatened them, Hecker defended access to offices for an accomplished and educated middle class. In both cases he was defending middle class rights in a state that would intervene as little as possible, permit the free play of forces, and at the same time hinder monopolies among large companies. Local self-administration and self-government and a decentralized state would create the conditions for this, a concept that recalled the "pre-industrial thinking" of German liberals. Hecker, precisely like Schurz, was much more concerned with white emancipation than with the uncompromising and consistent protection of black rights, which could be secured only at the price of a powerful expanding central government. Even his involvement in the American Civil War does not speak against this. Hecker's struggle was less to free slaves than it was to oppose slaveholders and, by extension, an economic system that contradicted the interests of the white middle class. The slave aristocracy of the South was identical to the new economic aristocracy in its impact on the opportunities of a middle class society; in both cases there was a one-sided concentration of power and capital at the expense of more egalitarian, broader development and distribution. Ultimately, Hecker's approval of the peaceful reintegration of the South and a general amnesty did not seek the restoration of the Southern aristocracy; rather, through new patterns of office-holding along the Northern model he was attempting to achieve a regulation of conditions and the development of a national common prosperity "of middling existences."[72]

1 FH to Elihu Washburne, Lebanon, St. Clair County, Ill., 22 December 1864, Washburne Papers.

2 Rudolph Müller married FH's daughter Malwina after the end of the Civil War, see his letters to FH, FHP, box 2, folder 27. See the letter from FH to Karl Blind, Summerfield, St. Clair County, 17 February 1865 on the "War in America," published in an unidentified German newspaper, FHP, box 4, folder 42. As early as the start of July, Franz Sigel, who along with Carl Schurz was one of those Germans who had not joined the radical cause, wrote to his wife Elise that FH had come out against Frémont. Sigel referred to a published letter or article in the *Baltimore Wecker* from the end of June or the start of July, 1864; Sigel to Elise Sigel, 3 July 1864, Sigel Papers; also printed in Nagler, *Fremont*, 272. Sigel himself held the split from the Republican Party to be reprehensible, see on this ibid., 233-41. John Austin Stevens, Jr., to FH, New York, 25 August 1864; idem, to the same, 16 September 1864, FHP, box 2, folder 29. FH's answer to Steven's first letter is not preserved, but it is described in Stevens' second letter, since the conference never took place due to the change of political circumstances. Butz,

"Erinnerungen an Friedrich Hecker," *DAM*, May, 1864, 468-72, is very thorough. Nagler, *Fremont*, 243; Wittke, 246 ff.

[3] "Ein Brief Hecker's nach Deutschland," *BZ* [n.d., July, 1865], FHP, box 4, folder 42.

[4] Nagler, *Fremont*, 253. Both quotations, letter 1, 2 December 1865, FH, *Gepfefferte Briefe über Kleinstaatler und Kleinstaaterei. Geschrieben in Frühling, 1867* (St. Louis, 1867); FH to Elihu Washburne, Lebanon, St. Clair County, Ill., 17 May 1862, Washburne Papers. "Ein Brief Hecker's nach Deutschland," as above.

[5] FH to Elihu Washburne, Lebanon, St. Clair County, Ill., 17 May 1862, Washburne Papers.

[6] Thesis of the book by Richard Franklin Bensel, *Yankee Leviathan: The Origins of Central State Authority in America, 1859-1877* (Cambridge, 1990).

[7] "Der neue Präsident," *BZ*, weekly, 4 May 1865.

[8] Eric Foner, "The Failure of Presidential Reconstruction. Andrew Johnson and Reconstruction," in idem, *A Short History of Reconstruction, 1863-1877* (New York, 1988), 104-23. Both quotations from ibid., 84.

[9] Foner, *Reconstruction*, 88.

[10] Lincoln only favored a limited right to vote for colored people in the South, see Foner, *Reconstruction*, 33.

[11] Foner, *Reconstruction*, 111-13. "Die neuen Parteien," *BZ*, weekly, 2 November 1865. FH to Emil Frey, 6 May 1866, Staatsarchiv Basel (Stadt), Sig. PA 485 DXI 165.

[12] Tucker, *Political Leadership*, 339, 340. The expression "King in a frock coat" derived from the ultra-radical Carl Heinzen, who wanted to abolish the presidency altogether, see Carl Heinzen, *Teutscher Radikalismus in Amerika*, 2 vols. (Milwaukee, 1880-98), here vol. 1, 250; see also Heinzen's article in *Pionier*, "Herr Schurz contra Grant," (Quoted in *BZ*, weekly, 24 August 1871.) "Der König im Frack," *BZ*, weekly, 18 July 1867. Summary of his arguments in "Vernichtende Anklage gegen Andrew Johnson," *ISZ*, quoted in *BZ*, weekly, 1 April 1867. FH, *Ministerverantwortlichkeit*, 131.

[13] *New Yorker Abendzeitung*, quoted in "Die republikanische Platform," *BZ*, weekly, 28 May 1868; Schurz's opening speech, ibid., weekly, 4 June 1868.

[14] Wittke, *Refugees*, 249. Körner, *Memoirs*, vol. 2, 481; the obsessed attacker took Körner to be a protagonist of the "bondholders." FH to a friend of Philip Welker, Summerfield, St. Clair Co., Ill., 12 October 1868, *Expreß*, Toledo, Ohio, weekly, quoted in *BZ*, weekly, 5 November 1868.

[15] *New Yorker Abendzeitung*, quoted in *BZ*, weekly, 28 May 1868. *Ibid.*, 30 July 1868.

[16] Carl Schurz to FH, Office of the *WP*, St. Louis, 8 May 1867, FHP, box 3, folder 35. FH to Carl Schurz, Lebanon, St. Clair Co., 9 May 1867, Schurz Papers.

[17] Schafer, *Schurz*, 184. Carl Schurz to FH, Office of the *WP*, St. Louis, 21 January 1869, FHP, box 3, folder 35.

[18] Carl Schurz to FH, United States Senate Chamber, Washington, 14 April 1869, FHP, box 3, folder 35.

[19] Schurz' Senate speech of 27 January 1871, printed in excerpts in *BZ*, weekly, 23 May 1871. On Schurz's unpleasant experience with the spoils system on his first visit to Washington in the 1850s, see Trefousse, *Schurz*, 183-84. See this expression in FH's calls and invitations to an anti-Grant convention of Republicans and Democrats, *Der Westbote*, Columbus, Ohio, 6 and 9 March, 6 and 17 April 1872; see Wittke, *Refugees*, 250; also in a speech on corruption printed in the *WP*, quoted in *BZ*, weekly, 4 April 1872, "cleaning the Augian Stables."

[20] In general see Foner, *Reconstruction*, 216, 241; from a German perspective, *BZ*, weekly, 23 April 1868, 30 March 1871; "Proklamation der Präsident an die Ku Kluxe" (1880), FHP, box 4, folder 42; for Illinois in general, Edgar F. Raines, Jr., "The Ku Klux Klan in Illinois, 1867-1875," *Illinois Historical Journal*, 77, no. 1 (Spring, 1985), 17-44; on Schurz, F. Bancroft, W. A. Dunning,

"Carl Schurz' politische Laufbahn 1869-1906, für deutsche Leser bearbeitet von Max Blau," in Schurz, *Lebenserinnerungen*, vol. 3, 341-488, here 359. Bancroft and Dunning, "Schurz' politische Laufbahn," 350-54. Carl Schurz to FH, Washington, 27 December 1870, FHP, box 3, folder 35.

21 FH to Carl Schurz, Summerfield, St. Clair County, Ill., 30 December 1870, Schurz Papers, underlining in the original.

22 Ibid. Schafer, *Schurz*, 192; see also on Schurz's speech, "Reform im Beamten Wesen," *BZ*, weekly, 23 May 1871. Schurz reported to FH on the movement in the Senate. Carl Schurz to FH, Washington, 23 December 1871, FHP, box 3, folder 35. FH to Carl Schurz, Summerfield, St. Clair Co., Ill., 30 December 1870, Schurz Papers.

23 Carl Schurz to FH, Washington, 9 February 1871, FHP, box 3, folder 35. Schafer, *Schurz*, 196-97. Carl Schurz to FH, St. Louis, 2 October 1871, FHP, box 3, folder 35. *BZ*, 24 August 1871; see also the article on Schurz's speech in Chicago from the traditional Republican camp, "Carl Schurz," *T ISZ*, 12 August 1871. Bancroft and Dunning, "Schurz' politische Laufbahn," 374-77. His lecture on "Die Beamten im Fürstenstaate und im Volksstaate" is also printed in FH, *Reden*, 47-70. FH to Carl Schurz, Summerfield, St. Clair Co., Ill., 7 October 1871, Schurz Papers, emphasis in the original.

24 Foner, *Reconstruction*, 211-12; see also the commentary of the *Missouri Democrat* in *WP*, 25 February 1870. *Missouri Democrat*, quoted in *WP*, 20 February 1870.

25 FH, *Reden*, 47-70. FH to Carl Schurz, Summerfield, St. Clair Co., Ill., 7 October 1871, Schurz Papers.

26 FH to Carl Schurz, Symmerfield, St. Clair Co., Ill., 7 October 1871, Schurz Papers.

27 Report of the *BZ*, weekly, 7 December 1871.

28 FH, *Reden*, 51-67. Ibid., 64.

29 There was an intense exchange of documents, see Carl Schurz to FH, St. Louis, 2 October 1871, FHP, box 3, folder 35; also FH to Schurz, Summerfield, 7 March 1872, Schurz Papers. Carl Schurz to FH, Washington, 23 December 1871, FHP, box 3, folder 35.

30 Butz, "Erinnerungen," part 2; see also Carl Schurz to FH, Washington, 23 December 1871, FHP, box 3, folder 35; also the report of the editors, *TISZ*, 15 April 1872: "Friedrich Hecker honored us yesterday with a visit. Despite considerable pain he is in the best of humors."

31 FH to Carl Schurz, Summerfield, St. Clair Co. Ill., 7 October 1871, Schurz Papers.

32 On Carl Schurz's protests against temperance agitation in Wisconsin, see, for example, *BZ*, weekly, 10 and 17 October 1867.

33 Yates repeated his speech in March, 1867, see on this Tucker, *Political Leadership*, 345-46. "Die demokratische Partei und die Temperenzfrage," *TISZ*, also printed in *BZ*, weekly, 4 July 1867; also see, "Ueber Gründung einer neuer Freiheitspartei, *Chicago Times* quoted in *BZ*, weekly, 11 July 1867. Caspar Butz to John M. Palmer, 26 January 1872, John Palmer Papers, Illinois State Historical Society, from Jörg Nagler, "Die Deutschamerikaner und das Liberal Republican Movement von 1872," *AS*, 33 (1988), 415-38, here 419, n. 10. "Deutschhasserei. Friedrich Hecker an die Deutschen Amerikas!" *BZ*, weekly, 18 January 1872.

34 See *AW*, quoted in *TISZ*, 19 January 1872.

35 "Friedrich Hecker über das Temperenzgesetz," *TISZ*, 20 January 1872, also in *BZ*, weekly, 29 February 1872. Wittke, *Refugees*, 239; Zucker, *Forty-Eighters*, 287; *DAG*, 32 (1932), 28. *TISZ*, 26 February 1872. Foner, *Reconstruction*, 209. FH, "Das Temperenzgesetz und die Chicago Tribune," *TISZ*, 15 March 1872, also printed in the *BZ*, weekly, 21 March 1872.

36 *TISZ*, 22 February 1872. "Friedrich Hecker über das Temperenzgesetz," as above.

37 "Friedrich Hecker über das Temperenzgesetz" my own emphasis. Friedrich Hecker, "Das Temperenzgesetz und die Chicago Tribune."

[38] *Katholische Kirchenzeitung*, quoted in *TISZ*, 22 April 1872. FH's response to Oertel's accusations, Summerfield, Ill., 25 April 1872, ibid., 27 April 1872. FH to Carl Schurz, Summerfield, St. Clair Co., Ill., 7 March 1872, Schurz Papers.

[39] "Die Massenversammlung in der Turnhalle," *TISZ*, 20 January 1871. Wittke, *Refugees*, 251. Georg Schneider's speech, *TISZ*, 20 January 1871. Schurz's saying, "Germany is my mother, but America is my bride" was well known, see Saalberg, *Westliche Post*, 286.

[40] The resolution passed in Chicago drew on the resolutions passed in St. Louis, see *TISZ*, 20 January 1871. See the report and the printed speech of Judge Stallo in Cincinnati, ibid., 28 January 1871.

[41] "Gegen die Waffenschacher. Die Massenversammlung in der Turnhalle," *TISZ*, 20 January 1871. On Schurz and the weapons trade, see also Trefousse, *Schurz*, 178-79. Jörg Nagler, "Liberal Movement," 421; on the entire discussion between Schurz and his opponents in the Senate, Bancroft and Dunning, "Schurz' politische Laufbahn," 362-73. Carl Schurz to FH, Washington, 1 March 1872, FHP, box 3, folder 35. FH to Carl Schurz, Summerfield, St. Clair Co., Ill., 7 March 1872, Schurz Papers.

[42] FH to Carl Schurz, Peoria, Ill., 19 January 1872, Schurz Papers. FH wrote on 27 April 1872 in *TISZ* that Palmer had doubtless lost many German votes by signing the temperance law.

[43] Nagler, "Liberal Movement," 422, is in error in giving 29 February; the Missouri Liberal State Convention in Jefferson City took place in 24 February, see Schafer, *Schurz*, 197; also Bancroft and Dunning, "Schurz' politische Laufbahn," 379; Trefousse, *Schurz*, 202. Nagler, "Liberal Movement," 422. FH, *Reden*, 65; see also Nagler, "Liberal Movement," 423; Friedrich Münch and Emil Preetorius published articles on the one-term principle in the *WP*. "Ein Brief von Friedrich Hecker," Summerfield, Ill., 25 April 1872, *TISZ*, 27 April 1872; see also his reform speech in Chicago in ibid., 16 April 1872.

[44] FH to Charles Söhner, Summerfield, Ill., 9 November 1872, FHP, box 3, folder 38. "Heckers Reformrede in Chicago," *TISZ*, 16 April 1872.

[45] FH, "Über Townshiporganisation," *BZ*, weekly, 19 October 1871; my own emphasis.

[46] Lyman Trumbull to FH, Washington, 3 April 1872, in FHP, box 3, folder 33. On Trumbull and his relationship to the Liberal Republicans, see Mario R. DiNuzio, "Lyman Trumbull, The States' Rights Issue, and the Liberal Republican Revolt," *JISHS*, 66 (1973), 364-75; in general on Lyman Trumbull, *DAB*, 19 (New York, 1939), 19-20. See FH, *Reden*, 69, and the mention of Trumbull's proposal in a letter FH to Carl Schurz, Summerfield, 7 October 1871, Schurz Papers. FH to Carl Schurz, Peoria, Ill., 19 January 1872, Schurz Papers. Körner, *Memoirs*, vol. 2, 542. "Hecker über Korruption," *WP*, quoted in *BZ*, weekly, 4 April 1872. FH to Carl Schurz, Summerfield, St. Clair Co., Ill., 9 March 1872, Schurz Papers; underlining in the original.

[47] "Hecker über Korruption," *WP*, quoted in *BZ*, weekly, 4 April 1872. FH to Carl Schurz, Summerfield, St. Clair Co., Ill., 9 March 1872, Schurz Papers; cf. the same expression by FH in the *WP*, quoted in *BZ*, weekly, 4 April 1872. *WP*, quoted in *BZ*, weekly, 4 April 1872. Carl Schurz to FH, Washington, 1 March 1872, FHP, box 3, folder 35.

[48] FH to Carl Schurz, Peoria, Ill., 19 January 1872, Schurz Papers.

[49] "Hecker-Versammlung," *TISZ*, 16 April 1872.

[50] FH to Carl Schurz, Summerfielf, St. Clair Co., Ill., 7 March 1872, Schurz Papers. Körner's declaration on this in *TISZ*, 8 May 1872; DiNunzio, *Trumbull*, 370; Tucker, *Political Leadership*, 361; Trumbull was also a promoter of Georg Schneider, FH's friend in Chicago, see Tucker, *Political Leadership*, 358. See FH to Gustav Körner, 10 March 1872, in English, Körner, *Memoirs*, vol. 2, 543; the German original is not in the Körner Papers, but the words are in FH's style. Körner gives the date as 10 March 1872, but since FH already writes to Schurz about this letter on 7 March, there could be an error in the date.

51 *BZ*, weekly, 11 April 1872. *Ibid.*, 25 April 1872.

52 On the considerable literature on the Liberal Republican Movement see Richard Allen Gerber, "The Liberal Republicans of 1872 in Historiographical Perspective," *JAH*, 62 (1975), 40-75, with an extensive bibliography; for German participation, see Nagler, "Liberal Movement." My narrative concentrates on Fh's participation and is based on new, unpublished material. On the composition and development of the movement, see also Wittke, *Refugees*, 250-56, and Zucker, *Forty-Eighters*, 148-51.

53 Nagler, "Liberal Movement," 426-28. "Lyman Trumbull," *DAB*, 20; Hecker's commentary on Trumbull's campaigning for the Democrats, see FH, "Lyman Trumbull," articles 1 and 2, *WP* (n. d., 1880), FHP, box 9.

54 Nagler, "Liberal Movement," 424, 427, n. 53. The true German favorite was FH's candidate, Lyman Trumbull. The *BZ* favored Trumbull for president and Adams as vice-president (see *BZ*, 2 May 1872); I; the same for the *New Yorker Abendzeitung* (see ibid.). Even after the nomination it was said, "We Germans would have preferred a Trumbull or an Adams for many reasons." (*BZ*, 9 May 1872); see also Körner's comment in *TISZ*, 8 May 1872; see also Gerber, *Liberal Republicans*, 61, n. 47 "Die Nomination von Cincinnati," *BZ*, 9 May 1872. Gerber, *Liberal Republicans*, 62. Matthew T. Downey, "Horace Greeley and the Politicians: The Liberal Republican Convention in 1872," *JAH*, 53 (March, 1967), 727-50. Butz, "Erinnerungen," part 2. FH to Wilhelm Rapp [n. d.], printed in excerpts in *TISZ*, 13 May 1872; emphasis in the original.

55 "Fritz Hecker über Gratz-Brown," *AW*, quoted in *TISZ*, 31 May 1872. Hecker saw Gratz-Brown as the representative of the most hypocritical puritanism. Butz, "Erinnerungen," part 2. *TISZ*, 31 May 1872; also the remarks in Nagler, "Liberal Movement," 428-29. "Hecker über die Greeleyschuhnagelfresser," *AW*, quoted in *TISZ*, 23 May 1872. Körner, *Memoirs*, vol. 2, 557. "Hecker und Greeley," *TISZ*, 8 May 1872.

56 German-American papers were quite open about the trouble with Greeley. *NYC* quoted in *TISZ*, 11 May 1872. FH to Charles Söhner, Summerfield, 17 May 1872, FHP, box 3, folder 38.

57 Nagler, "Liberal Movement," 423. Trefousse, *Schurz*, 205. Butz, "Erinnerungen," part 2. FH was not the only one to believe in a conspiracy theory. *New Yorker Abendzeitung* quoted in the *TISZ*, 11 May 1872.

58 Foner, *Reconstruction*, 214-15. Nagler, "Liberal Movement," 428. Carl Schurz, "Wahre Civil-Reform und Horace Greeley," *BZ*, weekly, 18 July 1872; the request was dated 26 June, the response 8 July 1872. *TISZ*, 13 May 1872; ibid., 11 May 1872. "Ein kräftig Wort von General Sigel," ibid., 8 October 1872; also "General Sigel über die Präsidentenwahl," ibid., 21 September 1872; Karl Heinzen also criticized the reform movement in his *Pionier*, "Der liberale Humbug," reprinted in ibid., 8 April 1872. "Franz Lieber zur Präsidentenwahl," ibid., 7 August 1872. Peter H. Olden, "Anton C. Hesing: The Rise of a Chicago Boss," *JISHS*, 35 (September, 1942), no. 3, 260-87; and Peter H. Olden, Harvey Wish, "The Influence of the Illinois Staats-Zeitung upon American Politics," *AGR*, 6 (February, 1940), 30-32, 39; on Hesing and FH, see FH to Hesing, *TISZ*, 2 May 1874. Since Raster was as "short tempered" as FH, their relationship was not always unclouded, see Olden, Wish, "The Influence"; Zucker, *The Forty-Eighters*, 329. Quotes from Olden, Wish, "The Influence," 31.

59 Rudolph Lexow, "Carl Schurz und der Waffenhandel," *TISZ*, 4 March 1872; on the relationship between Schurz and Raster, Olden, Wish, "The Influence," 39. Carl Schurz to FH, Washington, 1 March 1872, FHP, box 3, folder 35.

60 FH to Carl Schurz, Summerfield, St. Clair Co., Ill., 7 March 1872, Schurz Papers. See particularly FH's articles, "Wie der Handel gemacht wurde," on the Cincinnati Convention. "Kaltblutige Betrachtungen eines Unbefangenen, dem es mit der Reform Ernst war"; "Was diejenigen den politischen Comidianten gegenüber zu thun haben, die man verhöhnt, weil sie sich weder ausverkaufen noch beschwindeln lassen," *AW* [n. d., 1872], FHP, box 9. Nagler, "Liberal Movement," 429-30. After the end of the Civil War almost three-quarters of a million

Germans immigrated to the United States between 1865 and 1872, see Peter Marschalck, *Deutsche Überseewanderung im 19. Jahrhundert* (Stuttgart, 1973), 48.

[61] "Hecker und Greeley," *TISZ*, 8 May 1872; the article could have been written by Wilhelm Rapp.

[62] "Hecker – das 'Staatsticket' und die Grantpresse," *Chicago Union*, quoted in *BZ*, weekly edition, 29 August 1872; emphasis in the original is in spread type. *TISZ*, 21 June 1872. FH to Charles Söhner, Summerfield, 17 May 1872, FHP, box 3, folder 38. Körner, *Memoirs*, vol. 2, 562. FH to the *ISZ*, Summerfield, Ill., 25 April 1872, *TISZ*, 27 April 1872. FH to Charles Söhner, Summerfield, 14 September 1872, FHP, box 3, folder 38.

[63] Among other things it was stressed that Greeley's *New York Tribune* stood on the side of the Germans during the Franco-Prussian War, see *WP*, quoted in *Cincinnati Volksfreund*, 6 May 1872, 4; also Nagler, "Liberal Movement," 430. Nagler, "Liberal Movement," 436; among such newspapers were large-circulation papers such as the *New Yorker Staatszeitung* of Oswald Ottendorfer and the *Philadelphia Demokrat*. Butz, "Erinnerungen," part 2. See the end of one Hecker letter in *BZ*, weekly, 29 August 1872; also Hecker's article, "Körner, Oglesby und die teutsche Stimmgeber," *AW* [n. d., 1872], FHP, box 9. Wittke, *Refugees*, 252-54; also Nagler, "Liberal Movement," 436. FH, "Die Pflicht zu wählen," *AW* [n. d., 1872], FHP, box 9. FH to Charles Söhner, Summerfield, 14 November 1872, FHP, box 3, folder 38. Foner, *Reconstruction*, 215. "Uebertünchte Gräber," *ISZ*, quoted in *BZ*, weekly, 13 February 1872. FH to Charles Söhner, Summerfield, Ill., 9 November 1872, FHP, box 3, folder 35.

[64] Foner, *Reconstruction*, 216. Gerber, *Liberal Republicans*, 43-50.

[65] "The best men" quoted from the title of John G. Sproat, *"The Best Men": Liberal Reformers in the Gilded Age* (New York, 1968).

[66] The tendency to such a position can be seen already in 1867 in an article in the *BZ* (27 June 1867).

[67] The largest German-American newspaper in New York, Oswald Ottendorfer's *New Yorker Abendzeitung*, joined the movement and published Tweed's sins for German readers. Foner, *Reconstruction*, 210. See Carl Schurz to FH, Washington, 23 December 1871, FHP, box 3, folder 35. *GL* (1874, 9-11, 634) published an extensive account of the proceedings for German readers after Tweed was condemned to prison. FH had already written to Schurz after the announcement of Tweed's indictment in 1870, FH to Carl Schurz, Summerfield, St. Clair Co., Ill., 30 December 1870, Schurz Papers.

[68] Gerber, *Liberal Republicans*, 50; Eric P. Goldman, *Rendezvous with Destiny: A History of Modern American Reform* (New York, 1952), 18-19.

[69] Foner, *Reconstruction*, 211-12. Trefousse, *Schurz*, 188.

[70] James McPherson, "Grant or Greeley? The Abolitionist Dilemma in the Election of 1872," *AHR*, 71 (1965/66), 43-61. Foner, *Reconstruction*, 212-13.

[71] See Gerber, *Liberal Republicans*, 68; Patrick W. Riddleberger, "The Break in the Radical Ranks: Liberals vs. Stalwarts in the Election of 1872," *Journal of Negro History*, 44 (April, 1959), here 152-53.

[72] FH to Carl Schurz, Summerfield, St. Clair Co., Ill., 8 May 1879, Schurz Papers. *TISZ*, 13 May 1872. FH, "Kaltblütige Betrachtungen eines Unbefangenen, dem es mit der Reform Ernst war," *AW* [n. d., 1872], FHP, box 9. Foner, *Politics*, 130; of great interest for Schurz's economic policy views are the reports he made for the government from the South after the Civil War: Joseph H. Mahaffey, ed., "Carl Schurz's Letters from the South," *Georgia Historical Quarterly*, 35 (September, 1951), here 230-31. *VSB*, 107. öS, 12 July 1844, 324. Lothar Gall, "Liberalismus und 'Bürgerliche Gesellschaft.' Zu Charakter und Entwicklung der liberalen Bewegung in Deutschland," *HZ*, 220 (1975), 324-56, here 353.

VIII

GERMANY –
A COUNTRY WITHOUT A BILL OF RIGHTS

Judging from Afar

Hecker's interest in developments in Germany, indeed in all of Europe, never declined, even on his isolated farm in southern Illinois. The reason that he did not often express himself on events in his old fatherland in the first years after his emigration probably lay, as he told a friend in Mannheim, in his preoccupation with farming and the schooling that he provided for his sons. He also said that he had "become rather laconic in corresponding, since lines thrown down in a rush make the rounds through the German and foreign newspapers, which makes them look like a provocative pursuit of spectacle and notoriety."[1]

Hecker drew his information on developments in Germany from the German-American press and from personal correspondence with friends in Germany. England and Switzerland. The large German-American newspapers in the urban centers on the East Coast and in the Midwest were, as a rule, especially interested in integrating German immigrants successfully, but they were also concerned with maintaining the bridge to Europe with thorough reporting. As a result German and European news took up much more space in the columns on the title page of these newspapers than in any comparable American newspapers. Alongside the contracted contributions of several European correspondents – Arnold Ruge and Karl Blind, for example, wrote articles from England for German-American newspapers for more than twenty years – there were also pages of copy directly from pooled German newspapers, including the *Kölnische Zeitung*, the *Rheinische Zeitung*, the *Weser Zeitung*, the *Augsburger Allgemeine Zeitung*, the *Wiener Freie Presse*, the *Norddeutsche Allgemeine Zeitung* and even the *Neue Preussische Zeitung* (known as the *Kreuzzeitung*). Thus the complete printing of Bismarck's parliamentary speeches, for example, was no rarity. The commentaries on them were composed from a primarily American point of view, however, and until the founding of the *Reich* these were neither pejorative nor overly enthusiastic.

At the end of the 1850s Hecker published some commentaries in the *Illinois Staatszeitung* on the clear shift of power in old Europe. His "Considerations on the Situation in Europe" were written exclusively for the German-American public in America and appeared under the telling pseudonym of "Agricola" ["Farmer"]. This played not only on his own profession as a Latin Farmer but also perhaps on that of the original Agricola, the Roman so praised by Tacitus who had spent most of his life in Great Britain. Why Hecker bothered to use a pseudonym at all is unclear. Friedrich Münch, Hecker's colleague in nearby Warren County, Missouri, whose pseudonym was "Far West," is a generally known example. Fashion or whim cannot be excluded as reasons.

In his first "Considerations", written on the eve of the military confrontation between Austria and the alliance of France and Piedmont-Sardinia, Hecker was particularly interested with a possible intervention by Prussia and with the position of the South German states. He saw peril in the exploitation of the growing national enthusiasm of the German people for the political goals of monarchist governments, which could abuse the self-sacrifice and loyalty of the people with the bogeyman of external threat. There was great danger, he said, that the people would lose sight of the development of its own liberty.

> Committed men, like the radicals and republicans on the other side of the ocean, call to arms under the current warlike conditions to throw out the Paris bandits. South Germany rallies to the black and yellow banner of blood and sin, less out of fear of the French than out of hatred of Prussia. This seems as reprehensible as the advance of the national charger, which has been ridden or will be ridden everywhere to loud cheers.

To him an appeal "to the nation, nationality and national unity" was reprehensible because in the past it had always been used to pursue other goals, and it led away from the demands of liberty. "The friend of liberty and the German people, looking back on the last fifty years, will be filled with concern when he sees how unconditionally the German people has been forced to shout the war cry." According to Hecker, it was not a question of "moving the people to self-sacrifice," but rather of the people's binding its own thoughts indivisibly "with the idea of fighting the Russian-German-Italian-French alliance ...[when] it should fight only" to free itself from "despots, tyrants and usurpers" and "win for itself its own liberty."

Hecker's evaluation of the political situation of Germany had changed little since his emigration. That situation appeared marked by the dualistic concept of a reactionary monarchy on one side and a people striving for unity and freedom on the other. Hecker also believed that the oppressive mechanisms of reactionary states continued unabated; revolutionary actions would, he feared, be dealt with as harshly as ever. Hecker skeptically overestimated the forces of a monarchy that had in fact ceased to operate in a purely arbitrary way; but he was right to see the peril of the abuse of national feelings. For Hecker there was no question that Napoléon III badly needed this war. He was as deeply in debt as Austria, which "turned to the sympathy of the German people" for support. And "remarkably enough, even among the democrats of 1848 were to be found supporters of this appeal." Austria, which had been nothing more than a "hindrance to all national, religious, political and industrial development," remained for Hecker "the archenemy as much as the French despot." So far as Prussia was concerned, Hecker suppressed his admiration out of his own South German antipathy toward the Hohenzollerns "who were feeding on the rest of Germany," in keeping with the "favored phrase, that 'Germany must be dissolved into Prussia.'"

In 1859 Hecker still believed in the old traditional power politics of the great powers, in which the pentagon of Russia, France, England, Prussia and Austria dominated to the disadvantage of smaller states and communities. Hecker's political hopes continued to go in one direction – the establishment of a unity "from below,'" "only a people's war can fortify Germany's freedom within and without, and everything that can and must bring it about is welcome, even defeats." As Hecker had understood when he demanded a permanent pre-Parliament, a gathering point where "despite all particular interests, all equally committed interests [could] unite" – in other words, "a national assembly." Even though he would not place "exaggerated expectations" in such a parliament after the experiences of 1848-49, Hecker still saw it to be "in itself the sole means of preventing a reaction in the sense of 1815-20." Only a national assembly could ensure "that victory over an external enemy ... would [not] be exploited for suppression within." Hecker anticipated that, with the creation of a national assembly, "in the case of peril and need, men would rise from its midst as bold partisans, like Schill, like Garibaldi, to lead fearsome guerrillas into battle against the enemy."

In a later article Hecker compared the preliminary peace agreement of Villafranca between France and defeated Austria to a comedy by

Aristophanes, not least because France made sure that the expelled Austrian monarchs would be compensated in Modena and Tuscany. The creation of an Italian league of states under the presidency of the pope, of all people, to which league the Austrian emperor would also belong with his remaining land in Venice – he had lost and evacuated Lombardy – had to stimulate the national movement:

> The revolution begins its world course in Italy, Hungary and the Danube lands. ... Among the peoples it is cooking and fermenting like a fever. They look at this peace with concern, with distress, with shaking, with scorn and contempt. ...] Never have the hopes of a people been led to the edge of realization and then suppressed and stomped on with such cold mockery as in this lamentable act of Villafranca.

Italy now knew that "no ally stands at her side but the revolution of the peoples." Whoever knew a league of European manufacture, and particularly whoever knew that "sick tapeworm, the German League," knew all too well, Hecker wrote, that not only the Italians "but also the French are being insulted by this league. ...and this insult alone is worth both a July and a February Revolution." A federal state had a chance of survival under republican auspices, but a state league of dynastic families and hereditary personal interests was impossible over the long term.

So far as Germany was concerned, Hecker heard the cry for association and unity, the desire to be rid of "that cursed League and the debilitating small-statism," even from those who had few republican sympathies. He held the general dissatisfaction to be even greater than in 1846-47, and he declared the *current* agitation" to be *"much more general,* and despite all the constitutional nonsense, more widespread." Even the greatest reactionaries could already see "that the current economy cannot be very long-lasting." What Hecker hoped from this general dissatisfaction in 1859 was like a Utopia.

> Do you know what Germany lacks? It lacks nothing but one or two dozen men who do not fear prison and will intervene with rude hands into the movement, moving courageously forward, giving the signal that brings honor to treasonous speech. The whole people would cheer such a man. They do not have to begin with putsches and riots but with that agitation in word and writing that consumes like Greek fire and burns broader than a prairie fire.[2]

Certainly neither Hecker nor any other ex-revolutionary living overseas could take on this mission. His "effect would be of little significance, accomplish little, [bring] nothing immediate, [be] regarded by many with distrust, by others with indifference. The agitators could only arise from the midst of the people and pursue their goal fearlessly." Hecker regarded the chances for such action as not insignificant. He thought the North Germans, who had shown themselves "little saturated with revolutionary spirit" in 1848, to be now the most zealous followers of "the new movement," and "whatever the thoughtful, tough North Germans [had] once adopted," he would not let loose. And in South Germany, Hecker believed confidently, "the revolutionary spirit [still lives], and the lighter blood boils up quickly and wildly at the first opportunity." Hecker did not yet see the rising Bismarck.

A few years later, after the American Civil War, Hecker turned once more to German politics. Two of his letters appeared in the *Kölnische Zeitung* The first letter was composed on 2 December 1865, appearing before the Austro-Prussian War. The second was written on 2 September 1866, after the preliminary peace of Nickolsburg at the end of July 1866. Both were sent to a Mannheim friend who then passed it on to the newspaper. These two letters demonstrate, as the introductory commentary said, "that Hecker continues to have the same brave, fresh and solid heart that we knew in him, but that he has learned much, very much, since that splendid blonde lion's mane that he shook on the speaker's tribunal of St. Paul's Church in Frankfurt was bleached on American soil."[3]

Whoever spoke of Germany now had to speak of Bismarck – and Hecker did too. As he contemplated the development of affairs in the Old World, particularly in Germany, a horrible shudder descended on him, he declared in his December letter. He was unable to find "one iota of serious strength to act, no self-sacrifice" in his old fatherland. Everyone went about his business and sought to protect his own position:

> And in all the confusion only one man is standing, a man who knows what he wants, who has the recklessness, the slyness, the tyrannical push, along with a correct evaluation of his mulish opponents, and gives them the basically mocking disrespect they deserve; a man who obviously has Strafford before his eyes and of whom one would not marvel if he had Strafford's portrait hanging in his office. That is Bismarck.

Since the "Apple of discord of Gastein," the partitioning of the duchies of Schleswig and Holstein between Prussia and Austria after the German-Danish War, it had been clear that Bismarck knew precisely what he wanted, "and even worse…, Austria did not [know] from one day to the next what it wanted and should do." And the small states had not even grasped that the great powers had the solid intent "to throw them out, and only the time is not yet fixed." The people, however – and to him this was the real insult – regarded "this entire confused and dreadful activity like a herd of steers being driven across the wide-open prairie." There would be good chances to win liberty if the people simply had the will. The dissolution of Germany into Prussia, as it "has been and will be practiced by the professors and other members of the learned cattle class," was little to be desired. Here Hecker played on the founding of the National Society [*National-verein*], whose clear goal was propagating a German unity under Prussian leadership. The differences between the various regions and states made a federative form of state necessary, but if it continued "as before, with its hollow euphemism and professorial doctrinarianism, you and your princes will become as certainly Prussian as two times two equals four. If I were Bismarck," he judged with agreement but not with admiration, "no devil could prevent me from peacefully bagging the whole business. It would cost less than he himself believes, and he could easily put up a monument with the inscription, … 'You wanted it yourself, Michel.'"[4]

After the defeat of Austria at Königgrätz on 3 July 1866, Hecker felt that his predictions had been confirmed. It had corresponded entirely to the "logic of events":

> Austria's power has been broken, and not just toward Germany. It in fact falls as far from its zenith as England has (as mistress of the seas). But the situation of Austria is a dreadful process of decay through the nationalities principle, which is no Bonapartist invention.

Napoléon III had merely "given leave to the feelings and efforts of the peoples." Hecker thought that it was "one of the most fortunate events" that Austria's influence on Germany was gone. Its overwhelmingly reactionary influence on the politics of the German League had always been seen as "a national shame to the German nation."

> Even if Bismarck were the devil, one would still have to give him credit for breaking the omnipotence of this house over the concerns, the politics,

of the peoples, which was always the *Jud Süss* of Austrian absolutism as well as his baron.

Hecker continued by saying that all South German constitutionalism had been hated by every initiate as a "miserable puppet-show and vain hypocrisy," because everyone had understood the impossibility of any autonomous progress of the small states in their great dependency on Austria. This constitutionalism had, for that reason, become a "school of contempt and hate," "created by the 'uncompromising republicans.'"[5] Hecker laconically pushed aside the accusation made in America about the "fratricidal war" between Austria and Prussia; talk of fratricide "only unnerved the nation."

Yet while Hecker observed the rising influence of Prussia with distrust, he was just as unlikely to support the small states. On the contrary, he thoroughly discussed in the course of several letters the necessity of abolishing small-statism, supporting the saying, "that small-statism must *fall* if the nation is to *rise*" to show that, after the decline of small-statism, "we *must* arrive at freedom."[6] Discussion of small-statism was understandable against the background of the results of the War of 1866, with the creation of Prussian hegemony in northern and central Germany through the annexation of the duchies of Schleswig-Holstein, Hannover, and Hesse-Nassau and the Free City of Frankfurt. The preliminary peace of Nikolsburg had also bestowed complete sovereignty on the four South German states of Bavaria, Württemberg, Baden and Hesse-Darmstadt, which had participated on Austrian side in the war, with the option of forming their own South German League. Hecker believed in an autonomous existence for the South German states as little as many of his contemporaries; he regarded small-statism and separatism as merely a necessary transition.

> From the position of a republican I do not understand how any man with a healthy understanding could support the small states. The sooner these mini-kings are done away with, the faster the development of the nation to a greater unity and finally to freedom. ... What do the several "small ones" want beyond the Main line? What can they want? To experiment with chronic weakness at the expense of the whole nation. Cannot the North German League, actually Prussia, tie up all of their arteries through customs restrictions and a hundred thousand traffic chicaneries in such a way that they will be compelled for the sake of their own material prosperity to unite with the overwhelming portion of the nation? ...

Let them all, all come under one hat ... once Prussia has united South Germany in its projected Empire, the West, further advanced on its way to a republic in the days of '48, will be the Achilles heel of the new empire. One has only to wound it to throw it over and erect a republic.[7]

It was obvious that Hecker was in no way taking sides with Prussia by demanding that small-statism be ended. His statements on this were an irritant, particularly to Gustav von Struve, who expressed his displeasure in the newspapers, saying that he could not understand how anyone "could support the large states against the small states from the point of view of a republican." Many mini-kings had already been done away with, Struve observed, "without unity coming as a result." Austria itself was an example of how the elimination of the mini-kings did not necessarily lead to liberty, while classical Greece and the United States, with such small states as Rhode Island, Delaware and Vermont, were examples of fortunate popular development. "I really disapprove," he wrote, "that Friedrich Hecker, who once believed that Germany's liberation could come from little Baden, now has no other advice to the whole of Southwest Germany except to surrender."[8]

But Hecker did not support the large states either, and he especially did not support Prussian interests. For that reason he asked Struve to recall:

The men of 1848, who knew their goal, saw in small-statism the worm that was gnawing away the life and strength of the nation. And if our friend Struve supports small-statism today, that contradicts his own program announced then, according to which Germany was to be transformed into a large federal state of eight or twelve federated republics without regard to the existing small-state borders. No one was in doubt that if the movement of 1848 had succeeded, there would be more than one Old-Bavarian Vendee to fight.[9]

Hecker referred to the fact that all of the German republicans located in America, men such as Carl Schurz, Friedrich Kapp, Franz Zitz, Lorenz Brentano, Rudolph Lexow, Daniel Hertle, Emil Preetorius, Adolph Douai, Hermann Raster and Philip Weigel, "have [spoken] against small-statism as a man." Rudolph Lexow, a Forty-Eighter emigrant in New York and now owner of the *Criminalzeitung*, responded to Struve's objections with an answer similar to Hecker's saying that it was doubtless right that "unity does not necessarily [lead] to liberty" if the people itself did "not [strive] for liberty" and had "no concept of its essence." But it was still not possible to deny, in the case of Germany, that "it will be easier to be done with one dynasty than with dozens." In addition, Struve's reference to classical Greece and the United States completely ignored the fact that the "small states" there were republics and not monarchies. "It would be very pleasing to us to learn how Struve will undertake organizing the small states of South-west Germany in the immediate neighborhood of the Prussian Phillip so that they may be compared to Athens, Thebes, Rhode Island, Vermont, etc."[10]

Like many others, Hecker continued to harbor the hope of a successful development, "through unity to liberty." As a German-American he had a special interest in a greater German nation; the contempt in America for Germans would suddenly cease, he hoped, if respect for Germany rose in the world. He would be proven right by the euphoric celebration among Germans in America upon the foundation of the *Reich*, showing that national pride was also, or rather especially important overseas. In addition there were what he regarded as the economic advantages of a closed domestic market, which spoke for the necessity of unity and the democratizing tendencies that went with it. The hope for a unified German nation resulted, he said, from American experiences. "[H]ere we see every day, with our own eyes, the advantages of a greater whole in trade and travel as well as the advantages of a broad horizon." He was convinced that "trade and industry, art and science … [would make] every absolutism impossible in the long run." "Every assault on free economic development by state power is a rooting in their own guts – a suicide." Here he showed himself a representative of economic liberalism, which proposed self-regulation through the free play of forces.

Hecker expected nothing from the small states. As long as particularism ruled, the peril persisted that the princes of Germany would carry on intrigues with foreigners that were destructive to Germany, endangering the sought-after unity of the nation. Hecker recalled the conduct of the League of the Rhine in this connection. In addition he was convinced that a reduction in state debt could come only from the elimination of the whole army of sovereigns and officials of the middling and small states. A large state, in contrast, needed comparatively few officials and was more efficient and cheaper for the citizen, who would in the end become a citizen of a republic.

> [I]t was precisely this horde of bureaucrats of the many states and towns that was the main theme of the 1848 movement. A reduction in the number of officials is absolutely necessary and must come before

we can think about the founding of a republic, if it is to last; thus any annexation works for our principle.[11]

Although Hecker did not want to promote German unity under Prussian leadership, he could imagine unity only under these conditions. He had nothing with which to oppose Prussia's or Bismarck's lust for hegemony except the consciousness of a committed people that would reject subjection once unity had been achieved. "What arises logically from Prussianized unity?" he asked himself and warned, "If the [German people] is a people of subjects, then it deserves to be under one overseer's whip instead of thirty."

What he criticized about the constitution of the North German League – he called it a "modern knock-off of the Act of the League of the Rhine" – was the fact that no human rights were adopted.

> Bismarck knows full well ... what can be offered to a people when its belly is stroked and the political gases of the head are used for steam. The federal act has cared for the Philistines and their feeding instruments, but there is no trace of human rights. The short-term meat of trade and transportation is plentiful, but the man of the people and his liberty are in mourning. No one will accuse us of narrowness for believing that the House of Hohenzollern owes some sort of popular freedom ... We do not hold Count Bismarck to be a different man from the one he was twenty years ago ... The commercial and industrial interests get thrown some bait for the "soft-living flesh," as Münzer said of Luther; but the rights of the people, their Bill of Rights, is passed over in noble silence.

Bismarck had brilliantly understood how "to play on French alarms and Oriental Questions to burn up the future of the German people in raging haste for his modern Caesar." The people, living from one day to another, knew not and forgot too quickly "that dynasties and aristocrats do not live from hand to mouth, that they lay plans whose fulfillment is not bound up with today or tomorrow; they are made for gradual ripening and completion, even if they take decades."[12]

The Forty-Eighters in America complained particularly about the lack of any rights to liberty. Before his final departure from the *New Yorker Criminalzeitung*, Rudolph Lexow commented on the North German Constitution in much the same way as Hecker. He too placed his hopes in the autonomy of the people, which "cannot reasonably wait until Bismarck gives it a valuable gift; it must fight for it itself to be worthy of it. Until now only North Germany has been united, but it is inevitable that the South will come along soon." But Hecker distrusted "Bismarck's quiet lusts," was not misled about the controlling influence of Prussia in the North German League and was particularly upset about the "military budget [passed] without ministerial responsibility." Lexow, on the other hand, believed that the imposing position of the new League in international affairs would serve to guarantee the peace. Lexow believed this army would never be sent across the French frontier "unless there were a compelling provocation to do so, ... and Germany would never think of a war of conquest against France if France were not so frivolous as to attack Germany."[13]

Carl Schurz shared Lexow's view, but in May 1867, Hecker believed there was a clear interest on both sides in favor of war.[14]

> In truth the December Man [Napoléon III] wants war. In truth Bismarck wants war. In truth the French always want to play first violin, and in truth the Teutons would like to fiddle for a while, as well. But no one wants to be responsible. "He started it." One also has no idea how it would end, and for that reason they are looking for a "Karnikel did it." ... I am solidly convinced that Bismarck wants war with the sinking Caesar. This would cement the unity of Germany with blood under the House of Hohenzollern, and it would also serve the premier's other plans.

Bismarck's disinclination to any parliamentarism was obvious to Hecker. Hecker believed solidly that the German chancellor would tie a war against France to the intention of obliterating a "hearth of revolution," whose sparks could leap to Germany. Bismarck essentially planned a government in keeping with the "system of enlightened absolutism," with a "quite conservative national representation." For this he would harvest thanks even among liberals. Bismarck only played with German patriots for tactical reasons, because they would not give away a centimeter of German soil, and his calculations would be dropped "if there were any presumption that the German people possesses either the courage or the strength to win and keep national freedom for itself."

Hecker's concerned appeal to the courage of the people to free itself, his insistence not to doubt "the German people in this age of natural sciences and of universal suffrage," because such a trained and enlightened people would "no longer go back to the 'good old days' of the monarchical kennel" – shows the ambivalent position of almost all political refugees confronted with such a strong political personality as Bismarck, while they themselves were powerless and without influence. Hecker's comment was that it was a "consolation for the future" that "Bismarcks are not morel mushrooms" "that grow anew every year. There were "many ministers with his tendencies and desires" but "none … with his talent, energy, tenacity and slyness." Here Hecker merely demonstrated that he had given in to Bismarck. Such thoughts as Hecker expressed in his letters were no rarity in the German-American press. They expressed the general, growing acceptance of the coming events and the means by which unity could be achieved. Hecker understood that unity could not be achieved by republican means. It was not without reason that he approved the "eventuality of a war" in his last letter of May 1867, in hopes that "a nation enthused with national spirit, hardened in war, [could] not be enslaved, and that all aristocratic calculation would fail on that." And it sounded like rhetoric about himself when he ended his letter with the call, "No Bismarck, no god on earth will restrain the young giant [Germany]. Democracy will triumph, through unity to liberty, to a republic!"[15]

In the Frenzy of Founding the *Reich*

The first news of the victories of the German army was received by German-Americans with euphoria. The capitulation of a large part of the French army after the Battle of Sedan and the capture of the French emperor on 2 September 1870 made it clear to Hecker that the day had "finally [dawned] for Germany" too. He wrote shortly after the battle to August Becker.

> To explain the surrender to old Wilhelm is both easy and hard. It is easy if one says the army … had been destroyed, the remnants pushed against a neutral wall, the old emperor a sick, run-down, headless bum without ideals, encircled by the Teutons. It would not be advisable to flee to Paris, due to Vitellius – hence surrender. That is where the matter sits for every Philistine, like a stuffed sausage. But when one seeks behind the affair for a Mephistophelian element of obsession and revenge, it was a revenge on the plebiscite voters, 'who disappointed and cheated me," and for whom a sauce still has to be prepared. The matter is not at an end with the old bum's departure.[16]

Hecker had no doubt that the moment for the true people's war had only just begun, and that France would now mobilize other forces. Yet the final victory of Germany filled him, like all others at first, with pride. For a brief moment all cares and concerns over a Prussian hegemony moved into the background, although the time for worrying would not be long in coming. In a private letter to Germany written in March 1871, printed in the Mannheim National Liberal *Neue Badische Landeszeitung*, he praised the great future of the German nation.

> The new German Empire stands there, great and powerful through its *unity* toward which it had always worked. I have no doubt that the new Germany, despite the too narrow limits of the federal constitution up to now, will this time also achieve *liberty* as a prize of victory.

So far as the questions of war reparations and just territorial claims of the victor, as Caspar Butz later described it, Hecker pursued "no idealistic policy any more, but rather he took the practical position that a ... provoked war must be paid for by the conquered." In his March 1871 letter to Germany he made statements that he would repeat later at his victory celebration in St. Louis. Although he would never deny the good qualities of the French people and could never forget "what we owe this nation from the days of the Sorbonne to the present day in fine literature, in political and legal science, in philosophy, in natural sciences, etc.," he still saw that "a colossal disciplining was necessary" so that Germany would have peace in the future and not be disturbed in its internal development. To be sure, he would regard

> partitioning France into smaller kingdoms to be a great misfortune. But I would have no hesitation in taking back from the French what they have robbed us of, not only Alsace and Lorraine, but also Burgundy, the bishopric of Toul, Verdun, etc., and that part of Arelate (the Lyonnais with Lyon) only taken from Germany under the Emperor Charles IV.

In his victory celebration Hecker said that the peace negotiations should be oriented to the "natural ancient borders of Germany," which were currently identical with the German linguistic frontier. Alsace and Lorraine must "return home to their father's house." In his defense of German claims, Hecker was no different from a German in the old fatherland, impressed by the outcome of the war and by national greatness. "Even though he persisted in his old republican viewpoint and judged other things from only this basis," Caspar Butz wrote on Hecker's initial enthusiasm,

> the grandiose movement in the German Reich in 1870 bore him along, as well, despite the fact that it was led by princes. Although as a Badener he had been raised remembering the French Revolution, although he had known a few members of the Convention in his youth and was better informed about some of its active personalities than the history books tell us, although he preferred the French Code to the Prussian State Law, although the West German movement for liberty had joined with the French risings of 1830 and 1848 – now he felt the German blood running in his veins. Historical memories overweighed the abstract ideas of liberty that had never struck solid roots in France either, but merely shot up in the personality of an individual. For a time Francophilia vanished in him as in all of us; Germany's good rights outweighed all other considerations.

Hecker received invitation after invitation from German committees and associations to speak at German meetings and planned parades. The most famous and prominent of the speeches made in this context was an 1871 oration in St. Louis celebrating the peace, "one of the best speeches he ever gave, which was reprinted throughout Germany, even in the *Norddeutsche Allgemeine Zeitung*." This address found a good reception not only in Germany, but also in America. Years later it was translated into English and included in a collection of the world's best speeches given from antiquity to the present.[17]

Joy and skepticism alike marked this presentation. Conscious of the fact that the nationality principle had finally replaced "the scoundrel's formula and hollow phrase of 'European balance of power'" of traditional politics, Hecker went on in this speech to deal with the question of a lasting peace. First, he was completely hostage to the common perception that the Franco-Prussian War was the necessary result of a long-awaited conflict between the Romance and Teutonic peoples. The true precipitator of the war had not been Napoléon III, the unprincipled adventurer and usurper, the overthrower of the Republic. Hecker saw the "principal cause" in the "national character of the Gauls," which had been exploited by demagogues. To him it was obvious that the Franco-Prussian War had a longer prehistory than merely the dispute over the Spanish succession and the Ems Telegram. From Caesar to Machiavelli, from Polybius to Gregory of Tours, everyone had described the windy, faithless character of the Gauls. The "measureless lust for robbery" of French kings had contributed to the fact that the German *Reich* had declined to an "Imperial image of sorrow." The French people's "barbaric ignorance and elevated sensuality," their inclination to being puffed up and their overestimation of self had been exploited. A lasting peace was possible only if France would begin to recognize and respect "not only itself, but others as equally entitled," directing "its attention to instructing and educating the masses." In contrast Germany should now take the position of world power to which it had a right as a result of its achievements in the cultural heights.

But this address was not merely an occasion for unalloyed joy and back-slapping in Greater Germany. The manner of the proclamation of the emperor in Versailles, and the claim of the Prussian king "that he had set the German imperial crown on his head at the bidding of the *princes* and the free cities (hence the bearers of *sovereign* power), *which we now announce to the people*," had sounded in Hecker's ears like a military order of the day. A people of forty million had been reduced to the role of spectators. And Hecker's fears were already alive that the spirit of military subordination could also operate in the area of civil legal life.

Hecker also noted with pain the formation of the German national state through the simple joining of the South German states to the North German League, whose nearly unaltered constitution became the constitution of the *Reich*:

> Should a man who loves his people and his homeland, the law of nations and liberty, not be concerned when he sees a constitution that stands far below the old Magna Carta of Runnymede, and which has no Bill of Rights to protect the people against servitude? A constitution that is barely worth more than old Bassermann's representation of the people at the Federal Diet plus an emperor and minus Austria? A parliament without power, in which the poor knights of the spirit can find no place because they are not rich enough to pay their own expenses? A right to approve taxes with an iron, inalterable military budget, and a constitution with a double life of modern feudality: imperial vassalage and state sovereignty. And what guarantee exists for the empire's unified existence but this princely double life of imperial vassalage and state sovereignty?[18]

The new constitution of the *Reich* lacked all guarantees that Hecker regarded as indispensable for the democratic flourishing of a nation. It denied any guarantee to human rights. The bearers of sovereignty were not the German people but the community of princes and free cities, a point that had already raised his concern in the imperial proclamation in Versailles. The imperial executive was vested in the Prussian king, who was also supreme commander of the German armed forces in case of war, with the exception of Bavaria. There was no ministerial responsibility for the parliament, and a measured and balanced representation, in Hecker's eyes, was not provided because of the lack of pay for members. The legislative competence of the *Reichstag* was also restricted through the necessity of working with the Federal Council, in which the representatives of the princes and free cities took their places under the presidency of the *Reich* chancellor. The military command of the monarch remained alien to the *Reichstag,* and conflicts over the army budget were inevitable.

In a special way the establishment of German unity confronted the Forty-Eighters, and also the political refugees of the 1830s, with questions about the impact and the results of the Revolution of 1848. It obviously promoted attempts among them to avoid the devaluation of their own life stories, attempts to place their lives in a sensible and necessary relation to current events. Hecker, for example, sought to see himself in the role of a "birth helper." In a letter to New York's Society of German Patriots of 1848 and '49, whose president was Franz Sigel – a group that, in contrast to other Forty-Eighters, had not broken into jubilation but had always rejected the new German state in the memory of their comrades shot by Prussian troops – Hecker wrote in a less euphoric mood than his peace address:

> Even if our republican efforts in Germany have currently been adjourned (who knows for how long?), at least the German people has felt and measured its power and strength, and will also be able to use it domestically ... Nobody, not even our most understanding opponents, denies anymore that the years 1870-71 would not have been possible to the same extent without our efforts of 1848-49. We showed the nation the misery of small-statism, ... we proclaimed that we sought a great, powerful, common entity of the German nation. Our bodies were conquered, but our ideas have moved forward, conquering. We have not suffered in vain, even if we have not completely accomplished our desires and goals.[19]

The extent to which Hecker grew ever more comfortable with the events of 1848 is striking. More and more he spoke of the "rising" as a deed carried out consciously by him, and more and more he stressed that his emigration had been right despite the achievement of German unity. According to the account given by Friedrich von Weech, a historian who stressed only national unity, in his 1891 *Badische Biographien* that Hecker "in this time of patriotic excitement," looked back "with some regret on his own and his friends' political activity in the 1840s."[20] The National Liberal historians of a later generation thus sought additional confirmation of German unity. But there was little regret about the 1848 movement to be found in Hecker. When the old volunteers of 1848 sent Hecker a volume of poetry and spoke as if 1848 had been yesterday, he understood this as a sort of

> medal, but not a shooting medal like monarchical dog collars. That does a person good, truly good, deep down within, where no one can see or guess. The spirit of the time is democratic, republican. Monarchs cannot stand the new means of transportation of modern life. They tear him down until the king is only a tolerated doll with a crown and a scepter, and the sword is with the people. We came early. Not too early; but we did not understand, or we grasped in the twilight, and for that reason our ship sank, and now we build on a new beach. But we have remained men, and over there we would perhaps have deteriorated into kept dogs.[21]

Other emigrants also reconciled themselves to European developments without thinking of returning personally. Schurz shared Hecker's hope that the South German weight in the new federation would limit and ultimately restrain Prussia's lusts. Thus he wrote to Hecker:

> So we Germans have an emperor again. The manner in which we got him is suited to reconcile us to some extent to the fact. I cannot doubt that Germany will now quickly have its development of liberty. ... Besides, since South Germany finally belongs to the national association and can put in a word, the liberal force will not only become stronger in number but also win some fire. The cause has certainly come out differently from what we believed in '48, but I believe that the development is solid. So let's build on it.[22]

Tired of Europe or Tired of America? The Kapp Controversy

The result of the Franco-Prussian War – the rise of the old fatherland to the status of a "first-class power" – together with the return of such prominent Forty-Eighters as Friedrich Kapp, generated rumors that Hecker planned to return to Germany. "The old agitator of Forty-Eight … is tormented by homesickness," rumor said, and for that reason he wanted to "sell everything in America and return to the beloved fatherland with his sons." Not a word of this was true. The *Gartenlaube* denied these rumors and quoted a letter from Hecker. He wrote to Leipzig,

> I do not understand how this story gets told again, "I intend to return to live in Germany." What would I do there? Perhaps become a subject when I am already one of the two million sovereigns of Illinois? With sixty years soon on my back, one becomes too stiff to bend down to "subjecthood" and regard it as fortunate.[23]

In December 1870 Hecker also mentioned to Carl Schurz the rumors wafting around Germany and the attempts by some friends to entice him with a political office. "I have been encouraged to return to Germany," he wrote to Schurz, "to serve in the parliament, with an electoral district. I certainly could do no harm to the people there. But to take an oath as a subject and poor devil at the age of 60 is worse than *tria kakka kappa*."[24]

Hecker's return would have had a special impact in South Germany. It could easily have become a symbol of reconciliation between the past and the present, a recognition of developments by one of the most prominent leaders of the Revolution. But Hecker was far from giving the current Germany more recognition than he could with a clear conscience. In particular, an elevation of Germany did not mean any simultaneous downgrading of his adopted homeland. This would become clear in the conflict between Friedrich Kapp, a Forty-Eighter who finally returned to Germany in early 1870, and the old guard of his former colleagues, particularly Friedrich Hecker.

America had been a painful exile for Kapp. He quickly and successfully established himself in a New York law office, engaged in the decisive political struggles of the 1850s and 1860s, presided over several committees, serving the German population in America in several honorable posts. But he never felt at home on American soil. "The longer I am here," he wrote to his friend Eduard Cohen in Hamburg, "the less I feel at home. With few exceptions I dislike the country and the people and have no desire to go completely wild here. So far my private studies have kept me above the meanness of the goings-on here." The general amnesty in Prussia brought a cry of joy from Kapp, in contrast to Hecker. Kapp's plans to return took on more concrete form beginning in 1865, but he was not able until 29 April 1870 to take ship from New York in the direction of home. A year earlier Ludwig Bamberger sought to make reintegration easier for Kapp with an article in the *Gartenlaube*, "Citizen of Two Worlds." But Kapp had never understood himself as a citizen of two worlds; rather he was a *"Deutschländer,"* as his first biographer Rattermann called him from a German-American perspective. Kapp was regarded from then on as an expert on America, although, as he himself stressed once, few in Germany had read his writings. Kapp had already made his transition to Bismarck's *Realpolitik* in America. In the first two years of his new residence in Germany, the National Liberal euphoria continued, and he identified himself without restraint with German interests. Only later, when he was a deputy in the *Reichstag,* did he break again with Bismarck's policies. He criticized Bismarck's foreign trade and colonial policy, while he supported the *Kulturkampf* [Bismarck's campaign against the Catholic Church] from personal conviction and the anti-socialist laws out of "fear of the uncontrolled masses."

Hinners writes in his biography that Kapp "quickly distanced" himself from his old acquaintances in the United States after his return.[25] The distance was not merely from his acquaintances, but from the entire country, whose conditions he harshly condemned in his own publications. As early as the first edition of his book, *History of the Germans in the State of New York until the Beginning of the Nineteenth Century,* Kapp aroused criticism from many German-Americans, less for his narrative than for statements in his coda. "Whoever emigrates gives up his fatherland and is lost to it," Kapp asserted, and drew as a conclusion,

> You cannot have two fatherlands any more than you can have two fathers; thus, either German or American. The German-American is merely an in-between being who vanishes in two generations. Whoever wants to be German should remain home or return to the homeland, because for the individual the emigration that he seeks is a national death.[26]

Kapp condemned the rapid, unavoidable assimilation of Germans and denied that they had a decisive influence on American conditions. German-Americans saw this as "Kapp's uncomplimentary *cultural fertilizer theory* for the Germans here." They expended great effort portraying and proving the special role of Germans in and for America, claiming "that Germans are called here [in America] to function as priests at the altar of humanity." Such discussions as the "German Element in the United States" and "Emigration and National Feeling" received new life as Kapp renewed his criticism of the United States in further publications and presentations, generally questioning the rationale for German emigration and seeking to restrict it in the interest of the German nation.[27] In his 1871 book on *Frederick the Great and the United States of America*, Kapp directly confronted his exile home, in particular the part of the appendix entitled "The United States and the Law of the Sea," in which he dealt with clashing interests of Germany and America over the law of the sea. In his article "Government of the City of New York," published in the *Preussische Jahrbücher*, he flayed the machinations of the Tweed Ring. And in a speech in Berlin on 2 February 1871 he expressed his skepticism about prevailing emigration practice on economic grounds. Emigration, Kapp declared in his lecture, weighed down the "debit account of Germany" with amounts in the billions, while it entered these amounts in America's profit columns. Kapp denounced emigration as a "great national harm," because most emigrants did not simply take all of their financial means with them; the nation also lost the value of their education, labor and military service, while they provided "wealth unexpected because unearned" overseas.[28] His conclusion was that the causes of emigration should be eliminated through reforms.

Kapp's comments on emigration, in particular, encountered sharp criticism in America because they targeted the justification for the very existence of German-Americans. Not only did German-American newspapers rely on a steady stream of new German-speaking emigrants; immigration was also regarded as indispensable for the national welfare of the United States. Kapp's assault on American conditions, German-Americans feared, had a direct impact on the readiness of Germans in the old fatherland to emigrate. The *Illinois Staatszeitung* criticized Kapp's narratives as giving "a basically false impression" from someone who could not shake the feeling of having "sat out twenty years in America as if in a penitentiary." The newspaper continued:

> Kapp has a perfect right if he did not feel himself to be an American, not even a German-American, but only a German. But when he uses his

knowledge of American life, obtained as a supposed German-
American, to create German misunderstanding about and displeasure
with America, he has no right to be so upset that German-American
newspapers call him to account.

Kapp thus lacked the "correct feeling of the relationship between positive
and negative qualities" of the United States.

Kapp complained about the criticism from the German-American
press. In a letter to Carl Ludwig Bernays, editor of the *Anzeiger des Westens,*
the second-largest German-American newspaper in St. Louis behind the
Westliche Post, he stressed again that he was merely expressing what "every
thinking [American] editor repeats almost every day in his paper." One
could not prevent him, as a former American citizen, he said, from expressing "what the sparrows whistle from the rooftops."[29] But German-
Americans saw it differently. The editor of the *Philadelphia Demokrat* thought
that the National Liberal was discredited as a historian because Mr. Kapp
did not write like an impartial historical writer, led by the facts. Rather, he
wrote like as "a pamphleteer committed against America" who "feels himself driven by the lacks and failings of republicans to pay court to the
European caste system." Gustav Körner disputed Kapp's *Frederick the Great,*
accusing him of falsely reading sources, and described his statements in the
appendix as words that Kapp's "best friends must wish that he [had] never
written." What was surprising was the personal distress betrayed by this
exchange. Körner, for example, closed his considerations by saying that he
did not know

> what embittered Mr. Kapp about America ... I can only say that I very
> much regret that Mr. Kapp no longer displays the great worldwide
> character I had always been so glad to attribute to him. Such a charac-
> ter is never embittered because its standpoint is too high, this vision too
> broad, preserving a free and just judgment despite personal experi-
> ences and injuries.[30]

With all of this Hecker could not avoid mixing in the scenario. At the
dedication of the Turner flag in Trenton Illinois, on 4 July 1871, he gave what
the *Illinois Staatszeitung* reported as "an address ... that proves that he is not
one of those tired of America, 'sitting out' his twenty years in America in
order raise his nose about America in Germany" "without rejecting
American dollars." In fact the speech at Trenton grew into a hymn to

America and a sharp condemnation of America's critics. Hecker responded directly to Kapp's attacks, accusing him of applying his New York experiences to the whole country, although New York was not America. It was clear to every listener that Hecker, without naming Kapp, had him had in mind when he said, "There are certainly some who scratch after Mammon, returning to the Old World to pour out words of condemnation on this country and its people." But, he continued, it could happily be said that it was simply

> Those marveling over their own greatness and importance who stay away from our West. Kid gloves are so rare here and our unbound manner are so unironed and so much less chic than in the harbor cities of the East. There it is much more Europeanized, and it is simply easier – to pile up money. Your greatness was not marveled at. It felt itself exiled, put back. It saw the Union through Tammany glasses and ran home to mother.

America could do without such persons easily enough, Hecker assured his listeners. "We can watch them without pain or longing, rolling back, back whence they came. They will feel happier among chamberlains and court lackeys than among us." He did want to point out one thing to those people who were tired of America, however. "You have placed yourself between two chairs. People over there look at you in distrust, as not one of themselves, while we here want to know nothing about you. March! Away!"[31]

In a few weeks Hecker rose to considerably higher polemics in newspaper articles entitled "Contemporary Considerations from the Mississippi Valley," bearing the subtitle, "The Spirit of Servitude, Its Perils and Results for Germany." Here Hecker was in his highest form. In the face of "the excessive praises, the lists of splendid qualities and glittering virtues that were the exclusive possession the German emperor, the empress, the crown prince, the crown princess, all the members of their family, the *Reich* Chancellor, ... in short, all the first cabin on the German *Reich* ship of state as reported in journals and newspapers over the last three months," there was little wonder, Hecker wrote, that the rest of the population might doubt its own worth alongside such fabulous imperial heroism. When republics and republicanism were defined as "brooding places of anarchy, disorder, coarseness, corruption," he continued, whoever was irritated at Germany and began talking about basic rights, or a Bill of Rights, deserved at best a shrug of the shoulders. "How can anyone concern himself with bagatelles about basic rights in the presence of the hero emperor?" It is easy to find a diffident, patriarchal, even indifferent tone in "writers of court circulars and newspapers," said Hecker, the same tone now found in Kapp:

> Even our friend Friedrich Kapp, in whom we never detected any war-like inclinations even during 1861-65, has learned something about maneuvers. In his well-known letter to Carl Ludwig Bernays he says, "If the United States does not give up its injury of German interests with a good will, then we must compel it to do so." Aye-aye-aye! How brave! Warlike! Fit for an admiral! Friend Kapp! There sits Brother Jonathan and simply waits to be compelled, nothing to me, nothing to you.[32]

Hecker could hardly believe Kapp's turnaround, but he was even less prepared for the message of [the novelist] Gustav Freytag to Germans overseas. To Hecker, Freytag was the master of German nationalist grandiosity and pretention. Hecker had his own reason for upset with Freytag. Freytag, "the panegyrist of Carl Mathy," had denounced Hecker and his ilk as "rude boys," "mutineers," "traitors to country and fatherland," "foolish agitators," "wild kids," just to "cause the figure of the renegade Carl Mathy to appear as a shining hero against this hellish-Breughelian background." Now Court Counsel Freytag had written a sweet open letter to Germans overseas, assuring them of his majesty's protection with the words, "We will build fast-sailing corvettes to protect your trade and wish to care for your well-being overseas with all our strength. The victory of our armies should be to your benefit, etc." But Hecker simply threw his hands in the air and sent his answer back across the ocean. "Please! Do not trouble yourself to assure us high, higher and all-highest protection and police guard protection; we don't need it." Along with the obvious hatred and arrogant rhetoric, Hecker still showed here a concern about the consequence of his own life, a concern that shifts into self-stylization:

> Please, do not concern yourself. We are no subjects. We have also fought here in our adopted fatherland against oligarchy and servitude. We literally marched, literally suffered and froze, literally bled and many of us literally died on the field of honor, casting their failing eyes on the symbol of civic freedom. Their last sigh was, "Long live the republic!"[33]

Hecker asked Freytag what he had contributed to "the German people in terms of wealth, position, happiness at home and in life, to move him to assure us pioneers of Germanity in an alien land [of his] protection." Hecker's pride over remaining faithful to one principle his entire life arose, and he repeated with irritation, "Today we do not need your transatlantic protection and help any more today than we did a generation ago." In closing, Hecker showed himself a "good hater" by thanking Gustav Freytag for his historical writing. He ended his open letter with a nudge at German writers, cultural historians and journalists:

> But as you say "we," it is entirely proper for us who live overseas to ask, "Who then is the protective 'we' of all Teutons?" Without having the blessing of a restricted subject's perception, I have earnestly considered who that protecting "we" might be. I have come to the conclusion that under "we" can be only – the German emperor, Prince Bismarck and Gustav Freytag. Now, before this Nicene Council comes together and decrees and sanctions this trinity, onion plants will grow pineapples and the forests rooster-trees, with their roots in the air.

> Dear Jonathan may rest, my dear,
> The Freytag is not yet here.

> Now confess to me, Mr. Court Counsel, it was more than mere modesty that drove you to take us protection-chicks under your wings.[34]

Hecker's speech at Trenton quickly became public in Germany through German-American news pools. The *Weser Zeitung* devoted an article in response, "Hecker and Kapp." Taking Kapp's side, which was that of the National Liberals, the newspaper stated that the conflict between German-Americans and the Germans they had left behind had grown so intense because personal life choices had been placed in question by the glorious victories of the German nation. Emigrants could now enjoy German unity only from afar, because they had chosen to emigrate prematurely. Hecker did not forgive "his former fellow exiles for returning to the old fatherland both physically and spiritually, with their whole hearts, and he had caused a very negative opinion of the great transatlantic republic." Hecker's "irreconcilable mood," the newspaper continued, was easy to explain. "If Friedrich Kapp is correct, Friedrich Hecker has behind him a wasted life, and it is human enough to strive grimly against such a conclusion." Hecker believed

he "had found the principles of the democratic future of mankind," but had
been deceived and could not admit this deception; instead, he declared the
dreadful conditions in America to be marginal matters. But the truth, the
newspaper continued, was that during the period that the two refugees had
lived in America, "conditions in Germany have become continually better,
those in America continually worse." "The ascending line is on our side, the
declining on his," the newspaper asserted. Kapp had used his penetrating
insight, and he had drawn the consequences.

As far as the *Weser Zeitung* was concerned, good came only from
Germany. It was therefore interesting to observe how the paper built
bridges to the Liberal Republican movement, which began forming at this
time, with heavy participation from German-Americans. The *Weser Zeitung*
had already printed the platform of the movement, which was seen in
Germany as an effort against corruption and "disgust with politics."
According to the new argument of the newspaper, German-Americans had
been so influenced "by the powerful impression of the French war" that
they sought to organize with newly awakened self-awareness and "act on
the political life of the Union … purifying and improving." In other words,
even the impulse for betterment in America came from Germany, so positively had events in the fatherland influenced German-Americans. The
newspaper asked its readers, "Is it too proud to hope that it will be one of
the influences of our national revolution to bring the Teutons on the other
side of the ocean to salvation?"[35] This question was not very far from
Freytag's rhetoric.

In his open letter to Gustav Freytag, Hecker had already indicated how
little he thought of such reverse-influence, or of German national protection. But he feared negative results from such attacks as Kapp's both on the
attitude of Germans, and on the attitudes of German-Americans toward the
Union. It therefore appeared advisable to him to dedicate one of the lectures
that he prepared during the winter of 1871-72 to the theme of "Our
Republic, Its Critics and Opponents." As he said at the beginning of the lecture, he wanted "to compare the conditions in our republic that have been
made the object of the most violent attacks, with those in the Old World, and
show in short sketches that those [people] overseas are the least qualified to
speak against us like Pharisees." In this lecture Hecker disputed all of what
could be called the "classic" resentments and commonplaces about America.
These ranged from the romantic skepticism of a Nikolaus Lenau about
civilization to Kürnberger's "Tired of America" position. Offensive lack of
culture; commerce without poetry; moral coarseness and spiritual superfi-

ciality of the population; moral bankruptcy from the pursuit of the "almighty dollar," driven by the most conscienceless individualism and egoism and dictated by commercial interests alone – all of these characterizations were included in the spectrum of German criticism.

Against the accusation of gross materialism, Hecker raised the question whether such a thing might also exist in Europe. He then referred to American magnanimity, of which there was none in Europe. Regarding "moral coarseness," Hecker asked whether this phenomenon was to be found only on American soil. Concerning cultural superficiality, he pointed to a flourishing free press, a generally larger demand for newspapers, the intense political interests of Americans, which far exceeded those of Germans, and extensive schooling and popular instruction. America's regions and resources were so great that social questions could be experimented with and resolved in a manner without extensive conflicts. The effectiveness of American administration checkmated European shadow economies because state finances were regulated. Only England and America were currently repaying public debts. Hecker finally contrasted European subjects to free citizens under the integrated dynamism of the Bill of Rights. People became Americans voluntarily, and state membership was determined by neither ethnicity nor culture nor territory, but rested only on a political agreement. "Our [population] is a mixture of all nations. The medium of agreement is our constitution. It is a melting pot that creates a homogenous construct out of heterogeneous elements." When he summarized it, Hecker could proclaim, "I thank you over there for expelling me, for banning me. The free earth is the fatherland of the free."[36]

The Journey to Germany – Rip van Winkle Returns

After Grant's election victory in November 1872, Hecker's plans for a trip across the Atlantic gradually took shape. Before he began his great lecture tour for the winter, he wrote to his friend Charles Söhner, whom he expected to accompany him, saying he could come through Indianapolis and "discuss everything about how we will make out projected trip over the big water. I am for going in the middle of May, coming at the end of September. In that time a sea journey is not so nasty." Hecker also already had an idea of the sense and purpose of his journey.

I would observe the country, people, situation, economy there more precisely and also use the libraries to complete my long-assembled notes against priesthood … in order to crown my life with a survey of priesthood over 4000 years, so that every priest jumps when I pass, like a cat with catnip.

Although enthused about this idea, he confessed to Söhner:

I am extraordinarily sad that there are no immortality and no ghosts. How I would like to haunt the priests, sitting on their humps … tormenting them at camp meetings, goosing them while they preach, in short infesting their stale bread with all sorts of moldy stunts.

When Charles Söhner later had to tell him that business kept him from traveling along, Hecker was visibly disappointed. "It is fatal," he wrote to Söhner, "that you are not going to Europe. I had almost been counting on our sea-salting together." He added about German conditions, "It seems to me that the reaction is well underway in Germany, and the old darkness is again abroad. Prussians are incurable."[37]

By the end of March everything was confirmed. "[M]y departure for Europe has been set for 10 May, and with the *Berlin* to Bremen via Baltimore. If you rush," Hecker wrote to Söhner, still hopeful, "you could still get a place there, so hurry up." But before Hecker could finally take his great journey, he had to complete some lecture obligations that led him, among other places, to Chicago, where he stayed in the house of Caspar Butz. Butz asked whether Hecker planned a visit to Berlin on his journey, but Hecker responded that he did not know precisely. "Should you go there," Butz told "the old man," he believed "that through Kapp or someone else it would be easy to arrange a meeting between you and Bismarck." Bismarck had received Schurz, for example. But Butz had not figured on Hecker's attitude. Hecker blew up, declaring, "What are you thinking about? … how can I as a republican sovereign visit the servant of a sovereign?[38] Butz was unable to raise another objection to this "drastic argument."

On the evening of 5 May 1873, shortly before his departure, Hecker quickly wrote a last letter to Söhner, informing him of a small but ominous episode.

It occurs to me that I shall return more American than I go; although today, when I hung up my cloak, the picture of [Robert] Blum came off the wall and fell at my feet. The late August Becker would immediately *not* have traveled, because he was such a shy fellow but had a superstitious corner … If Old Nick takes me or other princely graces are practiced on me, I will think for a bit on this old restless fellow who was a friend to you, an honorable friend.[39]

Yet contrary to Hecker's deep-seated fear, which had once caused him to flee to Constance, conditions in Germany had decisively changed. The arrest of Hecker had long since ceased to be a political necessity.

Hecker departed St. Louis for Baltimore on 6 May in a comfortable sleeping coach of the Ohio and Mississippi Railway, arriving on 7 May. His sister Charlotte had come down from Philadelphia to say goodbye, and they celebrated a simultaneous reunion and farewell in Franz Gardner's wine cellar. As the Baltimore *Männerchor* sounded a farewell song on the quay on 10 May, Hecker went aboard the steamer *Berlin* with Dr. Berger, a physician friend from Lebanon. The *Berlin*, 300 feet long and 32 feet wide, was one of 32 ships of North German Lloyd out of Bremen. Under the command of the experienced Captain John Putscher, the passage lasted two weeks, ending with arrival in Bremen early on the Sunday morning of 25 May. Old Mannheim friends were already in Bremen to greet their old comrade and escort him back to Mannheim. They continued by night train through Hanover and Frankfurt. In Mannheim the news of Hecker's approach spread like wildfire. Because Hecker wanted to avoid a scene at the Mannheim train station, he and his companions left the train in Ladenburg, where eight open coaches were waiting. But a mass of people was already at Ladenburg to greet him. The news of Hecker's early departure from the train caused the people of Mannheim to move out of the city in the direction of the Chain Bridge. This developed into a crowd running for kilometers, with over 10,000 people gathered to greet him.

"On the journey from Frankfurt there were friendly demonstrations at some railway stations," Hecker described his reception later in a private letter to Wilhelm Rapp of the *Illinois Staatszeitung*.

> [B]ut in Ladenburg there was a great mass of people gathered for a jubilant welcome, and the population of the villages all the way to Mannheim formed a lane of people, so that the enthusiastic reception in Mannheim exceeded anything I had ever experienced. … the bridges over the Neckar were crammed with enthusiastic people, and the closer the city the thicker the crowd of people. The main street (*Breite Strasse*) was a true dark mass of people, the houses (windows, balconies) occupied. There was uninterrupted hurrahs, *Hoch*'s, songs, hat

swinging,, scarf waving, wiping of tears. It was not just isolated, interrupted waves of cries, but an uninterrupted drone of jubilation, coming spontaneously from the heart. You could imagine my feelings. It cost me great effort not to be overcome by the emotion.[40]

Hecker made a brief, simple speech of thanks in front of the house B 2, 101/2, where he was staying with relatives. The *Badische Landeszeitung* gave Hecker's words, saying he was the same in his political principles as he had been 25 years before. He had not come, however, to cause disturbance, and he reminded the people of the obligation to obey the laws. Hecker declared that the reason for his journey was the desire to visit his father's grave, see his relatives again and take the waters to restore his health. "After he had thanked them for the heartfelt reception," the *Mannheimer Tageblatt* reported, "he entered the house while thousands shouted hurrah, and the singing of the 'Hecker Song' responded to the words of the simple man."[41]

The attention paid to Hecker in Mannheim did not decline over the next few days, and earlier allies as well as former political enemies visited him. As soon as he was seen in Mannheim streets, he was surrounded by a mass of people. Even when he went out in a coach early on the morning after his arrival to visit the "graves of friends murdered by the courts" and the grave of his "unforgettable father, whose heart has suffered so much from their parting," there were some waiting for him to press his hand with emotion. "There I now stand," Hecker wrote to Rapp, "a helpless old child, before the blood martyrs of liberty."

From Mannheim Hecker traveled to Offenburg, where a greeting committee also awaited him at the train station. Then he went on to Freiburg, to his brother, Carl Hecker, professor of medicine. Here he composed his first contracted report for the *New Yorker* and the *Illinois Staatszeitung* and wrote his first private letter to his "old piano pal" Söhner, who had asked for an exact report on the political situation. What Hecker reported surprisingly often to his correspondents was the recognition from former political opponents, who now all confessed, "We have you Forty-Eighters to thank for everything we have achieved. You were in advance and recognized the needs of the time and what we needed. You came too early, but today we thank you." Whether Hecker actually heard this everywhere is unclear, but it shows that such recognition had a great value to him. He reported something similar to Söhner:

It is 11 p.m., hence about 5 p.m. for you. I have to write at night, because I have no time during the day. They come to me from all sides and all sorts to greet me. ... I can tell you confidentially that no emperor was ever received as I was in Mannheim. From Ladenburg on, there was a wall of people through the villages. ... Such demonstrations of interest, love and respect exceed all my expectations. I thought of ... Garibaldi. Six hours ago old General Boekk told me, "You were in advance of your time, you are right today," and Adolf Sander's son, a splendid man, reveled over memories of his great father. ... On the whole Germany has the appearance of prosperity, in the cities even luxury. The stock market and swindle flourish as usual. Much that already belongs to the past with us is still rising in splendor here. [There is] much industry, speculation, hunting after money and rushing for enjoyment. Freedom fighters are thinly spread, but still many and of good quality. A reaction such as before is impossible, and there is a feeling of discipline and strength that will make itself known.[42]

Hecker's journey into Switzerland, which began a little later, was supposed to serve his study of republican institutions. In Basel he met his former major in the 82nd Illinois, Emil Frey, now a member of the Swiss National Council and a lieutenant colonel.[43] Solothurn was celebrating the anniversary of the independent canton, and in Bern, the seat of the federal government, Hecker could see all of the laws, regulations and materials being prepared for the federal assembly. From such insight into the constitutional life of the Swiss Confederation he expected stimulation for the reform plans for the civil service of the United States, which he and Schurz had not yet completed.

When Hecker returned to Freiburg in the middle of June after his brief visit to Switzerland, he received an invitation from the festival committee of the American Club in Stuttgart. They asked him whether he was ready to come to Stuttgart to be the festival speaker on the ninety-seventh anniversary of Independence Day. Hecker responded elliptically that he would be glad to accept because during his lecture tour of the past winter in the United States he had spoken with a great crowd of "friends and acquaintances of German and English speech intending to travel to the Continent," who were presently in Germany or were expected soon. They had decided even then to gather on 4 July "in or near Stuttgart" to celebrate the national holiday together there. "If only half of those who promised come, then there will be an imposing gathering." He also told the committee at the end of his letter what he would say in his address. "The celebration of the ninety-seventh birthday of our great, splendid republic is made truly worthy by the fact that we citizens of a free republic meet on free soil and express sympathy through this gathering. What extra to-do is needed?"[44]

Hecker's hope for a generous stream of American citizens to the festival in Stuttgart was not disappointed. After the end of the Franco-Prussian War there was a sudden rise of visitors from America. Many German-Americans traveled back to their old homeland in the summer months to make personal discovery of the altered conditions of the country, as had Hecker. These "tourists" were the occasion for a dispute between the Berlin *Kreuzzeitung* and the Bremen *Weser Zeitung*, which will be briefly mentioned because it reflected the sensitive mood regarding emigration in that summer. The *Kreuzzeitung*, in an article on the growing emigration in 1873, stated its regret that no records were kept on returning emigrants, for whom things had gone poorly "over there"; there were certainly even more who were prevented from returning to their old homeland from America due to shame or a lack of travel money. Certainly, the *Weser Zeitung* replied, there were many who did worse in America than they would have done in Germany and finally went to their ruin there.

But if the Kreuzzeitung saw the numerous groups of German-Americans who come to visit their old homeland on the weekly Lloyd steamers, one would conclude that there is no more successful advertiser of emigration than these returning emigrants, who all bear the marks of prosperity and announce that they have succeeded in winning a social position far above what they would have had in their old homeland. Their example is much more seductive than any discouragement through the failure of those who return unsuccessful.

More than 500 American citizens responded to the invitation to celebrate the ninety-seventh anniversary of the Declaration of Independence, which, as the *Stuttgarter Neue Tageblatt* wrote, "had been so happily celebrated for years by the American citizens currently in Germany." This time the celebration received a "special significance" through Hecker's presence, and the celebration had a "particularly large draw from the West" due to the Vienna World Exhibition. Due to poor weather, the gathering had to be moved to the Stuttgart Liederhall, but it was hoped that the musical entertainment and the fireworks could still be held in the garden afterwards. Festivities began at noon. After the festival march from Wagner's *Tannhäuser,* Hecker gave the festival address. He knew, he said as he began, that people were curious to hear "my current confession of faith," and so he began with it. "He confesses himself to be a son of free earth alone, an American, the son of a country whose ideas and laws should serve as a model for the whole world." Then he passed on to the occasion of the festival, briefly portraying the history of the Union "in a language filled with images" from its origins to the present day, spending the most time on the great accomplishment of the abolition of slavery, the reduction of the army to 20,000 men after the Civil War and the simple return of the officers and soldiers to their civil professions, without endowments or decorations. Despite such a small military presence, the state cared for the wounded and dependents "splendidly," although part of this was supplied by private money, to which he referred anyone who thought that the term "American" was identical with the pursuit of the dollar. He himself had "never found it to be the case that the dollar was less beloved in the Old World than in the New." Hecker went on to speak of the principle of liberty that had conditioned all great American developments. He elaborated by saying that liberty meant more than anything else to an American; without liberty even unity meant very little, and respect for liberty was the principle for the development of the American nation. "[E]migration is a clear indication of a certain attraction of liberty, the idea that over there you can move your elbows, draws people to the west." The Union, Hecker concluded his address in simile, was "a giant tree with broadly spreading branches, casting a shadow under whose protection human rights and human happiness flourish. Three cheers for the principle of unity and liberty for all on earth, for the stars and stripes, the symbol of the equality of mankind!" The American national anthem was played, the Declaration of Independence was read out and a chorale ended the official part of the festivities.[45]

Hecker's speech had really dealt only with American conditions, but it had given the speaker many opportunities, as a correspondent who was present remarked, "to refer sentence for sentence to those states whose development was precisely opposite to liberty. The fact that Germany was very often the example was certainly not Hecker's fault." Naturally there was indirect criticism, as when Hecker compared the sizes of the standing armies in America and Germany, contrasted the modesty of American soldiers with the German mania for medals or referred to the presence of a free press. But while democratic newspapers were pleased with Hecker's speech, the National Liberal press could only swallow the unthankful American with difficulty. The *Schwäbische Merkur* noted "with pain" Hecker's attempt "to heighten the relief of his American images ... by placing them against the black background of his earlier homeland." One would have expected a few words of recognition for the great changes in his old fatherland. Even the way he began his speech was unpleasant, the *Merkur* declared, "in that he spoke of himself in the introduction exclusively as an American." In the end one would conclude "that he [would have had] more reasonable ideas in the backwoods of America than in Stuttgart in the atmosphere of the People's Party." Other newspapers were even less conciliatory. "Generally," said the commentary of the *Hamburger Nachrichten,* "it is thoroughly irrelevant as far as we are concerned, what a person so dedicated to pure rhetoric, to phrase and spectacle, as Friedrich Hecker, thinks or does not think about the new Germany."[46]

It was once again the *Weser Zeitung* that was perhaps the most pointed criticism of Hecker's speech. The *Weser Zeitung* was highly regarded among German-American newspapers as a "usually very noble and careful" pool newspaper, and it was available for export relatively rapidly and easily through the Bremen harbor. As early as 1873 newspapers suffered the dreaded "summer hole" for news, and it was because there was a "political vacation," the *Weser Zeitung* noted, that Hecker's speech received so much attention from the German press. "We would have believed that the words would have been forgotten within a few days. This, however, has not happened. The words already have a full week behind them, and still they are being zealously reviewed in the press – primarily in the South German press, of course." The *Weser Zeitung* saw it as a symptom of political progress that Hecker's speech had produced such lively opposition from the National Liberal press. The newspaper concluded from this that they had ceased "to celebrate a spokesman as long as he used freethinking slogans; they no longer tolerate that an individual, even a party man of the highest rank, sets himself above the nation to which he belongs and cancels the rest of them out as if they were a herd of stupid Philistines." If Hecker had settled for celebrating the advantages of the American republic on the occasion of the celebration of independence, no one would have objected. But the fact that he had attempted to compare Germany negatively with America, using "malignant insinuations" and "perfidious parallels," was "entirely unjustified and tasteless in the highest degree." That was fine with an exclusively American audience on American soil – this was certainly a jab at Hecker's Trenton speech, which had also been published in Germany and reviewed in the *Weser Zeitung* – but in front of a German audience and on German soil, was not only discourteous "but also a violation of the piety even an emigrated German owes his old fatherland and, fortunately, usually observes." In the end one could even have the impression that the new American Hecker wished to ask the forgiveness of native-born Americans for his German ancestry.

In a later article, written by the London correspondent of the *Weser Zeitung,* the paper dealt even more harshly with Hecker. The writer's thoughts concerning Hecker's biography were as difficult to overlook as the article's attempt to justify the National Liberals.

> After the Stuttgart declaration, Friedrich Hecker is neither necessary nor useful. When one reads these ways of speaking, it is possible to hear a Rip van Winkle who, after 25 years of magical sleep, now wants to start life over again where he left it a quarter century ago, and who is entirely incapable of even seeing the facts that lie between his going to sleep and awakening, not to mention understanding them. ... National Liberalism was a hard patriotic necessity to which men of the most various parties brought their inclinations, memories, even their principles and political ideals as sacrifices. Such sacrifices are hard and painful, and one may not presume that [knowledge from] a man who has lived in the primeval forests of America for 25 years to keep his ideals pure and unsullied. He has managed to persuade himself with moving self-deception, and contrary to all evidence against him in his horrid isolation, to believe that political life in the United States fulfills everything for which he agitated, fought and sinned in his youth. National Liberalism has also done much for the nation, precisely because it was a creation of necessity, the momentary need of the fatherland.[47]

The criticism of Hecker by liberals, that he had only been able to preserve his unworldly republican ideal only in isolation, without making adequate allowance for the important and proper changes in his old fatherland, without adequately understanding the necessary compromises and concessions, was received with shock by the German-American press on the other side of the ocean. In articles such as "Hecker and the 'Liberal' Gentlemen in Germany" and "The Howl in Germany against the Old Man," German-American newspapers defended his open speech and justified criticism. In fact the *Philadelphia Demokrat* was even of the opinion that "Hecker could [still] speak entirely differently if he had not held himself back as a German-American, and shown the restraint that the 'liberal' servants of Bismarck miss in him." The *Demokrat* wrote that Germany had become great "only from the top down, driven to it by the whip. It is great as a military power,

but small as a nation." In response to the accusation that Hecker had wanted to apologize for his German origin, the *Illinois Staatszeitung* countered
what the liberal gentlemen of the *Weser Zeitung* appeared to have missed –
that no one had fought nativism and temperance nonsense more in the last
few years than Hecker. And his other political activities must have been
completely hidden from the Germans, or no one could write him off as an
isolated backwoodsman. Concerning his supposed ingratitude, Hecker's
friend Wilhelm Rapp remarked in the *Illinois Staatszeitung* that Hecker owed
"Germany not a pipsqueak's worth of thanks." Thanks for what? And the
fact that Hecker had had a drink with "South German democrats [in
Wilhelmsbad]" was hardly an indication that he unreservedly supported
their politics, but rather reflected the fact that most of them were "old personal acquaintances and friends," with whom taking a glass could be seen
as a natural necessity. In addition Hecker had been as severe as the liberals
in his opinion of the democrats for allying with the Ultramontanes. As far
as the *Illinois Staatszeitung* was concerned, the matter was clear. "Hecker has
raised himself in our estimation through his manly appearance in Germany,"
and the time would come when "thinking and understanding people in
Germany will find no lack of German patriotism in Hecker's openness and
love of truth, but rather see in it true patriotism." As the *Westliche Post* laconically concluded about all of the disputing, "The new, strongly-awakened
national feeling has also made our old countrymen touchy."[48]

The fact that Hecker was defended by the German-American press, run
largely by Forty-Eighters, is no surprise. This support arose from the same
impulse as the criticism of Kapp. Further, Hecker was and remained the
symbol of the 1848 movement for liberty, and hence was the Forty-Eighters'
ambassador on German soil. The *Illinois Staatszeitung* expressed clearly that
Hecker owed German-Americans a precise portrayal and judgment of
German conditions. "[I]n him is celebrated not simply his person, but also
his cause and the cause of all the old German freedom fighters who came to
America as a result of the revolutions of 1848 and 1849." Hecker himself –
used to American press wars and unflustered by the accusation that he was
and remained a hopeless idealist, immune to the necessary and unavoidable
politics of reality – did not take the liberal criticism much to heart. "With my
speech held on 4 July in the American Club at Stuttgart," he wrote to
Söhner, "I brought all of the imperial toadies to arms at me, making them
whistle and growl against me like a rat king against a couple hounds. But
you know my leather is good, more like alligator. Nothing gets through."[49]

The fact that Hecker in no way regretted his Stuttgart speech was shown a few days later during a festival banquet in Leipzig. His speech there followed the same tenor. He had come to Germany "partly to view see for once, first hand, developments in our nation, and partly to press his old partisans once more to his heart before the trumpeter calls him into the final land of liberty." For, as Hecker confessed, he longed, "to rest over there in free soil." The ovations that he had received showed that he had merely done "what his teacher, the historian Rotteck, imparted to him as a young man, to act always without hesitation for what he saw as good and right." But he had not been the only one to do it; hundreds, even thousands had acted for liberty. So he merely wanted to respond "in the name of the noble dead, the martyrs who fought and suffered for us." The "memory of these men" was dearest to him. Concerning Germany, Hecker closed with the wish "that the Germanic nation, having begun its career as a world power, will be as great and strong in civil liberty as it is externally."[50] That was no unconditioned praise. And so the editor of the *Gartenlaube*, Ernst Keil, an earlier friend and comrade of Robert Blum, sought to interpret Hecker's words in a mollifying way for his many readers in order to answer his own question, which was whether Hecker had returned "as still a complete German." Keil considered that Hecker had departed "on the advent of severe conditions here and was an alienated" German. In the last 25 years he had not experienced or fought for the great events in Germany. To be sure, Hecker remained a German "of our national spiritual nobility"; but in "his political family feeling" he had

> become an American, not only because he is an enthusiastic republican from birth, but also *because his most significant experience lacks such a large piece of German history.* Such has been the last quarter century, with the abysmal humiliations and glorious revivals of the spirit of our people. *For that reason he is in no position to measure, with the full warmth of his heart, the scale of transformation that has taken place with us, and for that reason he cannot marvel at the greatness of this transformation, made through deeds of the spirit as well as with the sword.*[51]

This was merely a benign variant of the National Liberal critique, which disputed Hecker's right to judge German conditions because he could not judge them properly, from afar and without personal sacrifice of his own. What was significant in this declaration was the stress on the sacrifice made by all forces for the common goal. It showed how much Bismarck's appeal to the people's self-sacrifice had succeeded, and how

much the awareness of the unity of a great nation had made not only the
National Liberals but also earlier democratic forces want to participate,
"despite themselves."

Hecker wrote Söhner that he had been traveling "continually since the
25th of May," "whipped like a Whitsun ox, passed around like festival mut-
ton and shown off like a bear." After so much excitement Hecker had earned
his bath vacation twice over. With his brother Carl and Dr. Berger, he traveled to Wildbad in Württemberg's Black Forest. He arrived there on 16 July,
immediately running into "tall Gagern" [Heinrich von Gagern] on a path.
Gagern "marveled mightily over my appearance and bold nose." The
American wilderness and the Civil War had doubtless left traces, and the
Gartenlaube had already remarked that on encountering him on the street one
would at best take him to be a "handsome old farmer." In Wildbad Hecker
once again had time to write his dispatches for the *Illinois Staatszeitung* and
send Söhner a second "political atmosphere report." He told his friend that
there were only three kinds of people who were of importance.

> First are the soldiers, who are topic A number 1, then the Jews. They
> have the most money, the top businesses, lovely palaces in which they
> host the citizens. They sit in the first balcony seats and become "Herr
> von" and "Ritter." The third are the National Liberals, who ride about
> on clouds of glory and serve as horsies, park beasts and other conven-
> iences for Bismarck and old Wilhelm, with enthusiasm and out of fear
> of what would come otherwise. Republicans live only as rare speci-
> mens in dark caves, like the last dinosaurs, and democrats are thinly
> spread, only now and then visible like birds of passage. Social
> Democrats, who hate all principles, as well as all forms of property and
> those who own them, have free room and board behind closed doors,
> which they accept with the joy of martyrs.[52]

What Hecker wrote briefly and pungently to Söhner, he thoroughly
worked out in his reports. Directed to the German public in the United
States, these articles were willfully subjective and often written after first
impressions, but they reflected in almost every case what Hecker also said
in his private correspondence. Hecker concentrated on what he thought was
"German thought" and what best described the mood in the country. His
gaze was directed first and foremost to all central questions of the new
German *Reich*.

In a chapter on Prussian militarism, he guessed that a "state within a state" had been created, standing outside the *Reich* constitution, under the supreme military leadership of Prussia. It could be turned against not only external but also internal enemies, and in the long run it intended the "abolition of the shadow princes" of the small states. At the same time Hecker marveled at Prussian discipline as compared to his own experiences in the American Civil War:

> One remarks at the soldiers, their severe Prussian discipline. The fellows proceed, move and march in a way that does an old soldier good. There is nothing slow or stiff. Gymnastic training, bayonet fencing and so on give bodies a remarkable flexibility. You know by his posture and movement a man who has passed through this schooling, even in civilian clothing.[53]

Hecker found hostility toward Jews to be a matter of concern. He believed that the litany of "envy and hatred" could be encountered at all social levels, "from the nobility to the peasantry." When the revolutionaries promoted civil equality of Jews in the 1840s. they had confidently expected a "dissolving of the old prejudice, the old hatefulness." Now Jews were blamed for development that did not come from them, but from which they had best profited. "The Germans have squinted at one class of citizens and loaded on them all that happens to be a result of the industrialism of the current day," observed Hecker. The wealth of "Israelites," Hecker declared, came from the fact that they normally worked harder, pursued fewer pleasures, on the whole "lived more moderately, more at home, more economically than their Christian fellow citizens." Hecker confirmed that there was tension between educated urban, Jews and less educated, rural Jews, who were now streaming into the cities, prospered, and then sought to "make up their lack of intellectual general training through the display of their wealth." These newcomers "heat up the hostile feeling of the mob, both elite and common," Hecker wrote,"who shift their own vices onto others and feed themselves on prejudice and envy."[54]

In the *Reichstag* Hecker saw nothing but "Bismarck's yes men" and a "claque parliament." He numbered Eugen Richter and Eduard Lasker among the few talented and gifted members. In the case of Lasker, Hecker asked himself why this man did not more energetically "act on whatever human rights would be guaranteed by any Bill of Rights," except that perhaps he would be isolated and would stand together with only a few other people, receiving no hearing. Hecker could not discern a republican party, and the "apathetic" Democratic Party seemed to him to lose its weak influence the farther north one went. There were only two parties that were "active, loud and organized, ... the Social Democrats and the Blacks, or Ultramontanes. The latter merely use their mouths in the Reichstag, and often cuttingly enough, because they do have some talent, such as the sly, consistent, nasty and learned Windhorst." While the Ultramontane forces received a stimulus from events in France, Hecker predicted that the Social Democrats would not have as fortunate a fate. It was obvious that the "Social Democrats are to be silenced," he wrote, "which will of course give the National Liberals transports of joy." In a letter written soon afterward, Hecker stressed that the existence of the Social Democrats was not an indication of political liberty, no "proof of national tolerance," because people figured on their self-elimination. "They allow them [the Social Democrats] to serve as a dreadful example to keep the others in fear and trembling. They are certain that anarchists will kill one another off, and the correctness of their calculation is shown by the breakdown of the *Internationale*."[55]

Hecker's personal concern was clearly with the mainstream National Liberals. He wrote,

> It begins to dawn in their heads that there is no future in a National Liberalism without principles, living hand to mouth. It is hardly enough to drink beer at a Bismarck soiree, charmed by the frat-boy nonchalance of the chancellor, and say to lady wife at home, "What a great man I am that the Great Man spoke with me, even toasted me. Elise, consider what a husband you have!" You have to know them personally, these bourgeois factory owners and bloated bankers with ribbons in their buttonholes and their water-blue, empty eyes. You have to know these career riders, who hope in vain to make it to Prussian privy-councilor; these professors who rework history and scholarship according to imperial and Prussian applause; those pseudo-journalists, who lust for the moneys of the Welf Fund, etc., to understand that even the "master" can feel only contempt for such underlings.[56]

It was Hecker's solid conviction that a people could not be liberated from the top down; rather, a clear wish for liberty must be tied to a stubborn will to win and keep that liberty. He cast his gaze on the contemporary political consciousness of German society. He found the "great mass" to be politically indifferent, and it surprised him that in clubs and inns and other public places "public matters are much less the object of review and discussion than in the Union," which he found "characteristic of our American self-government and the participation of everyone in it." Even the fall of Thiers and the "saber government of Mac Mahon" was discussed mostly "by the people from the stock exchange." To be sure there were always a few fighters from 1830 and 1848; but the younger generation that had been "raised and trained in the reaction of 1851" showed itself uninvolved in idealistic undertakings and the erection of a "libertarian, legally guaranteed state life. *'Gloire'* absorbs one, making money the other."[57]

As ever, Hecker associated the idea of the will to liberty with the importance of a political opposition and the presence of a free, independent press. Both of them had to influence the decision process of the heads of state and government. But he found Germany poorly supplied. "One may assert with full truth," he wrote,

> that there are not a dozen political journals in the whole of Germany that equal or exceed any one of the great American German journals in content, form or attitude. And none of them achieves in terms of content, extent and multiplicity of material, the level of papers such as the *New York Times, Herald, Cincinnati Commercial, Chicago Tribune,* not even the most important of all of them, the *Wiener Freie Presse, Kölnerin,* or the *Neue Preussische Zeitung.* If the demand for reading newspapers were as large and general as in the Union, this phenomenon would not exist. Instead, the public is served by a large number of fish-wrappers that would not be able to survive four months over there.

Yet the newspapers did not bear the guilt themselves. A study of the bill being considered at the time for the new *Reich* press law gave sent up Hecker's spine. Paragraph 20 forbade every criticism of the state order "undermining morality, sense of law or love of country." "[E]very criticism of the status quo" would cease, observed Hecker, "not only opening the door and the gate to the falsification of history," but also protecting such falsification. Paragraph 19 would punish the owner or publisher of a printed work for knowingly giving a false name for the responsible editor, even if the article came from another source. This made the arrest of the actual author easier, and there was no doubt that it would place a burden on free journalism. What were these preventative measures other than censorship, Hecker asked. He found it to be inconceivable that anyone "still believes himself capable of placing the human spirit in such a pitiful straightjacket and smothering it in these times of rapid national and international travel and exchange of ideas."[58]

A quick look at the new penal ordinance led Hecker to conclude that it was also far behind what had already been achieved in South Germany in 1846, as far as the political part was concerned. "It might be progressive in Prussia in comparison with that time, but not in South Germany." Hecker saw the same development in the communal ordinance and constitution. Through the introduction of *Reich* citizenship, a general right of residency and the right to practice trades, differences between the old bourgeois communes and the new community of residents – "the child of the new conditions" – had become clear, particularly when it came to taxation, representation and election law. In South Germany, especially in Baden, the self-determination and self-administration of communes had always been seen as the essential foundation of the new state system, the most secure guarantee of constitutional rights and autonomous civil developments. Mayors and communal representatives could be chosen completely independently, freely elected by the citizens in a manner similar to American "self-government." But now there was talk of reintroducing the state's right to confirm the highest officers of the commune, as well as appoint commissars at urban expense. This seemed extremely questionable to Hecker. He warned that no modifications for new conditions should permit the government to intervene in and restrict political life. Just as Hecker defended township organization in the United States as the practice of "little republics in a [larger] republic," he believed that a communal ordinance in Germany would be "the sole correct measure for judging the development of liberty of a people and of all nations." Subjugation was "the foundation of despotism in centralized guardianship. A communal life under guardianship is a declaration that the people is incompetent."[59]

It was not merely that an autonomous administration of the communes was a "postulate for the new economic life of the nations." For Hecker bureaucratic control and guardianship meant a "national scandal" in the context of current development and movement of trade and transportation, and a restriction of the people's power of control. The results of the Baden urban congress and its resolutions accommodating and unifying the old communal civic law with *Reich* citizenship and freedom of movement in a clear, simple and pregnant manner received his complete approval. They rested on the complete integration of state citizenship and *Reich* residency into a communal association with equal rights and duties, retaining the autonomy of communal representative bodies.

The one point where Hecker could not doubt the existence of progress was the improvement in the quality of life arising from the developments of trade and transportation. He noted in a rather irritated manner the fact that one continuously heard that Germany had "made great progress," "only praise, praise, praise, finding only the most advanced progress." Yet this progress came from the economic sector above all else. Hecker was under the impression that the people were being called on to praise something that was not even the "product of an order from above." "[T]here is no progress specific to one or two nations," he wrote; rather, economic progress had taken the place of real political progress and had been marked down as a success for Bismarck. But this progress in fact derived from the "industrialism of our times." "[I]t is the new means of transportation. It derives from the growing closeness of nations, and the exchange of their products is the driving force."

On the whole the political laws did not correspond to Hecker's own concepts of republican and civic freedom. There was no Bill of Rights, genuine constitutional guarantees or consistent constitutional division of powers. "There might be some political progress when compared to the dark period of reaction in the 1850s," he summarized, but "I cannot see a continuation, a continual, free continuation of what was already accomplished in 1846, 1847, 1848."[60]

From Wildbad, Hecker first traveled with his brother to Freiburg and then alone to Mannheim, where the festival banquet had been postponed at his request until Sunday evening, 24 August. Because Hecker had passed the final weeks of his German visit with his brother in Freiburg, the festival in the Badener Hof, organized by his political friends and attended by more than 300 persons, had become his farewell banquet. His speech of more than an hour, as the *Neue Badische Landeszeitung* wrote, had "the significance of a political last will and testament," for it meant "the close of his political activity in Germany." The banquet proceeded in a solemn and simple manner because Hecker had forbidden all applause. When he entered the hall with the reception committee at 8 p.m., those present rose in silence from their chairs, and Hecker began his address after a brief statement by Privy Councilor Langeloth. The address was a panegyric for Mannheim, but it was also more. In it Hecker described the origins of his "ancient historical" republicanism in the humanistic Mannheim education he had enjoyed. He described the model, the inner necessity of his life and the ideals that had formed him. In Mannheim he had gone to school. There he had received the first "impressions of liberty"; heard about Gaius Sempronius [Gracchus]; read of the last Roman [Cato the Younger], who "pressed the dagger into his heart because he did not wish to experience the fall of liberty." He had promised then, "with a holy oath" "to become the tribune of my people, to fight for the good of the people, the liberty of the people and the education of the people, and by Almighty God, I have kept my oath." Hecker's life – as he wanted it to appear, as he himself believed it – was the consistent, concrete application of this ancient historical republicanism. What perhaps sounded like mere rhetoric was in truth a serious secularized confession of faith. The content of this confession was political and profane, but the feeling was profoundly religious. He could be dogmatic and even unworldly in applying these ideals, but it was still these ideals, these principles, that strictly and exclusively determined him.

In his address Hecker also responded to accusations that he was a man without a country and a betrayer of his country. Referring to his efforts to bring Germans "to honor" wherever he was, he recalled that he had celebrated the peace festival in St. Louis as a German. But he continued by saying that he needed "free earth and a free fatherland." "I am a democrat, I am a republican, and I pity the gentlemen who cannot bear that." Germans had been upset that he called himself an American; now he wanted to add the word "must" and call himself "a must-be-American," "and I am happy that I am one," he added.

In his Mannheim farewell address Hecker also proclaimed the peaceful struggle for the people's rights of liberty. Unity was only a body. What was this body without its soul, liberty? Basic rights were "the piece of bread necessary for daily nourishment," because "only the people that has not merely unity but also liberty is strong enough to protect itself against every assault." In the certainty that he is seeing his fatherland for the last time, Hecker closed with the words, "I am 62 years of age, I will never see my homeland again. But between us there exists a spiritual band ... every word that comes here across the ocean, every bale of goods ariving here, will contribute to supporting the spirit of liberty and promoting the cause of liberty." It starts to sound a little "imperialistic" when he assured his listeners that

> we [the German-Americans] will always communicate the experiences we have had for liberty and human rights ... We Germans in the Union are and remain Germans even on foreign soil; but we also remain true republicans and are good citizens of the great American fatherland. We believe in the solidarity of democratic principles and interests, and what we achieve over there can also be useful in the old German homeland.[61]

As with all other Hecker speeches, his Mannheim farewell address was published in German newspapers. The criticism was as vehement as at the beginning of his homecoming, even a littler harsher, because it was now apparent that Hecker's Stuttgart speech had been no error. "A man like Friedrich Hecker has already become an object for historical consideration," wrote the ever-vigilant *Weser Zeitung*, "because, isolated from our life, he has remained in America what he was in 1848. ... He has remained standing while we have moved. We can understand that we have moved because of our increased distance from him." The National Liberals were the progressive, modern forces, and Hecker's republicanism represented at best the dusty dogmatism of past times. He was totally out of tune with current conditions. To Hecker's accusation of a lack of liberty and a body without a soul, first already made in Stuttgart but now even clearer in Mannheim, the newspaper responded with conviction.

> A nation is still well served with a body, since one could turn this around and ask, what is a soul without a body? A body without a soul is at least a body, but a soul without a body is, at least here on earth, nothing at all. Which means that we are not so out of line in assuring ourselves of unity first.

In response to Hecker's somewhat "imperialistic" report that every bale of American goods exported to Germany promoted liberty, the *Weser Zeitung* raised indignant objections. Noting how Hecker had defended himself against the protectionist attacks of Gustav Freytag, the *Weser Zeitung* remarked that Germans well knew how to defend themselves. "We believe that the new Prussian regional ordinance will do more for the cause of liberty in one day than all of America's petrolium, cotton and tobacco in a hundred years." Weech's 1891 commentary on Hecker's visit shows that this attitude toward Hecker would establish itself in National Liberal historiography. It said in *Badische Biographien* that, during his visit to Germany, Hecker had fallen "back into the old bombastic tone of a pre-Revolutionary demagogue," "who had been taken in by the stormy jubilation of unreconstructed democrats in Mannheim and other German cities," but who had shown "that politicians of his sort, like the extreme ultras of the opposition ... have learned nothing and forgotten everything."[62]

On 20 September Hecker reached Frankfurt. Here he took his quarters in the Brüsseler Hof and visited old friends from earlier days. Hecker had always had a strained relationship with Frankfurt, conditioned by his memory of his failure in the pre-Parliament and his later exclusion from the National Assembly as a traitor. He had heard of the annexation of Frankfurt by Prussia in 1866 with a certain satisfaction. "Nothing so pleases him as the profound humiliation the Frankfurt pepper-bags, or rather moneybags, had to experience," Caspar Butz later wrote. Now it was just as well that Frankfurt left a less than stellar impression on Hecker. When a torch parade was planned in his honor, the torches were confiscated by the police, where-upon the crowd went straight to the Gallusgasse in front of the Brüsseler Hof and sent a delegation to Hecker. When he finally appeared at the door of the inn after long beseeching, intended to speak, a policeman interjected himself "with the snarling voice of a Prussian police commissar. 'no public meeting may be held here and there may be no speaking. In the name of the law I demand those present to disperse!'" In response Hecker vanished back into the inn without having said a word. He explained later to an acquaintance he still wondered, "How you can stand it? I am happy that I will soon be able to breathe free air. Three more days in Prussia and I would be smothered to death."[63]

On 30 September he departed once more on the steamer *Berlin* for Southhampton, where Hecker had arranged a rendezvous with Karl Blind. Blind came down from London but spent "three days at anchor" in the harbor town because Hecker's arrival was postponed, due to damage to the ship's screw, and the ship had to return to Bremerhaven. Blind, whom Hecker had defended as a lawyer in the 1840s and who later participated in the Baden uprisings, was well informed of Hecker's activities in Germany, but he was still curious to hear Hecker's own opinion. They discussed political questions and wallowed in reminiscences. Hecker declared at the close that the best description that anyone could give of himself was a "German nationalist republican."[64]

Hecker's arrival in Baltimore would prove as friendly and festive as his departure. Weeks before his arrival the *Baltimore Wecker* began issuing calls to the German-Americans of the city to stage a worthy reception for this "much-tried man." Once more the identifying motifs that German-Americans applied to Hecker included Christian associations:

> Do we Germans of Baltimore not wish to sweeten this joy [for country, family and friends] even more by preparing for him a worthy recep-tion? By doing this we could only honor ourselves, and there would be no better way of announcing German-American pride for Hecker as the best one from our ranks. Let's get underway, you singers, sharpshoot-

ers and Turners of Baltimore, all you citizens, let us go to work with zeal so that the day of his arrival does not find us unprepared.

On his arrival in Baltimore on Tuesday afternoon, 21 October 1873, Hecker was greeted formally by a citizens committee. Various addresses were presented in the ship's salon. The editor of the *Baltimore Wecker* presented Hecker with telegrams from his family and then greeted "the celebrated one especially in the name of the German progressive press, which saw in him one of its sharpest thinkers, one of its most intelligent fellow fighters for progress, a shining model for all." Everywhere in the Union German-Americans had followed his outstanding observations, his reports published in the *Illinois Staatszeitung*. They had "marveled at their responsible, non-partisan judgments," noting that "uncorrupted by the extreme splendor and aura," he had "given full justice to the republic on this side of the ocean." Hecker had been, without any doubt, the "spiritual advanced warrior of the German-Americans, who pride themselves in him." Hecker thanked them emotionally for the reception, which he had not expected in this form. He was glad to be able to hold uncensored speeches once more, and he mentioned the episode in Frankfurt before departing for his hotel. At about 11 p.m. the united singers of the *Liederkranz*, the *Germania Männerchor* and the *Arion* serenaded Hecker. They sang "Ich grüsse Dich" and "Am Rhein," and Hecker gave another speech in the courtyard of the hotel from the balcony. His praise of republican institutions and liberties was what the occasion demanded. But then, perhaps carried away by the moment, perhaps overtired from the long ocean voyage, both overwrought and over-stimulated, he spoke of the dominant inclination of the times to worship the success of the moment. Then he boldly declared in hyperbole, "that Prince Bismarck's name will fall into the same oblivion as Prince Kaunitz, who had accomplished even more." Then gave examples from popular life of the fact that the names of men of the people, such as Ulrich von Hutten and the leaders in the Peasants' War lived on in tradition, while the people no longer recalled the servants of princes.

This statement barely impressed those who were present that evening, but as soon as it was spread by the press, some German-Americans began to doubt Hecker's "responsible, non-partisan judgments" of things. The *Illinois Staatszeitung* wrote, "It will strike our readers as it does us that in the harmony of Hecker's reception in Baltimore, the old man's statement that 'Bismarck's name will fall into oblivion' sounded shrilly off tune." The paper judged as absolutely "monstrous" the comparison of Bismarck to a cabinet politician such as Kaunitz, and the prophecy that the German people would ever forget the man "who has done more than any other for the restoration of the honor and greatness of the nation" was described as absurd. The *Westliche Post* reacted to Hecker's statement in a similar way with the remark that his judgments were simply "not always right." "The two souls that live in the breast of Friedrich Hecker, the German and the American," the newspaper explained, "often express themselves indeed in unpredictable and even for his friends intolerable ways." Even the *Philadelphia Demokrat*, the greatest supporter and defender of Hecker's visit in Germany, offered criticism under the headline, "Young People Are Quickly Finished With the Word," that the proverb applied not only to youth, but also to "the old man" who preserved the fresh and impulsive nature of youth. To be sure they had long been used to Hecker's manner of not weighing every word of his intense, harsh speech, particularly not in balcony speeches; but the fact that he had gone too far this time was clear. The public had shown its rejection, crying protest and shouting "Long live Bismarck!"

While Hecker did not weigh every word on a scale, most German-Americans did, particularly when they were emigrated Forty-Eighters. The fact that he was seen as "their ambassador" – Carl Schurz was in Germany at the same time, but there were almost no articles about him – is shown by the commentary of the *Philadelphia Demokrat*. This paper wrote that any criticism of Hecker by "his American friends" was not proper "as long as the gallant warrior had to endure the crossfire of his critics in Germany." But, "when he is once more in our midst, one may well say that quieter language and an objective position in his speeches about Germany and his correspondence about Germany would have been more impressive over there and more instructive for us." And as for Hecker's statement about Bismarck, the *Demokrat* observed that Germany, like the United States and every other country only developed "from premises created by the entire nation." Bismarck was no more the creator of this development than were Grant or Napoléon III; he was "only the momentary representative of it." Hecker knew this at heart as well, and when calm would see that his statement was too rash. The *Westliche Post* had already reached this conclusion, for it declared that Hecker had been the one who had recognized Bismarck early, "when many did not yet know him." Recognizing Bismarck's accomplishments over Hecker's expressed contempt revealed a dilemma that impinged on every German-American. Even while praising and defending republican institutions and American liberty, German-Americans wanted a sovereign, strong German nation, and Bismarck, although a "servant of princes," remained a representative of this strength and success.[65]

Hecker himself was already aware as he composed his reports that some of his expressions would excite contradiction. "[A]ll of the Chauvins over there [in the United States] will again yelp over your correspondent" he observed, if he expressed skepticism about German greatness and unity. "There are not only religious but also political Syllabus-skulls that will go through thick and thin," he said in one report, "that [condemn] free and well-meaning criticism of German conditions, not just in Germany, but also over there in New York, St. Louis and Chicago." The high-wire act between necessary respect for and justified criticism of German conditions could never satisfy all sides, he believed. For that reason Hecker never attempted to orient himself to any view other than his own. The fact that he was now criticized in America as well as Germany pleased him, for here everyone could "have a sow's snoot." Returning to his farm, he immediately reported to his friend Söhner.

> Here I am again, where there are no little ribbons, ... no tips and privy councilors, no taking off of hats ... no princes or advocates of beggars. Everyone can have a sow's snoot, travel in the sleeping cars, and pick his nose with his fingers, and ... any ass can be president. Here I am again, and although parting with my beloveds and my brave friends over there was very hard, I am still glad that I once again can take a breath without a bridle in my mouth. If you knew of the innumerable trials for offending His Majesty, if you had seen this Dalai Lamaism, you would be as happy as I am.[66]

[1] FH, *Gepfefferte Briefe,* 2d ed. (Mannheim, 1868), 1-2 (2 December 1865).

[2] Agricola, "Betrachtungen über den Stand der Dinge in Europa," St. Clair County, Ill., 12 May [1859]. FHP, box 4, folder 42.

[3] F. Hoffmann to FH, Burghof bei Königswinter, 11 November 1866, FHP, box 3, folder 33. "Friedrich Hecker's 'Briefe uber Deutschlands Zukunft.' Aus Süddeutschland, 23. Oktober," *Kölnische Zeitung,* FHP, box 4, folder 42, later in FH, *Gepfefferte Briefe,* 1-18.

[4] FH, *Gepfefferte Briefe,* 3-4, 7-8 (2 December 1865).

[5] FH, *Gepfefferte Briefe,* 10-12 (2 September 1866).

[6] FH, *Gepfefferte Briefe,* 31 (14 February 1867); emphasis in the original.

[7] FH, *Gepfefferte Briefe,* 12-13 (2 September 1866).

[8] See the controversy in the *New Yorker Criminalzeitung,* quoted in *BZ,* weekly, 3 January 1867. Struve's objection is printed there in full.

[9] FH, *Gepfefferte Briefe,* foreword, X.

[10] FH, *Gepfefferte Briefe,* 19 (3 February 1867); Friedrich Lexow, *New Yorker Criminalzeitung,* quoted in *BZ,* weekly, 3 January 1867.

[11] On the Forty-Eighters in the years before the foundation of the *Reich*, see best of all Wittke, *Refugees*, 345-66; FH, *Gepfefferte Briefe*, 16, 20-21, 27, 53ff.; "Eine Erklärung Friedrich Heckers," *ISZ* [n. d., 1867], FHP, box 4, folder 42.

[12] FH, *Gepfefferte Briefe*, 84-85, 87.

[13] "Das norddeutsche Verfassungs-Werk," *New Yorker Criminalzeitung oder Belletristisches Jounral*, quoted in *BZ*, weekly, 11 April 1867; FH, *Gepfefferte Briefe*, 87-88.

[14] German-American newspapers were speculating on the possibility of a war against France starting in April, 1867, see Wittke, *Refugees*, 351. FH wrote to Carl Schurz on 5 May 1867, Lebanon, St. Clair County, "I do not agree with you about the war question in Europe. Michel [Germany] has to strike a blow if anything is to become of him. How much good has come of war? Without it we would be utterly southernized. Bismarck must have war. Parliamentarism is to be done away with, which is his goal, ... supported on the hilt of the sword." Schurz Papers.

[15] FH, *Gepfefferte Briefe*, 89-96 (7 May 1867), here 89, 91, 92, 93, 96.

[16] On German-American response to the Franco-Prussian War and the unification of the *Reich* in general, Hans L. Trefousse, "Die deutschamerikanischen Einwanderer und das neugegründete Reich," Frank Trommler, ed., *Amerika und die Deutschen: Bestandsaufnahme einer 300-Jährigen Geschichte,*(Opladen, 1986), 177-91; G. A. Dobbert, "German-Americans between Old and New Fatherland, 1870-1914," *American Quarterly* 19 (1967), 663-80; La Verne J. Rippley, "German Assimilation: the Effect of the 1871 Victory on Americana-Germanica," Hans L. Trefousse, ed., *Germany and America: Essays on Problems of International Relations and Immigration* (New York, 1980), 122-36; on the American attitude to German developments, John Gerow Gazley, *American Opinion of German Unification, 1848-1871* (New York, 1926). "News of the Battle of Sedan was being cried out in the streets of St. Louis with many details at 11 p.m. on the very day the battle occurred, earlier than in Berlin, Vienna or St. Petersburg." FH received the news on 3 September; see FH to August Becker, Summerfield, 4 September 1870, *TISZ*, 15 September 1870.

[17] "Friedrich Hecker über Deutschlands Zukunft," printed from a private letter to Germany *(Badische Landeszeitung)*, reprinted in the *TISZ*, 14 March 1871; emphasis in the text. Butz, "Erinnerungen, 2. Teil." FH, *Reden*, 6. David J. Brewer, ed., *The World's Best Orations from the earliest Period to the Present Time*, vol. 7 (1899), 2457-64.

[18] "Festrede zur St. Louiser Friedensfeier," printed in FH, *Reden*, 1-12.

[19] See Wittke, *Refugees*, 352; among the critics of German unity were the Boston radical Adolph Douai, Karl Heinzen and the "socialistically"-oriented Wilhelm Weitling, see Witke, *Refugees*, 355. FH to the Verein der deutschen Patrioten von 1848/49 in New York, Franz Sigel and others, Summerfield, St. Clair County, 18 April 1871, *BZ*, weekly, 11 May 1871; see also FH's letter to the arrangements committee for the peace festival to be held on Whitsun Monday in Milwaukee; FH was invited, but he could not participate. Printed in the *TISZ*, 5 June 1871; also in the *BZ*, weekly , 8 June 1871.

[20] "Friedrich Franz Karl Hecker," Friedrich von Weech, ed., *Badische Biographien*, vol. 4, (Karlsruhe, 1891), 166-71, here 171.

[21] FH to Charles Söhner, 14 November 1872, FHP, box 3, folder 38.

[22] Carl Schurz to FH, Washington, 3 February 1871, FHP, box 3, folder 35.

[23] Wittke, *Refugees*, 351; *GL*, 1870, 208; cf. the letter from Ernst Keil to FH, Leipzig, 6 March 1870: "Here and there in the newspapers the story of your return pops up. I will use your notification of finality in the *Gartenlaube* to stop the mouths of these people once and for all." FHP, box 3, folder 34.

[24] FH to a friend, Summerfield, St. Clair County, 111., 25 December 1870; original in Stadtarchiv

Mannheim, Kleine Erwerbungen, 127; also printed in the *Neue Badische Landeszeitung*, 6 November 1911. FH to Carl Schurz, Summerfield, St. Clair Co., Ill., 30 December 1870, Schurz Papers.

25 See particularly Hinners, *Exil*, 159, 254, 268-71, 273; Wehler, *Kapp;* Vagts, *Rückwanderung*, 182-86. Friedrich Kapp to Eduard Cohen, New York, 21 September 1861, quoted in Hinners, *Exil,* 166. Ludwig Bamberger, "Bin Burger zweier Welten. Friedrich Kapp," *GL* 1869, 341-44. H. A. Rattermann, "Friedrich Kapp," *Deutsch-Amerikanisches Magazin* part 1: no. 1 (October, 1886), 16-33; part 2, no. 2 (January, 1887), 226-38; part 3, no. 3 (April, 1887), 360-73, here part 2, 231.

26 Friedrich Kapp, *Geschichte der deutschen Einwanderung im Staate New York,* vol. 1, (New York, 1867), here 370; the first edition appeared with Quand und Handel in Leipzig, see Hinners, *Exil*, 217.

27 See *WP*, daily, 28 April 1870; my own emphasis. Gustav Korner's book, Das *deutsche Element in den Vereinigten Staaten von Nordamerika* (Cincinnati, 1880) also served the attempt to show the great gain of the United States through immigration of the Thirtyer generation. He dedicated this book to Friedrich Kapp, who had denied the significance of the Thirtyers in his essay on the Forty-Eighters in America, see Kapp, "Die Acht und Vierziger in den Vereinigten Staaten (1861)," idem, *Aus und über Amerika. Thatsachen und Erlebnisse,* vol. 1, (Berlin, 1876),307-30. , *TISZ* 15 April 1871.

28 Friedrich Kapp, *Friedrich der Grosse und die Vereinigten Staaten von Amerika,* (Leipzig, 1871); idem, "New Yorker Stadtverwaltung," *Preussische Jahrbücher* 28 (1871), 522-38; idem, "Über Auswanderung," lecture held on 2 February 1871 before the Berliner Handwerker Verein, *TISZ,* 6 March 1871; idem, *Über Auswanderung* (Berlin, 1871); idem, "Die Stellung und Zukunft des deutschen Elementes" (both essays 1868/69 from his *Geschichte der deutschen Auswanderung)* reprinted in idem, *Aus und über Amerika,* 331-35.

29 "Deutschtum und Deutschamerikanertum," *TISZ* 24 July 1871; see also the first criticism of Kapp, "Bin Amerikamüder," *TISZ* 22 June 1871. Friedrich Kapp to Carl Ludwig Bernays, printed in *AW* quoted in *TISZ* 24 July 1871.

30 *Philadelphia Demokrat,* quoted in *TISZ* 31 July 1871. "Gustav Körner über Friedrich Kapp," 1st and 2nd part in *TISZ,* 26 and 27 July 1871, also reprinted in *BZ*, weekly, 3 August 1871.

31 "Kein Amerikamüder," *TISZ,* 20 July 1871; Kapp had invested part of his wealth in American bonds; on his trans-Atlantic business, see Hinners, *Exil,* 265-67. FH's speech, "Unsere Republik, ihre Kritiker und Gegner," was printed in FH, *Reden,* 13-20.

32 FH, "Zeitbetrachtungen aus dem Mississippi-Thale," parts 1 and 2, *TISZ,* 10 and 11 August 1871.

33 Hecker, "Zeitbetrachtungen," part 1, 2; corresponding passages are not as violent as FH portrays them, see Freytag, *Mathy,* 247, 264-65; on Freytag's pejorative image of America in his earlier plays, see Vagts, *Rückwanderung,* 96-97.

34 FH, "Zeitbetrachtungen," part 2; the "restricted spirit of subjection" is a quote from Luther.

35 See, for example, the reaction of one editor of the *Newarker Freie Presse* in Germany at the time, *BZ*, weekly, 26 October 1871. *Weser Zeitung*, 11 August 1871, from the reprint in *BZ*, weekly, 19 October 1871. Earlier commentaries to this article of the *Weser Zeitung* in *TISZ,* 2 September 1871; also *BZ*, weekly, 7 September 1871.

36 FH, *Reden,* 21-46; see also the account in the *WP* on the lecture; quoted in *TISZ,* 13 November 1871. See also Dan Diner, *Verkehrte Welten. Antiamerikanismus in Deutschland. Ein historischer Essay,* (Frankfurt a. M.), 1993. FH, *Reden,* III.

37 FH to Charles Söhner, Summerfield, 11 November 1872, idem to idem, Summerfield, 29 December 1872, FHP, box 3, folder 38.

38 FH to Charles Söhner, Summerfield, 20 March 1873, FHP, box 3, folder 38. Butz,

"Erinnerungen, 2. Teil."

39 August Decker died on 26 March 1871. Hecker published his obituary in the *TISZ*, 17 May 1871; on Becker also see *TISZ*, 30 March 1871; Zucker, *Forty-Eighters*, 276. FH to Charles Söhner, Summerfield, 5 May 1873, FHP, box 3, folder 38, underlining in the original.

40 *WP*, daily, 6 May 1873; *TISZ*, 15 May 1873. On Dr. Berger, see *BZ*, weekly, 15 August 1867. For information see FH's first correspondence, Freiburg in Baden, 2 June 1873, printed in *TISZ*, 25 June 1873; excerpted in *WP*, daily, 27 June 1873; printed whole in *BZ*, weekly, 3 July 1873. See, for example, *Mannheimer Tageblatt. Anzeigeblatt für Baden und die bayerische Rheinpfalz*, no. 125, 29 May 1873, also found in FHP, box 4, folder 41; *Neue Badische Landeszeitung*, 28 May 1873, also printed in the *TISZ*, 19 June 1873; *Karlsruher Zeitung*, 29 May 1873, also *TISZ*, 19 June 1873; on FH's arrival in Bremen, *Weser Zeitung*, 26 May 1873, FHP, box 4, folder 41, also printed in the *BZ*, weekly, 19 June 1873. FH to Wilhelm Rapp, Freiburg, 2 June 1873, printed in *TISZ*, 25 June 1873.

41 *Neue Badische Landeszeitung*, 28 May 1873; *Mannheimer Tageblatt*, 29 May 1873.

42 FH to Wilhelm Rapp, Freiburg, 2 June 1873, printed in *TISZ*, 25 June 1873; FH to Charles Söhner, Freiburg i. B., 5 June 1873, FHP, box 3, folder 38.

43 Frey had been a prisoner of war in the Civil War, and FH worked for an exchange or release, see the correspondence, FHP, box 2, folder 28.

44 All quotations FH to the festival committee of the American Club in Stuttgart, Freiburg i. B., 18 June 1873, FHP, box 3, folder 33. The request to FH was dated 14 June 1873.

45 See, for example, on the obsession for travel to Europe by Americans that increased every year, *BZ*, weekly, 5 June 1873. Report of the *Kreuzzeitung (Neue Preussische Zeitung)* and the *Weser Zeitung*; *Neues Tageblatt*, Stuttgart, no. 155B, Sunday, 6 July 1873, FHP, box 4, folder 41. "Auszug aus Fr, Heckers Rede, die er am 4. Juli 1873 in Stuttgart hielt," in *BZ*, weekly, 7 August 1873; see also "Das amerikanische Unabhängigkeitsfest, Stuttgart, 4. Juli," *Frankfurter Zeitung und Handelsblatt*, Sunday, 6 July 1873, p. 2.

46 *Frankfurter Zeitung und Handelsblatt* (6 July 1873) praised the speech as a "masterpiece" in form and content, and the *Stuttgarter Beobachter* was happy to tell its readers that after the speech Hecker and his brother and Swabian friends, who all belonged to the democratic People's Party, traveled to Canstatt and celebrated wine-soaked rounds in Wilhelmsbad, "since Hecker had to do during his visit almost exclusively with members of the People's Party such as Carl Mayer, Hausmann, Vollmer, etc." *Schwäbischer Merkur*, quoted in *WP*, daily, 30 July 1873; see also *TISZ*, 2 August 1873. *Hamburger Nachrichten*, quoted in *WP*, daily, 4 August 1873.

47 See *TISZ*, 2 August 1873; *Weser Zeitung*, 11 July 1873; the volume *Reden und Vorlesungen von Friedrich Hecker* had already been published in Germany in 1872. On the occasion of Hecker's visit, however, the *Weser Zeitung* printed a review by C. Bentlage in which he reported the "panegyruc for the republic," and "that he still has something to learn," see the reprint from the *Weser Zeitung* in *Mississippi Blatter*, 15 June 1873. *Weser Zeitung*, "London," 10 July 1873, reprinted in *WP*, daily, 7 August 1873. *Weser Zeitung*, 11 July 1873.

48 "Hecker und die 'liberalen' Herren in Deutschland," *Philadelphia Democrat*, reprinted in the *TISZ*, 1 August 1873; "Das Geheul in Deutschland gegen den Alten," *TISZ*, 2 August 1873. "Politische Dornrosen," *WP*, daily, 4 August 1873.

49 *TISZ*, 25 June 1873; FH to Charles Söhner, Wildbad, 19 June 1873, FHP, box 3, folder 38.

50 FH's Leipzig speech, printed in *TISZ*, 5 and 8 August 1873.

51 See "Ernst Keil (1816-1878), der Gründer der Gartenlaube," Magdalena Zimmermann, ed., *Die Gartenlaube als Dokument ihrer Zeit*, (Munich, 1963), 9-12 (In 1870 the *Gartenlaube* had a distribution of 270,000). "Friedrich Hecker in Leipzig," *GL* 1873, 526; my own emphasis; see also the announcement of the visit *ibid.*, 17, 382; FH's letter of farewell to Ernst Keil, *ibid.*, 658.

52 FH to Charles Söhner, Wildbad, 19 July 1873, FHP, box 3, folder 38; he wrote in a similar tone to Emil Frey on 30 July 1873, Staatsarchiv Basel (Stadt), Sig. PA 485 DXI163. *GL,* 1873, 526.

53 "Briefe aus Deutschland von Friedrich Hecker. Ein Capitel vom preussischen Militarismus. Aus Süddeutschland, Anfangs September 1873," (11th correspondence), *TISZ,* 23 September 1873; additional material from Baden, 6 September 1873 (12th correspondence), *TISZ,* 25 September 1873. "Briefe aus Deutschland von Friedrich Hecker. Aus dem Badischen," 7 June 1873 (2nd correspondence), *TISZ,* 30 June 1873.

54 "Briefe aus Deutschland von Friedrich Hecker. Aus Süddeutschland," 20 September 1873 (14th correspondence), *TISZ,* 13 October 1873; see also his later essays, "Zur Judenhetze in Deutschland," *WP* [n. d., 1880], FHP, box 9.

55 "Briefe aus Deutschland von Friedrich Hecker," Mannheim, 30 June 1873 (4th correspondence), *TISZ,* 24 July 1873. FH to Ernst Keil, September 1873, *GL,* 1873, 658; also printed in the *TISZ,* 28 October 1873; also in *BZ,* weekly, 6 November 1873.

56 The mention of the Welf Fund was an attack on FH's earlier comrade Julius Fröbel, whose *Siiddeutsche Presse* in Munich was subsidized by Bismarck's "reptile fund." Correspondence 12.

57 Correspondence 2, 4, 5.

58 Correspondence 2, 6.

59 FH to Ernst Keil, September 1873, *GL,* 1873, 658; Correspondence 13.

60 FH to Ernst Keil as in the previous note; Correspondence 2, 7.

61 *Neue Badische Landeszeitung,* 26 August 1873, FHP, box 4, folder 41; "Heckers Mannheimer Abschiedsrede vom 24. August 1873," *Neue Badische Landeszeitung,* 26 August 1873, Hecker Papers, box 4, folder 41; also printed in *WP,* daily, 13 September 1873 and *TISZ,* 15 September 1873.

62 "Der deutsche Garibaldi," *Weser Zeitung* [n. d.], reprinted in *WP,* daily, 17 September 1873; Weech, *Badische Biographien,* 171.

63 Butz, "Erinnerungen, 2. Teil"; see on this also FH's statement on Frankfurt's "integration" in FH, *Gepfefferte Briefe,* 14; also correspondence 1. The entire incident is described by "O. H.," "Friedrich Hecker," *Frankfurter Zeitung und Handelsblatt,* 30 March 1881, morning edition; the episode was also described in German- American newspapers of 1873.

64 "Wiedersehen mit Friedrich Hecker," Karl Blind, London, 8 October, printed in *WP,* daily, 29 October 1873.

65 "Heckers Empfang in Baltimore," *Baltimore Wecker,* 19 September 1873, also FHP, box 4, 41; *WP,* daily, 22 October 1873; American newspapers also reported Hecker's arrival in Baltimore, see "Welcome Back to America – What He says of America and Germany," *Baltimore Sun,* 22 October 1873. "Ein wohlgemeinter Rüffel fur Hecker," *TISZ,* 28 October 1873. See "Nicht immer Richtig," *Mississippi Blatter,* 26 October 1873. 205 "Der alte Freischärler Hecker und der Befreier Kinkels auf einer Erholungsreise nach Deutschland," *BZ,* weekly, 22 May 1873; see also "Hecker und Schurz," [n. d.], FHP, box 4, folder 41. "Schnell fertig ist die Jugend mit dem Wort," *Philadelphia Demokrat,* quoted here in *TISZ,* 28 October 1873. Conversely the *Missouri Staatszeitung* defended Hecker against the "German- American Bismarck batteries, their cross-fire from New York *(Journal),* Philadelphia *(Demokrat)* and St. Louis *(Westliche Post),* praising his upright opinion and condemned the opinion of "Schurz & Co.," who would celebrate "the promised messiah of the German people" in Bismarck. "Zu Heckers Baltimore Rede," *Missouri Staatszeitung* [n. d.], FHP, box 4, folder 41.

66 Correspondence 12, 13; FH to Charles Söhner, Summerfield, 27 October 1873, Hecker Papers, box 3, folder 38.

Page honoring Friedrich Hecker as the "Grand Old Man of Fighters for Freedom and Justice" drawn in the 1870s by Joseph Keppler for the St. Louis journal *Puck*. Friedrich Hecker Papers, Western Historical Manuscripts, University of Missouri – St. Louis.

Josephine Hecker. Friedrich Hecker Papers, Western Historical Manuscripts, University of Missouri – St. Louis.

IX

LECTURES

German Lectures in America

German lectures in America had little hope for success so far as contemporary German-American newspapers were concerned. The largest potential audience was available to Anglo-Americans, who could present their lectures to an ethnically mixed public, while the number of people attending German-language events was limited. An additional difficulty was the greater variation of education of German immigrants; that of Anglo-Americans was more uniform due to their school system. The "immigration to the United States did not consist of a *proportional* number of *all* levels of German civil society; rather there were perhaps only about five thousand learned or highly trained German immigrants, or even fewer," a German-American newspaper urged. The German lecturer therefore had to "figure at least on a certain *average education* to find a bridge over which he could make himself understood to his listeners." Despite these problems there were efforts by such noted German-Americans as Emil Steiger of New York, the most successful German publisher in America, to advance "the systematic promotion of German intellectual life in America" through well-organized lecture series. [1]

On 10 August 1871 Hecker's brother-in-law Heinrich Tiedemann published a newspaper announcement of "Hecker's lectures in the cities of the Union." There he announced that Hecker had decided to hold a series of lectures during the coming winter, from December into the new year, in all towns and places where he could find an arrangement. Whoever had an interest in such lectures should get in direct contact with Hecker. Tiedemann sought "to secure the educating enjoyment of these lectures" through timely response to this call, which he asked other newspapers to copy.

This appeal was immediately registered and in fact reprinted in many German-American newspapers. Because there was a question of the themes of these lectures, Wilhelm Rapp, who was still editor of the *Baltimore Wecker* in 1871, published a letter sent to him by Hecker saying why Hecker wanted to take up lecturing.

The situation with the lectures is this. With the bad times and poor harvests, despite all of the sour sweat and superhuman labor, I am compelled to grab at something besides the hoe and the plow in order to stay afloat. My brother-in-law Teidemann has recommended that I take to the field of lectures in late autumn and winter. Comparative biographies in Plutarch's manner – Washington and Caesar, Lincoln and Cromwell, Augustus and Napoleon III – as well as civil-service reform, the journalist as a great power, the mechanism of his activity and influence, these and other themes swim in my head.[2]

Hecker made no secret in this letter of his difficult financial situation. The slowly emerging economic crisis, continued overproduction of American agriculture, high rates for shipping and railroads, and high labor wages at a time of sinking prices for agricultural products, all hit Hecker as hard as they did other farmers in the Midwest. In addition he had had to sell land during the Civil War in order to pay off debts. Because, as Caspar Butz wrote, he "had spurned the amassing of riches," he now had to look for another source of income. Lectures offered themselves as a solution. Hecker permitted Tiedemann to announce that he would hold a lecture in any town paying him $100 and travel costs. He was his own organizer, and he coordinated the travel plans himself with the individual arrangers. The ticket price charged for a lecture by Hecker was high; usually fifty cents, so that he stood in the "middle price class." Entirely unknown or lesser known speakers such as Amand Goegg could be heard for ten cents, while Carl Schurz's lectures demanded seventy-five cents per person. The success of such events depended on the theme selected and the reputation of the presenter. This could also be read from the response to the first appeal.

Hecker declared himself considerably surprised that he received many invitations from all parts of the Union. "I will travel first through St. Louis, Chicago, Cleveland, Pittsburgh, Philadelphia, New York and the cities between, from there to Baltimore, Wheeling, etc. via Indianapolis to home," he wrote to the editor of the *Indianapolis Telegraph* and added, "The lectures are of course no stump speeches in which I can do roundhouse blows. They presume an intelligent public and its consideration." The themes of the lectures Hecker prepared for the winter of 1871-72 were "Women's Rights and Womensrightsism [*Weiberrechtelei*]," "Lincoln and Cromwell," "Officials in a Republic and in a Principality," and "Our Republic, Its Critics and

Opponents." Because he held several lectures in a single location, it occasionally happened that he agreed spontaneously to present other subjects. "Hecker's lectures have aroused so much enthusiasm," the *Louisville Volksblatt* said, "that he had to agree to hold a second lecture on his return from his tremendous tour." He also held several lectures in St. Louis, Baltimore and Philadelphia, and he wrote to Wilhelm Rapp in satisfaction, "My lectures were entirely successful everywhere; I am quite moved by the applause and the loving reception."[3]

Hecker's first tour "paid rather well," and he undertook similar half-year winter tours in following years on themes worked out during the summer. During his first tour he had made a series of helpful organizational contacts such as Heinrich Metzner, the presiding leader of the North American Turner League (NAT), who arranged lectures for him. Metzner was especially interested in using Hecker's lectures to stimulate new respect for the original idea of the Turners, which was the simultaneous development of body and spirit. He had discovered that among the younger German immigrants Turners were seen only in terms of physical training, while the idea of "political Turners" was in decline, on its way to mere "sport." Hecker, whose visit to Cincinnati in 1848 had stimulated the establishment of the first Turner Society on American soil, was pleased at Metzner's offer for more reasons than this. He knew how much he depended as a speaker on the Turners. He wrote to Metzner,

> Without the Turner Societies, German lectures would be zero. Without the Turner Societies, often mostly people who earn their bread through hard work, we would hear no lectures in the German language at all. There are only a few "clubs," mostly consisting of rich people, who do anything in this direction. They are ready enough for songstresses, singers, princes and similar mutton with gilded horns, right there, but God forbid that they give anything for scholarly lectures.

With the Turners Hecker knew that there was an automatic interest in lectures that was not necessarily present in the rest of the German population. He compared the attitude of German-Americans negatively with that of the Anglo-American population, for whom "lectures are a necessity and an enjoyment." For that reason he planned to offer his lectures, produced with considerable expenditure of time and study, in English, as well.

Hecker did not see his lecturing as merely a way to earn money. In keeping with his earlier formulation of the role of the lawyer in enlightening and leading, he was committed to turning the caste knowledge commanded by a few into generally-known wisdom. This was in the interests of forming a general republican civic virtue, which he believed that his lectures would do. In this he was not so pessimistic as most German-American newspapers; the lectures held by many Americans "not only in scholarly societies," but directed at all levels of the population, had "contributed more to the enlightenment and promotion of the nation and political sciences than 100,000 books and pamphlets." They had "made into public property what had earlier been the caste possession of scholars." [4]

The lecture tours were trying undertakings. Hecker journeyed from west to east, from south to north through various climates. The first tour, in particular, which he had made too long out of ignorance, injured his already shaky health. The lecture tours planned for the following winter were repeatedly interrupted, delayed or cancelled by illnesses. Hecker wrote to Söhner in 1874, "I cannot stand for them to skin me *so*, as they did two years ago. The drunks after the lectures, especially, are no more." The lecture was by no means the end of the events; discussions followed, and often a moist, unofficial part, as well. Putting off lectures always distressed Hecker – "old fools should be beaten to death the moment they begin getting sick," he told Söhner – and a sudden cold brought him to despair since he still had to visit "the ice-bear states of Minnesota, Wisconsin and Michigan." But as soon as he was back on his legs, Hecker packed his bag, took off on his trip and organized his return in such a way that he always visited his piano buddy Sohner in Indianapolis. "[W]e sit once more at the table a quarter-hour before dinner is ready, to the joy of your ladies, and you lie to me about your farming and your virtue. That will be splendid." But the trying years left their traces. In early 1878 Hecker told Söhner that he would have to give up on touring in the winter altogether and thus "give up all lecturing." But this did not mean leaving public life. According to his own accounts his life had changed into that of a "private tutor" who intended to keep working through a plethora of newspaper articles. The fact that one of his planned lectures was to bear the title, "The Journalist, a Great Power, the Mechanism of his Activity and Influence" was perhaps an indication that he expected as much from this activity as from his lecturing.[5]

Women's Rights and Womensrightsism

One of the four lecture themes that Hecker presented in the winter tour of 1871/72 bore the title "Women's Rights and Womensrightsism," and dealt with the rising conflict over female suffrage. In many respects this discussion was more divisive in America than in Europe, American women had already found new forms of political agitation in the 1840s and 1850s through the organization of societies, whether against the abuse of alcohol or against slavery. In a republic where a general suffrage existed for men, where the Constitution had adopted general human rights and where the state was obligated to create conditions in which each individual could pursue happiness, the demand for the complete equality of women seemed more obvious to many people than it did, for example, in England, where the modalities of election continued to exclude certain male groups and where, as a result, a more general "female acceptance" of the complex inequality of their own society predominated. The various levels of equality achieved in different countries, as expressed in electoral rights, influenced the strategy of women's movements of those countries. For example, women's suffrage was stressed less in Germany or England than was the wish for general reforms in the social sphere of female life.[6] Robert von Mohl criticized the "excessive democratization" of suffrage in the United States in 1854, "with logical necessity."

> The concept of individual participation in government as an inborn, human right has forced the question of the participation of women into the first rank. Are they not people, too? Do they not belong to the people? Are they morally and intellectually less capable than many male voters? Do they not also have rights and interests in the state? Up until now natural feelings, a reluctance to be laughable, ... has always proved victorious; but it is very doubtful that this will always be the case.[7]

The unusual methods of female suffragist frequently harmed more than helped the fighters for women's rights in the United States, and they often became the target of mockery and criticism, as Hecker's lecture demonstrated. As early as the end of the 1850s, women's rights advocate Lucy Stone had freely adapted the slogan "no taxation without representation" to justify the non-payment of taxes. Stone argued against the proposition that women were good enough to pay taxes, but not to have the right of free representation. And in the 1870s Susan Anthony demonstratively registered and voted under the Fifteenth Amendment, which guaranteed to all citizens of the United States the right to vote and refused denial "on account of race, color, or previous condition of servitude." Her example was contagious, and the Supreme Court felt itself compelled in 1874 to put an end to this "nonsense" with a ruling. Anthony was sentenced to a fine, not to prison as her opponents demanded; such treatment would surely have given her the aura of a martyr. Differing strategies in the struggle for women's rights led to the formation of two separate women's organizations in 1869. In May 1869 the National Woman Suffrage Association was founded in New York under the leadership of Lucy Stone. Women's suffrage organizations were established all over the Union, including Belleville and St. Louis, in Hecker's immediate vicinity. One of the most peculiar phenomena complicating the women's rights campaign was the emergence of women's anti-suffrage societies. In 1871 an Anti-Woman Suffrage Society was founded, with spokeswomen from the most respected families, including the wives of General Sherman and Admiral Dahlgren, as well as a niece of Abraham Lincoln. Their objection was of a moral nature, because they felt the introduction of women's suffrage would lead to the decay of morals and the dissolution of the family.[8]

This was the situation into which Hecker injected himself with his rather unorginal contribution to the discussion. With the question of women's rights Hecker reached a point where his radicalism was at an end; here he pursued the traditional line of many liberals and conservatives without developing any original ideas. Over extensive stretches, his own contribution amounted to quotations from Welcker's essay on "Relations of the Sexes" in the *Staatslexikon*. In fact it could be asserted that Hecker merely took Welcker's basic argument and historical examples and enriched them with a few American elements. His presentation "Women's Rights and Womensrightsism" was based solely on an idea that was as old as the world itself, namely that the natural, physiological differences of the sexes made women unsuited for participation in public, political life on the basis of their bodies' biological operation. All of the philosophers who are most important to Hecker – Plato and Aristotle, Locke and Rousseau – declared themselves convinced on the natural, true dualism of the sexes. From this a particular feminine sphere of life was derived: reproduction, rearing children, household and family. Liberals such as Carl Theodor Welcker or, later,

Heinrich von Sybel, who made a presentation to his audience in Bonn "On the Emancipation of Women" in 1870 in complete agreement in its basic tone with the lectures given by Hecker in the large cities of the Union, included in their arguments this concept of economic division of labor and the division between the public and private spheres.

In both Hecker's and Sybel's lectures it was clear how much the natural sciences, particularly medical anatomy and biology, had achieved the position of a new theory of truth. The enumeration of the anatomical differences of the sexes was commonplace. What was really political was the seemingly permanent establishment of the area of female activities apart from the political arena. Hecker further formulated, "The *peripheral* in the construction of the man is directed toward the ocean of life, the *concentric* in the construction of the female turns inward, to the house, the family. ... His thought rules *understanding*, hers *feeling*." The weak power of woman's understanding, her emotional dependency, her easy influencing and her slight capacity, Hecker asserted in his lecture, showed her unsuited to political events. Aristotle had already derived the smaller capacity of women for virtue – significant for the existence of a republic – from their less-developed rationality, thus legitimizing the necessity of their exclusion from political life and their domination by men "for their own benefit." This was the source of the idea first stated by Aristotle and adopted by liberals, that equal rights could be given only to equals, but not to unequals such as women, slaves and house subordinates. They were all in a state of dependence, parts of that patriarchal great family whose political representation fell to the father of the house alone.

Also found in Welcker's article, as in Hecker's lecture, was the argument of equal rights and duties. But in the eyes of liberals, women were unequal not only in their physical constitution, but also in their incapacity – derived from these physical differences – to bear specific duties in the state, such as defending it. "The cardinal principle on which the entire *human* and *state community* turns, also containing the most important principle of liberty, is *that the sum of rights corresponds to an equal sum of duties*," said Hecker, repeating another idea adopted from Welcker. If woman did actually demand the exercise of all political rights, he continued, although she was entirely incapable of fulfilling the most difficult duties "because nature organized her differently," this would *constitute the most worthless and perilous aristocracy of all, the aristocracy of weakness.*" Hecker then revealed his true fear, that admitting women to the vote would be so dangerous because the women themselves would not be voting on their own; others would be voting through them. Women voters would be given over "to the influences of all political and ecclesiastical, secular and spiritual Jesuits and intriguers through the weakness of the sex, through the sensitivity of feeling." "With all of the troubles of our time." Hecker stated, "we at least do not have the cassock, the pulpit and the confessional, corruption and ambition, going to elections in and through petticoats."[9]

In his lecture Hecker proposed to women that they had already achieved complete equality in the private-law area. He mentioned rights of ownership and inheritance, reservations in case of bankruptcy, milder penalties for women in penal law and freedom of occupation. He played particularly on the situation in Illinois. Much of this enumeration reminds us of the German discussion of the emancipation of Jews, where in the same manner civil freedoms and rights were conceded, but political rights were reserved or denied. Because the civil equality of women was thought to be reasonable in economic and social terms, such rights were always defended by liberals with a gallantry intended to divert attention from the political rights being withheld.[10] Although Hecker expressly spoke of women having a liberty of occupation, most liberals stated that the chief female profession was wife and mother. Heinrich von Sybel told his Bonn audience in 1870, "Nature has dedicated a single great profession to women from about 20 to 40 years of age." Also, "No true mother will be inclined to exchange this condition with another, and no one will make the error that this leaves her the time or strength" to practice "any other autonomous life profession." According to liberal perceptions, professional women would remain exceptions; the alteration of the family structure through female occupations in the lower classes was a dreadful example that reinforced the defensive attitude of bourgeois liberals.

Certainly Hecker was a child of his times in his views on women's suffrage. There were few exceptions to this rule – such as Gustav von Struve or Karl Heinzen. Yet it is astonishing that Hecker did not defend women's suffrage as a consequence of the general concept of equality that he held to be true, as was the case with the suffrage that the Republican Party granted former (male) slaves. Instead Hecker went on to contradict a number of his own earlier statements. John Stewart Mill's 1869 work, *The Subjection of Women* – a book that was widely distributed in America by feminists and was translated into German in the same year – dealt above all with the concept of "birth as destiny," or the "fatality of birth." Mill criticized the "nature"-ideology of patriarchal society and argued that what was established to be the "eternal nature of the female" was in truth merely a socially deformed second nature of women, "artificially created through and through." No one could presume to make statements on the true destiny of the sexes as long as no one had attempted any other kind of relationship between the sexes. People took experiences from nature and declared the right of the strong as proof of the sensible structure of status quo. To Mill a higher order was being derived from a simple physical fact. Earlier Hecker, along with Rousseau, had denied the legitimacy of a "right of the strong" that was transferred into a legal right through custom or compulsion. He had never accepted inequality from birth, as expressed in a monarchy, and he had always defended the inborn, inalienable rights of all people, as formulated in the Enlightenment. Now, however, Hecker abandoned what was supposedly impractical abstractness of principle for real (state) life.

> Certain rights can be practiced only to the disadvantage of the whole, and so they must be restricted. ... Our knights of consistency, however, make it different. They climb into the clouds and do not concern themselves with life, reality, society or state. They take an ideal, abstract, legal principle of nature, stretch and expand it until it has the desired length and breadth, and shout down to me from cloud-cuckoo-land, "Isn't a female a person?"[11]

For Hecker women's suffrage was incompatible with the well being of the state; it was not a matter of "an abstract human right, but rather a matter of a state community, of one's right as a member of the state." He argued in a completely dogmatic way that everything had to be subordinated, even sacrificed, to the interest of the state, to the common good, even if it were a question of natural, inborn, inalienable rights. And women's suffrage was incompatible with the common good because it endangered the family and thus the state. Welcker had already formulated that unconditional equality would "have as its result the collapse of our present social order." In 1844 Hecker had argued quite differently from his position in the opposition.[12] But according to his new argument, women were condemned from birth to continue in "their" sphere, excluded from one of the most important liberal principles, which was to attain higher positions in life and to practice honorable occupations. "Every restriction of the field of election," as Mill had said, "robs the society of some opportunities of being served by capable persons, without protecting it against the incapable." Feminists were correct to point out that the variation of capacities and gifts was not a distinction of the sexes but of individuals. But Hecker's basic presumption that people were not born to a predestined place in life to which they were bound, and that they possessed the liberty to seek a place in life commensurate with their individual gifts, did not extend to women.

To be sure Hecker needed to have no fear that his lecture would bring him into discredit with the majority of the German-American population, or excite much contradiction. A glance at the German-American press, overwhelmingly dominated by former "radical" Forty-Eighters, showed that he was merely following a general rule. The rhetoric showed that commonly celebrated republicanism by no means included egalitarian connotations for female equality. When Hecker presented his lecture on women's rights in Belleville on 27 January 1872, the *Belleviller Zeitung* noted that he had "a rather good audience ... and the full appreciation of his listeners." Hecker himself called his lecture on "Women's Rights and Womensrightsism" a "vindication of nature against snake-oil artificiality." The *Illinois Staatszeitung* agreed, at the moment the book that was to spread Hecker's lectures to Germany appeared for sale at the bookseller Witter. The newspaper continued, "It is in fact a splendid defense of true German femininity and genuine German family life against female demagoguery and free love." According to the benevolent reviewer, the lectures showed that, despite his country life, Hecker still stood "at the apex of his times and at the apex of modern science."[13]

Fortunately not everyone was convinced of this. Both male and female critics of Hecker's views made themselves known, although they of course found little resonance. Wilhelm Spitznass, librarian of the Farmers' and Fruit Growers' Society in Belleville, who like Father Oertel often feuded with Hecker through open letters, was not convinced. Hecker's "primitive views, not restricted to this question," had to be opposed decisively, the resolute librarian declared, and for that reason he repeated the

> question already often posed to Hecker, which was whether he believed that states were made for people or people for states. And since Mr. Hecker has no other means of defense of his public rights than suffrage, how can he deny to women a right that he himself declared necessary to defend the rights for Negroes?

Hecker's assertion that women's suffrage was superfluous because "women are already in possession of all greater privileges and advantages" was simply false, Spitznass stressed. One could neither assert that "fifty cents is an inordinately high payment for twelve hours of sewing," nor forget "the unspeakable misery of women in the large cities." Thus the doughty fighter Spitznass offered his services to "demonstrate in the Turner Hall that there is no reasonable argument against women's suffrage in the democratic republic – after the Turners' masked ball, which currently is absorbing all the interest." But Spitznass was not Hecker, and the Belleville audience, primarily in agreement with Hecker's views, did not feel compelled to hear such an address. In 1870 even the ladies of St. Clair County had posted a series of signature-sheets in the "fashion shops of Belleville" to send a petition to "Belleville's representatives in Congress" and declared themselves opposed to any measure "that would give women the vote in Illinois."[14]

The German-American press created a broad distribution of Hecker's anti-suffrage lecture through repeated reprintings. The women's rights movement was supported more strongly in the urban centers of the large cities than in the rural regions of the Midwest. When the *New Yorker Journal* reported on the first public meeting of the German-American Society for Women's Rights in the German Turners' Hall in New York, in which Amand Goegg and Adolph Douai participated, among others, it was no surprise that the Baden revolutionary had become the very image of German opposition to women's rights. The New York ladies fully understood the appeal of the Latin Farmer in distant Illinois that they in their feminine spheres be faithful spouses and loving and, most of all, fruitful mothers. As a result the first speaker of the evening, Mrs. Auguste Lilienthal, "a large, powerful, blonde pillar in the temple of women's rights," as the hostile journalist ironically formulated, declared,

Oh, if they want to leave us alone with this sphere, this sphere that has made so laughable the famous Hecker, who once threatened to free Germany from the yoke of tyranny with his even more famous hat and his long boots! Oh Hecker, Hecker, if you had only remained in your sphere behind your plow in the West, it would have been better for you. Then the world would not have seen how dusty your famous hat has become, and how far your poor heart has fallen!

Even Hecker's most modern argument, the famous "three ounces" that the female brain lacked to make it capable of political life, was not left unmentioned. "Oh, the brain of a whale weighs two pounds more than that of a man," Mrs. Lilienthal declared. "Why then do the men not allow the world to be ruled by whales?"[15]

In America as in Great Britain and Germany, both conservatives and liberals feared in the 1870s and 1880s that the feminist movement would lead to increased female independence, encouraging women to deny their "biological destiny" and thus undermine the existence of the family. The visible decline of the birth rate and a rising rate of divorce – the latter visible only in the United States – particularly alarmed them. But Hecker was political strategist enough to reject women's suffrage for a reason other than the middle class birth rate. It was a generally recognized fact that the passage of the Fourteenth and Fifteenth Amendments by the majority of the Republican Party had been an electoral strategy. The hope of the secure gain of almost two million loyal colored votes guaranteed the party dominance in the South that would be hard to imagine otherwise. Allowing women to vote would negate this advantage because women were an unpredictable voting potential.

> Enfranchised women would constitute a larger and possibly less predictable political voting bloc than blacks; and given that the radicalism of the Republican coalition was limited, the safest course was to declare the postwar situation to be "the Negro's hour."

The unpredictability of the female voter accompanied Hecker's concept of a "bulwark of priests." Here his exaggerated view of the influence of the Catholic Church played a role. For him there could be no doubt that women stood under the influence of the Jesuits. The Catholic Church was identified with the Democratic Party. Ergo women's suffrage would merely work to the advantage of the Democratic Party. Hecker was not alone in the conviction that temperance and the women's movement were connected. Because the majority of women was opposed to women's suffrage, the *Illinois Staatszeitung* wrote, it was impossible to demand the political vote for women from men. This was good "because the victory of Susan & Co. would lead a sizeable reserve army to the ballot box for the dreadful temperance pack." For that reason German-American newspapers – solidly in the hands of radical Forty-Eighters – did not overlook any article reporting the absurd actions of puritanical American women who stationed themselves in front of saloons, tyrannizing saloonkeeper and guests with prayers, beseeching the barkeeper's conscience to leave his shameful profession, often even moving in to destroy barrels of beer and whiskey. This "prayer plague," as it was condemned in the press, was tied in newspapers with malice aforethought to the movement for women's rights. There can be no doubt that the borders between the women's movement and the abolitionist and temperance movements were not always easy to draw in the 1850s. But at the end of the 1860s and the start of the1870s they had crystallized, a fact that was manifest by the 1880s – the Women's Christian Temperance Union (WCTU) was founded in 1883. The majority of women joining the temperance movement rejected women's suffrage on strongly moral grounds, directly opposing the movement for women's rights.[16]

Railroad Monopolies and Markets

There can be no doubt that his discussion on railroad monopoly was the heart of Hecker's series of lectures. The *Illinois Staatszeitung* recommended this lecture in particular to its readers, because railroad monopolies were, it wrote, "the greatest practical reform question of our time," and it was obvious that "Hecker would treat it with primeval force and genius. As he sounds the alarm and storms against this perilous modern feudalism, he is doing a service for the entire country."

The world had changed, and America was approaching a major economic crisis after years of economic boom. Railroad construction had played a central role. The expansion of the rail system had set in motion a "transportation revolution," but it had also opened the way for unprotected speculative ventures. In September 1874, four months after the collapse of the Vienna stock exchange, the impact of the suspension of payments of the banking house of Jay Cook and Company was showing itself in New York when the Northern Pacific Railroad was no longer able to float millions of dollars in bonds. The stock market responded with a financial crisis and for a while came to a stop. Factories were forced to release workers, and for the first time there were questions about the free labor ideology of the Republican Party. Because the postwar boom derived essentially from railroad expansion – from 1865 to 1873 the railroad network doubled from

35,085 to 70,651 miles – the industrial branches dependent on it fell into crisis. As early as 1874 half of the blast furnaces in America were closed. While
a new generation of entrepreneurs began economic restructuring through
the rationalization of firms and factories, the number of workers in factories
continued to fall, "reflecting a growing concentration of capital and the triumph of large-scale mechanized production." Strikes became a medium of
protest for both factory workers and workers in the coal fields of
Pennsylvania. "The depression, it seemed, had brought European-style
class conflict to America and, ... fearfully deepened 'the antagonism
between rich and poor."[17]

Hard times also set in for the farmers of the Midwest. Agrarian production continued to climb, not least of all through the mechanization of agriculture promoted by the labor shortage after the Civil War. But prices for
agricultural products sank with the excessive production, followed by
declining land prices. In his article "Colonization Projects," Hecker said that
there was no question that overproduction was "a result of machines that
take labor out of human hands, making production easier, massive and
fast"; but without them one could "not survive, nor extract the riches lying
dead in nature." Since the beginning of the 1860s the problems of continual
agrarian overproduction had become a matter of public discussion. "Many
responded by calling for increased railroad regulation and currency inflation, to raise agricultural prices and enable indebted farmers to meet their
mortgage payments." The farmers' movements forming all over the
Midwest – secret farmers' lodges of Grangers and Patrons of Husbandry as
well as public farmers' associations, such as the State Farmer's Association
of Illinois with their statewide central associations – demanded at their
county and state conventions "the intervention of the state and federal
authority against the railroad monopoly and against the usurious transport
prices it demands." They wanted "control of railroad prices by law," "protection of honorable industry" and condemnation of the "miners of the
country."[18] The farmers' lodges of the various states joined together, organizing among themselves the exchange of various products, but not relenting
in their pursuit of state intervention.

Hecker made many efforts to approach the problem and publicize it.
He wrote articles in the newspapers and gave speeches and urged politicians to deal with the theme. Hecker specifically referred to the problem of
monopoly in the railroads as early as June 1872. He had discovered that the
total power of the railroads lay in a few private hands and that, instead of

competing with one another, the railroad companies dictated the prices for public transportation through mutual agreements. Hecker welcomed the creation of public commissions in some states to oversee railroad administration and limit abusive pricing. User rates had little relationship to the costs of transportation, and Hecker already began to discuss the possibility of a state takeover of private railroad companies. Such a takeover by the states would promote further centralization and the rule of bureaucracy, but Hecker saw as large a peril in too great a concentration of power in the hands of a few private entrepreneurs. Even when he could not yet offer ready answers to all these problem, he did present a general program in his winter lectures. He found the question of this monopoly and its impact on production and transportation to be more significant at the moment than civil-service reform and considerations "on the good or bad characteristics of some individual running for office." He continued to have no doubt about the railroads as a great power. Corporations and associations sought to avoid competition; wherever "cooperation was possible," he declared, "competition was impossible."[19] Every railroad company was also the holder of a patent, and whoever owned a railroad held a monopoly. This monopoly, Hecker now concluded, belonged in the hands of the state. The surest corrective to monopoly, which was free competition, was impossible in the case of railroads, since railroad companies were careful not to compete with one another over specific stretches. In addition much alternative water transportation vanished in the winter, and dependence – not least on the rapidity of shipping – forced almost all farmers, merchants and traders to use railroads alone.

With his consideration of state ownership of railroads and his proposals for a mediating or protecting intervention by the state in the freight rates of transport companies, Hecker for the first time departed from his liberal presumptions of a self-regulating market and became a representative of the large interests of Western farmers. Still, he did not break entirely from the economic views that he had held in Germany. As early as January 1848 he had described in the Baden State Assembly a situation in which the state was actually obligated to intervene. At that time he had stressed, "The rule stands that normally the state *should* not intervene actively, and it *can* do so only in the case of extremely obvious harm." Hecker now held this to be such a case. Of 13 million persons employed in the United States, 6.73 million were in agriculture and 2.13 million in industry. In the struggle with the railroad monopoly, the interests of the Western farmer conflicted with those of the Eastern ironworkers and coal miners, whose jobs and wages derived in part directly from the protective tariffs for domestic iron and coal and from the capacity growth of railroads. Hecker expected from state ownership the development of an indirect system of taxation that would replace other forms of direct taxation once debts were retired and the first profits were achieved; ideally it could even make all forms of direct taxation unnecessary. Railroads had in fact all been built and financed with contributions from cities, counties and states and finally with land and money from Uncle Sam; Hecker could not understand why the people now had to pay interest on its own capital. In an earlier article, "Railroad Monopoly in Illinois," Hecker had also conceived of the relationship between railroad and state juristically in favor of the state. Railroads constructed to the benefit of all were "roads, highways, military routes through the sovereign state territory," and they could be seen as "rights of way" and "easements to the land." Because the territory of the state was inalienable and permitted no transfer to third parties, a railroad enterprise was "a permit, tied to special conditions, to use a particular part of the sovereign, inalienable state territory that is the property of the people as a whole." Two consequences could be derived from this relationship. First, the use agreed upon dissolved if the party using the concession violated or misused the conditions that had been agreed to. Second, a control mechanism was required that continually monitored the services in terms of the purposes agreed upon. This control came from the state or the people as a whole. If the concession were being carried out to the disadvantage of the owner, it could be suspended.[20]

Hecker hoped that transition to a mixed system in which state-owned and private railroad systems would coexist, as in Belgium, would provide insight into the operation, craft mechanisms and transportation that would help the state in the just regulation of freight prices. Experience with its own railroads would permit the state to set just and economically viable rules for private railroads. Hecker recalled that railroads were commissioned in the interest of the community, and not a few. A reduction of freight prices had to be in everyone's interest because cheap freight increased volume, which would lead in turn to an increase in income. There was also a need for articulated farmer protest, with a clear demand for state intervention to assure the ability of farmers to compete on the world market.

It is hard to say whether Hecker's efforts had any effect. The *Illinois Staatszeitung* believed that Hecker, as "one of the first to deal with this matter, helped open the eyes of the German rural population to a significant degree." This, as the newspaper complained, was because there had been virtually "no German Grangers." The organizations of German farmers had been much slower and more restrained than among their Anglo-American colleagues.[21]

When Hecker left for Germany in May 1873, he promised Wilhelm Rapp, the editor of the *Illinois Staatszeitung*, "to study much over there, take notes, collect, make statistics, observe, investigate country and people," "giving special attention to the railroads, schools and civil service in Germany and Switzerland." On his tour of Germany, Hecker thought of himself as the special voice of the German farmer. He dedicated one of his dispatches exclusively to the agrarian situation in Germany and Europe, with attention to the discrepancy between pay demands and product prices, the lack of workers, the flight from the land, and especially increased competition from Russian grain on the world market. Through the construction of transportation arteries, grain produced in Russia and the Danube lands could be transported to Western Europe more quickly and cheaply than American grain, he established. The Union had not only long land routes, but also the sea voyage to take into account, and with its higher wages it was not competitive over the long haul, "for which reason other ways and means have to be found until [Americans] have grown to such a population that [internal] consumption corresponds to production." Hecker, however, did not want to rely on a growing population, whether through immigration or natural increase, any more than on chronic bad harvests in Europe that necessarily increased demand for American wheat. "In short, we have to *think about absolutely new markets,* we have to increase the number of consumers through internal development, we have to pay attention to the development of articles other than overproduced agrarian products, make internal transportation easier, or we will have to get ready for bad times." The crisis of 1873 forced the idea of a stronger public foreign trade policy ever more to the front. Hecker also addressed the pressure for new markets for American exports. "The boring or digging of the land routes of Panama or Darien appears to me one of the most pressing postulates." The functional necessity for expanded foreign trade was propagated ever more intensely at the end of the 1870s. "In an increasingly agitated, even hectic tone," Hans Ulrich Wehler writes,

> foreign trade was literally dogmatized as an ideology. In the horizon of many contemporaries, it was the sole promising therapy that was

sought from all responsible political instances. At last, the consensus of the agrarians and the industrial-financial complex was identical. Even if the free trade and protectionist concepts sharply diverged, the two camps still agreed completely on the high rank of the export question.[22]

Hecker's articles published in the second half of the 1870s showed how much he was occupied by questions and problems of economic expansion. These topics also took up increasing space in his letters to Charles Söhner and Carl Schurz. The subtitle of his 1876 work on the "Isthmus Canal" – "A way to lift our trade and hence lead to better times, particularly for the South and Northwest" – showed this. In this article Hecker considered the potential markets of certain goods produced in the United States and drew the moral that America should "think of new or easier routes ... as the Englishmen do" for a series of products. Not only the Atlantic, but also the Pacific Ocean, must be made into "an object of our commercial efforts, and indeed more than heretofore." England was the greatest competitor, with the Suez Canal now the greatest model; it was only English trade that could compete with the Union. The construction of an artificial canal across the Isthmus of Panama, which would be of enormous importance, an extension of the Mississippi, a "water route to the Pacific" for the Midwest. This was something Hecker favored from the beginning over building a Panama railway. From the connection to the West Coast, Asia and the islands of the Pacific through the canal he expected

a route of trade through which in a few decades this republic would become the first and most powerful trading nation of the world with its boundless treasures of the earth and industrial ability. Our West in particular will gain enormous growth, because all conditions are present; but now are mostly lying fallow.

Hecker followed his detailed discussion of all plans on particular routes, costs, digging projects, geological investigations and political factors with statistical material on the shortening of the voyages, the savings in time, the avoidance of perils and the expansion of trade. The article on the isthmus canal opened a long series of essays on the same theme. In other articles Hecker turned his attention to the United States as a trading nation and the need for regulation and legislation on neutral shipping in time of war., "[D]ue to the intertwined overlay of trade relations among all nations," neutrality was much more difficult than had been the case twenty years earlier. Hecker therefore demanded clear legal agreements to clarify these relationships.[23]

When the press began discussing a whole series of measures to reduce the unemployment created by the economic crisis, one of these proposals was to settle the unemployed on uncultivated land. Hecker had no regard whatsoever for this "state colonization project." To send the unemployed into the wilderness without any knowledge of what to do was at best a "temporary measure" that was certainly doomed to fail. It changed nothing about the true "illness of the time," which was "overproduction without markets." In this article, Hecker finally saw a solution in promoting the canal project, which would turn the Mississippi "into a stream draining our overproduction." Hecker's last large work, decorated with maps and tables, was an article "Various Projects for Inter Ocean Connections," in which he took a position on European and American discussions of the project. This article appeared in the *Westliche Post* three days after his death.

The extent to which Hecker conformed toward the end of his life with the ever stronger economically imperialistic attitude of the Republican Party was shown in a letter that he wrote to Elihu Washburne shortly before his death.

The Interoceanic Canal-routes have, for ten years, been the object of my studies and the Nicaragua-Canal ... should be pushed by all means. ... There is a great danger in a canal not built by americans and under full american Control, than most people know. The Canal will be built. ... For I have not the slightest doubt that our commerce would increase in such ways and proportions ... that the R[ail] R[oad] Comp[anies] would profit, perhaps profit more, than the Canal-Companies, as all more valuable articles and such one's, where the profit depends upon speedy arrival in the hands of the merchants, will use the overland-routes from shore to shore under all circumstances. ... Our commerce in the Interior and with and from foreign countries will take gigantic proportions after the construction of the interoceanic-canal.[24]

The Black Horde – *Kulturkampf* American Style

"The black Reich-piggery is in full swing," commented Hecker in 1873, outraged over German conditions. He added in warning, "The scope and results cannot be foreseen, particularly with the upheaval in France, Italy, in short in all Catholic regions. With one blow the black horde is at work with its unified organization." With German unification under Prussia's leadership, the apparent victory of Protestantism over Catholicism, the declaration of papal infallibility by the First Vatican Council in 1870 and the successful founding of the Center Party in 1870 as a "political organizational form of anti-Prussian, anti-liberal, primarily Catholic opposition," the discussion of the influence and position of the Catholic Church in the state revived and intensified. The notion that the Catholic Church endangered German national unity was a popular idea. Hecker approved wholeheartedly of Bismarck's effort to subordinate the Church to the state in all political questions and restrict its influence on the system of education as much as possible. This corresponded to the division of state and Church agreed on as absolutely necessary in assembly debates among liberals and radicals in the 1840s. But Hecker's approval of Bismarck's hard course in this question was still marked by a mixture of admiration for the consistent politician who declared he would not go to Canossa, and complaints about the issue of personal rights. "No one denies the accomplishments of the Reich chancellor," he said in one letter. "Everyone welcomes the strength with which he [Bismarck] threw down the gauntlet at the Jesuit and Roman priesthood." But Bismarck's opposition to the infallibility of the pope should not lead to Bismarck's own personal deification, Hecker believed,

> they pray to a single mortal as the bearer of the destiny of the Reich, and they place this opponent of papal infallibility in a tabernacle as the infallible leading spirit for 40 million people, spared from all opposition. If this man dies tomorrow, to whom would they move their yea-saying personal cult?

The strongest protection against "the black band" was to be found, in Hecker's well-known view, "in guaranteed basic rights of liberty." Unity alone did not make any nation strong outside and inside. The nation was truly served only if "the men of progress and liberty, besides supporting the Reich chancellor in his struggle against priesthood and crazy theorists and bombers, apply themselves to expanding the liberal legal structure instead of delaying it in mortal servility." The expulsion of the Jesuits that took place in 1872 suited Hecker's taste because he wanted nothing to do with any agreement with them. "A compromise with the Jesuits, who have driven the entire affair, is – as ever since the origin of the order – a defeat of the state, a Roman triumph." But he held that a conflict with the Jesuits was not simply one of the Roman Catholics against the state; rather it was "Jesuitism against all progress and every civil freedom." In addition the claim of absolutism deriving from the declaration of infallibility was binding for the Church in every case. "No pope," he believed, "will vary a hair's breadth from the infallibility established by the Council, with all its consequences. He cannot, he is not allowed to, according to the constitution of the See of Peter, constructed with iron consistency." In short, as far as Hecker was concerned, one should spare the effort at reconciliation. The interests of Church and state were diametrically opposed, and any attempt at reconciliation was condemned to failure. Hecker had little confidence in the influence of the Old Catholics, who did not recognize the infallibility dogma, and his conclusion was laconic and consistent. "Rome is not conquered with such half measures. One must break with the entire old See of Peter and completely cease being Roman Catholic if one wishes to combat Rome."[25]

Hecker's lectures in the following winter of 1873/74 stood entirely under the constellation of the *Kulturkampf*, and at the start of 1875 he was under way again on the East Coast with this theme. "Yesterday I gave a lecture before a splendid audience and a filled hall," he wrote to Söhner, "and after the end I was asked to give a second one on Monday the 12th." He stated the themes in his letter:

> 1) Limits of Church and state, or the struggle of priesthood against civil liberty. 2) Considerations on the current ecclesiastical conflict in Germany, the Vatican Council and papal infallibility. 3) Jesuitism and Jesuits.

Hecker saw as his principal mission in these lectures to "irritate the black horde and to awaken the sleeping Philistines, who cry 'Fire!' only when the house is already half or two-thirds burned down." He was pleased to report the first responses of the clergy, who cursed in such a way that it was a "primeval pleasure" to him.[26]

Hecker's lectures resulted in the pamphlet *Considerations on the Ecclesiastical Conflict in Germany and Infallibility*, appearing simultaneously through Carl Witters Buchhandlung in St. Louis and Edward Witters Verlag in Neustadt an der Haardt. First he sketched the more than 800-year conflict on infallibility, which had always been disputed and which could not be justified in

the Gospels or in the fathers or in Paul's *Letter to the Galatians*. The peril that
Hecker saw coming from Rome was the establishment of an "external state"
within the secular state and in the hierarchical form of the Catholic Church,
which had the council on one side and the blind, obedient masses on the
other. These masses would violate state laws in the case of conflict because
they recognized only one "lord and master," "the infallible vice-god in
Rome." All of the fundamental principles of the state were threatened with
upheaval by Rome because to the Vatican every means to sustain and realize the dogma of infallibility must be right. Here Hecker's concept of the
republican state and its security came forward. It was the conflict of loyal-
ties of the Catholic citizen, who in case of doubt would decide for the
Catholic Church rather than for the state.

The pamphlet also focused on the schooling and education of youth,
which formed the foundation of all "public civil morals." "[The Catholic
Church's] primary attack is against the free, non-confessional school,"
Hecker wrote. "They want to educate an ultramontane, priest-subjected
youth." Hecker did not even want to leave the training of seminarians to the
Jesuits, with their use of "blind faith, formulaic junk and thin, thoughtless
memory work." The only solution that he offered was the one that he had
promoted in the 1840s, "to preserve peace." Only Rome continually sowed
dispute. "There is only one great ally, the spirit of the new time. That is,
information, knowledge, science – school." In a state that stood "on the
watchtower of its rights against ecclesiastical societies," there would be

> no more inquisition of Urban VIII ruling against Galilei ... no condem-
> nation of Harvey's discovery of blood circulation as godless. His
> pupils, following his system, feel the fallible pulse of the infallible vice-
> Lord-God and in case of illness to help the god-on-earth back on to his
> infallible, shaky legs with purgatives and expectorants.[27]

Hecker, Caspar Butz wrote, "was notorious as a man of complete non-
faith, as far as religion went." He was loath "to penetrate into the inner
domain of people, to intervene in their relationship with God and divine
things." But it was precisely for the sake of tolerance, conscience and spiritual liberty that the state had to fight the "attempt of an infallible individual and his servants to dominate." Every intervention by the Church in the
state, Hecker declared in his lecture, made the state an "ecclesiastical institution of compulsion." But the Constitution had "nothing to do with heav-

en, with the interior of people, with conscience. Its kingdom is of *this* world. It is the law defining the state, the government."²⁸ And as a political entity the citizen was obligated by this law alone in the state community, not through compulsion but through a true love of his fatherland. This stimulus was in its emphasis, not unlike religious feelings, at least in Hecker's conception.

Hecker's distrust of what he thought to be the growing influence of the Catholic Church was so great that he was convinced that a *Kulturkampf* was coming sooner or later to American soil. "The struggle playing out in Europe is not a local, European one," he warned his audience. "It has worldwide significance. The citizen of every civilized states who loves liberty and confessional peace has an obligation to follow it and gather lessons for his own country." In his 1875 article on "Rome and the United States," Hecker saw the growth of the Catholics in America as threatening for two reasons. First, the European struggle between Church and state had driven "a mass of Roman faithful to these shores." Second, Roman Catholic families, for well-known reasons, had a "higher number of children," so that now "in the Union, as well, there are all of the conditions for a colossal expansion of the Vatican plenitude of power." In a further article, "The Vatican Council and the North American Union," Hecker interpreted the growing presence of Jesuits in Latin and South America as an indication that they were determined to "take up the struggle" in North America, as well, and not lose control over their faithful there. Concerning the conflict over public and parochial schools in America, Hecker wrote to Ernst Keil in Leipzig, "Believe me, the peril here is greater than over there, because here republican liberty is used for dark purposes and abused to throttle liberty." His tenor was similar years later, when he wrote his former major, Frey in Switzerland.

> You have no idea of the growth of Roman power in the U.S. In five years they have erected four new Church provinces and archbishoprics. All of the scum that you and Germany have run out nest here, and we have more nuns and monks here than in any country of mixed confession. With our poor laws against the Dead Hand they have already amassed a huge fortune (... certainly about 100 million) and innumerable associations and brotherhoods, all the way down to children! Associations for soul-infancy spread across the land.

The fact that Hecker feared Catholic influence for entirely pragmatic, electoral considerations was clear in these lines to Frey.

> None of their adherents is allowed to read any paper, pamphlet or book that has not received the blessing of the Church, on penalty of confession ... and *not even one* may vote anything but the Democratic ticket. Tammany Hall, that notorious robber band, leads this party.[29]

Together with the publisher of the *Westliche Post*, Emil Preetorius – Carl Schurz appeared as ever on the masthead of the paper as publisher and editor, but in truth he did not write a line for his newspaper and was in Germany again in 1875 – Hecker felt himself called to take up the fight with all of his zeal against the black horde in America. In the articles that flowed from Hecker's sharp pen directly into the columns of the *Westliche Post*, we see what Caspar Butz once called his "peculiar style," an "eschewed artistic form" that gave prominence and precedence to ideas. It was not that Hecker could not write in the loveliest, purest style; he could do that "quite well." But such efforts were suspended, as Butz wrote, "when he was fighting with the gentlemen in the black cassocks. Then he did not measure out any of his comments on a scale. Rather he wrote in the style of the age of the Reformation."[30]

The struggle for the public school system and against Jesuit arrogance and Catholic repression held Hecker in its grip for the whole year of 1875 and along with him the *Westliche Post*. It is possible that the 1875 condemnation by Pius IX of the May Laws, promoting the combativeness and solidarity of Catholics, brought with it a new quality of conflict. Rainer Doerries writes that, among German-American Catholics, the "news from afar on the *Kulturkampf* reported in their newspapers hardened their will for ethnic solidarity and with it their readiness to fight to preserve German Catholic usages in the New World." Hecker, however, appeared always either to overestimate Catholic influence in the United States or to allow himself to be influenced by the special situation in St. Louis, where there actually was a strong German Catholic rather than an Irish Catholic influence. Here a Jesuit seminary had been established that was later to become a college – St. Louis University. In this context it is instructive that the pious Catholic businessman Peter Paul Cahensly, who made it his mission to protect Catholic emigrants and to preserve their ties to Rome, described St. Louis as "the headquarters of Catholic Germanism" on his journey through the

United States in August 1883, showing that strong German Catholic influence in St. Louis was possible. In general, however, the Catholic Church played a reduced role as an immigrants' Church, and it was only gradually that bishops and Catholic clergy came into the country: they followed the wave of immigration, so to speak, and their mission was always to reduce the "dreadful losses" of Catholics as a result of Americanization. This was done by strengthening the relationship to Rome through stronger supervision and stricter transatlantic organization. The notion had existed since the first immigration of caring for them "with clergy of their own nationality and language, hence the idea of what were called *national* parishes," but they only became significant after the 1880s, at the time of the arrival of the extensive immigration from Southern and Eastern Europe. Under the motto, "Language saves Faith," they not only reinforced the structure of German-language Catholic churches, but also promoted German-language Catholic schools. All of this, however, was some time after Hecker's savage attacks against Catholicism and Vaticanism in the German-American press in 1875.[31]

"Old Fritz," recounted a critic of the anti-Catholic campaign of 1875, "rooted through the garbage heaps of the history of Europe to collect proofs that the Protestants, Jews and heathens of America were in peril and would be burned or massacred in droves by the evil Catholics." Depending on Hecker "as on a field battery," the *Westliche Post* took up the gauntlet and took the field with a sort of "wild guerrilla polemic" against the pope and the Catholic Church. The bellicose mood projected by the *Westliche Post* articles naturally provoked ecclesiastical organs. This time not Father Oertel but Father Becker of the Society of Jesus expressed the suspicion in one speech that Bismarck's "reptile fund" had now "croaked" all the way to Hecker. In response Hecker merely said that the father had missed the "the affection that monarchies (secular as well as spiritual) and their servants harbor for me." Hecker regretted in general that, when he looked at Catholic Church papers such as the ultramontane *Civiltà Cattolica* or the *Osservatore Romano*, not a single suitable opponent was to be found. The editorships of Roman papers were "laughably poorly" staffed.

If it is not a failed schoolmaster, then it is a student who failed examinations who was stuck here in a seminary. He was made over in a few months via theological quick tanning, had the bunghole in his roof shaved and now can go apostolizing. Or he is a Protestant with a warrant out for his arrest for whom the ground in Prussia grew too criminally hot, ... and now he has settled in the lap of the sole-saving Church to be remade like a "turned-out sack" in the Roman faith. So far has proud Rome fallen.

According to Hecker's own statement, it gave him "tremendous pleasure" when his criticism offended. He always wrote in a good mood that his articles were being read in Germany, and that he had received a letter from Johannes Ronge thanking him for his "priest-beating." And a few months later there was, "Have you read how I am skinning the priests? They are furious because I even produce irrefutable quotations from their own main works." Hecker's articles even received some recognition among a few strictly Catholic critics for his enormous knowledge of canon law and Church history. Thus the journalist Gottlieb Kellner, who had taken over the editorship of the *Philadelphia Demokrat*, spoke of the "polyhistorical, in part anecdotal, informative and at the same time entertaining articles of Hecker."[32]

But other German-American newspapers such as the *Westliche Post*'s competitor the *Anzeiger des Westens* or the *Illinois Staatszeitung*, published in Chicago, a town filled with Irish and German Catholics, found what was going on at the *Westliche Post* extremely questionable. For good reason the *Illinois Staatszeitung* refused "to work into the hands of hypocrites and temperance people through scandal and spectacle with the Catholics, without whose help throwing off the Sunday and temperance yoke is as little possible as it is in Chicago." In order to win influence over municipal politics, the *Staatszeitung* was perennially compelled into a difficult and fragile coalition with Irish, Polish, Italian and German Catholics, particularly when it was a question of preventing temperance or Sabbath laws. Because the *Staatszeitung* was led by different local political interests in Chicago from those of the *Westliche Post* in St. Louis, it also sought to act against this "handful of fools and crackpots who have sought to disturb political reform in the United States through launching an assault against the Catholics, a sixth of the total population." It went on to point out that "the pope [possessed] only a leaden sword without hilt or blade" and that, even while "religious struggles [resound] over there," "everything here [runs] quite friendly and heretically, neighborly and intermingled." The last was a quote from Hecker's own speech at the start of the 1870s, "Our Republic, its Critics and Opponents." It was intended to show that Hecker then defending the United States against Germany, asserted precisely the opposite of what he now declared, which was the possibility of a *Kulturkampf* on American soil. The passage was chosen with care because it obviously documented how much Hecker's rhetoric could be used for the political goal that he momentarily desired. But when the *Illinois Staatszeitung* then committed the *faux pas* of reprinting in good faith a speech that Hecker had supposedly given in Minnesota but that was not his, "the old man" really let loose in the *Westliche Post,* accusing the *Staatszeitung* not just of distributing false information but also of fearing a clear statement about the papacy,

> As long as the Illinois woman reads newspapers in her ordinary Church-state, we can satisfy ourselves with a mocking laugh of pity. She has only superficial knowledge and thus a sort of calendar-almanac – plus the wisdom and learning of journals.

The *Staatszeitung,* particularly its editor in chief Hermann Raster, revenged itself with the statement that the newspaper could not be accused of fear because Hecker's dispatches from Germany had been "provided with the most complete liberty" in its columns in 1873. Even his "often unjustified judgments of Prussian ecclesiastical measures and of the new praiseworthy accomplishments of Germany" had been published without censorship. But whatever was the case, the conflict between the two most influential German-American newspapers of the Midwest was a signal of the end of the common political era of the Forty-Eighters in the United States, a split that was completed in the campaign year 1876.[33]

The break was irreparable. Hecker never published in the *Illinois Staatszeitung* again. He wrote his numerous articles almost exclusively for Schurz's *Westliche Post,* and he wrote to Söhner regarding the *Illinois Staatszeitung* that it "has come out against me, mean as a dog." The tone of the *Staatzeitung* clearly hardened, and Hermann Raster revenged himself for Hecker's attacks with his own ruthless assaults on "the old man." Hecker's tirades merely served to confirm, Raster once wrote, "that animal rage through which he made such a bad name with his soldiers during the war." A year after the *Kulturkampf* campaign, the *Illinois Staatszeitung* was still condemning the "buffoonish attempt" by Preetorius and Hecker "to create a new 'burning question' for American national politics" and to transplant "with all their strength" the "imperial-royal Prussian *Kulturkampf* to American soil." And their review declared that this conflict would "always be one of the more repellent episodes in the history of the German-American press."[34]

Hecker's journalistic struggle against the Catholic Church never relented over the following years. Articles would recur in the old manner, if not always the concentrated form of 1875, interpreting both minor political events and great Church-policy decisions from Rome itself. It is little wonder that in the end Hecker regarded Bismarck's change of course in domestic politics as more than reprehensible. Through the death of Pius IX and the advent of his more amenable successor, Leo XIII, reconciliation between Berlin and Rome went to such an extent that Bismarck spoke of not actually suspending the May Laws, but delaying their execution, Hecker wrote a furious article about the "Chancellor's Skinning." To promulgate laws but then not regard them as binding appeared to him to be a "corpse of laws that are thrown ad lib into the toy box of the state marionette theater." It was remarkable, he went on, that this happened precisely at a time when the Bismarck press was full of complaints about contempt for law, lack of direction and moral coarsening among the people, so that under the "false flag of the anti-socialist laws" the government could repress the freedom of speech, press, assembly and association. Laws that were not carried out, or dead letters, were for him "monstrosities preserved in bureaucratic alcohol." Returning to Bismarck's policy, he wrote,

> Isn't it a pitiful show when one compares this begging-pilgrimage to the Vatican with the high-flying declarations, the proud turns of phrase, the rattling and ringing of 1872-73 and 1874? Making up with the Vatican is nothing more than begging for Center votes. Braun, the bear, puts on his pilgrim rags and begs pious Reinecke to pull his chestnuts of reaction out of the hot pan.

Rome, Hecker continued, was still precisely informed about everything that took place in Berlin court and government circles. It knew how Bismarck was completely sick of that "parrot Lasker," "as [he is] of the whole National Liberal herd." The Vatican also knew that

> it would take only the slightest lifting of a finger to see cuirassier hands and heads stretched out. ... The moment has come now when the man who boasted that he would not come to gates of Canossa seeking help

will go farther than Canossa to be rid of the Liberals and to pass his autocratic plan. He will be welcomed in the towers of the Vatican, seeking peace.

For Hecker, Bismarck's capitulation meant a complete victory for Rome. Ultramontanism had won tremendous prestige in the entire Catholic world.

> The great Bayard of the *Kulturkampf*, in the full confidence of his lord, surrounded by all his following and by his army, inured to victory in weapons and by pen, he bows and begs an alliance with the Vatican against – they hear and gape – Bebel, Liebknecht, Geil, the "parrot" and the rest of the "liberal band."

Hecker said in conclusion that "the drama would have been splendid, if it had not been so sad."[35] He believed, however, that Bismarck would find that trading iron for a wax candle was a bad bargain. In this matter as well, his private opinion did not differ from his public one. Hecker wrote to Söhner, disillusioned about Bismarck's change of direction and his entire policy.

> Over there is the most shameful oppression of all civil and human liberty, working according to a well-planned system. ... In order to carry out this "shameful plan of general subordination," slapping his own past of 1873/74 in the face, he hangs a rosary over this wax candle in his hand and goes pilgriming to Rome. ... The slaggy National Miserables ... are so endlessly cowardly that they have unlearned the ability to say "no." ... The year 1870 was the last strong expression of strength of the people's spirit of liberty, then not completely dead.[36]

[1] See "Deutsche Vorlesungen in den Vereinigten Staaten," *AW* also printed in *TISZ*, 11 April 1873; "Deutsche Vorlesungen," *Philadelphia Demokrat*, also in *TISZ*, 22 January 1873; "Deutsche Vorlesungen in Amerika," *TISZ*, 2 December 1872.

[2] H. Tiedemann, "Vorlesungen Heckers in den Städten der Union," Philadelphia, 10 August 1871, printed, for example, in *BZ*, weekend. 17 August 1871. FH to Wilhelm Rapp, Summerfield, St. Clair Co., Ill., 11 August 1871, *Baltimore Wecker*, 17 August 1871, also *BZ*, 24 August 1871.

3 See also FH's letter to a friend in Mannheim, Summerfield, St. Clair County, Ill., 25 December 1870: "the war has considerably reduced my mass property," Stadtarchiv Mannheim, Kleine Erwerbungen, 127; printed in *Neue Badische Landeszeitung, 6* November 1911. FH to a friend in Germany, Postoffice Lebanon, St. Clair County, Illinois, 28 April 1857, Stadtarchiv Mannheim, Kleine Erwerbungen, 127, 28,316. See FH to Heinrich Metzner, Summerfield, St. Clair County, Ill., 24 November 1874, Library of Congress, Manuscript Division. On FH: *Mississippi Blatter,* 4 January 1874; on Goegg, *TISZ,* 8 May 1872; on the Frauenwahlrechtsverein, see *TISZ,* 10 March 1871. FH to Goebel, editor of the *Indianapolis Telegraph,* Summerfield, St. Clair Co., Ill., 20 September 1871, reprinted among others by the *BZ,* weekly, 28 September 1871. See *BZ,* weekly, 28 September 1871; also *TISZ, 5* September 1872; all were printed in FH, *Reden. Louisviller Volksblatt,* quoted in *BZ,* weekly, 23 November 1871. See *TISZ,* 13, 23 November 1871; *BZ,* weekly, 30 November 1871; 7 December 1871. FH to Wilhelm Rapp, Philadelphia, 1 December 1871, printed in *TISZ, 7* December 1871 and *BZ,* weekly, 4 December 1871.

4 Butz, "Erinnerungen, 2. Teil." See Heinrich Metzner, ed., *Jahrbücher der Deutsch-Amerikanischen Turnerei,* vols. 1-3, New York, 1891-94); idem, *American Turnerbund. A Brief History of the American Turnerbund,* 2d ed., Pittsburgh, 1924; on FH's view of Turners, see his "Festrede zum 16. St. Louiser Bezirksturnfest" (1879), printed in *Hecker, Sein Antheil,* 62-71; excerpted as document 4 in Horst Ueberhorst, *Turner unter Sternenbanner,* (Munich, 1978), 239-40; also in *Amerikanischer Turner-Kalender,* year 3 (1882), 95-100. FH to Heinrich Metzner, Summerfield, St. Clair Co., Ill., 11 December 1872, Library of Congress, Manuscript Division. An English translation is in the Papers as a newspaper clipping, "Our Republic, its Critics and Opponents," so Hecker held at least this lecture in English as well as German, see FHP, box 9.

5 The extensive correspondence between FH and Charles Söhner documents this richly. FH to Charles Söhner, 17 January 1874, underlining in the original; 21 February 1874; 28 November 1874; 7 December 1875; 16 February 1878; 7 December 1875, all FHP, box 3, folder 38.

6 The Allgemeine Deutsche Frauenverein was thus more interested in reform in the social realm. This society was exemplary in promoting better chances in life for women through promotion and improvement of education and training, see "Die Frauenbewegung in Deutschland," *GL* 1871, 817-19, here 818.

7 Robert von Mohl, *Geschichte und Literatur der Staatswissenschaften. In Monographien dargestellt,* vol. 1, (Erlangen, 1855), 529.

8 See "Weiberrechte," *Mississippi Blatter,* 23 January 1858; Christine Bolt, *The Women's Movement in the United States and Britain from the 1790s to the 1920s,* (Amherst, Mass., 1993), 122, 151; see also the article "Die Martyrerin des Frauenstimmrechts," *TISZ,* quoted in *WP,* daily, 24 June 1873. There was a St. Louis County Woman's Suffrage Association; on a committee session, see *WP,* daily, 15 September 1873.

9 FH chose as motto for his lecture the passage by Goethe, "Man strives for liberty / The woman for morality"; quoted in Carl Theodor Welcker's article "Geschlechterverhaltnisse," *Staatslexikon,* vol. 6, 2d ed., Altona, 1845, 629-65, here 641; see also the proverb "Nunquam aliud natura, aliud sapientia docet" [There is no wisdom against nature] in FH, *Reden,* 93, in Welcker, "Geschlechterverhaltnisse," 635; see also the Luther quote in FH, *Reden,* 98, in Welcker, *Staatslexikon,* 644. Hecker's speech is printed in FH, *Reden,* 92-116. Complete analysis, with the corresponding texts, particularly with the social-political conceptions resulting from them in

Plato, Aristotle, John Locke, Jean-Jacques Rousseau and G. F. W. Hegel: Seyla Benhabib, Linda Nicholson, "Politische Philosophie und die Frauenfrage," Iring Fetscher, Herfried Münkler, eds., *Pipers Handbuch der politischen Ideen*, vol. 5, (Munich; Zurich, 1987), 513-62, esp. 524-25. Claudia Honegger, *Die Ordnung der Geschlechter*, (Frankfurt a. M., 1991), shows the establishment of this dualism by natural sciences. Heinrich von Sybel, "Ueber die Emancipation der Frauen," from a lecture presented in Bonn on 12 February 1870, reprinted in *Mississippi Blatter*, 27 March 1870; the fact that the *WP* reprinted this with approval shows how much people accepted this view and regarded it as applicable to America.

10 See his treatment in FH, *Reden*, 104; FH's views appear to be based on an article in *ISZ* on "Das rechtliche Verhaltniss von Eheleuten in Illinois" (also in *BZ*, weekly, 10 January 1870); the actual model before all else was Welcker, who dealt extensively in his article with the private-law area of women and also stressed their great freedoms and improvements, see Welcker, "Geschlechterverhaltnisse," 651 ff., same tone in Sybel, "Ueber die Emancipation"; "On the contrary it would be entirely perverse to place any legal restriction on [woman] in the area of private work, economic and industrial, literary and artistic activity." See Heinrich von Sybel, "Ueber die Emancipation."

11 Mill and his wife Harriet Taylor had published in the journal *Westminster Review* on the emancipation of women since 1851. Heinrich von Sybel deals with objections by Mill (Sybel, "Ueber die Emancipation"). Hecker only did this indirectly by accepting generally-formulated objections. John Stewart Mill, Harriet Taylor, Helen Taylor, *Die Hörigkeit der Frau* [*The Subjection of Women*] (Frankfurt am Main, 1976), here 156-211. Wolfgang Riedel, "English Liberalism and Nineteenth-Century American Feminism," *Amerikastudien* 36 (1991), 111-17. See FH, *Erhebung*, 15. FH, *Reden*, 107.

12 FH, *Reden*, 108. When Hecker defended the admission of women to public court proceedings, he referred to the *"free companion of the man* as the citizen, the educator of men. [...] Their dignity cannot suffer [by this admission]; for the *woman is a citizen of the state* as is the man." (*VSB*, 59. offtentliche Sitzung [30 April 1844], 249-50; my own emphasis. Cf. Welcker, "Geschlechterverhaltnisse," 650.

13 Mill, *Subjection*, 154. *BZ*, weekly, 1 February 1872. FH was a friend of the publishing and bookselling Witter family. Conrad Witter emigrated to St. Louis around the middle of the century, and his brother Eduard remained in Winzingen near Neustadt an der Haardt. Eduard Witter visited Hecker on his sixtieth birthday (28 September 1871) on his farm in Summerfield (see his description of the celebration in *GL*, 1872, 390). Conversely Hecker visited Eduard Witter during his visit to Germany in 1873. The book with his lectures is a "mutual product" of the German publishing firm run by both the Witter bookstore in St. Louis, Missouri, and that of Eduard Witter in Neustadt. *TISZ, 8* June 1872; the proclamation of "free love" was a specialty of Victoria Woodhull, who drew upon herself the criticism of other women's rights supporters as a result. *TISZ*, 8 June 1872.

14 *BZ*, weekly, 18 January 1872; see Spitznass's second letter, *BZ*, weekly, 1 February 1872. "Women's suffrage does not appear to have many friends among the Germans of Belleville," *WP*, daily, 15 April 1870. On the growing conservatism even within the movement for women's rights in Illinois, see Steven N. Buechler, *The Transformation of the Women's Suffrage Movment: The case of Illinois, 1850-1920* (New Brunswick, NJ, 1986), here especially chapters 2 and 4.

[15] See the article originally published in the *Pittsburger Volksblatt*, reprinted among other places by the *TISZ*, 24 November 1871; also *BZ*, weekly, 30 November 1871; it was certainly also found in the large New York dailies. *New Yorker Journal*, quoted in *TISZ*, 26 March 1872.

[16] See Bolt, *Women's Movement*, 136; 70 percent of divorce cases tried between 1867 and 1886 was won by women; on the German-American interpretation of these numbers, see "Ein Kapitel über amerikanisches Heirathen," *BZ*, weekly, 22 June 1871; also on the frequency of divorce in America, *TISZ*, 2 September 1871. Bolt, *Women's Movement*, 119, 133; see also Angela Davis, *Rassismus und Sexismus. Schwarze Frauen und Klassenkampf in den USA* (Berlin, 1982), here 70-84. *ISZ*, quoted in *WP*, daily, 24 June 1873. An example for the 1850's: "Weiber-Herrschaft," *BZ*, weekly, 22 April 1856; "Der Weiberkrieg in Indianapolis," *WP*, daily, 10 March 1874; "Das Bekehrungsfieber," *WP*, daily, 13 February 1874; see also the report of such events in Germany in the article "Amerikanischer Frauenkrieg gegen Trinkstuben," *GL*, 1874,210-13.

[17] *TISZ*, 5 September 1872. See on this Hans Ulrich Wehler, *Der Aufstieg des amerikanischen Imperialismus* (Göttingen, 1974), 19ff., 21. FH himself wrote to Chicago while on his German tour, "One has no idea [in America] what bad blood has been created by the 'Oregon Railroad Shares' and the swindle associated with it, and associated stocks, including the Erie scheme! And the monarchists are always immediately present with their kept press when it is time to accuse our republic or to discredit it." Correspondence 8; see also the typical article for Germany, "Der Eisenbahnschwindel in Amerika. Zur Warnung fur meine Landsleute in Deutschland," (G. O., New York, January, 1874), *GL*, 1874,110-12. Foner, *Reconstruction*, 218.

[18] In 1873 "farm product prices stood 30 percent below those for 1870/71," Wehler, *Imperialismus*, 21. Friedrich Hecker, "Colonizations Projecte," *WP* [n. d., 1877], FHP, box 9. Foner, *Reconstruction*, 218. Public farmers' associations pursued essentially the same goals as the secret farmers' lodges; see, for example, the articles in the *TISZ*, 2 August 1873, 2 October 1873; see also "Die Grangers von Illinois," *BZ*, weekly, 18 December 1873, in which 1838 lodges with 10,000 members are alleged, 800 lodges for Illinois without statement of members; *BZ* of 14 May 1874 numbered 1216 associations of the "Farmers' Party of Illinois."

[19] So he corresponded with Josiah Quincy, for example (letter to FH, Boston, MA, 3 October 1872, FHP, box 3, folder 33) on the "railroad system." FH, "Die Eisenbahn-Monopol," *TISZ*, 19 June 1872, also in *BZ*, weekly, 27 June 1872. *TISZ*, 19 June 1872. Quoted here from the complete reprinting of his speeches in the *TISZ*, I April 1873 (first presentation, Aurora Hall); ibid., 2 April 1873 (second presentation, Burlington Hall); see also *WP*, daily, 4 April 1873.

[20] *VSB*, 16. öS (28 January 1848), 283; emphasis is spread-type in the original. Wehler, *Imperialismus*, 20-21. The portion of agriculture in the national income in 1877/78 was 27.5 percent, of industry 17.1 percent. *BZ*, weekly, 3 May 1873; 11 September 1873. "Zum Kampf gegen die Eisenbahnmonopole in Illinois von Friedrich Hecker," [n. d., 1872], FHP, box 9.

[21] See *TISZ*, 31 April 1873. "Keine deutsche Grangers," *TISZ*, 26 August 1873; also "Bauernparteien in Illinois," *ibid.*, 16 August 1873; "Die Grangers von Illinois," *ibid.*, 11 November 1873.

[22] Excerpt from a letter to the editors of the *ISZ* [n. d.], *TISZ*, 3 May 1873. "Briefe aus Deutschland von Friedrich Hecker: Ein Kapitel vom Ackerbau drüben und hüben und von Russlands gewaltiger Conkurrenz mit der Union, Aus Deutschland im August 1873" (Correspondence 8, in *TISZ*, 30 August 1873, my own emphasis). See on this his correspon-

dence 9 from Germany; also the articles that his lectures summarized, "'Die zwolf ersten Bauern-Artikel.' Ein Wort an die Farmer von Fr. Hecker" [n. d.], FHP, box 4, folder 42; "Ein Wort zu meine Collegen, die Farmer!" *BZ*, weekly, 3 March 1870; these articles already contain all of Hecker's later proposals. Wehler, *Imperialismus*, 36.

23 He had statistical material on agricultural exports and other data from the Commerce Department through Schurz, see for example FH to Carl Schurz, 25 June 1879, Schurz Papers. FH, "Der Isthmuskanal. Ein Weg zur Hebung unseres Handels und damit zu besseren Zeiten im Allgemeinen und insbesondere für den Süden und Nordwesten," *WP* [n.d., 1876]; "Englands Stellung im Mittelmeer. Seine weitblickende Handelspolitik und Stellung in der orientalischen Frage," *WP* [n. d., 1876]; FH, "Der Panama-Kanal," *WP* [n.d., 1880]; "Torpedo-Kriegsfuhrung und der Panama-Kanal," *WP* [n.d., 1880]; "Weizenpreise und Spekulanten," *WP* [n.d., 1880], FH, "Unsere Neutralität," *WP* [n.d., 1877]; "Die Neutralen. Die Kriegs-Contrebande," *WP* [n.d., 1877], all in FHP, box 9.

24 FH, "Colonisations Projecte," *WP* [n. d., 1877], FHP, box 9; FH, "Die verschiedenen Projekte Interoceanischer Verbindungen," *WP*, daily, 27 March 1881. FH to Elihu Washburne, Summerfield, St. Clair, 111., 12 February 1881, Washburne Papers.

25 Correspondence 9, 10, 12; see the commentary on Bismarck's speech in the Reichstag on the "Kulturkampf": Peter Wende, *Politische Reden (1868-1914),* vol. 2 (Frankfurt a. M., 1990), here 701. Bismarck in the Reichstag, 14 March 1872; see Horst Kohl, ed., *Die politische Reden Fürst Bismarcks,* vol. 5, Stuttgart, 1893, 338.

26 In Hoboken and New York, see *TISZ,* 2 February and 2 March 1875. FH to Charles Söhner, 9/17 January 1874, FHP, box 3, folder 38; on his lectures in St. Louis, see also *Mississippi Blätter,* 4 January 1874; also *WP,* daily, 9 January 1874,10 January 1874,13 January 1874; on his lectures in Indianapolis, *TISZ,* 5 February 1873.

27 FH, *Betrachtungen Tüber den Kirchenstreit in Teutschland ud die Infallibilität* (St. Louis; Neustadt an der Haardt, 1874), here 4-6, 11, 16, 20, 27.

28 Butz, "Erinnerungen, 2. Teil." FH, *Kirchenstreit,* 27. "Heckers Vorlesung über 'Die Grenzen von Kirche und Staat," *WP,* daily, 9 January 1874; emphasis in the original.

29 FH, *Kirchenstreit,* 27. FH, "Rom und die Vereinigten Staaten," *WP,* daily [n. d., 1875]; FH, "Das vaticanische Concil und die nordamerikanische Union," *WP,* daily [n. d., 1875], FHP, box 9; FH to Ernst Keil [n. d., 1874/75], *GL,* 1881, 266. FH to Emil Frey [n. d., February 1877], Staatsarchiv Basel-Stadt, Sig. PA 485 DXI165; underlining in the original.

30 On Emil Preetorius (1827-1905), Zucker, *Forty-Eighters,* 327-28; also Nagler, *Fremont,* 195 ff.; Saalberg, *Westliche Post,* 123. Butz, "Erinnerungen, 2. Teil."

31 A large proportion of the articles written in this year in the *WP* is to be found in the FHP, box 9, for example, "Die Freischul-Hatz und die trugerischen Argumente der Hetz-Pfaffen" (articles 1 to 3); "Die Sprache der vaticanischen Organe und ihrer Gehiilfen"; "Humbug. über die New Yorker Tribune, die den Pfaffen Beifall zollt"; "Bonifacius, Apostel der Teutschen"; "Wissenschaft, Schule, Glauben und Dogmen im Kampfe"; "Die herrschende Macht in den Vereinigten Staaten ist der Vatican"; "Warum wird der erste Angriff von Seiten der Vaticanler auf das Freischulensystem gemacht." See Reinhard R. Doerries, "Zwischen Staat und Kirche: Peter Paul Cahensly und die Katholischen Deutschen Einwanderer in den Vereinigten Staaten

von Amerika," Alexander Fischer, Günter Moltmann, Klaus Schwabe, eds., *Russland, Deutschland, Amerika* (Frankfurter Historische Abhandlungen, 17)(Wiesbaden, 1979), 88-104; also Colman J. Barry, *The Catholic Church and German Americans* (Milwaukee, 1953), 5, 10. Olson, *St. Louis,* 120. See the informative article "Römisch-Katholische Kirche in den Vereinigten Staaten," *Deutsch-Amerikanisches Conversations-Lexicon,* vol. 9 (1873), 434-38. Carl Lüdeking, " St. Louis," *Deutsch-Amerikanisches Conversations-Lexicon,* here 595-96.

32 "Vom Culturkampf," *TISZ,* 23 August 1876. *Philadelphia Demokrat,* in *TISZ,* 15 May 1875. FH quoted from editions of the *Volksfreund,* 28 and 30 March 1874. "Ein 'Kraftschreiben' von Friedrich Hecker (Entgegnungen auf die Vorlesung des Pater W. Becker, S. J.), an Herrn J. S. Ellison, Redakteur der Buffalo Freien Presse, Summerfield, St. Clair Co., Ill., 12 April 1874," Hecker Papers, box 9; emphasis in the original. FH to Charles Söhner, 21 May 1875, 7 December 1875, FHP, box 3, folder 38. Ronge wrote from Darmstadt. *Philadelphia Demokrat,* in *TISZ,* 15 May 1875.

33 *TISZ,* 20 January 1875. See, for example, the election propaganda for local precincts in Chicago in English, Italian, German, Polish, Swedish and French in the *TISZ,* 1 November 1875. *TISZ,* 12 January 1875. FH, *Reden,* 46. *TISZ,* 12 January 1875; see also FH, *Reden,* 36-37, 44-45, for example, "that here the spring of upset and confusion does not flow because Church and school are separated, and through this tolerance is planted in young hearts," (here 37). See *WP,* daily, 15 May 1875, as well as the answer in *TISZ,* 17 May 1875. Hecker in *WP,* daily, 15 May 1875.

34 For FH's cooperation with Schurz on behalf of the *WP,* see the private correspondence: Carl Schurz to FH, St. Louis, 3 January 1877; 2 February 1877 and many more, FHP, box 3, folder 35. In the last three years of his life Hecker wrote more frequently for the *BZ.* FH to Charles Söhner, Summerfield, St. Clair County, 3 April 1875, FHP, box 3, folder 38. *TISZ,* 17 May 1875. *TISZ,* 23 August 1876. *WP,* daily, 23 August 1876. *TISZ,* 23 August 1876; the *Philadelphia Demokrat* took a practical position on this conflict, paying attention to the genuine situation, see for example, "Religions-Hetzereien," reprinted in the *TISZ,* 3 May 1875; see also FH's account of his break with the *ISZ* to Emil Frey [n.d, early 1877], Staatsarchiv Basel-Stadt, PA 485 DXI165.

35 The works in FHP, box 9, provide an overview of these articles, almost all printed in the *WP.* FH, "Nach Canossa gehen wir nicht! Bismarck 1873 – wohl aber nach dem Vatican. Bismarck, 1878," *WP* [n. d., 1878], FHP, box 9.

36 FH to Charles Söhner, Summerfield, 24 September 1878, FHP, box 3, folder 38.

X

APOLOGIST FOR THE REPUBLICAN PARTY
(1876-81)

The Campaign for Rutherford B. Hayes

In one matter Hecker's opponents in the *Kulturkampf* were correct; if the question of public schools had any role at all in the upcoming campaign, it was peripheral. Since 1873 the great questions of the day had all been economic. The question of finance, with its dispute in particular hard money and paper money, determined public debate. Adherents of both positions could be found in the Democratic as well as the Republican Party, so that a clear distinction between the parties was impossible in this question. As was the case with the overwhelming majority of German-Americans, Hecker was an uncompromising advocate of sound money. On his journeys through the country he sought to explain "what paper money is," how the distinction between nominal and real value of loans operated and how the credit of the United States could be recovered only through thrift and an uncompromising hard-money policy. Economic and financial integrity had, he believed, suffered so much through uncovered loan speculations that it was hard to get foreign lenders interested in the American market again. Although Hecker opposed Grant's policies, he still saw Grant's "best deed" to be his veto of the Inflation Bill passed by Congress at the start of 1874, which proposed to add $64 million to the circulation of greenbacks and national banknotes. "Without this veto," Hecker declared in Chicago,

> our credit overseas, which was already bleeding from the severe wounds that the swindle opened, would have received its coup de grace. They saw this expansion of our non-convertible paper money or paper-promises, to be an overextension of public credit.

This veto was also, as American historians stress, "a milestone in the process by which ... the 'slow, conservative sentiment' gained ascendancy in Republican circles and economic respectability replaced equality of rights for black citizens as the essence of the party's self-image."[1] As economic questions increasingly paralyzed political discussion, the radical elements of Republican Reconstruction policy increasingly faded. The economic crisis also altered the basic conditions for liberal politics for which the Republican Party had stood since its foundation, particularly since the Civil War. A turnabout that was not merely economic announced itself and began changing the image of the Republican Party. It became a pure representative of the interests of the middle and upper propertied classes, the party protecting industry and capital. It was only in the course of the 1870s that the party won its profile as the advocate of economic imperialism.

It appeared as if American voters first reacted to bad times by turning away from their previous party. With the congressional elections of 1874, power shifted in favor of the Democrats; the Republicans lost their majority in the House of Representatives, and gradually in the Senate as well. In general this shift produced a stalemate, with neither party controlling both houses at once. This marked the situation in the election of 1876. In opposition to a third term for Grant, the Republicans nominated Governor Rutherford B. Hayes of Ohio, a man who had not been involved in any corruption, had maintained good relations with all groups within the party and was regarded as a representative of sound money.[2] His Democratic opponent was the successful new governor of New York, Samuel J. Tilden, a man whose name had a good sound since his successful fight against the Tweed Machine in the largest city of the United States, and who was thought to be personally honest.

The stalemate of the parties was reflected in the decisions that German Forty-Eighters made about their support for candidates. The platforms at the national conventions in Cincinnati and St. Louis were not essentially different. Both parties made reform their central slogan, for now there was no grand criterion of distinction such as slavery. For that reason Carl Schurz remarked correctly that in this election it was no longer "about the platforms, but about the men standing on them." The *Illinois Staatszeitung* also stressed that

> In the national elections this year, there are no principled conflicts reaching deeply into the whole life of state and society as at the time of the Civil War or in the six or seven years following it. The difference between the confessions of the two parties is so small that it can hardly be detected.

Franz Sigel and Oswald Ottendorfer, both living in New York, now supported Tilden, although Sigel was really a Republican and Ottendorfer had
always been a Democrat. The same was the case with Friedrich Hassaureck,
Schurz's brother-in-law Edmund Jüssen and even Gustav Körner, who
returned to his "old love," the Democratic Party. Hecker, on the other hand,
went on the stump for Hayes, as did Carl Schurz, who had already had an
important role in Hayes's victory in the gubernatorial elections in Ohio.
With them were Lorenz Brentano (just returned to Chicago from his consular post in Dresden), Caspar Butz, Georg Schneider, Friedrich Münch and
Emil Preetorius.[3]

    Why did Hecker decide for the Republican Party? In 1874 everything
indicated that the reform forces continuing from the 1872 movement would
still be able to establish themselves, and a return to the old party seemed out
of the question for most. It was precisely the reform movement that had
made it possible for coalitions between Democrats and Republicans in local
county or state elections to come into existence, coalitions that operated
very successfully. For the Illinois legislative elections, Hecker had supported an ultimately victorious reform party initiated by Anton Hesing and
Hermann Raster consisting of "Democrats, liberals and all other opponents
to the Republican Party." In the speeches that he gave in this context in
Chicago, he condemned the corrupt nature of the Republican Party and disputed the notion of any reform efforts within its ranks. Nonetheless,
Hecker's vehement criticism of the Republican Party, a consistent continuation of the reform spirit of 1872, was silent in 1876. Instead of giving up on
the whole party, now he held it to be

> utterly, irresponsibly arrogant, offensive and rude ... that a handful of
> shopworn, office-hungry politicians blame the entire Republican Party,
> which includes all of the citizens belonging to it, for what one or two or
> even three dozen oafs in the party actually did.

With the phrase "shopworn, office-hungry politicians" Hecker meant that
group of former Republican German-Americans who, coming out of the
Liberal Republican Movement, now gathered under the Democratic banner
and actually presented themselves in a speech as "Tilden Republicans." The
degree to which this division of the German-American elite into Democratic
and Republican camps clarified what historical research has often called a
struggle for ethnic leadership could be seen from Hecker's criticism of the

Tilden Republicans. He thought it "utterly tasteless and laughable … when a handful of those fallen from or escaped from the party play themselves up as the sole-saving heralds of the Germans." His own function in this campaign – in Illinois alone there were 60-80,000 German votes – was nothing less.

Conversely Hecker, Schurz and all of those who returned to the Republican Party were exposed to the criticism of the Reform Democrats. Carl Schurz's brother-in-law, Edmund Jüssen, declared on behalf of the Tilden Democrats, in an open letter to Friedrich Hecker, that their address accusing others of corruption within the Republican Party did not mean Hecker, "nor the immovable messrs. Brentano, Butz or Schneider, nor any of the few other German-Americans still loyal to the Republicans." The corruptors, Jüssen continued, had all "only recently passed to the Republican Party. It has not been long that every one of them believed it necessary to shatter this party, corrupt to its innermost core, cost what it might." Jüssen recalled the common agitation of 1872 and accused those who had returned of inconsistency. "That is your sad, unexplainable blinding, colonel," he wrote to Hecker,

> that you have convinced yourself now to be able to shatter the political machine within the party, against which you could find only a point of attack outside the party. Have you no idea that this machine has grown larger, more complete, and is set on solid foundations in splendid well-oiled condition? And there you desire to halt the mighty swings of this machine with your pygmy strength, setting yourself against its fly-wheel. … How is your Mr. Hayes to succeed in forming an honorable cabinet, in the event of his election? … Or do you perhaps believe that Mr. Carl Schurz would go to a seat in the cabinet if he were named?[4]

Hecker and Schurz had, in the meantime, actually become convinced that neither forming a new party nor going over to the Democrats made any sense or promised any success. They considered it better to work for changes within the Republican Party and promote the political demands of reform forces there. In the case of Schurz, interest in an office might have played a role. In the case of Hecker, it appeared that intense efforts to win his support after the fatal defeat of the Republicans in the congressional elections of 1874 had borne fruit. Hecker continued to suspect the Democratic Party continued to be suspect to him for other reasons. In 1876 he had once declared, in his efforts for the legislative elections in Illinois,

> In 1874 I rejoined the reform movement in my own state, only to find
> myself after the victory in the midst of Irish whiskey bottles and Jesuit
> blessings. That was too dangerous a reform. I experienced that wherev-
> er the [Catholics] have their hand in the game, something is rotten.

In addition to his dislike for the Catholic element within the Democratic
Party, there was also what he saw as the dangerous development in the
Southern states. His letters to Söhner and Schurz, as well as his articles for
the *Westliche Post* and his election speeches made this clear. It was "arrogant," he declared of the Tilden Republicans, to assert "that salvation and
reform can come only from the old enemies of the Union. ... Traitors to the
Union and their country" had never yet figured in the ranks of the
Republican Party. Hecker's fear of a recovery of the old Democratic elites,
accompanied by a decline of the Republican element in the Southern states,
was justified. What Eric Foner has called "the waning of southern republicanism" was seen all over the South, contributing to later assertions that the
Republican Reconstruction policy had failed. When the Democrats emerged
as victors in the congressional elections of 1874, the committee chairman-
ships were half in the hands of Southern Democrats, although they actually
had less than half the electoral votes. In the same way colored members
once more disappeared from the committees, as well as from the local and
state political offices and positions that they had held for a brief time, in
modest but still impressive numbers, during the "Reconstruction Spring."[5]

Both the loss of congressional votes and the slow but continuous return
of Republican politicians to the Democratic camp – among them Lyman
Trumbull, whom Hecker had wanted to nominate as presidential candidate
of the Liberal Republicans in 1872 – made the Republicans take note. Their
appeal for help was shown by a letter from the Republican reformer G.
Hanigan that reached Hecker after the elections in December 1874. The
Chicago politician asked Hecker for his evaluation of German-American
opinion, as well as advice on how to mobilize the Germans for the
Republicans again in the presidential election of 1876.[6]

It was chiefly the presidential candidate nominated by the Republicans
in Cincinnati, Rutherford B. Hayes, who managed to reassemble the ram-
shackle party. Like Lincoln he had entered the ranks of the Republican Party
as a former Whig in 1856. He had participated actively in the Civil War and
stood close to the reforming forces of the Liberal Republican Movement, but
he had remained in the regular party under Grant in 1872. His nomination

had pleased both reformers and war veterans. What Hecker particularly liked about Hayes was his declared intention not to seek a second term as president. To be sure Hecker later viewed the temperance agitation of Hayes's wife Lucy with some distrust, when she managed to have the serving of alcohol in the White House stopped. But at the start of September 1876, a letter from Hayes reached Hecker asking whether he was ready "to aid us in Ohio with our people of German origin." Hayes was convinced that "a few days stump by you in Ohio will do great good."[7] And so Hecker set himself in motion for the last time to campaign actively for a Republican presidential candidate.

More than anything else, the small notices and sharp comments of the alienated German-American press reflected the remarkably divided situation of the Forty-Eighters in this campaign. "The Baden Forty-Eighters," read a notice in the *Illinois Staatszeitung*, "are now sharply divided. On Tuesday the Baden dictator Brentano obliterated Tilden in Cleveland, and two evenings later in the same Cleveland the Baden field commander Sigel annihilated Hayes." Another example of the often quite personal assaults was the report that "Brentano and Hecker are reported in Ohio German papers to be Republican stump speakers. If the Republicans there are smart, they will take care to have Brentano speak after Hecker; otherwise 'the old man' will mess up what Brentano makes good." The *Westliche Post* picked up the gauntlet thrown by its competitor in Chicago. It sent an arrow from St. Louis to Chicago, reporting Hecker's speech there with the words, "Hecker speaks today in Chicago. A hot day for the *Staatszeitung*." In response the *Illinois Staatszeitung* printed only a short reply, "Bah! Hot at least for a $300 orator!" The fact that such remarks were actually read is best witnessed by Hecker himself. In his Chicago speech he mentioned the accusation of his being a paid stump speaker, and he also defended Carl Schurz on the same theme.[8]

Hecker's stump speeches in Ohio, Indiana and Illinois all showed a similar construction. The arguments presented were at the same time responses to criticisms of the Republican Party. In addition to the latent accusations about corruption and closeness to the temperance and Know Nothing movements, there was the criticism that the party had caused the economic crisis and was pursuing a false Southern policy. As he had in 1856, Hecker attacked temperance and Know-Nothingism in 1876 before coming to his actual themes. The temperance movement was playing an especially important role again in the 1870s and 1880s. For the Germans and the Irish it was as ever a political theme. As in 1856, Hecker did not deny the connection between puritanical Republicans and their temperance agitation; but he argued that this was an electoral tactic to mislead the Germans. Hecker certainly played this aspect down. This was the only way that he could benefit the Republicans, who in this matter had the most uncompromising and believable speaker on their side. Hecker's anti-temperance agitation was well known. His tactic consisted of shifting the theme to what he felt was the most important question of the time. "There are national questions that are more important than the beer question." Hecker also had to deal with the reviving hostility to foreigners within the Republican Party. But as in 1856, he was not deflected; he played down nativism as a bogeyman and discounted it as a serious threat. "We men, thrown on these shores by the great migration of 1848, had to fight against other powers," he declared to his audience. He referred to the best elements within the party, the Forty-Eighters, whose historical significance he consciously exaggerated. "If we had not been, Negroes would probably still be sold in the South. I recall the time when the mob was ready to stone Schurz and me because we participated in the founding of the Republican Party." Finally he warned his audience that the Germans would only be used by the Democrats "to bring the Irish into office."

It was obvious that Hecker had to go into the accusations of corruption within the Republican Party. That was the chief source of the claim of the Democratic Party to basic reform. Because he had great difficulty here denying corruption, his arguments concentrated on weakening the opposition. At the same time they contained a personal confession. He told his listeners,

I concede that a band of rascals penetrated the Republican Party because the street wasn't good enough for them. No one expressed his shock more energetically than I. In 1872 I threw the first grenade into the Grant camp, and not one filled with rose oil either. I fought then, as now, for reform. But when I saw what company I had to keep to achieve this reform, I said thanks and left. There were a few good, convinced men in Cincinnati, along with worn-out, rejected, hungry politicians who were merely waiting for the right chance to snatch an office again.

Hecker had been excited about experimentation and ready for a new beginning in 1872. But there was still peril for him in the perennial slogan

"time for a change." The desire for change, for a change in government relations, would this time bring about the opposite of what was hoped for:

> One cannot experiment with the well-being of the people like trying on
> rows of boots in a shoe store to see which fits best. It may end like the
> soul in purgatory, who wants a change and ends up in hell.

Against the proposition that one should elect Tilden as president, but a
Republican Congress, Hecker reminded his audience of the president's
power of appointment. This could influence the entire public administration of the Union without any involvement by Congress because confirmation by the Senate was normally only a formality.

Hecker's position on the world crisis was already well known. The general depression could hardly be blamed on one party, and compared to the
European situation the American position was dramatic but not hopeless.
However, he did assign guilt for the war to the Democrats. "We would be
the richest and most powerful nation if 24,300 slaveholders had not compelled us to a bloody, trying war." To eliminate the depression Hecker
advised thrift, and it was exactly this appeal that betrayed his ambivalent
attitude on economic policy questions. On the one side there was Hecker's
liberal laissez-faire tone, which was not alien to economically imperialist
elements. He promoted the American ideology of self-help and free entre-
preneurialism. As a farmer he included himself as a small entrepreneur, and
he encouraged the pursuit of individual interests according to ability and
endowment. Like Thomas Paine, Hecker had already supported liberal capitalism as a strongly anti-aristocratic force in Germany, a force that promoted republican equality. Every bale of goods arriving in Europe from
America, he had declared in his 1873 Mannheim farewell address, contributed to spreading republican ideas.

At the same time, however, he maintained a pre-modern, basically pre-
industrial faith in the possibility of a virtuous republic, as well as the concept of the republic's endangerment from tensions between commerce and
virtue in the economically changing 1870s. Built on ancient examples, the
concept of the instability of republics as a result of corruption, faction and
luxury meant that pursuing individual interests seemed to endanger the
common good. "The best system is to build again a solid, civil life through
hard work, thrift, elimination of luxury and addiction to wasteful spending," Hecker declared to his listeners in Indianapolis.[9] Here he had in mind

less the ancient rulers' virtues than Montesquieu's *vertu publique*, the concept of political virtue developed in his *Esprit des lois*, which includes
"l'amour de la patrie et de l'égalité," ["The love of country and equality"] and
meant the commitment of each person to the common good, to country,
equality, *frugalité*, the most extreme material self-sufficiency. What is significant in this virtue, whose realization in "modern" republics Montesquieu
himself doubted, was that, unlike a concept of reason, it was accessible to
everyone as a "sentiment," a "passion." It described a particular relationship between personal virtue and simultaneous national prosperity.
Accomplishing *vertue publique* was to renounce individual interests, to
renounce one's own self – *"un renoncement à soi-meme,"* as Montesquieu had
called it. This only appeared possible under the precondition of the equality and self-sufficiency of all. Montesquieu had derived from this that wealth
should go to the state alone, not to its citizens.

It is precisely this relationship of national prosperity and the simplicity
of the virtuous citizen that we find in Hecker. He was entirely serious about
his call to thrift and the elimination of luxury. As pathetic, banal and
anachronistic as this sort of statement might seem, it formed the core of his
political views and was the reason for his own conscious, personal decision
to live on the land. Thomas Jefferson was convinced that "vicious morals
[were] unknown among the mass of farmers" and that corruption was a
particularly urban problem. Hecker adopted this view. "Nothing can
improve without farmers; cities are all corrupt, more or less," he stated.
Even the metaphors that he used for dangerous, corrupting luxury in 1876
were those used in Germany in the 1840s. Again there was talk of "oysters,"
whose enjoyment was supposed to cause gout in the rich citizen who had
plenty of money but was too sick to participate actively in the citizens'
guard. Hecker told his listeners in Indianapolis,

> I am still sleeping in the bed I bought 26 years ago when I came to this
> country. I lived here sixteen years without seeing an oyster. Now when
> I ask my hired hands where they are going and what they are doing on
> Saturday, they answer me, "I'm going to ...ville [sic] to have a meal of
> oysters." If we continue in this manner, we will all become bums.

It was precisely the problem of overproduction, for which Hecker had no
patent remedies other than creating new markets, that was the source of the
evil, so far as he was concerned. He wrote privately to Söhner,

with it goes and must go hand in hand a mass of hitherto unknown demands. Through overproduction and ... transportation, a mass of things become lower in price and available and more inviting to all classes. Where once pearl barley was eaten, now people eat oysters. Lobster, which in our area we barely knew from picture books and natural histories, is eaten by day laborers in the backwoods. ... Whoever wants to swim in such times has to be ready to reduce, get rid of demands and simply be satisfied; there is no other recipe.[10]

Hecker regarded "Existence and support" as the highest human goods, alongside "glory and honor." Securing an existence, however, was nothing more than rising above materialism and luxury. Hecker's entire life was determined by this attitude, and it was not without pride that he reported to Söhner that, when he unexpectedly inherited a considerable sum from his late brother in Freiburg, he passed the money immediately to his sons Erwin and Alexander to promote their business in East St. Louis, satisfied in the awareness of having everything he needed. "My books, maps, studies are enough, and in them I find what makes my evening of life pleasant."[11]

But the luxury that threatened the republic was not Hecker's sole concern. For him the situation in the South was just as worrying for the survival of the Union. Behind the call of Democratic reformers for reconciliation and termination of Reconstruction he suspected an effort to forget their own past. And with this forgetting, proclaimed as so necessary, he suspected that white Democratic supremacy would establish itself once more in the South, and thus all that the war had accomplished would be obliterated. He himself, Hecker wrote, had once operated on the presumption that the old rebel spirit had been brought to reason and that it would subordinate itself to the facts and to constitutional laws. But instead the Republican element in the South was being cowed, and there were zealous efforts to restrict the rights of colored people. Political calculation after the Civil War made Southern politicians act as if they were interested in equality, but Southern Democrats had always been interested in having the insult of the Civil War and the resulting humiliation be forgotten. There had never been a true Democratic interest in constitutional rights, he continued; the arrogance of the Southern aristocracy lived on.

Southern men have too much honor in their bodies to change their views and their long-treasured principles like cloaks and, in the manner of so many political weather vanes, servants of time and profit, remove them and throw them away. No! Cleverness and the weighing of the relations of power might cause them to conform to the new (or old) order of things. But a total change of views and feelings in the short time of ten years is as improbable as in the history of all restorations. They will seek to recover as much of what was lost as possible.

The votes of the freedmen were of great importance to the Republican Party. Discussions that one should "not immediately grant complete equality and suffrage to raw, ignorant slaves" indicated to Hecker that most Southerners regarded the Thirteenth, Fourteenth and Fifteenth Amendments, which were to guarantee the rights of freedmen in the South, as impositions passed without their approval. Hecker saw a danger in the possibility that states would "assault Negro equality and suffrage, attempting to go around the amendments by means of the limited right of a state to establish qualifications for suffrage and electibility." That is, through state regulation establishing the right to vote, such restrictions as in terms of residence, personal capacity or elementary knowledge could be prescribed. Hecker also prophesied that it would be no challenge to the sharpness and inventiveness of the Democratic Party to "cripple, to go around" the operation of the amendments "under the form of general legal rules that, in practice, are directed against the Negro and his suffrage." What Hecker formulated here was a hint of developments that would actually take place. In 1879 legislatures in various Southern states declared the Thirteenth, Fourteenth and Fifteenth Amendments not to be legally binding, and the need to reduce the budgets of individual Southern states led to reductions for public education and training, which in turn dramatically reduced the equality of opportunity for colored people.[12]

The Hayes campaign differed from earlier presidential campaigns in its more aggressive mood. For the first time Hecker reported disruptions of meetings, particularly in the states bordering the South. "In Fort Wayne they tried to mob me," he wrote to Söhner,

they attempted to break up meetings. But I stood firm, and so the louts finally quieted down and said that they would mob Schurz, who was speaking the next day. The matter went so far that 40 extra policemen had to be brought, in and 50 boys in blue agreed to protect the podium.[13]

Hardly any other presidential election was as uncertain in its result as that between Tilden and Hayes. Hayes himself believed on the evening of 7 November that he had lost the election, but on the following morning the surprising news of 185 electoral votes and with it a "one vote electoral college majority" arrived. The votes of Florida, South Carolina and Louisiana made the difference in a victory for Hayes and the Republican candidate for the offices of governor. The Democrats believed that there was electoral fraud and disputed the result: "Not elected, but bought off," wrote the *Illinois Staatszeitung*. The campaign, which had already proceeded to the tune of violent episodes and had even been marked by militant clashes between white Democrats and colored Republicans in the South, bringing the country to the edge of civil war. It would continue in a similarly confused manner. Because there were also disputes within the Republican Party – many doubted Hayes's will to reform – Congress decided to call an independent electoral commission to decide the disputed election. At the end of January 1877, they began to form the commission of 15 members. Ten members were from Congress (five Democrats and five Republicans), and five were justices of the Supreme Court. Four of the five justices had already been chosen, two Democrats and two Republicans, and together they were supposed to choose a fifth. It was expected that the non-partisan, independent justice David Davis would be chosen, but when he was unexpectedly elected senator by the Illinois legislature, he resigned his position in the commission. The Republican Joseph P. Bradley took his position, and so the disputed electoral votes were counted for Hayes by a vote of 8 to 7. There had already been negotiations with leading Democratic politicians from the Southern states, whose primary goal was achieving a policy of federal nonintervention. Hayes supported not only hard money but also the policy of local self-government. Democrats could agree with him who hoped for a greater measure of self-government in the South, and to whom it was a matter of indifference who ruled in Washington as long as the Southerners were conceded their own policies.[14]

In the course of commission's proceedings in January and February 1877, Hecker wrote and discussed with Schurz the details of the electoral mechanisms and whether the vice president of the United States, as president of the senate, had the last word in such decisions. When Hayes finally emerged as victor, Hecker was highly satisfied with the result. "So far so good," he wrote to Schurz.

If I find myself in a good mood about the end of the campaign, this is the highest reason. As I said before, no nation in the Old World could have resolved such a conflict in such a manner, and this prestige does our republic and republican institutions unlimited good. The second reason is that no harm was done to the surging economic development, which rapidly leads us to the pinnacle of peoples. Third, I am jubilant that the shame has been spared us of seeing conscious less, politically dishonorable, immoral rascals at the pinnacle of the nation. ... In the eyes of the world we would be drowned in the mud of contempt.[15]

Hecker, who was very proud "that I have worked to achieve this result of the election," now stepped forth in the press as a defender of Hayes's policies. Shortly after his entrance into office, the president removed the federal troops placed around the legislative buildings in South Carolina and Louisiana to protect elections, ordering them back to their barracks. "Hayes did not, as legend has it, remove the last federal troops from the South." A little later Hecker later supported this decision in a letter to the editor of the *Neue Freie Presse* in Chicago. The *Neue Freie Presse* had stated justifiable doubts about this action because the return of home rule in the South and the filling of public offices with Democrats could mean the beginning of gradual restriction of colored rights. Hecker, however, was so pleased with Hayes's election and the prevention of a Democratic president that he uncritically approved of actions that he would have considered extremely dangerous under a Democratic administration. This included leaving the South to its "natural leaders." Hecker did not understand the uproar over Louisiana and South Carolina, he wrote. It was not true that

the amendments and the freedmen have been given up through the withdrawal of the troops. ... An end had to be put to anarchy and to the organized economic ruination arising from it, if we were not to be become a mockery overseas and if the internal peace and economic development, ever growing, should not be placed in question.

Hecker, who seldom had any reason to believe in the goodness of people, now referred to the seemingly conciliatory mood in negotiations with the Southerners. He asserted that there had been assurances from the other side. He defended the earlier federal intervention by the Republican government after the Civil War, and its centralistic tendencies. "In that time of

Reconstruction, a strong hand and armed measures necessary to protect the freedmen were absolutely necessary which today are not needed." Now the legal protection of colored people was guaranteed by the federal Senate; it stood "like a brass wall," so that henceforth an "armed force in the South to keep watch" was no longer needed. If these rights were threatened, the federal government "would intervene in legal form." He depended on those with insight, "that those dealing with the economic development of the South keep the upper hand and leadership. The South has an absolute need for its colored element." But his hope for insight would not be fulfilled, and Hecker himself would doubt a few years later whether the colored element actually was "absolutely" necessary. With the recalling of the troops – or even earlier, with Grant's refusal on tactical grounds to commit federal troops in the tumultuous conflicts in Mississippi in 1875 – the freedman policy of Reconstruction vanished from the political agenda.[16]

Our Man in Office – Schurz as Secretary of the Interior

When Carl Schurz was called by Hayes to be secretary of the interior, the result was inevitable. The results of the election were no sooner known than the same hunt for office began among the Republicans with the sort of zeal that Hecker had conceded only to the Democrats. "I have no doubt," he remarked to Schurz, "that *you* are already being bombarded .... Even my own little hut will be visited by candidates' rockets. Since, praise God, I have *never* been a candidate *nor* will be one at the close, I can preserve my soul's and civic peace." Yet it was good for Hecker to know a German-American party friend in one of the most important positions of the American administration, and Schurz would prove able to do a thing or two for him. First Hecker's friends Georg Schneider and Caspar Butz turned to him with a request. He sent their requests on by the next mail to Washington, asking Schurz whether there might be a post for these two "faithful party colleagues."

> Schneider would like to be chargé d'affaires in Switzerland, specifically Bern, and Caspar a pension agent in Chicago ... I have written to them personally that I cannot apply directly to Hayes because I have never understood the manner of asking for things, and the few times that I have done it (never for myself, only for friends), it always fell through. But on top of that I let Hayes know that I went on the stump

in response to his letter request, and that he would not have to do anything for me. So that I should request a favor for that ... *Sela*.[17]

Schurz understood Hecker's hesitation and was happy to help in his
effort, even managing to get Georg Schneider offered a consular post. A
position for Caspar Butz was harder to arrange, but Schurz did honorable
service seeking something proper. In the end Butz remained in Chicago, as
did Schneider. It was only when Hecker approached Schurz with more candidates that Schurz had to point out that his possibilities were limited, particularly with positions that did not fall in his competence. "Naturally the
influence that I can exercize on another department is limited," he wrote to
Hecker, "as I permit no interventions into my own department."[18]

Under Hayes Schurz had the opportunity to organize the Department
of the Interior the way that he wanted. But he did not always hit on unrestrained approval, in addition to which many Republicans could never forgive his bolting the party in 1872. He was made to feel this particularly in
the Senate. Schurz stuck stubbornly to his civil-service reform, and one of
the first measures that he introduced to his department was the examination of candidates. "He was bound to make his department the best concrete
argument in favor of the ideas he had been advocating for many years,"
writes Schurz's biographer Joseph Shafer. And the hardbitten farmer from
distant Illinois sought to reinforce the "overloaded pack-animal of the U.S.
humanity" to the best of his ability and support him. "I marvel at your
endurance," Hecker wrote to Schurz, full of praise. " It would not be possible for me. I would rather chase through the fields as chief of the robbers
than be the servant of this thankless, often stupid species that so worthily
represents in the mass Darwin's ancestors in his *Descent of Man*." What
Hecker meant was not only the difficult high-wire act within the
Washington administration, but also the manifold obligations of the many
duties of Schurz's department, which was known to initiated mockers as
the "great miscellany." (Schurz's department included the Office of Indian
Affairs, the General Land Office, the Pension Office, the Patent Office and
the Bureau of Education). "Your letter of 24 July once more did my heart
good," Schurz wrote from Washington to Hecker when he had been in office
only four months. "I thank you heartily for the information about the mood
in the country," he said, and promised to strike "at the vitals of foolishness
solidly and mortally" and not miss.[19]

Civil-service reform had once more become the magic word. Because the concept was by no means closed and complete, Hecker worked with visible pleasure on its perfection. "I will get at once a report on the workings of the system from a friend (a member of the state assembly) in Switzerland," he told Schurz. Hecker wrote a letter to his former major, Emil Frey, in the meantime become a federal councilor in Basel. He requested information as detailed as possible on the entirely practical functions of the Swiss civil-service system. "Often in public addresses and journals I have set up your republic and constitution as a model and directed public attention there," he wrote to Frey and continued, "Now you must help with your information." Hecker had a very precise notion of the sort of information he needed for Schurz. The questions listed in the letter show what Hecker particularly wanted. He asked about the procedures for naming and promoting officials, membership in or independence of parties, pensions, removals, life tenure, controlling authorities, tests and examinations, and finally the legal anchoring of the civil-service system. He assured Frey that every patriot would listen to the information with curiosity because,

> despite the enormous extent of our country your healthy principles are all the more applicable. The [American] republic is also federal and decentralized, resting on the people's sovereignty and self-government. You will do the country, for which you have so bravely fought and suffered, a great service with your comprehensive information, and as long as I breathe I will work for these reforms.

Hecker composed this letter with the intention of passing the information to Schurz, as it was Schurz's time to get to work. "Every day I expect a thorough, basic presentation of the Swiss civil-service system, with commentary," he reported to Washington, "and I will give you notice of that *ad usum Delphini* ["in the style of Delphi"]." Hecker appeared to have received the desired information and passed it on to Schurz. He obviously enjoyed the role of informer to the German-American interior secretary, for he encouraged Schurz not to relent in his reform efforts, made judgments about the political situation of the country, accused various politicians of misdemeanor and kept Schurz informed of the course of the Republican Party. And naturally Hecker always had something on his heart that he had to tell Schurz without delay. "Are you not coming," he wrote the interior secretary, "for at least a few days to the West, once the stall of Congress has been cleaned out? Then let me know in advance. I would like to discuss something with you by word of mouth that is important to us in Illinois, and in which you must play an essential role."[20]

The policies of President Hayes and his administration during Hayes' four years in office won general support after the initial difficulties of 1877. To be sure Hayes did not succeed in achieving lasting civil-service reform; but "little by little his hard-working habits, conscientiousness, system, and responsiveness to moral forces impressed the nation; the original Democratic bitterness decreased; and he became generally esteemed." Hecker paid great respect to Hayes's well-intended efforts for civil-service reform, which made even Hecker to view the events of 1872 in a new, positive light. "Now our sentimentality of 1872," he wrote to Schurz, "has achieved a splendid, untoppable result. ... Now every ordinary Joe knows ... what we are about and how it was intended, and that is good, very good."[21]

It was not only Hayes's reform policy, but also his hard stance on the currency question that won Hecker's applause. In his inaugural address the new president promised a clarification of the unsatisfying "monetary situation" and expressed himself against the irresponsible paper-money economy. His uprightness put Hayes to the test when bills were presented by both parties in Congress – the question had been debated in both houses since autumn, 1877 – demanding the suspension of the law reintroducing specie payments on 1 January 1879 and the simultaneous free and unlimited minting of silver as full legal tender. Hayes vetoed the bill and hindered its passage in the Senate. He finally achieved the restoration of specie payments, so important for the national credit, by the set date. In a whole series on the currency question in the *Westliche Post*, Hecker sought to inform readers of the unpleasant results of "hard-money truths and paper-money errors," and he shared Hayes's economic views.[22]

Other decisions of the president met with Hecker's approval. In 1879 Hayes led a successful fight against the attempt by Congress to use amendments to two appropriations bills to subordinate the power of the executive and the president to Congress. Hayes, who saw in these measures "the first attempt in our History to break down the functions of the Executive by coercion," used his veto and declared the amendments to be unconstitutional. Congress finally had to give in and remove the two clauses from the bills. "If I were not an infidel," Hecker commented on Hayes's actions in a letter to Schurz, "after reading though the veto message I would have called out, 'God bless the president and his Cabinet.' But instead I will use the best wish an Arab can give another, including good fortune, health and long life

…: 'May your shadow never grow shorter.'" Hayes's steadfastness against the attempt by Congress to restrict the competence of the president and at the same time expand that of Congress, increased Hecker's admiration for the Republican president. If Hecker had regarded the Second Chamber in Germany as the true and only chamber of the people and the First Chamber as at best a useless and antiquated remnant of an aristocratic caste, this did not mean that he would automatically have voted for a unicameral system. Now, however, he had been an American long enough to endorse whole-heartedly the careful construction of the American Constitution – "the most splendid of all state constitutions," as he once called it – with its division of the legislature into two houses and with checks and balances that provided mutual security and control of the legislative, executive and judicial branch-es. As he wrote in another article, it was precisely this "sort of setting lim-its, a constitution of common sense and sober second thought," that had always prevented the development of a one-sided and dangerous predom-inance by one party. Quite differently from Grant's time, Hecker now stood without restriction on the side of the president, who was seeking to protect this balance and defend it against the false presumption and ruinous ambi-tion of Congress. "The gentlemen miscalculated with Hayes," Hecker wrote in satisfaction to Schurz a month after the presidential veto.

> If he had been Mephistopheles himself, he could not have done it better. … Suddenly it dawned on the masses that Hayes with his admin-istration was really a pillar of the original, constitutional idea and bulwark. This veto parade is a striking evidence for all students and scholars of public and constitutional law against the unicameral system and the abolition of the … veto.[23]

The Red Menace – General Strike and Communism

The first year of President Hayes's term, 1877, stands not only for the end of Reconstruction, but also for the first great national railroad strike in the history of the United States. The progress of the industrialization of postwar America had brought into disorder the Republican ideology of a balanced harmony between capital and labor. The hope of many workers that wage work was only a prelude to their own independence and eleva-tion into the comfortable middle class appeared increasingly questionable. The mass of propertyless workers continuously rose, and an intensification of class conflict was the result.

[T]he railroad strike shattered an even greater myth, that Americans could have industrialization without the dark satanic mills of Europe and a permanent wage-earning class, could have capitalism without class conflict. So, in the end, Reconstruction came full circle. It began with southerners trying to adjust to the northern system of free labor. It ended with northerners having to accept the reality of conflict between capital and labor – a reality that southerners, white and black, had understood all along.[24]

On 16 July 1877, with the strike of the workers of the Baltimore & Ohio Railroad because of wage cuts, a protest began that swiftly spread west across the entire land, with the exception of the New England states and the deep South. It expanded to other industries, as well. This general strike completely paralyzed cities such as Chicago and St. Louis, particularly after massive conflicts in Pittsburgh. Skilled and unskilled workers alike demanded the eight-hour day, a return to the wages before the economic crisis, the state seizure of railroads and the repeal of what were called "tramp ordinances" that made it possible to arrest unemployed workers. Finally federal troops were set against the strikers, often replacing the usual keepers of public order, who had refused to act against the workers. The strikes revealed how much social conditions had changed since the Civil War. Fear of communists spread, supported and intensified by agitators in the larger cities."[25]

In the midst of general hysteria, Hecker explained "The Groundlessness of Fear of Communism in the Union" in an entire series of articles. These essays clearly showed that Hecker's radicalism, which was first and foremost a consistent republicanism, never had anything in common with socialistic or communistic tendencies, even in his earlier years. Instead he was entirely committed to an economic liberal tradition that bound individualism of property to a premodern understanding of republics. The creed of his political views remained bound up with the liberal concept of man. The free-born, autonomous individual seeking to develop his individual talents could desire only such a governmental form that guaranteed him his own realization within the largest possible framework. Hecker profoundly distrusted the welfare state led from above. With its state regulation, much of it reminding him of the monarchical system. "The eternal doodledum, doodledee of state help, state support, state rescue" was, he wrote, "nothing other than 90 percent of all monarchism, born in Europe, drenched with

milk in meat and blood, and wandering around here in praise or rejection."
Hecker asserted something similar a year later in connection with the state
of siege laws planned by Bismarck. He did not condemn socialism because
it was the most dramatic contradiction to liberalism and "ancient democracy," but because it represented even more of an "injury to human dignity,"
a "contradiction of the conditions of the culture"; it was the epitome of the
guardian state. In that sense the socialist bureaucratic state and the monarchical form of state were not particularly distinct from each another.

> Socialist or communist state doctrines are the quintessence of abso-
> lutism. ... The state takes everything in hand. It is the *"faisseur général"*
> ["general doer"]. Industry, crafts, trade, marriage, children, work,
> property, food, drink, clothing – it holds everything in the center, pro-
> viding the general income-, outgo- and producer-state.[26]

In terms of cultural history, Hecker wanted to place the communist
state on the same level as nomadic life. It was surrendered as a social order
at the point when people became sedentary, and it was today at best a reactionary attempt to restore old conditions that had long since been left
behind by the progressive movement into modernity. Such a communist
state made sense only among nomadic peoples, who had no secure ownership and who relied to a great degree on mutual support and help. This
flight back into the earlier era of human social life gave Hecker the opportunity to present the essence of the liberal creed.

> The special development of individuals and the varying endowment of
> single persons, as well as the interior differences in strength, energy
> and impulsivity – this individuality cannot be pressed into communist
> uniformity and equality patterns, like bricks into a mold.

To make people "the same" meant for Hecker destroying every individual capacity and readiness for accomplishment, endangering all extraordinary human creativity. He argued, one could never say to communist leaders "that a Phidias, a Michel Angelo, a Homer, an Aristotle, a Kant, a
Herodotus, a Tacitus or a Schlosser ever came from their ranks." Because of
this, and because America had always promoted individualism, Hecker
held that all communist communes in the United States had quickly dissolved in spite and conflict, so that the creation of communist societies in

America "was excluded." The pragmatic attitude of Americans toward the state lay in a preference for self-help; the "born American" is educated "too much in terms of 'help yourself,'" according to Hecker. Communist societies would be alien to America's political institutions. Their creation "has not happened, and in that lies their condemnation. It did not happen because communism strives against individuality, against the free development of humanity." Hecker saw envy as the chief goad and motivation of all supporters of communist ideas. At the same time he believed that any flirting with communist ideas by the lower class would cease if the lower class passed over into the propertied classes. Communism was an expression of the longing of those who did not belong to those classes. Why precisely it was German-Americans, as distinguished from Americans, who showed themselves inclined to communist ideas, Hecker explained by saying that Germans had been damaged by the monarchical system. A German's hopes therefore depended too much on state leadership, while an American stood "on the soil of his republic" with both feet. The American does not "sway, mist or quake ... in unrealizable imported Utopias." In Europe the socialists were also an effective means of applying pressure. "The communists are very useful to the monarchies. The great mass of citizens would rather have a little more monarchical law-peace and order simply to avoid seeing the red tiger break loose."[27]

Returning to economic considerations, Hecker was certain that an economy controlled by the state would sooner or later collapse. Financial resources were insufficient to sustain the institutions of control that were necessary to administer trade, crafts and industry, and finally the society itself adequately. In addition, Hecker wrote, if everyone could demand the right to participate through universal suffrage, the way was opened to general political chaos and finally absolute corruption; no one would be in a position any longer to control the enormous state apparatus. Trade, depending on rapid reaction, simply would not tolerate "any state control, any state enterprise," Hecker warned in his article. As a farmer he was particularly concerned that an equal distribution of the soil would pay no attention to differing fertility and productivity, and further no one could practice an eight-hour day in agriculture. "The state is the free, best and happiest," sounded his political confession once again, "that is governed the least."[28]

Hecker's view that a fear of communists in America was groundless agreed completely with the evaluation of another German-American whom he could barely stand, Friedrich Kapp. In 1877 Kapp published an article in the *Preussische Jahrbücher* on the American July riots. With the current German situation before him, and calling on his "twenty-year experience" in America, came to the conclusion that European Social Democrats were in great error if they believed that the American strikes were the result of a "well-organized Social Democratic Party." To be sure, in the "large cities of the Union there are a few dozen, perhaps even hundreds of pupils of European communist leaders, crackpot pharmacists or schoolmasters"; but it was a long way from their proclamations and meetings, which "sound extremely harmless in the American air," to a party that can win serious hearing. Kapp explained why this was so, using the same arguments as Hecker.

> The inner reason for the lack of success of all these efforts lies in the fact that every American worker can make it to master and independent property owner in good times with some hard work, hence that it is relatively easy for a "proletarian" to become a "bourgeois" sooner or later – a change of estate to which he ... is certainly inclined. ... Besides, the formation of capital there [in America] is still too young, too little hardened by history; on the contrary, it is still in flux. In short, over there there is not yet the hostile confrontation between capital and labor as there is with us, and movement between the two classes, if they can even be spoken of, takes place without comment. He who is a worker today could be a capitalist tomorrow, and vice versa.

Even if Kapp intended his article in the *Preussische Jahrbücher* to be something different from Hecker's piece in the *Westliche Post* – Kapp was celebrating the American strikes as a "great moral and political defeat" for the United States – the two liberals actually came very close to each other in their basic evaluation of the situation. Kapp, unlike Hecker, sympathized with the actions of the railroad companies and condemned the Granger Movement of the early 1870s. He distinguished between the real workers striking for better wages and social advancement, on the one hand, and the "lazy scum," on the other, which "brought the entire movement into discredit through murder, arson and plunder." Such "scum" remained for him corrupted voting cattle from whom he feared an attack on "the property of others." Hecker shared precisely this class consciousness and this fear of the raw, uneducated masses. He wrote to Söhner,

> The communists here have no soil, and they can at most create trouble,

sowing nonsense and damage. The farmers (hence half the population) don't want to hear about it, and in the world of trade and business only ... drunken louts; among workers and craftsmen it is only found among ... the adherents of degraded rascals; associated ... with sleazy unmarried apprentices, thieves, ... robbers, losers and altogether, scum, Brother Jonathan [the United States] is by no means inclined to give up republic and government to this sulphurous band. Past experience has shown that the next attempt of this sort will be dealt with promptly and pitilessly, and they are armed to do it.[29]

Hecker's basic outlook, identical to Kapp's, was described by the *Illinois Staatszeitung*, which published Kapp's article in Chicago, as "the views of the so-called 'Manchester people' in Germany, that is, the promoters of unlimited competition and the opponents of any sort of intervention by the state in the relationships between capital and labor." A self-regulating market, with the specifically American variant that advancement into the broad middle class remained open to the worker – the landowning farmer already belonged to this middle class as an autonomous, small entrepreneur – continued to make sense to Hecker, despite riots and strikes. Kapp made a similar evaluation of the situation in America; however, he was more interested in the German problem of a more inflexible class society, whose propertied and educated bourgeoisie were seized by fear of the "uncontrollable masses."[30] For both Kapp and Hecker, as for many Forty-Eighters, the Republican Party had been attractive, particularly in its foundation phase in the 1850s, not least for its decidedly liberal free-labor ideology. For emigrants coming from Europe the moral aspect of slavery was not so central to their thinking as the economically liberal concept of free labor and the chance for individual advancement. This economic model and a specific image of mankind connected with it held both Kapp and Hecker despite their diverging lives.

As in many other political questions, Hecker showed no discrepancy between his public and private statements. He thus knew full well that his attitude toward socialism and communism would divide him from some of his friends and acquaintances. When Amand Goegg was back in America on a speaking tour during the winter of 1876/77, Söhner asked Hecker whether Goegg might visit him. Hecker responded, "Goegg has not visited me, and he will have trouble doing it because he knows what view I have of communism and the phrases of the *Internationale*. Here masses of such

fools are lacking to crown this nastiness." In his rejection of communism,
however, Hecker found himself – and this should be no surprise – totally at
one with another "liberal" Forty-Eighter, Carl Schurz, who read Hecker's
article in the *Westliche Post* and wrote him in approval.

> The "red menace" has not been as many wanted to make it. I believe
> that we here in Washington can be proud that we did not lose our heads
> for a moment in the general crying out for troops, volunteers, etc. And,
> elastic as the American character is, now they have almost too com-
> pletely forgotten the matter.

Kapp also asserted this. "Hardly six weeks after its end, the rebellion has
been as good as forgotten," he said in the *Preussische Jahrbücher*.[31]

The Exodus of the Colored People

If both Hecker and Carl Schurz showed themselves concerned about
conditions in the Southern states, it was partly from their fear of a dwindling influence of the Republican Party. In the summer of 1877, shortly after
entering office, Schurz expressed his concerns on this to Hecker. He feared
that the Republican Party had ceased "to be viable" in the South.

> All moral and intellectual conditions for existence are lacking. But as
> quickly as the Republican organization vanishes and the Democratic
> finds itself in undisputed possession of the field, what will be the
> result? Symptoms are already showing themselves in many places. ...
> The conservative Democrats are hauling the Republicans into their
> wake ... This might develop slowly, but it will develop.

Hecker made the same diagnosis a few years later. After the conflict
over Hayes's veto, Hecker declared himself convinced that the Democrats
had decided to regain their influence, but not through a war that they could
not afford. "The gentlemen rightly reject a rebellion with weapons. War and
rebellion require money, much money, and that is precisely what stamps
them as 'mild' beggars," he wrote to Schurz. Rather, Southerners would act
via the institutions of Congress, at the expense of the "longevity of the
American republic" and American politics, which depended on the "harmony of three factors." Hecker believed that what he was perceiving was a
creeping overthrow of the foundations of the Constitution. He also found

the "claims" of the South in Congress, which were to regulate damage from the Civil War, to be arrogant. "If you read the *Westliche Post*," he wrote to Schurz,

> you will have seen from my article "The Beginning of the Second Rebellion and Secession" that I hold the current political situation to be more dangerous than in 1860/65. That was an *actus eruptus* fever, today we are suffering from a creeping chronic illness. Those who act with constitutional paragraphs in hand and pursue conscious reaction with their debates are much more dangerous and worse than what was done with guns, grapeshot and grenades. The great mass understands quickly when its pelt is scorched, but it does not understand the detours, crooked ways and intrigues.[32]

If Hecker still believed after the election of Hayes in 1877 that the rights of the colored people would be secured in the South, all signs pointed to storm by 1879/80. In December 1878 he wrote to Söhner that he had a "work ready in my head in which I basically destroy that stupid saying, 'they shouldn't give civil rights and full liberty to the niggers right away.'" In the essay that appeared soon after in the *Westliche Post*, he involved himself in the disputed theme of the vote for colored people. The issue was perennially criticized not only in many Democratic Southern newspapers, but also in the newspapers of northern industrial cities that defended the interests of Northern workers against cheap freedmen labor. Questioning this right and the delaying attitude of the South reminded Hecker of European conditions and the argument that certain people must first be educated to liberty before they could achieve the vote:

> How can one educate anyone to liberty using whips and servitude? How can you educate republicans – citizens of free self-determination, subject to no one but the law and respecting the law – under the curse of no rights and of crippled rights, under laws that do not exist for them?

He responded with a quotation from the essay "Recollections on Mirabeau" by the British historian Thomas Babington Macauley. "It is not in swaddling bonds that we learn to walk. It is not in the dark that we learn to distinguish colours. It is not under oppression that we learn how to use freedom."[33]

The discussion of suffrage for colored people, in which Hecker participated for obvious reasons, did not take place in total abstraction. It was stimulated by a peculiar phenomenon that was quickly dubbed 'The Exodus of the Colored People" by the press. In order to escape the increasing reaction of what Eric Foner describes as the "redeemer counterrevolution," colored people sought at the beginning of 1879 to leave the Southern states and settle farther to the north and west. They were most interested in Kansas, which became the goal of tens of thousands of Southern freedmen and their families. Prominent black leaders such as Frederick Douglass criticized this Kansas migration because they feared that the westward movement was nothing but a silent capitulation in the struggle for the civil rights of colored people in the South. This exodus did, however, cause great excitement among many colored people, not least because it touched deep religious convictions and recalled the removal from Egypt of the Israelites seeking a new homeland far from pharaonic control. "To countless blacks," Eric Foner summarized this phenomenon, "Kansas offered the prospect of political equality, freedom from violence, access to education, economic opportunity, and liberation from the presence of the old slaveholding class – in sum, the 'practical independence' that Reconstruction had failed to secure."[34]

"Wherever possible," Hecker commented on this phenomenon in a newspaper article, "every dog avoids the place where he was beaten and mishandled; his existence is not secure, nor can he be happy there." He saw in the exodus of the colored people a chance to keep the peace and also preserve Republican voting potential. In the approaching presidential campaign, whose result was continually seen as extremely close, securing these potential votes was decisive. Hecker told Schurz of these considerations.

> The exodus of the colored people is a very important moment. It is assured that what has happened so far is only preliminary, and that in 1880 the movement ... will take on colossal dimensions. In any case, the emigration this year has already sent a large number of votes to the North, and I do not need to say what ticket they will vote for, as a man. The Republican Party should promote this exodus with all means and ways. The beggar barons and their following of white trash will either have to work or perish. In the place of the blacks an emigration of Northern labor will fill the gaps; new people and different ideas will establish themselves. I hold the exodus of the colored people to be the sole way for a pacification and genuine union of the two regions. The

work will have been completed in a generation. As things lie today, with the current living together of the two races, peace, quiet and concord between North and South will never be possible at any time. It is better for the colored people, and culturally more advantageous, to scatter among the Northern people. We have room enough in New Mexico, in the waterways of Arizona, in Colorado, Kansas, Nebraska and the territories; if there were workers there, particularly agricultural ones, much more land would already have been brought under cultivation.[35]

How much Hecker had become an apologist for the Republican Party, how much he was led by Republican Party interests and how much he had developed a class consciousness – at least over against the raw, work-shy mob, as Friedrich Kapp had branded it in the *Preussische Jahrbücher* – were clearly shown by his comments on the new stream of immigrants from Southern and Eastern Europe. For him immigration was no longer welcomed without restriction, nor was it in the interests of the general prosperity of the country as it had been at the beginning of the 1870s. Instead it meant a strengthening of the Catholic element, because these immigrants ran immediately to the Democratic camp. He expressed his concerns to Söhner without restraint.

Letters to me from Europe report of the enormous misery prevailing there and emigration will take ever more colossal proportions. I have to confess honorably that this is too much of a good thing, especially the Bohemians, Polacks, Italians, Slovaks, Irishmen – pure Roman Catholics, a lazy, drunken, thieving pack of beggars. The green Germans of the last round are not worth much: bloated, lazy, dumb, gluttonous and full of the drunken devil. Pure Democrat voting cattle.[36]

Hurrah for Garfield!

As a German journalist to the *Gartenlaube* in Leipzig reported on the beginning of the American election campaign of 1880, "Preparations for the big campaign ... had begun this time earlier than usual in all parties." In fact former President Grant had announced as early as 1879 his interest in being renominated, and some senators loyal to him had gone as far as working for his nomination in their own states. The greatest resistance to Grant's third term came first from the German camp under Schurz, which was joined a

little later by Americans of the same conviction, most of them earlier Reform
Liberals. On 6 May 1880 this group met as "Independent Republicans" in St.
Louis to express their opposition to Grant's renomination and to the danger
that it posed to the reforms successfully begun. Along with Schurz, Emil
Preetorius also participated in this meeting. Hecker had to pass on the meeting as early as March on the grounds of health. Yet months before the campaign, when Grant's intentions became known, Hecker had encouraged creating "anti third-term organizations in all states and every county." "If the
Chicago Convention on 2 June were left to a free, reasonable expression of
its will, then Grant would not be nominated," Hecker wrote to Schurz in
February 1880, and continued, "I still have not given up hope that we will
get over this baleful episode. If the Sherman and Blaine people set more
organized resistance in motion, then the Grantists will be lost."[37]

The reasons for Hecker's hostility to Grant's third term were the same
as in 1872: Grant was a soldier and no statesman. For Grant's presidency,
Hecker wrote to Söhner, he would "not move one finger." He had already
formulated this in a public declaration:

> Almost fifty years of study have convinced me that there is no greater
> peril and mismanagement for a republic than to bring victorious field
> commanders to the head of the state. ... They bring the style and man-
> ner of the headquarters into the leadership of the state.

The art of command, he continued, was "so complex that the general who
rises high in war [has] no time for the art of state." As in 1872 Hecker's rejection was not motivated by any personal dislike of Grant – he had always
eschewed this assumption – but by his presumption that Grant should be
placed where he could best use his capacities, in the military. Hecker wrote
frequently in public and private, that Grant could always be empowered by
the president to take command of the armed forces in the case of a threatening second rebellion, and "his fame would then be immortal and without a
Caesarean or dictatorial smell." Hecker passed over in silence the fact that
it was precisely Grant's corrupt government and administration that had
led many Republicans to leave the party and create a distinct party or return
to the Democrats, as well as the fact that Schurz in particular, and he himself, would lose all influence under a new President Grant. He summarized
his "filtered" views, dictated entirely by his apparently "objective" passion-
less considerations and by historical studies, in a letter to the English-
language *Belleville Republican*.[38]

Hecker naturally knew quite well that the German vote, which he thought would "give the signal" this time was "overwhelmingly anti-third term and anti-Grant." Carl Schurz had also expressed himself vehemently against a third term for Grant, and in an article in the *Westliche Post* he threatened that he would move over to the Democratic Party if Grant were nominated. Hecker criticized this announcement as an ill-considered *faux pas* by Schurz and reminded Schurz, who was still a serving member of the cabinet, that Grant could gain by such an attitude among all the anti-reform forces of his own party, who were Schurz's enemies. Hecker further wanted to make it clear to Schurz that going over to the Democrats would be political suicide. He urged the secretary of the interior to consider,

> The rash threat in the *Westliche Post* to go over to the Democratic camp if Grant is nominated helps him more than it harms him, but it gives you more severe injury than the *Post* suspected. ... But listen to what a friend says. Under no circumstances may you appear in the Democratic camp. That would be political suicide. Look at Adams, Palmer, Trumbull, etc. They are dead so far as political activity is concerned. The Democrats might galvanize you for reasons of the election, but once in position, never again; they didn't want you already in 1872, let alone today. You are still young and have legs! You are too good and capable to become upset over every problem. You must preserve yourself within the Republican Party and keep to it, outside there is *nulla salus* ["no salvation"] for C. Schurz. ... You are too good to be a Democratic lemon for copperhead-rebel-punch. You must save yourself for better times.[39]

It is hard to determine whether Hecker's warning helped to keep Schurz in the Republican Party, but it is clear how serious Schurz was about leaving. But Hecker had correctly grasped one thing: Schurz's own skepticism and the difficult position of the man who would soon be the former secretary of the interior. Schurz's influence in Republican circles and among German-Americans was still large, and he had gained much in reputation in the course of his tenure under Hayes. But the opposition of a series of party members was just as large, including significantly some German-Americans. Joseph Shafer has tried to explain why Schurz preferred being a "political free lancer" or, as Trefousse calls it, to be independently active as a "mugwump." "It is true," Shafer says, that "the Hayes-Tilden contest had

seriously disrupted all reform aggregations, the Germans among the rest, so
that Schurz would not in future be looked up to by his fellow countrymen
as their political high priest."[40] German-American disunity and their generally dwindling influence as a political pressure group were obvious to
Schurz's eyes.

According to Hecker, securing the administrative success of the Hayes
government depended more than ever on the election of a qualified Republican successor. That man would be in a position to advance the economic
improvement that was already obvious by 1879, and unite all of the elements
of the fragmented party behind him. Beyond that, he should be an attractive
candidate for Northern-oriented Democrats. If Republicans were reasonable enough not to nominate Grant, Hecker wrote to Söhner, he knew one
man "who would be certainly elected, the old watch dog of the treasury for
all the Germans. Many Democrats of the best sort would also vote for him,
and that is E. B. Washburne. ... I am as active as possible in this direction."

Elihu Washburne, the friend of Germans in difficult times, who had
never feared Hecker's anticlerical tone and whose honesty had earned him
the nickname of a "watchdog of the treasury" in Congress, was once again,
as in 1860, Hecker's favorite candidate for the office of president. What
Hecker wrote privately to Söhner and Schurz about Washburne he also promoted publicly in the newspapers. Yet Hecker's support would have as little success as that of his hated *Illinois Staatszeitung*, which also promoted
Washburne's candidacy. Washburne renounced his own nomination out of
loyalty to Grant, and Hecker and others found themselves poorer by one
hope. But the final result of the Republican National Convention from 2 to
8 June 1880 in Chicago, would make him more conciliatory. After balloting
lasting for days, it was not Grant but James Abraham Garfield who was
finally nominated on the thirty-sixth ballot, by 399 votes against 357.
Garfield had originally come to Chicago to lead the Ohio delegation for
Sherman, but he quickly became the leader of the anti-Grant Republicans.[41]
The convention finally declared his nomination to be unanimous.

Hecker was overjoyed at this prospect, which he had not expected.
"Hurrah for Garfield," he wrote enthusiastically to Söhner.

> One could hardly find a better man. Originally a pure worker, then and
> still today a progressive farmer, brave soldier in his best years, no hyp-
> ocrite, [but rather a] sharp-sensed and learned statesman, no ring man
> or boss – he will gather the entire party ... around him, and we will win
> a victory that we have not had since 1860.

Hecker publicly spoke "laud and praise" to the 399 delegates who made Garfield's election possible, and he celebrated Garfield's nomination "as the best since Lincoln." To Söhner he wrote,

> The 399 of the convention have done it. Three cheers and a tiger for them! If I were healthy I would climb down into the cellar and drink some of the white [wine] that makes your legs so dubious even in its feather-white garb of innocence. ... When the campaign gets under way, everything will go crazy. God, that I cannot participate! A true misery for me.[42]

Garfield was a candidate entirely to Hecker's taste. Like Lincoln he was a thoroughly self-made man, a Westerner who, after growing up in straightened circumstances, quickly made himself a good name on the political stage, particularly in national economic questions. In 1859 Garfield was first elected senator from Ohio. At the outbreak of the Civil War he initially served as colonel of a volunteer regiment, like Hecker, ultimately rising to the rank of major general. Since 1862 he had served in the House of Representatives from the same district nine times in a row. There he finally took over the undisputed leadership of the Republican Party. He could look back on more than twenty years of political experience.

Because of his physical condition Hecker was not able to participate actively in the campaign for Garfield. He had to decline by telegraph an invitation to New York, the Democratic citadel. His health compelled him, he told Schurz, to protect himself "against every breeze, every exertion," and a lung ailment caused him occasional spells of shortness of breath "so that I have to be treated like a baby, to my regret, until a friendly stroke of the heart, brain or lung suddenly rescues me." When Caspar Butz invited Hecker to accompany him to Wisconsin on a speaking tour for Garfield in autumn 1880, Hecker had to decline. "I am soon to be seventy, and I cannot dare it any more. It could be for me like for old Chandler, and you could find me one morning dead in the bed of an inn." Because Hecker could no longer go on campaign tours, there remained "to him in this most critical of all times only the pen" as a useful instrument, serving him for the last time on his isolated farm. Distressed over what was expected to be a "close contest," he proceeded to combat the Democratic candidate in his best campaign style. "We *must* work with all our strength," Hecker explained his strategy to Söhner.

A Democratic administration would once more place in question the system established with effort and persistence, and cause it to tumble. The business world must and should see that seven-eighths of the Democratic Party does *not* belong to it but consists rather of louts, swindlers, priests and tramps. [We] … must block their revenge, which I have already started in a few *articles* and I have hammered away there adequately. I have to attack with the pen, for speech making is out of all question due to my physical ability.[43]

Hecker had become such a "strict Republican" that Caspar Butz occasionally mocked him over his "virtuosity of conviction." Hecker's zeal produced an extraordinarily large number of political articles in 1880, all dealing with the approaching election. In them he denounced the Democratic Party as one "which numbers in its ranks the greatest mass of the unknowing, raw, consciousless and greedy mobs, therefore the most inclined to follow a leader blindly." In several extended articles entitled "Andrew Johnson's Conspiracy" he linked the Democratic presidential candidate General Winfield Scott Hancock to the supposedly conspiratorial plans of the vice president to "Southernize" the Union by exchanging generals who were loyal to the Union for those who would be more useful to his goals. Yet Hancock was as respectable a candidate as Garfield. Although a Southerner he had fought on the Northern side at the outbreak of the Civil War out of a conviction for the preservation of the Union. Congress had expressed its recognition for his bravery at the Battle of Gettysburg. Hecker knew how essentially clever Hancock's nomination was. It was "a strong one," he wrote to Söhner, "but not strong enough to beat us with this West Pointer and general in active service in the regular army."

Precisely because Hancock's nomination was such a "strong" one, Hecker had to strain to diminish Hancock's attractiveness. In his article "The Nomination of General Winfield Scott Hancock" for the *Belleviller Zeitung*, the German colonel reflected loosely on "the general tendency to make candidates out of West Pointers." It is no wonder that none of the presidents recruited from West Point gave any occasion for praise in his historical review. Remarking that one needed "an experienced statesman for domestic economic and political development and the relations to foreign powers," Hecker was merely repeating the skepticism that he had expressed about Grant, which he now transferred to Hancock. In an article entitled "All Sorts of Things from the Old Man," Hecker formulated what he saw as the most important question of the campaign. This time, he said, special care had to be taken with the effect of the nomination overseas, where the experience of the president in national economic questions played a large role. Naturally Garfield, after almost twenty years in the House of Representative, was superior to Hancock in his political experience and his knowledge as a statesman. In an article in the *Westliche Post* on "Hancock and Gettysburg," Hecker finally placed Hancock's military merit in question by strongly relativizing it, attributing to others just as much, if not more, credit for the successful result of the battle.[44]

In contrast to Hancock the businessman English, nominated by the Democrats to be vice president, offered more of a target for criticism. English, who came from Indiana, had been nominated as vice president for geographic reasons. As a "Westerner" he balanced Hancock, who came from the East. However, he was particularly suspect to the settlers in the West, who had not forgotten that, in the period of the conflict over the territories of Kansas and Nebraska, he had been the author of that "English Bill" on Douglas's behalf that public land be offered to settlers as a bribe if they ratified the pro-slavery constitution. English had supposedly always known that the population would reject this offer, which was ultimately supposed to resolve the matter. Hecker formally sought material to attack English and inquired of Söhner,

> English of Indiana indeed lives in Indianapolis. Give me precise details about him, *in confidence*. He is supposed to have been a Knight of the Golden Circle. Is that true and can it be proved? How are prospects in Indiana concerning the election? Do we have good prospects there, or what?

Because membership in a secret racist organization could not be proven against English, Hecker was well advised to avoid falsely accusing him in public. Instead he wrote a general article about secret organizations in order to present "the political master-labor means of the Solid South," with which the South had managed to consolidate the influence of the Democratic Party with the aid of the exclusive and intimidating tactics of secret organizations, bringing about "the total disappearance not only of earlier Republican majority, but also of the entire Republican vote" through disturbances and hindering actions.[45] He then recited all the acts of terror that could be brought into any connection with secret organizations. This tactic was more

than remeniscent of "waving the bloody shirt" in the 1850s. Likewise
Hecker had to return to party positions of the past because there was no
central, current campaign theme.

Garfield's clear victory – with a small majority of only 10,000 in the
popular vote the electoral vote was still clear at 214 votes against 155 – was
accompanied by the Republicans' regaining control in both houses of
Congress. On the very day of the election, Hecker wrote to Söhner, enthused
by the happy result. His state of health prevented him from celebrating otherwise than "in the spirit." He could drink no alcohol because of illness,
and so he lifted his glass in an imaginary toast to Garfield, simulating his
hiccups, caused by his chronic shortness of breath .

> I hear myself making a splendid, hick, speech, hick, ladies and gentle-
> men (hick), what a glorious day (hick). Hurrah for Garfield (hick, hick,
> hick) – that damned sucker (hick) Morrison has unfortunately been
> elected, but barely; … Our county is Republican, and my Summerfield
> district glorious.

The campaign between Garfield and Hancock, as contemporaries
noted, was remarkable for "the lack of major issues." Hecker's diverse articles were a good example of the randomness of campaign rhetoric and
themes. He had promoted Garfield, but all he could express at Garfield's
election was his basic desire that this man would guarantee the continuation of the Republican Party's economic policy. The party was not yet the
clear representative of the interests of industry and capital or the promoter
of imperialist expansion that it would be at the turn of the century, but
development in that direction was already clear, and Hecker's own course
appeared entirely determined by it. In a letter praising Garfield's presidency, Hecker described to Söhner why Garfield, and with him the Republican
Party, was so important to him. Many people in Germany, he wrote, had
sought information from him about how they could invest their wealth in
the United States in the event of Garfield's election and the Republican
Party's victory, since "over there [they live] in a gunpowder tower" and
"the burden of taxes is beyond all conception, so that people who want to
live from the interest on what they have saved can no longer make it."
"They write me," Hecker continued, "that people overseas will let their capital flow over here if we win. What paper other than USA's do you regard
as worth recommending?" he asked Söhner to discuss this with a few busi-

nessmen and "bankers" and give him their answers.[46] The United States was on its way to becoming the leading nation on earth, and its economic prosperity, which Hecker desired to protect and promote, would show the justice of the only political system that he respected, the republic.

1 Wittke, *Refugees*, 257; also Schafer, *Schurz*, 205. See, for example, his first reform speech held in Chicago in 1874, *TISZ*, 21 October 1874. Foner, *Reconstruction*, 221.

2 See also Schafer, *Schurz*, 205-6.

3 "Männer und Parteien," *TISZ*, 27 July 1876; emphasis in the original. Kenneth E. Davison, *The Presidency of Rutherford B. Hayes* (Westport, CT, 1972), 110; also Trefousse, *Schurz*, 228 ff. Wittke, *Refugees*, 258.

4 *TISZ*, 19 August 1874; reform speech 1; Hecker's second reform speech in *TISZ*, 23 October 1874. "'Hecker und die schwarzen Schimmel,' Brief an einen nicht genannten Parteifreund, Summerfield, 21. August 1876," FHP, box 9. Edmund Jüssen, "Eine höfliche Antwort auf Fr. Hecker's grobe Kritik," Chicago, 24 August 1876, *TISZ*, 25 August 1876.

5 Between 1874 and 1877 a number of letters reached FH from Republican politicians either asking for information or his help for future state, county or local elections, for example, D. L. Philips, editor of the *Illinois State Journal* to FH, Springfield, 25 May 1876; R. L. Oglesby to FH, 26 March 1877; Horace Rublee, Republican Central Committee, Madison, WI, to FH, 18 October 1877, all in FHP, box 3, folder 33. "Friedrich Hecker's Rede in der Washington Halle in Indianapolis," *Indianapolis Deutsche Zeitung* [n.d., 1876], FHP, box 9; later he once wrote, "let me add that unless one single hour in May 1872 I was radically and forever cured of all separate leagueings, (Sonderbuendeley is the pregnant German word)." "'Colonel Hecker defines the Duties of Patriots,' FH to Mr. T. W. Eckert, Editor of *Belleville Republican*, Summerfield, Ill.," 15 March 1880, FHP, box 9. Foner, *Reconstruction*, 227, 228-29.

6 G. Hanigan to FH, Chicago, 5 December 1874, FHP, box 3, folder 33.

7 "Rutherford Birchard Hayes," *DAB*, vol. 8, New York, 1932, 446-51, here 449. FH to Charles Söhner, Summerfield, St, Clair Cty, 5 March 1877, FHP, box 3, folder 38; also "Friedrich Hecker über die Hayes'sche Politik," FH to the editor of the *Chicago Neue Freie Presse*, Summerfield, 1 May 1877, FHP, box 9; also FH to Schurz, 4 March 1877, Schurz Papers; on Hayes's political considerations on the one term, see Davison, *The Presidency*, XV, 157-58. Rutherford B. Hayes to FH, Columbus, 30 August 1876, FHP, box 3, folder 33.

8 *TISZ*, 11 September 1876; *TISZ*, 4 September 1876; before he went to Dresden as American consul, Brentano was editor of the *Illinois Staatszeitung* in Chicago and a friend of Wilhelm Rapp; see also "Brentano's Ehrentag," *TISZ*, 2 November 1876; although he was a Republican, the *Staatszeitung* supported Brentano as a candidate for Chicago in the congressional elections. *WP*, daily, 27 October 1876; *TISZ*, 27 October 1876. Hecker's Chicago speech in *Chicago Freie Presse* [n.d., October, 1876], FHP, box 9; shortened version in *TISZ*, 28 October 1876.

9 Alongside his Chicago speech, see also "Friedrich Hecker's Rede in der Washington Halle in Indianapolis," *Indianapolis Deutsche Zeitung* [n. d., 1876]; also "Die drohende Gefahren. Ausfuhrungen einer in Summerfield, Ills., am 5. August 1876 gehaltenen Rede von Friedrich

Hecker," *WP* [n. d.], 1876; also "Friedrich Hecker's Rede, gehalten vor der republikanischen Massenversammlun, an der Eck von Race- u. 12. Strasse, am Samstag, 23 September 1876." All in FHP, box 9.

[10] The concept of sufficiency also played a role in the thought of some founding fathers, see on what follows the useful essay by Gerald Stourzh, "Die tugenhafte Republik. Montesquieus Begriff der 'vertu' und die Anfange der Vereinigten Staaten von Amerika," idem, *Wege der Grundrechtsdemokratie. Studien zur Begriffs- und Institutionsgeschichte des liberalen Verfassungsstaates,* (Vienna; Cologne, 1989),117-36, here 119. Montesquieu developed his idea of a *vertu politique* in his *Esprit des lois,* book 3, chapter 3; see on this also Arthur Fickert, *Montesquieus und Rousseaus Einfluss auf den vormärzlichen Liberalismus Badens* (Leipzig, 1914), 11; naturally FH already knew the "kalokagathia" of the Greeks, "Roman virtus" and the "the virtue of a Montesquieu," see *VSB,* 107. öS (12 July 1844), 326. As a survey, see James P. Young, "Amerikanisches politisches Denken: Von der Revolution bis zum Biirgerkrieg," Iring Fetscher, Herfried Münker, eds., *Pipers Handbuch der politischen Ideen* (Munich; Zürich, 1985), chapter 12, 617-53, on Jefferson here 639 (quoting from *Notes on the State of Virginia).* "Brief von Friedrich Hecker an die Illinois Staatszeitung" [n.d.], printed in *TISZ,* 3 May 1873; emphasis as spread-type in the original. *VSB.* 44. öS (28 March 1848), 335. Friedrich Hecker to Charles Söhner, Summerfield, 7 February 1877, FHP, box 3, folder 38. The connection between machinery, overproduction and the "addiction to enjoyment," "imaginary needs" and luxury goods, returns often in FH's letters, e.g. letter to Söhner, Summerfield, 14 April 1878, FHP, box 3, folder 38.

[11] FH to Charles Söhner, 28 February 1879, FHP, box 3, folder 38.

[12] See FH, "Das blutige Hemd," *WP*[n. d., 1876], FHP, box 9. "Die drohenden Gefahren. Rede von Friedrich Hecker," *WP* [n. d.], 1876. On the reduction of rights, see Foner, *Reconstruction,* 247-48; on savings in education, ibid., 249-51; also Rudolph Doehn, "Präsidentenwahlen in der Union. Streiflichter zum Verständniss des gegenwartigen Wahlkampfes," *GL,* 1880, 484-88, here 487.

[13] FH to Charles Söhner, 16 October 1876, FHP, box 3, folder 38.

[14] Foner, *Reconstruction,* 236-37, 242, 243-44; Schafer, *Schurz,* 212.

[15] See on this the two letters of FH to Carl Schurz, 9 January and 9 February 1877, Schurz Papers. FH discussed articles in the *New American Review* and more recent books dealing in general way with the Constitution; also see his letter to Emil Frey [n. d., February 1877], Staatsarchiv des Kantons Basel-Stadt, Sig. PA 485 DXI165. FH to Carl Schurz, Summerfield, 4 March 1877, Schurz Papers; see also FH to Charles Söhner, 5 March 1877, FHP, box 3, folder 38, where he uses almost the same words to describe the positive aspects of Hayes's election.

[16] FH to Charles Söhner, Summerfield, 5 March 1877, FHP, box 3, folder 38; also to Emil Frey [n. d., February 1877]: "Despite my 66 years I could not restrain myself from participating in the struggle with my last strength when I saw what elements desired to seize the ship of state. Wherever the fresh rebel office-hungry mutiny prevails, along with the Roman priests with their blindly-following sheep-herds, must be regarded as rotten and ruined, and there the flag I belong to does not stand." Staatsarchiv des Kantons Basel-Stadt, Sig. PA 486 DXI165. Foner, Reconstruction, 236-37, 244. "Friedrich Hecker iiber die Hayes'sche Politik, Friedrich Hecker an den Redakteur der *Chicago Neuen Freien Presse,*" Summerfield, 1 May 1877, FHP, box 9; emphasis in the original.

17 On Schurz's term as Interior Secretary, Trefousse, *Schurz*, 235-52. FH to Carl Schurz, Summerfield, 4 March 1877, underlining in the original; FH to Carl Schurz, Summerfield, 4 March 1877, Schurz Papers.

18 "George Schneider," *DAB*, vol. 16, New York, 1935, 446-47, here 447. Carl Schurz to FH, Department of the Interior, Washington, 22 April 1877, Carl Schurz to FH, Washington, 1 February 1878, FHP, box 3, folder 35; Caspar Butz to FH, Washington, 1 February 1878, FHP, box 3, folder 33.

19 Carl Wittke, "Carl Schurz and Rutherford B. Hayes," *The Ohio Historical Quarterly*, 65 (October, 1956), 337-55; also Davidson, *Presidency*, 109-12. Schafer, *Schurz*, 214. FH to Carl Schurz, Summerfield, St. Clair County, I11., 25 June 1879, Schurz Papers. Davison, *Presidency*, 111. Carl Schurz to FH, Washington, 29 August 1877, FHP, box 3, folder 35.

20 FH to Carl Schurz, Summerfield, 9 February 1877; FH to Carl Schurz, Summerfield, 4 March 1877, FH to Carl Schurz, Summerfield, St. Clair County, 25 June 1879, Schurz Papers. See FH's review of the constitutional treatise of Hermann von Hoist, *Verfassung und Demokratie der Vereinigten Staaten von Nordamerika*, in *TISZ*, 13 March 1874. FH to Emil Frey [n. d., February 1877], Staatsarchiv des Kantons Basel Stadt, Sign. PA 485 D XI, 165, printed in Frei, *Hecker in den USA*, 53-55; unfortunately the original has no date, but from the information in the letter itself it can be dated to February 1877. In the Papers are to be found the binding of a printed version of the Swiss constitution in German, French and Italian, and it is possible that the contents of the binding with additional material was either in FH's library and lost, or it was sent right to Schurz with additional information.

21 "Hayes," *DAB*, 451; FH to Carl Schurz, Summerfield, St. Clair County, I11., 8 May 1879, Schurz Papers.

22 On Hayes's financial policy, see the chapter, "The Money-Question," Davison, *Presidency*, 174-81; also Trefousse, *Schurz*, 230. See FH, "Hartgeld-Wahrheiten und Papiergeld-Irrthümer. Wie es kommen würde," articles 1-9, *WP* [n. d., 1878], FHP, box 9.

23 Hayes, *Diary*, 21 March 1879, quoted in Davison, *Presidency*, 163. FH to Carl Schurz, Summerfield, St. Clair County, I11., 8 May 1879, FH to Carl Schurz, Summerfield, St. Clair County, 25 June 1879, Schurz Papers. FH to Emil Preetorius, 7 March 1880, *WP* [n. d., 1879], FHP, box 9. FH, "Der Beginn der zweiten Rebellion und Secession eines echten vollblut-mexicanischen Pronunciamentos," *WP* [n.d., 1879], FHP, box 9. Hayes made more use of his veto than any previous president; on his successful effort to win a proper position for the executive, see "The Use of Executive Power," in Davison, *Presidency*, 155-73.

24 "The Great Railway Strike," Davison, *Presidency*, 145-54; Foner, *Politics*, 127.

25 See on this Foner, *Reconstruction*, 245-46.

26 FH, "Betrachtungen iiber den Communistenstaat," article 1-7, *WP* [n.d., 1877]; "Einige historische Betrachtungen iiber Communismus," *Neue Freie Presse*, Chicago [n. d., 1877]; "Grundlosigkeit der Furcht vor dem Communismus in der Union," *Neue Freie Presse*, Chicago [n.d., 1877]; FH, "Bedeutung der beabsichtigten Ausnahmsgesetzte in Teutschland trotz der bereits bestehenden Strafgesetze," article 1-3, *WP* [n. d., 1878], FHP, box 9.

27 FH, "Einige historische Betrachtungen über Communismus," "Grundlosigkeit der Furcht," as in the previous note.

28 FH, "Einige historische Betrachtungen über Communismus," as in the previous note.

29 Friedrich Kapp, "Der jüngste Aufstand der Eisenbahnarbeiter in den Vereinigten Staaten," *Preussische Jahrbücher*, 40 (1877), no. 4, 398-424. Kapp's view on the socialist laws, which he supported, Hinners, *Exil*, 254, 268-71; Hecker strictly rejected them. FH to Charles Söhner, Summerfield, 24 August 1877, FHP, box 3, folder 38.

30 Friedrich Kapp on the American July riots in *TISZ*, 19 November 1877. Hinners, *Exil*, 254.

31 FH to Charles Söhner, Summerfield, 21 December 1876, FHP, box 3, folder 38. Carl Schurz to FH, Washington, 29 August 1877, FHP, box 3, folder 35. Kapp, "Aufstand," 399.

32 Carl Schurz to FH, Washington, 29 August 1877, FHP, box 3, folder 35. FH to Carl Schurz, Summerfield, St. Clair County, Ill., 8 May 1879, Schurz Papers. FH, "Der Beginn der zweiten Rebellion ...," *WP* [n. d., 1879], FHP, box 9.

33 FH to Schurz, 8 May 1879, Schurz Papers. FH to Charles Söhner, Summerfield, 12 December 1878, FHP, box 3, folder 38. FH, "Das farbige Stimmrecht," *WP* [n. d., 1880], FHP, box 9; emphasis in the original. Macauley, *Recollections on Mirabeau*, quoted in ibid.; FH mentioned Macauley often in his letters, see, for example, FH to E. B. Washburne, Lebanon, St. Clair County, 9. December 1861, Washburne Papers.

34 Foner, *Reconstruction*, 252, 254.

35 FH, "Der Beginn der zweiten Rebellion ...," *WP* [n. d., 1879], FHP, box 9. FH to Charles Söhner, Summerfield, 4 April 1879, FHP, box 3, folder 38. FH to Carl Schurz, Summerfield, St. Clair County, III, 8 May 1879, Schurz Papers.

36 FH to Charles Söhner, Summerfield, St. Clair Co., Ill., 2 December 1880, FHP, box 3, folder 38.

37 Rudolf Doehn, "Prasidentenwahlen in der Union. Streiflichter zum Verständniss des gegenwärtigen Wahlkampfes," *GL*, 1880, 484-88. FH to Emil Preetorius, Summerfield, 7 March 1880, *WP* [n. d., March, 1880], FHP, box 9. FH, "Zur Frage des 3. Termins. Antwort auf den Artikel der New Yorker allgemeinen Zeitung vom 28. Januar des Jahres 1879," *WP*, daily [n. d., 1879], FHP, box 9. FH to Carl Schurz, Sumerfield, 14 February 1880, Schurz Papers; underlining in the original; Sherman and Blaine were both presidential candidates of the anti-Grant group.

38 FH to Charles Söhner, Summerfield, 22 April 1880, FHP, box 3, folder 38. FH, "Zur Frage des 3. Termins," as in the previous note; FH to Emil Preetorius, Summerfield, 7 March 1880, printed in *WP* [n. d., March, 1880, FHP, box 9; see also FH to Charles Söhner, Summerfield, 13 March 1880, FHP, box 3, folder 38. "Colonel Hecker defines the Duties of Patriots," FH to Mr. T. W. Eckert, editor of the *Belleville Republican*, Summerfield, Ill., 15 March 1880, FHP, box 9.

39 FH to Carl Schurz, Summerfield, 14 February 1880, Schurz Papers.

40 Schafer, *Schurz*, 224. Trefousse, *Schurz*, 253.

41 FH to Charles Söhner, Summerfield, 28 January 1880; also his letter to Söhner, Summerfield, 13 March 1880, both in FHP, box 3, folder 38. See *BZ*, 1 June 1871; during the Franco-Prussian

War Washburne was in Paris and took Germans living there, among others, under protection against French attack. FH to Schurz, 14 February 1880, Schurz Papers. FH, "Colonel Hecker defines the Duties of Patriots." Peter H. Olden, Harvey Wish, "The Influence of the Illinois Staats-Zeitung upon American Politics," *AGR*, 6 (Fenruary, 1940), 30-32, 39, here 32. "Elihu B. Washburne," *DAB*, vol. 19, New York, 1936, 504-6, here 505. "James Abraham Garfield," *DAB*, vol. 7, New York, 1931,145-50, here 147.

42 FH to Charles Söhner, Summerfield, 10 June 1880, FHP, box 3, folder 38. See the article, "Lob und Preis den 399 Delegierten der Chicago Convention von Friedrich Hecker," *Chicago Neue Presse* [n. d., 1880], FHP, box 9. FH to Charles Söhner, Summerfield, 10 June 1880, FHP, box 3, folder 38. FH to Elihu Washburne, Summerfield, 12 February 1881, Washburne Papers.

43 FH to Carl Schurz, 14 February 1880, Schurz Papers. FH to Carl Butz, here quoted from Butz, "Erinnerungen an Friedrich Hecker," *WP*, daily, 8 May 1881. FH, "Zur Frage des 3. Termins," *WP*, daily [n.d., 1879], FHP, box 9. FH to Charles Söhner, Summerfield, 28 June 1880, FHP, box 3, folder 38; emphasis and underlining in the original.

44 Butz, "Erinnerungen, 2. Teil." FH, "Die sich, in Zeiten nationaler Krise und Gefahr, 'Unabhängige' nennenden und ihre Verantwortlichkeit gegeniiber der Nation," articles 1-3, *WP*, daily [n. d., 1880], Hecker Papers, box 9. FH, "Die Verschwörung unter President Andrew Johnson, alle Resultate des Sieges über die Rebellion und Secession zu vernichten, seine Mitverschworenen und Helfershelfer, und die Rolle, welche General Hancock als Werkzeug Johnson's dabei spielte," articles 1-3, *St. Louis Tribüne* [n.d., 1880], FHP, box 9. FH to Charles Söhner, Summerfield, 28 June 1880, FHP, box 3, folder 38. FH, "Die Nomination von General Winfield Scott Hancock," articles 1-3, *BZ* [n d., 1880], FHP, box 9. "Allerlei vom Alten, Ansichten von Friedrich Hecker," *BZ* [n.d., 1880], FHP, box 9. FH, "Hancock & Gettysburg," *WP*, daily [n.d., 1880], FHP, box 9.

45 "William Hayden English," *DAB*, vol. 6, New York, 1931,167-68. FH to Charles Söhner, Summerfield, 28 June 1880, FHP, box 3, folder 38; underlining in the original. FH, "Die geheimen Organisationen der ehemaligen Rebellenstaaten, ihre Macht und Bedeutung," articles 1-2, *BZ* [n. d., 1880], FHP, box 9; also his article on the Ku Klux Klan, *WP* [n. d., 1880], FHP, box 4, folder 42.

46 The Republican electoral district had repeatedly elected the Democrat William Rails Morrison to the House of Representatives despite voting for a Republican president. Morrison was a member of the Congress from 1873 to 1887, "Morrison," *DAB*, vol. 13, New York, 1934, 232-33, here 232. FH to Charles Söhner, Summerfield, 4 November 1880, FHP, box 3, folder 38. "Winfield Scott Hancock," *DAB*, vol. 8, New York, 1932, 221-22, here 222.

Obverse of the Medallion commemorating Friedrich Hecker issued on the occasion of the 23rd National Turner Festival of the North American Turner League in St. Louis in 1881. Missouri Historical Society.

XI

THE PRINCIPLE OF LIBERTY:
COSMOPOLITAN UNITY VERSUS THE ETHNIC NATION

Farewell to Hecker

Hecker was not just anti-clerical, he was "notoriously a man of complete unbelief in religious matters." When he reflected on death, he felt that it was best accomplished in connection with illness, which seemed to him most suited to the act of dying. He himself hoped for a stroke because he expected that to be a sudden, painless end. Time and again he painted a picture of how wonderful the news of his death would be to Democrats and priests, who could jubilate "that the old oaf has finally been hauled away by the devil." He wanted to die in the manner common in his family. "My good mother departed with a word of wit ..., my unforgettable brother slept his last with a jest, and I think I will do that too." Otherwise Hecker expressed himself with peasant-like crudity on the subject of death, directly and often meanly. "In fact 999999 out of a million of humanity is nothing at the end but dung, muck, dust, dirt." Hecker the farmer reviewed the transitory nature of all that is earthly in a letter to Söhner.

> People would rather have joy in every little bit, drink, drop, etc., etc., that they enjoy at this beast-university of humanity and existence. I regret no madness, but rather the intellectual efforts exerted in heartless, pointless donkeys' bridges.

Hecker was as true to the Bible as his worst Catholic enemy in his interpretation – and at the same time a personal confession – of the text of Ecclesiastes from the Old Testament: "Everything has its season. To be a beast and to be spirit, and a reasonable mixture of both is the best."[1]

When Charles Söhner invited Hecker at the start of December 1880 to spend Christmas with his family in Indianapolis, Hecker immediately declared him to be insane; Hecker was barely able to go to St. Louis, and even then he had to pay for his short trip with a long turn in bed. Weak, infected lungs, which he sought to cure with a journey to Colorado, made breathing difficult. From the start of February 1881 he was continually

Friedrich Heckers Leichenbegängniß am 28. März 1881 bei Summerville, St. Clair Co., Illinois. — Herr Preetorius hält die Leichenrede. Nach einer Skizze von Armand Balder. (S. 279.)

"Friedrich Hecker's Funeral on 28 March 1881 in [Summerfield], St. Clair County, Illinois. Mr. [Emil] Preetorius delivers the funerary oration." Friedrich Hecker Papers, Western Historical Manuscripts, University of Missouri – St. Louis.

under a physician's care, but his health deteriorated during a "killing winter" marked by "colossal masses of snow." On 7 March Hecker informed Caspar Butz of his condition and wrote him, "the old machine is finished. March will take me. My pains in the heart and lungs are such that I have given up hope of recovery." Hecker's family and friends were concerned. "Dear Friend! Father is seriously ill and yesterday we thought he would die," Hecker's eldest son Arthur wrote to Charles Söhner on a postcard. He continued, "This morning it is a bit better but still in a critical condition. It is a lung infection. I will inform you how it goes tomorrow." Arthur kept his word, but the news that he sent from Summerfield to Indianapolis via Western Union held no good tidings. "Father died at half past eight this evening."[2]

St. Louis papers reported the news of the death the next morning. "To the Germans in America and to many of them in Europe, there could scarce be tidings more sorrowful, as Hecker was to them a demigod," wrote the English-language *Missouri Republican*. And the *Westliche Post*, which lost its most popular contributor with Hecker, placed "its pen to the most painful obituary that we have ever written in our life. … Even if we will bury many a good man and have many more alive, we have never lost a Hecker before, and a Hecker can never again die for us." In memory of the departed the flags on the courthouse in Belleville and on the building of the *Belleviller Zeitung* flew at halfstaff. Hecker's deeds on both sides of the ocean were laid again before the readers over the next few days in many German-American newspapers. So far his American years went, three accomplishments were chosen for particular recognition: his work in the founding of the Republican Party, his selfless commitment in the Civil War, and his journalistic activity. It was the last, in particular, that was extensively stressed. "His correspondence, signed 'F. H.' in the Westliche Post and other German papers, was widely read, and his reputation as a writer is scarcely second to that which he achieved as a speaker," said the *Missouri Republican*. The *Westliche Post* also saw Hecker's work as a writer as the greatest accomplishment of his "political activity." The *Belleviller Zeitung* especially thanked him for wielding such a "sharp pen" in the struggle against "temperance fanatics," just as "earlier [he had wielded] a sharp sword." Even in distant California, Hecker's Luther-like style of journalism was famous, as the *California Demokrat* reminded its readers.

Hecker was tirelessly active in German-American journalism, and in this area a gap has opened with his death that will be hard to fill. His style was earthy, ultra-earthy, often even baroque, and his arguments fell like club blows on the heads of his adversaries. Just as he could be a faithful and warm-hearted friend, he was a profound hater, and if ever sympathy or rejection were expressed in his writing, it occurred with an openness that eschewed cowardly phrases, steering straight for the target, neither complementing friends nor sparing an enemy. Hecker's influence on the form of politics in the republic cannot be set high enough.[3]

That Hecker was respected as a political personality at least in his own state of Illinois was shown by the fact that, on receiving news of his death, the legislature adjourned its session. The following resolution was passed unanimously:

Since we have just heard the sad news of the death of Colonel F. Hecker, it is resolved that we see in the death of this splendid and patriotic citizen and soldier the loss of one of its most magnificent sons, and out of respect for the memory of the outstanding departed the house adjourns.[4]

In the following days the Central Turner Hall in St. Louis became the place of negotiation for many German associations to agree on common resolutions and the course of the burial. As early as the evening of 25 March there was a meeting of the North American Turner League, which resolved that all members should participate in the burial "in person." That same evening the St. Louis Turner Society called a special meeting, resolving that, "we German Turners in particular mourn his loss most deeply as a man who promoted the life of our society through stimulating speeches and lectures, and who helped to make a permanent place for German Turnerism in America." They also resolved to send a mourning committee to Summerfield to express sympathy and to participate in the burial in large numbers. A day later many "of our most prominent German citizens met in the Central Turner Hall to make the arrangements necessary for the funeral of Friedrich Hecker. It was agreed to publish an appeal in the newspapers calling on all friends of the old fighter to participate in the burial and to convene on Monday, 28 March, on the 8 a.m. train from St. Louis to Summerfield.[5]

The burial was set for 1 p.m., and the return was to take place at 4 p.m. Not only Germans gathered in St. Louis; the French Revolutionary Union also met in its club to pay "proper tribute in eloquent words to the virtues of the immortal hero of freedom" and to select a "committee of five to represent the group at the burial the next day." While consultations were going forward in St. Louis, veterans of the 24th and 82nd Illinois Volunteers (The Hecker regiments) were meeting in Chicago to express their sorrow and to choose representatives to travel to Summerfield.⁶ In New York the Society of Forty-Eighters gathered a day before Hecker's burial under the presidency of General Franz Sigel for an "extraordinary meeting to pass resolutions concerning the death of Friedrich Hecker." The statement of this society, published by German newspapers in Southwest Germany, is interesting for the self-perception of its members, who had made it their mission to preserve the memory of 1848. Unlike many political refugees of the revolution who had remained in Europe, most German-American Forty-Eighters hesitated to discuss conditions in their old country. It appears instead that, like Hecker, those in New York and indeed in the whole of the United States, had lived long enough in a republic, away from Germany, not to have lost their faith in the justice of their cause or at least to cling to the justice of what they had done then. Without question this had been the true purpose of founding the society. In New York they now sought a positive relationship to their own revolutionary action in their old fatherland. For that reason one of the resolutions read,

> Resolved, that the striving, the open struggle for the rights of the people, for its unity and liberty, was the true and only method to respond to the rule of injustice and force; that it had opened the eyes not only of the people but also of the governments and contributed mightily to bringing about the important political changes that have been introduced since the years of 1848 and 1849.

As in many later speeches memorializing Hecker, it was not forgotten in New York to bestow special honor on the American Hecker. This was also a defense of one's own cause, for even if the Revolution of 1848 had failed, they wanted to see the struggle taken up on American soil in 1861 as a simply consistent continuation of the liberal strivings of yore; the victory of that "just cause" in 1865 was confirmation in retrospect for the veterans of 1848.

> Resolved, that we recognize the great services that our departed friend performed to such a high degree in his adopted fatherland through his splendid capacities, his pure, truly republican character, his agitation with word and writing, as well as his patriotic participation as a soldier and leader in the struggle for the Union. His name, his spirit and his

Tombstone of "Col. Frederic Hecker, 82nd Illinois Infantry" in Summerfield Cemetery. Photograph taken by Steven Rowan.

deeds, the example of a glorious and honorable life that he gave, are a great, unforgettable heritage and will live forever as a precious memory in our midst.

A transcription of the resolutions was sent to the family of the departed "as an expression of our pain and as a sign of our respect and sympathy for those left behind."[7]

The speeches at Hecker's burial, the memorials in his name and the two solemn unveilings later of monuments in St. Louis and Cincinnati were witness above all to his power as an identifier for the political refugees of the Revolution. But at the same time they were witness to the ambivalence that this group never resolved toward its old country, and to their effort to hang onto a republican tradition that had necessarily overpowered the ethnically determined nation-state. The resolutions, declarations and memorial letters of German-American societies and individual German-Americans were both political and cultural demonstrations. So also the entire burial itself – like a ritual – became a demonstration of the self-perception of the German-American Forty-Eighters. How much Hecker's burial was thought of as a self-dramatization of the German Forty-Eighters could be seen in the prose of the *Westliche Post*.

> The little cemetery in Summerfield, which receives on Monday the remains of Friedrich Hecker, will become even more than Uffnau in Switzerland, where the Hecker of the sixteenth century, Ulrich von Hutten, is buried, a place of pilgrimage for not only Germans, but for friends of liberty of all nations. But our immortal friend was also a true Teuton in his cosmopolitan elements that makes us Germans so sympathetic everywhere on the globe to those "who are troubled and burdened" and are being unjustly oppressed![8]

Hecker's burial in Summerfield was purportedly the largest ever to take place in St. Clair County. More than four hundred people left St. Louis at an early hour to travel to Summerfield on a train of the Ohio and Mississippi Railroad. All Turner societies were represented through large delegations. Several singing societies, such as the Social Sängerchor and the Germania Sängerbund, had sent groups. In addition private persons came, including of course many political companions from both the Old and the New World. Chicago was represented by Caspar Butz, Georg Schneider, and by veterans of the 24th and 82nd Illinois Volunteers. In Summerfield the

mourners from St. Louis met around seven to eight hundred other mourners from the neighboring towns of Belleville, Summerfield, Mascoutah and
Highland who had gone to the farm to take leave of the deceased. The
funeral procession from Hecker's farm to the cemetery, about two miles distant, consisted of 150 vehicles. It included Hecker's honor guard, who
accompanied the coffin on foot, followed by a carriage full of laurel wreaths
to be placed on the grave by various societies.[9] Only a few hundred people
were privileged to hear the speeches given at the grave. It was all the more
important, then, for the newspapers to print the addresses unabridged.

Emil Preetorius, publisher of the *Westliche Post*, started with his speech,
followed by Caspar Butz, who told the story of his friendship with Hecker.
Georg Schneider declared Hecker a part of the history of two hemispheres.
Carl Lüdeking praised Hecker's "self-selected exile" and stressed that the
"free man" always creates his own "fatherland." Judge Rombauer spoke for
the Hungarian republicans and praised the cosmopolitan Hecker in a
speech in English. Dr. Hugo Starkloff spoke for the North American Turner
League. J. G. Eberhardt took the podium for the Swiss republicans, followed
by Mr. Seguemor, who spoke in French for the French republicans, empha-
sizing for all present that cosmopolitan principle that must be stronger than
any one nation. *"Pour lui, il n'y avait pas de frontieres … pour ce grand coeur il
n'y avait pas de nationalité, il n'y avait qu'un principe."* ["For him, there were
no frontiers, for this great heart there was no nationality; he had only a principle."] Major Frank Backof laid on the grave a wreath of immortality with
a black-red-gold ribbon on behalf of the Forty-Eighters. Captain Erbe spoke
in the name of his old companions in the Hecker regiments. Christian Stifel
laid a wreath as a representative of the St. Louis Turner Society. Lorenzo
Anderlini laid a wreath on behalf of Italian republicans after a speech in
Italian. F. F. Fritzsche, a Social Democrat from Germany who happened to
be passing through at the time, spoke on behalf of oppressed Germans.
Lieutenant Governor Körner, asked to speak by Hecker's family, did not
ignore his political differences with Hecker in his speech, but he praised
Hecker's independence and consistency as a virtue rare in America. Hecker
was without a doubt, Körner stressed, "an earnest worker for the greatness
and prosperity of our country." It was, as the *Westliche Post* reported on the
ceremonies a day later, as "moving as it was a grand demonstration," and
the speeches at the grave became "a true contest of eloquence in the most
noble sense." The *Badischer Landesbote* wrote that Hecker's burial was "a
grandiose people's demonstration," an "elevating memorial" such "as only
a few men ever receive."[10]

On the basis of a strong demand from the old homeland, the *Belleviller Zeitung* printed several hundred extra copies of its weekly edition, and announcing in a businesslike manner, "Everything concerning the great departed and his burial is gathered in this edition, and we send it free to any address in Germany for five cents." Whether Hecker was really also first in the hearts of people "over there" might be doubted after a glance at the reaction in Germany to the news of his death. The German resonance to Hecker's death strongly recalled the conflicts during his German visit and also explained why subsequent false reports on Hecker's American life could establish themselves. While democratic papers, primarily from the Southwest German region, wrote friendly obituaries, the National Liberal press retained its chilly view that Hecker had already been "dead" for some time, which the German-American *Belleviller Zeitung* found rather "mean."[11]

Within Germany the number of obituaries rose as one went from north to south and from east to west. The *Neue Preussische Zeitung* stubbornly remained silent on the death of the Baden rebel with the exception of a short notice under the rubric "Telegraphic Reports" reading "New York, 25 March. The death of Friedrich Hecker was announced from St. Louis." No obituary, even a critical one, was to be found in its columns. This was no wonder, for the "*Kreuzzeitung*" had its hands full reporting on tainted American pork and defaming the departing President Hayes, as well as the newly-inaugurated Garfield. There was also extensive reporting on "The Doings of International Revolutionaries," in which the paper attacked the Social Democrats virtually every day. The *Norddeutsche Allgemeine Zeitung* was also restrained, as was the usually eager *Weser Zeitung*. The *Berliner Volkszeitung* took more trouble, correctly pointing out the difference in importance of Hecker for Germans and for German-Americans, although it must remain a puzzle how the editor knew so precisely Hecker's relationship to the German emperor. Hecker, he wrote,

> had warmer personal feelings for our Kaiser than one would have expected given his past. And Prince Bismarck always had an objective judge in him. ... In speaking with him one always immediately had the impression that one was dealing with a true masculine nature. In him the Germans of the United States have lost one of their best men.

In the Prussian Rhine Province the *Kölnische Zeitung* dealt with the old revolutionary, but in a manner that showed clear preferences. They stressed the "German nationalist" Hecker, who had greeted unity in 1871, and over-

FRIEDRICH HECKER

St. Louis Gedenkfeier

Memorial Ribbon for the dedication of the Hecker monument in Benton Park St. Louis, on 28 March 1886. Friedrich Hecker Papers, Western Historical Manuscripts, University of Missouri – St. Louis.

looked the Hecker who pressed for the expansion of personal rights. Stressing his voice in St. Louis in 1871, the *Kölnische Zeitung* declared that the Franco-Prussian War had "awakened his German patriotic feeling into full enthusiasm for Kaiser and Reich." Only when he traveled to Germany in 1873, "German conditions that he found did not entirely correspond to his views"; but Hecker "honorably" confessed, as apparently only that newspaper knew, "I have grown old and much over there I do not understand, but a fresh wind moves through the land that will lead to liberty." Finally the generous Cologne newspaper declared, "As with Arnold Ruge, Friedrich Hecker reconciled himself with the fatherland that rejected him and cleared the guilt of his past.'"[12]

The *Frankfurter Zeitung* published an entirely sympathetic and humorous obituary, obviously with a self-seeking purpose. This anti-Prussian, liberal newspaper recalled in its article with pleasure how in 1849 people had buried in the haystack or the garden Hecker pictures, Hecker-hats "along with the black-red-gold cockades and revolutionary writings so that the bumbling Prussians searching through their houses could find nothing." The newspaper also recalled Hecker's unfortunate conflict with the Prussian police in Frankfurt in 1873 and stressed how Hecker had sought contact with democrats during his visit in Stuttgart. Because the author knew Hecker personally, this obituary achieved a very effective image of the man's character.

> The manner in which he thought, acted and expressed himself always had something natural, direct, folksy about it. He was at odds with everything diplomatic, privy-councilish, sweet or slick. ... This man could certainly act, but he was not born to negotiate or broker. Hecker's eloquence was known to be considerable. But it was not the eloquence of an academic orator, nor that of a government minister or a trained parliamentarian, nor of a consistery officer, but an eloquence that comes from the heart and speaks to the heart.

Against the accusation often made in the National Liberal camp that Hecker had not been able to judge the changes in his country adequately, the *Frankfurter Zeitung* responded that Hecker had always followed "German conditions with high interest:"

> He took German newspapers and had books sent from Germany, and nothing happened in politics, literature, art or science of which he was

not informed. … The speeches on the burning questions of the day that he gave from time to time in St. Louis are proof that he remained fresh, and their echo sounded all the way back to the old fatherland.[13]

The democratic, anti-Prussian *Badischer Landesbote* also reported sadly on the death "of the old German man of liberty, great patriot" and "dear countryman Hecker." In their own behalf – since a few days before there had been bitter complaints about the high indirect taxes passed by the *Reichstag* that unjustly hit the lower classes – it recalled Hecker's refusal of taxes in 1847. It said, "The noble man will live unforgotten in the history as well as in the heart of those Baden people desiring liberty." The Vienna *Neue Freie Presse* summarized the German obituaries of Hecker in very laconic style. "Most German newspapers dedicate warm words to him and stress his purity of character and the selflessness of his efforts. With him one of the typical figures of 1848 has departed, whose basic drive was naive enthusiasm."[14]

In Hecker's home city of Mannheim the departed was commemorated on 23 April with a ceremony in which almost eight hundred persons participated. "Our fine, old friend, the great citizen and battler for liberty and right in two hemispheres, is now no longer among the living; *but his spirit will always remain with us!*" read the letter of condolence from Mannheim printed in newspapers and also sent to Summerfield. It was precisely this ceremony that gave the last occasion in Germany for dispute over Hecker, for the *Kölnische Volkszeitung* wrote, distressed over the address and the large participation in the festival, recalling the *Kulturkampf*, which Hecker had supported. "This is how to celebrate a barren man of revolution! German Catholics remain enemies of the state, even if it is not mentioned so often anymore." And the *Badische Landpost*, loyal to the Baden state government, critically made it clear in its criticism what could be found in all the obituaries: when one spoke of Hecker, one was basically speaking of his relationship to the German revolution of 1848/49. Once again his name served as a demonstration of one's own political conviction. And once again the entire country was confronted with its own political past in remembering Hecker and was compelled to take a position on it. The *Landpost* was distressed that the celebration for a man "who helped in his unhappy blindness to throw many fellow citizens into misfortune and drive them to rebellion and civil war" had been "blown up to [such] a great political action." One should no longer marvel "at the confusion of concepts of right and injustice, of loyalty and disloyalty, of true love of country and subject-loyalty and punishable blindness." The democratic *Badischer Landesbote* added its own views with these lines: "If the *Landpost* speaks of 'punishable blindness' then it proves nothing but a lack of knowledge of the conditions then, not only in Baden but in the whole of Europe. The justification for a revolution does not need to be derived from those times alone." The American and French revolutions had shown this justification clearly enough, the *Landesbote* continued. Against the statement by the *Badische Landpost* "that this glorification of a chief actor of the darkest period of our country of Baden should be greeted with joy in governmental circles," the *Landesbote* finally reponded that "to be sure no death commemoration could give any joy to the current government. If the *Landpost* warns that the democratic movement not be undervalued because it is still currently active, we respond in thanks to the praise this gives us."[15]

On 19 April 1881, three weeks after the burial, Hecker's English-language will was opened in the St. Clair County Courthouse. The will had been written by Hecker after his German tour, on 25 February 1874, and amended only once, on 19 January 1880. The last alteration dealt with the equal participation of all of his children in his financial estate. His wife Josefine was designated as heiress, Hecker's whole movable and immovable property was left to her use for life and after her death all of the children would inherit equally. His farm went to his eldest son, Arthur, who had farmed it exclusively over the last several years. It was also Arthur who inherited Hecker's library, his correspondence and his collection of newspapers, and who was to agree with his siblings over their distribution. The oddest clause of the will had to do with Hecker's heart. "My dead body shall be opened, the heart taken out, embalmed, put in a metal box, sent to Mannheim in Germany to be buried there by my relatives or friends in the vault of the cemetery where my father and 3 children rest. My skull shall be left intact by the surgeons opening my body." It is remarkable that Hecker, despite his great presence of mind shortly before his death, had not alerted the family to this and one other clause on the location of his grave. When the will was opened, the astonishment was great. "The family of the deceased had no knowledge of the content of the will," said the *Westliche Post* the next day, relying on the report of the *Belleville Stern* and the *Belleviller Zeitung*, "otherwise they would dutifully have carried out the instructions concerning the burial of the heart in his beloved old fatherland and of his body in the cemetery in Lebanon. Whether these instructions will be carried out after the fact is unknown to us." Now Hecker's heart would in fact not return across the ocean but remain under a small gravestone in the cemetery in Summerfield bearing the inscription, "Col. Frederic Hecker,

82nd ILL. INF." Yet the symbolically powerful act of wishing to be divided
certainly corresponded to Hecker's inner attitude. The fact that his "skull
[should be left] intact" clarifies one thing: he was an American by understanding, a "Must-be American," as he had said in 1873 in Mannheim. And
the wish to have his heart rest at the side of his beloved father and his three
dead children showed first of all his private, familial desire and only secondarily his love for his old fatherland. It was seen as the latter in Germany,
and at least the democratic *Landesbote* had no doubts that his desire should
be fulfilled. "If the condition of the corpse allows it, the heart must be
removed before it finds its permanent place in the cemetery at Lebanon,"
and be sent to its old homeland.[16]

After the burial solemnities in Summerfield, a number of men, including Caspar Butz and Georg Schneider, gathered in the Fremont House in St.
Louis to discuss in this more intimate circle the erection of a monument.
First there was talk of Tower Grove Park, where there were also monuments
to Shakespeare and Alexander von Humboldt. It was decided that money
would be collected under the leadership of Emil Preetorius and the
Westliche Post, and the location of the monument would be St. Louis. Even
the *Illinois Staatszeitung*, at odds with Hecker in life, emerged as a supporter of this plan and the placement of a monument in St. Louis, if only not to
prevent placement of the monument to the anti-clerical and pro-freedmen
Hecker in Chicago. The *Belleviller Zeitung* also spoke in favor of St. Louis
and desired "to follow the lead of the paper that always was the chief organ
of the great departed."[17]

In Belleville the Turner Society named an "agitation committee" to take
over the monument collection for St. Clair County. Selected men were called
from various communities of the county to collect donations. Receipts for
the contributions were to be published in the newspapers. The cost of a
monument was set at about six thousand dollars. Beginning in April the
first donations came to the *Westliche Post*, whose fund-raising was promoted by many German-American newspapers throughout the country. As
promised, every payment was acknowledged in the columns of the newspaper so that it could be seen from which parts of the States the donations
came.Along with newspapers, it was particularly German societies,
German businesses such as breweries and a whole series of private persons
who participated. The *Brooklyner Freie Presse* donated $50, writing, "To set a
monument to the hero of liberty and man of the people Friedrich Hecker,
who fought with sword and pen in both worlds for the highest good of
mankind ... would also be a sign of remembrance of the movement of

1848." The *Freie Zeitung* in New Jersey likewise believed that "a monument must be erected to brave old Hecker. The German-Americans owe it to him, they owe it to themselves." And a private donor wrote, "I, as a freethinking German, will contribute a stone, like any other freethinking and nobly minded friend of Hecker. If a quarter-dollar were donated [by each person], a palace could be built. Let' s go!" Dr. Philipp Weigel, Hecker's friend who had moved to Denver, gathered together $216 from friends and sent the money to the *Westliche Post* via the Denver, Colorado, *Journal*. Carl Schurz sent $175 from his friends in New York. They did not want to restrict themselves to donations; imagination was also demanded to raise money for the planned monument. Hence the *Westliche Post* was pleased to announce a benefit performance of the Social Dramatic Club in the Apollo Theater in St. Louis, "looking forward to a genuinely enjoyable evening, particularly as the roles are (as we are told) in the hands of the best local amateurs." And who could possibly pass up this enjoyment, if the musical accompaniment of the evening was in the hands of the Concordia Zither Club?[18]

At the beginning of May private initiative led to the minting of a Hecker memorial medal. Sponsors believed that the medal could also be sold in Germany without any difficulty, as a sign of the efforts of the German-American population to commemorate 1848. The project was undertaken with the intention, as one published private letter said, that "the dead Hecker, like the dead Cid, will still terrify his enemies, the enemies of liberty." The finished medal was sold for 25 cents from a special sales booth during the 23rd Federal Turner Festival in St. Louis from 4 to 7 June 1881. It was already sold out two days later, so that it had to be reminted in greater quantity. Hecker's brother-in-law Heinrich Tiedemann, chairman of the Hecker Memorial Committee, took orders for the medal, which would be sent on its way to all of Europe, including Germany, for 35 cents post paid. In order that this news be generally known, all "exchanging newspapers are asked in the most friendly manner to copy the notice."[19]

The Hecker Monument Committee published at the beginning of its undertaking a "call to the likeminded" showing great similarity to the resolution of the New York Society of Patriots of 1848/49. The general character of the monument was stressed as more than the mere place of remembrance for an individual man. Honoring one of its most prominent comrades in destiny dealt altogether with the place of the Forty-Eighters in America. Entirely in the sense of Kantian moral philosophy, the monument committee's call stressed that Hecker's life should be measured "by the standard not of success, but of striving; it was a great, a rare life." His proclamation of the republic in 1848, if premature, still that much less out of date," since "the republic has shown its practical worth," and "republican tendencies have emerged all over Europe." It was also "the duty of our contemporaries" to renew Hecker's memory in the present and keep it fresh for the future "to pass [his memory] on to the coming generation." In the last analysis this meant preserving in memory the life and striving of all emigrated Forty-Eighters.[20]

When the committee gathered in the Central Turner Hall in St. Louis on the occasion of Hecker's seventieth birthday on 28 September 1881, completion of the project was already certain. For that reason the main theme was not the discussion carrying out the project, but rather it was the committee's own self-definition. Only a little effort was needed to extract from Carl Lüdeking's speech the significance of the monument for German-Americans. Lüdeking stated at the very outset that they recalled Friedrich Hecker too well as a friend and person to need a celebration to refresh his memory. No, instead it was a question of the proper valuation of the "permanent essence and worth of Friedrich Hecker." This consisted in a "life for the whole and in the whole, the *res publica* of mankind." What is particularly striking in Lüdeking's speech was its great, unsurprising similarity to Hecker's own rhetoric. It was the rhetoric of an educated German elite that understood concepts such as morality – in Hegel's sense – the common good and civic virtue as thoroughly as Hecker had. It was a rhetoric that fed on the educational ideals of humanism and the Enlightenment. Lüdeking and many others shared with Hecker a similar political and biographic development, having internalized republicanism in theory long before they had any experience with an actual republic. Notions of popular opinion, civic virtue and selflessness from ancient history formed the political views they all shared. There was no question that their enthusiasm for the republican form of state, which they believed was necessary for the development of republican civic virtue, arose from the study of classical antiquity and the reception of its modern interpretation. Hecker, however, stood not simply for that common educational ideal and the political goals connected with it, but much more for the enthusiasm with which people clung to these ideals and goals. Hecker became the symbol of passion, the image of a political feeling that was not understood by many. The sponsors of his monument celebrated in Hecker the idea of the republic, the necessity of revolution and the unavoidable deed of revolution as a consequence of Hecker's own life story. Much points to the fact that in distant St. Louis the political refugees of old wanted to defend themselves against the objections of German political realists who asserted that they, like Hecker, had not read the signs of the times. In America these refugees asserted the contrary; it was only a question of time until the political vision of the German-American would realize itself in the old homeland, as well.

Republicanism, Lüdeking continued, had been Hecker's "morale," "the source of his activity and virtue to his last breath. … His proclamation of the German Republic in 1848 had been the deed of his conscience, his moral enthusiasm, his moral necessity, his moral subordination to an ideal." Hecker had been determined through and through by the idea of a German republic, and the rebellion in 1848 – which came from below, from the people – had been a "genuine German rising of the people." "It arose like a blossom from the total literary-philosophical development of the previous century." For the German-American Lüdeking – who would revisit this theme in his Cincinnati speech – the Revolution had never been discredited for owing its impulse to theoretical considerations. Much the contrary, this origin guaranteed greater universality and purity of principle, and dependence on sensual and material influence seemed smaller. The ideas that the revolutionaries had revered had not lost anything in attractiveness and validity; American experience had confirmed their correctness, even if the origin of the ideas had been purely theoretical. The principle of liberty was a general idea that embraced all of mankind and excluded any restriction to the "national" context. For that reason Lüdeking quoted not the nationalist Schiller, but the more skeptical German prince of poets, Goethe, and his *Faust*. "Standing on free ground with a free people," German-Americans were opposed to the "revolution in the bad sense, in our opinion," that began "from above" and had been "pressed downward with blood and iron." This Lüdeking of a further expression of *Faust*: "Only he who must conquer it every day earns liberty, like life."[21] This was the political exile's confession of faith against the accusation of treason and infidelity to the old homeland. The Forty-Eighters conceived of themselves as the true and genuine patriots who committed themselves selflessly and in a self-sacrificing manner for the fatherland, the common good. As Hecker had always insisted, a people must conquer its own liberty and concern itself without interruption for liberty's preservation. To that degree liberty "from above" was questionable to most Forty-Eighters in America, because as far as they were concerned the members of a political society had to agree on their laws, on justice, which in turn should regulate the relationship of the members of a political society to one another.The very act of resolving and establishing right, which is to secure the quest for goals of life and the external liberty of every individual in the political society, was excluded precisely where it was dictated by a few.

Through his insistence on the principle of liberty, Lüdeking was taking a stand on the dramatic change of view of the German public toward emigration since the foundation of the *Reich*. Emigration was no longer seen in Germany as the solution to impoverished overpopulation among rural peoples in the midst of an industrializing society. Instead the concept represented by Friedrich Kapp, of emigration as the loss of people and material goods, had prevailed. Even Bismarck's remarks on emigrants showed a change. As the chancellor of the North German League, he had supported the naturalization treaty that had been negotiated with Washington:

> Between this league and that on the other side of the ocean [has arisen a] bond of blood relationship ... [There exists] such a number of Germans, even Germans born in Germany, in no country outside of Germany. ... In no land in the world [have] Germans, who are found in all lands as visitors or emigrants, preserved so warm a dependence on their old homeland as there.

In June 1873, however, Bismarck complained that Germans overseas showed all too great an inclination to lose their ethnic identity. And about ten years later, during the conflict over protectionist policies, American exports and American pork that was supposedly infected with trichinosis, Bismarck expressed himself in completely negative terms.

> I am no friend of emigration in general, and certainly not the morbid promotion of emigration that we had in the first years of the German Reich. ... A German who strips off his fatherland as if it were an old coat is no longer a German to me; I have no more interest in him as a German.[22]

But as the German-American, who had never held a central position, increasingly vanished from the view of the German chancellor, the Forty-Eighters wanted to hold fast to a trans-Atlantic relationship and to keep their faith with the fatherland for the sake of their own life stories. They called on the tradition that raised itself above the ethnically determined national state, a tradition that was "rooted," as Lüdeking formulated it, "in the philosophy and republic of classical antiquity," swearing allegiance to "free thought and the free state." A monument for Hecker could have no other purpose than to "place in a correct light a period of history so often reviled and misunderstood as that of 1848."[23]

The solemn dedication of the monument in St. Louis that took place about a year later resembled a staged event. The festival procession, consisting of five divisions, began at the Central Turner Hall and moved along the main streets of the city. Decorated with American and German flags, it headed toward Benton Park, which bordered the splendid German quarter of Compton Heights, still in the process of construction. Old battle companions of Hecker from 1848 and 1861 led the parade, followed by invited guests such as Gustav Körner, the congressional representative from Hecker's district, a delegation from Chicago, members of the North American Turner League, the keynote speaker Carl Lüdeking, and the Hecker Memorial Committee. Sixteen singing societies and various Turner societies joined the parade, followed by members of the Free Congregation of North St. Louis and the St. Louis Sharpshooters Society. "Comrades of Hecker's conviction joined the splendid procession with a long row of carriages." Approximately five thousand persons awaited the procession in the park, despite the rain. Emil Preetorius spoke first as the monument's co-initiator. Today he fulfilled a promise that he had made at the grave, he declared to the assembly, and he compared Hecker to George Washington, "First in war, first in peace, first in the hearts of his people." Then Carl Lüdeking followed in his function as chairman of the Hecker Memorial Committee with his German festival oration. This was, he declared before the draped memorial, "a historical, a world-historical monument of liberty, to the blooming memory of two of the greatest struggles for freedom of this century,1848 and 1861," that were joined in Hecker's person. It was "a monument to the single, indivisible liberty joining together nations and continents, a monument of single, indeed intercontinental, 'Atlantic' liberty!"[24]

The joining of the two events of 1848 and 1861 was in fact a commonplace of the day's reminiscences and commemoration of Hecker. This had a reason of its own. The speakers raised the value of 1861, exaggerating their own service to the war, in order to make their claim on American citizenship clear, but also – and this was often overlooked – to raise the value of 1848. "The mighty movement of 1848, which appeared to vanish in the darkest abyss of reaction, continued its existence on the soil of the New World, and the seed that seemed drowned in blood ripened here to golden fruit." Stressing 1861 documented the position that the idea of 1848 had not died, had not been defeated; the political refugees were no losers in history, and the principle of liberty had not been discredited through defeat in the old fatherland. It had been born anew and achieved justice on American soil.

With all of their differences in historical causation, prospect and particularly final development, the risings in 1848 and 1861 bore the same
character of striving for unity and liberty, for the generalization of
equal rights and the welfare of all.

By calling on the one principle, the one liberty, Forty-Eighters not only
achieved the legitimation for their own presence in the United States; they
further signaled their desire to be ready to integrate into such a pluralistic
society as that of the United States. The call to a cosmopolitan republic was
turned against the nation of their origin and ancestry.

> The band of cosmopolitan citizenship ... not only binds together citi-
> zens of varying origins and language under the same law, with equal
> obligation; it also joins together the republics of the Old and New
> Worlds as natural allies, their citizens as "fellow citizens," one in their
> consciousness of the same liberty.

The speaker stressed that Hecker's monument expressed "the political and
progressive joining of the Old and the New Worlds." With this declaration
the political refugees could always feel themselves bound to Europe in their
way, because they were bound to the political tradition of the Enlightenment, rational thinking. In a country whose population could not call on a
common religion, all that remained as the basis of integration was the evo-
cation of political creeds. The formula of naturalization demanded nothing
else from immigrants. From the beginning it was no problem for most
Forty-Eighters to submit to this. The American Declaration of Independence
was a political creed that they could endorse without hesitation; it contained a clear denunciation of the monarchical principle and further established the sovereignty of the people. For that reason Lüdeking turned once
more in his speech to the accusations of all those to whom "the republic was
not fine or learned enough":

> The idea of the self-government of the people is as old as humanity
> itself and can only die with it. It is simple and generally understood.
> It requires no wit, that complicated "art of state" that deals with
> the guardianship, the exploitation, the alienation, the dumbing down
> and beastializing of the peoples. The art of self-government, of the
> republic, rests on the education and virtue of its citizens, and this in
> turn on the capacity of our race to achieve knowledge and virtue
> through education.

It could have been Hecker himself speaking here. The joining of popular sovereignty and the virtue of the citizens, the concept that a state based on the self-government of the people could be built only on the capacity of the people for education, and hence for virtue, was the foundation of all of Hecker's political convictions. But alongside the idea of an "education of mankind, derived from the Enlightenment and even celebrated in the pre-Revolutionary period" was the much more decisive fact that the principle of popular sovereignty had made the question of ethnic origin superfluous. Republican liberty was untouched by ethnic questions. Most Forty-Eighters warned against overstressing their German origins because ethnic separatism was not the goal pursued. Tolerance and the maintenance of certain cultural ways did not stand in the way of recognizing all citizens as equal in principle. But the first priority was to secure political recognition. Determining the nation on the basis of descent or origin could never be a serious program for political refugees, and it indeed contradicted the rational view of many Forty-Eighters of a "constitutional patriotism." Agreeing to a republican constitution was to guarantee the greatest possible individual liberty, beyond all ethnic definition. In this attitude German-American Forty-Eighters clearly distinguished themselves from revolutionary refugees who remained in Europe and who put aside the "liberty" that they had failed to achieve in 1848 in order to concentrate on the element of "unity." Some of these ex-revolutionaries, such as Julius Fröbel, approached the unity that they desired through theories about ancestry and the worth of various races. The disillusionment that set in among German-Americans after the euphoric hopes of 1870/71 – hopes that had been bound up with the faith that the unity created by the foundation of the *Reich* would level the way for the development of liberty as they defined it – would appear to have led to reconsideration of the original revolutionary goals of liberty. Ethnicity did not gain importance in this. On the basis of their own experiences with the threat of American nativism in the 1850s, which continued virulent, Lüdeking formulated expectations of German-Americans using Hecker as an aid.

> It is the name of a foreign-born man who has been marked on this monument by foreign-born persons, not because the bond of foreign origin joins them, but because they are joined by the common bond of equal citizens' rights, won through commitment and deed, and the equally fulfilled obligations of citizenship. This is no monument of nationalism and nativism after the European or the American style. We may not say with Charles Sumner that Americans form a nation in the etymological

sense of a common origin or language; but in the sense of the Declaration of Independence they do become a unity. There is a just nativism of those born with a good human nature, and of those obtaining the rights of a free citizen through fulfilling their duties – a nativism of moral birth in the spirit of the Declaration of Independence. If our monument proclaims nativism in this sense, it will serve all.

Even the solemn unveiling of the monument by a granddaughter of Hecker, who was described as "the image of *Germania*," underscored the double function of the monument. The united bands first played *"Hecker, hoch Dein Name schalle"* ["Hecker, high shall thy name sound"], immediately followed by the "Star-Spangled Banner," in keeping with the two dates carved on the monument, 1848 and 1861. Female Turners decorated the monument with wreaths, and Judge Robert Rombauer followed with an English-language speech. Rombauer recalled Hecker's eventful life and pointed out how many nations were represented at the cemetery in Summerfield to do tribute to the "widest expansion of humanity" and "general fraternity" embodied in Hecker. Attendees had put aside all "interests and parties" and "national animosity." Rombauer spoke particularly of Hecker's voluntary exile and formulated most clearly the attitude of all German-Americans to their country of origin and their present homeland, as exemplified by Hecker. "He utterly venerated the principle … that the land of our fathers had claims on our thankful memory, but that the land of our children was entitled to our active work." America had a claim on the integration of its foreign-born citizens. America was also the future of their children, and hardly any German-American could fool himself about the fact that the second generation had largely integrated itself into American society. Friedrich Kapp thus had been correct in describing the German-American as an in-between being.

A monument for Hecker as a message to coming generations, as all the speakers had been happy to stress, could only make a weak effort to witness to the origins of their fathers, the reason for their exile and of their reasons for remaining here. This was also Rombauer's intention. He recalled conditions in the old fatherland in his speech, making the impression that they could never be good enough to move the exile to return. When Hecker himself visited the land of his birth shortly after the Franco-Prussian War, Rombauer said, "even some of his old party comrades no longer heeded his words of warning; unfortunately he would see these words fulfilled." This recitation of the unsatisfactory conditions in the old fatherland were also part of the rhetoric of memorial speeches, and they also were to justify choosing to remain on American soil. The explanation of one's own position included making it clear how far one was from returning. The decline of immigration from Germany was not yet so striking that German-Americans were moved yet to reconsider their choice to emigrate, but improvements in Germany gave middle-class families continually fewer reasons to leave.[25]

Not all German-American newspapers and societies had contributed to the Hecker memorial in St. Louis. In Cincinnati, a similar citadel of German population, another German-American Hecker Memorial Society had been formed, and about nine months after St. Louis. On 24 June 1883, it invited people to a solemn dedication of its own Hecker memorial. Here as well the memorial was celebrated as a "triumph of the Germans," and here as well thousands of people, including many Americans, passed down streets decorated with black-red-gold and American flags to Washington Park. Here as well the procession, consisting of at least five thousand persons, included German bands, Turner Societies, male choirs, drum corps, members of Schleswig-Holstein, Prussian, Saxon-Thuringian, Baden, Bavarian, Swabian, Rhine-Palatine and German-Austrian support societies, 1848 and Civil War veterans from Cincinnati and Indianapolis.[26] Here as well maidens strewed flowers and there were wagons and coaches crowned with laurel. When the procession reached the north side of Washington Park, a large mass of people was already gathered about the platform built around the monument. On the entry of the guests of honor – Hecker's four sons Arthur, Erwin, Alfred and Alexander, and Mayor Stevens of Cincinnati – Brand's Band played "a potpourri of national melodies" with songs such as *"Was ist des Deutschen Vaterland"* ["What is the Fatherland of a German?"], immediately answered by "Yankee Doodle."

The first speaker of the day, Albert Springer, spoke on behalf of the German-American Hecker Memorial Society of Cincinnati. He greeted first of all the Forty-Eighter veterans, then his fellow fighters of 1861, then the Turners and singers, and in the end, "All of you citizens who have come to honor Hecker's political selflessness, sense of the people and civic virtue." Cincinnati's ceremonies showed many parallels to St. Louis. The monument, Springer said, was not simply for Hecker, but more importantly as tribute to "the principle of liberty in its purest and most perfect form" and to exercise a "positive influence on the coming generation." As Springer gave the monument swathed in an American flag to the citizens of Cincinnati, the Germania men's choir, with musical accompaniment, sang, *"Germania, du stolzes Weib"* ["Germania, you proud woman"]. Mayor Stevens thanked him in the name of the city and stressed on his part the "elevated thoughts" associated with it, "that Americans and Germans honor in this country him, the great departed, the apostle of liberty, who spilled his blood for this country as well."

The chief speaker of the day was Emil Rothe. He formulated in the most pregnant manner the intentions involved in erecting the monument:

> Fellow citizens! With the work we have done here, we honor more than the man whose face and name the chiseled stone bears. ... It is not he who needs our witness, we are the ones who want to show our world and the future that we hold high the name and memory of one who remained true to his people and dedicated his life's work to liberty, right and progress, on German or American soil or anywhere in the world.[27]

Here, as well, true patriotism was defined not by ethnic membership but by holding fast to the quest for liberty. Having wished the best for his people, independent of of success or defeat, had finally won him recognition, Rothe believed. Rothe stressed an ideal of civic virtue, enriched by Kant that was as familiar to him as it was to his listeners. When speaking of Hecker, Rothe naturally had to speak of the Revolution as well. In this context he referred to the concept of republican thought and the theoretical influence of doctrines disseminated by German universities:

> The movement of 1848 was a powerful outbreak of patriotic idealism developed at German universities, and it took place following the example of France at a time when the masses of the German people had almost no understanding of it. ... Whoever enthused and gloried in that patriotic May air, felt the glow of spirit filling his breast. There are many in this circle still whose old heads cannot forget until life's end the high feeling that possessed us.

In Cincinnati as in St. Louis, the speakers no longer conjured up the greatness of the German fatherland as they would have in the immediate aftermath of the Reich's founding, but rather they recited the reasons for their own exile. They, the true patriots of the country, had been expelled.

> Who could have thought then that we would be setting a monument to our venerated leader a whole generation later, far across the ocean? Who would have thought it possible that our fatherland would expel us, that many there would still curse us, many others laugh at us, some sympathize in silence, and only very few would understand!

Even in Cincinnati no one doubted that the Revolution was condemned to failure. The question about the reason led to the same answers as in St. Louis. Goals had been set too high, expectations had been too idealistic, and neither the times nor the people had been ripe for a republic. The difficult realization and preservation of a republic could be properly undertaken only in America. "Making Hecker responsible for the failure of the movement," Rothe asserted, "would be a great injustice. He was a child of the German idealism of the time, its genuine loyal representative." The "excessive rushing and clumsiness of which one might accuse him," "his violence and crudity" arose from the "glowing zeal" "with which he approached anything that appeared to him untrue or wrong." "Strict to himself and without a trace of self-seeking," Hecker had

> never sought or held a title or a paid official office other than his military rank ... but rather preferred to work with plow and shovel in his field, meadow and vineyard, leading a simple but independent life at the bosom of that nature that he loved above all else, the model of a self-sufficient citizen.

The frugal life of a virtuous Roman/American citizen, who actively fulfilled the needs of the will of the people and ignored his private advantage, also was part of the canon of republican rhetoric that would meet with general support. It stressed basic values that Americans and Germans accepted in the same way as an ideal and a standard. If Rothe took into account Hecker's choleric temperament and recalled his errors and misjudgments better than other orators, such objections could never obliterate Hecker's positive attributes, which everyone present understood.

The following passage showed how much one could use a shortened history to feel bound to great developments in the old homeland:

> Despite all errors and misjudgments that could be properly assigned to him, the justice of history will never permit that his invaluable contribution to his German fatherland should be disputed or reduced. ... He laid the first stone for the later formation of the Reich by directly creating the Pre-Parliament and indirectly creating the Parliament in Frankfurt. Thus for the first time, Germany could be spoken of as a single Reich. The building fell down again, but the German Reich was erected on this foundation wall, that mighty Reich that now forms the core and axis around which all Europe turns. ... Without '48 no '70 or '71 would come, and without the advance work of Hecker and his com-

rades neither the giant strength of a Bismarck nor the military genius of a Moltke would be able to protect Germany against the pressing power of its western neighbor.

The National Liberal press might interpret America's Liberal Republican movement as a positive echo of German developments. But in America German liberals saw themselves in a tradition that conversely saw the efforts of 1848/49 as necessary preconditions for the developments of 1870/71. The question of whether all German-American Forty-Eighters were actually deeply convinced of their role as preparers for German unity must be set aside here. Their rhetoric showed their efforts to ascribe to themselves the role of political midwives, making it possible to recoin failure into later victory.

In their recall of Hecker the Forty-Eighters were happy to stress their own services to their fatherland. And so what came to pass in St. Louis and Cincinnati was what Hecker had already expressed in his speech in Stuttgart, which seemed both disturbing but almost unavoidable: "fame attached itself to him in particular,"[28] his name stood for a great number of men who had all sought the same goal and failed, as he had. What made him famous, notorious but also beloved was an excess of temerity, lack of restraint, and the rigorism with which he disciplined himself to be a virtuous citizen. But most importantly it was his ability to bear "his heart on his tongue"[29] and say straight out what he had on his mind. He was, above all, that mixture of sensibility and understanding that is needed in any popular hero, that half "a beast" and half "spirit" who strove often futilely to make of it all "a reasonable mixture." Without the failed popular uprising in April, 1848, Hecker's symbolic power would certainly have been less; but for all anti-clerical Forty-Eighters, indeed for all adherents of the republican form of state, Hecker became the secularized answer to the difficult theological question of how the "Word became flesh," or rather, how to get from word to deed.

---

[1] Butz, "Erinnerungen, 2. Teil." FH to Charles Söhner, Summerfield, 12 December 1878, 28 February 1879, 13 March 1880, FHP, box 3, folder 38; also FH to Emil Frey, 6 May 1866, Staatsarchiv Basel Stadt, Sig. PA 485 DXI165: "the individual person is a more or less ordinary scum, mankind itself is splendid."

[2] FH to Charles Söhner, Summerfield, 2 December 1880, 16 March 1881, Arthur Hecker to Charles Söhner, Summerfield, 23 March 1881, telegram from Arthur Hecker to Charles Söhner, 24 March 1881, FHP, box 3, folder 38. FH traveled in the summers of 1874 and 1875 to the mountains of Colorado, whose climate was recommended for asthmatics; on his impressions see his article in the *TISZ*, 27 July 1874 ("Aus den Alpen Colorado's, Brief von Friedrich Hecker

vom 19. Juli 1874"); ibid., 5 August 1875, also his letters to Söhner of 6 June 1874,1 August 1874, 21 May 1875 and 2 September 1875, FHP, box 3, folder 38. FH to Caspar Butz, 7 March 1881, quoted in Butz, "Erinnerungen, 2. Teil."

3 *Missouri Republican*, 25 March 1881. *WP*, daily, 25 March 1881. *BZ*, daily, 25 March 1881. *California Demokrat*, 26 March 1881, also in *WP*, 2 April 1881.

4 *Mississippi-Blätter*, 27 March 1881.

5 *WP*, daily, 26 March 1881. *Mississippi-Blätter*, 27 March 1881 (resolutions and list of participants, including Emil Preetorius, R. G. Rombauer, Carl Witter, Eugen Weigel, Carl Lüdeking); the call had appeared in the same edition and following.

6 *Mississippi-Blätter*, 27 March 1881. *Neue Freie Presse*, Chicago, in *WP*, daily, 27 March 1881, see also the reports in FHP, box 4, folder 42. *New Yorker Staatszeitung*, 28 March 1881, also in *WP*, daily, 31 March 1881.

7 "Trauerbeschlüsse für Friedrich Hecker vom Verein der Patrioten von 1848/49," *Badischer Landbote*, no. 91, 20 April 1881.

8 *WP*, daily, 26 March 1881.

9 Detailed descriptions of the burial and the speeches made there in "Friedrich Heckers Bestattung zu Summerfield am 28. Marz 1881," Hecker Denkmal Comite St. Louis, eds., *Erinnerungen an Friedrich Hecker* (St. Louis, 1882), 2-12; *Friedrich Hecker und sein Antheil an der Geschichte Deutschlands und Amerikas*. Herausgegeben unter den Auspicien des Deutsch-Amerikanischen Hecker-Denkmal-Vereins von Cincinnati/Ohio (Cincinnati, 1881), 35-44; original reports are in *WP*, daily, 29 March 1881; in addition there were special editions with collected articles on Hecker's burial of the *BZ*; on the size of the event, see also Körner, *Memoirs*, vol. 2, 659. *Badischer Landesbote* spoke in its report of two thousand mourners, see "Hecker's Leichenbegängniss," *Badischer Landesbote*, no. 90, 17 April 1881.

10 On Lüdeking see Zucker, *Forty-Eighters*, 317. *Erinnerungen an Friedrich Hecker*, 10-11, 12. On the American visit of F. F. Fritzsche, deputy in the Reichstag, see for example *Weser Zeitung*, no. 12296, 31 March 1881 (morning edition): "at a reception in St. Louis, the German socialists Fritzsche and Viereck stated their disapproval of the murder of rulers." Czar Alexander II of Russia had fallen victim to an attack days before, and the news dominated everything else in conservative papers; also on Fritzsche in America, *Norddeutsche Allgemeine Zeitung*, no. 139, 24 March 1881 (morning edition). Körner, *Memoirs*, vol. 2, 659-60. *WP*, daily, 29 March 1881. The *Badischer Landesbote* selected Körner's speech as the "most remarkable," but also noted the fact that "Swiss, French, Hungarians and Italians could not restrain themselves from laying laurel wreaths on the grave of the old freedom fighter," see "Friedrich Hecker's Leichenbegängniss," *Badischer Landbote*. *Karlsruher Anzeiger*, no. 90, 17 April 1881.

11 *BZ*, daily, 31 March 1881.

12 *Neue Preussische Zeitung* (*Kreuzzeitung*), no. 74, 27 March 1881; it was the standard telegraphic dispatch also published, for example, in the *Badischer Landbote*, no. 73, 27 March 1881. On the "pig war," *Neue Preussische Zeitung*, 30 March 1881, 2d supplement to no. 76; on negative judgments on Hayes and Garfield, ibid., no. 77, 31 March 1881; on "Treiben der internationalen Revolutionäre," ibid., no. 75, 29 March 1881, and succeeding issues. Cf. Otto Pflanze, "Germany – Bismarck – America," Jürgen Elvert, Michael Salewski, eds., *Deutschland und der Westen im 19. und 20. Jahrhundert*. part 1: *Transatlantische Beziehungen* (Stuttgart, 1993), 67-84, here 74-76; from the American side, Louis L. Snyder, "Bismarck in American Caricature," *American-German Review*, 5 (September, 1939), 42-45, 52. *Berliner Volkszeitung*, quoted in *BZ*, daily, 16 April 1881. *Kölnische Zeitung*, no. 87, 28 March 1881 (page 3); my own emphasis.

[13] "Our esteemed friend and countryman O. H.," see *Badischer Landesbote. Karlsruher Anzeiger*, no. 77, 1 April 1881. O. H., "Friedrich Hecker" *Frankfurter Zeitung und Handelsblatt*, no. 89, 30 March 1881 (morning edition). The *Badischer Landesbote* reprinted the obituary of the *Frankfurter Zeitung*, see *Badischer Landbote. Karlsruher Anzeiger*, no. 77, 1 April 1881.

[14] *Badischer Landesbote*, no. 74, 29 March 1881; reports on unjust taxation, *Badischer Landesbote*, no. 70, 24 March 1881 and ibid., no. 71, 25 March 1881. *Wiener Neue Freie Presse*, quoted in *BZ*, daily, 16 April 1881.

[15] Report of the gathering in *Badischer Landesbote*, no. 97, 27 April 1881; also *BZ*, 12 May 1881. The original "An den theuren Hinterbliebenden Friedrich Heckers!" Mannheim, 23 April 1881, has about 200 signatures, FHP, box 5, folder 51; underlining in the original. The condolence sent to the Hecker family was also published in America, see "Die Heckerfeier in Mannheim," *BZ*, daily, 12 May 1881. *Kölnische Volkszeitung*, quoted in *Badischer Landesbote*, no. 99, 29 April 1881; emphasis in the original. *Badische Landespost*, reprinted in *Badischer Landesbote*, no. 100, 30 April 1881.

[16] The original will is to be found in the Illinois Regional Archives, Carbondale, Illinois; there is a microfilm copy of it in the County Court House in Belleville, Illinois (case no. 00106, roll 4, sequence no. 600 215); see Paul, *Freie Erde*, 204, n. 74; a copy of the original is in the Stadtarchiv Mannheim, Kleine Erwerbungen, 974. Arthur and Malwina had received $1200 on their weddings, which was to be taken into account at the division of the estate; FH cancelled this clause on 19 January 1880. FH spoke of his own three children who died young: one child born dead in 1840; Gabriele, a daughter born in 1841 who died in 1843, and a daughter born in 1848 who died in 1849. FH never saw this child. A few days after Hecker's death, Arthur's description of FH's last hours appeared in the newspapers. According to that, he precisely analyzed the symptoms of his illness and knew he would die. "Go over to the library," FH said to Arthur, "take the Richter [a book of medicine] and turn to page 710 – there you will find the symptoms of my illness described precisely. I know what is wrong with me and know that it is the end." Printed in the *BZ*, 26 March 1881; *Mississippi Blätter*, 27 March 1881. FH wished to be buried in Lebanon, not in Summerfield: "My earthly remains shall be buried in a vault to be buried in the cemetery of Lebanon, St. Clair County, Illinois and the vault so spacious as to leave room for the remains of my dear wife Josefine to be buried in time to come on my sides." *WP*, daily, 20 April 1881; the first two reports on the reading of Hecker's will were printed on the same day by the English *Belleville Stern*, 19 April 1881, and in the German-language *BZ*, 19 April 1881. There is no entry in the Mannheim cemetery register for any later deposit of a heart, courteous information from Friedrich Teutsch, Stadtarchiv Mannheim. "Das zu spät bekannt gewordene Testament Hecker's," *Badischer Landesbote*, no. 114, 17 May 1881.

[17] On the meeting and those present, *WP*, daily, 31 March 1881. Andreas Daum, "Celebrating Humanism in St. Louis. The Origins of the Humboldt Statue in Tower Grove Park, 1859-1878," *Gateway Heritage*, vol. 15, no. 2 (Fall, 1994), 48-58. *TISZ*, quoted in *WP*, daily, 29 March 1881. *BZ*, quoted in *WP*, daily, 2 April 1881.

[18] See *BZ*, daily, 20 April 1881. Newspapers that published the appeal in the first two months and sent money included the *Philadelphia Demokrat*, *Freiheitsfreund* (Pittsburgh), *Volksblatt* (Louisville), *Cincinnati Volksblatt*, *Neue Freie Presse* (Chicago), *Cleveland Anzeiger*, *New Yorker Zeitung*, *Buffalo Freie Presse*, *Washingtoner Journal*, *BZ*, *Belleviller Stern*, *New Jersey Freie Presse*, *Brooklyner Freie Presse*, *Davenport Demokrat*; *Milwaukee Freie Presse*; *Detroit Abendpost*, *Centraler Missourier*, *Denver Colorado Journal*, *Anzeiger des Südens* (Nashville). *Brooklyner Freie Presse*, quoted in *WP*, daily, 1 April 1881. *New Jersey Freie Presse* (Newark), quoted in *WP*, daily, 1 April 1881. Contributed by J. & C. B., *WP*, daily, 1 April 1881. *Denver Colorado Journal*, quoted in *WP*, daily,

22 April 1881. See the letter of Carl Schurz to Emil Preetorius, New York, 26 September 1881, *Erinnerungen an Friedrich Hecker*, 19-20. *WP*, daily, 30 April 1881.

[19] Tiedemann to P. F. C. Tiedemann, chair of the monument committee, O'Fallon, 14 April 1881, printed in *WP*, daily, 7 May 1881. Information on the memorial medal, *WP*, daily, 29 May 1881; 4 June 1881; 9 June 1881. The medal was of the size and with a silver wash similar in appearance to an American dollar, bearing on one side Hecker's portrait, on the other side the inscription "Bundesturnfest des Nordamerikanischen Turnerbundes zu St. Louis, 4-7 Juni 1881." *WP*, daily, 29 May 1881.

[20] The call was also published in Southwest Germany, see, for example, *Badischer Landesbote*, no. 93, 22 April 1881. "Aufruf des Hecker Denkmal Comites," quoted here from *BZ*, daily, 20 April 1881, also printed in *Erinnerungen an Friedrich Hecker*, 13-14.

[21] *Faust*, part 2, act 5, great court of the palace, line 11,580. *Faust*, part 2, act 5, great court of the palace, lines 11,575-76.

[22] Horst Kohl, ed., *Die politische Reden des Fürsten Bismarck*, 14 vols., (Stuttgart, 1892-1905), here Bismarck on 2 April 1868, vol. 4, 7-10; see on Bismarck's altered attitude to America after the founding of the Reich, Pflanze, "Germany – Bismarck," 73-74. Bismarck in the Reichstag, 9 June 1873, *Reden*, vol. 6, 61-62. Bismarck in the Reichstag, 26 June 1884, *Reden*, vol. 10, 208.

[23] All quotations Lüdeking's speech, *Erinnerungen an Friedrich Hecker*, 18; emphasis in the original.

[24] Thorough description in *WP*, daily, 2 October 1882; also printed in *Erinnerungen an Friedrich Hecker*, 27-48; see also the English-language account in *St. Louis Republican*, 2 October 1882 *WP*, daily, 2 October 1882. Lüdeking's festival speech quoted in *Erinnerungen an Friedrich Hecker*, 34.

[25] Only Guido A. Dobbert, *The Disintegration of an Immigrant Community: The Cincinnati Germans, 1870-1920* (New York, 1980), 668, pays attention to this in another context: "As such the goals of the Civil War were essentially more compatible with the aims of '48 transposed to the American Scene than was Germany's unification of 1870. This was particularly so because the new Empire had to be paid for to some extent with the freedom of the people." Robert E. Rombauer was a leading Missouri member of Butz's Radical Democracy Party, intitiated in 1864, see Nagler, *Fremont*, 374, n. 203. Schurz had also noted the rapid assimilation of the second generation, see Schurz, *Lebenserinnerungen*, vol. 3 (letter of 8 July 1867). See concerning St. Louis also Saalberg, *Westliche Post*, 285. Audrey L. Olson, *St. Louis Germans, 1850-1920: The Nature of an Immigrant Community and its relation to the Assimilation Process* (New York, 1980), here chapter 9 (Conclusion). The rapid process of assimilation, that is, the Americanization of Germans, in Cincinnati, is shown by Dobbert, *Disintegration*, even if the title of his work does not imply it. Decline was only palpable after 1890; until then the German-American newspapers also continued to experience growth and improvement, see for example Dobbert, *Disintegration*, 663.

[26] There were similar gatherings, speeches, donations, correspondence, appeals before this dedication of the monument in Cincinnati, see the newspaper notices in FHP, box 9; on the following *Cincinnati Free Press*, 25 June 1883; also *Cincinnati Volksblatt*, 25 June 1881; and the brochures distributed by the Deutsch-Amerikanischer Hecker Denkmal-Verein. The *Cincinnati Freie Presse* presents the procession in various divisions, distributed into two long columns, see Dobbert, *Disintegration*; Olson, *St. Louis*.

[27] *Cincinnati Freie Presse*, 25 June 1883. Zucker, *Forty-Eighters*, 333; DAG, 11 (1911), 222 ff.

[28] Stuttgart speech in *Frankfurter Zeitung und Handelsblatt*, 6 July 1873.

[29] Hausser, *Gegenwart*, 358.

Sources and Literature

1. Unprinted Sources:

Friedrich Hecker Papers, Western Historical Manuscript Collection, University of Missouri – St. Louis (cited as FHP); on microfilm, also available in the Bundesarchiv, Abteilung Frankfurt a. M.

Individual documents in the Missouri Historical Society, St. Louis, Mo. Papers on Hecker's treason trial and press-law violations due to his editing of the "Volksfreund," Generallandesarchiv Karlsruhe.

Individual letters and documents in Stadtarchiv Mannheim, Kleine Erwerbungen.

Individual Hecker letters in Emil Frey-Nachlass and Carl Brenner-Nachlass, Staatsarchiv des Kantons Basel-Stadt.

Materials on Hecker's participation in the American Civil War in the National Archives, Washington, DC.

Hecker's letters to Heinrich Metzner, Library of Congress, Manuscript Division, Washington, DC.

Friedrich Hecker to F. S. Jucho, 16. January 1846, Jucho-Nachlass, Sig. FS9 1/116, Bundesarchiv, Abteilung Frankfurt a. M.

Further collections with materials about and letters by Hecker
(letters completely attributed in the notes):

Karl Blind Papers, British Library, London.

Lorenz Brentano Papers, Chicago Historical Society, Chicago.

Adam von Itzstein Nachlass, Bundesarchiv Abteilungen Potsdam, Zug.-Nr. 168/58; individual copies also in Bundesarchiv, Abteilung Frankfurt a. M., Sig. FSg. 1/17.

Friedrich Kapp Papers, Library of Congress, Manuscript Division, Washington, D.C.

Franz Lieber Papers, Huntington Library, San Marino, CA. Franz Lieber Papers, Library of Congress, Manuscript Division, Washington, DC.

Georg Schneider Papers, Chicago Historical Society, Chicago. Carl Schurz Papers, Library of Congress, Manuscript Division, Washington DC.

Franz Sigel Papers, New York Historical Society, New York. Gustav von Struve Nachlass, Bundesarchiv, Abteilung Frankfurt a. M.

Lyman Trumbull Papers, Library of Congress, Manuscript Division, Washington, DC.

Elihu Washburne Papers, Library of Congress, Manuscript Division, Washington, DC.

Richard Yates Papers (Yates Family papers), Illinois State Historical Library, Springfield, Illinois

2. Printed Sources

Congressional Globe. Containing Debates and Proceedings, Washington D.C. 1861ff.

Deutsch-amerikanisches Conversations-Lexicon, ed. Alexander Schem, 11 vols., New York 1869-1874.

Dictionary of American Biography, ed. Alien Johnson, Dumas Malone, 16 vols., New York 1936 - 1988 (cited as DAB).

Dokumente zur deutschen Verfassungsgeschichte, ed. Ernst Rudolf Huber, vol. 1, Stuttgart 1961.

Historical Aspects of the Immigration Problem. Selected Documents, ed. Edith Abbott, Chicago, 1926.

Lincoln-Douglas Debates of 1858, ed. Robert Johannsen, New York 1965. Selected *Speeches of Abraham Lincoln*, ed. Herbert Mitgang, New York 1992.

Staatslexikon. Encyklopädie der sämtlichen Staatswissenschaften fiir alle Stände, in *Verbindung mit vielen der angesehensten Publizisten Deutschlands*, ed. Carl von Rotteck, Carl Welcker, 1st ed., Altona, 1934 ff., 2nd ed. Altona, 1845 ff.

Stenographischer Bericht über die Verhandlungen der deutschen constituierenden Nationalversammlung zu Frankfurt am Main, ed. Franz Wigard, Frankfurt a. M., 1848-50.

The Collected Works of Abraham Lincoln, ed. Roy P. Easier, 5 vols., New Brunswick, NJ, 1953, Supplement 1972.

The War of the Rebellion: A Compilation of the Official Records of the Union and Confederate Armies, 128 vols., Washington, 1880-1901 (cited as OR).

Verhandlungen der Standeversammlung des Grossherzogtums Baden von 1842 bis 1848, Protokolle und Beilagen der zweiten Kammer, Karlsruhe (cited as VSB).

Verhandlungen des deutschen Parlaments, ed. F. S. Jucho, Frankfurt a. M., 1848.

Newspapers
German Newspapers:

Badischer Landesbote, Karlsruhe; *Badische Landpost*, Karlsruhe; *Berliner Volkszeitung*, Berlin; *Frankfurter Journal*, Frankfurt; *Frankfurter Zeitung und Handelsblatt*, Frankfurt; *Kölnische Zeitung*, Cologne; *Kölnische Volkszeitung*, Cologne; *Mannheimer Tageblatt*, Mannheim; *Neue Badische Landeszeitung*, Mannheim; *Neue Preussische Zeitung (Kreuzzeitung)*, Berlin; *Norddeutsche Allgemeine Zeitung*, Berlin; *Weser Zeitung*, Bremen

German-American Newspapers:

(Neuer) Anzeiger des Westens, St. Louis, Missouri; *Baltimore Wecker*, Baltimore, Maryland; *Belleviller Volksblatt* (weekly), Belleville, Illinois; *Belleviller Zeitung*, Belleville, Illinois; *Chicago Neue Presse*, Chicago, Illinois; *Misissippi-Blatter, Sonntagsausgabe der Westlichen Post*, St. Louis, Missouri; *Neue Freie Presse*, Chicago, Illinois; *New Yorker Abendzeitung*, New York; *New Yorker Criminalzeitung und Belletristisches Journal*, New York; *New Yorker Staatszeitung*, New York; *Philadelphia Demokrat*, Philadelphia, Pennsylvania; *Tägliche Illinois Staatszeitung*, Chicago, Illinois; *Tägliche Westliche Post*, St. Louis, Missouri

American Newspapers:

Belleville Advocate, Belleville, Illinois ; *Belleville Republican*, Belleville, Illinois; *Missouri Republican*, St. Louis, Missouri; *St. Louis Republican*, St. Louis, Missouri

Publications by Friedrich Hecker
Independent Publications

Betrachtungen über den Kirchenstreit in Deutschland und die Infallibilität (St. Louis, Missouri; Neustadt a. H., 1874) (cited as FH, Betrachtungen*). Deutschland und Danemark. Für das deutsche Volk (Schaffhausen, 1847) (with Georg Lornmel).*

Die Erhebung des Volkes in Baden fur die deutsche Republik im Frühjahr 1848 (Basel 1848; 2nd ed. Strasbourg 1848) (cited as Hecker, *Erhebung*).

Die staatsrechtlichen Verhaltnisse der Deutschkatholiken mit besonderern Hinblick auf Baden (Heidelberg 1845; 2nd ed. 1846) (cited as Hecker, *Deutschkatholiken*).

Gepfefferte Briefe über Kleinstaatler und Kleinstaatlerei. Geschrieben im Frühling 1867 (St. Joseph, Missouri, n.d.) (1867; a further edition appeared in 1868 in Mannheim under the title of *Gepfefferte Briefe. 12 Briefe von 1865-67*, 2nd ed. in the same year (cited as Hecker, *Gepfefferre Briefe*).

Ideen und Vorschläge zu einer Reform des Gerichtswesens (Mannheim, 1844).

Reden und Vorlesungen, St. Louis (Missouri; Neustadt a.H., 1872). Contains the following texts, all from 1871 (cited as Hecker, Reden): "Festrede zur St. Louiser Friedensfeier"; "Rede, gehalten am 4. Juli bei der Turnfahnenfeier in Trenton, Illinois: Unsere Republik, ihre Kritiker und Gegner"; "Die Beamten im Fürstenstaate und im Volkstaate"; "Lincoln und Cromwell"; "Weiblichkeit und Weiberrechtelei."

Speeches and Smaller Articles:

"Ansprache an die deutsch-arnerikanische Bevölkerung der Vereinigten Staaten", *Belleviller Volksblatt* (weekly), No. 26: 16. August 1856 (introduction); No. 27- 23. August 1856; No. 28: 30. August 1856; No. 29 : 6. September 1856; No. 30 :13. September 1856; No. 31 : 20. September 1856; No. 3127. September 1956; No. 33: 4. October 1856 (conclusion).

"Advokat. Der deutsche Advocatenstand," in: *Staatslexikon*, ed. Carl von Rotteck, Carl Welcker, vol. 1, 2nd ed. (Altona, 1845), 355-69.

"Itzstein", in: *Vorwärts. Volkstaschenbuch auf das Jahr 1844*, ed. Robert Blum, Friedrich Steger (Leipzig 1844), 234-44.

"Aus einer Rede Heckers, gehalten zu St. Louis im Februar d. J. bei einer Geldsammlung für den Centralausschuß der deutschen Dernokraten in Berlin", *Der Voksfreund. Eine Wochenschrift für Westfalen*, Nr. 31 (3.8.1949), 128f,Nr.32 (10.8.1849), 132-33.

"Aus meinem Leben. 1. Wie die geheimen Wiener Conferenzbeschlüsse an das Tageslicht gezogen wurden", *Die Gartenlaube*, no. 35 (1869), 552ff.

"Aus meinern Leben. 2. Der Hexenmeister der Prarie", *Die Gartenlaube*, no. 20 (1870), 313f.

Blankenhorn, Adolph, ed., *Über den Weinbau der Vereinigten Staayen von Nordamerika und die Bedeutung der amerikanischen Reben fiir die Erhaltung des europaischen Weinbaues. Briefwechsel zwischen Adolph Blankenhorn und Friedrich Hecker in den jahren 1872-1880 (= Mitteilungen des önologischen Institutes Karlsruhe-Blankenhornsberg)*, (Darmstadt 1883); available in the Bibliothek der Forschungsanstalt Geisenheim im Rheingau.

"Das politische Lied," Karl Heinrich Schnauffer, *Neue Lieder fiir das teutsche Volk. Mit einem Vorwort von Hecker* (Rheinfelden, 1848), 3-6.

"Der badische Landtag von 1842," Georg Herwegh, ed., *Einundzwanzig Bogen aus der Schweiz*, l.Teil (Zurich; Winterthur 1983), 33-55.

Die Friedensglocke. prophetischer Mahnruf an das deutsche Volk aus Amerika (Munich, 1866) (includes "Wiedergabe einer miindlichen Stellungnahme Heckers zugunsten der Triasidee zur Losung der Deutschen Frage," 5-15, of doubtful authenticity).

Preface to Thomas Paine, *Die Rechte des Menschen. Eine Antwort auf Burke's Angriff gegen die Franzosische Revolution und zugleich eine Kritik des Wesens und des Wertes der verschiederien bestehenden Regierungsformen, mit einer Biographie des Verfassers und einer Vorrede von Friedrich Hecker* (Leipzig, 1851), VII-XIV.

Many speeches printed in *Verhandlungen der Ständeversammlung des Grossherzogtums Baden von 1842 bis 1848, Protokolle und Beilagen der zweiten Kammer.*

Printed Hecker Letters

FH to Sebastian Straub, n. p. (= Mannheim), 6 October 1845; 20 March 1847, Helmut Eckert, "Heckerbriefe," ZGO 93 (1941), 279-85.

FH to Emma Herwegh, Muttenz, 11 July 1848,1848. *Briefe von und an Georg Herwegh*, ed. Marcel Herwegh (Paris; Leipzig; Munich, 1896), 247-50.

FH to Josefine Hecker, New York, 7 October 1848, *AGR* 26 (1960), 18-19; from the *Kaiserlauterner Wochenblatt* no. 52 (1848), no. 1 (1849) without sequel; there is a complete reprint in *Der Volksfreund*, no. 28 (30.12.1848) 140ff.

FH to his family, St. Louis. 9 November 1848, *Der Volksfreund* no. 9 (6 March 1849).

FH to unknown friends in the United States and Switzerland (excerpts), Le Havre n. d. (July, 1849), *Die republikanische Partei in Baden und ihre Führer, beurteilt und gerichtet in der schriftliche Hinterlassenschaft von Hecker, Struve und Brentano. Als Beilage zum Heidelberger Journal separat gedruckt* (Mannheim, 1849), 9ff.

FH to the author, Le Havre, 30 June 1849, *Eine Notwendigkeit, für Deutschland. Worte aus voller Brust an die Ehrfichen aller Parteien, mit einem Brief e als Vorwort von Friedrich Hecker* (Herisau, 1849), 111 -12.

FH an seine Schwester Henriette Cron, Lebanon, St. Clair County, 111., 18 July 1858; 8 November 1858, in Hansmartin Schwarzmaier, "Auswanderbreife aus Nordamerika," *ZGO* 126 (1978), 327-332.

FH to Gustav Struve, Lookout Valley, Tennessee, 21 December 1863, printed by P.P. Kenkel, "Ein Brief Friedrich Heckers an Gustav Struve als Beitrag zur Geschichte des Bargerkrieges," *DAG* 3 (1903), Heft 3,53-56; also printed in *Die Gartenlaube*, Jahrgang 1865, 56ff.

"Friedrich Hecker an den deutschen Eidgenossen (Der Krieg in Amerika), 17. Februar 1865," *Der deutsche Eidgenosse*, 15. Marz 1865, London; Hamburg 1865,43-47.

"Friedrich Hecker to the State Department in Washington, Lookout Valley, Tennessee, December 21st, 1863," printed in Horace White, *The Life of Lyman Trumbull* (New York, 1913), 215.

FH to the editor of *Die Gartenlaube* (Ernst Keil), n. d., n. p., *Die Gartenlaube*, 1869, 416 (excerpts).

FH to the editor of *Die Gartenlaube* (Ernst Keil), n. d., n. p., *Die Gartenlaube*, 1870, 208 (note, "Blätter und Bluthen").

FH to the editor of *Die Gartenlaube* (Ernst Keil, April-May, 1873), *Die Gartenlaube*, 1873,17 (excerpts).

FH to the editor of *Die Gartenlaube* (Ernst Keil), n. d., n. p., *Die Gartenlaube*, 1873, 658.

FH to an unnamed friend, Summerfield, St. Clair County, 111., Friedrich Walter, "Bin Brief Friedrich Heckers aus dern Jahre 1870," *Mannheimer Geschichtsblätter* 12 (1911), 225-29.

FH to Max A. F. Haas, n. p., 5. Dezember 1877 (a characteristic letter by Friedrich Hecker, with an introductory explanation by Wilhelm Rapp), *DAG* 5 (1905), no. 1,47-48.

Hecker's Letters from Germany, 1873 (for the *Illinois Staatszeitung*, Chicago):

1: Freiburg, Baden, 2 June 1873, TISZ, 25 June 1873.

2: Baden, 7 June 1873, TISZ, 30 June 1873.

3: Black Forest, 19 June 1873, TISZ, 15 July 1873.

4: Mannheim, 30 June 1873, TISZ, 24 July 1873.

5 : Wildbad, 19 July 1873, TISZ, 6 August 1873.

6: Germany, start of August 1873, TISZ, 21 August 1873.

7: Germany, 7 August 1873, TISZ, 26 August 1873.

8: Germany, August, 1873, TISZ, 30 August 1873.

9: Germany, 18. August 1873, TISZ, 5 September 1873.

10: From the Baden Highlands, 26 August 1873, TISZ, 16 September 1873.

11: From South Germany, start of September, 1873, TISZ, 23 September 1873.

12: Baden, 6 September 1873, TISZ, 25 September 1873.

13: Freiburg, September, 1873, TISZ, 1 October 1873.

14: From South Germany, 20 September 1873, TISZ, 13 October 1873.

Publications about Hecker

Anonymous [Gustav Pfizer], *Die Glorie Heckers*, 2nd edition (Stuttgart, 1848). Anonymous, *Ein freies Wort über die Ausweisung der badischen Abgeordneten v. Itzstein und Hecker aus Preussen* (Leipzig, 1845).

"Friedrich Hecker," *GL*, 1881, 264-266.

"Friedrich Hecker," *Der Freidenker. Organ der Freidenker von Nordamerika und des Nordamerikanischen Turnerbundes*, vol. 10, no. 14, continuous no. 448, 3 April 1881,4.

"Friedrich Hecker," *Frankfurter Zeitung und Handelsblatt*, 30 March 1881, no. 89.

"Hecker," *Deutsch-amerikanisches Conversations-Lexicon. Mit specieller Rücksicht auf das Bedürfnis der in Amerika lebenden Deutschen*, ed. Alexander J. Schem, vol. 5 (New York, 1871), 223-24.

"Colonel Friedrich Hecker," *The United States Biographical Dictionary and Portrait Gallery of Eminent and Self- made Men* (Urbana, Illinois, 1876).

"Frederick Karl Franz Hecker," *The World's Best Orations from the Earliest Period to the Present Time*, ed. David J. Brewer, volume 7 (1899), 2457-2464.

"Friedrich Hecker," *History of St. Clair County, Illinois*, ed. St. Clair County Genealogical Society (Dallas, Texas, 1988), 291-292.

"Friedrich Hecker. Der Liebling des Volkes," Ruetenik (ed.), *Berühmte Deutsche Vorkämpfer*, 338-342, identical with the article "Friedrich Hecker. Der Liebling des Volkes," *Deutsche Amerikaner in Kirche und Staat von 1626 bis zur Gegenwart* (Cleveland, 1892), 270-274.

"Ein Volkstribun von Achtundvierzig," *GL*, 1872, 390-392.

"Friedrich Hecker in Leipzig," *GL*, 1873, 526.

"Begrüssung Heckers in Deutschland," *GL*, 1873, 382.

Assion, Peter, "'Es lebe Hecker! Stosset an!' Die Popularität und Verehrung Friedrich Heckers von 1848/49 bis zur Gegenwart," Frei, ed., *Hecker in den USA*, 117-134.

Assion, Peter, Der Heckerkult. Bin Volksheld von 1848 im Wandel seiner geschichtlichen Präsenz," *Zeitschrift fur Volkskunde* 87 (1991), 53-76.

Bohrne, Albrecht, "Der Deutschamerikaner Friedrich Hecker," *Die Gegenwart* 4 (1873), 7-11.

Braun, Karl, "Friedrich Hecker, der Sterne- und Streifenbanner-Schwärmer," idem, *Zeitgenossen. Erzahlungen, Charakterisitiken und Kritiken. Gesammelte Feuilletons*, vol. 2 (Braunschweig, 1877), 230-281.

Butz, Caspar, "Erinnerungen an Friedrich Hecker," *WP*, daily, parts 1 and 2, 1,8. May 1881.

Erinnerung an Friedrich Hecker. Herausgegeben vom Hecker-Denkmal-Comite, St. Louis, Missouri, 1882, includes "Friedrich Heckers Bestattung zu Summerfield ..."; "Das Heckerdenkmal in St. Louis (Planung, Geldsammlung)"; "Friedrich Heckers siebenzigster Geburtstag in der Central-Turnhalle zu St. Louis gefeiert am 28.9.1881"; "Hecker-Denkmal Enthüllungs-Feierlichkeit im Benton-Park zu St. Louis am 1.10.1882."

Faust, Albert Bernhard, "Friedrich Hecker," *DAB*, vol. 4/2 (New York, 1931), 493ff.

Frei, Alfred G., ed., *Friedrich Hecker in den USA. Eine deutsch-amerikanische Spurensicherung* (Konstanz, 1993).

Freitag, Sabine, "Friedrich Hecker. Der republikanische Souverän," idem., *Die Achtundvierziger. Lebensbilder aus der deutschen Revolution 1848/49* (Munich, 1998), 45-62.

Friedrich Hecker und sein Antheil an der Geschichte Deutschlands undAmerikas. Herausgegeben unter den Auspicien des Deutsch-Amerikanischen Hecker Denkmalvereins von Cincinnati/Ohio (Cincinnati, 1881).

Haass, Wolfgang, *Friedrich Hecker. Leben und Wirken in Dokumenten und Wertungen der Mit- und Nachwelt* (Angelbachtal n. d. [1981]).

Hecker Reynolds, Alice, "Friedrich Hecker," *AGR* 12 (1946), no. 4,4-7.

Hecker Reynolds, Alice, "Hecker Lore," *AGR* 14 (1947/48), no. 5, 7-11.

Hofer, J. M., "Preparatory Material for a Biography on Friedrich Hecker," *DAG* 33 (1933), 124-45 (has only known, printed sources).

Horn, Eva, "Das Heckerle," *FAZ*, 22 January 1992, no. 18, page N3.

Kaiser, Leo M., "'Symbolic Obelisk'": The Hecker Monument in Benton Park," *Bulletin of the Missouri Historical Society*, 17 (July 1961), 352-356.

Klingelschmidt, Klaus-Peter, *Vivat hoch! – Die freie Republik! Friedrich Hecker – ein deutscher Mythos* (Stuttgart, 1982).

Krimm, Konrad, "Friedrich Hecker (1811-1881)," *USA und Baden-Württemberg in ihren geschichtlichen Beziehungen, Beiträge und Dokumente* (Stuttgart, 1976), 85-87.

Luck, Andreas, *Friedrich Hecker. Rolle, Programm und politische Möglichkeiten eines Führers der radikal-demokratischen Bewegung von 1847/48 in Baden*, Ph. D, dissertation. Berlin 1979.

Muhs, Rudolf, "'Wie die geheimen Konferenzbeschlüsse an das Tageslicht gezogen wurden.' Zur Publikation des Schlussprotokols von 1834 und zur Rolle des Hallgarten-Kreises fur die vormarzliche Opposition," *Archiv fur Sozialgeschichte* 26 (1986), 321-343.

Muhs, Rudolf, "Heckermythos und Revolutionsforschung," *ZGO* 134 (1986), 422-441.

Paul, Roland, "'Freie Erde und freies Vaterland/ Friedrich Hecker in den USA," Frei ed., *Hecker in den USA*, 15-41.

Rowan, Steven, Friedrich Hecker Papers, Inventory, Western Historical Manuscripts, University of Missouri – St. Louis 1987.

Scharp, Heinrich, *Friedrich Hecker, ein deutscher Demokrat*, Ph. D. dissertation, typescript, Frankfurt a. M., 1923.

Schieder, Wolfgang, "Friedrich Franz Karl Hecker," *NDB*, vol. 8, Berlin 1968, 180-82.

Strack, Paul, "Friedrich Heckers Herkunft," *Beiträge zur Familien- und Heimatkunde in Baden*, no. 2 (Grafenhausen bei Lahr/Baden, 1959).

Struve, Gustav, "Friedrich Hecker," idem and Gustav Rasch, eds., *Zwölf Streiter der Revolution* (Berlin, 1867), 7-33.

Struve, Gustav, "Friedrich Hecker in Amerika," *GL*, 1865, 56-59.

Trefousse, Hans Louis, "Carl Schutz und Friedrich Hecker," Frei, ed., *Hecker in den USA*, 97-106.

Voigt, Frederick M., *A Study of Selected Speeches of Friedrich Hecker in the United States*, University of Southern Illinois-Carbondale 1964 (unpublished dissertation, in the first instance a linguistic study of Hecker's *Reden und Vorlesungen* in English translation; in general a very weak analysis).

Vollmer, Franz X, "Der Hecker-Nachlass von St. Louis/USA," *ZGO* (1988), 349-415.

Weech, Friedrich von, "Friedrich Franz Karl Hecker," idem., *Badische Biographien*, part 4, Karlsruhe 1891, 166-171.

Weech, Friedrich von," Friedrich Hecker," *ADB*, vol. 50,1905, 93-95.

Zilling, Bernhard, *Helfen kann nur die grosse That. Die Radikalisierung in Baden 1848*, vol. 1 (Freiburg i. Br., 1984).

Zimmermann, Wilhelm, "Friedrich Hecker," *Zeitgenossen in Biographien und Porträts. Ein Volksbuch*, 2nd ed. (Jena, 1849), 83-88.

Contemporary Printed Sources and Literature

Andlaw, Heinrich von, *Der Aufruhr und Umsturz in Baden als einenatürliche Folge der Landesgesetzgebung, mit Rücksicht auf die "Bewegungin Baden" von J.B. Bekk, damaligen Vorstand des Ministeriums desInnern, dargestellt*, 3 vols. (Freiburg, 1850/51).

Bassermann, Friedrich Daniel, *Denkwürdigkeiten*, ed. Friedrich von Bassermann-Jordan (Frankfurt a. M., 1926).

Bekk, J.B., *Die Bewegung in Baden vom Ende des Februar 1848 bis zur Mitte des Mai 1849* (Mannheim, 1850).

Bernays, Carl Ludwig, "Betrachtungen iiber die Metamorphose der deutschen Einwanderung in das Amerikanerthum," *DAM*, year 4, [1867] May issue, 386-399.

Bernays, Carl Ludwig, "Der deutsche Sonntag in Amerika," *DAM* (Lexow), year 3, vol. 1, 1866, June issue, 509-519.

Bernays, Carl Ludwig, "Die Tugendhaften in der Politik," *DAM*, year 3, 1866, December issue, 311-523.

Bernays, Carl Ludwig, "Bin Beitrag zur Geschichte der Metamorphose der eingewanderten Deutschen in Amerikaner," *DAM*, year 4 [1867], vol. 1, February issue, 91-108.

Beseler, Georg, *Volksrecht und Juristenrecht* (Leipzig, 1843).

Blum, Hans, *Die deutsche Revolution 1848/49. Eine Jubiläumsgabe fur das deutsche Volk* (Florence; Leipzig, 1898).

Börnstein, Heinrich, *Fünfundsiebzig jahre in der Alien und Neuen Welt. Memoiren eines Unbedeutenden*, 2nd ed. (Leipzig, 1884) [English translation and edition of the American portion by Steven Rowan, published as Henry Boernstein, *Memoirs of a Nobody: The Missouri Years of an Austrian Radical* (St. Louis, 1998)].

Bromme, Traugott, *Rathgeber für Auswanderungslustige. Wie und wohin sollen wir auswandern. Eine umfassende Beleuchtung* (Stuttgart, 1846).

Busch, Moritz, *Wanderungen zwischen Hudson und Mississippi, 1851 und 1852*, 2 vols. (Stuttgart; Tubingen, 1854).

Butz, Caspar, "Abraham Lincoln," *DAM*, January 1864,11-21; March, 1864, 224-229; May, 1865, 468-472.

Butz, Caspar, "Das Finale des Wahlkampfes," *DAM*, 371-378.

Butz, Caspar, "Die neue Partei," *DAM*, July, 1864, 74-86.

Butz, Caspar, "Unser Urteil über Lincoln," *DAM*, February, 1864, 125-129.

Der Deutsche Pionier (Monatszeitschrift) ed. Pionier-Gesellschaft (Cincinnati 1869-88).

Deutsch-Amerikanische Monatshefte fur Politik, Wissenschaft und Literatur, ed. Caspar Butz, Chicago 1864-1866 (cited as *DAM*)

Die Deutschen in Amerika. Jahrbuch der Deutschen in Amerika für das Jahr 1873, ed. Verlag Emil Steiger (New York, 1873).

Die Gegenwart. Eine encyklopädische Darstellung der neuesten Zeitgeschichte fiir alle Stände (Leipzig: F.A. Brockhaus, 1848-55).

Douai, Adolf, *Land und Leute in der Union* (Berlin, 1864).

Fester, Richard, "Bismarcks Gespräch mit Carl Schurz am 28. Januar 1868," *Süddeutsche Monatshefte* 11, no. 1, 363-368.

Fröbel, Julius, *Aus Amerika. Erfahrungen, Reisen und Studien*, 2 vols. (Leipzig, 1857-58).

Fröbel, Julius, *Die deutsche Auswanderung und ihre culturhistorische Bedeutung, 15 Briefe* (Leipzig, 1858).

Fröbel, Julius, *Ein Lebenslauf. Aufzeichnungen, Erinnerungen, Bekenntnisse,* 2 vols. (Stuttgart, 1890-91).

Gervinus, Georg Gottfried, *Die Mission der Deutschkatholiken* (Heidelberg, 1845).

Hausser, Ludwig, *Denkwürdigkeiten zur Geschichte der badischen Revolution* (Heidelberg, 1851).

Hausser, Ludwig, "Baden vor den Ereignissen von 1848," *Die Gegenwart,* vol. 2 (Leipzig, 1849), 321-359. Hausser, Ludwig, "Baden im Friihjahr 1848," *Die Gegenwart,* vol. 3, Leipzig, 1849,443-486.

Hagenmeyer, Karl, *Die Revolutionsjahre 1848/49. Schilderungen auf Grund eigener Anschauung und persönlicher Erlebnisse,* Karlsruhe 1899, on Hecker, 23-39.

Heinzen, Karl, *Teutscher Radikalismus in Amerika. Ausgewählte Abhandlungen, Kritiken und Aphorismen aus den Jahren 1854-1879,* 2 vols. (Milwaukee, 1898).

Hertle, Daniel, *Die Deutschen in Nordamerika und der Freiheitskampf in Missouri,* (Chicago, 1865).

Kapp, Friedrich, *Geschichte der Deutschen im Staate New York bis zum Anfang des 19. Jahrhunderts,* 3d ed. (New York, 1869).

Kapp, Friedrich, *Über Auswanderung. Ein Vortrag* (Berlin, 1871).

Kapp, Friedrich, *Aus und über Amerika: Thatsachen und Erlebnisse,* 2 vols. (Berlin, 1871).

Knortz, Karl, "Francis Lieber," *DP,* September 1873, year 5, no. 5, 203-207.

Kohler, Carl, *Briefe aus Amerika für deutsche Auswanderer* (Darmstadt, 1852).

Kohler, Manfred, ed., "Aus dem Land des Republikanismus, der Sklavenbefreiung und des Nützlichkeits Prinzips. Briefe von Franz Zitz an Julius Frobel," *Mainzer Zeitschrift,* 84/85 (1989/90),167-199.

Körner, Gustav, "Beleuchtung des Duden'schen Berichtes uber die westliche Staaten Nordamerikas (geschrieben im Jahre 1834)," *DAG* 16 (1916), 280-333.

Körner, Gustav, *Das deutsche Element in den Vereinigten Staaten von Nordamerika (1818-1848)* (Cincinnati, 1880).

Kroger, A. E., "Die Regierungsform der Vereinigten Staaten," *DAM,* May, 1865, 397-413.

Lexow, Friedrich, "Das Jahr der Deutschen," *DAM,* September, 1866, 313-19.

Lexow, Friedrich, "Die Deutschen in Amerika, Zweiter Artikel," *DAM,* March, 1866, 255-261.

Lexow, Friedrich, "Graf Bismarck," *DAM,* year 3, July, 1866, 65-69; Oktober, 1866, 399-406.

Lexow, Friedrich, "Herr Bernays und das Deutschthum in Amerika," *DAM,* March, 1867, 235-44.

Lexow, Friedrich, "Unsere Sympathie," *DAM,* August, 1866,184-190.

Lexow, Rudolf, "Andrew Johnson," *DAM,* April, 1866, 349-360. Lexow, Rudolf, "Die Situation," DAM , May 1866, 465-473.

Mathy, Ludwig, ed., *Aus dem Nachlass von Karl Mathy. Brief aus den Jahren 1846-1848 mit Erläuterungen,* Leipzig 1898.

McCormack, Thomas J. (ed.), *Memoirs of Gustave Koerner, 1809-1896. Life Sketches Written at the Suggestion of his Children,* 2 vols. (Cedar Rapids, Iowa. 1909) (cited as Körner, *Memoirs*).

Mögling, Theodor, *Briefe an seine Freunde* (Solothurn, 1858).

Münch, Friedrich, *Der Staat Missouri geschildert mit besonderer Berücksichtigung auf teutsche Einwanderung* (New York; St. Louis, 1859).

Münch, Friedrich, "Die künftige deutsche Auswanderung nach Nordamerika," *DP,* year 3, September 1871, no. 7, 203-12.

Münch, Friedrich, "Ist die Erhaltung des deutschen Elementes innerhalb der Vereinigten Staaten für die Fortenrwicklung derselben erforderfich oder nicht? Rede auf das Jahr 1857," repr. in: Münch, Friedrich, *Gesammelte Schriften*, St. Louis 1902, 384-391.

Münch, Friedrich, "Zur Geschichte der deutschen Einwanderung," *DAM*, June, 1864, 481- 495.

Münch, Friedrich, "Zur Geschichte der Emanzipation in Missouri," *DAM*, February, 1864, 97-110; March, 1864,193-203.

Perry, Thomas Sergeant, ed., *The Life and Letters of Francis Lieber* (Boston, 1882).

Pichler, Karoline, "Ueber weibliche Bildung und Bestimmung," *DP*, year 5, March, 1873, no. 1, 7-11.

Poesche, Theodor, "Anzahl der Deutschen in den Vereinigten Staaten im Jahre 1870," *DP*, year 5, August 1873, no. 6, 173-179.

Posche, Theodor, "Die Deutschen in den Vereinigen Saaten nach dem Census von 1870," *DP*, year 4, December 1872, no. 10, 348-349.

Preetorius, Emil, "Die Neubildung der Parteien," *DAM*, vol. 1, Mai 1864, 435-440.

Preetorius, Emil, "Missouri," *DAM*, vol. 1, January, 1864, 4-8.

Preetorius, Emil, "Prasidentliche Selbstnachfolge," *DAM*, vol. 1, April, 1864, 289-294.

Rasch, Gustav, "Heimgekehrt aus dem Exil. Zur Begrüssung Gustav

Struves," *GL*, 1865, 453. "Resume iiber Aus- und Einwanderung," *DP*, year 4, February, 1873, no. 12,410-416.

Rousseau, Jean Jacques, *Vom Gesellschaftsvertrag oder Grundsätzes des Staatsrechts* (Stuttgart, 1991).

Ruetenik, H.J., ed., *Berühmte Deutsche Vorkämpfer fur Fortschritt, Freiheit und Friede in Nord-Amerika van 1626- 1898. Einhundert und fünfzig Biographien* (Cleveland, 1899).

Rümelin, Carl, "Das verklagte Deutschland," *DAM*, year 3, vol. 1, April 1866, 327-32.

Schafer, Joseph, *Intimate Letters of Carl Schutz, 1841-1869* (Wisconsin Historical Publications, No. 30) (Madison, WI, 1928).

Schnake, Friedrich, "Geschichte der deutschen Bevölkerung und der deutschen Presse von St. Louis und Umgegend," *DP*, September 1872, year 4, no. 7, 226-236; *Der DP*, year 4, Mai 1872, no. 3 , 85-88; ibid., year 4, no. 2, April 1872, 46-49; *DP*, year 3, no. 12, Februar 1872, 378-382

Schurz, Carl, *Lebenserinnerungen*, 3 vols. (Berlin, 1909-1912).

Schurz, Carl, *The Reminiscences of Carl Schurz*, 3 volumes (New York, 1907-08).

Stallo, Johann B., *Reden, Abhandlungen und Briefe* (New York, 1893).

Struve, Amalie, *Erinnerungen aus den badischen Freiheitskämpfen* (Hamburg, 1850).

Struve, Gustav von, *Dieseits und jenseits des Oceans. Zwanglose Hefte zur Vermittlung der Beziehungen zwischen Amerika und Deutschland*, 4 fascicles (Coburg, 1863-1864).

Struve, Gustav von, *Wegweiser fur Auswanderer* (Bamberg, 1866).

Struve, Gustav von, *Geschichte der drei Volkserhebungen in Baden* (Bern, 1849).

Tocqueville, Alexis de, *Über die Demokratie in Amerika*, 2 vols. (Zurich, 1987).

"Unsere deutschen Schulen," *DP*, year 4, no. 3, Mai 1872, 100-106.

Wagner, Maria, ed., *Mathilde Franziska Anneke in Selbstzeugnissen und Dokumenten* (Frankfurt a. M., 1980).

Wagner, Philipp, *Ein Achtundvierziger. Erlebtes und Gedachtes* (Brooklyn, 1882).

Wagner, William, *History of the 24th Illinois Volunteer Infantry Regiment (Old Hecker Regiment)*, Chicago (August) 1864, Chicago Historical Society Library.

Wehler, Hans Ulrich, ed., *Friedrich Kapp: Vom radikalen Frühsozialisten des Vormarz zum liberalen Parteipolitiker des Bismarckreich, Briefe 1843-1884* (Frankfurt a. M., 1969).

Welcker, Carl Theodor, "Association," *Staatslexikon*, vol. 1, 2nd ed. (Altona, 1845), 723-747.

Welsch, Dr., "Deutsch-Amerikaner, aber keine arnerikanisierte Deutsche," *DAM*, year 4, April, 1867, 348-356.

Zimmermann, Wilhelm, Die deutsche Revolution (Karlsruhe, 1848). "Zur Erinnerung an August Becker," *DP* year 4, no. 3, May 1872, 82-85.

Secondary Literature

Adams, Willi Paul, ed., *Die deutschsprachige Auswanderung in den Vereinigten Staaten. Berichte über Forschungsstand und Quellenbestande* (John F. Kennedy Institut für Nordamerikastudien, Materialien 14) (Berlin, 1980).

Adams, Willi Paul, ed., *Die Vereinigten Staaten van Amerika* (Frankfurt a. M., 1977).

Adams, Willi Paul, "Ethnische Führungsrollen und die Deutschamerikaner," Trommler, ed., *Amerika und die Deutschen*, 165-175.

Andreas, Willy, *Geschichte der badischen Verwaltungsorganisation und Verfassung in den Jahren 1802-18*, vol. 1 (Leipzig, 1913).

Angermann, Erich, "Der Deutsche Frühkonstitutionalismus und das amerikanische Vorbild," *HZ* 219 (1974), 1-32.

Arndt, Karl J. R., Olson, May E, eds., *German American Newspapers and Periodicals, 1732-1955*, 2d ed. (Heidelberg, 1965).

Ashton, Rosemary, *Little Germany. German Refugees in Victorian Britain* (Oxford; New York, 1989).

Barclay, Thomas, *The Liberal Republican Movement in Missouri, 1865-1871* (Columbia: State Historical Society of Missouri, 1926).

Barry, Colman J., *The Catholic Church and the German Americans* (Milwaukee, 1953).

Bartlett, Ruhl J., *John C. Fremont and the Republican Party* (Columbus, 1930).

Bauer, Sonia-Maria, *Die Verfassungsgebende Versammlung in der Badischen Revolution von 1849* (Dusseldorf, 1991).

Baumgart, Franzjörg, *Die verdrängte Revolution. Darstellung und Bewertung der Revolution von 1848 in der deutschen Geschichtsschreibung vor dem 1. Weltkrieg* (Dusseldorf, 1976).

Bensel, Richard Franklin, *Yankee Leviathan: The Origins of Central State Authority in America, 1859-1877* (Cambridge, 1990).

Bergquist, James M., "The Forty-Eighters and the Politics of the 1850s," Trefousse, Hans L, ed., *Germany and America*, 111-121.

Bergquist, James M., "The Forty-Eighters and the Republican Convention of 1860," Brancaforte (ed.), *The German Forry-Eighters*, 141-155.

Bergquist, James M., *The Political Attitudes of the German Immigrant in Illinois 1848-1860*, Ph.D. dissertation, typescript., Northwestern University, 1966.

Betz, Gottlieb, "Die deutsch-amerikanische patriotische Lyrik der Achtundvierziger und ihre historische Grundlage," *Americana Germanica* 22 (1916), S. 18ff; 93ff.

Bios, Walter, *Badische Revolutionsgeschichte aus den Jahren 1848 und 1849* (Mannheim, 1910).

Brancaforte, Charlotte L, ed., *The German Forty-Eighters in the United States* (New York; Bern; Frankfurt; Berlin, 1989).

Brandt, Hartwig, ed., *Restauration und Friihliberalismus 1814-1840* (Darmstadt, 1979).

Brandt, Hartwig, *Landständische Representation im deutschen Vormärz. Politisches Denken im Einflussfeld des monarchischen Prinzips* (Berlin, 1968).

Bruncken, Ernest, "German Political Refugees in the United States during the Period from 1815-1860," *DAG* 111 (1903), no. 3/4, 33-48; *DAG* IV (1904), no. 1, 33-59.

Cole, Arthur C, "President Lincoln and the Illinois Radical Republicans," *Mississippi Valley Historical Review* 4 (1918), 417ff.

Conzen, Kathleen Neils, "Germans," *Harvard Encyclopedia of American Ethnic Groups*, ed. Stephan Thernstrom et al. (Cambridge, MA 1980), 402-425.

Conzen, Kathleen Neils, "Deutschamerikaner und die Erfindung der Ethnizität," Trommler ed., *Amerika und die Deutschen*, 149-163.

Conzen, Kathleen Neils, "Die Assimilierung der Deutschen in Amerika," Adams, ed., *Die deutschsprachige Auswanderung*, 33-65.

Curran, Thomas, *Xenophobia and Immigration 1820-1930* (New York, 1975).

Deuchert, Norbert, *Vom Hambacher Fest zur badischen Revolution. Politische Presse und Anfänge deutscher Demokratie1832-1848/49* (Stuttgart, 1983).

Detjen, David W., *The Germans in Missouri,1900-1918. Prohibition, Neutrality and Assimilation* (Columbia: University of Missouri Press, 1985).

Dobbert, Guido Andre, "German-Americans between New and Old Fatherland," *American Quarterly* 19 (1967), 663-680.

Dobbert, Guido Andre, *The Disintegration of an Immigrant Community. The Cincinnati Germans, 1870-1920* (New York, 1980).

Dobert, Eitel W., *Deutsche Demokraten in Amerika. Die Achtundvierziger und ihre Schriften* (Göttingen, 1958).

Doerries, Reinhard R., "Soziale Eingliederungsprozesse von Iren und Deutschen in den Vereinigten Staaten. Ein Vergleich," *Amerikastudien*, Band 27, Heft 3 (1982), 259-273.

Doerries, Reinhard R., "Zwischen Staat und Kirche: Peter Paul Cahensly und die Katholischen deutschen Einwanderer in den Vereinigten Staaten," Alexander Fischer, Gunter Moltmann, Klaus Schwabe eds., *Russland, Deutschland, Amerika* (Frankfurter Historische Abhandlungen 17) (Wiesbaden, 1979), 88-104.

Doerries, Reinhard R., *Iren und Deutsche in der Neuen Welt: Akkulturationsprozesse in der amerikanischen Gesellschaft im späten neunzehnten Jahrhundert* (VSWG suppl. 76) (Stuttgart, 1986).

Doerries, Reinhard R., "Organization and Ethnicity. The German-American Experience," *Amerikastudien* 33 (1988), 309-317.

Dorpalen, Andreas, "The German Element and the Issues of the Civil War," *Mississippi Valley Historical Review* 29 (June 1942), 55-76.

Dreyer, Michael, "Die Verfassung der USA. Ein Modell fur deutschen Verfassungsentwürfe des 19. Jahrhunderts?" Elvert, Salewski, *Deutschland und der Westen im 19. und 20. Jahrhundert, part 1: Transatlantische Beziehungen* (Stuttgart, 1993), 225-246.

Elvert, Jiirgen, Salewski, Michael (Hrsg.), *Deutschland und der Westen im 19. und 20. Jahrhundert, part 1: Transatlantische Beziehungen* (Stuttgart, 1993).

Ericson, David F., *The Shaping of American Liberalism: The Debates over Ratification, Nullification and Slavery* (Chicago; London 1993).

Faust, Albert Bernhard, *Das Deutschtum in den Vereinigten Staaten in seiner Bedeutung fur die amerikanische Kultur*, 2 vols. (Leipzig, 1912).

Fickert, Arthur, *Montesquieus und Rousseaus Einfluss auf den vormärzlichen Liberalismus Badens* (Leipzig, 1914).

Flexner, E., *Hundert Jahre Kampf. Die Geschichte der Frauenbewegung in den Vereinigten Staaten* (Frankfurt a. M., 1978).

Foner, Eric, *A Short History of Reconstruction 1863-1877* (New York, 1990).

Foner, Eric, *Free Soil, Free Labor, Free Men: The Ideology of the Republican Party before the Civil War* (Oxford, 1970).

Foner, Eric, *Politics and Ideology in the Age of the Civil War* (Oxford; New York, 1980).

Franz, Eckhard G, *Das Amerikabild der deutschen Revolution von 1848/49. Zum Problem der Übertragung gewachsener Verfassungsformen* (supplement to *Jahrbuch fur Amerikastudien* 2) (Heidelberg, 1958).

Freitag, Sabine (Hrsg.), *Die Achtundvierziger. Lebensbilder aus der deutschen Revolution von 1848/49* (Munich, 1998).

Gall, Lothar, *Bürgertum in Deutschland* (Berlin, 1989).

Gall, Lothar, "Das Problem der parlamentarischen Opposition im deutschen Frühliberalismus," K. Kluxen, W. J. Mommsen, eds., *Politische Ideologien und nationialstaatliche Ordnung* (Munich, 1968), 153-170.

Gall, Lothar, *Der Liberalismus als regierende Partei in Baden. DasGrossherzogtum Baden zwischen Restauration und Reichsgründung* (Wiesbaden, 1968).

Gall, Lothar, "Liberalismus und 'Bürgerliche Gesellschaft.' Zu Charakter und Entwicklung der liberalen Bewegung in Deutschland," *HZ* 220 (1975), 324-356.

Ganter, E., *Karl von Rotteck als Geschichtsschreiber*, Ph. D, dissertation, Freiburg 1908.

Gazley, John Gerow, *American Opinion of German Unification, 1848-1871* (New York, 1926).

Gerber, Richard, "The Liberals of 1872 in Historical Perspective," *Journal of American History*, 62 (June 1975), 40-75.

Gerhard, Hermann, *Das Deutschtum in der amerikanischen Politik* (Leipzig, 1909).

Gienapp, William E., *The Origins of the Republican Party 1852-1856* (Oxford, 1988).

Glossy, Karl, *Literarische Geheimberichte aus dem Vormärz* (Vienna, 1912).

Goebel, Julius, *Der Kampf der deutschen Kultur in America: Aufsätze und Vorträge zur deutschamerikanischen Bewegung* (Leipzig, 1914).

Goldman, Eric F., *Rendezvous with Destiny: A History of Modern American Reform* (New York, 1951).

Grimm, Dieter, *Deutsche Verfassungsgeschichte 1776-1866* (Frankfurt a. M., 1988).

Hamerow, Theodore S., 'The Two Worlds of the Forty-Eighters," Brancaforte, ed., *The German Forty-Eighters*, 19-35.

Hansen, Marcus Lee, "The Revolutions of 1848 and the German Emigration," *Journal of Economic and Business History* 2 (1929/39), 630-658.

Hansen, Marcus Lee, *The Atlantic Migration 1607-1860: A History of the Continuing Settlement of the United States* (Cambridge, MA, 1945).

Harper, James F., "The Arrival of the Europamüde: Germans in America after 1848," Brancaforte, ed., *The German Forty- Eighters*, 1-17.

Harper, Richard Conant, *The Course of the Melting Pot Idea to 1910* (New York, 1980).

Hecker, George S., Gleichert, James E., "Lincoln writes to Friedrich Hecker. A New Letter," *Lincoln Herald* 69 (1967), 159-60.

Herriott, F. I., "The Conference in the Deutsches Haus, Chicago, May 14-15, 1860: A Study of some of the preliminaries of the National Republican Convention of 1860," *Transactions of the Illinois State Historical Society for the year 1928*, 101-194.

Herriott, F.J., "The Germans of Chicago and Stephen A. Douglas in 1854," *DAG* 12 (1912), 381-404.

Higham, John, *Strangers in the Land. Patterns of American Nativism 1860-1925* (New Brunswick; New York, 1955).

Hinners, Wolfgang, *Exil und Rückkehr. Friedrich Kapp, Amerika und Deutschland* (Stuttgart, 1987).

Hinrichs, Beare, *Deutschamerikanische Presse zwischen Tradition und Anpassung* (Frankfurt a. M., 1989).

History of St. Clair County, Illinois, 2 vols., ed. St. Clair County Genealogical Society (Dallas, 1992).

Huch, C. F., "Die Deutsch-Amerikaner und die deutsche Revolution," *DAG* ll (1911),44ff.

Kamphoefner, Walter D., "St. Louis Germans and the Republican Party 1848-1860," *Mid-America* 57 (April 1975), 69-88.

Kamphoefner,Walter, "Dreissiger and Forty-Eighter. The Political Influence of two Generations of German Political Exiles," Trefousse, ed., *Germany and America*, 89-102.

Kaufmann, Wilhelm, *Die Deutschen im amerikanischen Bürgerkriege, Sezessionskrieg 1861-1865* (Munich; Berlin, 1911). [English translation by Steven Rowan, *The Germans in the American Civil War*, Carlisle, PA, 1999]

Koch, Rainer, *Demokratie und Staat bei Julius Fröbel 1805-1894. Liberales Denken zwischen Naturrecht und Sozialdarwinismus* (Wiesbaden, 1978).

Langewiesche, Dieter, "Republik, konstitutionelle Monarchie und 'soziale Frage'. Grundprobleme der deutschen Revolution von 1848/49," *HZ* 230 (1980), 529-548.

Langewiesche, Dieter, "Die deutsche Revolution von 1848/49 und die vorrevolutionäre Gesellschaft. Forschungsstand und Forschungsperspektiven," *AfS*, 21 (1981), 458-498.

Levine, Bruce, *The Spirit of 1848. German Immigrants, Labor Conflict, and the Coming of the Civil War* (Urbana; Chicago, 1992).

Luebke, Frederick, ed., *Ethnic Voters and the Election of Lincoln* (Nebraska, 1971).

Luebke, Frederick C, "German Immigrants and American Politics: Problems of Leadership, Parties, and Issues," Randell Miller, ed., *Germans in America: Retrospect and Prospect. Tricentennial Lectures delivered at the German Society of Pennsylvania in 1983* (Philadelphia, 1984), 57-74.

Luthin, Reinhard H., "Lincoln appeals to German American voters," *AGR* (June/July 1959), 4-6, 15.

McPherson, James M,, "Grant or Greeley? The Abolitionist Dilemma in the Election of 1872," *The American Historical Review* 71 (1965/66), 43-61.

McPherson, James, *Für die Freiheit sterben. Die Geschichte des amerikanischen Burgerkriegs* (Munich, 1992).

Metzner, Henry (Heinrich), *A Brief History of the American Turnerbund*, 2d. ed. (Pittsburgh, 1924).

Meyer, Hildegard, *Nordamerika im Urteil des deutschen Schrifttums bis zur Mitte des 19. Jahrhunderts* (Hamburg, 1929).

Moltmann, Günther, *Atlantische Blockpolitik im 19. Jahrhundert: Die Vereinigten Staaten und der deutsche Liberalismus während der Revolution von 1848/49* (Diisseldorf, 1973).

Moltmann, Giinther, ed., *Deutsche Amerikaauswanderung im 19. Jahrhundert* (Amerikastudien vol. 44) (Stuttgart, 1976).

Moltmann, Giinther, "German Emigration to the United States during the First Half of the Nineteenth Century as a Social Protest Movement," Trefousse, ed., *Germany and America*, 103-110.

Monagham, Jay, "Did Abraham Lincoln receive the Illinois German Vote?" *Journal of the Illinois State Historical Society*, 35 (March 1942), 131-139.

Nagler, Jörg, '"Ubi libertas, ibi patria' – Deutsche Demokraten im Exil. Die politische Tätigkeit der Achtundvierziger in den USA," Frei, ed., *Hecker in den USA*, 61-71.

Nagler, Jörg, "Deutschamerikaner und das Liberal Republican Movement 1872," *Amerikastudien* 33 (1988), 415-438.

Nagler, Jörg, *Fremont contra Lincoln. Die deutsch-amerihnische Opposition in der Republikanischen Partei während des amerikanischen Bürgerkrieges* (Frankfurt; Bern, 1984).

Nagler, Jörg, "Politisches Exil in den USA zur Zeit des Vormärz und der Revolution von 1848 /49," Elvert, Salewski, eds., *Deutschland und der Westen*, 267-293.

Nagler, Jörg, "The Lincoln-Fremont Debate and the Forty-Eighters," Brancaforte, ed., *The German Forty-Eighters*, 157- 178.

Nipperdey, Thomas, *Deutsche Geschichte 1800-1866- Bürgerwelt und starker Staat* (Munich, 1983).

Nolte, Paul, "Bürgerideal, Gemeinde und Republik, 'Klassischer Republikanismus' im frühen deutschen Liberalismus," *HZ* 254 (1992), 609-656.

Nolte, Paul, "Gemeindeliberalismus. Zur lokalen Enstehung und sozialen Verankerung der hberalen Partei in Baden 1831- 1855, " *HZ* 252 (1991), 57-93.

Nolte, Paul, *Gemeindebürgertum und Liberalismus in Baden: 1800-1850. Tradition, Radikalismus, Republik* (Kritische Studien zur Geschichtswissenschaft 102) (Göttingen, 1994).

O'Connor, Richard, *The German-Americans: An informal History* (Boston, 1968).

Oberndorf, Ludwig, "The German Press in the United States," *AGR* 6 (December 1939), 14-16.

Olson, Audrey L, *St. Louis Germans, 1850-1920. The Nature of an Immigrant Community and its Relation to the Assimilation Process* (New York, 1980).

Parenti, Michael, "Ethnic Politics and the Persistence of Ethnic Identification," *American Political Science Review* 61 (September 1967), 717-726.

Peiser, Jurgen, *Gustav Struve als politischer Schriftsteller und Revolutionär*, Ph.D. dissertation, typescript, Frankfurt a. M., 1973.

Pflanze, Otto, "Germany - Bismarck - America," Elvert, Salewski, op. cit., 67-84.

Reiter, Herbert, *Politisches Asyl irn 19. jahrhundert. Die deutschen politischen Flüchtlinge des Vormärz und der Revolution van 1848/49 in Europa und den USA* (Berlin, 1992).

Riddleberger, Patrick W., "The Break in the Radical Ranks: Liberals vs Stalwarts in the Election of 1872," *Journal of Negro History* 44 (April, 1959).

Rippley, La Vern John, *The German-Americans* (Boston, 1976).

Rippley, La Vern John, "German Assimilation: the Effect of the 1871 Victory on Americana-Germanica," Trefousse, ed., *Germany and America*, 122-136.

Rosskopf, Josef, *Johann Adam van Itzstein. Ein Beitrag zur Geschichte des badischen Liberalismus*, Ph. D. dissertation, typescript, Mainz 1954.

Rowan, Steven, ed., *Germans for a Free Missouri. Translations from the St. Louis Radical Press 1857-1862* (Columbia, Missouri, 1983).

Saalberg, Harvey, *The Westliche Post of St. Louis*, Ph.D. dissertation, typescript, University of Missouri-Columbia 1964.

Sauter, Udo, "Zur Vorgeschichte des Amerikanischen Burgerkriegs," *Historische Mitteilungen* 10 (1997), Heft 1, 1-13.

Schafer, Josef, *Militant Liberal - Carl Schurz*, Publication of the State Histroical Society of Wisconsin, 1930.

Scharf, Thomas J., *History of St. Louis and County*, 2 vols. (Philadelphia, 1883).

Schneider, Otto C, "Abraham Lincoln und das Deutschthum," *DAG* 7 (1907), 65-75.

Schoberl, Ingrid, *Amerikanische Einwanderungswerbung in Deutschland 1845-1914*, Stuttgart 1990.

Schrader, Franklin Frederick, *The Germans in the Making of America* (Boston, 1924).

Selby, Paul, "Lincoln and German Patriotism," *DAG* 12 (1912), 510-535.

Siemann, Wolfram, Die deutsche Revolution von 1848/49 (Frankfurt a. M., 1985).

Skal, Georg von, *Die Achtundvierziger in Amerika* (Frankfurt a. M., 1923).

Sproat, John G., *"The Best Men": Liberal Reformers in the Gilded Age* (New York, 1968).

Stadler, Ernst A., "The German Settlement of St. Louis," *Midcontinent American Studies Journal*, University of Kansas, Lawrence, 6 (Spring 1965),16-29.

Stolleis, Michael, *Geschichte des öffentlichen Rechts in Deutschland*, vol. 2 (Munich, 1992).

Trefousse, Hans L., "Die deutschametikanischen Einwanderer und das neugegriindete Reich," Trommler, ed., *Amerika und die Deutschen*, 177-191.

Trefousse, Hans L. , ed., *Germany and America: Essays on Problems of International Relations and Immigration* (New York, 1980).

Trefousse, Hans L., "Abraham Lincoln and Carl Schurz," Brancaforte, ed., *The German Forty-Eighters*, 179-201.

Trefousse, Hans L., *Carl Schurz. A Biography* (Knoxville, 1982).

Trefousse, Hans L., "Die deutschamerikaniscben Einwanderer und das neugegründete Reich," Trommler ed., *Amerika und die Deutschen*, 177-191.

Trommler, Frank, ed., *Amerika und die Deutschen: Bestandsaufnahme einer 300 jährigen Geschichte* (Opladen, 1986).

Trommler, Frank, "The Use of History in German-American Politics," Brancaforte ed., *The German Forty-Eighters*, 279- 295.

Tucker, Marlin Timothy, *Political Leadership in the Illinois-Missouri German Community, 1836-1872*, Ph. D. dissertation, typescript, University of Illinois 1968.

Überkorn, Horst, *Turner unterm Sternenbanner. Der Kampf der deutschamerikanischen Turner fur Einheit, Freiheit und soziale Gerechtigkeit 1848-1918* (Munich, 1978).

Vagts, Alfred, *Deutsch-Amerikanische Rückwanderung. Probleme – Phänomene – Statistik – Politik – Soziologie – Biographie* (supplement to *Jahrbuch für Amerikastudien* 6) (Heidelberg, 1960).

Valentin, Veit, *Geschichte der deutschen Revolution von 1848-1849. vol. 1: Bis zum Zusammentritt des Frankfurter Parlamentes* (Cologne; Berlin,1970).

Vossler, Otto, *Die Revolution von 1848 in Deutschland* (Frankfurt a. M., 1967).

Wagner, Maria, "Das Bild Amerikas in der deurschen Presse 1828-1865," Trommler, ed., *Amerika und die Deutschen*, 314-325.

Walker, Mack, *Germany and the Emigration 1816-1885* (Cambridge, MA, 1964).

Walter, Friedrich, *Geschichte Mannheims vom Übergang an Baden (1802) bis zur Gründung des Reiches*, repr. of 1907 (Frankfurt a. M., 1978).

Wehler, Hans Ulrich, *Der Aufstieg des amerikanischen Imperialismus 1865-1900. Studien zur Entwicklung des Imperium Americanum, 1865-1900* (Kritische Studien zur Geschichtswissenschaft 10) (Göttingen, 1974).

Wehler, Hans Ulrich, *Deutsche Gesellschaftsgeschichte*, vol. 2 *(1815-1845/49)* (Munich, 1987).

Wellenreuther, Hermann, "Die USA. Ein politisches Vorbild der bürgerlich-liberalen Krafte des Vormärz," Elvert, Salewski, op. cit., 23-41.

Wende, Peter, "Der Revolutionsbegriff der radikalen Demokraten," W. Klotzer, D. Rebentisch, R. Moldenhauer, eds., *Ideen und Strukturen der deutschen Revolution von 1848* (Archiv für Frankfurts Geschichte und Kunst, Heft 54) (Frankfurt a. M., 1974), 57-68.

Wende, Peter, "Radikalismus," *Geschichtliche Grundbegriffe*, vol. 5 (Stuttgart, 1984), 113-133.

Wende, Peter, *Radikalismus im Vormärz. Untersuchungen zur politische Theorie der frühen deutschen Demokratie* (Wiesbaden, 1975).

White, Horace, *Life of Lyman Trumbull* (New York, 1913).

Wiltberger, Otto, *Die deutschen politischen Flüchtlinge in Strassburg 1830-49*, Freiburger Abhandlungen zur mittleren und neueren Geschichte 17 (Berlin; Leipzig, 1910).

Wittke, Carl, *Against the Current. The Life of Karl Heinzen (1809-80)* (Chicago, 1945).

Wittke, Carl, "Carl Schurz and Rutherford B. Hayes," *The Ohio Historical Quarterly*, 65, no. 4 (Okrober 1956- 337-355.

Wittke, Carl, *Refugees of Revolution. The German Forty-Eighters in America* (Philadelphia, 1952).

Wittke, Carl, "The German Forty-Eighters," O. Fritiof Ander, ed., *The John H. Hanberg Historical Essays*, Rock Island, I11., 1954.

Wittke, Carl, *The German-Language Press in America* (Lexington, KY, 1957).

Wittke, Carl, *The Utopian Communist. A Biography of Wilhelm Weitling, Nineteenth-Century Reformer* (Louisiana, 1950).

Zarefsky, David, *Lincoln, Douglas and Slavery in the Crucible of Public Debate* (Chicago; London 1990).

Zucker, Adolf E., ed., *The Forty-Eighters. Political Refugees of the German Revolution of 1848* (New York. 1950).

Abbreviations used throughout the notes

ADB Allgemeine Deutsche Biographie

AGR *American German Review*

AHR American Historical Review

AfS Archiv für Sozialgeschichte

AW Anzeiger des Westens, St. Louis, Missouri.

BV Belleviller Volksblatt, Belleville, Illinois.

BZ Belleviller Zeitung, Belleville, Illinois.

DP Der deutsche Pionier

DAB Dictionary of American Biography

DAG Deutsch-Amerikanische Geschichtsblätter

DAM Deutsch-Amerikanische Monatshefte

FH Friedrich Hecker

FHP Friedrich Hecker Papers

GL Die Gartenlaube

HZ Historische Zeitschrift

ISZ Illinois Staatszeitung, Chicago, Illinois.

JAH Journal of American History.

NDB Neue Deutsche Biographie

TISZ Tägliche Illinois Staatszeitung, Chicago, Illinois.

TWP Tägliche Westliche Post, St. Louis, Missouri.

VSB Verhandlungen der Ständeversammlung des Großherzogtums Baden von 1842 bis 1848, Protokolle und Beilagen der Zweiten Kammer (Karlsruhe); *gS*=geheime Sitzung; *öS*=öffentliche Sitzung.

ZGO Zeitschrift für die Geschichte des Oberrheins

Index of Names